Marketing Strategy and Competitive Positioning

Visit the Hooley, Piercy and Nicolaud: *Marketing Strategy and Competitive Positioning, Fourth Edition* Companion Website at **www.pearsoned.co.uk/hooley** to find valuable **student** learning material including:

- Annotated weblinks to relevant specific Internet resources to facilitate in-depth independent research
- Additional classic cases that allow you to apply theory to recognisable real-world brands and products

We work with leading authors to develop the strongest educational materials in marketing, bringing cutting-edge thinking and best learning practice to a global market.

Under a range of well-known imprints, including Financial Times/Prentice Hall we craft high quality print and electronic publications which help readers to understand and apply their content, whether studying or at work.

To find out more about the complete range of our publishing, please visit us on the World Wide Web at: **www.pearsoned.co.uk**

Graham J. Hooley   Nigel F. Piercy   Brigitte Nicoulaud

Marketing Strategy and Competitive Positioning

fourth edition

FT Prentice Hall
FINANCIAL TIMES

An imprint of **Pearson Education**
Harlow, England • London • New York • Boston • San Francisco • Toronto • Sydney • Singapore • Hong Kong
Tokyo • Seoul • Taipei • New Delhi • Cape Town • Madrid • Mexico City • Amsterdam • Munich • Paris • Milan

Contents

Part 3 Identifying Current and Future Competitive Positions 203

Part 6 Conclusions 539

Supporting resources
Visit **www.pearsoned.co.uk/hooley** to find valuable online resources

Companion Website for students
- Annotated weblinks to relevant specific Internet resources to facilitate in-depth independent research
- Additional classic csaes that allow you to apply theory to recognisable real-world brands and products

For instructors
- PowerPoint slides, including key figures from the book
- Extensive Instructors Manual, with guidelines on how to get the most out of the book in your teaching

Also: The Companion Website provides the following features:

- Search tool to help locate specific items of content
- E-mail results and profile tools to send results of quizzes to instructors
- Online help and support to assist with website usage and troubleshooting

For more information please contact your local Pearson Education sales representative or visit **www.pearsoned.co.uk/hooley**

Preface

Marketing Strategy and Competitive Positioning

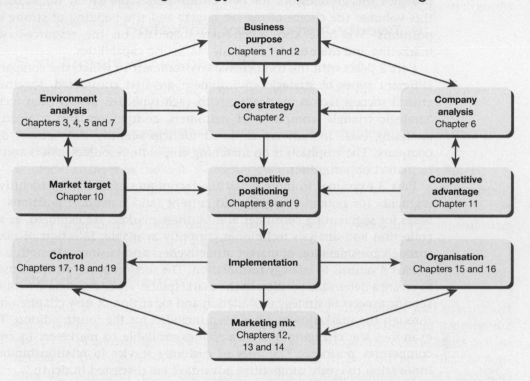

This book is about creating and sustaining superior performance in the marketplace. It focuses on the two central issues in marketing strategy formulation – the identification of target markets and the creation of a differential advantage. The book includes new developments in strategic thinking that have emerged in recent years. In particular, our approach emphasises the very different role that organisations are defining for marketing as a strategic force rather than just as an operational department. It also represents our goal of reaching a broader audience to include strategic decision-makers as well as marketing specialists.

Some of the topics include service quality and relationship marketing, networks and alliances, innovation, internal marketing and corporate social responsibility. Greater emphasis is given to the development of dynamic marketing capabilities, together with the need to reassess the role of marketing in the organisation as a critical process and not simply as a conventional functional specialisation.

Abbreviations

ACORN	A Classification of Residential Neighbourhoods
ATM	automatic telling machine
CAPM	capital asset pricing model
CD	compact disc
CEO	chief executive officer
CRM	customer relationship management
DFMA	Design For Manufacturing and Assembly
DIY	do it yourself
DMU	decision-making unit
EB	*Encyclopaedia Britannica*
ECR	Efficient Consumer Response
ESP	unique emotional proposition
EU	European Union
GATT	General Agreement on Tariffs and Trade
GDP	gross domestic product
GP	general practitioner
HRM	human resource management
IT	information technology
JIT	just in time
KFS	key factors for success
MDSS	marketing decision support systems
MIS	marketing information system
OPEC	Organisation of Petroleum Exporting Countries
PC	personal computer
PEST	political and economic, social and technological [environment]
PIMS	Profit Impact of Marketing Strategy [study]
R&D	research and development
RBV	resource-based view
ROI	return on investment
SBU	strategic business unit
SIC	Standard Industry Classification
SOEs	state-owned enterprises
SPACE	strategic position and action evaluation [analysis]
SWOT	strengths, weaknesses, opportunities, threats [analysis]
TGI	Target Group Index
TQM	total quality management
USP	unique selling proposition
VALS	Values and Lifestyles
VCR	video cassette recorder
WTO	World Trade Organisation

part one

Marketing Strategy

The first part of this book is concerned with the role of marketing in strategy development and lays the groundwork for analysing the two critical issues of competitive positioning and market choices.

Chapter 1 discusses the modern challenges to the conventional view of marketing as simply a specialised function in an organisation, and the move towards examining marketing as a process of value creation and delivery to customers that transcends traditional departmental boundaries. We examine the issue of our growing understanding of market orientation as a way of doing business that places the customer at the centre of operations, and aligns people, information and structures around the value-creation process. We also recognise the role of organisational resources in creating sustainable competitive advantage. The chapter concludes with a set of fundamental marketing principles to guide the actions of organisations operating in competitive markets, and by identifying the role of marketing in leading and shaping strategic management.

Chapter 2 presents a framework for developing a marketing strategy that is then adopted throughout the rest of the book. A three-stage process is proposed. First, the establishment of the core strategy. This involves defining the business purpose, assessing the alternatives open to the organisation through an analysis of customers, competition and the resources of the organisation, and deciding on the strategic focus that will be adopted. Second is the creation of the competitive positioning for the company. This boils down to the selection of the target market(s) (which dictates *where* the organisation will compete) and the establishment of a competitive advantage (which spells out *how* it will compete). Third, implementation issues are discussed, such as the achievement of positioning through the use of the marketing mix, organisation and control of the marketing effort.

The ideas and frameworks presented in Part 1 are used to structure the remainder of the book, leading into a more detailed discussion of market analysis in Part 2, segmentation and positioning analysis in Part 3, the development of competitive positioning strategies in Part 4, and strategy implementation issues in Part 5.

chapter one

Market-led strategic management

The successful organization of the future will be customer-focused, not product or technology focused, supported by a market-information competence that links the voice of the customer to all the firm's value-delivery processes . . . Successful marketing organizations will have the skills necessary to manage multiple strategic marketing processes, many of which have not, until recently, been regarded as within the domain of marketing.

Webster (1997)

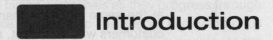 Introduction

As the third millennium unfolds there is continued debate about whether marketing, as an approach to business and as a business function, has come of age, has reached maturity or is in decline. While a decade ago marketing was misunderstood by many senior managers and typically thought to be just a new name for selling and advertising, today most senior managers could offer passably accurate textbook definitions of marketing, centring on identifying and satisfying customer requirements at a profit, and most would probably also claim that their businesses were 'market oriented'. In Greyser's terms, marketing has successfully 'migrated' from being a functional discipline to being a concept of how businesses should be run (Greyser, 1997). Similarly, marketing is talked of as a key function in organisations other than the conventional commercial company – in not-for-profit enterprises such as charities and the arts, in political parties, and even in public sector organisations such as the police service.

Table 1.1 The fabric of the new marketing concept

1	Create customer focus throughout the business.
2	Listen to the customer.
3	Define and nurture the organisation's distinct competencies.
4	Define marketing as market intelligence.
5	Target customers precisely.
6	Manage for profitability, not sales volume.
7	Make customer value the guiding star.
8	Let the customer define loyalty.
9	Measure and manage customer expectations.
10	Build customer relationships and loyalty.
11	Define the business as a service business.
12	Commit to continuous improvement and innovation.
13	Manage culture along with strategy and structure.
14	Grow with partners and alliances.
15	Destroy marketing bureaucracy.

Source: Webster (1994)

An interesting attempt to 'reinvent' the marketing concept for a new era of different organisational structures, complex relationships and globalisation, which may be relevant to overcoming the barriers to market orientation, is made by Webster (1994). He presents 'the new marketing concept as a set of guidelines for creating a customer-focused, market-driven organization', and develops 15 ideas that weave the 'fabric of the new marketing concept' (Table 1.1).

Webster's conceptualisation represents a useful attempt to develop a pragmatic operationalisation of the marketing concept.

We can summarise the signs of market orientation in the following terms, and underline the links between them and our approach here to marketing strategy and competitive positioning:

- Reaching marketing's true potential may rely mostly on success in moving past marketing activities (tactics), to marketing as a company-wide issue of real customer focus (culture) and competitive positioning (strategy). The evidence supports suggestions that marketing has generally been highly effective in tactics, but only marginally effective in changing culture, and largely ineffective in the area of strategy (Day, 1992; Varadarajan, 1992; Webster, 1997).

- One key is achieving understanding of the market and the customer throughout the company and building the capability for responsiveness to market changes. The real customer focus and responsiveness of the company is the context in which marketing strategy is built and implemented. Our approach to competitive market analysis in Part 2 provides many of the tools that can be used to enhance and share an understanding of the customer marketplace throughout the company.

- Another issue is that the marketing process should be seen as inter-functional and cross-disciplinary, and not simply the responsibility of the marketing department. This is the real value of adopting the process perspective on marketing, which is becoming more widely adopted by large organisations (Hulbert *et al.*, 2003). We shall see in Part 4 on competitive positioning strategies that superior service and value, and innovation to build defensible competitive positions, rely on the coordinated efforts of many functions and people within the organisation. Cross-functional relationships are also an important emphasis in Part 5.

● It is also clear that a deep understanding of the competition in the market from the customer's perspective is critical. Viewing the product or service from the customer's viewpoint is often difficult, but without that perspective a marketing strategy is highly vulnerable to attack from unsuspected sources of competition. We shall confront this issue in Part 3, where we are concerned with competitive positioning.

● Finally, it follows that the issue is long-term performance, not simply short-term results, and this perspective is implicit in all that we consider in building and implementing marketing strategy.

A framework for executives to evaluate market orientation in their own organisations is shown in Box 1.1. However, it is also important to make the point at this early stage that marketing as organisational culture (the marketing concept and market orientation) must also be placed in the context of other drivers of the values and approaches of the organisation. A culture that emphasises customers as key stakeholders in the organisation is not inconsistent with one that also recognises the needs and concerns of shareholders, employees, managers, and the wider social context in which the organisation operates.

Market orientation assessment   Box 1.1

1 CUSTOMER ORIENTATION

	Strongly agree	Agree	Neither	Disagree	Strongly disagree	Don't know
Information about customer needs and requirements is collected regularly	5	4	3	2	1	0
Our corporate objective and policies are aimed directly at creating satisfied customers	5	4	3	2	1	0
Levels of customer satisfaction are regularly assessed and action is taken to improve matters where necessary	5	4	3	2	1	0
We put major effort into building stronger relationships with key customers and customer groups	5	4	3	2	1	0
We recognise the existence of distinct groups or segments in our markets with different needs and we adapt our offerings accordingly	5	4	3	2	1	0

Total score for customer orientation (*out of 25*)

▶

2 COMPETITOR ORIENTATION

	Strongly agree	Agree	Neither	Disagree	Strongly disagree	Don't know
Information about competitor activities is collected regularly	5	4	3	2	1	0
We conduct regular benchmarking against major competitor offerings	5	4	3	2	1	0
There is rapid response to major competitor actions	5	4	3	2	1	0
We put major emphasis on differentiating ourselves from the competition on factors important to customers	5	4	3	2	1	0

Total score for competitor orientation (*out of 20*)

3 LONG-TERM PERSPECTIVES

	Strongly agree	Agree	Neither	Disagree	Strongly disagree	Don't know
We place greater priority on long-term market share gain than short-run profits	5	4	3	2	1	0
We put greater emphasis on improving our market performance than on improving internal efficiencies	5	4	3	2	1	0
Decisions are guided by long-term considerations rather than short-run expediency	5	4	3	2	1	0

Total score for long-term perspectives (*out of 15*)

4 INTERFUNCTIONAL COORDINATION

	Strongly agree	Agree	Neither	Disagree	Strongly disagree	Don't know
Information about customers is widely circulated and communicated throughout the organisation	5	4	3	2	1	0
The different departments in the organisation work effectively together to serve customer needs	5	4	3	2	1	0
Tensions and rivalries between departments are not allowed to get in the way of serving customers effectively	5	4	3	2	1	0
Our organisation is flexible to enable opportunities to be seized effectively rather than hierarchically constrained	5	4	3	2	1	0

Total score for interfunctional coordination (*out of 20*)

5 ORGANISATIONAL CULTURE

	Strongly agree	Agree	Neither	Disagree	Strongly disagree	Don't know
All employees recognise their role in helping to create satisfied end customers	5	4	3	2	1	0
Reward structures are closely related to external market performance and customer satisfaction	5	4	3	2	1	0
Senior management in all functional areas give top importance to creating satisfied customers	5	4	3	2	1	0
Senior management meetings give high priority to discussing issues that affect customer satisfaction	5	4	3	2	1	0

Total score for organisational culture (*out of 20*)

Summary

Customer orientation (*out of 25*)
Competitor orientation (*out of 20*)
Long-term perspectives (*out of 15*)
Interfunctional coordination (*out of 20*)
Organisational culture (*out of 20*)
Total score (*out of 100*)

Interpretation

80–100 indicates a high level of market orientation. Scores below 100 can still, however, be improved!

60–80 indicates moderate market orientation – identify the areas where most improvement is needed.

40–60 shows a long way to go in developing a market orientation. Identify the main gaps and set priorities for action to close them.

20–40 indicates a mountain ahead of you! Start at the top and work your way through. Some factors will be more within your control than others. Tackle those first.

Note: If you scored '0' on many of the scales you need to find out more about your own company!

1.2　The resource-based view of marketing

While academic researchers and managers in marketing have been obsessed over the last decade or so with understanding what being 'market oriented' means (how to measure it and how to build it), a revolution has been taking place in the field of strategic management.

The dominant view of strategy in the 1980s had been that propounded by, among others, Michael Porter of the Harvard Business School (Porter, 1980, 1985). Under this view the key to strategy was deemed to lie in industry dynamics and character-istics. Porter suggested that some industries were inherently more attractive than others, and that the factors driving industry competition were the key determinants of profitability. Under the new approach, however, the focus for explaining perform-ance differences shifted from outside the firm (the industries in which it operated) to within the firm itself.

Termed the resource-based view of the firm (Wernerfelt, 1984) or the focus on 'core competencies' (Prahalad and Hamel, 1990) this new approach suggested that performance was essentially driven by the resource profile of the organisation, and that the source of superior performance lay in the possession and deployment of distinctive, hard to imitate or protected resources.

Current views on strategy and marketing suggest that these two approaches can be combined to the benefit of both (see Hooley *et al.*, 1998). They do, however, throw into stark relief the different approaches to strategy in general and marketing in particular still evident in many organisations today. Three main alternative approaches are apparent (see Figure 1.3):

● **Product push marketing:** Under this approach firms centre their activities on their existing products and services and look for ways to encourage, or even persuade, customers to buy. This is a myopic interpretation of the resource-based view – we have a resource (our product or service) that we are good at producing and is different from what competitors offer. The key thing is to make customers want what we are good at. Day (1999) identified this approach in the IBM state-ment of goals in 1983. Under that statement the firm set out objectives to grow the industry, to exhibit product leadership across the entire product line, to be most efficient in all activities undertaken, and to sustain profitability. What is remarkable about these goals is that customers are not mentioned once. The entire focus was on what IBM did then (1983) and how it could be done more efficiently. Interestingly, IBM's performance in the 1980s was poor.

● **Customer-led marketing:** The other extreme is customer-led marketing (Slater, 1998). Under this approach organisations chase their customers at all costs. The goal is to find what customers want and, whatever it is, give it to them. This can also lead to problems. In the 1980s Procter & Gamble was being hit by increas-ingly aggressive competitors and squeezed by increasingly powerful retailers. It reacted by giving customers more choice, heavy promotions and deals to stimu-late purchases, and aggressive salesforce targets. The result was product prolifera-tion on a grand scale (there were at one time 35 variants of the Bounce fabric conditioner!). Customers were confused by the over-complex promotions (deals, coupons, offers, etc.) and retailers became angry at having to stock a wide variety of choices on their shelves. In the production process the product line extensions caused chaos and logistics nightmares (Day, 1999). Being excessively customer led can lead to a short-term orientation resulting in trivial incremental product development efforts and myopic R&D (Frosch, 1996). Christensen and Bower (1996) go further, suggesting that 'firms lose their position of industry leadership . . . because they listen too carefully to their customers'.

● **Resource-based marketing:** In this book we advocate a middle ground between these two extremes. In this approach firms base their marketing strategies on equal consideration of the requirements of the market and their abilities to serve it. Under this approach a long-term view of customer requirements is taken in the context of other market considerations (such as competitor offerings and strategies, and the realities of the supply chain), together with mapping out the assets, competencies and skills of the organisation to ensure they are leveraged to the full. By the late 1980s IBM had recast its approach in its market-driven quality campaign along the lines: 'if we can be the best at satisfying the needs and wants of customers in those markets we choose to serve, everything important will follow'. The newer approach recognised the centrality of the customer, but also the need to be selective in which markets to serve, ensuring they were markets where IBM's resources (its assets and capabilities) gave it the chance of leadership.

Resource-based marketing essentially seeks a long-term fit between the requirements of the market and the abilities of the organisation to compete in it. This does not mean that the resources of the organisation are seen as fixed and static. Far from it. Market requirements evolve over time and the resource profile of the organisation must be continuously developed to enable it to continue to compete, and indeed to enable it to take advantage of new opportunities. The essential factor, however, is that opportunities are seized where the organisation has an existing or potential

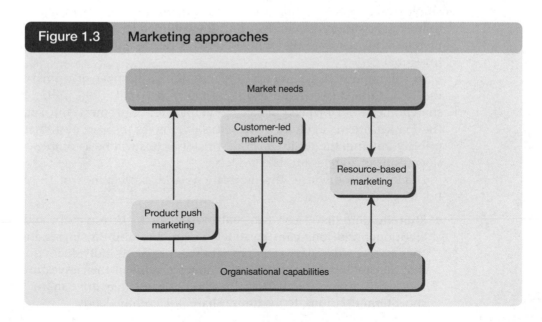

Figure 1.3   Marketing approaches

advantage through its resource base, rather than just pursued ad hoc. These points will be returned to when we discuss the assessment of company marketing resources (Chapter 6) and the criteria for selecting those markets in which to operate (Chapter 10).

First, however, we need to explore how market orientation and marketing resources impact on organisational performance. To do this we introduce the idea of organisational stakeholders.

1.3   Organisational stakeholders

Why do organisations exist? The simple answer for commercial organisations may be to earn returns on their investments for shareholders and owners of those organisations. For non-commercial organisations, such as charities, faith-based organisations, public services and so on, the answer may lie in the desire to serve specific communities. But organisations, both commercial and non-profit, are rarely driven by such simple goals. Often there are many demands, sometimes complementary, sometimes competing, that drive decisions. For example, James Dyson's decision to move production of his household appliances out of the United Kingdom to the Far East in early 2002 for cost reasons (responsibility to shareholders to operate efficiently) resulted in a considerable backlash from the local community over the impact on jobs and livelihoods in the region (responsibility to employees and the local community).

All organisations serve multiple stakeholders (Harrison and St John, 1994; Mitchell *et al.*, 1997). Some, however, will be given higher priority than others in the way decisions are made and resources allocated (Rowley, 1997; Ogden and Watson, 1999). Research into the transition economies of Central and Eastern Europe, for example, found that in many state-owned enterprises (SOEs) the major stakeholders were the employees, and organisational objectives centred on providing continuity of employment (Hooley *et al.*, 2000). This orientation persists in many former SOEs following privatisation and sell-off to the commercial sector. For many of the commercial firms surveyed the prime objectives centred on profitability and return on investment.

In the context of commercial organisations a number of primary stakeholders can be identified (see Figure 1.4) (Greenley and Foxall, 1996, 1997). These include shareholders and owners, managers, employees, customers and suppliers. While the market-oriented culture discussed above serves to place customers high in the priority ranking, the reality for most organisations will be a complex blend of considerations of all relevant stakeholders.

Doyle (2000) discusses the motivations and expectations of the various stakeholder groups as follows:

● **Shareholders** may be of two main types. First, there may be individuals with emotional and long-term personal ties to the business. Increasingly, however, shareholders nowadays are financial investors, both individual and institutional, that are seeking to maximise the long-term value of their investments. Paradoxically, this desire for long-term shareholder value may drive many firms to make short-term decisions, to maximise share price or dividends.

Figure 1.4 Organisational stakeholders

- **Employees** may also have long-term commitment to the firm. Their priorities are generally some combination of compensation (through wages and salaries), job satisfaction and security (of employment). These may be at odds with the value of the firm to shareholders. Few employees would agree that their personal job loss through 'downsizing' is a price worth paying for increasing shareholder value! Some firms, however, put a great deal of effort into understanding employee motivations. Skandia, the Swedish insurance company, for example, regularly surveys employees with a view to aligning their personal and corporate goals (*Fortune*, 11 March 2002). The John Lewis Partnership, the UK retail group operating 26 department stores, an online business – John Lewis Direct – and 183 Waitrose supermarkets with a turnover in excess of £5 billion, involve their 68,000 employees in decision making through meetings between management and elected staff representatives. Staff turnover is low and employees share in profits and have entitlement of sabbatical breaks.

- **Managers** are also concerned with personal rewards in the form of salaries and prestige. Professional managers may have less long-term commitment to the firm and see their roles as temporary staging posts on their longer-term career journeys. Managerial 'success' is often measured by short-term gains (in sales, for example, or efficiency), which may not necessarily equate to longer-term performance improvement for the firm.

- **Customers** are the ultimate source of shareholder value. As Doyle (2000) points out, 'even the most focused financial manager understands that the source of a company's long-term cash flow is its satisfied customers' (p. 23). There is, however, an inherent danger of pursuing customer satisfaction at the expense of all other considerations. Customers might be 'delighted' by lower prices or higher quality offerings than competitors, but if the underlying costs exceed the prices that customers are prepared to pay the firm will not remain in business very long. In this respect the blind pursuit of customer satisfaction may be at odds with longer-term shareholder value creation. Many of the ill-fated extravagant customer offers made by the Internet-based dot.coms in recent years underline the fact that customer value creation must be balanced with other issues.

- **Suppliers and distributors** also have a stake in the business. Suppliers rely on the firms they serve to ensure the achievement of their own goals. Again, suppliers may be looking for security, predictability and satisfactory margins. When the UK retailer Marks & Spencer (M&S) hit financial problems in 1999–2000 many of the long-term relationships they had with their suppliers such as Courtaulds became casualties. M&S began to source materials wider afield to cut costs and the trust and relationships built over a long period of time with their suppliers were quickly eroded, ending in legal action in some instances. Distributors too are stakeholders in the business. In the automobile industry, car distributors are normally closely allied to individual car makers through franchise agreements. The success or otherwise of the manufacturer in developing and marketing the right cars for the market will impact directly on the distributor. Again, the distributor may be seeking predictability and continuity at satisfactory margins.

For non-profit organisations the identification of stakeholders and their requirements may be even more complex:

- **Owners** of the organisation may be hard to identify and their interests difficult to define. For example, who 'owns' the Catholic Church, or Greenpeace, or the Labour Party? Many might argue that the owners are those who support such organisations, the churchgoers, the activists and the members. Or are employees (such as the Pope and the clergy) the owners? In the case of organisations such as the Health Service, or the police service, or education, are the owners society in general, the taxpayers who foot the bill, or the government of the day that sets priorities and performance targets?

- **Customers** may be defined as those the organisation seeks to serve. The customers of the Catholic Church may be those who attend mass on Sundays. They may also, however, extend to others the Church wishes to appeal to and whose behaviour and beliefs it seeks to influence. Who are the customers of the Health Service – the patients? Or those who avoid the service through heeding health warnings? Who are the customers of higher education? The students? Their parents who fund them? Or the employers who seek their skills on graduation? Who are the customers for the police service? Society in general that needs protection from criminals? The criminals themselves? Or the taxpayers who fund them? Different definitions of customers may result in different interpretations of what they are looking for, what their expectations and requirements are. Failure to identify and meet the needs of different customers destroys market position. For example, while doctors and police officers struggle with the idea that they exist to provide customer value, their position is being eroded by the growth of alternative medicine and private security services.

- **Employees**, we might conclude, are relatively easy to identify. Their motivations, however, may be far more complex than in the commercial sector. What motivates nurses to work such long, hard hours for relatively little financial reward? Why do people volunteer to staff charity shops for no payment? Why do activists risk their lives to prevent the dumping of oil platforms or nuclear waste at sea? In the non-profit sector employees may or may not receive financial rewards. Often their prime motivators, however, are not financial but centre far more on satisfaction derived from contributing to a cause they cherish or value.

While the considerations of many of the above stakeholders may be complementary they may also conflict at times (Clarkson, 1995). For example, the desire of shareholders for long-term value creation may be at odds with the demands of suppliers and distributors for continuity, security and satisfactory margins. The demands placed on a firm through being customer led may have significant impacts on the roles and activities of managers and employees, not all of them welcome. This confusion may be compounded when individual stakeholders assume more than one role. For example, managers and employees may also be shareholders in commercial organisations. They could also, from time to time, be their own customers!

In any organisation there will be a blend of orientations towards the various stakeholders. We would argue, however, that a strong orientation towards the market, as discussed at the outset of this chapter, can be a unifying force that helps achieve other stakeholder goals.

1.3.1 The contribution of marketing to stakeholder objectives

There is increasing evidence that firms which do well in the marketplace also do well financially, adding to the value of the firm for shareholders. Homburg and Pflesser (2000), for example, have shown that firms adopting a market-oriented culture perform better financially than those that do not. Many other studies have also shown direct links between market orientation, customer satisfaction and firm financial performance (see Lafferty and Hult (2001) for a summary).

Figure 1.5 shows the effects of market-oriented culture on firm activities and performance. The degree of market orientation, as discussed above, is a deeply embedded cultural aspect of any firm (Deshpandé et al., 1993). Where market orientation is

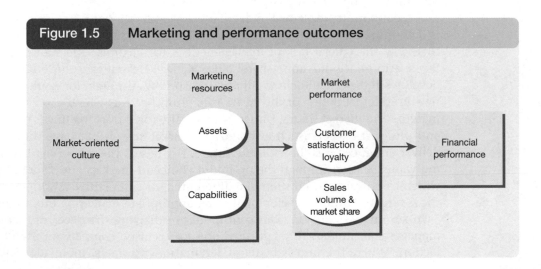

Figure 1.5   **Marketing and performance outcomes**

high all organisational functions are focused on their role in, and contribution to, creating superior customer value. This in turn affects the way those functions are managed, and the priorities they pursue. For example, human resource management and training is often directed towards customer awareness and service, and reward structures are designed to encourage customer satisfaction generation. Where market orientation is high, employee job satisfaction and commitment have also been demonstrated to be high (see Siguaw *et al.*, 1994; Selnes, 1996; Piercy *et al.*, 2002) creating a motivated workforce focused on the needs of customers (see Heskett *et al.*, 2003). Sir Stuart Hampson, Chairman of the John Lewis Partnership, puts it this way: 'It's a virtuous circle. Happy, fulfilled partners [employees] take pride in their jobs and give better service, which in turn leads to contented customers and better service' (*The Guardian*, 18 March 2002).

High levels of market orientation also lead to an emphasis on developing marketing assets such as company and brand reputation (Aaker, 1991), market innovation capabilities (Slater and Narver, 1995; Han *et al.*, 1998) and the development of customer relationship management (CRM) skills (Gummesson, 1999).

Well-developed marketing resources (assets and capabilities), when deployed in the marketplace, can lead to superior market performance. Satisfied and well-motivated staff (a prime marketing asset), for example, can make a significant contribution to creating satisfied and loyal customers (Bowen and Lawler, 1992; Payne, 1993; Heskett *et al.*, 2003) and subsequently increased sales volume and market share. Reputational assets, such as well-known and respected brands, together with well-developed marketing capabilities such as CRM and market innovation skills, also affect market performance directly.

The link between market performance and financial performance is also well established. Customer satisfaction and loyalty leads to greater sales volume and market share (Hart *et al.*, 1990; Anderson and Sullivan, 1993; Rust and Zahorik, 1993; Wells, 1994/5), which in turn leads to financial performance. One suggested route is through the impact of economies and advantages of scale. The PIMS project (Profit Impact of Marketing Strategy) has shown that firms with higher market shares perform better financially due to the economies they enjoy in purchasing, production, operations and marketing (see Buzzell and Gale, 1987).

A second route, explained in detail by Doyle (2000), notes that shareholder value is determined by anticipated future cash flows, adjusted for the cost of capital. In this view the crucial task of management is to maximise the sum of future cash flows, and hence maximise shareholder value. Marketing's contribution will be to develop strategies that deliver enhanced cash flows through, for example, successful new product launches, or the creation of strong brands which can command high margins and market shares. Under this view the focus of marketing is on developing and protecting assets (such as brands or market share) that have the potential to deliver enhanced cash flows in the future. Doyle sees the role of marketing as driving value creation through the optimum choice of markets and target segments in which to operate, the creation of a differential, or competitive advantage in serving those targets, and the development of an appropriate marketing mix for delivery.

In summary, marketing can contribute to satisfying the needs of employee and manager stakeholders through providing for security, compensation and job satisfaction. Where the firm is better at serving its customers, more adept at winning orders in the face of competition, it is more likely to survive into the future. There is also evidence that where firms are more market oriented their employees get more satisfaction out of their jobs (Slater and Narver, 1995). This in turn can lead to a virtuous circle of improvement as happy, motivated staff generate increasingly satisfied customers, so that organisational performance improves, and staff become more satisfied, etc. Similarly, the most effective route to achieving the profit and performance desires of supply chain partners is through market success. Heightened success through partnerships and alliances can serve to bond organisations together, creating more stability and predictability in the supply and distribution chain. Nonetheless, concerns of customers and employees for the environment, for social justice, for fair employment, and other social priorities have led to renewed emphasis on corporate social responsibility and good corporate citizenship. However, importantly, we shall see in Part 5, thinking has changed from altruistic behaviour to meet moral obligations to pursuing social initiatives as part of the value proposition and a source of competitive advantage (see Chapter 18).

1.4　Marketing fundamentals

Following from the underlying marketing concept outlined above, the considerations of alternative stakeholders, and the logic of resource-based marketing, we can distil a set of basic and very pragmatic marketing principles that serve to guide marketing thought and action. The principles follow the logic of value-based processes described by Webster (1997). Each of these principles seems so obvious as not to require stating. However, recognition of these principles and their application can revolutionise how organisations respond to, and interact with, their customers.

Principle 1: Focus on the customer

A first principle of marketing that emerges from our comments throughout goes back to the marketing concept itself. This recognises that the long-run objectives of the organisation, be they financial or social, are best served by achieving a high degree of customer focus – but not a blind focus! From that recognition flows the need for a close investigation of customer wants and needs, followed by a clear definition of if and how the company can best serve them.

It also follows that the only arbiters of how well the organisation satisfies its customers are the customers themselves. The quality of the goods or services offered to the market will be judged by the customers on the basis of how well their requirements are satisfied. A quality product or service, from the customers' perspective, is one that satisfies or is 'fit for purpose' rather than one that provides unrequired luxury.

As Levitt (1986) demonstrates, adopting a market-led approach poses some very basic questions. The most important include:

- What business are we in?
- What business could we be in?
- What business do we want to be in?
- What must we do to get into or consolidate in that business?

The answers to these fundamental questions can often change a company's whole outlook and perspective. In Chapter 2 we discuss more fully business definition and show how it is fundamental to setting strategic direction for the organisation.

Principle 2: Only compete in markets where you can establish a competitive advantage

Market selection is one of the key tasks for any organisation – choosing where to compete and where to commit its resources. Many factors will come into the choice of market, including how attractive the market appears to the firm. Especially important, however, in competitive markets will be the question: do we have the skills and competencies to compete here? The corporate graveyard is littered with firms that were seduced into markets which looked attractive, but when competition got tough they found they had no real basis on which to compete. Many of the dot.com failures of the early 2000s were firms that saw an opportunity but did not really have the skills and competencies to establish an advantage over other dot.coms or 'bricks and mortar' firms.

Principle 3: Customers do not buy products

The third basic marketing principle is that customers do not buy products, they buy what the product can do for them – the problem it solves. In other words customers are less interested in the technical features of a product or service than in what benefits they get from buying, using or consuming the product or service.

For example, the do-it-yourself enthusiast putting up book shelves will assemble the tools for the job. One of these could be a drill bit to make the holes in which to screw the shelf supports, on which to place the shelf. However, the DIYer does not want a quarter-inch drill bit, but a quarter-inch hole. The drill bit is merely a way of delivering that benefit (the hole) and will only be the solution to the basic need until a better method or solution is invented (Kotler, 1997). We can go further – what is really wanted is storage for books (or indeed in the longer term possibly alternative ways of storing knowledge and information in electronic media). Competition will not come just from other manufacturers of drill bits, but from laser techniques for making holes in the wall; wall designs that incorporate shelving studs in their design; adhesives that will support shelves; or alternative ways of storing books. This is the difference between an industry – firms with similar technology and products – and a market – customers with a problem to solve or a need to meet. In this sense, white goods manufacturers may see themselves as an industry – they all produce white boxes with electric motors – but the markets they serve are the laundry market, the food storage market, and so on. Similarly, gardeners don't really want a lawnmower. What they want is grass that is 1 inch high. Hence a new strain of grass seed, which is hard-wearing and only grows to 1 inch in height, could provide very substantial competition to lawnmower manufacturers, as could artificial grass substitutes or fashions for grass-free garden designs.

This is far from mere academic theorising. One trend in retail marketing in the grocery business is category management. Retailers are defining categories around customer needs, not manufacturers' brands. For example, one common category is 'ready-meal replacement' – the challenge to manufacturers is to prove to the retailer what their products and brands add to the value of the category. Putting category definition at its simplest:

The manufacturer makes	*potato crisps.*
The retailer merchandises	*salty snacks.*
The customer buys	*lunch!*

Looking at a market from the customer's perspective may suggest a very different view of market opportunities and the threats to our competitive position.

It is critical that marketers view products and services as 'bundles of benefits', or a combination of attractions that all give something of value to the customer.

One mission for the marketing executive is to ensure that the organisation gears itself to solving customers' problems, rather than exclusively promoting its own current (and often transitory) solutions.

Principle 4: Marketing is too important to leave to the marketing department (even if there still is one)

It is increasingly the case that marketing is everyone's job in the organisation. The actions of all can have an impact on the final customers and the satisfaction the customer derives.

King (1985) has pointed to a number of misconceptions as to what marketing is. One of the most insidious misconceptions he terms 'marketing department marketing', where an organisation employs marketing professionals who may be very good at analysing marketing data and calculating market shares to three decimal points, but who have very little real impact on the products and services the organisation offers to its customers. The marketing department is seen as the only department where 'marketing is done', so that the other departments can get on with their own agenda and pursue their own goals.

As organisations become flatter, reducing layers of bureaucracy, and continue to break down the spurious functional barriers between departments, so it becomes increasingly obvious that marketing is the job of everyone. It is equally obvious that marketing is so central to both survival and prosperity that it is far too important to leave only to the marketing department.

However, it is clear that we must avoid simply stating that marketing is 'everyone's job' and leaving it at that. If marketing is 'everyone's job' it may become 'no one's job'. Greyser (1997) points to the need for simultaneous upgrading of market orientation and downsizing of the formal marketing function as two sides of the same issue:

While the marketing function ('doing marketing') belongs to the marketing department, becoming and being marketing-minded is everybody's job. What happens when (almost) everybody is doing that job? As companies have become more marketing-minded, there have been substantial reductions in the formal 'marketing departments' which do marketing. In short, a corollary of the trend to better organisational thinking about marketing is the dispersion of the activity of marketing, e.g. via task forces.

Principle 5: Markets are heterogeneous

It is becoming increasingly clear that most markets are not homogeneous, but are made up of different individual customers, sub-markets or segments. While some customers, for example, may buy a car for cheap transport from A to B, others may buy for comfortable travel, or safe travel, and still others may buy for status reasons or to satisfy and project their self-image. Products and services that attempt to satisfy a segmented market through a standardised product almost invariably fall between two or more stools and become vulnerable to more clearly targeted competitors.

Picking up on Principle 2, it is evident that a basic way of segmenting markets is on the basis of the benefits customers get in buying or consuming the product or service. Benefit segmentation (see Chapter 8) has proved to be one of the most useful ways of segmenting markets for the simple reason that it relates the segmentation back to the real reasons for the existence of the segments in the first place – different benefit requirements.

Market heterogeneity has another effect. Concentration in the customer base – facilitated by mergers and acquisitions and attrition rates – has become a daily reality for companies in business-to-business marketplaces. The emergence of powerful, dominant customers underlines the importance of strategic sales capabilities and strategic account management approaches to give specialised attention to customers who can leverage the seller's dependence on them. It is difficult to consider marketing strategy in business-to-business markets without recognising the deep-seated implications of this factor. We devote Chapter 15 to this topic.

Principle 6: Markets and customers are constantly changing

It is a truism to say that the only constant is change. Markets are dynamic and virtually all products have a limited life that expires when a new or better way of satisfying the underlying want or need is found; in other words, until another solution or benefit provider comes along.

The fate of the slide rule, and before that logarithmic tables, at the hands of the pocket calculator is a classic example where the problem (the need for rapid and easy calculation) was better solved through a newer technology. The benefits offered by calculators far outstripped the slide rule in speed and ease of use.

This recognition that products are not omnipotent, that they follow a product life cycle pattern of introduction, growth, maturity and decline, has led companies to look and plan more long term; to ensure that when the current breadwinners die there are new products in the company's portfolio to take their place.

Also evident is the need for constant product and service improvement. As customer expectations change, usually becoming more demanding in the benefits they expect from a given product or service, so organisations need continuously to upgrade their offerings to retain, let alone improve, position.

There are two main processes of improvement. The first is through innovation, where a relatively large step is taken at one point in time. The advent of the pocket calculator was a significant innovation that virtually wiped out the slide rule industry overnight. Other step changes in technology such as the advent of colour television and the compact disc have served to change whole industries in a similarly short period of time.

The second approach to improvement is a more continuous process whereby smaller changes are made but on an insistent basis. This approach has been identified by a number of writers (e.g. Imai, 1986) as a major contributor to the success of Japanese businesses in world markets since the early 1950s. The Japanese call continuous

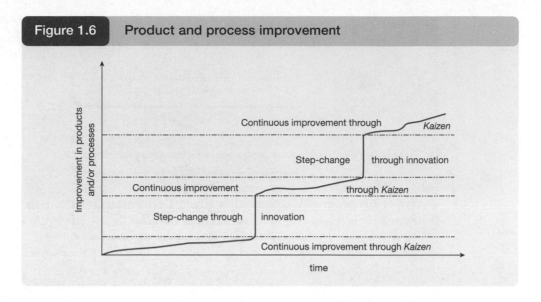

Figure 1.6   Product and process improvement

improvement **Kaizen** and see it as an integral part of business life. Increasingly, organisations are attempting to marry the benefits of step change innovation with continuous (*Kaizen*) improvement. Figure 1.6 illustrates this process diagramatically.

The impact of technological change has been felt most, perhaps, in the computer industry. It is sometimes hard to remember that computers were invented *after* the Second World War because they are now such a pervasive part of both business and home life. Toffler (1981) noted in *Computer World* magazine:

> *If the auto industry had done what the computer industry has done over the last thirty years, a Rolls Royce would cost $2.50, get around 2,000,000 miles to the gallon and six of them would fit on the head of a pin!*

If that was true over 20 years ago just think what the analogy would be today!

1.5   The role of marketing in leading strategic management

In order for strategic management to cope with the changing marketing environment there is a need for it to become increasingly market led. In taking a leading role in the development and the implementation of strategy the role of marketing can be defined in the way shown in Figure 1.7. That role is threefold.

1.5.1   Identification of customer requirements

The first critical task of marketing is to identify the requirements of customers and to communicate them effectively throughout the organisation. This involves conducting or commissioning relevant customer research to uncover, first, who the customers are and, second, what will give them satisfaction.

Figure 1.7 The role of marketing in the organisation

Identify and communicate customer wants and needs throughout the organisation

Determine the competitive positioning to match the needs of the customers with company capabilities

Marshal all relevant organisational resources to deliver customer satisfaction

Who the customers are is not always obvious. In some circumstances buyers may be different from users or consumers; specifiers and influencers may also be different. Where services are funded, for example, by central government the suppliers may be forgiven for the (mistaken) view that government is their customer.

Customers may expect a degree of benefit from purchasing or using a product or service. They may actually want something more, but believe they have to settle for second best because of budget or other constraints. The organisation that can give customers something closer to what they want than what they expect has an opportunity to go beyond customer satisfaction and create 'customer delight'.

Customer expectations, wants and needs must all be understood and clearly communicated to those responsible for designing the product or service, those responsible for creating or producing it, and those responsible for delivering it. Identifying what customers require is discussed in Chapter 4.

1.5.2 Deciding on the competitive positioning to be adopted

Recognising that markets are heterogeneous and typically made up of various market segments each having different requirements from essentially similar offerings leads to the need to decide clearly which target market or markets the organisation will seek to serve.

That decision is made on the basis of two main sets of factors: first, how attractive the alternative potential targets are; and second, how well the company can hope to serve each potential target relative to the competition. In other words, the relative strengths or competencies it can bring into play in serving the market. These two related issues are discussed at length in Part 4.

1.5.3 Implementing the marketing strategy

The third key task of marketing is to marshal all the relevant organisational resources to plan and execute the delivery of customer satisfaction. This involves ensuring that all members of the organisation are coordinated in their efforts to satisfy customers, and that no actual or potential gaps exist between offer design, production and delivery.

In the field of services marketing there has been a great deal of work aimed at identifying the factors that can create gaps in the process from design through to delivery of offer to customers. Parasuraman *et al.* (1985), for example, have studied each of the potential gaps and concluded that a central role of marketing is to guide design so as to minimise the gaps and hence help to ensure customer satisfaction through the delivery of high quality (fit for the purpose) services (see Chapter 14).

Chapters 15, 16 and 17 address implementation and coordination issues more fully.

Summary

This chapter has sought to review the marketing concept and demonstrate its importance in providing a guiding approach to doing business in the face of increasingly competitive and less predictable marketing environments. This approach we term market-led strategic management. A number of marketing principles were discussed, together with the role of marketing in strategic management. The remainder of Part 1 presents a framework for developing a market-led approach.

Psion Case study

Laurie Knight

Over the past 20 years Psion has had more than a few difficult moments when it has questioned its future as a maker of handheld electronic organisers.

It could innovate its way out of trouble but now it has admitted the handheld market has changed

too much and even innovation will not save it. What matters is not differentiation but scale.

For David Levin, the cerebral chief executive of Psion, one of the most telling signs of change was a recent advertisement by Dixons, the retail group, designed for the Nokia 9210, a new smartphone product: 'The advert described the Nokia as having all the functionality of a Psion organiser and a phone, too. It indicated in stark relief the issues for us.'

Psion faced a dilemma. It lacked the scale to compete with cut-throat global rivals, such as Palm, Handspring of the US or Sony, for cheaper organisers that were becoming commodity items.

However, it saw the high-end organiser market was being invaded by a new generation of smartphones – phones with organiser capabilities built in.

'We knew the standalone organiser had a finite lifespan,' Mr Levin said. 'Our route forward was to create a connected device. That is why we did a strategic deal with Motorola, to penetrate the market for integrated devices.' However, that fell through in January, when Motorola pulled the plug as part of a cost-cutting agenda.

'We spent the last five months going through every option to see what other ways there were to preserve that strategic thrust,' says Mr Levin.

Those efforts coincided with excess capacity. Rivals such as Palm of the US have huge warehouses of unsold organisers.

Palm recently wrote off about $300m, representing more than 5m unsold units. Handspring has done the same. Prices have dived. Faced with that deteriorating scenario, Mr Levin said, 'It would have been commercially naive to press on.'

The decision to pull out is costly – both financially and emotionally. Psion will take a £29m restructuring charge, of which £10m is a cash charge. The exceptional costs include £3m related to 250 redundancies, and about £15m for inventory write-downs, representing about 20,000–30,000 unsold devices.

Even though it will stop making handheld organisers, Psion intends to keep exploiting the intellectual property it has gleaned from more than 20 years of producing them.

Mr Levin said existing products, such as the Psion Revo, would continue to be sold, but admitted: 'We do not expect them to be a big seller by Christmas 2002.'

So what will be left of Psion after restructuring?

The answer is twofold. It retains its 28 per cent stake in Symbian, the consortium that controls Epoc, the operating system for wireless devices. For many investors that stake has long been a good reason to hold Psion shares. Hopes remain that Epoc will be the operating system of choice for the next generation of mobile phones. But Psion's core business – as even Mr Levin admits – is in a less sexy area than consumer electronics, selling services and gadgets for the enterprise wireless market.

'The industrial wireless market does not hit those buttons, but it does in terms of making money,' says Mr Levin.

Psion said underlying revenue growth in this market was in the high teens – low when compared with the 40 per cent growth Psion had last year for its handheld devices – but solid.

This enterprise business was bolstered by the acquisition last year of Teklogix, a Canadian company, which already provides the bulk of Psion's revenues.

Provisional revenues from the combined enterprise division would be £63m in the first half of 2001, against £36m from Psion Digital, which includes handheld sales. However, the move into wireless enterprise, although less risky than staying in the consumer market, is not without hazard. Psion said Teklogix had grown in line with expectations until June. Then, it was hit by the slowdown in IT spending in the US.

Although there have been few signs of that slowdown spreading to Europe, Psion believes European demand could see a 'similar slowdown to those in North America during the second half'. Mr Levin, though, has few doubts the prospects in enterprise are far better than Psion's chances in the consumer market.

Source: Caroline Daniel, 'Psion opts to close its future in handheld organisers', *Financial Times*, 12 July 2001, p. 18.

Discussion questions

1 Evaluate and comment on Psion's market orientation using the market orientation assessment form (Box 1.1).

2 Based on a resource-based view of marketing, what best describes Psion's stance in the market and to what extent is their current dilemma a result of that stance?

3 Should Psion become more market oriented? What would they need to do to become more market oriented?

Strategic marketing planning

2

Strategy is the matching of the activities of an organisation to the environment in which it operates and to its own resource capabilities.

Johnson and Scholes (1988)

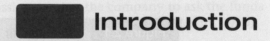

Introduction

The essence of developing a marketing strategy for a company is to ensure that the company's capabilities are matched to the competitive market environment in which it operates, not just for today but into the foreseeable future. For a commercial organisation this means ensuring that its resources and capabilities match the needs and requirements of the markets in which it operates. For a non-commercial organisation, such as a charity or a public utility, it means achieving a fit between its abilities to serve and the requirements of the publics or causes it is seeking to serve. At the heart of strategy lies a need to assess critically both the organisation's resource profile (often referred to as its strengths and weaknesses) and the environment it faces (its opportunities and threats).

Strategic planning attempts to answer three basic questions:

Figure 2.2   Components of mission

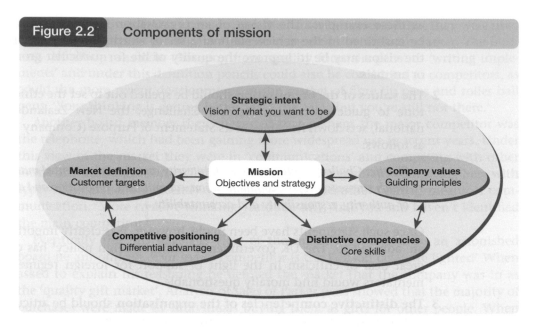

The second question posed at the start of this section – What business do we want to be in? – is often more difficult to answer. It requires a thorough analysis of the options open to the organisation and an understanding of how the world in general, and the company's markets in particular, are changing.

2.2   The marketing strategy process

Once the purpose of the organisation has been defined the marketing strategy can be crafted to help achieve that purpose. We can view the development of marketing strategy at three main levels: the establishment of a core strategy, the creation of the company's competitive positioning, and the implementation of the strategy (see Figure 2.3).

The establishment of an effective marketing strategy starts with a detailed, and creative, assessment both of the company's capabilities – its strengths and weaknesses relative to the competition – and the opportunities and threats posed by the environment. On the basis of this analysis the core strategy of the company will be selected, identifying marketing objectives and the broad focus for achieving them.

At the next level, market targets (both customers and competitors) are selected and/or identified. At the same time the company's differential advantage, or competitive edge, in serving the customer targets better than the competition is defined. Taken together the identification of targets and the definition of differential advantage constitute the creation of the competitive positioning of the organisation and its offerings.

At the implementation level a marketing organisation capable of putting the strategy into practice must be created. The design of the marketing organisation can

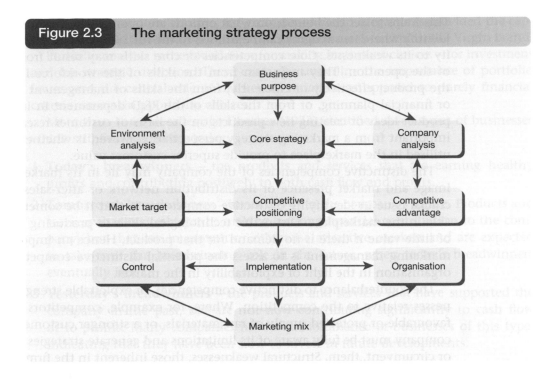

Figure 2.3   The marketing strategy process

be crucial to the success of the strategy. Implementation is also concerned with establishing a mix of products, price, promotion and distribution that can convey both the positioning and the products and services themselves to the target market. Finally, methods of control must be designed to ensure that the strategy implementation is successful. Control concerns both the efficiency with which the strategy is put into operation and the ultimate effectiveness of that strategy. Each of the three main levels of strategy is now considered in more detail.

2.3   Establishing the core strategy

The core strategy is both a statement of the company's objectives and the broad strategies it will use to achieve them. To establish the core strategy requires a detailed analysis of both the resources available and the market in which the organisation will operate, both within the context of achieving the overall business purpose or mission.

2.3.1   Analysis of organisational resources

Any organisation could create a long list of the resources it has at its disposal. Not all of those resources, however, will be equally useful in crafting a marketing strategy. Similarly, if it is honest, any organisation could list many weaknesses, but not all of those will be fatal. In defining the core strategy, organisations attempt to define the distinctive resources (assets and capabilities) that serve to define the organisation.

with, or competitive activity designed to change the balance of power within the market.

A changing world requires constant intelligence gathering on the part of the organisation to ensure that it can keep abreast of customer requirements. Keeping up with technological developments can be particularly important in many markets. The pocket calculator destroyed the slide rule market in the early 1970s and the digital watch caused severe (if temporary) problems for Swiss watch manufacturers in the mid-1970s; now music downloads are leading to the demise of the CD. Changes also occur in customer tastes. Fashions come and go (many of them encouraged by marketers), but in markets where fashion is important keeping up is crucial. Chapter 4 deals in more detail with customer analysis.

The second major type of threat an organisation may face is from its competition. Increasing competition, both from domestic and international sources, is the name of the game in most markets. As competitors become more sophisticated in seeking out market opportunities and designing marketing programmes to exploit them, so the company itself needs to improve its marketing activities. In the United Kingdom many industries have failed or have been unable to respond adequately to increased international competition and have suffered the consequences. It is telling, for example, that in the highly competitive laptop computer market the first sub-3-pound lightweight computers – demanded by business users weary of carrying heavier machines around the world – did not come from existing PC manufacturers, but from Sony leveraging their core competence of making things smaller. In the more sophisticated marketing companies rigorous competitor analysis commands almost as much time as customer and self-evaluation. Substantial effort is geared to identifying competitors' strengths and weaknesses and their likely strategies (see Chapter 5).

2.3.3 SWOT analysis

The above analysis of organisational strengths and weaknesses (essentially an internal focus) can be brought together with the analysis of the market (an external focus) to create a SWOT (strengths, weaknesses, opportunities and threats) analysis (see Figure 2.8).

The purpose of SWOT is twofold. First, it seeks to identify the most significant factors, both internal and external, affecting the organisation and its markets. It provides a quick, executive summary of the key issues. Second, however, by looking at where strengths and weaknesses align with opportunities and threats it can help strategy formulation (see Figure 2.9). The organisation can begin to see where its strengths might be best deployed, both offensively and defensively, as well as where its weaknesses leave it vulnerable to market change or competitor action.

2.3.4 Core strategy

On the basis of the above analysis the company seeks to define the key factors for success (KFS, sometimes termed critical success factors) in its particular markets. Key factors for success in the industry are those factors that are crucial to doing business (see Ohmae, 1982). The KFS are identified through examining the differences between winners and losers, or leaders and also-rans in the industry. They

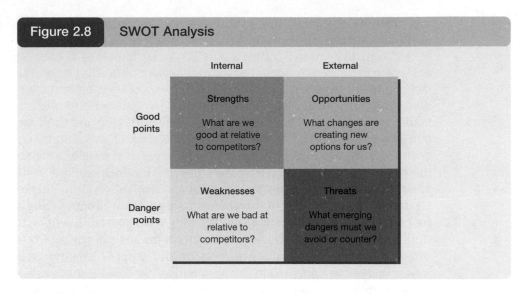

Figure 2.8   SWOT Analysis

	Internal	External
Good points	**Strengths** What are we good at relative to competitors?	**Opportunities** What changes are creating new options for us?
Danger points	**Weaknesses** What are we bad at relative to competitors?	**Threats** What emerging dangers must we avoid or counter?

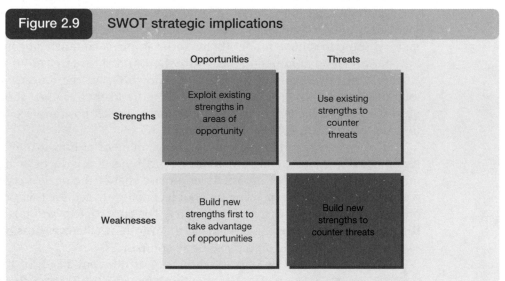

Figure 2.9   SWOT strategic implications

	Opportunities	Threats
Strengths	Exploit existing strengths in areas of opportunity	Use existing strengths to counter threats
Weaknesses	Build new strengths first to take advantage of opportunities	Build new strengths to counter threats

often represent the factors where the greatest leverage can be exerted, i.e. where the most effect can be obtained for a given amount of effort.

In the grocery industry, for example, the KFS can centre on the relationships built up between the manufacturer and the retailer. The power of the major multiples (less than half a dozen major food retail chains now account for around 80 per cent of food sales in the United Kingdom) is such that if a new food product does not obtain distribution through the major outlets a substantial sector of the potential market is denied. In commodity markets the KFS often lie in production process efficiency, enabling costs to be kept down, where pricing is considered the only real means of product differentiation. As Ohmae (1982) points out, for the Japanese elevator business the KFS centre on service – it is essential that breakdown is rectified immediately as the Japanese hate to be stuck in lifts!

A further consideration when setting the core strategy for a multi-product or multi-divisional company is how the various corporate activities add up, i.e. the role in the company's overall business portfolio (see Chapter 6) of each activity.

Having identified corporate capabilities, market opportunities and threats, the key factors for success in the industry in which the firm operates and the role of the particular product or business in the company's overall portfolio, the company sets its marketing objectives. The objectives should be both long and short term. Long-term objectives indicate the future overall destination of the company: its long-term goals. To achieve those long-term goals, however, it is usually necessary to translate them into shorter-term objectives, a series of which will add up to the longer-term goals. Long-term objectives are often set in terms of profit or market domination for a firm operating in the commercial sector. Non-profit-making organisations, too, set long- and short-term goals. The long-term goal of Greenpeace, for example, is to save the world's environment. Shorter-term goals in the mid 2000s centred on single, high-profile campaigns, such as making Apple computer greener, to global issues, such as stopping world climate change.

Often short-term and long-term goals can become confused, and there is always the danger that setting them in isolation can result in a situation where the attainment of the short-term goals does nothing to further the long-term objectives and may, in some instances, hinder them. For example, a commercial company setting long-term market domination goals will often find short-term profit maximisation at odds with this. Many of the managers, however, will be judged on yearly, not long-term, performance, and hence will be more likely to follow short-term profit objectives at the expense of building a stronger market position (see the discussion in Chapter 1 on stakeholder motivations).

The core strategy of the organisation is a statement of how it intends to achieve its objectives. If, for example, the long-term objective is to be market leader in market X, with a share of market at least twice that of the nearest competitors, the core strategy may centre on using superior technology to achieve this, or it may centre on lower prices, or better service or quality. The core strategy will take advantage of the firm's core competencies and bring them to bear wherever possible on the KFS to achieve the corporate objectives of the company.

The core strategy to be pursued may vary at different stages of the product or service's life cycle. Figure 2.10 shows alternative ways in which a company may go about improving the performance of its products or services.

A basic choice is made between attempting to increase sales or improve the level of profitability achieved from existing sales (or even reduced sales in a declining market). When the objectives are to increase sales, again two fundamental approaches may be taken: to expand the total market (most easily, though not exclusively, achieved during the early, growth stages of the life cycle) or to increase share of the existing market (most often pursued during the late growth/maturity phases).

Expand the market

Market expansion can be achieved through attraction of new users to the product or service, identifying new uses for the product or developing new products and services to stimulate the market. New users can be found through geographical expansion of the company's operations (both domestically and internationally).

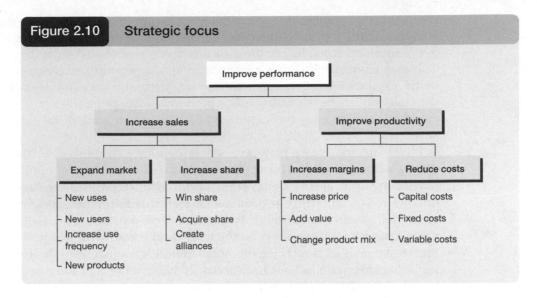

Figure 2.10   Strategic focus

Asda (now owned by Wal-Mart), for example, pursued new customers for its grocery products in its move south from the Yorkshire home base while Sainsbury's attacked new markets in its march north from the south-east. Alternatively, new segments with an existing or latent need for the product may be identifiable. Repositioning Lucozade as a high-energy drink found a new segment for a product once sold exclusively to parents of sick children.

The spectacular growth of the 'no-frills' airlines, easyJet and Ryanair, is founded not simply on taking market share but on growing the market – i.e. 'more people fly more often'. Ryanair, in particular, with its carefully chosen routes where it is the only flyer, has on occasion experienced fourfold traffic growth.

Land-Rover, manufacturer of the Freelander, Discovery and Range Rover brands, aimed to increase the demand for 4 × 4 vehicles by encouraging drivers of other types of car to switch. It first identified those car drivers who were keen on adventure through leaflets and direct mail. This was followed up by a campaign of tele-marketing, direct mail and dealer contact, offering extended test drives without the dealer present. In 12 months the campaign added 80,000 high-quality prospects to the database, and generated 10,000 test drives of which 28 per cent were converted into sales. The company estimates that its investment of just under £1 million has resulted in £100 million worth of extra sales (RoyalMail.com, November 2001).

For some products it may be possible to identify new uses. An example is the use of the condom (largely abandoned as a means of contraceptive for the more popular pill and IUD in the 1960s and 1970s) as a defence against contracting HIV-AIDS. In household cleaners Flash was originally marketed as a product for cleaning floors, but now is also promoted as an all-purpose product for cleaning baths and basins.

Increase share

Increasing market share, especially in mature markets, usually comes at the expense of existing competition. The main routes to increasing share include: winning competitors' customers; merging with (or acquiring) the competitors; or entering into strategic alliances with competitors, suppliers and/or distributors. Winning competitors' customers requires that the company serves them better than the competition. This may come about through identification of competitor weaknesses, or through better exploitation of the company's own strengths and competencies. Each of the elements of the marketing mix – products, price, promotion and distribution – could be used to offer the customer added value, or something extra, to induce switching.

Increasing usage rate may be a viable approach to expanding the market for some products. An advertising campaign for Guinness (the 'Guinnless' campaign devised by the ad agency Ogilvy & Mather) sought to convert irregular users (around one bottle per month) to regular use (at least one bottle per week). Colman's has attempted to encourage more frequent use of mustard, and Hellmann's more varied use of mayonnaise beyond the traditional accompaniment to summer salads. Breakfast cereals are now being promoted as healthy, any time of day snacks or, even, slimming aids (such as Kelloggs' Special K). Lastminute.com has run a 'get 5 a year' campaign aimed at encouraging people to book five holidays a year through them.

The UK children's charity Barnardo's set out in 1999 to increase its share of charitable donations. The £1 million spent on advertising and promotion around the theme 'Giving Children back their Future' was aimed at 35–54-year-olds. Over a six-month period to April 2000 its share of donations went up 66 per cent, while that of other children's charities fell. The core target (35–54-year-old, ABC1 adults with children) rose from 19 per cent of donors to 34 per cent. An associated website attracted over 2,000 visits per week (compared with 700 before the campaign), and a controversial advertisement showing a baby affected by heroin misuse generated an additional £630,000 worth of media coverage (*Marketing Business*, July/August 2001).

Improving profitability

With existing levels, or even reduced levels, of sales, profitability can be improved through improving margins. This is usually achieved through increasing price, reducing costs, or both. In the multi-product firm it may also be possible through weeding of the product line, removing poorly performing products and concentrating effort on the more financially viable. The longer-term positioning implications of this weeding should, however, be carefully considered prior to wielding the axe. It may be, for example, that maintenance of seemingly unprofitable lines is essential to allow the company to continue to operate in the market as a whole or its own specifically chosen niches of that market. They may be viewed as the groundstakes in the strategic game essential to reserve a seat at the competitive table.

2.4 Creation of the competitive positioning

The competitive positioning of the company is a statement of market targets, i.e. where the company will compete, and differential advantage, or how the company will compete. The positioning is developed to achieve the objectives laid down under the core strategy. For a company whose objective is to gain market share and the broad approach to that is to win competitors' customers, for example, the competitive positioning will be a statement of exactly how and where in the market that will be achieved.

2.4.1 Market targets

While the discussion of core strategy required an analysis of customers and competitors to identify potential opportunities and threats, competitive positioning selects those targets most suited to utilising the company's strengths and minimising vulnerability due to weaknesses.

A number of factors should be considered in choosing a market target. Broadly, they fall into two categories: assessing market attractiveness, and evaluating the company's current or potential strengths in serving that market (see Robinson *et al.*, 1978; Porter, 1987).

Market attractiveness is made up of many, often conflicting, factors. Other things being equal, however, a market will generally be more attractive if the following hold:

It is large.

It is growing.

Contribution margins are high.

Competitive intensity and rivalry are low.

There are high entry and low exit barriers.

The market is not vulnerable to uncontrollable events.

Markets that possess all these features do not exist for long, if at all. They are, almost by definition, bound to attract high levels of competition and hence become less attractive to other entrants over time. For small or medium-sized companies small and/or static markets, which do not attract more powerful competitors, may be more appealing. In a market where high entry barriers (such as proprietary technology, high switching costs, etc.) can be erected the company will be better able to defend its position against competitive attack (see Chapter 11).

All markets are vulnerable to some extent to external, uncontrollable factors such as general economic conditions, government legislation or political change. Some markets, however, are more vulnerable than others. This is especially true when selecting among international market alternatives. In the international context one way UK companies assess vulnerability to external political events is through the Department of Trade and Industry's Export Credit Guarantee Department. The department operates the UK's official export credit guarantee agency, helping to arrange finance facilities and credit insurance. Under the scheme advice about the risks involved in entering a particular market is freely available and insurance against default in payments is made available. Recently the scheme has underwritten export business valued at over £2 billion on a yearly basis.

Domestically, the company must weigh the power of various pressure groups in determining market vulnerability. The company's strengths and potential strengths in serving a particular market must be considered relative to customer requirements

long-term market domination, short-term financial performance may suffer. Where managers are rewarded (i.e. promoted or paid more) on the basis of short-term financial performance it is likely that long-term marketing objectives may be sacrificed to short-term profit. In comparing the strategies pursued in a number of UK markets by Japanese firms and their UK competitors, Doyle *et al.* (1986) found that the Japanese were more prepared to take a longer view of market performance, compared with the short-term profit orientation pursued by many of the UK firms.

Recent attention has focused on the development of 'marketing metrics' as a better way of linking marketing activities and financial returns to the business (Ambler, 2000). Ambler reports the most important marketing metrics used by companies:

- relative perceived quality;
- loyalty/retention;
- total number of customers;
- customer satisfaction;
- relative price (market share/volume);
- market share (volume or value);
- perceived quality/esteem;
- complaints (level of dissatisfaction);
- awareness;
- distribution/availability.

Ambler argues that linking marketing to business performance requires that such metrics be reported to top management regularly, compared with forecasts and compared with competitors, with the drivers of buyer behaviour clarified and monitored.

A final important element in implementation is contingency planning, i.e. answering the question: 'What will we do if?' Contingency planning requires a degree of forecasting competitive reaction to the plans developed should they be implemented and then estimation of the likely competitive moves. Forecasting a range of likely futures and making plans to deal with whichever occur is termed scenario planning.

Summary

Strategic marketing planning involves deciding on the core strategy, creating the competitive positioning of both the company and its offerings, and implementing that strategy.

The above is equally true of the one-product firm as it is of the large conglomerate containing many different businesses. For the conglomerate, however, there is an added dimension to planning. That extra dimension consists of portfolio planning, ensuring that the mix of businesses within the total corporation is suitable for achieving overall corporate objectives.

iPhone

Case study

Getty Images News

The throngs of Apple fans who crowded into the Moscone convention centre in San Francisco to hear Steve Jobs give his annual MacWorld keynote address went into the room with high expectations.

Judging by their response their expectations were more than met.

The unveiling of the iPhone, Apple's long-awaited entry into the mobile handset market, was greeted by rapturous applause, gasps of disbelief, and occasional whoops of joy from the Apple faithful.

Six years after Apple transformed the market for digital music players with the introduction of the iPod, the company had attempted a repeat performance in the market for mobile handsets with the iPhone – a slim, sleek handset that relies on an innovative touch-screen interface.

'This thing is amazing,' says Van Baker, an analyst at Gartner, who had a chance to try the iPhone himself during an analyst briefing by Apple. 'It's the biggest home run for them I've seen yet.'

Apple is far from the first company to try to crack the so-called smartphone market. Microsoft, Apple's arch-rival, has been talking about such devices for years, but its mobile windows effort has slumped – in part because mobile carriers were wary of Microsoft and kept out.

Just 6m smart phones were sold in the US last year, compared with more than 1bn mobile handsets sold worldwide.

Two million of them operated on Windows software, with the rest of the market split between Research In Motion, makers of the Blackberry; Palm, maker of the Treo handset; and a handful of others. Shares of RIM fell 7.9 per cent yesterday while Palm stock fell 5.7 per cent.

Charles Golvin, analyst at Forrester, cautions that, even with Apple's impressive device, the market for phones that integrate voice calls, e-mail, web browsing and music will remain a small part of the overall handset market.

Miro Kazakoff, senior associate at Compete, an industry analyst group, says his research shows that 'it's unlikely that any phone, no matter how good, is going to get people to pay a high price and up to $200 in early termination fees on their current contract.'

'Wireless shoppers are hooked on free phones as carriers have subsidized better and better devices over the years.'

Apple is betting that the iPhone's unique user interface – the result of years of research – will reinvent the entire smartphone category, just as the Macintosh redefined computers and just as the iPod redefined what customers came to expect from their digital music players.

'Apple is going to reinvent the phone,' was Mr Jobs' bold pronouncement at MacWorld.

The early signs are encouraging.

Ralph Simon, MEF Americas Chairman Emeritus of the Mobile Entertainment Forum, says that the iPhone represents a 'quantum leap in innovation' for the entertainment industry.

'You can't overlook the strides already made by competitors like Nokia and Motorola, but the seamless marriage of the iPod's kudos to the mobile phone is a key step evolution of the mobile to becoming an all-round entertainment device,' says Mr Simon. With the least expensive iPhone models priced at $499, price remains a concern. 'How many people will be out there willing to pay that kind of premium?' Mr Golvin asks.

However, he says there are some encouraging signs in Motorola's recent experience with the Razr, its ultra-thin premium mobile phone. 'The

Razr is now several years old – they were able to keep their premium prices for quite a while,' Mr Golvin says.

Mr Jobs was keen to signal Apple's intention to become a leading player in consumer electronics yesterday. At the close of his MacWorld speech, he announced the company had decided to drop the word 'computer' from its name now that its brand has spread well beyond the Macintosh to include other devices.

Even the most jaded observers would be hard pressed to deny that, with the iPhone, the newly christened Apple is off to a great start.

Source: Kevin Allison, 'Apple faithful smitten to the core with iPhone', *Financial Times*, 10 January 2007.

Discussion questions

1 What is driving Apple's entry into the mobile phone market?

2 Is the move consistent with Steve Jobs' vision for Apple?

3 What strategic focus does the move signify? What alternatives are open to Apple and how could Apple pursue them?

part two

Competitive Market Analysis

Part 2 examines the analysis of competitive markets in finer detail. This is pursued through the five chapters described below.

Chapter 3 commences with a discussion of the changing market competitive environment facing many firms and organisations in the 2000s. Frameworks such as PEST analysis for analysing change in the broader macro-environment are introduced and strategies for operating in changing markets discussed. The chapter then focuses on the competitive, or industry environment. This begins with a discussion of the Five Forces Model of industry competition and an introduction of the product life cycle, followed by a review of strategic groups and industry evolution. Environmental stability is assessed, together with SPACE analysis. Finally, the Advantage Matrix is reviewed as a means of assessing the key characteristics of an industry when forming strategy.

Chapter 4 considers customer analysis. Information requirements are first discussed, followed by sources of customer information. The variety of marketing research techniques available to aid customer analysis is examined. The discussion then turns to the processes by which customer data are collected and how those data can be turned into information to aid marketing decision making.

Chapter 5 addresses competitor analysis. Following a discussion of competitive benchmarking the dimensions of competitor analysis are discussed, together with techniques for identifying competitor response profiles. The chapter concludes with a review of sources of competitor information.

Chapter 6 is concerned with the internal analysis of an organisation's resources, assets and capabilities that can be leveraged in its target markets. Starting from a broad, resource-based view of the firm and the

identification of its core competencies, the chapter moves to the more detailed issues of auditing resources and itemising specific marketing assets, such as brands, reputation, supply chain strengths and partnerships. The chapter concludes with a framework to build a profile of a company's marketing capabilities.

Chapter 7 looks at methods and techniques for forecasting future demand. These include methods based on current demand, historical analysis of demand patterns and experimentation. Finally, subjective forecasting methods are presented and the various approaches compared to assess their relevance to specific forecasting goals.

chapter three

The changing market environment

3

'The road goes ever on and on, down from the door where it began. Now far ahead the road has gone, and I must follow if I can. Pursuing it with weary feet, until it joins some larger way, Where many paths and errands meet. And whither then? I cannot say.'

Frodo Baggins, in *The Fellowship of the Ring*, by JRR Tolkien

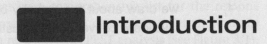 **Introduction**

Of central importance in developing and implementing a robust marketing strategy is awareness of how the environment in which marketing takes place is changing. At its simplest, the marketing environment can be divided into the **competitive environment** (including the company, its immediate competitors and customers) and the **macro-environment** (the wider social, political and economic setting in which organisations operate). Competition between firms to serve customers is the very essence of modern, market-led economies. During the earlier stages of the twentieth century competition is intensifying as firms seek to create competitive advantage in ever more crowded markets and with increasingly demanding customers. This chapter provides a number of tools for understanding the competitive environments in which firms operate and recognising the opportunities and threats they present. It can provide no simple rules for achieving competitive success, but can

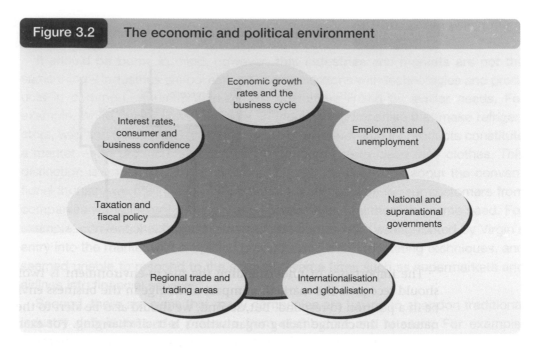

Figure 3.2   The economic and political environment

such as profitability, are now becoming more important. Market choices may be affected radically: Farley (1997) ranks the most attractive international markets for the year 2003 not as the United States or the European marketplace, but as India, China, Brazil, Indonesia and Nigeria.

Figure 3.2 shows a number of key considerations of which firms need to be aware when assessing the political and economic environments in which they operate.

The European Single Market and its enlargement

January 1992 saw the realisation of the dream of many Europeans with the creation of the European Single Market. The Single Market of over 320 million consumers was created to allow the free flow of products and services, people and capital between the member states. As such it was intended to improve economic performance by lowering costs of trading across national borders within the European Union (EU), and to encourage economies of scale of operation rivalling the US internal market. By January 2002 a single European currency, the euro, had been introduced into all but a handful of the EU member states, further facilitating trade and exchange across the old political borders.

In October 2002 a referendum in the Irish Republic paved the way for the enlargement of the European Union through the accession of ten new states: the three Baltic states, Hungary, Poland, the Czech Republic, Slovakia, Cyprus, Malta and Slovenia. That enlargement will have significant implications for many organisations, both commercial and non-commercial, as Europe expands. The population of the European Union will rise by around 20 per cent while GDP will rise by only 5 per cent (Fishburn and Green, 2002). Significant differences in labour costs, for example, are likely to raise questions of location for many firms. In 1992 hourly labour costs were £1.60 in Hungary compared with £14 in Germany.

Internationalisation and globalisation

The continuing North–South divide between the rich and poor nations, the developed and the less developed, is accompanied by a growing recognition by raw materials producers of the power they hold over the Western, developed economies. This was sharply demonstrated by the formation of OPEC in the early 1970s and the immediate effect on world energy prices. At that time energy costs soared and other Third World countries with valuable raw materials realised the power their resources gave them.

The 1990s saw dramatic changes in East/West relationships. The dismantling of the Berlin Wall, the liberalisation of the economies of Central Europe (Poland, Hungary, the Czech Republic, Slovakia) and the break-up of the Soviet Union signalled many potential changes in trading patterns.

While the political barriers have been coming down in Europe, there is some concern that the emergence of regional trading blocs ('free trade areas') will have a dramatic impact on the future of free world trade. The European Single Market post-1993, closer economic relations in the Asia–Pacific region (Australia, Singapore, Thailand, South Korea, etc.) and the North American Free Trade Alliance zone (the United States, Canada and Mexico) are emerging as massive internal markets where domestic-based, 'international' trade will become freer.

At the same time, trade between trading blocs or nations outside them may become more restricted. Major trading partners such as the United States and Japan are increasingly entering into bilateral trade deals (e.g. the US–Japan deal on semi-conductors). While most politicians espouse the goals of free international trade (see, for example, Sir Leon Brittan, 1990, EC Competition Commissioner, speaking at the EC/Japan Journalists' Conference), the realities of the 1990s were a concentration of trade within blocs and reduced trade between them.

3.3 The social and cultural environment

Coupled with the changing economic environment has been a continuous change in social attitudes and values (at least in the developed West) that are likely to have important implications for marketing management (see Figure 3.3). Examples include the following.

Demographic change

The Western 'demographic time bomb' has started to have an impact on diverse businesses. With generally better standards of living, life expectancy has increased (across the world, according to Kofi Annan, Secretary-General of the United Nations, average life expectancy has risen by 10 years over the last 30).

The grey market

In the developed West the over-60s age group currently makes up around 20 per cent of the population, and is predicted to rise to nearer one-third by 2050. These 'grey' consumers are relatively rich. The over-50s own around three-quarters of the world's financial assets and control half of the discretionary budget. Perhaps

the company had sales of £320 million, but was issuing repeated profit warnings, and its shares had lost three-quarters of their value in 12 months. The loss-making manufacturing units started to declare redundancies. The death of the founder in 1985 had marked a turning point. The loss of vision for the company at that point was accompanied by losses in most of the following 12 years. Ann Iverson (then chief executive) faced the problem of turning the company around and reclaiming its position with the affluent 35–50-year-old female fashion buyer. City comment-ators pointed to the strength of new competitors such as Ralph Lauren in this core market and concluded that 'Its management must decide what to be, preferably before the money runs out' (*Daily Telegraph*, 1997; Olins, 1997a).

3.5.2 The role of marketing

The role of marketing in the modern corporation has been subject to far-reaching reappraisal (e.g. Webster, 1992). It is possible to argue that the marketing function has a major role to play in keeping the company up to date with changes in its broader environment and the competitive environment. However, the way that role is fulfilled is likely to reflect major forces of change, such as: increasingly sophistic-ated customers; the move from an emphasis on single sales transactions to long-term customer relationships; the role of information technology (IT) in changing how markets and organisations work; and the development of the network organisation consisting of a group of companies collaborating to exploit their core competencies linked together by a mix of strategic alliances, vertical integration and looser partner-ships (Webster, 1994). The implications for how marketing will operate are profound (see Chapter 16).

3.6 New strategies for changing macro-environments

In reaction to the above a number of critical issues are emerging for marketing management and theory.

First, and central to developing a sustainable competitive advantage in rapidly and often unpredictably changing circumstances, is the ability to learn fast and adapt quickly (Dickson, 1992). A major challenge for any organisation is to create the combination of culture and climate to maximise learning (Slater and Narver, 1995).

Slow to change has been the high-street retailer W.H. Smith. Almost every UK high street and rail station has a W.H. Smith retail outlet, selling magazines and newspapers, books, stationery, cassettes/compact discs and videos. Its bookstalls first appeared in 1792, and W.H. Smith had a market value of £1.1 billion in 1997 with 10 million customers a week buying in its stores. However, during the 1980s and 1990s, W.H. Smith's traditional core market was attacked by strong competitors. On the one side there was a growth in specialist retailers such as Dillons, and on the other was a dramatic expansion by the main supermarket groups in selling books, newspapers and music/videos. W.H. Smith had bought its own specialists, such as Dillons and Our Price, but the commercial position of the core retail chain continued to decline. Many of the peripheral businesses were sold by Bill Cockburn, the chief executive who spent the mid-1990s trying to position the company as a 'world-class retailer' before resigning in 1996. Management at the problematic retail chain claim that W.H. Smith is a middle-of-the-market variety chain, serving consumers who are not Dillons customers or Tesco customers. The retail business is struggling to find a role and has been left behind by market change. Some commentators in the city accuse W.H. Smith of smugness. Analysts suggest that the underlying retail concept and trading format has had its day, leaving the business with no credible growth strategy in its core business (Olins, 1997b; Weyer, 1997).

In increasingly demanding, crowded and competitive markets there is no substitute for being market oriented. This does not, however, imply oversophisticated marketing operations and elaborate marketing departments. Staying close to the customer, understanding his or her needs and requirements and marshalling the firm's resources, assets and capabilities to deliver superior value is what counts. Here the resource-based view of the firm (see Hamel and Prahalad, 1994) can add important new insights into achieving the necessary fit between firm and market (Day, 1994a).

The shift from transactions-based marketing to relationship marketing will likely intensify in many markets as firms seek to establish closer bonds with their customers (see Payne, 1995). They will need to realise, however, that for any relationship to last requires benefits on both sides. Too many early attempts at 'relationship building' have been simply mechanisms to buy temporary loyalty. Relationship building will need to become far more sophisticated.

Firms are also increasingly practising 'multi-mode marketing' – pursuing intense relationship-building strategies with some customers, less intense strategies with others and arm's length strategies with yet others, depending on the long-term value of the customer and their requirements.

3.6.1 Marketing strategies

However, to suggest that firms need to develop new strategies as times change may not go far enough. The problem may not just be that we need to develop new strategies, but that we have to develop wholly new approaches to strategy. For example, at the 1997 Academy of Marketing Science conference two leading marketing thinkers (Jag Sheth and David Cravens) spoke of the trends in strategic development that they believe have to be confronted.

Sheth challenged conventional marketing thinking along the following lines:

- **Global positioning**: Sheth urges strategists to think about globalisation and focus on core competencies, instead of thinking about the domestic market and a portfolio of business and brands. He suggests the need for a different approach to delivering shareholder value (see Figure 3.4).

- **The master brand**: Sheth argues that strength comes from a brand identity that links all parts of the business – this is the fundamental strength of Toyota and Honda compared with the dozens of brands operated by General Motors.

- **The integrated enterprise and end-user focus**: the challenge of managing people, processes and infrastructure to deliver value to an end user.

3.7.3   The threat of substitutes

New entrants may use the existing technology of the industry, or they may attempt to revolutionise the market through leapfrogging. Indeed, technological substitution may come from new entrants or from existing firms doing things in new ways. Substitution can increase competitiveness of an industry for a number of reasons:

- **By making existing technologies redundant.** Classic examples include the decimation of the slide rule industry by the advent of pocket calculators, the overtaking of mechanical timepieces by electronic technologies, and the advent of digital television replacing analogue. Where technologies are changing rapidly, competition between firms to stay ahead also tends to be intense.

- **By incremental product improvement.** Even where industries are not revolutionised overnight by step-changes in technology, existing market offerings may become quickly dated. Technological development in the computer industry, for example, proceeds apace, with personal computers becoming out of date almost as soon as they have been shipped! The advent of e-mail as a means of communication has not (yet) made the letter obsolete, but it has had a significant impact on postal services. E-mail is simply a letter posted down the telephone wires rather than in a letterbox.

3.7.4   Bargaining power of suppliers

The balance of power between the members of an industry, its suppliers and its customers can significantly affect the level of competitiveness experienced by all. Where suppliers and/or customers have greater power than the members of the industry competition within the industry for scarce suppliers or scarce customers tends to be more intense. Suppliers tend to have more bargaining power where the following hold:

- **Suppliers are more concentrated than buyers.** Where there are few organisations capable and willing to supply, their power over their buyers tends to be greater. Similarly, where buyers are more fragmented, and purchase in relatively small quantities, their power relative to their suppliers is likely to be low.

- **Costs of switching suppliers are high.** If the supplier provides a key ingredient for the purchaser that is difficult or costly to source elsewhere, their bargaining power is likely to be greater. Where the supplier provides commodity products that can be easily purchased elsewhere, they will have less bargaining power. Welsh sheep farmers, for example, have found that their individual bargaining power with the supermarkets and butchers' chains that sell their meat is low, but when they band together in collectives their power increases.

- **Suppliers' offerings are highly differentiated.** Where suppliers' products are distinct and different, either through tangible differences in standards, features or design, or through less tangible effects such as branding and reputation, they are likely to hold more bargaining power. The power of Intel, for example, as a supplier of computer chips (which are increasingly commodity products) is enhanced through the reputation and branding of Intel among the ultimate customers for computers. This pull-through effect enhances the power of Intel in supplying to computer manufacturers and assemblers.

Intel Inside

Courtesy of Intel

3.7.5 Bargaining power of buyers

The buyers or customers of the output from an industry also exert pressures that can affect the degree of competition within it. Buyers tend to be more powerful in the supply chain where the following is true:

- **They are more concentrated than sellers.** Fewer buyers than sellers, especially where individual buyers account for large volumes of purchases and/or the sellers produce relatively small amounts each, means greater bargaining power for the customer. In grocery retailing, for example, a handful of major multiples command such a large percentage of total sales that they can practically dictate terms to their suppliers.
- **There are readily available alternative sources of supply.** Especially in the supply of commodity products or services, it may be relatively easy for buyers to buy elsewhere.
- **Buyer switching costs are low.** Where the inconvenience or cost of switching suppliers is low, greater power resides with the buyer who can 'shop around' more to get better deals.

3.7.6 Competitiveness drivers

Taken together, these five forces offer a useful framework for assessing the factors likely to drive competition. They also suggest ways in which the players in the industry – current incumbents, suppliers and buyers – might seek to alter the balance of power and improve their own competitive position. We can summarise as follows. Where the following industry characteristics are present, expect greater levels of competition:

There is little differentiation between market offers.

Industry growth rates are low.

High fixed costs need to be recovered.

High supplier switching costs.

Low buyer switching costs.

Low entry barriers.

High exit barriers.

As we shall see later (Chapter 11), one of the most successful ways of countering a highly competitive environment is to differentiate your offering from that of competitors, in a way of value to customers. That creates buyer switching costs, higher entry barriers, and helps create a defensible position in the market irrespective of industry growth rates or costs of supply.

3.8 The product life cycle

The product life cycle (PLC) is an insightful tool into an industry's competitive environment (Cravens, 2006, p. 171) and market dynamics. Its premises are that:

- All products have a limited life span until a better solution to the customer's problems comes along.
- Life cycles of products follow more or less predictable patterns or phases (see Figure 3.6).
- Market conditions, opportunities and challenges vary over the life cycle.
- Strategies need to adapt over the life cycle.

Chapter 12 will address this last point, while each of the four key stages (introduction, growth, maturity and decline) will be introduced here.

Introduction stage

The product is launched into the market and generally sales are slow to pick up because customers and distribution have to be found and convinced. If the product is new to the world (e.g. the first HD DVD player) it will face little or no competition and the company will have a pioneer advantage and appeal to innovators. If it is an addition (e.g. Motorola Razr in the fashion phone market) it will be targeted at a new segment and fit the 'ideal' of that segment better than alternative solutions. The key question here has to do with how quickly competitors will launch a variant. This is normally the stage for build strategies (see Chapter 11).

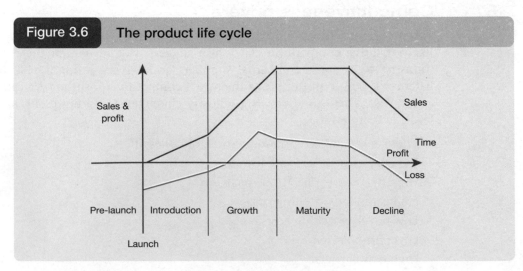

Figure 3.6 The product life cycle

Growth stage

The growth stage is characterised by a rapid increase in sales as the product starts to attract different types of customers and repeat purchases may start. Critically, it is at this stage that competitors assess the product's market and profit potential and decide on their competitive moves. They may decide to modify or improve their current offerings or enter the market with their own new products (e.g. Microsoft Zunes as the 'Ipod killer'). If not, they may use the other elements of the mix to detract attention away from the product, i.e. an advertising campaign or a price promotion. It is possible that defensive attacks may be required to prevent the curve from flattening.

Maturity stage

At this stage the rate of growth slows down significantly. This stage tends to last longer than the previous ones and is, probably, the most challenging one: it is a fact of life for most marketers that the markets they have to deal with are mature! This is a stage of severe competition, market fragmentation and declining profits, due to overcapacity in the industry. Indeed, competitors will try to uncover untapped niches and/or enter price wars. This leads to a clear-out and the weaker competitors will exit, possibly becoming suppliers to the stronger ones or being bought by them (as we are currently seeing in the car industry). The survivors will be either companies supplying the bulk of the market, competing on a high volume–low margin basis, or market nichers. Many firms will try to buck the trend and revamp their PLCs (not always successfully as both KitKat and Barbie experienced after unsuccessfully launching new variants of their products) or expand the market by creating a new segment, and hence extra demand overall, as Swatch did.

Decline stage

This stage is marked by a slow or rapid decline of the sales of the product. Decline may be due to better solutions (e.g. new technology such as the flash pen replacing floppy and zip-disks) supplanting weaker ones, a change in consumer tastes or an increase in competition, be it domestic or international.

3.9 Strategic groups

Within industries a useful basis for analysis can be the strategic group. A strategic group is composed of firms within an industry following similar strategies aimed at similar customers or customer groups. Coca-Cola and Pepsi, for example, form a strategic group in the soft drinks market (Kay, 1993). The identification of strategic groups is fundamental to industry analysis since, just as industries can rise or fall despite the state of the overall business environment, so strategic groups with the distinctive competencies of their members can defy the general fluctuations within an industry.

Indeed, understanding the dynamics of existing strategic groups can be productive to understanding their vulnerability to competitive attack. For example, pursuing the Coca-Cola and Pepsi illustration, these firms compete on the basis of massive advertising spend on image and packaging to position against each other. They will respond to each other's advertising and promotion with anything except one thing – price. Coca-Cola and Pepsi have experienced price wars and they do not like them. This made the big brands highly vulnerable to attack by cheaper substitutes – Sainsbury's own label and Virgin Cola have taken significant market share in the UK market, driven mainly by lower prices.

The separation of strategic groups within a market depends on the barriers to mobility within the industry. For instance, all the companies within the UK ship-building industry tend to compete with each other for high value-added defence contracts, but their lack of cheap labour and resources means that they are not in the same strategic group as the Korean or Japanese suppliers or bulk carriers. Other barriers may be the degree of vertical integration of companies, as in the case of British Gypsum and its source of raw materials for making plasterboard within the United Kingdom, or Boots Pharmaceuticals with its access to the market via Boots retailing chain. At a global level, geopolitical boundaries can also cause differences. For instance, the fragmented buying of the European military and the small production runs that result tend to position European defence contractors in a different strategic group from their US counterparts. Similarly, the differences in technology, reliability and safety standards form barriers between Russian and Western aerospace manufacturers.

As well as the barriers surrounding them, strategic groups also share competitive pressures. Within the US defence industry firms share similar bargaining power with the Pentagon and influence through the political lobbying system. This can help protect them from non-US suppliers, but does not give them an advantage within their home market. The threat from substitutes or new entrants may also provide a unifying theme for strategic groups. Within the computer industry suppliers of low-cost products such as Compaq are facing intense competition from inexpensively manufactured alternatives including desktop, laptop and even palmtop machines. Companies within the higher value-added mainframe businesses are under less threat from low-cost mainframe manufacturers, but are being squeezed by increasingly sophisticated and networked PCs. Finally, strategic groups often share common competitors because they are often competing to fulfil similar market needs using similar technologies.

The map of strategic groups within the US automobile market shows their dynamics (Figure 3.7). The presentation is simplified into two dimensions for ease of discussion but in reality a full analysis may use more. In this case the strategic groups show their clear geographical and historic origins. The Big Three – GM, Ford and Chrysler – remain dominant in supplying a broad range of cars with high local content. In this they retain some technological and styling expertise in the supply of regular and luxury sedans, but until recently had the common basic defence of promoting import restrictions.

Another group is the Faded Champions, which were once the major importers into the US market. Both are European companies whose US ventures have either seen better days, in the case of Volkswagen/Audi, or much better days, in the case of the Rover Group. Once suppliers of a relatively broad range of vehicles, both these companies retreated towards the luxury car sector where they appeared to have little competitive edge. When Rover was acquired (and then rapidly sold off again)

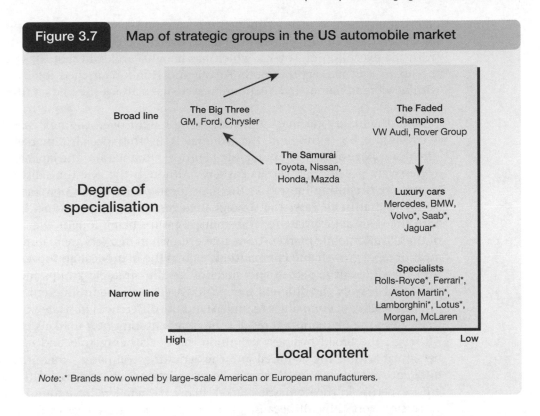

Figure 3.7   Map of strategic groups in the US automobile market

Note: * Brands now owned by large-scale American or European manufacturers.

by the German luxury car manufacturer BMW it reconfirmed its positioning at the cheaper end of the market, complementary to, rather than in direct competition with, the BMW range. The demise of the Faded Champions in the United States is not due to the Big Three, but to the entry of the Samurai into the US market. Initially the quality and low cost of the Japanese strategic group gave them an advantage over the European broad-range suppliers, but now the Japanese are gaining even more power by becoming local manufacturers and therefore overcoming the local content barriers.

High European labour costs have meant that they operate in strategic groups selling high added-value luxury cars or specialist cars, the luxury cars being supplied by relatively large-scale manufacturers with moderately wide product ranges (e.g. the German firm Mercedes-Benz), or specialist manufacturers producing the very expensive, small-volume products (e.g. the British Morgan cars).

The strength of the barriers surrounding the industry is reflected by recent shifts that have taken place. Although the Samurai have never attacked the hard core of the Big Three, they have continued to nibble away at the weaker imports: first the Faded Champions with cheap, reliable family cars and more recently the luxury car makers with the advent of the Lexus and other luxury offerings. Even though they are very large, the Big Three have found it difficult to defend their position by developing their own luxury cars and so have been seeking to defend their flanks against the Samurai by purchasing European manufacturers such as Jaguar, Volvo, Saab, Lamborghini, Aston Martin and Lotus. After years of the Big Three and the Samurai avoiding direct competition, the luxury car market has become the point where the two meet. Although the Samurai have not found it appropriate to purchase European companies in order to overcome entry barriers to those sectors (with the exception of Toyota, which has bought, and sold, Lotus), so distinct are the luxury car markets that both Toyota and Honda launched totally new ranges with new brand names and distribution systems to attack the market (the Acura and the Lexus).

With the luxury car market already being fought over, the next stand-up battle between the Big Three and the Samurai is in the specialist market where the Americans have again been purchasing European brands and the Japanese have been aggressively developing 'Ferrari bashers'. Although the one-time distinct strategic groups are becoming blurred as the main protagonists enter new markets, it is to be noted that in all cases the strategy involves establishing distinct business units with the skills appropriate for the strategic groups being fought over. Examination of the US automobile market shows that even when markets are mature there can be areas of rapid growth and competition, such as the luxury car and specialist markets. And the different expertise and situation of the strategic groups means that the protagonists from the different groups may well compete in different ways.

The inability of companies to understand the differences in strategic groups is one that causes the frequent failures of companies entering new markets by acquisition. Although the broad business definition, products being sold and customers may be similar within the acquired and the acquiring company, where the two are in different strategic groups there can be major misunderstandings. Although having great expertise in the domestic market, many UK retailers have found international expansion very difficult because of the competition they face in the new markets and their failure to understand the strategic groups they are entering. Examples include Boots' acquisition in Canada and Dixons' in the United States where, although their international diversification was into the same industries as those with which they were familiar in the United Kingdom, those skills that allowed them to beat competition within their strategic groups at home did not transfer easily internationally. Were the companies facing the same competition within the European markets it is likely that their ventures would have been more successful. In a sense that is what the Japanese have been doing, as their industries have rolled from country to country across the world, where their major competitors are their own compatriots whom they have faced in many markets in the past.

3.10 Industry evolution and forecasting

The critical issues to be addressed within an industry depend on its evolutionary stage. Porter (1980) discusses the evolution of industries through three main stages: emergence, transformation to maturity and decline (see Figure 3.8). These stages follow in much the same way as products are represented as following more or less identifiable life cycle stages (see O'Shaughnessy, 1995, for a comparison of the product life cycle and Porter's Industry Evolution Model). However, industry evolution is to the product what the product life cycle is to the brand. For example, whereas in the music industry the product life cycle may relate to vinyl records or CDs, industry evolution embraces the transition from cylinders to 78s, 45s, vinyl

Figure 3.8	Industry evolution

Stage	Issues	Strategies
Emergence	Technological uncertainty Commercial uncertainty Customer uncertainty Channel uncertainty	Locate innovators and early adopters Establish standard Reduce switching cost risk Encourage trial
Transition to maturity	Slow growth, falling profits Excess capacity, intense competition Increased customer power Extended product line	Marketing mix marketing Customer retention, segmentation Efficiency focus Coordination
Decline	Substitution by newer technologies Demographic change	Focus or divest

Source: Adapted from O'Shaughnessy (1988).

albums, 8-track cartridges, cassettes, compact discs, digital audio tape and subsequent technologies.

Uncertainty is the salient feature within emerging industries. Recent developments in broadcasting show this most clearly. There is no technological uncertainty about the basic technologies involved in achieving the direct broadcasting of television programmes by cable or satellite, but there are vast uncertainties about the combination of technologies to be used and how they should be paid for. In the early 1980s the discussion was about cable and the terrific opportunities offered for industrial redevelopment by cabling declining UK cities such as Liverpool. In the United States many cable channels emerged, but with no particular standard and with numerous channels that had a short life. In only a few years the vast infrastructure requirements of cable have been replaced by the equally capital-intensive but more elegant solution of satellite television. Even there, however, there is uncertainty about whether to use high-, low- or medium-powered satellites and the means of getting revenue from customers. In the United Kingdom to that brawl has been added uncertainty concerning British regulations, those of the European Union and the activities of the broadcasting channels, which were once the oligopolistic supplier. It is not surprising that with this uncertainty consumers have shown reluctance in adopting the new viewing opportunities open to them.

The high losses that can be associated with the emergent stage of an industry are shown by the losses incurred by the pioneers of the competing technologies in the video industry. Out of three competing video disc and video cassette recording technologies in the mid-1980s only one, VHS, has survived. Two of the losers in that round (Philips with the laser disc and V2000 VCRs, and Sony with the BetaMax format) managed the emergence of laser-based reproduction in the late 1980s and 1990s more carefully. The two industry leaders collaborated in the development of a compact disc (CD) standard and licensed the technology widely in order to accelerate its diffusion and reduce customer uncertainty. With the establishment of a single technology the compact disc was less prone to the software shortages that made video discs so unattractive to customers. Customers still faced potentially high switching costs if they traded in their existing album collection for CDs, but the impact of this was reduced by focusing on segments that were very conscious of hi-fi quality and heavy users. The CD was also capable of being integrated into existing hi-fi systems and quickly became an established part of budget rack systems.

In the transition to maturity uncertainty declines but competition intensifies. Typically the rapid growth, high margins, little competition and apparent size of industries within the late stage of emergence attract many competitors. Those who sought to avoid the uncertainty in the early stages now feel the time is right for them to enter the market. This decision usually coincides with a transition to maturity within a marketplace where competition increases, profits fall, growth slows and capacity is excessive as more producers come on stream. Also, by now a dominant design has typically emerged, and hence competitors are forced to compete on a basis of price or the extended/augmented product. In technological terms, there is a switch to process technology; in marketing terms, a switch from entrepreneurship to the management of the marketing mix; that is, towards efficiency, coupled with the careful identification of market segments with a marketing mix to address them.

Not unexpectedly, companies that fail to notice this transition from entrepreneurial to more bureaucratic management find things difficult. Take, for instance, Sinclair, which was still seeking to differentiate the market in the mid-1980s with the QL microcomputer after the emergence of the IBM PC had established industry standards. Equally, examine the increasing difficulties that Amstrad faced once its entrepreneurial, cost-cutting and channel strategies had been followed by industry leaders such as IBM and Olivetti.

An industry's decline is usually caused by the emergence of a substitute or a demographic shift. Two main strategies are usually appropriate: either divest or focus on the efficient supply of a robust segment. Although the basic options are few, industries often find this decision a difficult one because of the vested interests within the sector declining. It is extraordinary that at this last stage there seem to be more organisational choices about how to implement the basic strategies than at any other stage in an industry's evolution. At a clinical level there can be the decision to divest or milk a company within a declining sector. There is the option of carefully nurturing a long-lasting, lingering target market; or for the entrepreneurial zest of an opportunist who can take advantage of the shifting needs. There is certainly much money to be made in the remnants of industries as AEM, a subsidiary of RTZ, has found. It specialises in aviation engineering and maintenance of products that are no longer the main focus of the leading airframe and aeroengine manufacturers.

Industry evolution shows the violent shifts that occur within an industry as it progresses from stage to stage. Not only do the major issues change, but the management tasks and styles appropriate are equally shifting. Industry evolution also shows that their very success can lead to failure for some firms that do not adapt their approaches and styles to changing conditions. Firms that have been highly successful in entrepreneurial mode during emergence may find it difficult to make the transition to a more bureaucratic way of operating. Similarly, those that have learned to live with stability and maturity may find difficulty managing the business during industry decline where a highly focused, cost-restrained way of operating is appropriate. Understanding the stage of industry evolution is essential if a company is to avoid managing in an environment with which it is unfamiliar, with an inappropriate management style.

3.11 Environmental stability

A limitation of Porter's Industry Evolution Model is the rigid association of technological and marketing uncertainty with only the emerging stage of an industry. This may not be so. For instance, the UK grocery trade has certainly been mature for generations, but the growth of supermarkets and hypermarkets, the removal of retail price maintenance and the move towards out-of-town shopping have meant the market has faced great turbulence, despite its maturity. Ansoff's (1984) theory is that environmental turbulence is fundamental to understanding industries, but it should not be seen as relating only to the early stages of industry life cycle.

A distinction is drawn between marketing and innovation turbulence (Table 3.1). The reason for this is apparent when one considers many industries, such as the automobile industry, where competition has been rapidly changing but for which the competing technologies have changed little. The determinants of environmental turbulence parallel industry evolution in relating uncertainty to the stage of the product life cycle for both marketing and innovation turbulence. However, along with the emerging stage, decline and the transition from stage to stage can spell danger for the unwary company. And in some markets the antecedents of marketing and innovation turbulence are quite different.

Figure 3.9 provides a mechanism for combining two dimensions of turbulence and shows how two strategic groups in the same industry can be facing different environments. Within the UK food retailing trade the environment for the leading grocers, such as Sainsbury's and Tesco, is **developing** in terms of both marketing and innovation. The shift out of town is continuing (though there are signs that concerns for the environmental impact of out-of-town shopping may lead to a slowdown of this trend), as is the move towards larger establishments; but the pattern is well understood, as is the position of the main protagonists within the industry. Similarly, major changes with electronic point of sale (EPOS) and stock control technologies have been absorbed by this sector and are now a well-established part

Table 3.1 Determinants of environmental turbulence

Association of high marketing turbulence	Association of high innovative turbulence
High % of sales spent on marketing	High % of sales spent on R&D
Novel market entrant	Frequent new products in the industry
Very aggressive leading competitor	Short PLCs
Threatening pressure by customers	Novel technologies emerging
Demand outstripping industry capacity	Many competing technologies
Emergence, decline or shifting stage of PLC	Emergence, decline or shifting stage of PLC
Low profitability	Low profitability
High product differentiation	Creativity is a critical success factor
Identification of latent needs a critical success factor	

Figure 3.9	Environmental turbulence

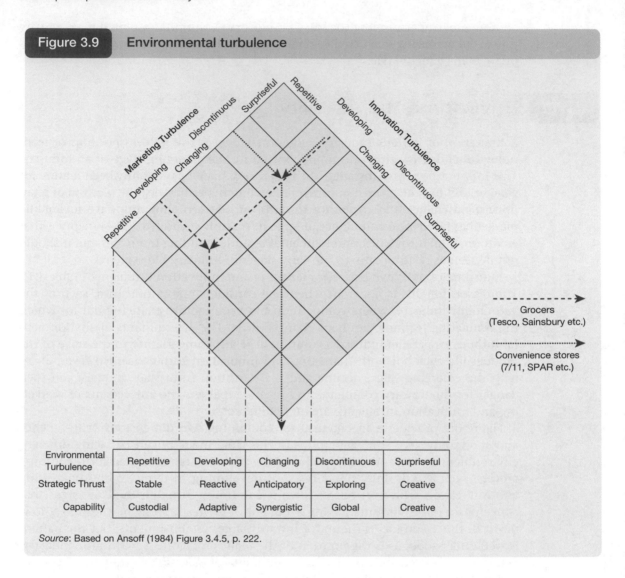

Environmental Turbulence	Repetitive	Developing	Changing	Discontinuous	Surpriseful
Strategic Thrust	Stable	Reactive	Anticipatory	Exploring	Creative
Capability	Custodial	Adaptive	Synergistic	Global	Creative

Source: Based on Ansoff (1984) Figure 3.4.5, p. 222.

of their activities. The intersection of the developing market turbulence and developing innovation turbulence not surprisingly indicates that the overall environmental turbulence is appropriately classified as developing.

The situation of the leading grocers contrasts with the convenience stores, which form another strategic group within the same industry. Although their innovation turbulence is similar to leading grocers, they face **discontinuous marketing** turbulence. This is due to their not yet having faced the shift from in-town to out-of-town shopping, and their existence within the emergent phase of an industry in which many new entrants are appearing. Although in the same industry as the leading grocers the convenience stores, therefore, face **changing environmental** turbulence.

Ansoff draws broad strategic and managerial conclusions from the differences in environmental turbulences that companies face. Whereas, he suggests, the leading retailers see the need to be *reactive* in terms of their strategic thrust and have the ability to adapt, he would suggest that the convenience stores need a more dynamic management style, where they *anticipate* shifts in the environment and look for synergistic opportunities. Within that context the convenience stores have concentrated on a series of goods for which their position is critical, such as alcoholic beverages, milk and soft drinks, which constitutes a very large proportion of their sales. Many have also opened video libraries.

From a marketing point of view there is great importance in correctly assessing environmental turbulence. A firm must try to match its capability to appropriate environments or develop capabilities that fit new ones. The Trustee Savings Bank (TSB) and many other retailing banks in the United Kingdom have shown the dangers of believing their resources can enable them to operate in unfamiliar style. TSB in particular almost epitomised custodial management, where it provided an efficient service in a standard way to a very stable market for a long time. Even more than other banks it meant the company was built around closed systems and operations where there was little need for entrepreneurship. The privatisation of TSB gave it a dangerous combination of a large amount of money and wider opportunities, together with a massively changed banking environment. Two almost inevitable developments have occurred: (a) the bank has shown its inability to manage businesses with a more dynamic environment; and (b) it has found itself unable to work out what to do with its cash mountain. A solution was eventually found in the merger with Lloyds Bank, which could provide the necessary capabilities. Similar examples within the UK financial market are legion, where the very mentality paramount in providing security and correct balances at the end of each trading day left management with completely inappropriate skills to manage modern, fast-moving trading houses. The conversion into banks of some of the leading building societies such as Alliance & Leicester and the Halifax will be watched with interest as they begin to come to terms with very different operating environments.

3.12 SPACE analysis

SPACE (**s**trategic **p**osition and **a**ction **e**valuation) (Rowe *et al.*, 1989) analysis extends environmental analysis beyond the consideration of turbulence to look at industry strength and relates this to the competitive advantage and financial strength of a company. Like Shell's Directional Policy Matrix and other multi-dimensional portfolio planning devices it is a method of summarising a large number of strategic issues on a few dimensions. One of the dimensions is of environmental stability (Table 3.2), which includes many of the facets of environmental turbulence. But with SPACE analysis environmental instability is seen as being counterbalanced by financial strength, a company with high liquidity or access to other reserves being able to withstand environmental volatility.

Industry strength is the second environmental dimension considered. This focuses on attractiveness of the industry in terms of growth potential, profitability and the ability to use its resources efficiently. For a company within the industry these strengths are no virtue unless a company has a competitive advantage. SPACE analysis, therefore, opposes industry strength by competitive advantage (Figure 3.10) to provide a gauge of a company's position relative to the industry.

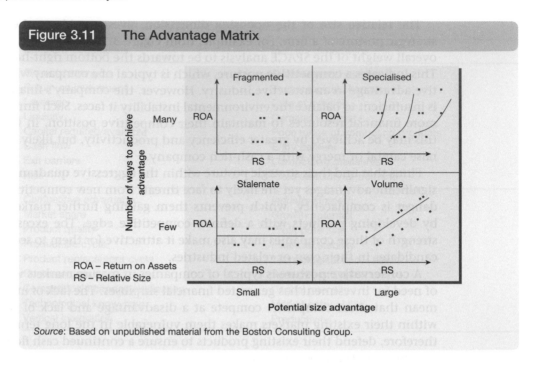

| Figure 3.11 | The Advantage Matrix |

Source: Based on unpublished material from the Boston Consulting Group.

manufacturers are using overseas suppliers, and consumers are well able to compare product with product. Attempts to differentiate the market, as tried by IBM with its PS$_2$, have failed. Therefore competitors are forced to compete mainly on the basis of efficient manufacturing and distribution.

The **volume** quadrant represents markets where the opportunities for differentiation remain few yet where potential size advantages remain great. This has occurred within some of the peripheral markets that support desktop computers. In particular, the printer industry has come to be dominated by Canon, Hewlett-Packard and IBM. The reason for this is the convergence in needs of users of printers and the mass production of the intrinsically mechanical printer units. Unlike microcomputers, where the manufacturing process is one of assembly of basically standard components in a very fixed fashion, as any user of printers will know there are numerous ways of solving the printing and paper-feed problems. This results in an industry where large economies of scale can be achieved by a few dominant suppliers. Where there are markets of this form, battles to achieve volume and economies of scale are paramount. Dominant companies are likely to remain dominant for some time once their cost advantage is achieved, although there is always a threat from a new technology emerging that will destroy the cost advantage they have fought to obtain. In this way Hewlett-Packard joined the band of leaders within the printer market by becoming the industry standard in the newly emerged market for laser printers.

Specialised markets occur when companies within the same market have differing returns on scale. This occurs most conspicuously among suppliers of software for microcomputers. Within the overall market for software there are clear sub-sectors with dominant leaders. It is also apparent that the market leaders, because of their familiarity and proven reliability, are able to charge a price premium. Microsoft

Office, for example, is fast establishing leadership of the integrated office software sector at prices ahead of its major competitors. Within the games sector Atari is less able to command premium prices, although its dominance does mean it is reaping size advantages within its own segments. The result in these specialised markets is therefore a series of experience curves being followed by different companies. Within these specialised markets the most successful companies will be those that dominate one or two segments. Within the market for microcomputer software this has often meant that they will be the companies creating a new generic class of product, as Microsoft achieved with its Windows products – making the IBM PC as user friendly as its Apple Mac rival.

Fragmented markets occur when the market's requirements are less well defined than the stalemate, volume or specialised cases. Several parts of the computer peripheral market conform to this pattern. In contrast to the demand for printers, the specialised users of plotters have a wide variety of requirements and the opportunities for colour and high resolution mean that an unlimited variety of differentiated products can be made. Similarly, in the provision of accounting software, alternative specifications are numerous and therefore many different prices and products coexist in the same market. Where this fragmentation has occurred, success depends on finding niches where particular product specifications are needed. Each niche provides little opportunity for growth; therefore, a company hoping to expand depends on finding a multiplicity of niches where, hopefully, some degree of commonality will allow economies to be achieved.

Summary

Several broad conclusions can now be drawn and their implications for marketing management identified.

First, in many industries the days of fast growth are gone forever. In those where high rates of growth are still possible competition is likely to be increasingly fierce and of an international nature. It is no longer sufficient for companies to become marketing oriented. That is taken for granted. The keys to success will be the effective implementation of the marketing concept through clearly defined positioning strategies.

Second, change creates opportunities for innovative organisations and threats for those who, Cnut-like, attempt to hold it back. It is probable that there will be a redefinition of 'work' and 'leisure', which will provide significant new opportunities to those companies ready and able to seize them. The changing demographic profile, particularly in terms of age, marital status and income distribution, also poses many opportunities for marketing management.

Third, the speed of change in the environment is accelerating, leading to greater complexity and added 'turbulence', or discontinuity. Technological developments are combining to shorten product life cycles and speed up commercialisation times. The increasing turbulence in the market makes it particularly difficult to predict. As a result, planning horizons have been shortened. Where long-range plans in relatively

chapter four

Customer analysis

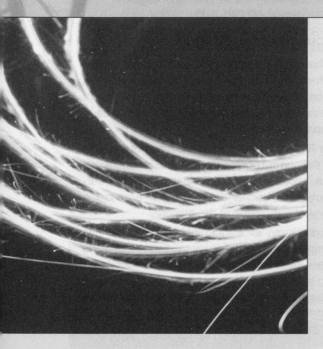

. . . when the future becomes less visible, when the fog descends, the forecasting horizon that you can trust comes closer and closer to your nose. In those circumstances being receptive to new directions becomes important. You need to take account of opportunities and threats and enhance an organisation's responsiveness.

Igor Ansoff, quoted by Hill (1979)

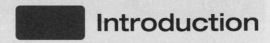

Introduction

Information is the raw material of decision making. Effective marketing decisions are based on sound information; the decisions themselves can be no better than the information on which they are based. Marketing research is concerned with the provision of information that can be used to reduce the level of uncertainty in decision making. Uncertainty can never be eliminated completely in marketing decisions, but by the careful application of tried and tested research techniques it can be reduced.

The first section of this chapter looks at the information needed about customers to make effective marketing decisions. This is followed by a brief discussion of the various research techniques available for collecting data from the marketing environment. The use of these techniques in a typical marketing research study aimed at creatively segmenting a market and identifying current and potential product/ service positions is then discussed. The chapter concludes with a discussion of how marketing-related information can be arranged within an organisation and the development of marketing decision support systems (MDSS).

4.1   What we need to know about customers

Information needed about customers can be broadly grouped into current and future information. The critical issues concerning current customers are: (1) Who are the prime market targets? (2) What gives them value? (3) How can they be brought closer? and (4) How can they be better served?

For the future, however, we also need to know: (1) How will customers and their needs and requirements change? (2) Which new customers should we pursue? and (3) How should we pursue them?

4.1.1   Information on current customers

The starting point is to define who the current customers are. The answer is not always obvious as there may be many actors in the purchase and use of a particular product or service. Customers are not necessarily the same as consumers. A useful way to approach customer definition is to recognise five main roles that exist in many purchasing situations. Often several, or even all, of these roles may be conducted by the same individuals, but recognising each role separately can be a useful step in more accurately targeting marketing activity (see Figure 4.1).

The roles are as follows:

1 **The initiator**: This is the individual (or individuals) who initiates the search for a solution to the customer's problem. In the case of the purchase of a chocolate bar it could be a hungry child who recognises her own need for sustenance. In the case of a supermarket the reordering of a particular line of produce nearing sell-out may be initiated by a stock controller, or even an automatic order processing system.

2 **The influencer**: Influencers are all those individuals who may have some influence on the purchase decision. A child may have initiated the search for a chocolate bar, but the parents may have a strong influence (through holding the purse

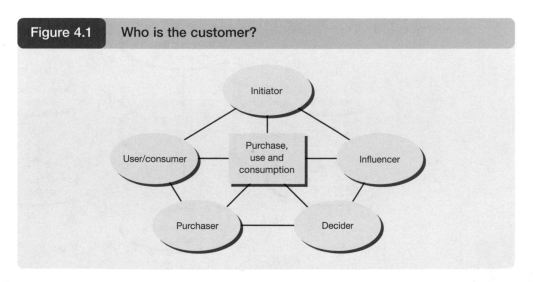

Figure 4.1   Who is the customer?

strings) on which product is actually bought. In the supermarket the ultimate customers will have a strong influence on the brands ordered – the brands they buy or request the store to stock will be most likely to be ordered.

3 **The decider**: Taking into account the views of initiators and influencers some individual will actually make the decision as to which product or service to purchase. This may be back to the initiator or the influencer in the case of the chocolate bar. In the supermarket the decider may be a merchandiser whose task it is to specify which brands to stock, what quantity to order, and so on.

4 **The purchaser**: The purchaser is the individual who actually buys the product or service. He or she is, in effect, the individual that hands over the cash in exchange for the benefits. This may be the child or parent for the chocolate bar. In industrial purchasing it is often a professional buyer who, after taking account of the various influences on the decision, ultimately places the order attempting to get the best value for money possible.

5 **The user**: Finally comes the end user of the product or service, the individual who consumes the offer. For the chocolate bar it will be the child. For the goods in the supermarket it will be the supermarket's customers.

What is important in any buying situation is to have a clear idea of the various actors likely to have an impact on the purchase and consumption decision. Where the various roles are undertaken by different individuals it may be necessary to adopt a different marketing approach to each. Each may be looking for different benefits in the purchase and consumption process. Where different roles are undertaken by the same individuals different approaches may be suitable depending on what stage of the buy/consume process the individual is in at the time (see Figure 4.2).

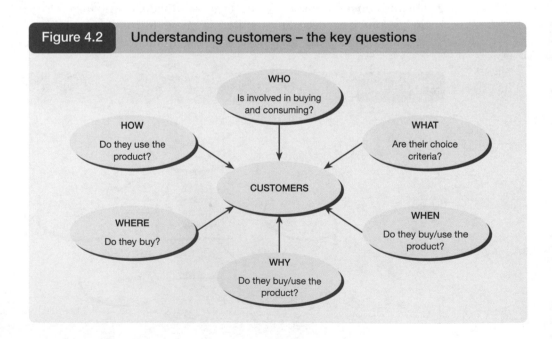

Figure 4.2   Understanding customers – the key questions

A central theme of this book is that most markets are segmented; in other words different identifiable groups of customers require different benefits when buying or using essentially similar products or services. Identifying who the various customers are and what role they play then leads to the question of what gives them value. For each of the above members of a decision-making unit (DMU), different aspects of the purchase and use may give value.

For example, in the child's purchase of a chocolate bar a number of benefits may emerge. The child/initiator/decider/user gets a pleasant sensory experience and a filled stomach. The parent/influencer gets a feeling of having steered the child in the direction of a product that is nutritious and good value for money. In a business purchase, such as a tractor, the users (drivers) may be looking for comfort and ease of operation, the deciders (top management) may be looking for economical performance, while the purchaser (purchasing officer) may be looking for a bulk purchase deal to demonstrate his/her buying efficiency. Clearly the importance of each actor in the decision needs to be assessed and the benefits each gets from the process understood.

Having identified the motivators for each actor attention then shifts to how they can be brought closer to the supplier. Ways of offering increased benefits (better sensory experiences, enhanced nutritional value, better value for money) can be examined. This may involve extending the product service offering through the 'augmented' product (see Levitt, 1986).

For business purchases a major route to bringing customers closer is to develop mutually beneficial alliances that enhance value for both customer and supplier. A characteristic of Japanese businesses is the closeness developed with suppliers so as to ensure continuity of appropriate quality supply of semi-finished material 'just in time' for production purposes.

Better service is at the heart of improving customer relations and making it difficult for customers to go elsewhere. Surveys in the United States have shown that, of lost business, less than 20 per cent is down to poor products and only 20 per cent down to high (relative) prices. The major reason for losing business is predominantly poor service – more than 40 per cent of cases.

4.1.2 Information on future customers

The above issues have been concerned with today's customers. Of importance for the future, however, is how those customers will change. There are two main types of change essential to customer analysis.

The first is changes in existing customers: their wants, needs and expectations. As competition intensifies so the range of offerings open to customers increases. In addition, their experiences with various offers can lead to increased expectations and requirements. A major way of dealing with this type of change is continuous improvement (or the *Kaizen* approach of the Japanese).

In the hi-fi market continuous product improvements, coupled with some significant innovations such as the MP3 player, have served to increase customer expectations of both the quality of sound reproduction and the portability of equipment. A manufacturer still offering the products of the 1980s or even 1990s in the 2000s would soon find its customers deserting in favour of competitors' offerings.

The second type of change comes from new customers emerging as potentially more attractive targets. Segments that may be less attractive at one point in time might become more attractive in the future. As social, cultural and economic change has affected living standards so has it affected the demand for goods and services. There is now, for example, increased demand for healthy or organically grown foods, green energy equipment and services such that markets which might have been less attractive in the 1990s or even the beginning of the 2000s are now booming or starting to grow.

The main ways in which organisations go about analysing their customers is through marketing research (to collect relevant data on them) and market modelling (to make sense of that data). Each is discussed below.

4.2 Marketing research

The use of marketing research services by a variety of organisations, from commercial firms to political parties, has increased dramatically in recent years. The sector is worth more than £500 million annually in the United Kingdom alone. Not only large companies and organisations benefit from marketing research. It is possible, through creative design of research studies, for organisations with smaller budgets to benefit from marketing research studies. Commercial research organisations will conduct studies for clients costing as little as £2,000, depending on the research being undertaken.

The advent of the Internet and the ubiquitous e-mail have opened the way for new marketing research methods and approaches. These are discussed in Chapter 12.

Figure 4.3 shows the range of marketing research activities engaged in by research agencies. In the United Kingdom there are currently over 200 agencies providing research services. Some companies, such as NOP and AGB, offer a wide variety of services. Others specialise in particular types of research (e.g. A.C. Nielsen specialises in retail audits). For a full listing of companies in the United Kingdom providing marketing research services, and where appropriate their specialisations, see the Market Research Society Yearbook. Each type of research is discussed below.

4.2.1 Company records

An obvious, but often under-utilised, starting point for gathering marketing data is through the effective use of the company's own records. Often large amounts of data that can be used to aid marketing decisions (both strategic and tactical) are held in unlikely places within the company (e.g. in the accounts department). Data on factors such as who purchases and how much they purchase may be obtained from invoice records. Similarly purchase records may show customer loyalty patterns, identify gaps in customer purchasing and highlight the most valuable customers.

The value of internally collected data is dependent, however, on how it is collected in the first place. Unfortunately sales data are often not collected or maintained in a form that facilitates use for marketing decision making. As a general rule it is desirable to collect routine data on as detailed a basis as possible to allow for unforeseen data analysis requirements. For example, sales records should be kept by customer,

Figure 4.3   Marketing research methods

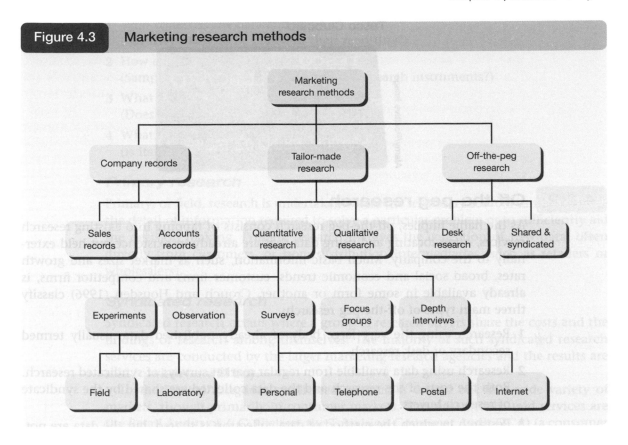

customer type, product, product line, sales territory, salesperson and detailed time period. Data of this type would allow the isolation of profitable and unprofitable customers, territories and product lines, and identify trends in the marketplace.

In direct marketing it is said that the best customer prospects are often existing customers. Adequate sales records should reveal frequencies of purchase, latent and lapsed customers, and may suggest alternative products that could be of interest. In the mail order business, catalogue companies keep records of the types of product customers have bought from them. This enables additional catalogues, more specialist in nature, to be targeted at the most likely prospects.

The British supermarket Tesco is successfully using its loyalty card – Clubcard – to build profiles of its customers so that it can 'generate a map of how an individual thinks, works and, more importantly, shops. The map classifies consumers across 10 categories: wealth, promotions, travel, charities, green, time poor, credit, living style, creature of habit and adventurous' (*The Guardian*, 20 September 2005). Still in the UK, ASDA does not have a loyalty card but still manages to hold a lot of information on how their customers spend their money. For example, the retailer discovered that the purchase of champagne is likely to be accompanied by that of a gift bag: the result is that gift bags are now located next to the champagne in the stores (*The Sunday Times*, 19 December 2004).

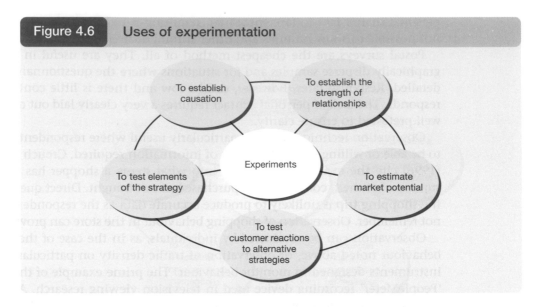

Figure 4.6 Uses of experimentation

syndicated sources and specially commissioned surveys it was estimated that in the
18 months of the test unit sales had increased by 16 per cent over and above what
would have been expected. Both initial purchase and repeat purchase rates were
shown to have increased. The campaign was judged to have turned the negative
(mess) into a positive (delicious morsels of Flake) through the humour of the ads and
was extended on a limited basis to other areas.

Cadbury Flake

Courtesy of Cadbury Trebor Bassett

There have been several recent innovations in test marketing. Full-scale testing,
as described above, suffers from a number of problems. It is costly, time-consuming
and alerts the competition to changes in marketing strategy or new products about
to be launched. As a result there has been an increase in other, smaller-scale testing
methods.

Mini-test markets, such as the Taylor Nelson 'Model Test Market' and the RBL 'Minivan', offer the opportunity to introduce products into the real market on a limited and controlled distribution basis. They are good at estimating initial and repeat purchase rates but poor at evaluating the overall impact of the complete marketing mix.

Simulated supermarket tests make grocery products available in a simulated environment. They can be helpful in estimating trial rates, testing purchase intents created by exposure to test advertisements and testing individual elements of the marketing mix such as packaging, pricing and branding. Supermarket panels, recruited within the shoppers of a particular chain, have their purchases recorded through laser scanning and related to purchase card numbers. These panels can be particularly useful in the limited market testing of new brands.

As with off-the-peg research, the variety of tailor-made research available is very wide. There are a great many market research agencies with varying expertise and skills. While it is still true to say that the majority of expenditure on marketing research comes from the larger, fast-moving consumer goods companies, it is possible for smaller companies to take advantage of the research services and sources available (especially off-the-peg research).

Market research techniques are also increasingly being used to investigate non-commercial problems. Research was used heavily, for example, to investigate drug abuse by young people prior to an advertising campaign designed to tackle the problem. The Oxfam charity has used survey research to help it understand the motivations behind charity donations and to help identify 'prime donor segments'. During the run-up to the 2001 General Election in the United Kingdom both major political parties spent heavily on market and opinion research to gauge the mood of potential voters. Opinion poll results (sponsored by the media and political parties) were published almost daily in the three-week run-up to the election.

In the context of competitive positioning, market research provides the raw data with which it is possible to segment the market creatively and it can help to identify current and potential product positionings. For example, Customer Care Research, which draws on the techniques mentioned above but follows the story of a purchase (a case study), is helping marketers refine their positions in 'job-to-be-done' segments. One such marketer discovered that his milkshakes were not just competing with other milkshakes but also with donuts, bagels, bananas and, more importantly, boredom, and was then able to improve his product to do the job better (see Christensen *et al.*, 2007; also Berstell and Nitterhouse, 2005).

4.3 The marketing research process

A typical segmentation and positioning research project might combine the use of several of the techniques described above to investigate a particular market. Figure 4.7 shows the various stages.

Problem definition

The first step is to define clearly the problem to be tackled. Typically, a series of discussions between marketing research personnel (internal or external to the

resembles the showroom of a Dixons or Circuit City store than the next big thing in domesticity. P&G uses the front room, dominated by a plasma-screen NEC television set, to test consumer responses to websites. The kitchen is a hub of indecision, stuffed with competing Internet machines – although the refrigerator does contain real food.

P&G hopes that the Future Home Lab will reveal consumers' preferences and that the company will be able to discover which gadgets will dominate the household of the future.

In an ideal world, data about consumers would complement an instinct for new products. However, the fear is that, at P&G, information is a substitute for inspiration.

P&G has introduced useful small changes – selling washing powder in tablet form, adding a fancy dispenser to liquid detergent – to keep key brands fresh. Its consumer research lends itself to incremental tweaking.

But other new products from P&G look less nimble. It recently launched a $44 tooth-whitening kit in the US under the Crest brand. Users wear flexible strips on their teeth for an hour a day over two weeks so the peroxide can seep in. A fabric spray that is supposed to release wrinkles from clothes looks equally fiddly and unconvincing.

P&G knows that it takes more than just listening to consumers to generate products that completely redefine a category. The company's recent history sorely lacks a big bang innovation in the mould of Pampers, first test-marketed in Peoria, Illinois, in 1961, or Tide, which was introduced in 1946. The initial sales boost from some of its more promising launches, such as Dryel, has not been sustained.

Moreover, by parading its plans to beef up traditional strengths such as consumer research, P&G is vulnerable to criticism that it is neglecting issues that are more pressing: the need to restore consistent earnings growth while managing huge lay-offs, the inevitable rise of own-label goods in US supermarkets and a perceived weakness in retaining the best female managers.

Burt Flickinger, a former P&G executive, says: 'P&G over-researches instead of concentrating on what is critically important.'

Mr Flickinger, now managing director of Reach Marketing, a consultancy, thinks P&G is 'fiddling, to a certain degree, while Cincinnati is burning'. One sign of the lack of innovation is P&G's recent acquisitions. In the absence of new blockbuster products, the company has been buying growth. The Clairol deal follows the purchase of Iams, the pet food group, in 1999, which followed the purchase of Tambrands, the maker of Tampax, in 1997.

'Growth through acquisition' is a less attractive slogan than 'understanding the consumer of the future', which is perhaps why P&G has been so keen to emphasise its consumer research efforts instead.

The new tools have the potential to pay their way by cutting travel bills, speeding up research projects and generating income from third parties keen to buy the research.

In the longer run, though, there is a threat to the P&G approach. The company's model of research-led product development assumes the continued participation of consumers.

Francis may be keen to allow P&G into his life – but his children, conditioned to be more sceptical of brands and consumption in general, may not.

Source: Adam Jones, 'Consumed by the consumer', *Financial Times*, 23 May 2001.

Discussion questions

1 What type of customer information is Procter & Gamble likely to obtain from the types of customer research mentioned in the case study?

2 Is Procter & Gamble's intensive use of customer research the cause of, or incidental to, the company's failure to develop blockbuster products? Since consumer research is only a means of gathering customer information, how can it stop the firm developing radical innovations?

3 What forms of consumer research could Procter & Gamble use to facilitate new product innovation and how should the information be used?

chapter five

Competitor analysis

> *A horse never runs so fast as when he has other horses to catch up and outpace.*
>
> **Ovid**, The Art of Love, *AD8*

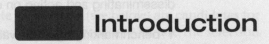

Introduction

Sun Tzu (see Clavell, 1981, for a lucid and readable translation), the great fourth-century BC Chinese general, encapsulated the importance of competitor analysis:

> *If you know your enemy as you know yourself, you need not fear the result of a hundred battles. If you know yourself but not the enemy, for every victory you gain you will suffer a defeat. If you know neither the enemy nor yourself, you will succumb in every battle.*

What was true of war in the fourth century BC is equally true of business today. However, the complexity facing the modern business is that its main competitor, customer and collaborator may be the same company! For example, Kodak and Fuji are intense rivals in the photographic film business, yet in 1996 they collaborated to bring the Advanced Photographic System to market while at the same time

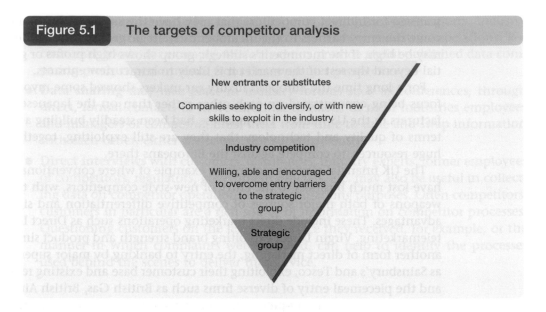

Figure 5.1   The targets of competitor analysis

New entrants or substitutes

Companies seeking to diversify, or with new skills to exploit in the industry

Industry competition

Willing, able and encouraged to overcome entry barriers to the strategic group

Strategic group

Lehmann and Winer (1991) suggest four main stages in competitor analysis (Figure 5.2):

1 **Assessing competitors' current and future objectives**: Understanding what the competitor is setting out to achieve can give clues as to the direction it will take and the aggressiveness with which it will pursue that direction.

2 **Assessing the competitors' current strategies**: By understanding the strategies used by competitors in pursuit of their goals and objectives the firm can identify opportunities and threats arising from competitor actions.

3 **Assessing competitors' resources**: The asset and capability profile of competitors shows what they are currently able to do. Those resources may not be fully deployed at present but can give further clues into how the competitor will move in the future, or how the competitor will react to threats.

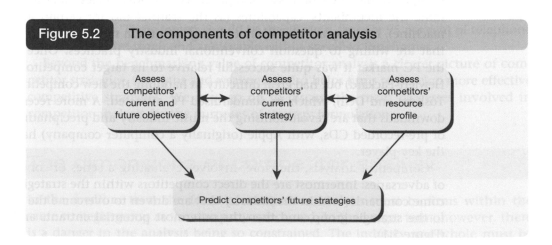

Figure 5.2   The components of competitor analysis

Assess competitors' current and future objectives

Assess competitors' current strategy

Assess competitors' resource profile

Predict competitors' future strategies

4 **Predicting competitors' future strategies**: By combining the above analyses the firm can begin to answer perhaps the most fundamental question in competitor analysis: what is the firm likely to do in the future?

Each of the above is now discussed in detail. In particular, potential sources of information are suggested, together with ways in which the analyses might be conducted. The aim of the analysis is not just to describe the competitor, but to be able to gauge the competitor's future intentions or, more importantly, what the competitor is likely to do in response to the evaluating firm's own actions.

5.2.1 Assessing competitors' current and future objectives

Understanding the goals or objectives of competitors can give guidance to strategy development on three levels (see Figure 5.3). Goals can indicate where the company is intending to develop and in which markets, either by industry or internationally, major initiatives can be expected. The areas of expansion could indicate markets that are to be particularly competitive but may simultaneously signify companies not so committed.

Where the intention is profitable coexistence it is often better to compete in areas that are deemed of secondary interest to major companies rather than to compete directly. Such was the opportunity created when both General Motors and Ford declared that the small car markets in the United States and Europe were intrinsically unprofitable and therefore of little interest to them. Interestingly, both are now actively pursuing this market as its full potential has become fully apparent. Pressures on the environment from automobile pollution and road crowding are leading governments to implement measures to encourage smaller cars with more efficient engines. Ford's initial response in Europe has been the launch of the Ka, a small, fuel-efficient, commuter and family second car. This illustrates that goals change as circumstances change and competitors need to be constantly monitored for shifts in strategic direction.

Goals may also give a guide to the intensity of competitor activity and rivalry. When the likes of Procter & Gamble or General Electric declare that they are only interested in being the number 1 or the strong number 2 in markets in which

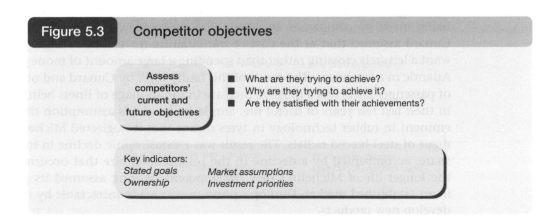

Figure 5.3   Competitor objectives

Assess competitors' current and future objectives

- What are they trying to achieve?
- Why are they trying to achieve it?
- Are they satisfied with their achievements?

Key indicators:
Stated goals
Ownership
Market assumptions
Investment priorities

Analysis of competitor pricing strategies may identify gaps in the market. For example, a firm marketing vodka in the United States noted that the leader offered products at a number of relatively high price points but had left others vacant. This enabled the firm to position its own offerings in a different market sector.

Both the message and the media being used by competitors warrant close analysis. Some competitors may be better than others at exploiting new media such as satellite or cable. Others may be adept at their use of public relations. Again, analysis will show where competitors are strong and where they are vulnerable.

Finally, understanding the distribution strengths and weaknesses of competitors can also identify opportunities. Dell, for example, decided to market its PCs direct to businesses rather than distribute through office retail stores where its established competitors were already strong.

Competitors' marketing organisation

Consideration of organisation is important because of the way that it can dictate strategy. For a long time Procter & Gamble's brand management structure was held up as a marketing ideal. This was probably the case when the US market was dominant and lessons learned there were relatively easily transferred downstream to less developed parts of the world. However, with the United States' relative economic decline compared with the rest of the world, Unilever's more flexible structure allowed them to transfer ideas across boundaries more easily and be more flexible to emerging local needs. Indeed, Procter & Gamble itself has now moved away from its product management structure.

Understanding the competitors' organisational structure can give clues as to how quickly, and in what manner, the competitor is likely to respond to environmental change or competitive actions. Competitors where responsibility for products is clearly identified are often able to respond more quickly than firms where responsibility is vague or confused. Firms organised around markets, rather than products, are most likely to spot market changes early and be in a position to lead change rather than simply react to it.

The position of marketing within the organisational structure can also provide clues to current and future strategy. In many traditional companies marketing is considered merely part of sales, responsible simply for advertising and other promotional activities. In such cases the voice of marketing may not be easily heard at the strategic decision-making level. In still other firms marketing may be seen as a guiding philosophy that will ensure a much more market-responsive set of actions. Clues to the position of marketing may lie in the background of the CEO, the visibility within the firm of senior marketing executives and, indeed, their previous career tracks. The appointment of a new marketing director from fast-moving consumer goods at Madame Tussaud's, the waxworks, signalled a far more customer-responsive and aggressive approach to the marketing of the attraction.

A useful tool for analysing current activities of competitors is the value chain.

Value-chain analysis

Porter (1985) identifies five primary activities that add value to the final output of a company (Figure 5.5).

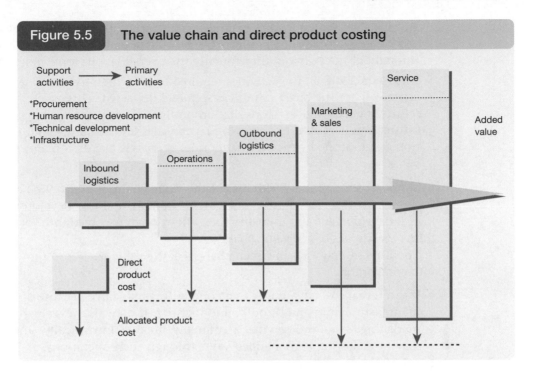

Figure 5.5   The value chain and direct product costing

1 **Inbound logistics** involves managing the flow of products into the company. Recent attention to just-in-time manufacturing has shown how important this can be to the efficient operation of a company and how by management of its suppliers and their quality a company can add to the quality of its final products.

2 **Operations** have long been seen as the central activity of businesses. These comprise the processes whereby the inbound items are changed in form, packaged and tested for suitability for sale. Traditionally this has been seen as the area where value is added to a company's products. At this stage value can be added beyond the normal capital and manpower inputs by the maintenance of high quality, flexibility and design.

3 **Outbound logistics** carry the product from the point of manufacture to the buyer. They therefore include storage, distribution, etc. At this stage value can be added through quick and timely delivery, low damage rates and the formulation of delivery mechanisms that fit the operations of the user. Within the fertiliser industry, for instance, ICI has added value to its products by offering blends that fit the specific needs of farmers at certain times of the year and delivery modularisation which fits the farmers' own systems. Taking it a stage further, deliveries can be taken to the field rather than to the farm or go even as far as spreading being undertaken by the supplier.

4 **Marketing and sales** activities inform buyers about products and services, and provide buyers with a reason to purchase. This can concern feedback, which allows the user company to fit their operation's outbound logistics to user requirements or by helping customers understand the economic value of products that

are available. Taking the ICI example again, part of its marketing activity involves showing how some of its products can be used to equalise the workload on a farm throughout the year and therefore use the overall labour force more efficiently.

5 **Service** includes all the activities required to keep the product or service working effectively for the buyer, after it is sold and delivered. This can involve training, return of goods policies, consultation hotline and other facilities. Since customer satisfaction is central to achieving repeat sales and word-of-mouth communication from satisfied customers, after-sales service is clearly a major part of added value.

In support of the primary activities of the value chain, Porter (1985) also identified support activities. These are procurement, human resource development, technological development and infrastructure. These, of course, feed into each stage of the primary activities of the value chain.

There are several ways in which analysis of the value chain can provide an insight into competitors.

● It can reveal cost advantages that competitors may have because of their efficient manufacture, inbound or outbound logistics. It may also reveal why, with better marketing, sales and service, a company making intrinsically similar products may be achieving higher added value through their operations.

● Many conventionally oriented companies perceive operations as their primary source of added value and therefore leave opportunities for competitors that take a more extended view of the value they can add in the customer's eyes.

● Where the value added is costed effectively it can help locate economical ways of adding value to the customer. There are often numerous ways of achieving this, such as in the efficient management of single sourcing and just-in-time inbound logistics; total quality being incorporated in the operations, thus reducing the service requirements and maybe adding to the appeal of the marketing and sales activity by offering extended warranties; well-targeted marketing and sales activities which assure that maximum perceived added value is communicated to the customer while incurring lower marketing and sales activity than if blanket sales activity was attempted.

A company's assumptions about how its costs are allocated across products and elements of the value chain can provide clear competitive guidelines. For instance, many companies add most of their overheads to manufacturing operations where inputs can usually be measured. This occurs despite products having vastly different inbound logistics, outbound logistics, marketing, sales and service expenditures. The result can be that the final price of the products in the marketplace has little bearing on the overall inputs and the value chain.

Similarly, where the overheads are allocated equally across products, direct product pricing can show where some products are being forced to carry an excessive burden of overheads, so allowing a competitor to enter the market and compete effectively on price. When a company is competing in many different markets it is very likely that its allocated product costs are completely out of line with some of the markets in which it is competing. This can act as an overall constraint upon its intention to support those products or give it little commitment to them. IBM encountered this problem in its PC marketing, where the margins were incapable of carrying the allocated overheads that were borrowed from its mainframe and mini-PC business. This became particularly true in IBM's venture into the home computer market with the 'Peanut', which was launched with a totally inappropriate performance:price ratio.

5.2.3 Assessing competitors' capability profiles

The above discussion has highlighted what the competitor is seeking to achieve and what it is doing now. Also critical, of course, are the degrees of freedom open to the competitor. What might it do in future?

The assessment of a competitor's resources involves looking at their strengths and weaknesses. Whereas a competitor's goals, assumptions and current strategy would influence the likelihood, time, nature and intensity of a competitor's reactions, its resources, assets and capabilities will determine its ability to initiate and sustain moves in response to environmental or competitive changes (see Figure 5.6).

Competitor resource profiles (see Section 5.1 above on benchmarking) can be built in much the same way as a firm conducts an analysis of its own assets and capabilities. A useful starting point is to profile competitors against the key factors for success in the particular industry. Among these could be operational areas (such as research and engineering or financial strength) or generic skills (such as the company's ability to grow, quick response capability, ability to adapt to change, staying power or innovativeness).

Lehmann and Winer (1991) suggest concentrating the analysis under five key competitor abilities.

1 **Ability to conceive and design**: Assessing the ability of a competitor to innovate will help the firm to predict the likelihood of new products being brought to market, or of new technologies being employed to leapfrog existing products. Indications of this type of ability come from assessing technical resources (such as patents and copyrights held), human resources (the calibre of the creative and technical staff employed) and funding (both the total funds available and the proportion devoted to research and development, relative to industry average).

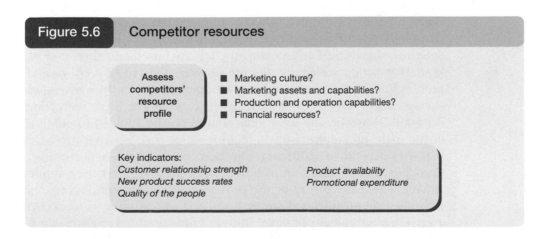

Figure 5.6 Competitor resources

page 129

2 **Ability to produce**: In manufacturing industries this will include production capacity and utilisation, while in service industries capacity to deliver the service will be critical. Firms with slack capacity clearly have more opportunities to respond to increased demand. Similarly, service firms that can manage their resources flexibly by, for example, calling on temporary but sufficiently skilled and motivated staff may enjoy more flexibility than those with a fixed staff with rigid skills. Ability to produce is signalled by physical resources (such as plant and equipment) together with human resources (including the skills and flexibility of the staff employed).

3 **Ability to market**: Despite strong innovation and production abilities a competitor may be relatively weak at marketing its products or services to customers. Assessing marketing capability is best accomplished through examining the elements of the marketing mix. Central to this analysis, however, will be the assessment of the skills of the people involved in sales, marketing, advertising, distribution, and so on. Also important will be the funds available and devoted to marketing activities. How well does the competitor understand the market? The answer to this question may lie in the extent and type of marketing research being undertaken.

4 **Ability to finance**: Financial resources act as a constraint in any organisation. In Hungary, for example, a major constraint on marketing activity for indigenous firms during the transition period of the 1990s was the limited funding available for investment. Many successful Hungarian firms overcame this problem through joint ventures with Western firms seeking entry into the market. The Hungarian firms provided the local market knowledge and contacts while the Western partners provided capital and managerial expertise. Examination of published accounts can reveal liquidity and cash flow characteristics of competitors. Again, however, such hard data should be supplemented with assessments of the qualities and skills of the human resources available within finance.

5 **Ability to manage**: The characteristics of key managers can send clear messages on strategic intentions. Indicators include the previous career paths and actions of powerful managers, the reward systems in place, the degree of autonomy allowed to individual managers, the recruitment and promotions policies of the firm.

Figure 5.7 shows a summary sheet a company has used to assess the relative capability of 'self' against three competitors: A, B and C. In this, six dimensions have been determined as critical and a company has rated itself and three competitors on each key factor using a scale ranging from –2 (very poor) to +2 (very good). The result are profiles that suggest the companies are quite similar in their overall capabilities and average scores, which clearly identify the company on a par with competitors A and B overall. However, the total score should not be allowed to cloud the differences of the main protagonists in the market, since their relative strengths clearly show that they may move in different directions given similar opportunities. For instance, Company A could build on its European strength in marketing applied technology, whereas Company B may be forced to depend on differentiation achieved through technological breadth and strength in R&D to maintain its market position. However, if the technology or market shifts in a direction that requires major expenditures,

Figure 5.7	Competitor capabilities

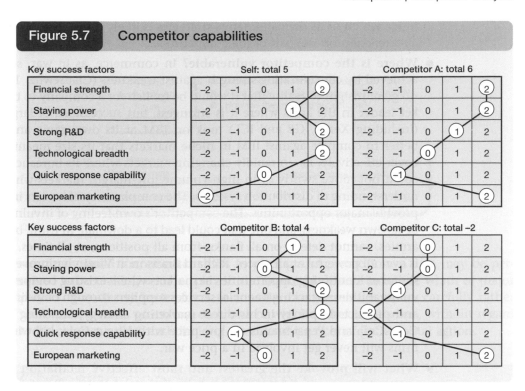

Company B may be weaker compared with A or 'self'. An inspection of the competitive capabilities also suggests that, although Company C looks weak overall, it could be a good acquisition by 'self'. Although weak in the financial and technological areas it has a strong European marketing presence and therefore may be capable of providing 'self' with rapid access to the European markets.

5.2.4 Predicting competitors' future strategies

The ultimate aim of competitor analysis is to determine competitors' response profiles – that is, a guide to how a competitor might behave when faced with various environmental and competitive changes. This covers such questions as the following:

- **Is the competitor satisfied with the current position?** One that is satisfied may allow indirect competitors to exploit new markets without being perturbed. Alternatively, one that is trying to improve its current position may be quick in chasing market changes or be obsessed by improving its own short-term profits performance. A knowledge of a company's future goals will clearly play an important part in answering this question.

- **What likely moves or strategy shifts will the competitor make?** History can provide some guide as to the way that companies behave. Goals, assumptions and capabilities will also give some guidance as to how the company can effectively respond to market changes. After looking at these a company may be able to

The competitively mature company understands the market it is operating in and enhances, rather than destabilises, the environment of the strategic group. The good competitor can help promote the industry's stability by understanding the rules governing the market and by holding realistic assumptions about the industry and its own relative position. In this way it is unlikely to embark on strategies that are unprofitable and which result in zero-sum competition, such as precipitating price wars or unprofitable practices. Among the UK clearing banks in the late 1980s both Midland and Lloyds introduced interest-bearing current accounts. This gave them a short-term competitive edge but, once the market leaders followed, the result was everyone losing money on this major part of their business. Once locked in it was difficult for any of the banks to extricate themselves from this self-defeating position.

A good competitor can support industry structure if it invests in developing its own product and enhancing quality differentiation and market development rather than confrontational price-cutting or promotional strategies. In that way barriers to entering the industry are enhanced because the market becomes relatively fragmented and the impact of one company or new entrant is diminished. The global pharmaceutical industry tends to have this structure, where legislation and the differentiation of drugs allow a large number of medium-sized companies to survive in many of the world's leading markets.

A further advantage of a competitively mature company is that it can provide a steady pressure towards the efficient operations of those with which it is competing. It can provide respectability and standards in the way that IBM did in the PC market, and ensure that the market does not become too comfortable for the incumbents. The danger, then, as many state monopoly industries have shown, is that once the protection is removed, or competition is allowed, they find themselves too weak, fat or rigid to change. Pressure increases when the leading competitor has a thorough understanding of industry costs and therefore sets standards for cost-efficient services.

Finally, the existence of the credible and viable large company within the strategic group can act as a deterrent to other entrants. A good competitor, therefore, can provide both pressure to keep its competitors lean and an umbrella under which the industry can develop steadily.

A good competitor is a company that has a clear understanding of its own weaknesses and therefore leaves opportunities for others in the market. Within the UK banking market after the 'Big Bang' there was clearly a shortage of good competitors when, once the market was deregulated, many clearing banks acquired diverse activities and offered excessive salaries in areas they did not understand. The result was over-capacity, collapsing profits and a weakening of the UK banking industry generally. A wiser competitor would have been more aware of its strengths and weaknesses and would have avoided ventures that would not only weaken its profitability but also damage the market generally. In that sense a company with a limited strategic concept or a clear idea of the business it is in is a better competitor than one with wider or more vague statements about its intent.

A good competitor will have reconcilable goals that make it comfortable within the market it operates, less likely to make massive strategic shifts and tolerant of moderate intrusion. Where its strategic stake is moderate a good competitor may not see market dominance or the maintenance of its own market position as a principal objective. If under pressure it may be willing to retreat from the market or, when faced with greater opportunities, may choose to grow elsewhere.

Moderation in desired profitability is also an advantageous characteristic of a competitor. If driven by the need to increase the returns it is obtaining, the industry's ability is likely to be disturbed by major investments in new products, promotional activity or price cutting. A company that accepts its current profitability will be a seeker of stability rather than of new opportunities.

The desire of a competitor to maintain its cash flow can have a further impact on promoting an industry's stability. Most ventures that involve destabilising an industry depend on investing in research and development, marketing and/or construction of new cost-cutting plant. A company with strict cash requirements is therefore less likely to embark on such costly ventures.

The reconcilable goals of a good competitor can also provide a beneficial, steady pressure on the other companies within the industry. If a competitor has comparable return on investment targets to its stakeholders, it will face similar competitive pressures to the rest of the industry. In contrast, a state-owned competitor, which does not face the same profitability requirements, or one that is funded from markets with different expectations from one's own, can be unhealthy. Within the European Union the British Steel Corporation for a long time faced a regulated market against European competitors that were heavily subsidised by their respective state governments. Rather than competing with these, however, it chose to concentrate on speciality steels where the competitors were often in the private sector and therefore faced similar expectations. In a global context, many firms have found it very difficult competing with the Japanese, who have a lower cost of money from their home stock market, which is also less volatile and responsive to short-term changes than its Western counterparts.

A feature of many Western companies that made them good competitors for the Japanese has been their short time-horizon. This means that when faced with adversity the Western companies that the Japanese face have often cut back investment to maintain short-term profitability or have taken a fast route to corporate success rather than investing for internal growth. In the UK market for dried milk products Cadbury found Carnation a particularly attractive competitor, because its US owners were seeking a quick return on their investment while Cadbury, which had a longer-term commitment to the market, was willing to invest to gain market share. Risk aversion can also lead to a competitor's being more attractive. Where there is a fear of making errors there are likely to be followers within an industry, which gives more agile companies a chance to gain an advantage when the technology or market changes.

Clearly, finding a market in which the competitors are good on all fronts is unlikely, just as it is impossible to find a market that is completely attractive and consistent with a company's own strengths. But by examining competitors and looking for markets where they tend to be good rather than wayward a company is likely to face a more stable environment and one in which opportunities are there to be taken.

The diversity of competition makes it difficult to draw generic classes of companies that are likely to be good competitors. Some groups can be identified as likely to be the good or bad competitors but, in all these cases, there are likely to be many exceptions to the rule. Porter (1985) identifies smaller divisions of diversified firms as one likely group of good competitors. These may not be viewed as essential to the long-term corporate strategy and they often face tough profitability targets. In a global sense, this is particularly true of US multinationals, which have shown a remarkable willingness to retreat home when faced with adversity. They are also often given particularly tough profitability objectives with little support or understanding in the overseas market. Part of this stems from the belief that what is good enough for the home market is good enough for the overseas subsidiaries, and that all the major lessons can be learned at home (Wright *et al.*, 1990).

Another group of potentially good competitors can be old-established companies with a dynastic interest in the industry. This can be because the companies are strong and set high standards but are careful (as in the case of Sainsbury's in the United Kingdom) or because they are moderate in their expectations (as many UK textile companies have been).

Among groups that are more difficult to compete with, and hence not 'good competitors' for the incumbent firm, could be new entrants from other industries that break the mould of established competition in the markets. They could also be new entrants in a market that have made major investments and therefore have a large stake in terms of ego and money in making a venture a success. By not understanding, or not choosing to understand, the market they may destabilise competition and be willing to forgo profits for a long time. Amazon.com was not a good firm for Barnes & Noble to compete with when it first entered the book retailing market. These can be very large companies at times, such as Unilever in the US market, which has a number 3 position in terms of household products and a desperation to grow in order to become viable; or Japanese automobile companies in Europe and the United States that have been building industrial capacity which requires their taking a huge market share in both continents. To the incumbents these are bad competitors.

Of course, the issue here is not good or bad from an ethical point of view. They are just bad competitors to compete with, although the new standards they bring to an industry and the services they provide to the consumer can do great good to the consumers and the economies concerned. Moreover they *are* good at competing, just not good to be competing against. Marc Andreessen, founder of Netscape (the Internet's first commercial browser) is reported to have said: 'Everyone should be in a business once in their lives that competes with Microsoft, just for the experience.' He added that once was enough though (*The Economist*, 9 March 2002).

5.4 Obtaining and disseminating competitive information

The inability of commanders to obtain and use military intelligence is one of the major reasons for displays of military incompetence (Dixon, 1976). The same is true of competitive intelligence. Also, given the competitive nature of both war and commerce, it is not surprising that the means of gathering information on an enemy or the competition are similar in both method and ethics. And, in both cases, the legality of methods has not been a barrier to their use. The final section of this

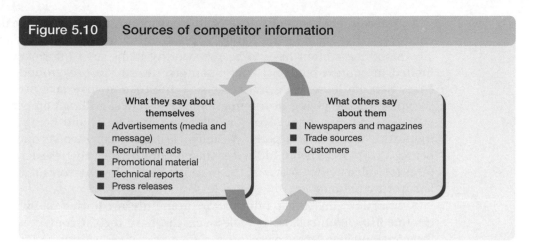

Figure 5.10 Sources of competitor information

What they say about themselves
- Advertisements (media and message)
- Recruitment ads
- Promotional material
- Technical reports
- Press releases

What others say about them
- Newspapers and magazines
- Trade sources
- Customers

chapter draws together the alternative means of gathering competitive information (see Figure 5.10). In doing so it follows a sequence of declining morality, but seeks to make no judgement about the ethics of many approaches mentioned.

At the most basic level a company can collect **published statistical information** on competitors and markets. Many companies will have such information on their records from market studies or from published sources on public companies. A problem with many of these sources is their disaggregation and the frequent inconsistency between various government statistics and those provided by a range of market research companies. Some of this is due to sampling problems, particularly in some government statistics, such as Business Monitors, where the respondents are little controlled. Although factual and quantitative, this sort of information is limited by its historic basis. Increasingly, use of the Internet can provide much background information. Search engines such as Yahoo and Hotbot allow investigators to rapidly search very wide sources to obtain up-to-date information on competitors and markets.

A company's own **publicity material** such as brochures, corporate magazines and websites can also be a source of useful background information. Sales brochures show the range of products on offer, and sometimes include price lists, while websites often give more insight into the strategies and philosophies of firms. Typically designed with customers or employees in mind, these publications need critical scrutiny but can be a mine of useful background information.

A company's own **propaganda** – in other words, its public relations activities – can add texture to background statistical information. The need to communicate to shareholders and intermediaries in markets means that frequent marketing or technological initiatives are broadcast widely. A danger here, clearly, is the credibility of the public relations involvement of the competitors. Investigative journalism can lead to more open disclosures but here again usually the press is dependent on the goodwill of a company in providing information. Nevertheless such sources can give a splendid feel for a company's senior executives. In that light it can be akin to the information that great generals try to gather on each other.

An increasingly frequent source of information on a company is **leakages** from employees that get into the hands of press, either intentionally or unintentionally. Since these often have to be newsworthy items such information is usually limited in context but, once again, can give texture to background information. Firms that are more aggressive seekers of information may take positive steps in precipitating the giving of information: for instance, grilling competitors' people at trade shows or conferences, or following plant tours and being a particularly inquisitive member of a party. Although leakages may involve one of the competitor's employees being indiscreet they do not involve the researching company in unethical activities. Many of the practices that follow hereon may be deemed as less worthy by some.

A company can gather information from **intermediaries** or by posing as an intermediary. Both customers and buyers can have regular contact with competitive companies and can often be a source of valuable information, particularly with the salespeople or buyers from a researching company with whom they have regular contact. It is also possible to pose as a potential buyer, particularly over the phone, to obtain some factual information, such as price, or to obtain performance literature.

Many industries have policies of not recruiting between major companies or, as in the United States, have regulations regarding the nature of an individual's work after he or she has moved from one company to another. However, a company would be naive if it did not thoroughly debrief **competitors' former employees** if they did join the company and, where there is a strong market leader, it is very frequent for that company's employees to be regularly recruited by smaller companies. For a long time in the United Kingdom Procter & Gamble and Unilever, for instance, have been a training ground for marketing people in many other industries. When they move they carry with them a great deal of useful information on their previous employers' products, methods and strategies. Many such large employers are very aware of this and often request that people who are leaving clear their desks and leave within minutes once their intention to move is known. Even if competitors' employees are not eventually recruited the interviewing process itself can often provide useful information, particularly since the person being interviewed may be eager to impress the potential employer.

Surveillance is widely used within counter-espionage, but is less common as a means of gathering competitive business information. Some of the methods used can be quite innocuous, such as monitoring competitors' employee advertisements or studying aerial photographs. Others are very sensible business practices, such as reverse engineering, i.e. tearing apart the competitors' products for analysis. Less acceptable, and certainly less hygienic, is the possibility of buying a competitor's garbage to sift for useful memoranda or components. Bugging is a controversial means of surveillance that is becoming more common now equipment is inexpensive, reliable and small enough to be concealed. Not only were Richard Nixon's presidential campaign organisers found using this method, but also the retailer Dixons, during their acquisition of Currys.

Dirty tricks have always been a danger of test marketing, but with the current availability of mini-test markets (Saunders *et al.*, 1987) a new dimension has emerged.

Their speed means that while a company is test marketing its products over a matter of months a competitor can buy supplies, put them through a mini-test market, find their market appeal and maybe experiment with alternative defensive strategies, before the test-marketed product is launched fully. Unilever's subsidiary Van den Bergh is reputed to have done just this when Kraft launched its Carousel margarine. Using mini-test markets it was able to find that, although the Kraft product had a high trial rate, few people adopted it in the long term and therefore it was of no great danger to Unilever's leading products.

A final means of gathering information is the use of **double agents**, either placed in a competitor's company purposely or recruited on to the payroll while still working for the competitor. One can easily imagine how invaluable such people could be over the long term. We know that such individuals are common within military espionage, although few examples have come to light in business circles. One wonders how many leading companies would be willing to admit that they have been penetrated, even if a double agent was found within them.

Disseminating competitor intelligence

Intelligence itself is an essentially valueless commodity. It becomes valuable only when it researches the right people within the organisation and is subsequently acted on. Successful dissemination requires two things. First, the destination must be clearly identified. Basically the question is: Who needs to know this? Second, the data must be presented in a manner that the recipient can understand and assimilate. Too many competitive intelligence reports, such as market research reports, are far too detailed and cumbersome for busy executives to extract and use the relevant information.

Bernhardt (1993) suggests the use of a hierarchical approach to dissemination. For senior management (including CEOs and strategy formulation groups) intelligence should be limited to that which is of high strategic value. There is little point burdening top managers with the minutiae of everyday operations. Indeed, too much operational detail in their menu of intelligence may mask the really important issues they need to act on.

Information to senior managers should include special intelligence briefings, typically one- or two-page reports identifying and summarising specific issues and showing where more detailed information can be obtained. Senior managers may also require regular (monthly or quarterly depending on the rate of change in the industry and market) intelligence briefings, which address regularly occurring issues systematically, so that trends can be identified and priorities made.

Middle and junior managers at a more operational level may require more detailed information to enable them to formulate tactical decisions. Here, more detailed profiles of competitor products and services will be required, together with detailed analysis of competitor marketing mix strategies. Increasingly, middle management (where it has survived the downsizing of the 1990s!) is becoming conversant with database manipulation, enabling managers to directly interrogate intelligence data rather than simply relying on information specialists to extract and present relevant information (see Fletcher, 1996).

Summary

Over the last few years competitive strategy has emerged as one of the major foundations of business strategy. Just as understanding markets is fundamental to business success, so is a complete understanding of competitors, their strengths, weaknesses and likely responses. This chapter suggests that the focus of competitor analysis should be on strategic groups, but should not neglect other firms within the industry with the ability to overcome entry barriers or be potential entrants to the industry. It provides some frameworks for analysing competitors and suggests the importance of thinking through their likely responses. It also suggests that when entering markets and instituting strategies firms should be looking for 'good' competitors that can stabilise markets, provide opportunities and apply downward pressure on performance. Finally, means of gathering and disseminating competitive information are presented. Ultimately the goal is to learn from competitors – their successes and their mistakes – as well as working out how to compete more effectively (Figure 5.11).

Although as important as market information, data on competitors are rarely gathered systematically or comprehensively. There is also such a multiplicity of sources which have to be assessed that there is little chance of doing so on an ad hoc basis. There is therefore good reason for incorporating a competitive information system within any marketing information system that exists, and having people responsible for ensuring its maintenance. In competitive strategy, just as in war, it is impossible to exaggerate the importance of gathering information on the adversaries a company faces. As Sun Tzu says: 'An army without spies is like a man without ears or eyes' and, because of this, 'to remain in ignorance of the adversary's condition simply because one grudges the outlay of a few hundred ounces of silver in honours and emoluments, is the height of inhumanity'.

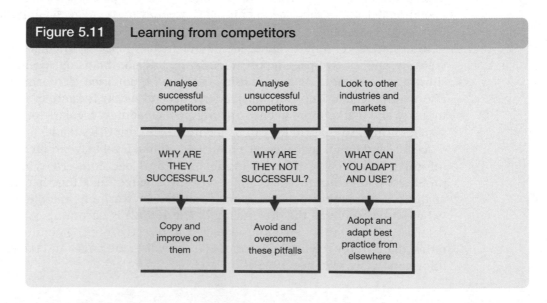

Figure 5.11 Learning from competitors

Emap

FT **Case study**

Courtesy of Smashhits TV

In the beginning there was music television and MTV was a global brand that had musical youths jiving to its beat, whether it was pop, dance, heavy metal or rock.

Now however, a new rival claims to be challenging for the top of the UK charts. Following the launch of its fourth new music TV channel in a year, Smash Hits TV, Emap Performance says it took 50 per cent of the music TV audience in SkyDigital homes for the week commencing 13 May.

With digital cable carriage deals promised and another new channel, Magic TV, due to launch on 11 September, the message is that the company is preparing a serious assault on the TV hit parade.

'I think that most people that advertise on TV have up until now thought that MTV equalled music TV. Well we've got news for you, it doesn't any more,' claims Emap Performance chief executive Tim Schoonmaker. He expects Magic TV to add a further 0.2 percentage points to Emap Performance's audience share when it launches later this year.

MTV, which has seven channels, disputes the numbers and points to the fact that, following the first week of Smash Hits TV, Emap's share has dropped back. Most weeks, it claims, Emap performance is usually around 20 per cent behind.

It's a row that's attracting attention for two reasons. First, there's nothing like a media catfight, a couple of suits having their own Robbie-versus-Liam-style spat.

'I'm told that they've got someone full time watching our channels writing down every video that we play,' alleges Schoonmaker.

'Emap are obviously quite desperate at the moment,' hits back Michiel Bakker, MTV Networks UK and Ireland's managing director. 'It's a small piece of hype aimed at propping up the share price.'

The second, and perhaps more important reason for all the attention is that the two companies have very different philosophies as to what a music TV channel should be.

Emap's vision of music TV is 'radio with pictures' while MTV is a firm believer in the 'music is a way of life' school of thought. Emap's five stations, which also include The Box, Q TV, Kiss TV and Kerrang TV, work on the basis that viewers are offered a limited choice of music videos and can vote for the track they want to see by ringing a premium rate phone line. It does make a limited amount of original programming, but nothing that's longer than a music video.

'People do not sit and watch music TV for an hour at a time,' says Schoonmaker. 'The idea that music channels will ever be appointment to view for other than a tiny minority is crazy.'

With the exception of The Box, all Emap's channels are extensions of its other media properties. And this is what has enabled it to expand its portfolio so quickly.

'Brands mean we do not need to market [the channels] with the same kind of mouth-watering budgets as you do when it's a new proposition,' he says.

MTV rejects this approach, putting its faith in programming investment. It employs around 80 people in programming and production compared to Emap's 25 dedicated TV staffers.

'We want our channels to be part of our audience's lives,' says Bakker. 'We will continue to drive investment in programming. We will see increased investment from our side on programming to create an absolute, clear blue water between our channels and any other channels that are out there.'

He disputes Schoonmaker's argument that music TV is never appointment to view, citing the fact that *Daily Edition*, a news show that airs at 7.00 p.m. on its premier channel, MTV UK, attracts a significantly higher share than the channel's average performance.

'It's all about connection with your audience, we do that by breathing life into our channels rather than running them as brand extensions,' he says. The reason why the market can support so many music channels is that someone else is supplying the programming.

'Music TV is very cheap to make because you've got someone else doing the work for you in terms of making videos,' observes Steve Gladdis, associate director at media planning and buying agency MediaCom.

However, given the difficulty of effectively monitoring such a small audience, the numbers in themselves are not the only factor in deciding where to buy advertising time.

'I do not think we really buy these channels from a numbers viewpoint, we are buying them for the environment. It's almost like buying a magazine schedule,' he adds.

Source: Alastair Ray, 'A different tune: Emap Performance is challenging MTV's dominance in music television – aggressively and with a slimmed-down approach', *Financial Times*, 3 July 2001, p. 9.

Discussion questions

1 How does Emap's market entry strategy take into account its knowledge of MTV?

2 How is MTV likely to respond to Emap's attack and what can Emap do to ready itself for MTV's counter-moves?

3 Since 'Music TV is very cheap to make because you've got someone else doing the work for you in terms of making videos,' does Emap's lower cost structure offer it a long-term competitive advantage over MTV? With such cheap content, what are the barriers to a flood into the market if Emap is successful?

chapter six

Understanding the organisational resource base

6

The most important assets a company has are its brand names. They should appear at the head of the assets list on the balance sheet.

Marketing Director, International Food Marketing Company

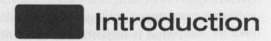

Introduction

The attractiveness of opportunities open to the firm depends on the resources available to exploit them. Organisational resources include both tangible and intangible assets, capabilities and competences. This is the base from which organisations build their competitive position, and any marketing strategy needs to be firmly grounded in these resources. Strategies that are not built on resource strength are unlikely to be sustainable in the longer term, and underutilised resources represent potential wastage. To succeed in a particular market the firm will need specific resources, the key factors for success in that market. If it does not have these, or cannot acquire them, the strategy is likely to fail at the implementation stage.

This chapter is structured around the following issues which provide a framework for assessing organisational resources:

- customer-based and reputational assets;
- supply chain assets;
- internal or marketing support assets;
- alliance-based assets.

6.4.1 Customer-based marketing assets

Customer-based marketing assets are those assets of the company, either tangible or intangible, valued by the customer or potential customer. Often they exist in the mind of the customer and they are essentially intangible in nature. They may, however, be one of the most critical issues in building a defensible competitive position in the marketplace.

Company name and reputation

One of the most important customer-based assets a company can possess is its reputation or image. Companies such as Mercedes, BMW and Rolls-Royce have a clear image of supplying a particular set of customer benefits (reliability, durability, prestige, overall quality) in the markets in which they operate.

Company name confers an asset on all products of the company where it is clearly identified. Indeed, in many cases where the company identity is a strong asset it has been converted into a brand name for use on a wide variety of products (e.g. Virgin, Kodak and Sainsbury are not only company names but also brands with strong customer franchises).

Image and reputation can also, however, be a negative asset or a liability. This may go far beyond what customers think about product quality. An Ogilvy & Mather study in 1996 contrasted the views of consumers of some companies as 'efficient bastards' compared with the 'Mr Cleans' at the other end of the scale. The top end of the ethical scale was occupied by companies like Marks & Spencer, Boots, Virgin Atlantic, Cadbury and The Body Shop. The other end of the scale was occupied by Camelot (the UK lottery operator), *The Sun* newspaper, Yorkshire Water utility, William Hill and Ladbrokes (bookmakers) and Sky TV (Bell, 1996). The seriousness of this issue is underlined by evidence that consumers are increasingly reluctant to deal with companies they regard as unethical (Bernoth, 1996). (See Chapter 18 for more detailed consideration of this issue.)

Also important is how firms deal with bad publicity. The reputation of Firestone, the tyre manufacturer, was, for example, badly damaged by public wrangling with Ford over the cause of 170 traffic deaths and hundreds of accidents in the USA involving the Ford Explorer, fitted with Firestone tyres. Ford eventually recalled 13 million tyres at a cost of $3 billion (*Marketing Business*, July/August 2001).

Skoda cars were best known in Britain in the mid-1990s as the butt of bad jokes, reflecting a widespread but erroneous belief that the cars were poor quality. In 1995, Skoda was preparing to launch a new model in the UK, and did 'blind and seen' tests of the consumers' judgement of the vehicle. The vehicle was rated as better designed and worth more by those who did not know the make. With the Skoda name revealed, perceptions of the design were less favourable and estimated value was substantially lower. Subsequent advertising made a joke of this image, showing customers happy with the cars but embarrassed at buying a Skoda. By also showing that Skoda had the strength of VW behind it (visually shown in poster advertisements as a VW shadow behind the Skoda) following acquisition, positive brand values were steadily built.

This leads us from company name and reputation to brands.

Brands

The identity and exploitation of brands remain central to many views of marketing. For example, the Interbrand agency annually reports the ten most valuable brand names in the world. The results are presented in Table 6.1 (and are regularly updated by the company on their website http://www.interbrand.com).

Not surprisingly, American brands dominate the lists with 73 per cent of the value behind the global brand rankings. Next highest country is Japan with 6 per cent, followed by Germany (also 6 per cent) and the UK (4 per cent) (Ambler, 2001). Such lists are, of course, limited, in that the 'winners' are selected by the nature of the criteria chosen more than the real value of the brand in question.

More importantly, for companies where corporate identity is a liability or a nonexistent asset, more emphasis is placed on building or acquiring individual brand names as assets. Beechams, for example, deliberately set out to acquire brands with a marketable reputation. The Bovril brand was purchased to ease the company's launch into the stock cubes market (Bovril being an established brand property in the similar meat extracts market). Companies with little customer-based corporate identity, such as Rank Hovis MacDougal (RHM), have developed their various brands into major assets: the Bisto brand, famous as the UK market leader in gravy making, for example, has been used to good effect by RHM in its move into the soups and sauces market.

The British car industry is perhaps one of the best examples of assets based in brand names or marques. Over the years Rover Group and its predecessors have had valuable assets in marques such as Rover, Wolsey, MG, Austin Healey and Jaguar. During the short period of ownership by BMW of what became referred to in the

Table 6.1 The top ten brand names

Rank*	1990	1996	2001	2006 (value in US$bn)
1	Coca-Cola	McDonald's	Coca-Cola	Coca-Cola (67)
2	Kellogg	Coca-Cola	Microsoft	Microsoft (57)
3	McDonald's	Disney	IBM	IBM (56)
4	Kodak	Kodak	General Electric	General Electric (49)
5	Marlboro	Sony	Nokia	Intel (32)
6	IBM	Gillette	Intel	Nokia (30)
7	American Express	Mercedes Benz	Disney	Toyota (28)
8	Sony	Levis	Ford	Disney (28)
9	Mercedes Benz	Microsoft	McDonald's	McDonald's (28)
10	Nescafé	Marlboro	AT&T	Mercedes (22)

Note: * Ranking based on: (1) weight – dominance of the market, (2) length – extension into other markets, (3) breadth – approval across age, religion or other divides, and (4) depth – customer commitment.

Source: Interbrand (1996, 2001, 2006).

years the product failed to show a profit (Mitchell, 1995). The Unilever-owned competitor Walls 'owns' the distribution channel that matters: small convenience stores. Indeed, Walls quite literally does own the freezers and display cabinets in many of these outlets, and does not share them with competitors. The critical marketing asset is distribution channel control.

Pockets of strength

Selective but close relationships between a company and its distribution outlets can lead to pockets of strength. Where a company is unable, through size or resource constraints, to serve a wide market, concentrating effort, either geographically on specific regions of the market (Wm Morrisons supermarkets were particularly strong in Yorkshire but spread nationally through acquisition of the Safeway chain of stores), or through specific outlets, can enable a pocket of strength to be developed.

Companies adopting the latter approach of building up a strong presence with selective distributors, or even end users in many industrial markets, often achieve that pocket of strength through key account marketing, i.e. giving full responsibility for each key account development to a specific, normally quite senior, executive. Pockets of strength are typically built up on the basis of strong relationships with those selected distributors and hence require a proactive relationship marketing strategy to ensure their development (see Chapter 16).

Distribution uniqueness

Further distribution-based assets can be built through uniqueness, reaching the target market in a novel, or innovative way. For instance, Ringtons sells tea and coffee door to door in the north of England and the Avon Cosmetics company has built a strong door-to-door business in cosmetics sales through the 'Avon Calling' campaign.

Similarly, Dell computers has achieved a uniquely strong position in the personal computer market by using a direct distribution approach, which enables most of the computers sold to be built to the specifications of the customer, while at the same time giving Dell a much faster stock-turn than its competitors. Dell has been growing at 50 per cent a year in a market growing at 20 per cent a year, and by the mid-1990s was the fifth largest computer manufacturer in the world (*Economist*, 5 October 1996). By 2006 Dell employed around 64,000 people worldwide and was the 25th biggest company in the USA. Product quality problems have, however, affected Dell profitability in 2006/7.

Delivery lead-time and security of supply

Delivery lead-time is a function of at least three main factors – physical location, order through production systems and company delivery policy. In an increasing number of situations the ability to respond quickly, at no compromise to quality, is becoming more important. Deliberately creating a rapid response capability can constitute a significant marketing asset (see Stalk, 1988).

Similarly, particularly in volatile markets, where the supplier's offering is on the critical path of the customer company, the ability to guarantee supply can be a major asset. As with lead-time that ability will be a function of several factors, but perhaps central is the desire on the part of the supplier to meet agreed targets.

The competitive success of fashion clothing retailers such as Primark, Zara and Hennes & Mauritz (H&M) is in large part based on supply chain strengths. These companies can identify fashion catwalk trends and have them in stores within a few weeks, sourced from low-cost suppliers, at attractive high-street prices. While they have different competitive positions, these companies are linked by their efficient supply chains and ability to manage the velocity of stock movement rather than focusing on stock levels. They are simply incredibly fast, and their customers expect no less.

Supplier network

At the other end of the supply chain, well-developed or unique links with key suppliers can be important marketing assets. These can help to secure continuity of supply of raw or semi-finished materials at required standards for negotiated prices. For example, Nissan, the Japanese car producer, operates a computerised supply chain, linking itself to its suppliers and distributors. The company claims it has increased by 80 per cent the number of customers who get exactly the car specifications they want from the dealer within 48 hours of deciding what they want. This precision in meeting exact customer needs is a potential competitive advantage that results in no increase in stock in the supply chain (Tighe, 1997).

6.4.3 Internal marketing support assets

A resource becomes an asset when it is actively used to improve the organisation's performance in the marketplace. Consider the following examples.

Cost advantages

A cost advantage brought about by employing up-to-date technology, achieving better capacity utilisation than competitors, economies of scale or experience curve effects can be translated into lower prices for products and services in the marketplace. Where the market is price-sensitive, for example, with commodity items, lower price can be a major asset. In other markets where price is less important, cost advantages may not be translated into marketing assets; rather they are used to provide better margins.

Information systems and market intelligence

Information systems and systematic marketing research can be valuable assets in that they keep the company informed about its customers and its competitors. Information is a major asset which many firms guard jealously but until it is utilised to make better decisions it does not convert to a marketing asset.

Of particular note is the use of 'data warehouses' of customer information – collected in loyalty schemes or as part of the purchase process, to develop very specific offerings to customers based on their interests and key characteristics. This is why Virgin Atlantic knows which newspapers and seats its frequent fliers prefer.

As well as understanding customers better than competitors do, the owners of data warehouses can create marketing strategies that exploit this resource as a differentiating capability. For example, Nestlé's attack on the pasta market in the UK involved major brand-building activities around the Buitoni subsidiary, entailing the creation of a large database of consumers attracted to traditional Italian cuisine, and the launch of the Casa Buitoni Club. To overcome the problems of a market where consumers were not well educated about pasta products and were confused by the variety on offer, as well as the problem of being cut off from the consumer by retailers, Nestlé used direct response advertising to establish the customer database, and the Casa Buitoni Club as a communications channel with its chosen market segment, allowing one-to-one marketing.

Existing customer base

A major asset for many companies is their existing customer base. Particularly where a company is dealing with repeat business, both consumer and industrial, the exist-ence of a core of satisfied customers can offer significant opportunities for further development.

This has been especially noted in the recent development of the direct marketing industry (accounting for around half of all marketing expenditure in the US), where it is recognised that the best customer prospects for a business are often its existing customers. Where customers have been satisfied with previous company offerings they are more likely to react positively to new offers. Where a relationship has been built with the customer this can be capitalised on both for market development and employed as a barrier to competitive entry.

The converse is, of course, also true. Where a customer has been dissatisfied with a product or service offering they may not only be negative towards new offers, but also may act as 'well poisoners' in relating their experiences to other potential customers. There is an old marketing adage: 'Each satisfied customer will tell three others, each dissatisfied customer will tell 33!'

The issue of customer retention and customer loyalty has become extremely important, and we will consider this in more detail in Chapter 15.

Technological skills

The type and level of technology employed by the organisation can be a further asset. Technological superiority can aid in cost reduction or in improving product quality. For example, the high rate of growth of a company such as Amersham International (specialising in high-technology medical products for diagnosis of cancers) is largely based on its ability to stay ahead of its competitors in terms of new product development, but also the capability for distributing highly toxic sub-stances safely throughout the world – many of the products are radioactive and extremely dangerous. In the automotive industry, German manufacturers of BMW, Audi and Mercedes Benz are successfully positioned at the high-quality end of the spectrum on the basis of their superior design, technical engineering excellence and quality controls. The strategy was encapsulated in the Audi slogan 'Vorsprung durch Technik' (leading through technology) which also emphasised the German engineering heritage of the cars (country of origin effect).

Production expertise

Production know-how can be used to good effect as a marketing asset. Mars, for example, are particularly good at producing high-quality nougat (a great deal of effort has been put into quality control at Mars, developing their production processes as a core competence). This asset has been turned into a marketing asset in a number of leading products such as Mars Bar, Milky Way, Topic and Snickers, all of which are nougat based.

Copyrights and patents

Copyright is a legal protection for musical, literary or other artistic property, which prevents others using the work without payment of an agreed royalty. Patents grant persons the exclusive right to make, use and sell their inventions for a limited period. Copyright is particularly important in the film industry to protect films from illegal copy ('pirating') and patents are important for exploiting new product inventions. The protection of copyrights and patents, in addition to offering the holder the opportunity to make and market the items protected, allows the holder to license or sell those rights to others. They therefore constitute potential marketing assets of the company.

Franchises and licences

The negotiation of franchises or licences to produce and/or market the inventions or protected properties of others can also be valuable assets. Retailers franchised to use the 'Mitre 10' name in hardware retailing in New Zealand, for example, benefit from the strong national image of the licenser and extensive national advertising campaigns.

Similarly, in many countries American Express cards and products are marketed under licence to the American Express Company of the US. The licence agreement is a significant asset for the licensee.

Partnerships

As we shall see in more detail in Chapter 16, increasingly companies are going to market in collaborative or alliance-based strategies. We should not neglect the importance of existing partnerships as marketing assets, and also the management capability to manage marketing strategy in alliance-based networked organisations.

Corporate culture

One of the resources that is least easy for competitors to imitate and particularly distinctive of a company is its culture. The formation of culture and the capacity to learn are complex issues. None the less, for many successful companies culture represents one of the most unique resources. For example, Hewlett-Packard (HP) has a culture which encourages teamwork and cross-functional and cross-divisional working. This has allowed HP to use its core technologies in many diverse products – printers, plotters, computers, electronic instruments – and to make these products compatible. Competitors can imitate HP's technology relatively easily, but it is far less straightforward to imitate the culture and organisation that underpins HP's marketing effectiveness (Barney, 1997). Despite a boardroom spying scandal, the loss of a chief executive, a problematic merger with Compaq and drastic restructuring, exploiting its underlying strengths in 2007 HP aims to be the first IT company to top

- **Crown Jewels.** These are the resources where the organisation enjoys an edge over its competitors and are instrumental in creating value for customers. As the source of differentiation these resources need to be guarded and protected to maintain the competitive edge. At the same time, however, managers need to constantly question whether these resources alone can ensure continued success. The danger lies in resting on the laurels of the past while the world, and customer requirements, move forward.

- **Black Holes.** Black holes are resources where the organisation has an edge but which don't contribute to customer value creation. These may be resources that provided customer value in the past but are no longer important. The world and customers may have moved on, rendering them less important at best and obsolete at worst. Managers need to take a long hard look at black holes resources and assess the costs of maintaining them. It could well be that some pruning, or downsizing, of such resources will free up efforts and even cash that can then be deployed more effectively elsewhere.

- **Achilles' Heels.** Where competitors are strong but the organisation is weak, and at the same time the resources are important in customer value creation, the clear implication is that resources need to be strengthened. These are resource deficiencies that could prove fatal if not corrected.

- **Sleepers.** Finally, resources that neither constitute a competitive advantage nor are important in customer value creation could be termed sleepers. They are unimportant today but managers do need to watch that they do not become more important in the future.

The resource portfolio model offers a useful summary of the organisation's resources which can be used to highlight areas for attention and development.

6.8 Developing and exploiting resources

While the emphasis above has been on identifying existing resources, organisations also need to ensure they are developing and nurturing the resources that will be required in the future. This involves a degree of forecasting how markets and customers will change over time. Figure 6.9 shows four strategies for development.

The two dimensions shown in Figure 6.9 represent choices open to the organisation in developing and exploiting both the markets in which it operates and the resources it employs.

In the lower left quadrant the focus is on utilising existing resources as effectively as possible in existing markets. The 'fill the gaps' strategy involves looking for better ways of serving existing customers, using the existing strengths of the organisation. In many ways this may be seen as a defensive strategy used to protect existing positions from competitor encroachment. For example, the major high-street banks have attempted to retain their customer base through offering additional services (such as longer opening hours, faster counter service, more widely available ATMs) using their existing resource base more effectively.

In the top left quadrant the organisation retains its focus on existing markets and customers but recognises that the resources it will need to serve them in the future

Figure 6.9	Developing and exploiting resources

Source: Adapted from Homel and Prahalad, 1994.

will need to change. This requires the 'next generation' of resources to be built and nurtured. Many traditional, 'bricks and mortar' firms, have found that to continue to serve their existing customers they need to develop online, Internet-based services (see Chapter 15). This often requires a new set of capabilities to be developed, not just those associated with Internet technology. These new resources do not necessarily enable the firm to reach new customers or markets, but are required to enable it to continue to serve its existing client base. Under this strategy the organisation stays with the markets that it knows and the customers it has built relationships with, but recognises that it must adapt to continue to serve them effectively. Tesco, the UK food retailer, is now among the largest online retailers in the world, having exploited the opportunities for serving existing customers more effectively through the Internet.

In the bottom right quadrant the organisation seeks new markets and customers where it can 'exploit current skills' more effectively. This quest for new customers, or new markets, is, however, guided by the existing capabilities of the organisation. The acquisition of the UK retailer Asda by the American firm Wal-Mart is a case in point. This enabled WalMart to further exploit its merchandising and purchasing capabilities in the new markets of the UK.

Finally, at top right the organisation looks to serve new customers with new resources through 'diversified opportunities'. This option takes the organisation simultaneously away from its existing markets and its existing resources – a more risky strategy and one that should not be pursued lightly. Firms that go this route often do so through acquisition or merger.

Summary

We started this chapter with a summary of the resource-based view of the firm and the recent development of ideas surrounding dynamic capabilities. Our focus on competitive positioning (i.e. the choice of target markets and the competitive advantage exploited) provides a mechanism for reconciling the internal focus of the

chapter seven

Forecasting future demand and market requirements

*What's small, dark and knocking at the door?
The future.*

Greek proverb

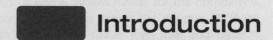

Introduction

The economist Ralph Harris defined a forecast as 'a pretence of knowing what would have happened if what does happen hadn't'. People are rightly cynical about forecasting, but forecasting is at the heart of marketing strategy and competitive positioning. As part of the marketing information system in Chapter 4, forecasting feeds into many of the stages of marketing strategy formulation. There is little point in developing strategies to fit the past, so forecasting needs to extend the environment and industry analyses of Chapter 3 into the future. Portfolio analysis (Chapter 2) starts with historic information, but ends by projecting the portfolio forward to help decide what to do. From that stage onwards plans depend upon forecasts. Target markets are chosen because of what markets are forecast to be (Chapter 10) and new product development programmes (Chapter 13) build upon market and technology forecasts.

Companies that have not mastered forecasting are likely to build positions that defend against yesterday's competitors or appeal to yesterday's customers. Yet forecasting is often neglected or done naively. Why? The perceived complexity and sheer variety of forecasting methods are two reasons. These barriers have risen as people try to develop ever more sophisticated ways of doing the impossible: looking into the future.

Fortunately, forecasts do not have to complicated to be good, although the methods do have to be understood if they are to be useful. This chapter introduces the forecasting alternatives for sales, markets, technology and society. It gives examples of their use and suggests what to use and when.

7.1 Forecasting what?

Market demand measurement calls for a clear understanding of the market involved. A **market** is the set of all actual and potential buyers of a product or service. A market is the set of buyers, and an **industry** is the set of sellers. The size of a market hinges on the number of buyers who might exist for a particular market offer. Potential buyers for something have three characteristics: interest, income and access.

Companies commonly use a three-stage procedure to arrive at a sales forecast. First, they make an **environmental forecast**, followed by an industry **demand forecast**, followed by a company **sales forecast**. The environmental forecast calls for projecting inflation, unemployment, interest rates, consumer spending and saving, business investment, government expenditure, net exports and other environmental events important to the company. The result is a forecast of gross national product used, along with other indicators, to forecast industry sales. Then the company prepares its sales forecast assuming a certain share of industry sales.

Companies use many techniques to forecast their sales. All are built on one of four information bases: what there is, what has happened, what happens when, or what people think will happen. There are numerous forecasting methods for each use with each information base (Saunders *et al.*, 1987). Figure 7.1 shows the important ones.

7.2 Forecasts based on current demand

Companies have developed various practical methods for estimating total market demand (Barnett, 1988). We illustrate three.

7.2.1 Market build-up method

The **market build-up** method identifies all the potential buyers in each market and estimates their potential purchases.

Suppose EMI wants to estimate the total annual sales of recorded compact discs. A common way to estimate total market demand is as follows:

$$Q = n \times q \times p$$

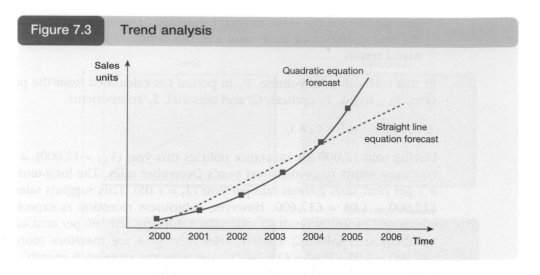

Figure 7.3   Trend analysis

The basic question of trend analysis, and many other statistical forecasting tools, is the estimation of the unknown coefficients. Regression analysis is the most common way of doing this. It calculates the values of the coefficient that minimise the sum of the squares of the differences between actual and forecast sales, minimising:

$$\sum_{Y=2000}^{2005} u_Y^2,$$

where u_Y is the error term, $F_Y - S_Y$.

The approach gives the equation:

$$F_Y = 0.14 + 1.65 \times T + u_Y$$

$$R^2 = 0.987$$

The R^2 value indicates a reasonably good fit since its value can range between 1, meaning a perfect fit to the data, and 0, meaning no fit at all.

This statistically excellent result reveals the dangers of trend analysis. The result is naive; only a fool would expect DVD sales to increase linearly with time for ever! Visual inspection also shows that the sales trend is not a straight line but one that curves upwards. Trend analysis can overcome this problem by fitting a more complex equation. A quadratic equation allows regression analysis to produce an equation with a better fit and shape:

$$F_Y = 0.44 + 1.05 \times T + 0.15 \times T^2 + u_Y$$

$$R^2 = 0.999$$

substituting $T = 5$, for 2005 and $T = 6$, for 2006. The results also give upper and lower limits (95 per cent) of the estimate – figures that are a useful by-product of regression analysis.

The linear and quadratic forms are two of many equations that can be used to fit trends. Other forecasts could be:

Log quadratic $RF_Y = EXP(-0.67249 + 1.1727 \times T + 0.13112 \times T^2)$, $R^2 = 0.999$
Exponential $F_Y = 0.66348 \times EXP(0.64821 \times T)$, $R^2 = 0.945$
Modified
hyperbola $F_Y = 1/(1.5006 - 0.4181 \times T)$, $R^2 = 0.730$

The fits are good but what do they forecast? The quadratic and exponential forms both forecast sales growing increasingly rapidly, but the exponential form at such a rapid rate that it produces a forecast of over 30,000,000 units in 2006 – more than one per household in the United Kingdom. Unfortunately the two curves with the best fit give the most contrasting forecasts. While quadratic suggests a reasonable exponential increase, the log quadratic forecasts declining sales after 2004.

The results show the danger of collapsing the shape and curve fitting parts of trend analysis. Curve fitting using regression analysis should only be attempted after the desired shape and expression have been chosen. If in doubt, use a straight line to fit the series. It may be obviously wrong, but at least its limitations are known. Alternatively, the careful choice of series to be analysed and the use of constrained trend analysis can overcome some of the problems with wayward curves.

Despite its limitations there are several useful applications of trend analysis. Sales are the most common but the adoption rate of new products, the substitution of one technology for another and technology forecasting are other areas where trend analysis is effective. Trend analysis also inherits several advantages from regression analysis. It is relatively quick and easy to use and, because it is based on a well-understood technique, it provides statistical measures of the reliability and validity of the results.

The S-curve

S-shaped time series, or curves that saturate to an upper limit, are particularly suited to time-series analysis. In technology and sales forecasting there is often an upper limit beyond which performance or sales can never go. Take, for example, the motor car engine. There is a theoretical limit to the thermal efficiency that the internal combustion engine can ever achieve, so it is expected that gains from spending on R&D would decline as the theoretical limit is approached. Similarly, for DVD sales, there is obviously some upper limit to the sales that can be made. By taking into account these rational or practical constraints the quality and reliability of trend analysis can be significantly increased.

When forecasting the potential of a new product group, such as the DVD was, it is easier and more reliable to forecast penetration rather than sales. This is because penetration always follows a particular type of curve that has an upper limit. For domestic appliances the absolute upper limit must be 100 per cent of households, although there are some goods, such as dishwashers, that appear to have saturated at a much lower level.

Figure 7.4 contains penetration figures and a forecast for DVDs. The forecast is produced using a Gompertz curve that is S-shaped and saturates. The expression has the form:

$$F_T = a_0 \times a_1^{a^{T2}}$$

where a_0, a_1 and a_2 are parameters to be estimated and T is time. After solution a_0 is the saturation level, the level beyond which sales will never go, and $a_0 \times a_1$ is the

Figure 7.4	S-curve penetration forecast

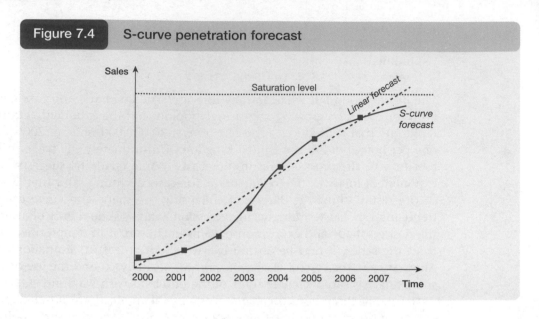

forecast when $T = 0$. Unfortunately, the Gompertz equation has to be solved using non-linear estimation techniques rather than regression. These are iterative procedures that use rules to guide the search for the coefficients that would otherwise be estimated using regression analysis. There is a wide range of procedures, but they are not all robust.

The Gompertz equation for the DVD penetration series is:

$$DVDF_Y = 59.2 \times 0.0420^{0.647^T}$$

where T = the year 2000.

This suggests a saturation level of penetration to be 59.2 per cent of households, with sales declining after 2004. As an alternative to using non-linear estimation to estimate an S-curve, the Gompertz equation, or a similar **logistic model**, can be solved using regression analysis if saturation level (a_0) is assumed.

These transformations allow reliable S-shaped expressions to be estimated, but if an inappropriate saturation level is chosen the results will provide a poor fit to the data. When this occurs alternative saturation levels should be tried until a more satisfactory result is obtained. If the search procedure is conducted systematically the process would become one of non-linear estimation. The following specialised cases of the diffusion of innovations and technology substitution provide other examples of where constrained trend analysis can be profitably used.

The similarity between the S-shaped curve explaining the adoption of a product and a plot of the early stages of the product life cycle is misleading. The S-curve tracks first uses of a product and leads to a saturation level when all users have adopted the product. In contrast, the product life cycle tracks sales that include repeat purchases as well as first-time uses. These curves are often out of phase. For example, in Europe almost everyone has travelled by bus so the S-curve of the adoption has levelled off and will not go up and cannot go down. Conversely, the product life cycle for buses is declining as more people take to their cars. An opposite case occurs for US wine consumption. Again the S-curve for adoption has levelled out as most people who are willing and able to try wine have done so. However, the product life cycle curve for wine in the United Kingdom continues to increase as people consume more table wine.

The 'market build-up' model discussed above (Section 7.2.1) links the adoption and product life cycle curves. In this the S-curve plot closely follows 'the number of buyers in the market' while the product life cycle represents 'total market demand'.

Diffusion of innovations

Some insights into the mechanism of the diffusion of innovations have led to trend analysis models with some behavioural detail. Bass (1969) has produced a new product growth model for consumer durables that is based on the innovative and imitative behaviour of consumers. For DVDs this suggests that I_T, the increase in penetration in time T, will be:

$$I_T = r(M - P_T) + p(M - P_T)P_T/M$$

where:

$r(M - P_T)$ is the *innovation effect*, proportional to the untapped potential;

$p(M - P_T)P_T/M$ is the *imitation effect*, proportional to the potential already tapped;

M is the final potential achieved as a fraction of the maximum potential;

P_T is the penetration achieved at time T.

This makes the realistic assumption that some individuals make their adoption decision independently (innovators), while others (imitators) are influenced by the number of people who have already adopted. The shape of the cumulative penetration curve depends on the relative magnitudes of the **innovation rate** (r) and the **imitation rate** (p). If the *innovation rate* is larger than the *imitation rate*, sales will start quickly then slowly approach saturation. However, if *imitation rate* dominates, an S-shaped curve will occur. Once sufficient data have been collected r and p can be calculated using regression analysis.

The diffusion equations are a useful variation on conventional trend analysis. Unlike other time-series methods, they are based on ideas about consumer behaviour. Actual diffusion processes are obviously far more complex than the simple dichotomy into innovators and imitators suggests, but the resulting equations are robust and can produce reliable forecasts.

There have been attempts to produce more sophisticated diffusion models by adding extra dimensions. These have had limited success. Most add the effect of one or two marketing variables (usually advertising and promotion), but there is no unified theory of how to incorporate marketing or exogenous variables. The few comparisons that have been made tend to show that the extra sophistication offers little improvement over the simple models. A major limitation of the more sophisticated models is their need to be estimated early in a product's life when few data are available.

Technology substitution

Technology substitution is a special case of the diffusion of innovation that occurs when a new technology replaces an old one; for example, the substitution of air for sea/rail travel, or the replacement of vinyl albums by prerecorded tapes or compact discs. Substitution can be forecast in the same way as conventional diffusion processes by the very neat method devised by Fisher and Pry (1978).

The Fisher–Pry method represents a series showing a new idea replacing an older one, in this case the per capita consumption of margarine and butter where:

$$f_T/(f_T - 1) = e^{d+bT}$$

where:

f_T is the fraction of people having adopted the new technology (margarine) at time T, d and b need estimating.

Regression analysis gives the result:

$$f_T/(f_T - 1) = e^{-0.261+0.284T}, \quad R^2 = 0.928$$

Although an equation can be solved using regression, the beauty of the substitution process is its regularity, which allows a clever transformation to show the process as a straight line that can be projected without resorting to statistics. This result shows the proportion of margarine consumed continuing to increase from 81 per cent in 1995 to 91 per cent by 2005.

The Fisher–Pry method is a simple way of looking at a very complex process. Over the decades covered by the substitution the economic, trade and health reasons for the change must have undergone many changes. An attempt to model the change causally would have to find some way of representing all the mechanisms involved. Like the other trend analysis methods, the Fisher–Pry approach observes the aggregate effect of all the influences and assumes that together they will produce the same pattern of substitution in the future as they did in the past. However, sometimes one of the major influences does undergo a major change and affect the rate of substitution.

Technology trend analysis

Technology trend analysis seeks to forecast changes in technological performance rather than sales. It has grown out of the realisation that, for most of the time, technological progress proceeds at a steady pace. Figure 7.5 shows how this is true for computational speeds that have changed dramatically over the last 40 years.

The trend analysis of technological progress appears to be at odds with the popular view of unexpected scientific progress, but unexpected breakthroughs are much rarer than commonly supposed. The much-quoted example of penicillin is the exception rather than the rule. Most of the innovation in the early decades of the new millennium will be based on scientific and technological knowledge existing now. The pattern of technological progress tends to be uniform because it is usually achieved as the result of designers selecting and integrating a large number of innovations from diverse technological areas to produce the higher performance achieved.

Often the impact of a radically new innovation is swamped by the steady progress of evolutionary developments in related areas. This is shown by the change

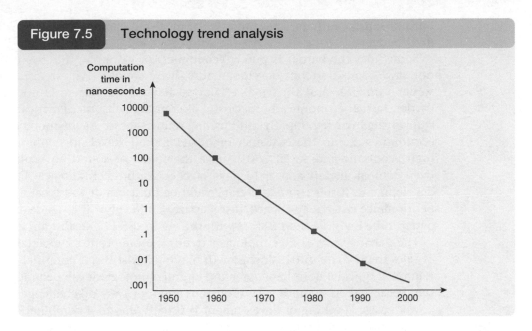

Figure 7.5 Technology trend analysis

of computational speeds. The period covers major discontinuous innovations (from vacuum tubes in 1950 to transistors in 1960, silicon chips in 1970 and gallium arsenide in 1980), but the progress is regular. The transistor itself provides a good example of the relative impact of breakthroughs. It is often credited with being responsible for the size reduction in electronic equipment, yet without the parallel development of ancillary technologies it is estimated that transistor-based electronic equipment would be only marginally smaller (about 10 per cent) than a vacuum tube version.

So, technological trend analysis is based on the same assumption as the Fisher–Pry approach to technological substitution. Both are the result of very complex processes, but their cumulative effect tends to be regular, and the past trends can be a good indication of the immediate future.

The recognition of the S-shaped path of technological progress is a major feature of technology trend analysis. Initially technological progress is slow, maybe because few people are involved, basic scientific knowledge must be gained and engineering obstacles cleared. Conventional wisdom and the establishment can hold back development for a long time. Combat aircraft technology progressed rapidly in the First World War, but then became almost frozen for 20 years as military budgets were cut and the senior services resisted flying machines. Advances start to accelerate exponentially once the importance of a technology is realised and technological effort and funds are expanded. The threat of the Second World War stimulated the rapid increase in combat aircraft performance and this continued after the war and the introduction of radically new jet engine technology.

Finally, technological advances cease to accelerate and may stop growing altogether. There are two reasons why rapid technological progress ends. First, there may be an absolute limit to the technology. For example, the maximum speed of operational helicopters has saturated at just above 350 kph. Above that speed either the forward moving rotor becomes supersonic (so loses lift), or the rearward moving rotor stalls (also losing lift). By using radically new technology the barrier can be overcome, but not satisfactorily or economically for most helicopter roles, even with military R&D budgets.

Sometimes the barrier is purely economic. For example, the 'sound barrier' did not slow combat aircraft development, so why should civil aircraft not be supersonic? Concorde and the Tu-144 (maybe) have shown there is no technological barrier, but all economically successful aircraft are subsonic. Practical technologies stop advancing when rapidly diminishing returns set in. At the moment the limited economic value to the customer of supersonic air travel, in conjunction with its high economic and social costs, make the speed of sound an economic barrier. Even combat aircraft appear to have reached a non-technological barrier to their development. Faster combat aircraft could be built but at too great a cost to other performance criteria, and speed, just like size, isn't everything! These days it is much better to be invisible than fast, as with the B-2 and F-117 stealth aircraft.

The S-shaped curve of technological trends is more prone to uncertainty than that of sales trends. The initial slow growth may not exist if the potential of a new idea is grasped quickly. Both helicopter and laser technology developed rapidly from the start because their significance was obvious and they were no challenge to established power bases. Levelling of development is usually due to a combination of technological and economic factors. Often the trend line continues across several major technological innovations but new technologies can sometimes cause rapid changes, as is now occurring in telecommunications where satellites and deregulation have destroyed the relationship between the distance of phone calls and cost, if not price.

The normally regular pace of technological development makes technology trend analysis a useful planning tool. It can help set realistic performance targets for new developments and prevent heavy expenditure on technologies when the likely returns are diminishing. However, it is a tool that can be dangerous if used thoughtlessly.

Often it is not obvious which performance trends are central. US aero engine manufacturers, and the UK government, initially rejected jet engines for transport aircraft because some experts were preoccupied with specific fuel consumption as the criterion for comparing aero engines. Relative to piston engines, jet engines still have poor specific fuel consumption, but they are supreme in terms of passenger miles per unit cost. To overcome this myopia, identifying at least half a dozen attributes or, more likely, twice that, is necessary. The criteria should then be used, compared and reviewed periodically.

Technology trend lines are often fitted manually rather than using regression analysis. Regression analysis is limited because transformations are often unable to follow the rapid saturation that sometimes occurs. It provides a good statistical fit to the data but produces a shape that overshoots natural or economic barriers. A second disadvantage of regression is the need to envelop data points rather than fit a line of best fit through them. It is usually the extremes of performance, rather than the average, that are tracked. However, developments in envelope methods are overcoming this problem (Bultez and Parsons, 1998).

The direction and limits of trends should be explored carefully. It is easy to neglect the limits to performance improvement when competition has focused attention on a particular criterion for a long time. Potential technical, economic, social, political and ecological reasons for barriers should be considered. Often, as was the case with Concorde, the actual limit is not due to one factor but to a combination of factors.

7.3.3   Leading indicators

Many companies try to forecast their sales by finding one or more **leading indicators**: that is, other time-series that change in the same direction but ahead of company sales. For example, a plumbing supply company might find that its sales lag behind the housing starts index by about four months. An index of housing starts would then be a useful leading indicator. Other leading indicators, such as birth rates and life expectancy, show huge shifts in markets in the next millennium. Many developed countries, including France, Germany and Japan, will have huge problems funding the greying population's pensions. Other countries with funded pension schemes, including the Netherlands, the United States and the United Kingdom, will have an increasingly wealthy ageing population. Despite the wide difference in countries' preparedness for this easy to forecast demographic shift, all will enjoy one rapidly growing market over the next few decades: the funeral market.

It can be dangerous to assume that the indicators that served in the past will continue to do so in the future, or will transfer from one market to another. For example, Disney places great stress on a model of concentric circles around its theme park sites, in which travel time and population numbers indicate demand. Part of the initial failure of EuroDisney (now Disneyland Paris) was because the company clung to this model, ignoring the fact that Europeans have different vacation spending and travel behaviour from Americans.

Getty Images/AFP

7.3.4   Multivariate statistical analysis

Time-series analysis treats past and future sales as a function of time rather than as a function of any real demand factors. But many real factors affect the sales of any product.

Statistical demand analysis

Statistical demand analysis uses statistical procedures to discover the most important real factors affecting sales and their relative influence. The factors most commonly analysed are prices, income, population and promotion. It consists of expressing sales (Q_T) as a dependent variable and trying to explain sales as a function of a number of independent demand variables $X_1, X_2, \ldots, X_n$. That is:

$$Q_T = f(X_1, X_2, \ldots, X_n)$$

Using multiple-regression analysis various equations can be fitted to the data to find the best predicting factors and equation.

For example, the South of Scotland Electricity Board developed an equation that predicted the annual sales of washing machines (Q_T) to be (Moutinho, 1991):

$$Q_T = 210{,}739 - 703P_T + 69H_T + 20Y_T$$

where:

P_T is average installed price;

H_T is new single-family homes connected to utilities;

Y_T is per capita income.

Thus in a year when an average installed price is £387, there are 5,000 new connected homes, and the average per capita income is £4,800, from the equation we would predict the actual sales of washing machines to be 379,678 units:

$$Q_T = 210{,}739 - 703(387) + 69(5{,}000) + 20(4{,}800)$$

The equation was found to be 95 per cent accurate. If the equation predicted as well as this for other regions it would serve as a useful forecasting tool. Marketing management would predict next year's per capita income, new homes and prices and use them to make forecasts. Statistical demand analysis can be very complex and the marketer must take care in designing, conducting and interpreting such analysis. Yet constantly improving computer technology has made statistical demand analysis an increasingly popular approach to forecasting.

Multivariate sales forecasting

Information gathered by the company's marketing information systems often requires more analysis, and sometimes managers may need more help in applying it to marketing problems and decisions. This help may include advanced statistical analysis to learn more about both the relationships within a set of data and their statistical reliability. Such analysis allows managers to go beyond mean and standard deviations in the data. In an examination of consumer non-durable goods in the Netherlands, regression analysis gave a model that forecast a brand's market share (B_t) based on predicted marketing activity (Alsem *et al.*, 1989):

$$B_t = -7.86 - 1.45P_T + 0.084_{T-1} + 1.23D_T$$

where:

P_T is relative price of brand;

A_{T-1} is advertising share in the previous period;

D_T is effective store distribution.

This, and models like it, can help answer marketing questions such as the following:

- What are the chief variables affecting my sales and how important is each one?
- If I raised my price 10 per cent and increased my advertising expenditure 20 per cent, what would happen to sales?
- How much should I spend on advertising?
- What are the best predictors of which consumers are likely to buy my brand versus my competitor's brand?
- What are the best variables for segmenting my market and how many segments exist?

Information analysis might also involve a collection of mathematical models that will help marketers make better decisions. Each model represents some real system, process or outcome. These models can help answer the questions *What if?* and *Which is best?* During the past 20 years marketing scientists have developed numerous models to help marketing managers make better marketing mix decisions, design sales territories and sales-call plans, select sites for retail outlets, develop optimal advertising mixes and forecast new-product sales.

7.4 Forecasting through experimentation

Where buyers do not plan their purchases or where experts are not available or reliable, the company may want to conduct a direct test market. This is especially useful in forecasting new-product sales or established-product sales in a new distribution channel or territory. New-product forecasting methods range from quick and inexpensive concept testing, which tests products before they even exist, to highly expensive test markets that test the whole marketing mix in a geographical region.

7.4.1 Concept testing

Concept testing calls for testing new-product concepts with a group of target consumers. The concepts may be presented to consumers symbolically or physically. Here, in words, is *Concept 1*:

> An efficient, fun-to-drive, electric-powered subcompact car that seats four. Great for shopping trips and visits to friends. Costs half as much to operate as similar petrol-driven cars. Goes up to 90 km per hour and does not need to be recharged for 170 km. Priced at £6,000.

In this case a word or picture description might be sufficient. However, a more concrete and physical presentation of the concept will increase the reliability of the concept test. Today marketers are finding innovative ways to make product concepts more real to concept-test subjects.

After being exposed to the concept consumers may be asked their likelihood of buying the product. The answers will help the company decide which concept has the strongest appeal. For example, the last question asks about the consumer's intention to buy. Suppose 10 per cent of the consumers said they 'definitely' would buy and another 5 per cent said 'probably'. The company could project these figures to the population size of this target group to estimate sales volume. Concept testing offers a rough estimate of potential sales, but managers must view this with caution. They must recognise that the estimate is only a broad pointer and is uncertain largely because consumers do not always carry out stated intentions. Drivers, for example, might like the idea of the electric car that is kind to the environment, but might not want to pay for one. It is, none the less, important to carry out such tests with product concepts so as to gauge customers' responses as well as identify aspects of the concept that are particularly liked or disliked by potential buyers. Feedback might suggest ways to refine the concept, thereby increasing its appeal to customers.

7.4.2   Pre-test markets

Companies can also test new products in a simulated shopping environment. The company or research firm shows, to a sample of consumers, ads and promotions for a variety of products, including the new product being tested. It gives consumers a small amount of money and invites them to a real or laboratory store where they may keep the money or use it to buy items. The researchers note how many consumers buy the new product and competing brands. This simulation provides a measure of trial of the commercial's effectiveness against competing commercials. The researchers then ask consumers the reasons for their purchase or non-purchase. Some weeks later they interview the consumer by phone to determine product attitudes, usage, satisfaction and repurchase intentions. Using sophisticated computer models the researchers then project national sales from results of the simulated test market.

Simulated test markets overcome some of the disadvantages of standard and controlled test markets. They usually cost much less (£25,000–£50,000), can be run in eight weeks, and keep the new product out of competitors' view. Yet, because of their small samples and simulated shopping environments, many marketers do not think that simulated test markets are as accurate or reliable as larger, real-world tests. Still, simulated test markets are used widely, often as 'pre-test' markets. Because they are fast and inexpensive one or more simulated tests can be run to assess a new product or its marketing programme quickly. If the pre-test results are strongly positive the product might be introduced without further testing. If the results are very poor the product might be dropped or substantially redesigned and retested. If the results are promising but indefinite the product and marketing programme can be tested further in controlled or standard test markets.

7.4.3   Mini-test markets

Several research firms keep controlled panels of stores that have agreed to carry new products for a fee. The company with the new product specifies the number of stores and geographical locations it wants. The research firm delivers the product to the participating stores and controls shelf location, amount of shelf space, displays and point-of-purchase promotions, and pricing according to specified plans. Sales results are tracked to determine the impact of these factors on demand.

Controlled test-marketing systems are particularly well developed in the United States. Systems such as Nielsen's Scantrack and Information Resources Inc.'s (IRI)

BehaviorScan track individual behaviour from the television set to the checkout counter. IRI, for example, keeps panels of shoppers in carefully selected cities. It uses microcomputers to measure TV viewing in each panel household and can send special commercials to panel member television sets. Panel consumers buy from cooperating stores and show identification cards when making purchases. Detailed, electronic scanner information on each consumer's purchases is fed into a central computer, where it is combined with the consumer's demographic and TV viewing information and reported daily. Thus BehaviorScan can provide store-by-store, week-by-week reports on the sales of new products being tested. And because the scanners record the specific purchases of individual consumers the system can also provide information on repeat purchases and the ways that different types of consumers are reacting to the new product, its advertising and various other elements of the marketing programme.

Controlled test markets take less time than standard test markets (six months to a year) and usually cost less. However, some companies are concerned that the limited number of small cities and panel consumers used by the research services may not be representative of their products' markets or target consumers. And, as in standard test markets, controlled test markets allow competitors to get a look at the company's new product.

7.4.4 Full test market

Full test markets test the new consumer product in situations similar to those it would face in a full-scale launch. The company finds a small number of representative test cities where the company's salesforce tries to persuade retailers to carry the product and give it good shelf space and promotion support. The company puts on a full advertising and promotion campaign in these markets and uses store audits, consumer and distributor surveys, and other measures to gauge product performance. It then uses the results to forecast national sales and profits, to discover potential product problems and to fine-tune the marketing programme.

Standard market tests have some drawbacks. First, they take a long time to complete – sometimes one to three years. If the testing proves to be unnecessary the company will have lost many months of sales and profits. Second, extensive standard test markets may be very costly. Finally, full test markets give competitors a look at the company's new product well before it is introduced nationally. Many competitors will analyse the product and monitor the company's test market results. If the testing goes on too long competitors will have time to develop defensive strategies and may even beat the company's product to the market. For example, prior to its launch in the United Kingdom, Carnation's Coffee-Mate, a coffee whitener, was test marketed over a period of six years. This gave rival firm Cadbury ample warning and the opportunity to develop and introduce its own product – Cadbury's Coffee Complement – to compete head on with Coffee-Mate.

There are other dangers. In 1997 Sainsbury's was conducting price tests by charging different prices at different stores to gauge customer response. When discovered, this made headline news, with the company criticised for the unfairness of differential pricing even in market tests. Market testing that endangers brand equity is unlikely to be pursued by many companies.

Furthermore, competitors often try to distort test market results by cutting their prices in test cities, increasing their promotion or even buying up the product being tested. Despite these disadvantages standard test markets are still the most widely used approach for significant market testing, although many companies are shifting towards quicker and cheaper, controlled and simulated test marketing methods.

Full test marketing tests its entire marketing programme for the product – its positioning strategy, advertising distribution, pricing, branding and packaging, and budget levels. The company uses it to learn how consumers and dealers will react to handling, using and repurchasing the product. The results can be used to make better sales and profit forecasts. Thus a good test market can provide a wealth of information about the potential success of the product and marketing programme.

The cost of a full test market can be enormous and test marketing takes time that may allow competitors to gain advantages. When the costs of developing and introducing the product are low, or when management is already confident that the new product will succeed, the company may do little or no test marketing. Minor modifications of current products or copies of successful competitors' products might not need standard testing. But when the new-product introduction requires a large investment, or when management is not sure of the product or marketing programme, the company should do a lot of test marketing. In fact some products and marketing programmes are tested, withdrawn, changed and retested many times during a period of several years before they are finally introduced. The costs of such test markets are high, but often small compared with the costs of making a serious mistake.

Whether or not a company test markets, and the amount of testing it does, depends on the cost and risk of introducing the product on the one hand, and on the testing costs and time pressures on the other. Test marketing methods vary with the type of product and market situation, and each method has advantages and disadvantages.

7.4.5 Test marketing business-to-business goods

Business marketers use different methods for test marketing their new products, including product-use tests; trade shows; distributor/dealer display rooms; and standard or controlled test markets. These various methods are explained below:

- **Product-use tests:** Here the business marketer selects a small group of potential customers who agree to use the new product for a limited time. The manufacturer's technical people watch how these customers use the product. From this test the manufacturer learns about customer training and servicing requirements. After the test the marketer asks the customer about purchase intent and other reactions.

- **Trade shows:** These shows draw a large number of buyers to view new products in a few, concentrated days. The manufacturer sees how buyers react to various product features and terms, and can assess buyer interest and purchase intentions.

- **Distributor and dealer display rooms:** Here the new industrial product may stand next to other company products and possibly competitors' products. This method yields preference and pricing information in the normal selling atmosphere of the product.

● **Standard or controlled test markets:** These are used to measure the potential of new industrial products. The business marketer produces a limited supply of the product and gives it to the salesforce to sell in a limited number of geographical areas. The company gives the product full advertising, sales promotion and other marketing support. Such test markets let the company test the product and its marketing programme in real market situations.

7.5 Forecasting through intentions and expert opinion

7.5.1 Buyers' intentions

One way to forecast what buyers will do is to ask them directly. This suggests that the forecaster should survey buyers. Surveys are especially valuable if the buyers have clearly formed intentions, will carry them out and can describe them to interviewers.

Several research organisations conduct periodic surveys of consumer buying intentions. These also ask about consumers' present and future personal finances and their expectations about the economy. Consumer-durable goods companies subscribe to these indexes to help them anticipate significant shifts in consumer buying intentions, so that they can adjust their production and marketing plans accordingly. For **business buying**, various agencies carry out intention surveys about plant, equipment and materials purchases. These measures need adjusting when conducted across nations and cultures. Overestimation of intention to buy is higher in Southern Europe than it is in Northern Europe and the United States. In Asia, the Japanese tend to make fewer overstatements than the Chinese (Lin, 1990).

7.5.2 Salesforce opinions

When buyer interviewing is impractical the company may base its sales forecasts on information provided by the salesforce. The company typically asks its salespeople to estimate sales by product for their individual territories. It then adds up the individual estimates to arrive at an overall sales forecast.

Few companies use their salesforce's estimates without some adjustments. Salespeople are basically observers. They may be naturally pessimistic or optimistic, or they may go to one extreme or another because of recent sales setbacks or successes. Furthermore, they are often unaware of larger economic developments and do not always know how their company's marketing plans will affect future sales in their territories. They may understate demand so that the company will set a low sales quota. They may not have the time to prepare careful estimates or may not consider it worthwhile.

Accepting these biases, a number of benefits can be gained by involving the salesforce in forecasting. Salespeople may have better insights into developing trends than any other group. After participating in the forecasting process the salespeople may have greater confidence in their quotas and more incentive to achieve them.

absorbing external information or quickly responding to step changes. In contrast, **trend analyses** outperform **judgemental methods** when there is plenty of historic sales data or when regular increases in sales are large (Sanders and Ritzman, 1992).

Econometric methods, including **multivariate demand analysis** and **multivariate sales forecasting**, are useful in exploring the impact of influences that are known and modelled. In these cases the influences have to be large and direct otherwise the margins of error swamp variations. **Econometric methods** do outperform **trend analyses** and **expert judgement** when changes are large. Once again, trend analyses suffer from their inability to learn quickly and 'experts' find it hard to imagine dramatic changes.

Comparative results for **new-product forecasting** are particularly convenient. Forecasting new-product sales is hard – an early estimate suggesting the average error is 65 per cent (Tull, 1967). Luckily the error does not increase with the earliness of forecasts. Relatively unrealistic but inexpensive **pre-test marketing** forecasts as well as full **test markets. Concept testing** also gives results as good as test marketing if the product being tested is an incremental change. This changes the role of new-product forecasting. Rather than checking what sales will be with the product in hand, managers can test what sales would be if it existed! If a concept does not work it is easy and quick to try an alternative. Developments in **conjoint analysis** have made it relatively easily to test and refine several product concepts simultaneously. From these conjoint experiments it is even possible to forecast the likely sales of some concepts not even tested (Cattin and Wittink, 1992).

Part of the answer to the difficult question of which forecasting method to use is not to choose just one. Combining forecasts irons out some of the problems with individual methods. In particular, combine forecasts derived using different approaches, such as econometric and subjective methods (Blattberg and Hoch, 1992). Do not worry about the weighting used in combining them, equal weighting is as accurate as any other schemes (Clemen, 1989).

A few simple guidelines can be suggested in choosing forecasting methods:

- Use the simple methods you understand rather than complex methods that few people do.
- Simple methods are often as good as complicated ones.
- Do not choose a forecasting method based on its past forecasting accuracy but on its fitness for the job in hand.
- Use different methods and combine them.
- Expensive does not necessarily mean good.
- Before making decisions based on forecasts, be aware of the way they were produced, and the limitations and risks involved.

When making forecasts it is useful to remember that for existing markets, where there is not major change, it is hard to beat a naive model that assumes that tomorrow will be like today (Brodie and de Kluyver, 1987). We should also remember that the past is unlikely to contain the information that forecasts major changes, so we need to scan the environment for these. Finally, if the environment is uncertain, flexibility not forecasting is the key to business success!

Boeing*

Case study

Alamy/The Flight Collection

Boeing, the world's leading aircraft maker, is forecasting annual growth of 4.7 per cent a year in air travel during the next 20 years and a market worth $4,700bn for new aircraft and aviation services.

Airline investment in new aircraft alone is forecast at $1,700bn over 20 years.

As a result of the continuing high growth, the world jet airliner fleet will more than double by 2020 from 14,500 to 33,000 aircraft, placing huge demands on strained airport capacities.

The Boeing 2001 Current Market Outlook released in Paris yesterday forecasts 18,400 new aircraft will be needed to meet the growth in air travel with a further 5,100 to replace existing aircraft. Around 9,500 aircraft flying today will still be in the air in 20 years.

Growth rates in Asia–Pacific of around 6.4 per cent a year will mean that the region will rival North America in traffic volumes by 2020 with traffic in the more mature markets of the US and

Canada forecast to grow at only 3.1 per cent. Latin America is the fastest growing market, averaging 7.7 per cent a year.

The global market forecast underpins Boeing's belief that there will be a growing fragmentation of air travel, with passengers preferring more frequent, non-stop flights and short trip times, rather than flying on main trunk routes between congested hub airports.

Note: * US airlines experienced their worst revenue decline on record in May, analysts said yesterday, and June could be the second worst month on record, writes Andrew Edgecliffe-Johnson in New York. Samuel Buttrick of UBS Warburg said revenues fell 10 per cent in May – the steepest decline since records began in 1976.

Source: Andrew Edgecliffe-Johnson, 'Boeing predicts fleets to double', *Financial Times*, 21 June 2001, p. 32.

Discussion questions

1 What is the likely basis for Boeing's long-term forecast of the world's airline market?

2 What accounts for the conflicting news from the Paris Air Show, where Boeing predicted fleets would double, and the report by UBS Warburg in New York that US airlines had their second worst month on record?

3 Within 18 months of making its bullish forecast Boeing closed plants in its home town of Seattle and discontinued its Sonic Cruiser project, a 250-seat long-range challenger to Airbus's 555-seat A380 super jumbo. Does this turn of events indicate major problems with market forecasting in support of strategic decision making?

part three

Identifying Current and Future Competitive Positions

The third part of the book addresses in more detail the issues and techniques behind segmentation and positioning research.

Chapter 8 discusses the underlying principles of competitive positioning and market segmentation, and their impact on the choice of target markets. The chapter continues by discussing in detail the logic of segmentation as an approach to identifying target markets, and by comparing the alternative bases for segmenting both consumer and business markets. The chapter closes by considering the benefits of identifying and describing market segments, but also the importance of integrating market segment-based strategies with corporate characteristics and competencies, as well as external factors.

Chapter 9 examines the techniques of segmentation and positioning research in detail. Two fundamentally different approaches are discussed. Under the first, termed a priori, the bases for segmenting are decided in advance and typically follow product/brand usage patterns or customer demographic characteristics. The second approach, *post hoc* or cluster based, searches for segments on the basis of a set of criteria, but without preconceived ideas as to what structure in the market will emerge. The chapter then discusses methods for collecting segmentation data (relating back to the marketing research methods discussed in Chapter 4), ways of analysing those data to identify and describe market segments, and addresses the issue of validating empirically the segmentation structure uncovered. The chapter next discusses both qualitative and quantitative approaches to positioning research. In the former the use of focus groups and depth interviews to identify images and positions is examined. The chapter concludes with a discussion of quantitative approaches to creating perceptual maps.

Chapter 10 discusses choice of target market following the analysis of options above. Two key dimensions are suggested for making the selection of target markets. First, the relative attractiveness of each potential segment. This will be dependent on many factors, including size, growth prospects, margins attainable, competitive intensity, and so on. The second key dimension is the strength of the organisation in serving that potential target market. This is determined by the resources of the organisation, its current and potential marketing assets and the capabilities and competencies it can call on and deploy relative to competitors.

chapter eight

Segmentation and positioning principles

Focussed competitors dominate their target segments – by fending off broad-coverage competitors who have to compromise to serve the segment, and outperforming rivals with the same focus . . . Focussed strategies also gain meaning from the differences between the segments covered and the rest of the market.

Day (1994)

Introduction

Our approach to marketing analysis so far has rested largely on the identification and exploitation of key differences – in marketing capabilities and competitive strengths, for example. Our attention now focuses on two particularly important areas of differentiation: the differences between alternative market offerings as far as customers are concerned, i.e. the **competitive positioning** of suppliers, products, services and brands; and the differences between customers – in terms of their characteristics, behaviour and needs – that are important to marketing decision-makers in developing strong marketing strategies, i.e. **market segmentation**.

The distinction between competitive positioning and market segmentation is illustrated in Figure 8.1, which suggests that the key issues are as follows:

● **Competitive positioning:** concerned with how customers perceive the alternative offerings on the market, compared with each other, e.g. how do Audi, BMW

Table 8.1 UK socio-economic classification scheme

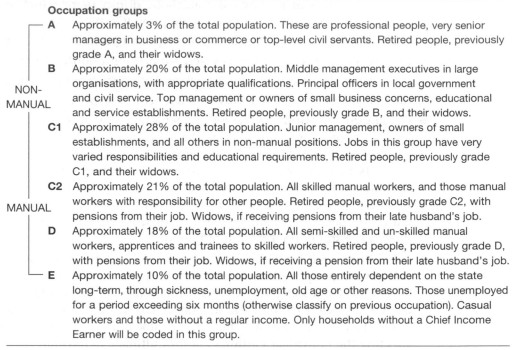

Occupation groups

NON-MANUAL

A   Approximately 3% of the total population. These are professional people, very senior managers in business or commerce or top-level civil servants. Retired people, previously grade A, and their widows.

B   Approximately 20% of the total population. Middle management executives in large organisations, with appropriate qualifications. Principal officers in local government and civil service. Top management or owners of small business concerns, educational and service establishments. Retired people, previously grade B, and their widows.

C1   Approximately 28% of the total population. Junior management, owners of small establishments, and all others in non-manual positions. Jobs in this group have very varied responsibilities and educational requirements. Retired people, previously grade C1, and their widows.

MANUAL

C2   Approximately 21% of the total population. All skilled manual workers, and those manual workers with responsibility for other people. Retired people, previously grade C2, with pensions from their job. Widows, if receiving pensions from their late husband's job.

D   Approximately 18% of the total population. All semi-skilled and un-skilled manual workers, apprentices and trainees to skilled workers. Retired people, previously grade D, with pensions from their job. Widows, if receiving a pension from their late husband's job.

E   Approximately 10% of the total population. All those entirely dependent on the state long-term, through sickness, unemployment, old age or other reasons. Those unemployed for a period exceeding six months (otherwise classify on previous occupation). Casual workers and those without a regular income. Only households without a Chief Income Earner will be coded in this group.

Source: The Market Research Society.

adopt different lifestyles. These lifestyles are, in turn, relevant to marketing-related activity, such as propensity to buy certain goods and services. Socio-economic measures are best seen in the use of social class groups.

Marketing researchers use several social class stratification schemes. The scheme used in the United Kingdom by the Market Research Society is presented in Table 8.1.

For many marketing purposes the top two and bottom two classes are combined to give a four-group standard classification by social class: AB, C1, C2, DE. In the United States several alternative social class schemes have been used for segmentation purposes (see Frank *et al.*, 1972). The most widely adopted, however, is that proposed by Warner (see Table 8.2).

Social class has been used as a surrogate for identifying the style of life that individuals are likely to lead. The underlying proposition is that consumers higher up the social scale tend to spend a higher proportion of their disposable income on future satisfactions (such as insurance and investments) while those lower down the scale spend proportionately more on immediate satisfactions. As such, socio-economic class can be particularly useful in identifying segments in markets such as home purchase, investments, beer and newspapers.

The financial services industry makes extensive use of socio-economic groups for marketing, such as developing pensions and life assurance products aimed at particular social groups. One company is launching an occupational annuity to pay a higher pension to those in stressful or unhealthy jobs. Premiums and terms for private health insurance are partly determined by social class groupings (Gardner, 1997).

Table 8.2 The Warner index of status characteristics

Class name	Description	Consumption characteristics
Upper-upper	Elite social class with inherited social position	Expensive, irrelevant, but purchase decisions not meant to impress; conservative
Lower-upper	*Nouveau riche*; highly successful business and professional; position acquired through wealth	Conspicuous consumption to demonstrate wealth, luxury cars, large estates, etc.
Upper-middle	Successful business and professional	Purchases directed at projecting successful image
Lower-middle	White-collar workers, small businesspeople	Concerned with social approval; purchase decisions conservative; home and family oriented
Upper-lower	Blue-collar workers, technicians, skilled workers	Satisfaction of family roles
Lower-lower	Unskilled labour, poorly educated, poorly off	Attraction to cheap, 'flashy', low-quality items; heavy exposure to TV

However, as with the demographic characteristics discussed above, it is quite possible that members of the same social class have quite different purchase patterns and reasons for purchase. Consider, for a moment, your peers – people you work with or know socially. The chances are they will be classified in the same social class as you. The chances are also that they will be attracted to different sorts of products motivated by different factors and make quite different brand choices.

Concern has been expressed among both marketing practitioners and academics that social class is becoming increasingly less useful as a segmentation variable. Lack of satisfaction with social class in particular and other non-marketing-specific characteristics such as segmentation variables has led to the development of marketing-specific measures such as stage of customer life cycle, geodemographics such as the ACORN classification system and the development of lifestyle research.

Consumer life cycle

Stage of the family life cycle, essentially a composite demographic variable incorporating factors such as age, marital status and family size, has been particularly useful in identifying the types of people most likely to be attracted to a product field (especially consumer durables) and when they will be attracted. The producers of baby products, for example, build mailing lists of households with newborn babies on the basis of free gifts given to mothers in maternity hospitals. These lists are dated and used to direct advertising messages for further baby, toddler and child products to the family at the appropriate time as the child grows.

Stage of family life cycle was first developed as a market segmentation tool by Wells and Gubar (1966) and has since been updated and modified by Murphy and Staples (1979) to take account of changing family patterns. The basic life cycle stages are presented in Table 8.3.

Table 8.3 Stages of the family life cycle

Stage	Financial circumstances and purchasing characteristics
Bachelor Young, single, not living at parental home	Few financial burdens, recreation oriented; holidays, entertainments outside home
Newly wed Young couples, no children	Better off financially, two incomes; purchase home, some consumer durables
Full nest I Youngest child under 6	Home purchasing peak; increasing financial pressures, may have only one income earner; purchase of household 'necessities'
Full nest II Youngest child over 6	Financial position improving; some working spouses
Full nest III Older married couples with dependent children	Financial position better still; update household products and furnishings
Empty nest I Older married couples, no children at home	Home ownership peak; renewed interest in travel and leisure activities; buy luxuries
Empty nest II Older couples, no children at home, retired	Drastic cut in income; medical services bought
Solitary survivor Still in labour force	Income good, but likely to sell home
Solitary survivor Retired	Special needs for medical care, affection and security

In some instances segmentation by life cycle can help directly with product design, as is the case with package holidays. In addition to using age as a segmentation variable, holiday firms target very specifically on different stages of the life cycle, from the Club Med emphasis on young singles, to Center Parcs family holidays, to coach operators' holidays for senior citizens.

Centre Parcs

Courtesy of Centre Parcs

In the United Kingdom the Research Services Ltd marketing research company has developed a segmentation scheme based on a combination of consumer life cycle, occupation and income. The scheme, termed SAGACITY, defines four main life cycle stages (dependent, pre-family, family and late), two income levels (better off and worse off) and two occupational groupings (white collar and blue collar – ABC1 and C2DE). On the basis of these three variables, 12 distinct SAGACITY groupings are identified with different aspirations and behaviour patterns (see Crouch and Housden, 1996).

Some analysts have pointed out that the Baby Boomer generation is set to make a significant impact on marketing to the over 50s (Paul Fifield in *Marketing Business*, January 2002). Thirty years ago the 'Boomers' changed the way marketers dealt with the youth market, as they demanded more individualised and tailored products and services. Having now raised families and paid off mortgages they are approaching the 'empty nester' stage of the life cycle but are likely to have very different expectations from previous generations of 50+ consumers. Generally fitter, well educated and more affluent, they pose very significant marketing opportunities for the future.

ACORN and related classificatory systems

As a direct challenge to the socio-economic classification system the geodemogarphic ACORN system was developed by the CACI Market Analysis Group. The system is based on population census data and classifies residential neighbourhoods into 36 types within 12 main groups (see Table 8.4). The groupings were derived from a clustering of responses to census data required by law on a ten-yearly basis. The groupings reflect neighbourhoods with similar characteristics.

Early uses of ACORN were by local authorities to isolate areas of inner-city deprivation (the idea came from a sociologist working for local authorities), but was soon seen to have direct marketing relevance, particularly because the database enabled postcodes to be ascribed to each ACORN type. Hence its use particularly in direct mail marketing.

Other 'geodemographic' data sources are provided by such firms as Marketing Information Consultancy, Equifax Europe and The Data Consultancy (Cramp, 1996).

Table 8.4 ACORN – a classification of residential neighbourhoods

ACORN group	Description
A	Agricultural areas
B	Modern family housing, higher incomes
C	Older housing of intermediate status
D	Poor quality older terraced housing
E	Better-off council estates
F	Less well-off council estates
G	Poorest council estates
H	Multiracial areas
I	High-status, non-family areas
J	Affluent suburban housing
K	Better-off retirement areas

Personality characteristics

Personality characteristics are more difficult to measure than demographics or socio-economics. They are generally inferred from large sets of questions often involving detailed computational (multivariate) analysis techniques.

Several personality inventories have been used by segmentation researchers. Most notable are the Gordon Personal Profile (see Sparks and Tucker, 1971), the Edwards Personal Preference Schedule (see Alpert, 1972), the Cattell 16-Personality Factor Inventory (see, for example, Oxx, 1972) and the Jackson Personality Inventory (see Kinnear *et al.*, 1974). All were developed by psychologists for reasons far divorced from market segmentation studies and have, understandably, achieved only varied levels of success when applied to segmentation problems.

Perhaps the main value of personality measures lies in creating the background atmosphere for advertisements and, in some instances, package design and branding. Research to date, however, primarily conducted in the United States, has identified few clear relationships between personality and behaviour. In most instances personality measures are most likely to be of use for describing segments once they have been defined on some other basis. As with the characteristics discussed above, behaviour, and reasons for behaviour, in personality-homogeneous segments may be diverse.

Lifestyle characteristics

In an attempt to make personality measures developed in the field of psychology more relevant to marketing decisions, lifestyle research was pioneered by advertising agencies in the United States and the United Kingdom in the early 1970s. This research attempts to isolate market segments on the basis of the style of life adopted by their members. At one stage these approaches were seen as alternatives to the social class categories discussed above.

Lifestyle segmentation is concerned with three main elements: activities (such as leisure activities, sports, hobbies, entertainment, home activities, work activities, professional work, shopping behaviour, housework and repairs, travel and miscellaneous activities, daily travel, holidays, education, charitable work); interaction with others (such as self-perception, personality and self-ideal, role perceptions, as mother, wife, husband, father, son, daughter, etc., and social interaction, communication with others, opinion leadership); and opinions (on topics such as politics, social and moral issues, economic and business–industry issues and technological and environmental issues).

A typical study would develop a series of statements (in some instances over 200 have been used) and respondents would be asked to agree or disagree with them on a 5- or 7-point agree/disagree scale. Using factor analysis and cluster analysis groups of respondents are identified with similar activities, interests and opinions. Examples include the following:

● In early lifestyle studies Segnit and Broadbent (1973) found six male and seven female lifestyle segments on the basis of responses to 230 statements. These have been used to segment markets by publishers of newspapers (such as the *Financial Times* and *Radio Times*) and manufacturers (Beechams used the technique successfully to segment the shampoo market in the mid-1970s).

- Martini advertising has been directed at individuals on the basis of what lifestyle they would like to have. It appeals to 'aspirational lifestyle' segments.

- Ford Motor Company identified four basic lifestyle segments for their cars: Traditionalists (who go for wood, leather and chrome); Liberals (keen on environmental and safety features); Life Survivors (who seek minimum financial risk by going for the cheapest options); and Adventurers (who actually like cars and want models to suit their own self-images) (*The Economist*, 30 September 1995).

- Marketing strategy at the House of Fraser department stores group relied on attracting three types of women clothes shoppers to the stores: the 'Follower of Fashion', the 'Smart Career Mover' and the 'Quality Classic – The Woman of Elegance'. The company deliberately decided not to target the 'Young Mum' and other buyers. In the mid-1990s there was some concern that House of Fraser products and merchandising did not attract the target segments (it was found that they tended to shop at House of Fraser only for the concession areas such as Oasis, Alexon and Morgan) (Rankine, 1996).

- B&Q, the UK DIY store, is targeting style-conscious consumers with its portfolio of bedroom and office furniture branded 'it'. The range, created by interior designer Tara Bernerd, is modular, allowing customers to choose according to their taste and the dimensions of their home (*Marketing*, 24 January 2002).

The most significant advantages of lifestyle research are again for guiding the creative content of advertising. Because of the major tasks involved in gathering the data, however, it is unlikely that lifestyle research will supplant demographics as a major segmentation variable.

Summary of background customer characteristics

The background customer characteristics discussed above all examine the individual in isolation from the specific market of interest. While in some markets they may be able to discriminate between probable users and non-users of the product class they can rarely explain brand choice behaviour. Members of the same segments based on background characteristics may behave differently in the marketplace for a variety of reasons. Similarly, members of different segments may be seeking essentially the same things from competing brands and could be usefully grouped together. While traditionally useful for the purposes of media selection and advertising atmosphere design, these characteristics are often too general in nature to be of specific value to marketers. They are essentially descriptive in nature. They describe who the consumer is, but they do not uncover the basic reasons why the consumer behaves as he or she does.

8.5.2 Customer attitudinal characteristics for segmenting markets

Attitudinal characteristics attempt to draw a causal link between customer characteristics and marketing behaviour. Attitudes to the product class under investigation and attitudes towards brands on the market have both been used as fruitful bases for market segmentation.

Benefit segmentation

Classic approaches (e.g. Haley, 1968, 1984) examine the benefits customers are seeking in consuming the product. Segmenting on the basis of benefits sought has been applied to a wide variety of markets such as banking, fast moving consumer products and consumer durables. The building society investment market, for example, can be initially segmented on the basis of the benefits being sought by the customers. Typical benefits sought include high rates of interest (for the serious investor), convenient access (for the occasional investor) and security (for the 'rainy day' investor).

Nokia, the largest maker of mobile phone handsets, has recognised that phones are now seen by many customers as fashion accessories. The Nokia 5510, for example, was aimed at fashion-conscious young people who used their phones for text messaging and music. While the market in the late 1990s was dominated by first-time purchasers of phones, replacement purchases in Western Europe accounted for 60 per cent of sales in 2001 and were predicted to rise to nearer 99 per cent by 2006. The Samsung A400 phone had a flip-up lid in a red 'feminine' version, called the 'Ladyphone', with special features such as biorhythm calculator, a fatness function that calculates height-to-weight ratio, and a calorie count function which estimates calories burned for everyday activities such as shopping, cleaning and cooking. Nokia has even launched a subsidiary named 'Vertu', which is marketing platinum-cased handsets with sapphire crystal screens for the very rich (they retail at $21,000) (*Economist*, 26 January 2002).

Benefit segmentation takes the basis of segmentation right back to the underlying reasons why customers are attracted to various product offerings. As such, it is perhaps the closest means yet to identifying segments on bases directly relevant to marketing decisions. Developments in techniques such as conjoint analysis make them particularly suitable for identifying benefit segments (Hooley, 1982).

Perceptions and preferences

A second approach to the study of attitudes is through the study of perceptions and preferences. Much of the work in the multidimensional scaling area (Green *et al.*, 1989) is primarily concerned with identifying segments of respondents who view the products on offer in a similar way (perceptual space segmentation) and require from the market similar features or benefits (preference segmentation). This approach to market segmentation is discussed further in Chapter 9, where we are concerned with segmentation research.

Summary of attitudinal bases for segmentation

Segmentation on the basis of attitudes, both to the product class and the various brands on offer, can create a more useful basis for marketing strategy development than merely background characteristics. It gets closer to the underlying reasons for behaviour and uses them as the basis for segmenting the market. The major drawback of such techniques is that they require often costly primary research and sophisticated data analysis techniques.

8.5.3 Customer behavioural characteristics for segmenting markets

The most direct method of segmenting markets is on the basis of the behaviour of the consumers in those markets. Behavioural segmentation covers purchases, consumption, communication and response to elements of the marketing mix.

Purchase behaviour

Study of purchasing behaviour has centred on such issues as the time of purchase (early or late in the product's overall life cycle) and patterns of purchase (the identification of brand-loyal customers).

- **Innovators**: because of their importance when new products are launched, innovators (those who purchase a product when it is still new) have received much attention from marketers. Clearly during the launch of new products isolation of innovators as the initial target segment could significantly improve the product's or service's chances of acceptance on the market. Innovative behaviour, however, is not necessarily generalisable to many different product fields. Attempts to seek out generalised innovators have been less successful than looking separately for innovators in a specific field. Generalisations seem most relevant when the fields of study are of similar interest.

- **Brand loyalty**: variously defined, brand loyalty has also been used as a basis for segmentation. While innovators are concerned with initial purchase, loyalty patterns are concerned with repeat purchase. As such, they are more applicable to repeat purchase goods than to consumer durables, though they have been used in durables markets (see the example below). As with innovative behaviour, research has been unable to identify consumers who exhibit loyal behaviour over a wide variety of products. Loyalty, as with innovativeness, is specific to a particular product field.

    Volkswagen, the German automobile manufacturer, has used loyalty as a major method for segmenting its customer markets. It divided its customers into the following categories: First Time Buyers; Replacement Buyers – (a) Model-loyal replacers, (b) Company-loyal replacers, and (c) Switch replacers. These segments were used to analyse performance and market trends and for forecasting purposes.

In the context of e-marketing, companies such as Site Intelligence have devised methods of segmenting website visitors and purchasers using combinations of behavioural (visits) and demographic characteristics.

Consumption behaviour

Purchasers of products and services are not necessarily the consumers, or users, of those products or services. Examination of usage patterns and volumes consumed (as in the heavy user approach) can pinpoint where to focus marketing activity. There are dangers, however, in focusing merely on the heavy users. They are, for example, already using the product in quantity and therefore may not offer much scope for market expansion. Similarly they will either be current company customers or customers of competitors.

Cook and Mindak (1984) have shown that the heavy user concept is more useful in some markets than in others. In the soap market they note that heavy users of soap account for 75 per cent of purchases. However, heavy users account for nearly half the population and constitute a very diverse group. By contrast bourbon whiskey is consumed by around 20 per cent of adults only, and the heavy users account for 95 per cent of consumption, making this a much tighter target market.

In the latter case brand loyalty patterns may be set and competition could be fierce. Companies may be better advised to research further the light or non-users of the product to find out why they do not consume more of the product. In the growth stage of the product life cycle the heavy user segment may well be attractive, but when the market reaches maturity it may make more sense to try to extend the market by mopping up extra potential demand in markets that are not adequately served by existing products.

Product and brand usage has a major advantage over many other situation-specific segmentation variables in that it can be elicited, in the case of many consumer products, from secondary sources. The 'heavy users' of beer, for example, can be identified through the Target Group Index (see Chapter 4) and their demographic and media habits profiled. For this main reason consumption is one of the most popular bases for segmenting consumer markets in the United Kingdom.

Communication behaviour

A further behavioural variable used in consumer segmentation studies has been the degree of communication with others about the product of interest.

Opinion leaders can be particularly influential in the early stages of the product life cycle. Recording companies, for example, recognise the influence that disc jockeys have on the record-buying public and attempt to influence them with free records and other inducements to play their records. In many fields, however, identifying opinion leaders is not so easy. As with innovators, opinion leaders tend to lead opinion only in their own interest areas. A further problem with satisfying opinion leaders is that they tend to have fairly strong opinions themselves and can often be a very heterogeneous group (the 'pop' disc jockeys providing a good example).

In addition to information-giving behaviour (as displayed by opinion leaders) markets could be segmented on the basis of information-seeking behaviour. The information seekers may be a particularly attractive segment for companies basing their strategy on promotional material with a heavy information content.

Response to elements of the marketing mix

The use of elasticities of response to changes in marketing-mix variables as a basis for segmentation is particularly attractive as it can lead to more actionable findings, indicating where marketing funds can best be allocated. Identifying, for example, the deal-prone consumer or the advertising-responsive segment has immediate appeal. There are, however, methodological problems in research in identifying factors such as responsiveness to changes in price.

Relationship-seeking characteristics

A related characteristic for segmentation that is attracting some attention in the light of the move towards relationship marketing (see Chapter 4) is the relationship requirements of customers (Piercy, 1997). One initial model suggests that the relationship-seeking characteristics of customers differ in the type of relationship customers want with suppliers (for example, long term versus short term and transactional) and the intimacy customers want in the relationship (for example, close or distant). This suggests the potential for segmenting markets into such groups as the following, and linking this to other variables:

● **relationship seekers**, who want a close long-term relationship with the supplier or retailer;

● **relationship exploiters**, who want only a short-term relationship with the supplier, but are happy with a close relationship, which they will exploit for any advantages on offer;

● **loyal buyers** – those who want a long-term relationship, but at a distance;

● **arm's-length transaction customers**, who do not want close relationships with suppliers and will shop around for the best deal because they see no value in a long-term relationship.

An example of an integrated study of consumer characteristics on a global scale is work done by the US agency Roper Starch (Shermach, 1995). International business has much interest in whether consumer segments cut across national boundaries and may be more useful than traditional geographical approaches to planning marketing. The study identified the following segments from 40,000 respondents in 40 countries:

● **deal-makers**: well-educated, aged in the early 30s, with average affluence and employment (29 per cent of the sample);

● **price-seekers**: a high proportion of retirees and lowest education level with an average level of affluence and more females than males (23 per cent of the sample);

● **brand loyalists**: mostly male, aged in the mid-30s, with average education and employment, and the least affluent group (23 per cent of the sample);

● **luxury innovators**: the most educated and affluent shoppers, mostly male in professional and executive employment; they seek new, prestigious brands (21 per cent of the sample).

The proportions of consumers in these groups varied in interesting ways across the geographic areas: deal-makers predominate in the United States, Asia, Latin America and the Middle East; price-seekers exist mainly in competitive developed markets such as Europe and Japan. Although producing only stereotypes, the study suggests that consumer behavioural and purchase characteristics may be stronger predictors of purchase behaviour than the traditional country-market definitions used in export and international marketing.

Summary of behavioural bases for segmentation

Many variables have been tested as bases for consumer segmentation, ranging from behaviour, to attitudes, to background characteristics. The most often used characteristics are product and brand usage and demographics/socio-economics, primarily because of the ease of obtaining this sort of data from secondary sources. Ultimately, however, for a segmentation scheme to be useful to marketing management it should seek not only to describe differences in consumers but also to explain them. In this respect attitudinal segmentation can offer better prospects.

8.6 Segmenting business markets

As with consumer markets, a wide variety of factors has been suggested for segmenting business markets, but in fact business segmentation variables can be considered under the same headings as those for consumer markets:

- background company characteristics;
- attitudinal characteristics;
- behavioural characteristics.

It should be noted, however, that market segmentation is substantially less well developed in business marketing than consumer marketing, which may affect both the acceptability of different approaches to companies and the availability of information and support to use a particular approach. It should also be noted that in business-to-business marketing it is far more common to find a one-to-one relationship between supplier and customer. In this situation the segmentation approach may best be applied inside the customer organisation. The segmentation structure below follows the model developed in Shapiro and Bonoma (1990).

8.6.1 Background company characteristics

Demographic characteristics of companies can be a useful starting point for business segmentation; indeed, they characterise the approaches most commonly used by business marketing companies. Factors that can be considered here include demographics such as industry type, customer size and location, but also operating variables such as customer technology and capabilities, different purchasing policies and situational factors including product application.

Industry type

Factors such as the Standard Industry Classification (SIC) provide a first stage of analysis, both for identifying target industries and subdividing them into groups of companies with different needs or different approaches to buying. This may be the basis for vertical marketing to industry sectors. Retailers and hospitals, for example, both buy computers, but they have different applications and different buying strategies.

Company size

Size may also be highly significant if, for instance, small companies have needs or buying preferences that are distinctly different from those of larger companies. Typical measures would be variables such as number of employees and sales turnover.

Size may be very significant because it impacts on issues such as volume requirements, average order size, sales and distribution coverage costs and customer bargaining power, which may alter the attractiveness of different segments as targets. Company size may be analysed alongside other demographics. Companies, for example, selling ingredients for paint manufacture in the United Kingdom could initially segment the market by SIC to identify paint manufacturers, then by size of company as indicated by number of employees (there are only seven companies employing more than 750 employees and together they account for over 60 per cent of the paint market).

Customer location

The geographic location of customers may be a powerful way of segmenting the market for a business product for several reasons. Domestically, location will impact on sales and distribution costs and competitive intensity may vary if there are strong local competitors in some regions. Product demand may vary also – the demand for chemicals for water softening in operating cooling equipment in factories will vary according to local water hardness conditions. Internationally, product preferences may also be different by location – medical diagnostic products sell to the National Health Service in the United Kingdom, but to private testing agencies and medical practices in the United States, and to hospital laboratories in the developing world, all of whom display very different product and price requirements.

Company technology

The customer's stage of technology development will impact directly on its manufacturing and product technology, and hence on its demand for different types of product. Traditional factories operating mixed technologies and assembly methods require different product and sub-assembly inputs (e.g. test equipment, tooling, components) compared with the automated production unit. High-technology businesses may require very different distribution methods – Tesco requires suppliers to have the capability to cooperate in electronic stock control and cross-docking to avoid retail stockholding. Increasingly, high-technology firms require that their suppliers are integrated to their computer systems for all stages of the purchase process.

Customer capabilities

Business customers may differ significantly in their internal strengths and weaknesses, and hence their demand for different types of product and service. For example, in the chemicals industry customers are likely to differ in their technical competencies – some will depend on their suppliers for formulation assistance and technical support far more than others. For many years in the computer business Digital Equipment specialised in selling minicomputers to customers who were able to develop their own software and systems, and did not need the full-service offering of IBM and others: it targeted a segment on the basis of the customers' technical strength in computing.

Purchasing organisation

How customers organise purchasing may also identify important differences between customers. For example, centralised purchasing may require suppliers to have the capability to operate national or international account management, while decentralised purchasing may require more extensive field sales operations. Depending on a supplier's own strengths and weaknesses, the purchasing organisation type may be a significant way of segmenting the market. IBM, for example, has always maintained a strong position in companies with a centralised Information Technology department, while other suppliers have focused on companies where IT is less centralised.

Power structures

The impact of which organisational units have the greatest influence may also be effective in segmenting a market to identify targets matching a supplier's strengths. Digital Equipment traditionally targeted engineering-led customers, where its strengths in engineering applications gave it a competitive edge.

Purchasing policies

The way different customers approach purchasing may also be a source of targeting information. Customers might divide, for example, into: those who want a lease-based deal versus those who want to purchase; those with affirmative action policies versus those dominated by price issues; those who want single supply sources versus those who want to dual source important supplies; public sector and similar organisations where bidding is obligatory versus those preferring to negotiate price; those actively pursuing reductions in their supplier base compared with others. Indeed, the model proposed above of the customer's relationship requirements as a basis for segmenting may be even more useful in the business market, where the demand for partnership between suppliers and customers characterises many large companies' approaches to purchasing.

Product application

The product application can have a major influence on the purchase process and criteria and hence supplier choices. The requirements for a small motor used in intermittent service for a minor application in an oil refinery will differ from the requirements for a small motor in continuous use for a critical process.

8.6.2 Attitudinal characteristics

It is possible also to segment business markets on the basis of the benefits being sought by the purchasers. As we saw, benefit segmentation in the consumer market is the process of segmenting the market in terms of the underlying reasons why customers buy, focusing particularly on differences in why customers buy. Its strength is that it is segmentation based on customer needs. In the business market, the same logic applies to the purchasing criteria of different customers and product applications (see above).

This may be reflected, for example, in urgency of order fulfilment – the urgency of a customer's need to keep a plant in operation or to solve a problem for its own customers may change both the purchase process and the criteria used. Urgent replacements may be bought on the basis of availability, not price. A chemical plant needing to replace broken pipe fittings will pay a premium price for a supplier's applications engineering, flexible manufacturing capacity, speed of delivery and installation skills, while a plant buying pipe fittings to be held in reserve would behave quite differently.

One corporate bank struggled to find a way of segmenting the UK market for corporate financial services; they concluded that the most insightful approach was to examine their customers' own strategies as a predictor of financial service product need and purchasing priorities.

An added complication in business markets, however, is the decision-making unit (see Chapter 4). For many business purchases decisions are made or influenced by a group of individuals rather than a single purchaser. Different members of the DMU will often have different perceptions of what the benefits are, both to their organisation and to themselves.

In the purchase of hoists, for example, the important benefit to a user may be lightness and ease of use, whereas the purchasing manager may be looking for a cheaper product to make his purchasing budget go further. Architects specifying installations for new plant may perceive greater benefit in aesthetically designed hoists and maintenance personnel may look for easy maintenance as a prime benefit.

Benefit segmentation is at the centre, however, of conventional wisdom on selling in business markets. Here the emphasis is on selling benefits rather than features of the product or service. In communicating with the different members of the DMU different benefits may be emphasised for each.

8.6.3 Behavioural characteristics

Behavioural issues relevant to segmenting business markets may include buyers' personal characteristics and product/brand status and volume.

Buyers' personal characteristics

Although constrained by company policies and needs, business products are bought by people in just the same way that consumer products are. Business goods markets can be segmented by issues such as the following:

- **buyer–seller similarity**: compatibility in technology, corporate culture or even company size may be a useful way of distinguishing between customers;
- **buyer motivation**: purchasing officers may differ in the degree to which they shop around and look at numerous alternative suppliers, and dual source important products and services, as opposed to relying on informal contacts for information and remaining loyal to existing personal contacts;
- **buyer risk perceptions**: the personal style of the individual, intolerance of ambiguity, self-confidence and status within the company may also provide significant leverage.

For example, for many years in the computer industry IBM focused on IT buyers in major corporates, providing training information and career development support, to build the 'IBM closed shop' where other suppliers were largely excluded.

Product/brand status and volume

The users of a particular product, brand or supplier may have important things in common that can make them a target. For example, customers may differ in the rate and extent of the adoption of new safety equipment in plants. Companies loyal to a specific competitor may be targeted – for instance to attack that competitor's weaknesses in service or product. Current customers may be a different segment from prospective customers or lost customers.

High-volume product users may be different from medium and low users in how they purchase. Even more than in consumer markets the 80/20 rule (80 per cent of sales typically being accounted for by only 20 per cent of customers) can dominate a business market. Identifying the major purchasers for products and services through volume purchased can be particularly useful. Also of interest may be the final use to which the product or service is put. Where, for example, the final consumer can be identified, working backwards can suggest a sensible segmentation strategy.

The paint market, for example, can be segmented at various levels. At the first level it can be divided into 'decorative paints', mainly used on buildings, and 'industrial paints', used in manufactured products. General industrial paints by volume represented 24 per cent of the UK market, the automobile industry 14 per cent, professional decorative 42 per cent and DIY decorative 22 per cent. Demand for vehicle paints relates to automobile sales (derived demand) and relates closely to demand in this market. In the general industrial paints sector there are various specialist segments such as marine coatings. Here ultimate product use dictates the type of paint and its properties and is the basic method for segmentation.

8.6.4 Summary of bases for segmenting business markets

The segmentation bases available for business marketing follow business buying behaviour as those in consumer marketing follow consumer buying behaviour. Because of the presence, however, of particularly large individual customers in many business markets usage-based segmentation is often employed. For smaller companies geographic segmentation may be attractive, limiting their markets to those that are more easily served. Ultimately, however, in business and consumer markets the basic rationale for segmentation is that groups of buyers exist with different needs or wants (benefits sought) and it is segmentation on the basis of needs and wants that offers the closest approach to implementing the marketing concept.

8.7 Identifying and describing market segments

It will be clear from the above that the first task the manager faces is to decide on what bases to segment the market. If product usage or background characteristics are selected in many markets the segmentation can be accomplished from secondary sources (e.g. from TGI or AGB/TCA in UK consumer markets, or from SIC or Kompass in business markets). Where segmentation is based on attitudes, however, there will often be insufficient data available from secondary sources. In these cases primary research will be necessary.

A typical primary research segmentation study could include initial qualitative research to identify major benefits to users and purchasers of the product or service under consideration. This would be followed by quantitative research to estimate the size of the potential segments and to describe them further in terms of other background characteristics. This methodological approach is described in the seminal work by Haley (1968).

8.7.1 First-order and second-order segmentation

There is a frequent misconception among marketing managers as to what constitutes a market segment.

In consumer marketing, in particular, many managers will describe the segmentation of their market and their selected market targets in terms of customer background characteristics. Thus, for example, a marketer of quality wines might describe the segmentation of the market in terms of social class, the prime target being the ABC1 social classes. From our discussion above, however, it can be seen that this way of segmenting the market is adequate only if all members of the ABC1 group purchase quality wine for the same reasons and in the same way. Where use/benefits of wine purchase differ substantially within a given social class there is the opportunity to segment the market in a more fundamental way.

In reality the most fundamental way of segmenting markets is the market-oriented approach of grouping together customers who are looking for the same benefits in using the product or service. All other bases for segmenting markets are really an approximation of this. The wine marketer assumes that all ABC1s have similar benefit needs from the wines they purchase. Hence use/benefit segmentation can be referred to as **first-order segmentation**. Any attempt to segment a market should commence by looking for different use/benefit segments.

Within identified use/benefit segments, however, there could be large numbers of customers with very different backgrounds, media habits, levels of consumption, and so on. Particularly where there are many offerings attempting to serve the same use/benefit segment concentration on sub-segments within the segment can make sense. Sub-segments, for example, who share common media habits, can form more specific targets for the company's offerings. Further segmentation within use/benefit segments can be termed **second-order segmentation**. Second-order segmentation is used to improve the ability of the company to tailor the marketing mix within a first-order segment.

In the wine example the marketing manager may have identified a first-order segmentation in terms of the uses to which the wine was being put (e.g. as a meal accompaniment, as a home drink, as a social drink, as a cooking ingredient). The quality level of the wine might suggest use in the first segment as a meal accompaniment. Further research would then reveal within this segment further benefit requirements (e.g. price bands individual customers are prepared to consider, character of the wine preferred, etc.).

Having further refined the target through matching the company's offerings to specific customer group requirements the marketer may still find a wide variety of potential customers for his or her wines. Within the identified first-order segment sub-segments based on demographic characteristics could be identified (e.g. AB social class, aged 35–55, male purchaser), enabling a clearer refinement of the marketing strategy.

8.8 The benefits of segmenting markets

There are a number of important benefits that can be derived from segmenting a market, which can be summarised in the following terms:

- Segmentation is a particularly useful approach to marketing for the smaller company. It allows target markets to be matched to company competencies (see Chapter 6), and makes it more likely that the smaller company can create a defensible niche in the market.

- It helps to identify gaps in the market, i.e. unserved or underserved segments. These can serve as targets for new product development or extension of the existing product or service range.

- In mature or declining markets it may be possible to identify specific segments that are still in growth. Concentrating on growth segments when the overall market is declining is a major strategy in the later stages of the product life cycle.

- Segmentation enables the marketer to match the product or service more closely to the needs of the target market. In this way a stronger competitive position can be built (see Jackson, 2007, for the importance for companies of determining their strategic market position). This is particularly important in the Internet age where companies compete in a large and heterogeneous community (see Barnes *et al.*, 2007).

- The dangers of not segmenting the market when competitors do so should also be emphasised. The competitive advantages noted above can be lost to competitors if the company fails to take advantage of them. A company practising a mass marketing strategy in a clearly segmented market against competitors operating a focused strategy can find itself falling between many stools.

8.9 Implementing market segmentation

It should also be noted that there is evidence that companies often struggle with the implementation of segmentation-based strategies, and fail to achieve the potential benefits outlined above (see, e.g., Piercy and Morgan, 1993; Dibb and Simkin, 1994) – this is the difference between segmentation as a normative model and as a business reality (Danneels, 1996).

8.9.1 The scope and purpose of market segmentation

There is growing recognition that conventional approaches may pay insufficient attention to identifying the scope of market segmentation (Plank, 1985). Indeed, a seminal paper by Wind (1978) proposed that in selecting segmentation approaches it is necessary to distinguish between segmentation that has the goal of gaining a general understanding of the market and use for positioning studies, and segmentation concerned with marketing programme decisions in new product launches, pricing, advertising and distribution. These are all valid and useful applications in segmentation analysis, but they are fundamentally different.

8.9.2 Strategic, managerial and operational levels of segmentation

One approach to making the scope of market segmentation clearer is to distinguish between different levels of segmentation, in the way shown in Figure 8.5 (Piercy and Morgan, 1993).

This approach is similar to the first-order and second-order segmentation distinction made above, but goes further in relating the levels of segmentation to organisational issues as well as customer issues. The nature of the different levels of segmentation can be described as follows:

- **Strategic segmentation** is related to management concerns for strategic intent and corporate mission, based on product/service uses and customer benefits.
- **Managerial segmentation** is concerned primarily with planning and allocating resources such as budgets and personnel to market targets.
- **Operational segmentation** focuses on the issue of aiming marketing communications and selling efforts into the distribution channels that reach and influence market targets (and their subdivisions).

These differences are important to gaining insight into what segmentation can contribute to building marketing strategy and competitive positioning, but also to understanding the sources of implementation problems with segmentation-based strategies. For example, when the manager responsible for marketing replacement car exhausts to car owners groups his or her customers in terms of their fears, ignorance and transport dependence, rather than their requirements for different product specifications and engineering, he or she is concerned with creating a new understanding

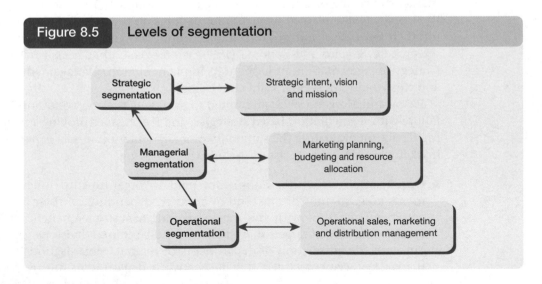

Figure 8.5   Levels of segmentation

of the market (strategic segmentation), not a model for the detailed application of marketing resources (operational segmentation).

When the corporate banker looks at the corporate banking market in terms of the strategic financial services needs of customers, based on their own corporate strategies (Carey, 1989), the goal is to create a framework for strategy, not a mechanism for advertising and salesforce allocation.

On the other hand, when advertisers and sales managers describe buyers in terms of socio-economic groups, geographic location or industrial sector, they are concerned with the effective targeting of advertising, sales promotion, selling and distribution resources, rather than describing customer benefit-based market segments. Market segmentation studies describing consumer groups in terms of their media behaviour – for example as 'mainstream media rejecters', 'genteel media grazers', '30-somethings', and so on (Laing, 1991) – are concerned with operational effectiveness, not strategic positioning.

Confusing these very different roles for segmentation may be why segmentation is sometimes seen as a failure in organisations:

> *Failed segmentation efforts tend to fall into one of two categories: the marketer-dominated kind, with little data to support its recommendations, or the purely statistical type that identifies many consumer differences that aren't germane to the company's objectives.*
>
> (Young, 1996)

The implication is that clarifying the role and purpose of an approach to segmentation may be important to avoid unrealistic expectations. However, it is clear that segmentation-based strategies do sometimes fail at the implementation stage.

8.9.3 Sources of implementation problems

The recognition of implementation problems with segmentation-based strategies may be traced back over the years: Wind (1978) noted that little was known about translating segment research into marketing strategies; Young *et al.* (1978) accused marketers of being preoccupied with segmentation technique rather than actionability; Hooley (1980) blamed segmentation failures on the use of analytical techniques for their own sake and poor communication between managers and marketing researchers. Shapiro and Bonoma (1990) wrote: 'Much has been written about the strategy of segmentation, little about its implementation, management and control', and this would still seem a valid conclusion.

Piercy and Morgan (1993) attempted to catalogue the sources of implementation failure with segmentation-based strategies, and these issues provide a further screening device for evaluating the suitability of a segmentation model generated through market research. Issues to assess include the following:

● **Organisation structure**: Companies tend to organise into functional departments and sub-units of one kind or another, depending on their task allocation and how they deal with the outside world. A customer benefits approach to establishing market targets may cut across these internal divisions – they may not 'fit' with the jurisdiction of departments or regional organisations for sales and marketing. Segment targets that fall between departments and regions may be neglected and lack 'ownership', and the strategies built around them will fail. We need to map carefully how segment targets will match the internal organisation structure.

● **Internal politics**: Young (1996) argues that strategic segmentation is essentially a cross-functional activity, requiring expertise and involvement by many functional specialists. If functions cannot collaborate or work together because people are vying for power and withholding their knowledge and expertise, the segmentation strategy is likely to fail. If our segmentation-based strategy relies on internal collaboration and cooperation, we need to be sure this can be achieved or the strategy will fail.

● **Corporate culture**: In some circumstances customer benefit segmentation is unacceptable to people inside an organisation, because it is not how they understand the world. Organisations dominated by strong professional groups frequently have struggles with customer benefit segments – examples are traditional financial service companies and professional service firms such as law and accountancy. The problem may be in overcoming bankers' preferences for 'prudent banking' to develop customer focus.

● **Information and reporting**: Novel segmentation schemes may not fit with existing information systems and reporting systems. This may mean it is difficult to evaluate the worth of segment targets, or to allocate responsibilities and monitor performance in doing business with them.

● **Decision-making processes**: If segmentation schemes identify new market targets that are not recognised in plans (they are not currently part of the served market, they are spread across existing segment targets for which responsibility has been allocated, or they are subsumed within an existing segment), then they may be ignored in the planning process and when plans are implemented. Similarly, segment targets that are not recognised by existing resource allocation processes may face difficulty in getting a marketing budget. We should examine carefully how a new segmentation approach can be integrated with planning and budgeting and in evaluation systems.

● **Corporate capabilities**: It is all too easy for marketing researchers and analysts to develop attractive market targets, but a company may have little basis for achieving a competitive advantage simply because it lacks the capabilities for dealing with this type of customer (see Chapter 6).

● **Operational systems**: Segmentation strategy may fail because it underestimates the problems faced at the operational level in translating segmentation strategy into effective reality: Can salespeople deal with this target customer? Do we have access to the distribution channels we need? Do we have the expertise to develop and operate segment-based advertising and promotion? Do we have market research organised around the segment targets so we can identify them, measure opportunities and evaluate progress? Do we have the technical facilities to price differently to different customer types if this is required? We should look very carefully at the operational capabilities we have in sales, advertising, promotion and distribution, and question their ability to adapt to a new segmentation-based strategy.

Figure 8.6 Market segment attractiveness and organisational resource strength

Organisational resource strength

		High	Low
Market segment attractiveness	**High**	**Best prospects** Attractive segments that fit well with organisational resources	**Build strengths first** Attractive markets but with poor fit with organisational resources
	Low	**Poor prospects** Unattractive segments that fit well with organisational resources	**Worst prospects** Unattractive segments with a poor fit with organisational resources

Many of these issues are covert and hidden inside the organisation, yet to ignore them is to place the strategy at risk. One proposal is that in addition to the conventional evaluation of market targets each potential target should be tested for internal compatibility, as suggested in Figure 8.6.

This analysis may suggest that some market targets are unattractive because they have a poor 'fit' with the company's structures and processes, or even that the company is not capable of implementing a segmentation-based strategy at the present time, or it may identify the areas that need to be changed if the segment target is to be reached effectively.

Summary

In increasingly fragmented markets, marketers in both consumer and business markets are turning more and more to segmentation methods to identify prime market targets. In approaching market segmentation, companies must confront the sometimes quite sophisticated methodology of segmentation, test the market targets identified and make the strategic segmentation decision of how to use a segmentation model in developing its market strategy.

This suggests that one of the major decisions faced is: 'What bases to segment on?' We have seen that there are a great many potential bases for segmentation in consumer and business markets, and for product and service (and non-profit) marketing.

Arguably the segmentation approach closest to extending the marketing concept is use/benefit segmentation originally suggested some 40 years ago by Haley (1968). While it does require considerable primary investigation, understanding the benefits customers derive in buying and/or consuming products and services is central to designing an integrated marketing strategy.

There are substantial potential benefits to be gained from basing marketing strategy on rigorous market segmentation. However, the organisational issues impacting on the implementation of segmentation-based strategies should also be evaluated to test for the internal compatibility of segment targets and the costs of organisational change that may be involved in segmentation-based marketing strategies.

The next chapter, on segmentation research, concentrates on the methodology for developing bases for segmentation.

Internet Exchange Case study

Alamy/Fredik Renander

Internet advertisers, wake up and smell the coffee! No, really. The fumes might lead marketers to one of the few places where the in-vogue theory for mixing on- and offline media can be tested.

Internet cafés have what standard Internet service providers or portals too often lack – 'captive' visitors, a proven charging model and physical assets with which to reinforce the messages of on-screen branding.

Many cafés, particularly independents, have struggled to gain scale and customer footfall to justify relatively fixed start-up and running costs. The spread of Internet access, at home or work, together with the advent of unmetered-access pricing, was supposed to sound their death-knell.

In fact, large café chains appear to be thriving. Internet Exchange, the international network of 171 franchised and wholly owned cafés, says it will go into operating profit 'within the next few weeks'.

easyEverything, the chain of giant cafés started by Stelios Haji-Ioannou, the low-cost airline entrepreneur, now provides 9,500 seats in 21 stores across eight countries. It recently signed a deal to open its first franchised operation, in

Athens, probably to be followed by Budapest.

The two chains claim to deliver, respectively, an average 1m and 2.2m Internet sessions across their outlets every month, although a user might buy several sessions during one visit. (The numbers are not audited by ABC Electronic, though easyEverything has plans to do so.) According to a report from Allegra Strategies, the consultancy, just under 60 per cent of people named web cafés as the best place to surf outside work or home. Allegra forecasts 54 per cent compound annual growth in the number of UK chain outlets opened between June 2000 and December 2002. And with claims to marry the captive audience of cinema or in-flight advertising with high-street shop frontage, the chains are going after media spend.

Both chains argue that even in a tight advertising climate they are delivering better results than online-only properties. Internet Exchange says in-store promotions have driven click-throughs on some screen campaigns for Mars and Virgin to between 5 and 50 per cent. easyEverything gives a typical rate for an online campaign as £1 a click, higher than market rates. Homepage channel sponsors pay from £2,000 to £10,000 for a three-month tenancy across the easyEverything network.

The reasons for these high rates, according to Maurice Kelly, chief executive of easyEverything, are distinctly low-tech. 'The most valuable space in the UK for McVities will be the one on a wall at the supermarket because the branding opportunity is as close as possible to the point of sale,' Kelly says. 'I have a million websites to choose from. A dotcom that buys ambient media in an easyEverything outlet can direct a customer to its website.'

Slots for sale range from stickers on mouse mats, screens and phones (used for international calls made via the Internet), to window and wall posters. BT and Consignia (formerly the Post Office) are among future poster clients.

Mike Roberts, general manager at ee-media sales, the joint venture set up with Spafax, the WPP-owned specialist in in-flight content and marketing, is responsible for selling easyEverything media space. To him, the entire 540-seat branch at Tottenham Court Road, central London, is a series of branding opportunities.

'We can replace selected keys on the keyboards with branded ones. Our staff could be wearing branded T-shirts. We can have stickers on the floor, on the coffee cups . . .' he says.

Before this vision goes into overdrive, it should be stated that easyEverything's core business has not changed. It still sells seats in front of Internet screens in much the same way as easyJet sells seats on planes. To cover costs, it needs to ensure a minimum average occupancy rate. This was first set at 40 per cent of all seats on the assumption that cafés stayed open 24 hours a day and charged an average of £1 per hour.

Adapting the 'yield' model applied by airlines for flight tickets, stores continually alter basic access prices to manage the trade-off between volume and margin. The model has been changed: price parameters are now fixed at between £1 and £3 an hour and the 580-seat High Street Kensington store, some of its most expensive real estate, now closes at night because of lack of demand. But the emphasis is still on volume. And in an online medium that is supposed to deliver personalised communications, is that what advertisers want? Kelly says: 'If we ran this business entirely for its advertising income, then I guess we would be data mining.

'We are only interested in the business as an advertising vehicle because of the numbers and because of the age group of our customers. That is what makes us an appropriate medium for some brands.' According to easyEverything, its users are aged 16–24 and predominantly local, if temporary, residents.

An average visit lasts 50 minutes, and about 40 per cent walk through the doors three times a week. Online, they exhibit the same 'tunnel' vision as everyone else, with a strong propensity to use e-mail and chat forums rather than surf multiple sites, where they might be exposed to advertising.

Mary Keane-Dawson, managing director of Spafax UK, describes the audience as 'notoriously difficult to reach, but valuable'. One thing they clearly want, she says, is cheap and fast access to the Web.

Kelly adds: 'If you advertise on a portal, you are mostly getting access to their customers for the minute or so before they get to the sites they want to visit. For the entire time a person is sitting in easyEverything, we can deliver inventory to them.'

The contrast with online portals is made even more directly by Simon Henderson, chief executive of Internet Exchange, which is less price-focused, more mass market and whose cafés are usually less centrally situated than easyEverything's. Henderson cites a Merrill Lynch report comparing the cost of customer acquisition and media sales at Internet Exchange and a variety of online portals.

Merrill Lynch estimates that Internet Exchange spends £4.20 in marketing to acquire each customer, compared to Liberty Surf, which spends £98.61. The chain's annual media sales per customer were £25.57, compared to £5.28 at Freeserve and £4.20 at Yahoo! Such figures clearly exclude the huge costs a café chain needs to sink before it can create the infrastructure to acquire customers in the first place. Cafés could not possibly compete on reach or scalability with online properties. The New York easyEverything branch alone cost around $3m to open and market, and although it has run campaigns for Nokia, Warner Bros and Virgin, many international youth brands have yet to make the leap. Jeffrey Young, of Allegra Strategies, questions whether café chains will ever have a big enough audience to deliver mainstream campaigns.

Both easyEverything and Internet Exchange also admit that it is still rare for British buyers and agencies, used to separate budgets, to buy on- and offline media in one go.

Henderson argues that what matters to advertisers is a comparison of effectiveness of marketing spend across media.

'I don't know anyone in this market who isn't looking at what they are getting for their marketing pounds and judging spending by results,' he says.

Source: Carlos Grande, 'Internet Advertisers, Wake Up and Smell the Coffee!' *Financial Times*, Creative Business, 10 July 2001, p. 8.

Discussion questions

1 Since users of Internet cafés are such a small portion of the population, what is the point in using them for advertising? Have other media similarly narrow user bases?

2 Using a range of criteria, describe the segments who are likely to be heavy users of Internet cafés. How can users be further segmented based on their use of the Internet?

3 Given the Internet café user segments and the nature of Internet advertising, what products are appropriate for advertising using the medium and what are suitable advertising objectives?

chapter nine

Segmentation and positioning research

Researchers are anxious to find a magic formula that will profitably segment the market in all cases and under all circumstances. As with the medieval alchemist looking for the philosopher's stone, this search is bound to end in vain.

Baumwoll (1974)

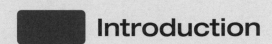 **Introduction**

While the last chapter was concerned with the underlying concepts and principles for the key strategic issues of competitive positioning and market segmentation, the subject of this chapter is the research and modelling techniques that can be applied to evaluate these issues operationally.

The first section of the chapter focuses on segmentation research, and in particular the critical questions of whether or not to pursue a segment-based approach, and if so whether these are based a priori on some predefined segmentation scheme or developed *post hoc* on the basis of creative, empirical research. The second part of the chapter turns to positioning research, which may often be carried out in parallel to segmentation research, applying both qualitative techniques such as focus groups and depth interviews, together with quantitative modelling methods such as perceptual mapping through multidimensional scaling.

The process of identifying potential market targets can be one of the most creative aspects of marketing. There is no single 'right way' to segment any market. Different competitors may adopt different approaches in the same market. All may be intrinsically valid, but each may lead to a different conceptualisation of the market, and subsequently a different marketing approach and a different strategy. The creative aspect of segmentation research lies in finding a new way to conceptualise your market, a way that will offer some competitive advantage over the ways competitors choose.

Two broad approaches to segmentation research are typically pursued. First, the a priori approach. This entails using an 'off-the-peg' segmentation scheme, such as socio-economic or geodemographic classifications. Central to this approach is that the segmentation scheme is known in advance and the number of segments predetermined by the scheme chosen. By its very nature **a priori segmentation** uses schemes that are in the public domain and hence also available to competitors.

The second approach is a *post-hoc* or **cluster-based** approach to segmentation. In this approach the final segmentation scheme is not known in advance, nor is the appropriate number of segments. The criteria on which to segment are defined in advance, but may typically be multidimensional (e.g. usage and attitude data). Data are then collected on these criteria (through the use of qualitative and/or quantitative marketing research) and analysed to identify underlying patterns or structure. The segmentation scheme emerges from the data analysis reflecting patterns identified in response. The data analysis itself is part science (using statistical techniques) and part art (employing judgement on which criteria to include and how to interpret the output). In this way the segmentation scheme emerging is likely to be unique to the specific analysis. This offers potential for looking at the market afresh and identifying new opportunities not necessarily seen by competitors. It also, of course, requires that any segmentation scheme created be rigorously tested to ensure that it is not merely an artefact of the specific dataset or the analytical technique employed.

Following the discussion of segmentation approaches the chapter goes on to discuss alternative methods for researching and presenting positions in the marketplace. Two broad approaches are discussed. First, the use of **qualitative** research methods to uncover brand, product and company images. These approaches are particularly popular in the development of advertising programmes. Second, **quantitative** approaches to modelling positions are explored, from simple profiling on semantic or similar scales, through the more complex modelling available to multidimensional scaling and correspondence analysis techniques.

To segment or not to segment? That is the question

Although a central part of most marketing programmes, there are circumstances in which segmentation may be inappropriate. It could be, for example, that customer needs and wants in a particular market are essentially homogeneous, and hence similar offerings can be made to appeal across the whole market, or that the costs associated with pursuing individual market segments with tailored marketing programmes outweigh their longer-term economic value.

A company following a segmented approach has either to choose a single market segment at which to aim, and therefore have a marketing mix that is inappropriate for other customers, or develop a series of marketing mixes appropriate for customer segments with different needs. Within UK retailing the two approaches have clearly been used by Next, which expanded its retailing chains to cater for the growing needs of young professionals, and the Burton Group, which has used the differently positioned Top Shop, Evans, Harvey Nichols stores, etc. to appeal to a variety of segments.

Both these approaches have limitations depending on the company's longer-term objectives. A single-focus company has limitations to its potential because the market segment itself is limited. If the company has expansion and growth objectives these may be constrained by the size of its target market. This, of course, would be less of a problem for a small or medium-sized company following the dictum *think small – stay small*. A company taking the multiple segment approach may face diseconomies in managing, supplying and promoting in a different way to each of the segments it has chosen. In some cases an economic alternative is to use an undifferentiated mix designed to appeal to as many segments as possible. The company does not fine-tune its offering to any one segment but hopes to attract a sufficient number of customers from all segments with one mix. The company can, therefore, benefit from economies of scale in a simple operation but may be damaged by the 'sameness of the mix', not appealing to the customers in each segment completely, or by better targeted competitors.

The appropriateness of segmenting or not segmenting depends on economies of scale, the cost of developing separate marketing mixes and the homogeneity of the needs of different markets – issues that are pursued further in Chapter 10. Such are the similarities in demand for petroleum, for example, that the products being supplied by competitors converge as they all seek to develop a mix with broad market appeal. Certainly segments do exist, but not of significant magnitude or difference to justify separate appeals. The aerospace industry and automobile industry have markets that are diverse but in which development and manufacturing costs are such that it is not feasible to develop products to fit all market needs exactly. The successful companies, therefore, focus on a relatively small product range with variations that appeal to individual customer preferences.

Even in markets whose main body does not demand segmentation, however, there are often small-scale opportunities where companies can thrive by pursuing a focus strategy. Examples include Aston Martin (now owned by Ford) and Morgan Cars in the sports car market. Therefore, even in markets where the major players may be using a mass strategy, segmentation offers an opportunity for some smaller participants. For small market share companies in particular, the advice is: segment, segment, segment!

Whereas the previous chapter concentrated on the concept of segmentation and possible bases for segmentation, this chapter follows the process of identifying usable market segments. First we discuss a priori approaches to segmentation. The chapter then goes on to discuss *post-hoc*, cluster-based approaches. For the latter we follow a model developed by Maier and Saunders (1990), which takes segmentation research from initiation through to eventual tracking. Within this framework the wide range of approaches and techniques for segmentation are discussed.

9.1   A priori segmentation approaches

9.1.1   Single variable segmentation

A priori, or off-the-peg, methods are the easiest way of segmenting markets. In their original form this involved searching among demographic or socio-economic characteristics and identifying which of these form significant and useful splits within the marketplace. Usually the search for appropriate criteria would be guided by some expectation of how the market could be divided.

The major advantage of this approach is that it can be undertaken from secondary sources and can be related directly to advertising media and messages. In the UK, consumer markets studies such as the Target Group Index enable managers to identify heavy users of a product group and relate this directly to their media usage. Crimp (1990) cites an example from TGI which shows that the proportion of wine users is higher among *Daily Express* readers and lower among *News of the World* readers than the national average. Wine users are also shown to be light viewers of television. A marketing manager responsible for wine sales may have segmented the market on wine use and can then use the TGI data to help select appropriate media.

There are some clear cases where a priori segmentation has proved a powerful tool. The successful toy company Lego, for example, has carefully developed assembly toys to fit the development of children from birth to mid-teens, segmenting the market on the basis of age. Duplo, their pre-school product, starts with rattles and manipulative toys, which are not immediately intended for assembly but do have fixture mechanisms that allow the child to progress into Duplo proper (chunky and brightly coloured bricks and shapes which can be assembled into all manner of toys). Duplo overlaps with Lego, a system of building bricks upon which the Lego empire was formed. Almost identical to Duplo parts in every other way, the Lego units are half the size, and therefore suitable for a child's enhanced manipulative ability, and allow more detail in construction. They are also cleverly designed to link with the Duplo units and therefore allow relatively easy progression from one to the other. As the children get older so they can progress to Legotechnic, and other specialist variants, which again build on the manipulative, assembly and design skills inculcated with earlier sets.

Age is also used as a powerful segmentation variable in the package tour market. ClubMed and Club 18–30 are aimed at the single or young couples market, while Saga Holidays are aimed at the over-50s.

Despite their ease of use and intuitive appeal, attempts to validate demographic and socio-economic bases in terms of product preferences have met with little success. One of the earliest reported attempts to validate this approach was by Evans (1959), who sought to use demographic variables to distinguish between Ford and Chevrolet owners in the United States. He concluded that:

> *demographic variables are not a sufficiently powerful predictor to be of much practical use . . . [they] point more to the similarity of Ford and Chevrolet owners than to any means of discriminating between them. Analysis of several other objective factors also leads to the same conclusion.*

In other markets the conclusions have been similar. Some relationships were found, but no more than could have been expected to occur by chance if the data were random. Unfortunately study after study throws doubt on the direct usefulness of demographic characteristics as a predictor for product purchase.

These findings do not dispute the certainty that some products with clearly defined target consumers depend heavily on demographic characteristics. For instance, nappies are purchased by families with babies, incontinence pads by older people and sanitary towels by women. However, evidence does seem to show that demographic characteristics alone are incapable of distinguishing between the subtle differences in markets that are not explained by the physiological differences between human beings. Perhaps most limiting, they have been found to be poor differentiators of individual products within the broad categories identified (i.e. brand of nappy or sanitary towel).

In business markets perhaps the most often used segmentation variable is the Standard Industrial Classification code. The industry classification can be very specific. Hindle and Thomas (1994) cite the SIC in the United States for manufacturers of a pair of pliers. The full code is '342311', made up as follows:

- '34' indicates a classification for fabricated metal products.
- '2' shows the industry group as cutlery, hand tools and hardware.
- '3' indicates the specific industry of hand and edge tools.
- '1' shows the product class of mechanics' hand service tools.
- '1' shows the product – pliers.

By selecting appropriate SICs a business marketer can identify the other businesses that may be most receptive to its offerings. Again, however, for businesses selling products and services that can be used across industry classifications (such as stationery, machine tools or consultancy services) SIC may be of little practical value as a segmentation base. While giving the impression of detail (six-figure classifications), the codes do not offer many clues as to why specific products are purchased or what is likely to appeal to individual customers.

9.1.2 Multiple variable a priori methods

Recently the traditional demographic and socio-economic means of off-the-peg segmentation have been supplemented by more sophisticated methods being promoted, in consumer marketing at least, by advertising and market research agencies.

These encompass the subjective methods and the marketing-specific objective measures discussed in Chapter 8. The distinction between these and the approaches discussed above is that multiple criteria are considered simultaneously and segments created on the basis of these multiple measures. A number of different consumer classification schemes have been suggested, such as ACORN, MOSAIC, VALS. These schemes have been created through analysis of large datasets (in the case of the former, two official census data) using cluster analytical techniques. They are still considered a priori because once formed they are then available for any users off the peg from the agencies concerned.

Earliest of the multiple variable a priori techniques was the extensive use of personality inventories in the 1960s and 1970s. At that time, researchers were seeking to identify personality typologies that could be related, in much the same way as socio-economic factors were, to purchase decisions and consumption patterns. Techniques of personality measurement were borrowed by marketing from psychologists. Set psychological tests such as the Edwards Personality Preference Schedule and the Catell 16 PF Inventory were tested in a marketing context. Unfortunately these tests showed them to be of little more discriminating power than the less sophisticated demographic and socio-economic methods.

Compared with demographic and socio-economic off-the-peg methods, personality inventories have a slight but insubstantial advantage. They do appear to be able to discriminate to a small extent between some high-involvement products, but even in these cases they leave the majority of variance unexplained. As with demographic and socio-economic methods, they seem to have most power to discriminate in markets where their measurement has a clear role, such as smoking, which reflects a drug dependency, and deodorants, which suggest anxiety. However, the subtlety of personality measurement renders it less useful as an off-the-peg measure in most cases because the personality differences are less strong and obvious than the physiological differences that demographics can measure: introversion and dependency are well-defined personality traits, but they are nowhere near as easily measured or as linked to behaviour as gender or age.

At the same time that personality traits were being explored as potential bases for segmentation, marketers were also experimenting with combining demographic characteristics to create the idea of the consumer life cycle. Under this model, age, marital status and family size were combined to identify a life cycle stage. This approach has been used for the marketing of holidays, insurance, housing, baby products and consumer durables. A more recent development is the SAGACITY classification scheme, developed by the Research Services Ltd marketing research agency. This scheme combines life cycle (dependent, pre-family, family, late) with income (better off, worse off) and occupation (blue collar, white collar). Crouch and Housden (1996) list 12 resulting SAGACITY segments and show the types of products the different segments are considered likely to purchase.

The introduction of CACI's ACORN geo-demographic database represented one of the biggest steps forward in segmentation and targeting techniques. Its basis was segments derived from published census information that provides a classification of neighbourhoods based on housing types. Although the measure is crude, the great strength of the service depends on CACI's own research linking the neighbourhood groups to demographics and buyer behaviour, together with the ability to target households. The system, therefore, provides a direct link between off-the-peg segmenting and individuals, unlike earlier methods that provided indirect means only of contacting the demographic or personality segments identified.

Like the other a priori techniques, the limitations of CACI's approach is the variability within neighbourhoods and the dissimilarity in their buying behaviour for many product classes. English (1989) provides an example of this where five enumeration districts (individual neighbourhood groups of 150 households) are ranked according to geo-demographic techniques. Of the five, two were identified as being prime mailing prospects. However, when individual characteristics were investigated, the five groups were found to contain 31, 14, 10, 10 and 7 prospects respectively: the enumeration districts had been ranked according to the correct number of prospects, but neighbourhood classifications alone appeared to be a poor method of targeting. With only 31 prime target customers being in the most favoured enumeration district, 119 out of 150 households would have been mistargeted. To be fair, as with other means of off-the-peg segmentation discussed, geo-demographics are powerful when related to products linked directly to characteristics of the neighbourhood districts; for instance, the demand for double glazing, gardening equipment, etc. Even in the case provided, targeting the best enumeration districts increases the probability of hitting a target customer from less than 10 per cent to over 20 per cent, but misses are still more common than hits. More recent developments have included CCN's MOSAIC, Pinpoint's PIN and SuperProfiles, all based on census data but using different items and different clustering techniques (Crimp and Wright, 1995).

Lifestyle segmentation provides an opportunity to overlay geo-demographic data with lifestyle characteristics. In this descriptive form they have existed for some time and have been associated with the original success of Storehouse's Habitat chain or the success of the Conservative Party in the 1986 British General Election. These have sometimes been used in conjunction with demographics and form the second part of two-stage segmentation. Third Age Research has done this after first identifying the over-65s as a target market and then breaking them up into lifestyle segments of apathetic, comfortable, explorer, fearful, organiser, poor me, social lion and status quo. To anyone who has contact with more than one older person it is clear that these labels provide a much more powerful way of putting a face on the over-65 customer than does their age alone.

Stanford Research Institute in the United States developed a lifestyle segmentation scheme called Values and Lifestyles (VALS) that has seven categories: **belongers** (patriotic, stable traditionalists content with their lives); **achievers** (prosperous, self-assured, middle-aged materialists); **emulators** (ambitious young adults trying to break into the system); **I-am-me group** (impulsive, experimental and a bit narcissistic); **societally conscious** (mature, successful, mission-oriented people who like causes); **survivors** (the old and poor with little optimism for the future); **sustainers** (resentful of their condition and trying to make ends meet). A similar scheme has been developed for use in pan-European marketing including: **successful idealists**; **affluent materialists**; **comfortable belongers**; **disaffected survivors**; and **optimistic strivers** (Hindle and Thomas, 1994).

Further developments have linked lifestyle segments to customer databases. In the United Kingdom there are several of these (Coad, 1989).

- **The Lifestyle Selector:** A UK database started in 1985 by the American National Demographics & Lifestyle Company. The Lifestyle Selector collects data from questionnaires packed with consumer durables or from retailers and holds over 4.5 million returned, self-completed questionnaires.

- **Behaviour Bank:** The UK service provided by the American Computerized Marketing Technologies company. This collects data from syndicated questionnaires distributed directly to consumers via magazines and newspapers, and holds over 3.5 million returned questionnaires.

- **Omnidata:** This is a result of a joint venture between the Dutch Post Office and the Dutch *Reader's Digest*. The company mails its questionnaires to all Dutch telephone subscribers and tries to induce them to respond by arguing that by doing so they would receive less junk mail. Twenty-three per cent of consumers responded, and Omnidata has 730,000 households on file from a total of 5 million in Holland.

- **Postaid:** This is a Swedish organisation by PAR, a subsidiary of the Swedish Post Office. It was started in the early 1980s and, similar to the Dutch system, was based on the thesis that people should be given the chance to determine the kind of mail they want to receive. The result is a database containing 1 million of Sweden's 3.7 million households.

Most research carried out so far has been on generalised lifestyle typologies and their comparative use in discriminating consumer attitudes and behaviour (Wilmott, 1989). The results are mixed, but one study (O'Brien and Ford, 1988) suggests that such generalised typologies are less efficient than traditional variables such as social class or age as discriminators. While the relative merit of demographic variables and lifestyle tends to vary from situation to situation overall, in the comparisons that have been conducted lifestyle comes out worst. It must therefore be concluded that, as with their less sophisticated demographic brethren, lifestyle segments are no panacea for marketing. Although, when added to databases, they provide a powerful means of shifting from target markets to individual customers, their low coverage renders them of limited value. On the other hand, lifestyle segments, where valid, do provide a more graphic portrayal of customers than do demographics, and hence can give suggestions for advertising copy platforms. As with single demographic variables, it is too much to hope that a single classification will work beyond markets for which they are particularly well suited.

To return to Lego, which has been so successful in using age as a way of discriminating between sectors in the market for construction toys. Once the individuality of children starts to develop Lego has found it necessary to develop a wide range of products covering the different needs of children: Lego Basic for 3–12-year-olds, which specialises in using the original Lego components as they were initially contrived; Fabuland, aimed at 4–8-year-old girls, which revolves around a fantasy theme based on animal characters; Legoland for 5–12-year-olds, which are sub-themes of space, medieval life, pirates and modern suburbia; and Legotechnic for 7–16-year-olds, which has a focus on engineering mechanisms. Although the company found demographics as the first basis of segmentation, to go further depended on identifying customer characteristics specific to the product in question.

All the above approaches are in the public domain and hence, even where they do offer reliable segmentation schemes of a market, they will rarely offer the marketer any originality in viewing it. The essence of a competitively useful segmentation scheme is that it is fresh, new, original and provides insights into the market that competitors do not have. To achieve this originality requires primary research, where preconceptions about the market structure are put on one side and patterns sought from the original data.

9.2 Post-hoc/cluster-based segmentation approaches

Unlike the methods discussed above for segmenting markets, the *post-hoc* approach does not commence with a preconception of market structure. The analysis is undertaken with a view to uncovering naturally existing segments rather than shoehorning customers into predefined categories.

The remainder of this chapter discusses how firms can go about this more creative approach to segmentation. In doing so it follows a model developed by Maier and Saunders (1990) (see Figure 9.1). The process flows from initiation of the desire to segment the market creatively through to the tracking of continuing segment usefulness.

9.2.1 Setting the boundaries

Original and creative segmentation research needs both market and technical expertise. This often necessitates a dialogue between a manager commissioning a segmentation study and an agency or individual conducting the necessary research. The value of the final segmentation results will depend on the effort the individuals concerned have taken in bridging the gap between the technical requirements of segmentation methods and the practical knowledge of marketing and sales management. It is customary to see this bridge-building role as a responsibility of the researcher (who will typically be a modeller or marketing scientist) but, since the marketing manager is going to depend on the results and is going to be responsible for implementing them, he or she has a clear vested interest in ensuring a mutual understanding is achieved. Whereas the expert or modeller faces rejection if the technical gap is not bridged, the marketing manager may face failure in the marketplace if the relationship fails. When employing an agency the marketing manager will certainly need to know how to cross-examine the agency to ensure their methods are appropriate and their assumptions valid.

The entry of the marketing researcher or marketing modeller into the segmentation process is similar to opening a sale. If good initial relationships are not formed the chance of further progress is slight. The researcher has to establish credibility by showing relevant expertise while fitting into the client's culture. As in selling, the prior gathering of information about the industry, the company and the personnel is beneficial. A grasp of terminology popular in the company is particularly useful.

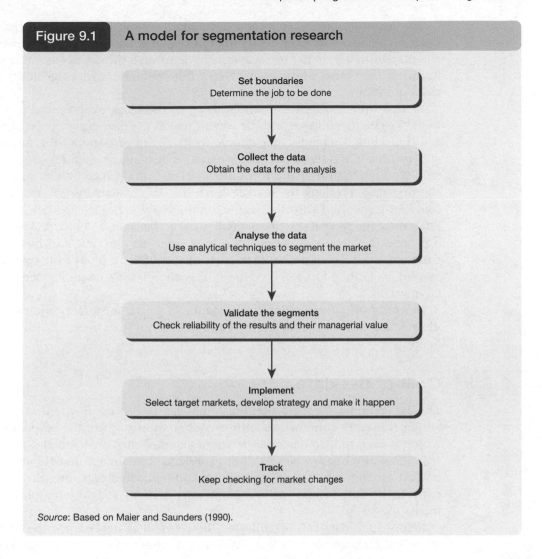

Figure 9.1 A model for segmentation research

Set boundaries
Determine the job to be done

Collect the data
Obtain the data for the analysis

Analyse the data
Use analytical techniques to segment the market

Validate the segments
Check reliability of the results and their managerial value

Implement
Select target markets, develop strategy and make it happen

Track
Keep checking for market changes

Source: Based on Maier and Saunders (1990).

This preparation accelerates the formation of the mutual understanding necessary for successful model implementation.

The roles of the salesperson and the marketing researcher should be different because, although a salesperson usually has a limited set of products to sell, the marketing researcher should theoretically be able to choose without bias from a wide portfolio of appropriate techniques. Unfortunately this perspective is an ideal, for many marketing research agencies have a predisposition towards techniques with which they are familiar, or may even have developed in-house. So, in commissioning segmentation research, the marketing manager has to have sufficient knowledge to resist being supplied from a limited portfolio of solutions. Beware the researcher adopting the *'have technique – will travel'* approach!

The major lessons for starting a segmentation project are that the first contact is critical and that successful segmentation depends on the marketing manager and the marketing researcher being sympathetic to each other's needs – not necessarily knowing each other's business perfectly, but certainly having the ability to ask the right questions.

At this initial stage it is essential to agree the focus of the project, the product market to be investigated and the way in which the results are intended to be used. Multi-product companies may choose to start with one application and proceed to others if the trial is successful. There may also be market structures – such as the division between industrial and consumer markets – that suggest a two-stage approach: the first stage breaking the market down into easily definable groups, and the second being involved with the segmentation analysis proper. In their segmentation analysis of the general practitioner (GP) market, Maier and Saunders (1990) used such a process by first dividing doctors into general practitioners and hospital doctors, this distinction being necessary because of the different jobs of the two groups. The second stage then focused on determining the product usage segments within the GP markets.

Agreeing on a focus reduces the chance of initial misunderstandings leading to dissatisfaction with the final results and maximises the chances of the results being actionable.

9.2.2 Collect the data

The data required for segmentation studies can be broken down into two parts: that which is used in conjunction with cluster analysis to form the segments, and that which is used to help describe the segments once they are formed. Cluster analysis will allow any basis to be used, but experience has shown that the most powerful criteria are those that relate to attitudes and behaviour regarding the product class concerned. These could include usage rate, benefits sought, shopping behaviour, media usage, etc.

Before such data can be collected, however, it is necessary to be more specific about the questions to be asked. Typically, qualitative techniques, such as group discussions, are used to identify the relevant attitudes, or benefits sought, prior to their incorporation in representative surveys.

For effective benefit segmentation, in particular, it is vital that exhaustive prior qualitative research is undertaken to ensure that all possible benefits of the product or service are explored in depth. The benefits that the firm believes the product offers may not be the same as the ones the customers believe they get. For the subsequent analysis to be valid the customers' perspective is essential, as is the use of the customers' own language in subsequent surveys.

Following qualitative research a segmentation study will usually involve a quantitative survey to provide data representative of the population, or market, under study. The method of data collection depends on the usage situation. Where the aim is to define target markets based on attitudes or opinions the data collection is usually by personal interviews using semantic scales that gauge strength of agreement with a number of attitude statements. The results then provide a proxy to the interval-scaled data, which is the usual basis for cluster analysis.

By contrast, where the segmentation in a study is to be used in conjunction with a database that can rely on direct mailing the data sources are much more limited. For example, the lifestyle classifications mentioned earlier use simple checklists so that consumers can be classified according to their interests. In the database segmentation study conducted by Maier and Saunders (1990) the basis was product usage reports by general practitioners. It is clearly a limitation of database methods that their data collection is constrained by the quality of data that can be obtained from a guarantee card or self-administered questionnaire. There inevitably tends to be an inverse correlation between the coverage in segmentation databases and the quality of the data on which they are formed.

Where surveys are conducted to collect data for segmentation purposes these data are usually of two main types. The primary focus is on the data that will be used to segment the market: the benefits sought, usage patterns, attitudes, and so on. In addition, however, the survey will also collect information on traditional demographic and socio-economic factors. These can then be related back to the segments once formed (they are not used to form the segments) to enable a fuller picture of the segments to be painted. For example, a benefit segmentation study may find that a significant segment of car purchasers is looking for economical and environmentally friendly cars. To enable a marketing programme to be directed to them, however, requires a fuller picture of their purchasing power, media habits and other factors. Often age and social class are used as intermediary variables; where these factors discriminate between segments they can be used to select media.

9.2.3　Analyse the data

Once the data on which the segments are to be based have been collected they need to be analysed to identify any naturally occurring groups or clusters. Generically, the techniques used to identify these groups are called **cluster analysis** (see Saunders, 1999).

It should be realised that cluster analysis is not a single analytical technique but a whole class of techniques that, while sharing the same objective of identifying classifications with homogeneity internally but heterogeneity between them, use different methods to achieve this. This diversity of approach is both an opportunity and a problem from the practitioner's point of view. It means that the approach can be tailored to the specific needs of the analysis, but requires a degree of technical expertise to select and implement the most appropriate technique. Not surprisingly, it has been found that cluster analysis is relatively little used and understood among marketing practitioners, but is much more widely used by marketing research companies. In a recent set of surveys Hussey and Hooley (1995) found that across the top European companies only one in seven (15 per cent) reported regular use of cluster analysis in their marketing analysis, whereas the usage figures rose to three out of five (60 per cent) among specialist marketing research companies. The techniques are particularly widely used among researchers in the Netherlands (73 per cent), France (68 per cent) and Germany (67 per cent), but less so in Spain (47 per cent) and the United Kingdom (52 per cent).

The most common approach to clustering is called hierarchical clustering. Under this approach all the respondents are initially treated separately. They are then each joined with other respondents who have given identical or very similar answers to the questions on which the clustering is being performed. At the next stage the groups of respondents are further amalgamated where differences are small. The analysis progresses in an interactive fashion until all respondents are grouped as one large cluster. The analyst then works backwards, using judgement as well as the available statistics, to determine at what point in the analysis groups that were unacceptably different were combined.

Even within hierarchical clustering, however, there is a multiplicity of ways in which respondents can be measured for similarity and in which groups of respondents can be treated. Grouping can be made, for example, on the basis of comparing group averages, the nearest neighbours in two groups or the furthest neighbours in each group. Table 9.1 summarises the main alternatives.

Comparative studies consistently show two methods to be particularly suitable for marketing applications: Ward's (1963) method, which is one of the minimum

Table 9.1 Clustering methods

Favoured name	Method	Aliases
Hierarchical methods		
Single linkage	An observation is joined to another if it has the lowest level of similarity with at least one member of that cluster	Minimum method, linkage analysis, nearest neighbour cluster analysis, connectiveness method
Complete linkage	An observation is joined to a cluster if it has a certain level of similarity with all current members of that cluster	Maximum method, rank order typal analysis, furthest neighbour cluster analysis, diameter method
Average linkage	Four similar measures that differ in the way they measure the location of the centre of the cluster from which its cluster membership is measured	Simple average linkage analysis, weighted average, centroid method, median method
Minimum variance	Methods that seek to form clusters which have minimum within-cluster variance once a new observation has joined it	Minimum variance method, Ward's method, error sum of squares method, H GROUP
Interactive partitioning		
K-means	Starts with observation partitioned into a predetermined number of groups and then reassigns observation to cluster whose centroid is nearest	Non-hierarchical methods
Hill-climbing methods	Cases are not reassigned to a cluster with the nearest centroid but moved between clusters dependent on the basis of a statistical criterion	

Source: Based on Punj and Stewart (1983).

variance approaches listed in Table 9.1; and the K-means approach of interactive partitioning. In fact, an analyst does not have to choose between these two, because they can be used in combination, where Ward's method is used to form the initial number of clusters, say seven, and the K-mean approach used to refine that seven-cluster solution by moving observations around. If desired, after finding the best seven-cluster solution, Ward's method can then be re-engaged to find a six-cluster solution that is again optimised using K-mean, etc. This may seem a computationally cumbersome approach, but fortunately packages are available to allow this process to be used. The leading package is now the PC version of the popular SPSS package, at the time of writing in Version 11. So, at a stroke, by realising that Ward's method in conjunction with K-means is the best approach for forming cluster-based segments, the analyst has removed the necessity to sort among numerous cluster alternatives and is able to choose between the clustering programs that are available.

While there is plenty of advice available on which techniques to use, the determination of the most appropriate number of segments to select following the analysis is very much more judgemental. The statistics produced will offer a guide as to where amalgamation of groups results in two quite dissimilar groups being joined. The internal homogeneity of the group will suffer. This is a starting point and in some circumstances, where segmentation is very clear-cut, will be the best choice.

Figure 9.2 shows an example where there are three fairly clearly defined segments on the basis of the two dimensions studied. In this case 'eyeballing' a plot of the positions of each object (in segmentation studies the objects are usually individual respondents) shows three clusterings of objects scoring similarly, but not identically, on each of the two dimensions.

| Figure 9.2 | Clustering of objects in two-dimensional space |

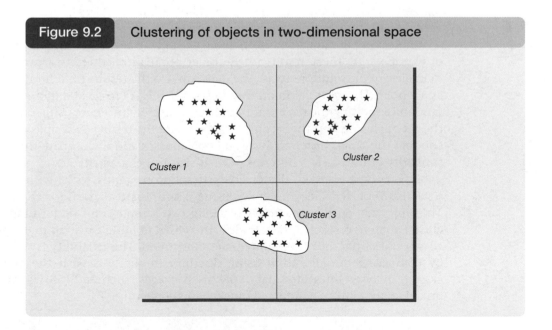

In most situations, however, there will be several dimensions on which the clustering is being conducted, and several candidate solutions, possibly ranging from a three-group to a ten-group solution. After narrowing down through examination of the statistics the analyst will then need to examine the marketing implications of each solution, basically addressing the question: If I treat these two groups separately rather than together, what differences will it make to my marketing to them? If the answer is 'little difference' the groups should usually be amalgamated. This is the creative element of segmentation where judgement is crucial!

Finally, it should also be noted that lifestyle and geo-demographic databases depend on some form of cluster analysis to group customers who are alike. The results obtained for ACORN and MOSAIC, for example, are based on judgement as to how many clusters are needed to represent the population adequately, just as tailor-made approaches are.

Once the segments have been identified, and described across other criteria, there is a need to validate the segments found.

9.2.4   Validate the segments

One of the beauties and problems of cluster analysis is its ability to generate seemingly meaningful groups out of meaningless data. This, and the confusion of algorithms, has frequently led to the approach being treated with scepticism. These uncertainties make validation an important part of segmentation research.

One favoured method of validation was mentioned above. Where product class behaviour or attitude was used to form the clusters, the extent to which those clusters also vary on demographic or psychographic variables is a measure of the cluster's validity. If the cluster is found to describe people with different beliefs, attitudes and behaviour it would be expected that they could also have different demographic or psychographic profiles. Equally, from an operational point of view, if the market segments are demographically and psychographically identical it is going to be very difficult to implement any plan based on them.

Where sample data have been used to suggest segments and there is a hope of extrapolating those results to the fuller population, there is a need to test the reliability of the solution, to ask the question: Do the results hold for the population as a whole? The most common way to test for this is cross-validation. This involves randomly splitting the data that have been collected into two, using one set to form the set of clusters and the second set to validate the results. A simple approach is to conduct the same cluster analysis on both samples and to compare them to see the similarity of the clusters in terms of their size and characteristics.

Since comparing two cluster analysis solutions tends to be rather subjective, several authors have recommended using discriminate analysis for cross-validation. This approach once again involves taking two samples and performing a separate cluster analysis on each. One sample is then used to build a discriminate model, into which cases from the other samples are substituted. The reliability is then measured by comparing the allocation using discriminate analysis with the allocation by cluster analysis. Integrated data analysis packages, such as SPSS PC, enable such linked analyses to be conducted quickly and efficiently.

It is necessary to supplement this statistical validation mentioned above with operational validation, which checks if the segments have managerial value. At a first level this means the segments having face validity and appearing to provide marketing opportunities. If further endorsement is needed an experiment can be run to test if the segments respond differently or not. For example, Maier and Saunders (1990) used a direct mailing campaign to a sample of GPs to show their segments captured major differences in the doctors' responses to certain self-reported activity.

9.2.5 Implement the segmentation

Implementation is best not viewed as a stage in segmentation research, but should be seen as the aim of the whole research process. Implementation has become one of the central issues in market modelling. A successful (validated) model adequately represents the modelled phenomena, and implementation changes decision making, but a successful implementation improves decision making. In many cases it is worth going beyond the concept of implementation to implantation. By this we mean the results of the exercise not just being used once, but adopted and used repeatedly once the marketing scientist has withdrawn from the initial exercise. This again suggests that implementation not only begins at the start of the segmentation research process, but continues long after the results have been first used by the marketing manager.

Successful implementation, therefore, depends on more than the correct transfer of a model into action. The whole model-building process needs to be executed with implementation in mind. In particular, the segmentation researcher must be involved with the potential user in order to gain their commitment and ensure the results fit their needs and expectations. An unimplemented segmentation exercise is truly academic in its more cynical sense.

Segment selection and strategy development are two critical stages that follow the technical activity of segmentation research. These are managerial tasks that are central to marketing strategy and on which successful implementation depends. Chapter 10 focuses upon these and links them to the broader issues of strategic positioning.

9.2.6 Tracking

A segmentation exercise provides a snapshot of a market as it was some months before the results were implemented. Inevitable time delays mean that, from the start, the results are out of date and, as time goes on and consumers change, it will inevitably become an increasingly poor fit to reality. Modelling myopia (Lilien and Kotler, 1983) occurs when successful implementation leads to the conviction that market-specific 'laws' have been found that make further analysis unnecessary. The converse is true: success means modelling should continue. Customers and competition change. Successful implementation itself may also change the market and competitors' behaviour.

Tracking of segmentation schemes for stability or change over time is essential in rapidly changing markets. As segmentation and positioning strategies are implemented they inevitably change the pattern of the market and customer perceptions, wants and needs. Through tracking the impact of various campaigns on segmentation it may be possible to refine and detail the sort of promotional activity that is appropriate for them. If the segments do not prove to be stable, either showing gradual changes or a radical shift, that itself can create a major opportunity. It may indicate a new segment is emerging or that segment needs are adjusting, and so enable an active company to gain a competitive edge by being the first to respond.

Positioning research is often carried out in parallel with segmentation research. Indeed, the quantitative approaches discussed below typically have as their aim the development of a multidimensional model representing both the positioning of objects (typically brands or companies) and customer segments.

9.3 Qualitative approaches to positioning research

The images of brands, products, companies and even countries have long been of interest to marketing researchers. Qualitative research approaches to this are semi-structured techniques aimed at gaining a more in-depth understanding of how respondents view aspects of the world (or more specifically markets) around them. They include focus groups and depth interviews (see Chapter 4).

Calder (1994) relates a qualitative research study into the image of a for-profit hospital in the United States. The hospital chain was opening a new 100-bed facility in a town with two existing and much larger hospitals. The problem was how to position the new hospital given its relatively small size and lack of established reputation. A number of focus group sessions were held which showed that the relative size was known by respondents but not seen as necessarily negative. Indeed, the smaller size led to expectations of a friendlier, more personalised service. Comments during the discussions included:

> *Very friendly and you get a lot of good care there. The others are a little big for that kind of care.*
> *From what I hear it has a more personalized service. Mealwise and otherwise. You even get wine [with meals]. It's more of a personalized hospital.*
> *I understand it has quite an excellent menu to choose from. Wine. They have the time to take care of you.*

The researchers concluded that the new hospital could be positioned very differently from the existing ones and it built on the friendly, caring image in subsequent marketing.

Through the use of projective techniques during qualitative research images can be uncovered that serve to show how the brand product of the company is positioned in the mind of the respondent. Some of the most popular techniques include the following:

- **The brand or company as animal or person**: Under this approach respondents are asked to name a person or an animal that embodies their view of the product or company under study. Calder (1994) cites the use of the technique to uncover the image of the US Army among potential recruits. Respondents were asked: 'If you were to think of the Army as an animal, which would it most be like?' The answers were, in order: tiger, lion, bull, wolf, bear. The Army was not seen as: mule, horse, dog, squirrel, elephant or cow! The researchers concluded that the Army was symbolised (positioned) as strong, tough, aggressive, powerful and dominating. This positioning had some negative effects on potential recruits who feared failure in the training/induction period. It is interesting to note that more recent recruitment advertising in the United Kingdom has served to stress the 'family' and 'team' nature of military service – an attempt at some repositioning.

- **Role-play**: In role-playing the respondent is asked to assume the role or behaviour of another person, or of an object under research. Tull and Hawkins (1993) give an example of research for a premium brand of Canadian whisky marketed by Schenley, called O.F.C. During a group discussion a member of the group was asked to role-play a bottle of O.F.C. and explain his feelings. The player explained that he didn't think anyone could like him as he didn't have a real name and hence no real identity. Further probing and discussion resulted in the name 'Old French Canadian' being suggested (using the letters of the original name, building on the origin of the liquor in the French-Canadian area of Quebec, and on the favourable image of 'Canadian Club'). The brand was relaunched with the new name, a stronger personality and a clearer positioning in the market.

- **The Friendly Martian**: In this approach the interviewer or group moderator assumes the role of an alien recently landed from space and asks members of the group to explain a particular product and how it is used. By acting as an alien the moderator can ask basic questions to which the respondents would normally assume the moderator knew the answers. In a group discussion for the British Home Sewing and Needlecrafts Association the researcher (a male in a female-dominated market) was able, through use of this technique, to discover that knitting was 'positioned' as a craft hobby that could be undertaken as a background activity while doing other sedentary activities such as watching television. Sewing, on the other hand, was 'positioned' as a thrift activity, undertaken primarily to save money, especially with children's garments, and required full attention to the exclusion of other activities.

A number of stimuli can be used to prompt respondents and aid them in articulating the images they hold of objects. These include the following:

- **Association techniques**: Here respondents are asked for associations with a particular stimulus. They may, for example, be asked what words, or values, or lifestyles, they associate with a BMW car. The words elicited can then be further explored through discussions and other techniques.

- **Concept boards**: Boards with pictures of the brand or the brand logo on them. These are shown to respondents and their reactions sought through probing.

- **Animatics**: Drawings of key frames from a commercial with 'bubble' speech. Respondents are then asked for their reactions and helped to describe the feelings they have towards the items being advertised.

- **Cartoon and story completion**: Cartoons of situations, such as the purchase of a specific brand, where the speech 'bubbles' are left blank for the respondent to fill in. Tull and Hawkins (1993) relate the use of story completion in researching changing drinking habits for Seagram. The unfinished scenario used was:

  Sarah hadn't seen Jane for a long time. She seemed very sophisticated and self-assured these days. At the bar she ordered . . .

  Completion of the scenario by female drinkers most often had Jane ordering a glass of wine reflecting, as the researchers interpreted it, her higher level of knowledge of drinks and general sophistication. Based on this and further qualitative research the company developed a wine-based drink with a twist of citrus to liven it up – 'Taylor California Cellar's Chablis with a Twist'.

- **Visual product mapping**: This is a qualitative form of the perceptual mapping approaches discussed below under quantitative techniques. Here respondents are given a large piece of paper – the size of a flip-chart – with two dimensions drawn at right-angles to each other. Respondents are then given a number of objects (such as brands or companies) on small cards, or in the case of small pack products such as shampoos they may even be given a number of real packages. They are then asked to position the cards or packs on the chart with similar brands close to each other but far apart from dissimilar brands. The dimensions that can be used to explain these differences are then discussed and written on to the maps. Alternatively, the identity of the dimensions may have been elicited from earlier parts of the interview (such as 'price', 'quality', etc.) and respondents are asked to 'position' the objects on the dimensions directly.

Qualitative approaches to uncovering the images and positions of objects in the minds of respondents have been particularly popular among advertising agencies who value the in-depth, rich data that can be derived. The images and positions articulated are in the respondents' own language and hence offer insights for direct communication with them as customers.

The classic concern of qualitative research, however, remains. That is, how representative of the population in their normal everyday shopping and consumption experiences are the responses of a relatively small number of respondents in often very artificial settings completing strange and unfamiliar tasks? In most instances positioning research needs to go beyond the qualitative to develop models of images and positions based on more representative samples in a quantitative study.

9.4 Quantitative approaches to positioning research

While qualitative approaches to image research often focus on the core object (brand, product, company, etc.) in isolation, the more quantitative approaches typically consider positioning relative to the positioning of major competitors and relative to the desires, wants and needs of target customer segments.

As a starting point, therefore, it is necessary to define the competitive set that will be analysed along with the focal brand, product or company. While positioning studies can focus at the level of the company or the product, most typically focus at the brand level.

For example, a company analysing the market for hover-mowers might be interested in how customers perceive competitors' brands (i.e. Flymo, Qualcast and Black & Decker) and the products they sell. When buying such a product a customer is likely to have a reasonable idea about the likely size and cost of the item they wish to buy and, therefore, give most attention to products within that price performance envelope. Among the competitors the customer is likely to see various dimensions of importance, such as value for money, reliability, safety, convenience, etc., and it is the relationships between the direct competitors with which positioning is particularly involved. If the direct competitors have not been correctly identified the researcher may include within the survey manufacturers of sit-on mowers, i.e. Lawnflight, Laser or Toro. This would not only add to the burden of respondents whose perceptions are being sought, but could also change the perceptions since, when compared with sit-on mowers, conventional hand-mowers may all look similarly inexpensive, time-consuming and compact.

The mower market is relatively simple compared with some others. Consider the problem faced by a company wishing to launch a low alcohol lager. Should the competitors be other low alcohol lagers or should it include low alcohol beers as well? Or maybe the study should be extended to include other low alcohol drinks such as shandy, cider or wine. In the United Kingdom the rapid increase in the consumption of soft drinks which has been associated with the concern for the health and safety of alcohol consumption may suggest that they too should be considered as an alternative to low alcohol lagers, but should diet and caffeine-free versions also be considered? Maybe it is a matter of just taste, and it is more appropriate to low alcohol drinks with variants with normal alcohol content. Production orientation is a danger when trying to reduce the number of product alternatives. A brewer may well consider low alcohol lagers or other lagers as the direct competitors, but certain customer groups may easily associate low alcohol drinks with colas or other beverages. It is clearly necessary to take a customer-oriented view of the direct competitors.

One way of defining direct competitors is to look at panel data to see what customers have done in the past. By tracking the past purchases of customers it may be possible to identify product alternatives when switching takes place. The danger in this approach is the dissociation of the purchasers with the usage situation and the user. For instance, a buying pattern that shows the purchase of low alcohol lagers, lemonade, beer and cola could represent products to be consumed by different people at different times, rather than switching between alternatives. Another approach is to determine which brands buyers consider. For consumer durables customers might be asked what other brands they considered in their buying process. For low involvement products it may be inappropriate to ask a buyer about a particular purchase decision, so instead they could be asked what brands they would consider if their favourite one was not available.

Day *et al.* (1979) proposed a more exhaustive process as a cost-effective way of mapping product markets. Termed *Item by Use Analysis*, the procedure starts by asking 20 or so respondents the use context of a product, say a low alcohol lager. For each use context so identified, such as the lunchtime snack, with an evening meal, or at a country pub, respondents are then asked to identify all appropriate beverages. For each beverage so identified the respondent has to identify an appropriate use context. Once again the process is continued until an exhaustive list of contexts and beverages is produced. A second group of respondents would then be asked to make a judgement as to how appropriate each beverage would be for each usage situation, the beverages then being clustered on the basis of their similarity of their usage situation. For instance, if both low alcohol lager and cola were regarded as appropriate for a company lunchtime snack but inappropriate for an evening meal they would be considered as direct competitors.

Rather than using consumers, it can be tempting to use a panel of experts or retailers to guide the selection of direct competitors. This could be quicker than using customers, but is likely to lead to a technological definition of preference. There can be a vast difference between what is perceived by experts and what is perceived by customers. Since the focus of positioning is to gauge customers' images of offerings and their preferences for them it is difficult to justify using any other than customers to define competitors.

9.4.1 Attribute profiling methods

One of the simplest ways of collecting quantitative position data is through the use of attitude or attribute scaling. Under this approach the dimensions that respondents use to differentiate and choose between alternative offerings are included in a survey (usually personally administered, though it is also possible to collect these data by mailed or telephone surveys) and presented as semantic scales for respondents to give their views on.

An example from a survey of store images and positioning is given in Figure 9.3. Here respondents were asked to rate two competing stores on six attributes identified as important in prior qualitative research: quality, price, staff attitudes, range of goods, modernity and ease of parking. Results are shown from one respondent only. Also shown is that respondent's ideal store profile – what he or she would ideally like in terms of the features listed. For most purposes the responses from the sample would be averaged* and those averages used to show the differences in positioning and requirements. Where ideal requirements differ across the sample they could be

---

* Note that where there is wide variation in the evaluations from individual respondents it may be necessary first to group respondents by perceptual segments, i.e. those sharing a common view of the market, prior to analysing alternative segment requirements.

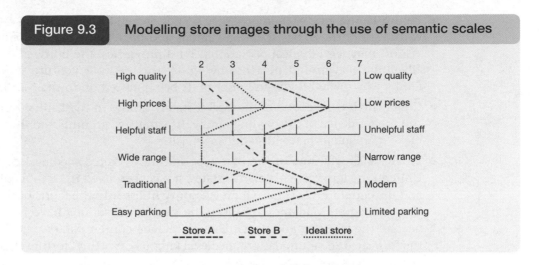

Figure 9.3   Modelling store images through the use of semantic scales

first grouped together (using cluster analysis – see above) to identify alternative segment requirements.

This approach examines each dimension separately, bringing them together in the diagram to enable a more complete image to be drawn. Some dimensions may, however, be more important to particular market segments than others. For instance, in the store positioning example above it might well be that for one segment price considerations outweigh convenience, range and other factors. It is therefore essential to examine the relative importance of the dimensions, either through weighting them differently to reflect importance or through assessing the dimensions simultaneously such that more important dimensions come to the fore.

9.4.2   Multidimensional positioning analysis

Increasingly researchers and managers are seeking to create multidimensional models of the markets in which they are operating. The essence of these models is that they seek to look at a number of dimensions simultaneously, rather than separately, in an attempt to reflect more closely the way in which customers view the market.

To explain this approach we shall follow a case involving the positioning of leisure facilities accessible from the East Midlands. For the sake of simplicity only the major attractions and segments are considered in this case. Interviews with respondents revealed six leisure centres that, although very different in their provision, were all seen as major attractions. These were:

- **The American Adventure theme park**: a completely modern facility, with a Wild West emphasis but also including other US themes such as GI and space exploration.
- **Alton Towers**: acquired by Madame Tussaud's, this is a large leisure facility based around a derelict country house. It has inherited several natural features, such as the house itself, the gardens and lakes, but particularly focuses on dramatic white-knuckle rides.

- **Belton House:** one of many country houses owned by the National Trust and, as with most of these, has splendid gardens and furnished accommodation, which visitors may see. Atypical of National Trust properties, the house also has a large adventure playground in a nearby wood, this being a venture started by the family who owned the house prior to its being passed on to the National Trust.

- **Chatsworth House:** one of the largest stately homes in the United Kingdom and still the residence of the owning family. Its extensive grounds and the house itself make it a popular place for families to visit.

- **Warwick Castle:** one of the best-kept and most visited medieval castles in the United Kingdom. As with many estates, it has been lived in from medieval times and the current owners have built a country house into the fabric of the building. Now owned by Madame Tussaud's, the castle's attractions have been extended beyond the building and its gardens, to include contemporary waxworks within the furnished accommodation, medieval knights cavorting, torture chambers, etc.

- **Woburn Abbey and Safari Park:** like Chatsworth, still the residence of the family owning the estate. However, the family in this case have developed two distinct attractions, the house and the safari park, the latter also having a fairground, etc.

Although widely different in their appeals, ownership and background, the respondents' interviews clearly indicated that these were direct competitors and were alternatives they would choose between when deciding on an outing.

The positioning research process (Figure 9.4) shows the determination of competitive dimensions, competitors' positions and the customers' positions as parallel phases. This is because there are certain techniques that can be used to extract all

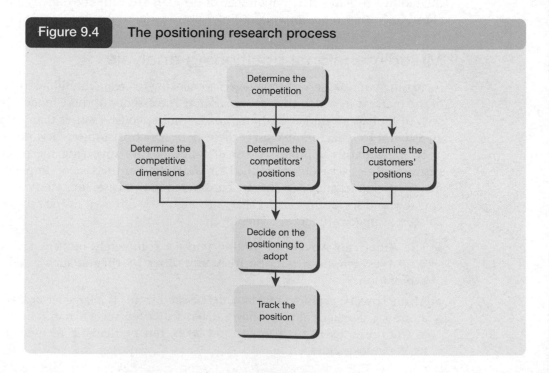

Figure 9.4   The positioning research process

these simultaneously. In this case the phases are taken in sequence. Details of other approaches that are available are given later.

Identifying product positions

It is an odd feature of many of the techniques used in positioning research that the competitors' positions can be determined before it is understood how the customer is differentiating between them. Such an approach was used to represent the leisure park market in the East Midlands. The approach is called similarities-based multi-dimensional scaling. In this, respondents were given a shuffled stack of cards that contained all possible combinations of the six leisure parks. There were 15 pairs in all, ranging from American Adventure linked to Alton Towers, to Warwick Castle linked with Woburn Safari Park. The respondents were then asked to rank the pairs in accordance with their similarity, the pair most alike being on the top and the pair least alike being on the bottom. Since this can be a rather cumbersome process it is sometimes advisable first to ask respondents to stack the cards into three piles representing those pairs that are very similar, those pairs that are very unalike and a middling group. The respondent then has to rank the pairs within each group.

Figure 9.5 presents the ranking from one such process. It shows that this particular respondent (one of many) thought Belton House and Woburn Safari Park were the most similar. As the next most similar, the pair of Belton House and Chatsworth House were chosen, and so on, until the least similar pair of the American Adventure and Chatsworth House. An indication that the respondent is using different criteria to judge each pair is shown by the judgement that Belton is similar to Woburn and Chatsworth, but Woburn and Chatsworth are not alike. Such are the permutations and combinations of pairs each respondent can choose that it is almost inevitable that each individual's similarity matrix is different.

The objective from this point is to develop a plot of the stimuli (leisure parks) which shows those that respondents said were similar close together, and those that respondents said were dissimilar far apart. Although this is a difficult task to conduct manually, computers are particularly adept at finding such solutions, and researchers in the field of multidimensional scaling have produced many computer packages that can be used (for a recent summary, see Green *et al.*, 1989). A multidimensional scaling package called KYST can be used to produce perceptual maps from the similarities matrix provided and many other data formats (Kruskal *et al.*, 1973). The map produced (Figure 9.6) shows some of the detail from a similarity matrix (Figure 9.5). Chatsworth House, Alton Towers and Woburn Safari Park are some distance apart,

Figure 9.5	Individual similarity matrix of leisure facilities

	(A)	(T)	(B)	(C)	(W)	(S)
American Adventure (A)	–					
Alton Towers (T)	3	–				
Belton House (B)	4	11	–			
Chatsworth House (C)	15	13	2	–		
Warwick Castle (W)	5	12	7	8	–	
Woburn Safari Park (S)	6	10	1	14	9	–

The map also shows the dangers of product positioning without consideration of market segments. The positions of the leisure centres suggest there may be an opportunity to develop one that excels in the provision of an educational experience for the pre-teens, or for all the family. Vacant that position may be, but it is dangerously away from the needs of the three major segments that have been identified in this case. Maybe the mums and dads would have liked such a leisure centre, but the kids would be happier with a less pretentious, synthetic attraction providing fun and games.

9.4.3 Alternative algorithms

In developing positioning maps researchers are spoilt by the number of alternative approaches that can be used (see Green *et al.*, 1989). For instance, PREFMAP allows the stage where segments were formed from individuals to be missed out and so produces a map representing the ideal point of each individual. Rather than the picture seen in Figure 9.8, which presents the ideal points of each segment, the map would then show the product positions, the market dimensions and the position of each individual relative to the product. From there it may be possible to eyeball the positions of individual respondents to identify a group that are worthy of being targeted. Another package, MDPREF (Chang and Carroll, 1969), can be used to combine the identification of the perceptual map of product positions and underlying dimensions. This would have required respondents to have rated leisure parks along each of the dimensions, such as 'for all the family' or 'sophisticated', and then aggregating the results to arrive directly at a map similar to Figure 9.7.

A further approach is offered through correspondence analysis. Correspondence analysis (see Carroll *et al.*, 1986, 1987) is a multivariate method for analysing tables of categorical data in order simultaneously to identify relationships between the variables (both rows and columns). It can therefore operate with commonly collected data, such as usage and attitude data, to produce perceptual maps that simultaneously show the positions of objects (brands or segment ideals) and attributes (dimensions). Originally developed in France as an alternative approach to multidimensional scaling, correspondence analysis is now available in leading MDS packages such as that provided by Smith (1990).

Anyone who starts to use this diversity of approaches will find that the map produced depends on the approach used. This is because of the differences in the data-gathering techniques and the assumptions and methods used to optimise the results. In that way the use of multidimensional scaling to produce perceptual maps is similar to cluster analysis, where the results depend on the clustering algorithm used. But, just as in cluster analysis, this should not be seen as a defect but the realisation that there are numerous ways of looking at a market. Life would be more convenient if there was just one map that represented a market, but any attempt to compress the richness of a market into so simple a perspective is likely to result in opportunities being lost, or never seen.

Only a few years ago the access to the packages was difficult, and the programs themselves were poorly documented and hard to use. Now the situation has changed completely. They, along with other reasonably user-friendly data analysis packages, are available in PC form (Smith, 1990) and are routinely used by leading market research companies.

Summary

Considerable research has shown that the naive practitioner of segmentation and positioning research can be easily confused and disappointed. The traditional a priori, off-the-peg methods of segmentation have proved to be a poor guide to segmenting markets other than those that have a direct and immediate link to the markets concerned, e.g. gender-, age- or race-based products. Although more expensive, and providing a much more graphic view of the marketplace, the more modern off-the-peg psychographic methods appear to provide little advantage. As with demographic bases for segmentation, they do work in certain circumstances, but only when the product class or form and the segmentation criteria are very closely related. Within a product class or a product form, however, they rarely differentiate between brands.

The need to find segmentation bases which are closely associated with the product market in question means that successful implementation often involves a company developing product-specific bases. Here there is a potential barrier because of the perceived complexity of the approach and the confusion that researchers have created by their own misunderstandings. Although once a major block to implementation, sufficient case law on using cluster analysis in marketing has been accumulated to allow some of the confusion to be removed. Comparative studies come down firmly in favour of Ward's (1963) method in conjunction with iterative partitioning. Few of the computer packages available can do this, so a selection of clustering algorithms and the computer package used to run it becomes routine.

There is rightly much scepticism about the results from cluster analysis. This is justifiable, given the confusion of the algorithms used, the tendency of cluster analysis to produce results even if the data are meaningless, and the lack of validation of those results. Being aware of these dangers it is vital that validation – both statistical and operational – has a central role within segmentation research. In particular, tests should be done to see if the segments formed can be replicated using other data, that the segments are managerially meaningful and respond differently to elements of the marketing mix.

As with segmentation research there is a wide variety of positioning research approaches and techniques available. Typically they require the collection of primary data relating to brand images and customer requirements. Multidimensional scaling techniques can be used to summarise the mass of data collected in visually appealing and easily communicable ways. They are perhaps best seen as visual models of the customer's mind. As such, they should be treated with caution, as any model is a simplification of reality, and used with care. They can never replace the individual manager's insights, which are central to creative marketing decision making. At best they are an aid to that process.

Segmentation and positioning researchers have indeed failed to find a single criterion that will fit all markets, despite the claims of those selling lifestyle segmentation.

However, rather than finding a single criterion, researchers have found consistently reliable methods of using product market data to segment customers into groups that are of managerial significance and to represent their views and opinions in visually communicable ways. While Baumwoll (1974) was right in predicting that no philosopher's stone would be found, researchers have perhaps discovered how to make philosophers' stones!

Asianet, Zee TV, Namaste and more   Case study

Alamy/Diondia Images

Is the UK's ethnic minority population big enough to sustain a strong media industry? On the face of it, the economics look difficult to work out. While the US's large ethnic minority population can support enough media to make Johnson a billionaire, it seems unlikely that a black entrepreneur with a similar business plan would reach those dizzy heights in the UK.

Ethnic minorities made up 7.1 per cent of the UK population in 2000, amounting to just over 4m people in total. That figure has been growing steadily for many years, up from 6.5 per cent between 1997 and 1999, and 5.7 per cent between 1992 and 1994. But the population is very diverse.

For instance, the black community, in which the two biggest single groups are the Afro-Caribbeans and black Africans, makes up 1.274m people. The Asian community divides into Indians (984,000), Pakistanis (675,000) and Bangladeshis (257,000). Chinese people make up one of the smaller ethnic groupings with 149,000 people, and about 219,000 other people belong to none of these bigger communities. White people total 53m.

These numbers ensure that any media exclusively targeting ethnic minorities will be catering to a small market. Look at the audience figures for existing ethnic minority cable TV channels: in 2001, according to the Independent Television Commission, Zee TV attracted 60,000 viewers and Namaste 51,436. Asianet fared better, with 230,530 viewers, but that lags behind other minority interest channels.

However, while the proportion of the UK's population coming from ethnic minorities is slowly rising, the media catering to them is proliferating faster, which could end up further fragmenting an already fragmented market. Plus, media targeting ethnic minorities face the additional problem that the groups on whom they focus have an increasingly diverse range of interests: an elderly black African immigrant may share few tastes with his young mixed-race granddaughter.

Attracting advertisers to such a heavily segmented market can be difficult. Saad Saraf, managing director of Media Reach Advertising, an ethnic marketing consultancy, says US advertisers are much keener than their UK counterparts on using ethnic media: 'US advertisers are much more willing to segment their markets, because they see that it makes their dollar go further. Brands in London still spend 100 per cent of their budget targeting 60 per cent of the people.' The prevailing attitude among advertisers is that their ads in the mainstream media already reach minorities, says Anjana Raheja, managing director of Media Moguls, an ethnic PR specialist. But she argues that, as people from ethnic minorities are increasing their spending power, advertisers are gradually growing more interested.

Tim Schoonmaker, chief executive of Emap Performance, believes advertisers and media buyers are getting more used to the fragmented audience of digital broadcast channels, which will benefit ethnic media.

And Michael Williams, director of marketing at Focus Consultancy, an ethnic change management agency, adds that advertisers should think influence, rather than size: 'Everyone talks about size, but that's not all there is to it. Ethnic minorities can be very influential on fashion – black kids had mobiles long before white kids.'

Source: Fiona Harvey, 'Creative Business: Could It Work Here?' *Financial Times*, 1 October 2002.

Discussion questions

1 'The prevailing attitude among advertisers is that their ads in the mainstream media already reach minorities' in the UK. Is this assumption reasonable? Why may such mass marketing fail?

2 Examine how the marketing for clothes, cosmetics, telephone services and air travel may vary with the ethnic group targeted.

3 Although mass marketing may fail to appeal to ethnic minorities, a firm may choose to accept that risk rather than face the cost of developing campaigns for each of the groups. What are the dangers of such an approach?

chapter ten

Selecting market targets

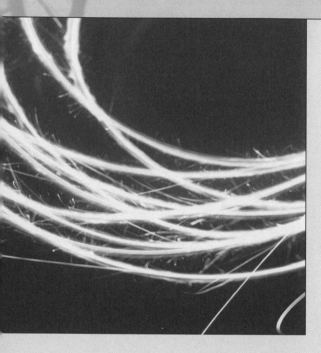

Attacking a fortified area is an act of last resort.

Sun Tzu (c. 500 BC)

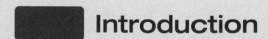 **Introduction**

One of the most fundamental decisions a company faces is its choice of market or markets to serve. Unfortunately, many firms enter markets with little thought as to their suitability for the firm. They are entered simply because they may appear superficially an attractive market for the firm's products or services. As we shall see in this chapter, a strong case can be made for choosing markets and industries where the prospects are attractive, and also where we can take a strong position. Figure 10.1 suggests that if we compare, in general terms, the attractiveness of markets and the strength of the competitive position we can take, then there are several traps to be avoided:

● **Peripheral business:** areas where we can take a strong and secure competitive position, but where the market simply does not deliver the benefits that the company needs. It is easy for those with great enthusiasm for a product or service in

Figure 10.1	Market attractiveness and competitive position

Source: Adapted from Piercy (1997).

which they specialise to drive us into these areas, but they will never deliver the margin and growth that we need and will absorb resources and management time.

- **Illusion business**: areas where the market appears very attractive to us, because it is large, dynamic, expanding, and so on. However, these are areas where we can only ever hold a weak position – perhaps because these are typically the markets defended most fiercely by entrenched competitors. It is easy for managers to be seduced into entering these markets because of the potential they offer, without acknowledging that we can never reach that potential.

- **Dead-end business**: markets that are not attractive and where we can only take an 'also-ran' position. Few managers will deliberately take us into these markets, but this may describe markets from which we should exit – they may have been attractive in the past, but have declined, or our competitive position may have been undermined by new competitors and technologies.

- **Core business**: markets offering the benefits we want, where we should take a strong position. Clearly these are the highest priority for investment of time and resources. The major issue here is how well we understand what makes a market attractive for a particular company, and what makes a competitive market strong (Piercy, 1997).

While these strategic traps are easily described, the importance of the issue is underlined by the fact that market choices are just that – choice may mean that we turn our back on some markets and some customers and some ways of business, to focus on the areas where we can achieve superior performance and results. Making such choices may be difficult. Michael Porter has suggested the heart of the problem:

> *To put it simply, managers don't like to choose. There are tremendous organisational pressures toward imitation and matching what the competitor does. Over time this slowly but surely undermines the uniqueness of the competitive position.*
> (Porter, quoted in Jackson, 1997)

273

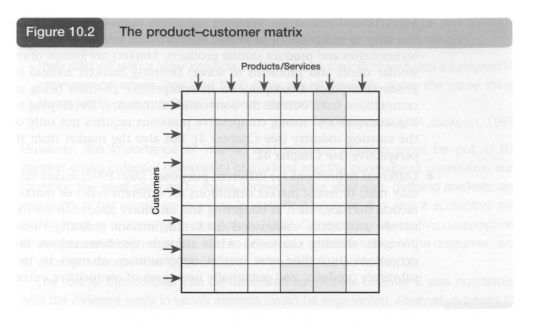

Figure 10.2   The product–customer matrix

- **products/services** – in terms of what they do for customers, not in terms of how they are produced or by whom;
- **customers** – in terms of important differences between groups in needs, preferences, priorities or ways of buying.

For example, vast arrays of retail financial services products provided by banks and their competitors can be reduced to six categories of products by considering what customer benefits they provide. Rather than hundreds of products, the market consists of only six groups of products and services to: provide access to cash; provide security of savings; buy-now pay-later; make cashless payments; get a return on assets such as savings; and acquire a range of specialist services. The same process of reduction can be applied to products/services. For example, do not describe the market as 'computers', but as what different mixes of computer hardware, software and services actually deliver to customers in a particular market, such as accounting systems, internal communications, management information, and so on.

This approach provides a start in defining markets in such a way that we move past the core market of similar products, to find the extended market:

> *to encompass all competitive possibilities for satisfying customer needs, including substitutes and potential entrants. [because] this latter perspective is especially needed to help understand why some markets are attractive and others are not.*

(Day, 1990)

This analysis can be used for a variety of purposes, but one advantage of this type of initial approach is that it starts to identify the way a market divides into distinctly different segments.

10.2 Defining how the market is segmented

As discussed in Chapter 8, there are many ways in which markets can be segmented. Often a useful starting point is to ask how management views the market, on the basis of their experience in the marketplace. Management definition of market segments may typically be on the basis of products/services offered or markets served.

10.2.1 Products or services offered

Describing segments on the basis of products or services offered can lead to broad-based segmentation of the market. John Deere, for example, competing against the much larger Caterpillar company in the US crawler tractor (bulldozer) market initially segmented the market into 'large' and 'small' bulldozers. On the basis of its marketing assets (defined in terms of better service support through local dealer networks and lower system price) Deere decided to concentrate its efforts in the small bulldozer market, thus avoiding head-on competition with Caterpillar, which was stronger in the large bulldozer market (where market requirements centred around spare parts availability).

Many market research companies operating in the service sector define their market segments in terms of the services they offer, e.g. the market for retail audits, the market for telephone surveys, the market for qualitative group discussions, the market for professional (industrial) interviewing.

Underlying this product- or service-based approach to identifying markets is a belief that segments defined in this way will exhibit the differences in behaviour essential to an effective segmentation scheme. The strategy adopted by Deere made sense, for example, only because the requirements of purchasers and users of large and small bulldozers were different. Where the requirements of customers are essentially the same, but satisfied by different products or services, this segmentation approach can lead to a myopic view of the market.

10.2.2 Market or markets served

Many companies now adopt a customer-based or markets-served approach to segmenting their markets. Segments are defined in terms of the customers themselves rather than the particular products they buy. In consumer markets, management may talk in terms of demographic and socio-economic segments while in industrial markets definitions may be based on SIC or order quantity. A particularly useful approach in many markets is to segment on the basis of the benefits the customer is seeking in consuming the product or service and/or the uses to which the product or service is put.

Van den Berghs (a subsidiary of Unilever) has been particularly successful in segmenting the market for yellow fats on the basis of the benefits sought by consumers (see Broadbent, 1983). The market, which comprises butter, margarine and low-fat spreads, stood at £600 million at retail selling price in 1979. It was a static market with no overall growth. Within the market, however, there were some important changes taking place. There had been a marked trend away from butter to margarine, primarily because of the increasing price differential (butter and margarine were roughly equivalent prices in the mid-1970s but since then butter prices had increased more rapidly, widening the gap). Coupled with this came increased price sensitivity as the UK economy entered the recession of the late 1970s/early 1980s. Van den Berghs was quick to spot a market opportunity as it segmented the market. There were at least five benefit segments identified:

- **Segment 1** consisted of customers who wanted a 'real butter taste' and were not prepared to forego that taste at almost any price. This segment chose butter, the top-selling brands being Anchor, Lurpak and Country Life.

- **Segment 2** were customers who wanted the taste, feel and texture of butter but were concerned about the price. They were typically not prepared to sacrifice on taste, etc., and not convinced that existing margarines could satisfy them. These customers would typically choose the cheapest butter available, such as supermarket own label.

- **Segment 3** were ex-butter users who were prepared to accept existing margarines as a substitute and even found they offered additional benefits over butter, such as softness and ease of spreading. Also attractive to this segment was tub packaging and larger packs. They were more price sensitive than Segment 2. The leading brand in this segment was Stork margarine.

- **Segment 4** was a growing minority segment concerned with diet and weight control. In particular they were concerned with calories and with fat content. Outline was a leading brand. More recently St Ivel Gold has been particularly successful in appealing to this segment.

- **Segment 5** were concerned with health in general and particularly the effects of cholesterol. Of special appeal to this segment were spreads low in cholesterol and high in polyunsaturated fats. The market leader in this segment was Flora.

Van den Berghs had achieved around 60 per cent of the total market in 1980 through recognising the segmentation described above and positioning its brands such that they attracted specific individual segments. Segment 1 was deliberately not targeted specifically. Krona, a block margarine with (in blind tests) a very similar taste to butter, was launched at a premium price and high margins to attract Segment 2 customers as they traded down from butter. Segment 3 was secured by Van den Berghs' leading brand, Stork, while Segments 4 and 5 were served by Outline and Flora respectively. During the 1980s and 1990s competition to serve Segment 2 intensified. Following the initial success of Krona, Dairy Crest launched Clover in 1983 as a dairy spread. In 1991 Van den Berghs launched the amazingly named 'I Can't Believe It's Not Butter' as a brand that gave a butter taste but with much lower fat intake levels. Within just nine months of its launch, ICBINB (as it became to be known in the trade), took 2.3 per cent of the margarine low-fat spreads market. In 1995 it was followed by St Ivel's new brand, positioned directly in opposition, 'Utterly Butterly'. More recently the emergence of 'cholesterol buster' spreads such as Benecol presented a new challenge to Van den Berghs' domination of the market. The launch of Flora Pro-Activ into this part of the market ensured continued overall leadership. Since its launch in 2000 the brand has gone from strength to strength, outselling its nearest competitor 3 to 1. In 2004 the Pro-Activ range was enlarged to include a spread with olive oil, a milk drink and low-fat yoghurts.

Central to the success of Van den Berghs and other creative marketers has been an unwillingness merely to accept the segmentation of the market adopted by others. In many fast-moving consumer products markets, and in grocery marketing in particular, there has been a tendency to over-segment on the basis of background customer characteristics or volume usage. By looking beyond these factors to the underlying motivations and reasons to buy, companies can often create an edge over their competitors.

Once the segments have been identified the alternatives need to be evaluated on the basis of market attractiveness and company strength, or potential strength, in that particular market segment. This evaluation is carried out across a number of factors.

10.3 Determining market segment attractiveness

It is clear that many factors may be considered in evaluating market, or specific segment, attractiveness. In Chapter 2 we discussed multi-factor approaches to evaluation in the context of assessing the portfolio of product offerings, while here they are discussed as strategic tools for deciding which markets to enter in the first place. There have been many checklists of such factors, but one way of grouping the issues is as follows:

- market factors;
- economic and technological factors;
- competitive factors;
- environmental factors.

However, it should be noted at the outset that a general checklist of this kind is only a starting point – the factors important to making a market attractive or unattractive to a specific company are likely to reflect the specific characteristics of that company and the priorities of its management. For example, one company may see a market segment that is growing as highly attractive, while in the same industry another company may look for slower rates of growth to avoid stretching its financial and other capacities. Similarly, a company that has cost advantages over its rivals may see a price-sensitive segment as highly attractive, while its competitors do not. In fact, there is a group of factors that impact on judgements of market attractiveness which are wholly subjective.

10.3.1 Market factors

Among the market characteristics that influence the assessment of market attractiveness are the following (Figure 10.3).

Size of the segment

Clearly, one of the factors that make a potential target attractive is its size. High-volume markets offer greater potential for sales expansion (a major strategic goal of

Figure 10.3	Factors affecting market segment attractiveness

Market factors Size; growth rate; life cycle stage; predictability; price elasticity; bargaining power of buyers; cyclicality of demand	Economic & technological factors Barriers to entry and exit; bargaining power of suppliers; technology utilisation; investment required; margins
Competitive factors Intensity; quality; threat of substitution; degree of differentiation	Business environment factors Economic fluctuations; political and legal; regulation; social; physical environment

many companies). They also offer potential for achieving economies of scale in production and marketing and hence a route to more efficient operations.

Segment growth rate

In addition to seeking scale of operation many companies are actively pursuing growth objectives. Often it is believed that company sales growth is more easily achieved in growing markets.

The market for colas within the carbonated drinks market is declining in many Western markets, making it a less attractive market than it has been. In the US, for example, the cola share of the market has declined from 72 per cent in 1990 to 60 per cent in 2000. Meanwhile sales of bottled water, juices and sports drinks have doubled. This is worrying for Coca-Cola which generates 65 per cent of its sales volume from colas and accounts for one-third of the soft drinks sold in the world (*Financial Times*, 19 September 2001).

Stage of industry evolution

We looked earlier (see Chapter 3) at the characteristics of markets at different stages of evolution. Depending on the company's objectives (cash generation or growth) different stages may be more attractive. For initial targeting, markets in the early stages of evolution are generally more attractive as they offer more future potential and are less likely to be crowded by current competitors (see competitive intensity below). Typically, however, growth requires marketing investment (promotion, distribution, etc.) to fuel it so that the short-term returns may be modest. Where more immediate cash and profit contribution is sought a mature market may be a more attractive proposition, requiring as it does a lower level of investment.

Predictability

Earlier we stressed the predictability of markets as a factor influencing their attractiveness to marketers. Clearly the more predictable the market, the less prone it is to discontinuity and turbulence, the easier it is to predict accurately the potential value of the segment. The more certain, too, is the longer-term viability of the target.

Price elasticity and sensitivity

Unless the company has a major cost advantage over its main rivals, markets which are less price sensitive, where the price elasticity of demand is low, are more attractive than those that are more sensitive. In the more price-sensitive markets there are greater chances of price wars (especially in the mature stage of industry evolution) and the shake-out of the less efficient suppliers.

Bargaining power of customers

Those markets where buyers (ultimate customers or distribution chain intermediaries) have the strongest negotiating hand are often less attractive than those where the supplier can dominate and dictate to the market.

In the UK grocery market the buying power of the major supermarket chains is considerable. Together the top five chains supply around 70 per cent of the nation's food shopping needs. Food manufacturers and processors compete vigorously for shelf space to make their products available to their ultimate consumers. Indeed, some supermarket chains are now moving towards charging food manufacturers for the shelf space they occupy.

Similarly, in the market for military apparel a concentration of buying power (by the governments) dictates to potential entrants on what basis they will compete.

Seasonality and cyclicality of demand

The extent to which demand fluctuates by season or cycle also affects the attractiveness of a potential segment. For a company already serving a highly seasonal market a new opportunity in a counter-seasonal market might be particularly attractive, enabling the company to utilise capacity all year round.

The Thompson publishing group found the package tour market highly attractive, primarily for cash flow reasons. The company needed to bulk purchase paper for printing during the winter months and found this a severe drain on cash resources. Package holidays, typically booked and paid for during the winter months, provided a good opportunity to raise much needed cash at the crucial time. Thomson Holidays, founded originally as a cash flow generator, has gone on to become a highly successful package tour operator.

10.3.2 Economic and technological factors

Issues reflecting the broader economic characteristics of the market and the technology used include the following.

Barriers to entry

Markets where there are substantial barriers to entry (e.g. protected technology or high switching costs for customers) are attractive markets for incumbents but unattractive markets for aspirants. While few markets have absolute barriers to entry in the long term, for many companies the costs of overcoming those barriers may make the venture prohibitively expensive and uneconomic.

Barriers to exit

Conversely, markets with high exit barriers, where companies can become locked into untenable or uneconomic positions, are intrinsically unattractive. Some new target opportunities, for example, may have substantial investment hurdles (barriers to entry) that, once undertaken, lock the company into continuing to use the facilities created. In other markets powerful customers may demand a full range of products/services as the cost of maintaining their business in more lucrative sectors. When moving into high-risk new target markets a major consideration should be exit strategy in the event that the position becomes untenable.

Bargaining power of suppliers

The supply of raw materials and other factor inputs to enable the creation of suitable products and services must also be considered. Markets where the suppliers have monopoly or near-monopoly power are less attractive than those served by many competing suppliers (see Porter, 1980).

Level of technology utilisation

Use and level of technology affects attractiveness of targets differently for different competitors. The more technologically advanced will be attracted to markets which utilise their expertise more fully and where that can be used as a barrier to other company entry. For the less technologically advanced, with skills and strengths in other areas such as people, markets with a lower use of technology may be more appropriate.

Investment required

Size of investment required, financial and other commitment will also affect attractiveness of market and could dictate that many market targets are practically unattainable for some companies. Investment requirements can form a barrier to entry that protects incumbents while deterring entrants.

Margins available

Finally, margins will vary from market to market, partly as a result of price sensitivity and partly as a result of competitive rivalry. In grocery retailing margins are notoriously low (around 2–4 per cent) whereas in other markets they can be nearer 50 per cent or even higher.

10.3.3 Competitive factors

The third set of factors in assessing the attractiveness of potential market targets relates to the competition to be faced in those markets.

Competitive intensity

The number of serious competitors in the market is important. Markets may be dominated by one (monopoly), two (duopoly), a few (oligopoly) or none ('perfect competition') of the players in that market. Entry into markets dominated by one or a few key players requires some form of competitive edge over them that can be used to secure a beachhead. In some circumstances it may be that the existing players in the market have failed to move with changes in their markets and hence create opportunities for more innovative rivals.

Under conditions of perfect, or near-perfect, competition price competitiveness is particularly rife. The many small players in the market offer competitively similar products so that differentiation is rarely achieved (the stalemate environment – see Chapter 3), and it is usually on the basis of price rather than performance or quality. To compete here requires either a cost advantage (created through superior technology, sourcing or scale of operations) or the ability to create a valued uniqueness in the market. In segments where there are few, or weak, competitors there may again be better opportunities to exploit.

In the early 1980s Barratt Developments made a major impact on the house-building market. Its segmentation of the market identified the need for specialist housing at various consumer life cycle phases. The first venture was Studio Solos, designed for young, single people. In the first year of sales Barratt sold over 2,000 (2 per cent of total new home sales). In the United States the same strategy was adopted to spearhead the company's international expansion (70 per cent of Barratt's US sales coming from solos). At the same time in the United Kingdom the company successfully developed retirement housing for pensioners, one- and two-bedroom apartments in blocks featuring communal facilities and wardens. In both retirement homes and solos housing Barratt was among the first to pursue aggressively the markets it had identified. Indeed, it would argue it was among the first to recognise that the housing market was segmented beyond the traditional product-based segmentation of terraces, semis and detacheds.

Quality of competition

Chapter 5 discussed what constitutes 'good' competitors – those that can stabilise their markets, do not have over-ambitious goals and who are committed to the market. Good competitors are also characterised by their desire to serve the market better and hence will keep the company on its toes competitively rather than allow it to lag behind changes in the environment. Markets that are dominated by less predictable, volatile competitors are intrinsically more difficult to operate in and control and hence less attractive as potential targets.

Threat of substitution

In all markets there is a threat that new solutions to the customers' original problems will be found that will make the company's offerings obsolete. The often quoted example is substitution of the pocket calculator for the slide rule, though other less dramatic examples abound. With the increasing rate of technological change experienced in the 1990s and 2000s it is probable that more products will become substituted at an accelerating rate.

In such situations two strategies make sense. First, for the less technologically innovative, seek market targets where substitution is less likely (but beware being lulled into believing substitution will never occur!). Second, identify those targets where your own company can achieve the next level of substitution. Under this strategy companies actively seek market targets that are using an inferior level of technology and are hence vulnerable to attack by a substitute product. Hewlett-Packard's success with laser printers followed by ink jet printers in the PC peripherals market (attacking dot matrix printers) is a classic example.

Degree of differentiation

Markets where there is little differentiation between product offerings offer significant opportunities to companies that can achieve differentiation. Where differentiation is not possible often a stalemate will exist and competition will degenerate into price conflicts, which are generally to be avoided.

10.3.4 The general business environment

Lastly, there is the issue of more general factors surrounding the market or segment in question.

Exposure to economic fluctuations

Some markets are more vulnerable to economic fluctuations than others. Commodity markets in particular are often subject to wider economic change, meaning less direct control of the market by the players in it. For example, the New Zealand wool export industry was badly affected in mid-1990 by an Australian decision, in the face of declining world demand and increasing domestic stockpiles, to lower the floor price on wool by 20 per cent. Australia is such a dominant player in the essentially commodity world market that New Zealand exporters were forced to follow suit.

Exposure to political and legal factors

As with exposure to economic uncertainty, markets that are vulnerable to political or legal factors are generally less attractive than those which are not. The exception, of course, is where these factors can be used positively as a means of entering the markets against entrenched but less aware competitors (e.g. when protection is removed from once government-owned monopolies).

Degree of regulation

The extent of regulation of the markets under consideration will affect the degrees of freedom of action the company has in its operations. Typically a less regulated market offers more opportunities for the innovative operator than one that is closely controlled.

Again there is an exception, however. Regulated markets might afford more protection once the company has entered. This might be protection from international competition (e.g. protection of European car manufacturers from Japanese car imports by quotas), which effectively creates a barrier to (or a ceiling on) entry. The warning should be sounded, however, that experience around the world has generally shown that protection breeds inefficiencies and when that protection is removed, as is the current trend in world trade, the industries thrown into the cold realities of international competition face major difficulties in adjusting.

Social acceptability and physical environment impact

Increasingly, with concern for the environment and the advent of 'green' politics, companies are looking at the broader social implications of the market targets they choose to go after. Especially when the company is widely diversified the impact of entering one market on the other activities of the company must be considered.

With increasing concern for the natural world, its fauna and flora, some cosmetics companies are now looking to non-animal ingredients as bases for their products and manufacturers of aerosols are increasingly using non-ozone-depleting propellants in place of CFCs. The Body Shop, a cosmetics and toiletries manufacturer and retailer, has built its highly successful position in the market through a clear commitment to the use of non-animal ingredients, just as Innocent trades on 'natural' values with fruit (and nothing but fruit) drinks.

The Body Shop

Alamy/UK Retail Alan King

accepted, the wisdom of such an approach in all but markets where preferences are strongly concentrated has been called into doubt.

10.6.2 Differentiated marketing

Differentiated marketing is adopted by companies seeking to offer a distinct product or service to each chosen segment of the market. Thus a shampoo manufacturer will offer different types of shampoo depending on the condition of the hair of the customer. The major danger of differentiated marketing is that it can lead to high costs, both in manufacturing and marketing a wide product line.

Depending on the company's resources, however, differentiated marketing can help in achieving overall market domination (this is the strategy pursued in the yellow fats market by Van den Berghs – see above).

10.6.3 Focused marketing

For the organisation with limited resources, however, attacking all or even most of the potential segments in a market may not be a viable proposition. In this instance concentrated or focused marketing may make more sense. Under this strategy the organisation focuses attention on one, or a few, market segments and leaves the wider market to its competitors. In this way it builds a strong position in a few selected markets, rather than attempting to compete across the board (either with undifferentiated or differentiated products).

The success of this approach depends on clear, in-depth knowledge of the customers served. The major danger of this strategy, however, is that over time the segment focused on may become less attractive and limiting on the organisation.

The Lucozade brand of soft drink was first marketed in the 1920s. It was originally developed by a Newcastle chemist as an energy drink for his son, who was recovering from jaundice. The brand was bought by Beechams in 1938 and marketed in a distinctive yellow cellophane wrapper, with the slogan 'Lucozade Aids Recovery'. During the 1950s and 1960s it was Beechams' biggest selling brand. By the 1970s, however, lower levels of sickness, less frequent flu epidemics and price increases had contributed to a decline in sales. From 1974 to 1978 sales fell by 30 per cent. The company decided that the brand needed to be repositioned.

The first repositioning was as an in-house 'pick-me-up' for housewives in the late 1970s. Sales initially increased by 11 per cent, but growth was not maintained, and by the end of 1979 sales had levelled out. In 1980 a new 250 ml bottle was launched and the new slogan 'Lucozade Replaces Lost Energy' was developed. But by 1982 a usage and attitude survey showed that the brand character had not changed significantly – it was still used primarily for illness recovery.

More radical repositioning was considered. In the carbonated soft drinks market Lucozade was competing head-on with well-established brands such as Coca-Cola and Pepsi. Lucozade also suffered from a poor image at the younger end of the market – it had been given to them by their mums when they were ill! A new positioning was developed around the theme: 'Lucozade is not only delicious and refreshing but can quickly replace lost energy'. The potential of the sports market became apparent and in July 1982 the advertising started to use Daley Thompson, an Olympic decathlete. Initially, however, the target customers liked Daley, but did not connect him with the brand.

The next phase of repositioning was the 'traffic lights' TV commercial, using Daley and the heavy metal music of Iron Maiden to 'portray' rather than 'explain' the message. The advertisements graphically conveyed the energy replacement message in a way younger users immediately identified with. In the first year of the new campaign, sales volume increased by 40 per cent. Qualitative research showed the message getting across to existing users and, crucially, to the younger target market.

Since then Lucozade has enjoyed continued success, and new flavour variants have been launched. The years 1988 saw the launch of the Lucozade Sport isotonic drink and 1995 the launch of the NRG teen drink. The same positioning strategy has been pursued successfully in Ireland, Asia and Australasia. From 1985 to 1995 worldwide sales had grown from £12 million to £125 million (Salmon, 1997). In 2002, the brand was promoted through the Lara Croft/Tomb Raider association.

The most effective strategy to adopt with regard to target market selection will vary from market to market. Certain characteristics of both the market and the company, however, will serve to suggest the type of strategy that makes most sense in a given situation.

The classic statement on how to approach the segmentation strategy choice comes from Frank *et al.* (1972). They propose that the choice of strategy should be based on:

- segment size – to determine its value and prospects;
- the incremental costs faced in differentiating between segments – which may be small, or may be high enough to undermine a full segmentation strategy;
- the extent and durability of segment differences – if segments are only marginally differentiated they may not be worth taking as separate targets, and if the differences are transitory then the viability of a segmentation strategy may be questionable;
- the stability and mutual compatibility of segment targets;
- the 'fit' between segment characteristics and company strengths (see Chapter 8); and
- the level and type of competition in the prospective segment targets.

Summary

The selection of which potential market segment or segments to serve is the crucial step in developing a robust and comprehensive marketing strategy. Until the targets have been clearly identified, their requirements and motivations fully explored, it is not possible to develop a robust competitive positioning.

Discussion questions

1 How do you explain that B&O has remained successful in the face of tougher competition? What is their competitive advantage?

2 How would you define the market B&O are competing in and which segment are they serving?

3 What targeting strategy is B&O currently pursuing? Is this sustainable?

part four

Competitive Positioning Strategies

Part 4 looks at the main ways in which firms strive to create a competitive advantage.

Chapter 11 discusses ways of creating sustainable competitive advantage once the target market has been decided. Routes to achieving cost leadership and differentiation are examined, both as alternative and as complementary strategies. The dangers of falling between these strategies, and not executing either effectively, are also addressed. The chapter then goes on to discuss how competitive positions can be effectively communicated to customers, as well as the characteristics of sustainable competitive advantage through positioning. It concludes by examining strategies for building position, holding position, harvesting, niching and divesting.

Chapter 12, a new chapter for this fourth edition, considers the new marketing mix including recent developments in e-business and e-marketing and their potential for impact on marketing strategies. Following the early hype of the dot.com boom, and the equally spectacular dot.com bust (or dot.bomb as it is being referred to), the chapter takes a more measured view of the opportunities and threats the newer, Internet-based technologies have to offer organisations and looks at how they integrate with the more traditional elements of the marketing mix.

Chapter 13 assesses the role of innovation and new product/service development in creating competitive positions. The critical factors for success in new product development are identified, together with common reasons for failure. The processes of new product development are discussed along with suggestions for speeding up and enhancing the likelihood of success. The chapter concludes by considering organisational issues in new product development and innovation.

Chapter 14 looks at the role of service and relationship marketing in building stronger competitive positions. The goods and services spectrum is introduced to show the increasing importance of the service element in the marketing implementation mix, even for goods marketers. Relationship marketing is discussed in the context of building and maintaining long-term relationships with key customers and customer groups. Techniques for monitoring and measuring customer satisfaction are presented with particular emphasis on the use of gap analysis to track problems in customer satisfaction back to their root causes.

chapter eleven

Creating sustainable competitive advantage

Competitive Strategy is the search for a favourable competitive position in an industry. Competitive Strategy aims to establish a profitable and sustainable position against the forces that determine industry competition.

Porter (1985)

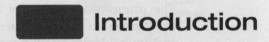

Introduction

Chapter 10 discussed the choice of target market suited to the strengths and capabilities of the firm. This chapter focuses on methods for creating a competitive advantage in that chosen target market. While few advantages are likely to last forever, some bases of advantage are more readily protected than others. A key task for the strategist is to identify those bases that offer the most potential for defensible positioning.

11.1 Using organisational resources to create sustainable competitive advantage

In Chapter 6 we assessed organisational resources. These we classed as three main types: organisational culture; marketing assets; and marketing capabilities. Any

the danger of losing clients when key staff move to competing agencies has been long recognised and agreed codes of practice have been drawn up, including 'golden handcuffs' to minimise the damage caused by lost resources.

In Chapter 6 the ways of protecting resources from competitor copy, or isolating mechanisms, were discussed. These include enhancing causal ambiguity (making it hard for competitors to identify the underlying value-creating resources in the first place), building economic deterrence (making resource acquisition uneconomic), establishing legal protection (through patents and copyrights) and creating path dependency (the need to devote time and effort to the establishment and/or appropriation of resources). In the longer term, however, few resources can be effectively protected against all competitor attempts to imitate.

11.2 Generic routes to competitive advantage

As noted in Chapter 2, Porter (1980) has identified two main routes to creating a competitive advantage. These he termed cost leadership and differentiation. In examining how each can be achieved Porter (1985) takes a systems approach, likening the operations of a company to a 'value chain' from the input of raw materials and other resources through to the final delivery to, and after-sales servicing of, the customer. The value chain was discussed in the context of competitor analysis in Chapter 5 and was presented in Figure 5.5.

Each of the activities within the value chain, the primary activities and the support functions, can be used to add value to the ultimate product or service. That added value, however, is typically in the form of lower cost or valued uniqueness. These options are shown in Figure 11.3.

Figure 11.3 Generic routes to competitive advantage creation

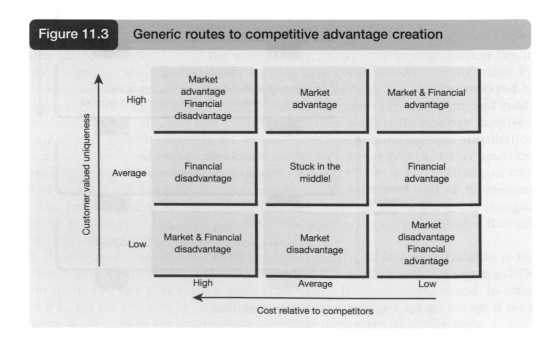

304

11.3 Achieving cost leadership

Porter (1985) has identified several major factors that affect organisational costs. These he terms 'cost drivers'; they are shown in Figure 11.4 and each is reviewed briefly below.

11.3.1 Economies of scale

Economies of scale are perhaps the single most effective cost driver in many industries. Scale economies stem from doing things more efficiently or differently in volume. In addition, sheer size can help in creating purchasing leverage to secure cheaper and/or better quality (less waste) raw materials and securing them in times of limited availability.

There are, however, limits to scale economies. Size can bring with it added complexity that itself can lead to diseconomies. For most operations there is an optimum size above or below which inefficiencies occur.

The effects of economies of scale are often more pronounced in the manufacturing sector than in services. While manufacturing operations such as assembly lines can benefit through scale the advantages to service firms such as advertising agencies are less obvious. They may continue to lie in enhanced purchasing muscle (for the ad agency in media purchasing for example) and spread training costs.

Figure 11.4   Cost drivers

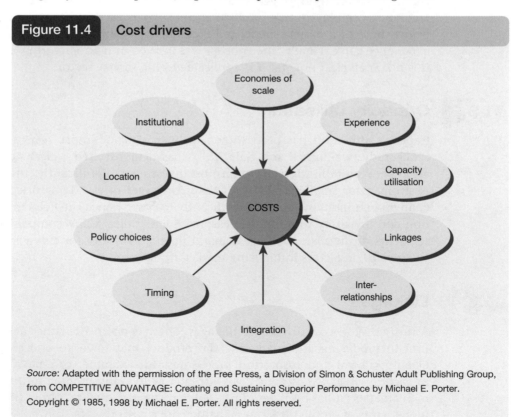

Source: Adapted with the permission of the Free Press, a Division of Simon & Schuster Adult Publishing Group, from COMPETITIVE ADVANTAGE: Creating and Sustaining Superior Performance by Michael E. Porter. Copyright © 1985, 1998 by Michael E. Porter. All rights reserved.

11.3.2 Experience and learning effects

Further cost reductions may be achieved through learning and experience effects. Learning refers to increases in efficiency that are possible at a given level of scale through an employee's having performed the necessary tasks many times before.

The Boston Consulting Group extended the recognised production learning curve beyond manufacturing and looked at the increased efficiency that was possible in all aspects of the business (e.g. in marketing, advertising and selling) through experience. BCG estimated empirically that, in many industries, costs reduced by approximately 15–20 per cent each time cumulative production (a measure of experience) doubled. This finding suggests that companies with larger market share will, by definition, have a cost advantage through experience, assuming all companies are operating on the same experience curve.

Experience can be brought into the company by hiring experienced staff, and be enhanced through training. Conversely competitors may poach experience by attracting away skilled staff.

The experience curve as an explanation of costs has come under increasing scrutiny. Gluck (1986) argues that when the world changed from a high growth, 'big is beautiful', mentality to low growth, 'big is bust', realisation the experience curve fell into disfavour. He concludes that in today's business environments competitive advantages that rely too heavily on economies of scale in manufacturing or distribution are often no longer sustainable. In addition, a shift in the level or type of technology employed may result in an inexperienced newcomer reducing costs to below those of a more experienced incumbent, essentially moving on to a lower experience curve. Finally, the concept was derived in manufacturing industries and it is not at all clear how far it is applicable to the service sector.

11.3.3 Capacity utilisation

Capacity utilisation has been shown to have a major impact on unit costs. The PIMS study (see Buzzell and Gale, 1987) has demonstrated a clear positive association between utilisation and return on investment. Significantly, the relationship is stronger for smaller companies than for larger ones. Major discontinuities or changes in utilisation can add significantly to costs, hence the need to plan production and inventory to minimise seasonal fluctuations. Many companies also avoid segments of the market where demand fluctuates wildly for this very reason (see Chapter 10 on factors influencing market attractiveness).

11.3.4 Linkages

A further set of cost drivers are linkages. These concern the other activities of the firm in producing and marketing the product that have an effect on the costs. Quality control and inspection procedures, for example, can have a significant impact on servicing costs and costs attributable to faulty product returns. Indeed, in many markets it has been demonstrated that superior quality, rather than leading to higher costs of production, can actually reduce costs (Peters, 1987).

External linkages with suppliers of factor inputs or distributors of the firm's final products can also result in lower costs. Developments in just in time (JIT) manufacturing and delivery can have a significant impact on stockholding costs and work in progress. Beyond the cost equation, however, the establishment of closer working links has far wider marketing implications. For JIT to work effectively requires a very close working relationship between buyer and supplier. This often means an interchange of information, a meshing of forecasting and scheduling and the building of a long-term relationship. This in turn helps to create high switching costs (the costs of seeking supply elsewhere) and hence barriers to competitive entry.

11.3.5 Interrelationships

Interrelationships with other SBUs in the overall corporate portfolio can help to share experience and gain economies of scale in functional activities (such as marketing research, R&D, quality control, ordering and purchasing).

11.3.6 Degree of integration

Decisions on integration, e.g. contracting out delivery and/or service, also affect costs. Similarly the decision to make or buy components can have major cost implications. The extent of forward or backward integration extant or possible in a particular market was discussed in Chapter 10 as one of the factors considered in assessing target market attractiveness to the company.

11.3.7 Timing

Timing, though not always controllable, can lead to cost advantages. Often the first mover in an industry can gain cost advantages by securing prime locations, cheap or good quality raw materials, and/or technological leadership (see Chapter 13). Second movers can often benefit from exploiting newer technology to leapfrog first mover positions.

As with other factors discussed above, however, the value of timing goes far beyond its impact on costs. Abell (1978) has argued that a crucial element of any marketing strategy is timing, that at certain times 'strategic windows' are open (i.e. there are opportunities in the market that can be exploited) while at other times they are shut. Successful strategies are timely strategies. An example was the impact of the more economical and 'honest' German and Japanese cars in the US market after the oil crisis and subsequent price rise, while Detroit kept 'gas guzzling juke-boxes on wheels' (Mingo, 1994).

11.3.8 Policy choices

Policy choices, the prime areas for differentiating (discussed below), have implications for costs. Decisions on the product line, the product itself, quality levels, service, features, credit facilities, etc. all affect costs. They also affect the actual and perceived uniqueness of the product to the consumer and hence a genuine dilemma can arise if the thrust of the generic strategy is not clear. The general rules are to reduce costs on factors that will not significantly affect valued uniqueness, avoid frills if they do not serve to differentiate significantly, and invest in technology to achieve low-cost process automation and low-cost product design (fewer parts can make for easier and cheaper assembly).

11.3.9 Location and institutional factors

The final cost drivers identified by Porter (1985) are location (geographic location to take advantage of lower distribution, assembly, raw materials or energy costs), and institutional factors such as government regulations (e.g. larger lorries on the roads can reduce distribution costs but at other environmental and social costs). The sensitivity of governments to lobbyists and pressure groups will dictate the ability of the company to exercise institutional cost drivers.

11.3.10 Summary of cost drivers

There are many ways in which a company can seek to reduce costs. In attempting to become a cost leader in an industry a firm should be aware, first, that there can only be one cost leader and, second, that there are potentially many ways in which this position can be attacked (i.e. through using other cost drivers). Cost advantages can be among the most difficult to sustain and defend in the face of heavy and determined competition.

That said, however, it should be a constant objective of management to reduce costs that do not significantly add to ultimate customer satisfaction.

11.4 Achieving differentiation

Most of the factors listed above as cost drivers could also be used as 'uniqueness drivers' if the firm is seeking to differentiate itself from its competitors. Of most immediate concern here, however, are the policy choices open to the company. These are summarised in Figure 11.5.

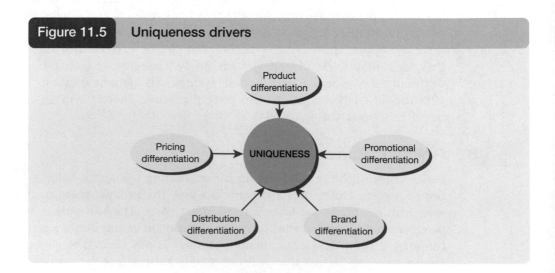

Figure 11.5 Uniqueness drivers

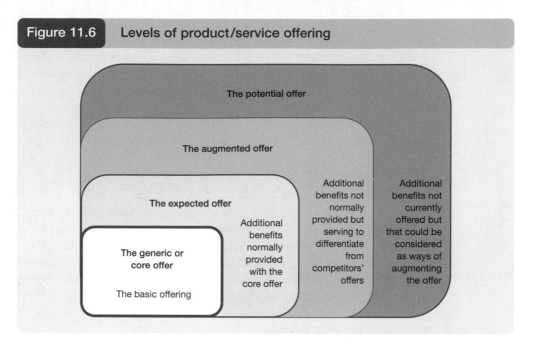

Figure 11.6 Levels of product/service offering

11.4.1 Product differentiation

Product differentiation seeks to increase the value of the product or service on offer to the customer. Levitt (1986) has suggested that products and services can be seen on at least four main levels. These are the core product, the expected product, the augmented product and the potential product. Figure 11.6 shows these levels diagrammatically. Differentiation is possible in all these respects.

At the centre of the model is the core, or generic, product. This is the central product or service offered. It is the petrol, steel, banking facility, mortgage, information, etc. Beyond the generic product, however, is what customers expect in addition, the expected product. When buying petrol, for example, customers expect easy access to the forecourt, the possibility of paying by credit card, the availability of screen wash facilities, air for tyres, radiator top-up, and so on. Since most petrol forecourts meet these expectations they do not serve to differentiate one supplier from another.

At the next level Levitt identifies the augmented product. This constitutes all the extra features and services that go above and beyond what the customer expects to convey added value and hence serve to differentiate the offer from that of competitors. The petrol station where, in the self-serve 2000s, one attendant fills the car with petrol while another cleans the windscreen, headlamps and mirrors, is going beyond what is expected. Over time, however, these means of distinguishing can become copied, routine, and ultimately merely part of what is expected.

Finally, Levitt describes the potential product as all those further additional features and benefits that could be offered. At the petrol station these may include a free car wash with every fill-up, gifts unrelated to petrol and a car valeting service. While the model shows the potential product bounded, in reality it is only bounded by the imagination and ingenuity of the supplier.

Peters (1987) believes that, while in the past suppliers have concentrated on attempts to differentiate their offerings on the basis of the generic and expected product, convergence is occurring at this level in many markets. As quality control, assurance and management methods become more widely understood and practised, delivering a performing, reliable, durable, conforming offer (a 'quality' product in the classic sense of the word) will no longer be adequate. In the future he predicts greater emphasis on the augmented and potential product as ways of adding value, creating customer delight and hence creating competitive advantage.

Differentiating the core and expected product

Differentiation of the core product or benefit offers a different way of satisfying the same basic want or need (see Figure 11.7). It is typically created by a step change in technology, the application of innovation. Calculators, for example, offered a different method of solving the basic 'calculating' need from the slide rules they replaced. Similarly the deep freeze offers a different way of storing food from the earlier cold stores, pantries and cellars. A new strain of grass that only grows to 1 inch in height could replace the need for a lawnmower.

Augmenting the product

Differentiation of the augmented product can be achieved by offering more to customers on existing features (e.g. offering a lifetime guarantee on audio tape, as Scotch provides, rather than a one- or two-year guarantee) or by offering new features of value to customers. There are two main types of product feature that can create customer benefit. These are performance features and appearance features.

Analysis of product features must relate those features to the benefits they offer to customers. For example, the introduction of the golf ball typewriter did not change

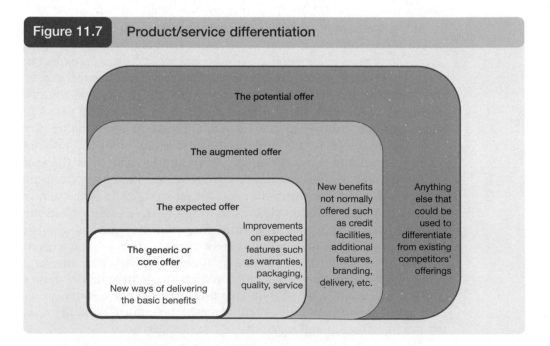

Figure 11.7   Product/service differentiation

The potential offer

The augmented offer

The expected offer

The generic or core offer

New ways of delivering the basic benefits

Improvements on expected features such as warranties, packaging, quality, service

New benefits not normally offered such as credit facilities, additional features, branding, delivery, etc.

Anything else that could be used to differentiate from existing competitors' offerings

the core benefit (the ability to create a typewritten page of text or numbers). It did, however, allow different typefaces and different spacing to be used, thus extending the value to the customer who wanted these extra benefits. The ink jet printer extended those benefits even further, offering virtually unlimited fonts, sizes and other effects.

In estimating the value to the consumers of additional product features and their resulting benefits, conjoint measurement (see Green and Wind, 1975) can be particularly useful. This technique has been successfully applied, for example, to decisions on product features by companies operating in the audio market and to service features offered by building societies in high-interest accounts.

In the lawnmower market Flymo introduced the rotary blade hover mower as a means of differentiating from the traditional rotating cylinder blade. In some markets, especially where lawns were awkwardly shaped or steeply sloping, the ease of use of the hover mower made it a very attractive, differentiated product. In other markets, however, the market leader, Qualcast, was able to retaliate by showing the advantage of the conventional mower in having a hopper in which to catch the grass cuttings. Under the Flymo system the cuttings were left on the lawn. More recent developments have seen the introduction of rotary hover mowers with hoppers.

Quality

A prime factor in differentiating the product or service from that of competitors is quality. Quality concerns the fitness for purpose of a product or service. For manufactured products that can include the durability, appearance or grade of the product while in services it often comes down to the tangible elements of the service, the reliability and responsiveness of the service provider, the assurance provided of the value of the service and the empathy, or caring attention, received (see Parasuraman *et al.*, 1988). Quality can reflect heavily both on raw materials used and the degree of quality control exercised during manufacture and delivery.

Of central importance is consumer perception of quality, which may not be the same as the manufacturer's perception. Cardozo (1979) gives an example of where the two do not coincide:

> *The marketing research department of a manufacturer of household paper goods asked for consumer evaluation of a new paper tissue. The reaction was favorable but the product was not thought to be soft enough. The R&D department then set about softening the tissue by weakening the fibers and reducing their density. In subsequent usage tests the product fell apart and was useless for its designed purpose. Further tests showed that to make the product 'feel' softer required an actual increase in the strength and density of the fibres.*

Quality has been demonstrated by the PIMS project to be a major determinant of commercial success. Indeed, Buzzell and Gale (1987) concluded that relative perceived quality (customers' judgements of the quality of the supplier's offer relative to its competitors) was the single most important factor in affecting the long-run performance of a business. Quality was shown to have a greater impact on ROI level and be more effective at gaining market share than lower pricing.

Closely related to perceptions of quality are perceptions of style, particularly for products with a high emotional appeal (such as cosmetics). In fashion-conscious markets such as clothes, design can be a very powerful way of differentiating. Jain (1990) notes that Du Pont successfully rejuvenated its market for ladies' stockings by offering different coloured tints and hence repositioned the stockings as fashion accessories – a different tint for each outfit.

Packaging

Packaging too can be used to differentiate the product. Packaging has five main functions, each of which can be used as a basis for differentiation.

1 Packaging **stores** the product, and hence can be used to extend shelf life, or facilitate physical storage (e.g. tetra-packs for fruit juice and other beverages).
2 Packaging **protects** the product during transit and prior to consumption to ensure consistent quality (e.g. the use of film packs for potato crisps to ensure freshness).
3 Packaging **facilitates use** of the product (e.g. applicator packs for floor cleaners, wine boxes, domestic liquid soap dispensers).
4 Packaging helps **create an image** for the product through its visual impact, quality of design, illustration of uses, etc.
5 Packaging helps **promote** the product through eye-catching, unusual colours and shapes, etc. Examples of the latter are the sales of wine in carafes rather than bottles (Paul Masson California Wines) and the sale of ladies' tights in egg-shaped packages (L'eggs).

Branding

A particularly effective way of differentiating at the tangible product level is to create a unique brand with a favourable image and reputation. As discussed in Chapter 6, brand and company reputation can be powerful marketing assets for a company.

Brand name or symbol is an indication of pedigree and a guarantee of what to expect from the product – a quality statement of a value-for-money signal. Heinz baked beans, for example, can command a premium price because of the assurance of quality the consumer gets in choosing the brand. Similarly, retailers such as Tesco and Sainsbury's are able to differentiate their own branded products from other brands because of their reputation for quality that extends across their product ranges. Branding is also a highly defensible competitive advantage. Once registered, competitors cannot use the same branding (name or symbol).

Service

Service can be a major differentiating factor in the purchase of many products, especially durables (both consumer and industrial). Certainly enhanced service was a major factor in the success of Wilhelm Becker, a Swedish industrial paints company. Becker developed 'Colour Studios' as a service to its customers and potential customers to enable them to experiment with different colours and combinations. Volvo, the Swedish auto manufacturer now owned by Ford, used the service in researching alternative colours to use on farm tractors and found that red (the colour used to date) was a poor colour choice as it jarred, for many farmers, with the colours of the landscape. Changing the colour scheme resulted in increased sales.

In domestic paints, too, there has been an attempt to add service, this time provided by the customers themselves. Matchpots were introduced by a leading domestic paint supplier to allow customers, for a small outlay, to try different colours at home before selecting the final colour to use. In this case, however, unlike Becker's Colour Studios, copy by competitors was relatively easy and the advantage quickly eroded.

Service need not be an addition to the product. In some circumstances a reduction can add value. The recent growth in home brewing of beers and wines is a case where a less complete product (the malt extract, hops, grape juice, yeast, etc.) is put to market but the customer is able to gain satisfaction through self-completion of the production process. Thus the customer provides the service and becomes part of the production process.

Providing superior service as a way of creating a stronger link between supplier and customer can have wide-reaching consequences. In particular, it makes it less likely that the customer will look for alternative supply sources and hence acts as a barrier to competitor entry.

To ensure and enhance customer service Peters (1987) recommends that each company regularly conducts customer satisfaction studies to gauge how well it is meeting customers' expectations and to seek ways in which it can improve on customer service.

Further elements of the augmented product that can be used to differentiate the product include installation, credit availability, delivery (speedy and on time, when promised) and warranty. All can add to the differentiation of the product from that of competitors.

Deciding on the bases for product differentiation

Each of the elements of the product can be used as a way of differentiating the product from competitive offerings. In deciding which of the possible elements to use in differentiating the product three considerations are paramount.

First, what do the customers expect in addition to the core, generic product? In the automobile market, for example, customers in all market segments expect a minimum level of reliability in the cars they buy. In the purchase of consumer white goods (fridges, freezers, washing machines, etc.), minimum periods of warranty are expected. In the choice of toothpaste, minimum levels of protection from tooth decay and gum disease are required. These expectations, over and above the core product offering, are akin to 'hygiene factors' in Hertzberg's Theory of Motivation. They must be offered for the product or service to be considered by potential purchasers. Their presence does not enhance the probability of consumers choosing products with them, but their absence will certainly deter purchase.

The second consideration is what the customers would value over and above what is expected. In identifying potential 'motivators' the marketer seeks to offer more than the competition to attract purchasers. These additions to the product beyond what is normally expected by the customers often form the most effective way of differentiating the company's offerings. Crucial, however, is the cost of offering these additions. The cost of the additions should be less than the extra benefit (value) to the customers and hence be reflected in a willingness to pay a premium price. Where possible an economic value should be placed on the differentiation to allow pricing to take full account of value to the customer (see Forbis and Mehta, 1981).

The third consideration in choosing a way of differentiating the product from the competition is the ease with which that differentiation can be copied. Changes in the interest rates charged by one building society, for example, can easily be copied in a matter of days or even hours. An advantage based, however, on the location of the society's outlets in the major city high streets takes longer and is more costly to copy.

Ideally, differentiation is sought where there is some (at least temporary) barrier precluding competitors following. The most successful differentiations are those that use a core skill, competence or marketing asset of the company which competitors do not possess and will find hard to develop. In the car hire business, for example, the extensive network of pick-up and drop-off points offered by Hertz, the market leader, enables them to offer a more convenient service to the one-way customer than the competition. Emulating that network is costly, if not impossible, for smaller followers in the market.

Peters (1987) has argued that many companies overemphasise the core product in their overall marketing thinking and strategy. He suggests that, as it becomes increasingly difficult to differentiate on the basis of core product, greater emphasis will need to be put on how to 'add service' through the augmented (and potential) product. This change in emphasis is shown in Figure 11.8, which contrasts a product focus (core product emphasis) with a service added focus (extending the augmented and potential products in ways of value and interest to the customer).

A focus away from the core product towards the 'outer rings' is particularly useful in 'commodity' markets where competitive strategy has traditionally been based on price. Differentiation through added service offers an opportunity for breaking out of an overreliance on price in securing business.

In summary, there are a great many ways in which products and services can be differentiated from their competitors. In deciding on the type of differentiation to adopt, several factors should be borne in mind: the added value to the customer of the differentiation; the cost of differentiation in relation to the added value; the

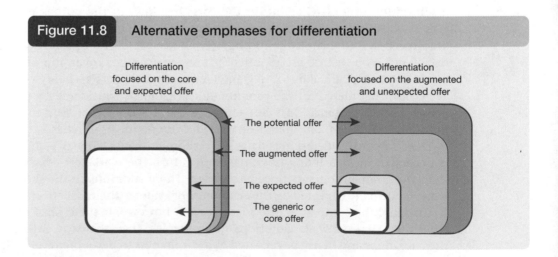

Figure 11.8   Alternative emphases for differentiation

Differentiation focused on the core and expected offer

Differentiation focused on the augmented and unexpected offer

The potential offer

The augmented offer

The expected offer

The generic or core offer

probability and speed of competitor copy; and the extent to which the differentiation exploits the marketing assets of the company.

11.4.2 Distribution differentiation

Distribution differentiation comes from using different outlets, having a different network or a different coverage of the market.

Recent developments in direct marketing are not only related to creating different ways of promoting products. They also offer new outlets for many goods. Shopping by phone through TV-based catalogues has yet to take off in any big way, but there are certainly opportunities for innovative marketers.

The advent of the Internet has made significant changes to the distribution strategies of many firms. Particularly for firms offering bit-based products such as information, or music, direct distribution to customers through their Internet connections is now possible (see Chapter 12). Again, first mover advantages afforded short-term differentiation but competitor copy has been rapid. Protecting an advantage in e-marketing, be it a distribution advantage or a communications advantage, is proving particularly difficult and innovative companies such as Amazon.com are having to constantly find new ways to add value for their customers in an attempt to remain differentiated.

11.4.3 Price differentiation

Lower price as a means of differentiation can be a successful basis for strategy only where the company enjoys a cost advantage, or where there are barriers to competing firms with a lower cost structure competing at a lower price. Without a cost advantage, starting a price war can be a disastrous course to follow, as Laker Airways found to its cost.

Premium pricing is generally only possible where the product or service has actual or perceived advantages to the customer and therefore it is often used in conjunction with, and to reinforce, a differentiated product.

In general, the greater the degree of product or services differentiation, the more scope there is for premium pricing. Where there is little other ground for differentiation, price competition becomes stronger and cost advantages assume greater importance.

11.4.4 Promotional differentiation

Promotional differentiation involves using different types of promotions (e.g. a wider communications mix employing advertising, public relations, direct mail, personal selling, etc.), promotions of a different intensity (i.e. particularly heavy promotions during launch and relaunch of products) or different content (i.e. with a clearly different advertising message).

Many companies today make poor use of the potential of public relations. Public relations essentially consists of creating relationships with the media and using those relationships to gain positive exposure. Press releases and interviews with key executives on important topical issues can both help to promote the company in a more credible way than media advertising.

A small, UK-based electronics company brilliantly exploited a visit by Japanese scientists to its plant. The company gained wide coverage of the event, presenting it as an attempt by the Japanese to learn from this small but innovative firm. The coverage was in relevant trade journals and even the national media. The result was a major increase in enquiries to the company and increasing domestic sales of its products. The PR had two major advantages over media advertising. First, it was very cheap in relation to the exposure it achieved (the company could never have afforded to buy the exposure at normal media rates). Second, the reports appearing in the press attracted credibility because they had been written by independent journalists and were seen as 'news' rather than advertising. (*Source*: *The Marketing Mix*, television series by Yorkshire TV.)

Using a different message within normal media advertising can also have a differentiating effect. When most advertisers are pursuing essentially the same market with the same message an innovative twist is called for. Most beers are promoted by showing gregarious groups of males in public houses having an enjoyable night out. Heineken managed to differentiate its beer by using a series of advertisements employing humour and the caption 'Heineken refreshes the parts other beers cannot reach'. Similarly an innovative campaign for Boddington's Bitter, emphasising the down-to-earth value of the beer and its creamy, frothy head, served to mark it out from the crowd.

When Krona was launched by Van den Berghs into the margarine market (see Chapter 10) it was aimed at consumers who were increasingly sensitive to the price of butter but who still required the taste of butter – and the company had a major communications problem. Legislation precluded it from stating that the product tasted like butter (Clark, 1986) and the slogan 'Four out of five people can't tell the difference between Stork and butter' had already been used (with mixed success) by one of the other company brands. The solution was to use a semi-documentary advertisement featuring a respected reporter (René Cutforth) which majored on a rumour that had circulated around a product of identical formulation in Australia (Fairy). The rumour had been that the product was actually New Zealand butter being dumped on the Australian market disguised as margarine to overcome trade quotas. The slogan selected was 'The margarine that raised questions in an Australian parliament' and the style of the advertisement, while never actually claiming taste parity with butter, cleverly conveyed the impression that people really couldn't tell the difference.

More recently Van den Berghs has promoted the margarine Flora as the spread bought by women who care about the health of their men, while their originally branded 'I Can't Believe It's Not Butter' returns to Stork's old taste appeal.

11.4.5 Brand differentiation

Brand positioning places the customer at the centre of building a maintainable hold on the marketplace. It shifts from the classic idea of companies developing a 'unique selling proposition' (USP) to establishing a 'unique emotional proposition'.

Competing products may look similar to the hapless parent buying a pair of Nike trainers, but not to their children. They want Nike trainers, and the parent is pressured to pay the extra to get them. Nike's success at brand differentiation flowed from its Air Jordan range, which built upon the USP of air cells in the heels and their unique emotional proposition of being associated with top athletes. So powerful did this combination become that even in crime-free Japan people paid huge price premiums for their Air Jordans but would not jog in them for fear of being mugged (called jugging) for their Nikes. Adidas and Reebok promote their products using athletes and air in their heels, but Nike has won the battle for the minds of teenagers and their parents' pockets.

Nike is an exemplary case of gaining market strength by using Ries and Trout's (1986) ladder of awareness. Even though there may be numerous products on the market consumers are rarely able to name more than a few. This was the problem faced by Audi when they realised that people mentioned Mercedes, BMW and Volkswagen as German cars, with all the connotations of quality and reliability that entails, but often omitted Audi (now owned by VW). The result was the 'Vorsprung Durch Technik' campaign which concentrated on the German pedigree of the product and, through rallying and the Quatro, on their technical excellence.

Alamy/Coverspot

Ries and Trout noted that the second firm in markets usually enjoys half the business of the first firm, and the third firm enjoys half the business of the second, etc. This flows through into profitability and return on investments where, in the long term, profitability follows the market share ranking of companies. Leading companies can also achieve major economies in advertising and promotion (Saunders, 1990). Part of the reason for this is the tendency for people to remember the number 1. When asked who was the first person to successfully fly alone across the Atlantic most people would correctly answer Charles Lindbergh, but how many people can name the second person? Similarly with the first and second people to set foot on the moon, or climb Mount Everest.

The importance of being number 1 is fine for market leaders such as Nike in sports shoes, Mercedes in luxury cars, Coca-Cola in soft drinks and Nescafé in coffee, but it leaves lesser brands with an unresolved problem. Positioning points to a way of these brands establishing a strong place in the minds of the consumer despite the incessant call for attention from competing products. This involves consistency of message and the association of a brand with ideas that are already held strongly within the consumer's mind.

11.4.6 Summary of differentiation drivers

Where the route to competitive advantage selected is differentiation the key differentiating variables, those that offer the most leverage for differentiation using the company's skills to the full, should be identified. Where possible, differentiation should be pursued on multiple fronts for its enhancement. In addition, value signals should be employed to enhance perceived differentiation (e.g. building on reputation, image, presence, appearance and pricing of the product). Barriers to copying should be erected, through patenting, holding key executives and creating switching costs to retain customers.

11.5 Sustaining competitive advantage

It will be clear from the above that there are a variety of ways companies can attempt to create a competitive advantage for themselves. Some of these will be easier for competitors to copy than others. The most useful ways of creating defensible positions lie in exploiting the following.

11.5.1 Unique and valued products

Fundamental to creating a superior and defensible position in the marketplace is to have unique and valued products and services crafted through the use of scarce and valuable organisational resources to offer to customers.

Dow Jones maintains high margins from unique products. *The Wall Street Journal* is a product that customers want and are willing to pay for. Central to offering unique and valued products and services is the identification of the key differentiating variables – those with the greatest potential leverage.

Uniqueness may stem from employing superior, proprietary technology, utilising superior raw materials, or from differentiating the tangible and augmented elements of the product.

Unique products do not, however, stay unique forever. Successful products will be imitated sooner or later so that the company which wishes to retain its unique position must be willing, and indeed even eager, to innovate continually and look for new ways of differentiating (see Chapter 13). This may mean a willingness to cannibalise its own existing products before the competition attacks them.

11.5.2 Clear, tight definition of market targets

To enable a company to keep its products and services both unique and valued by the customers requires constant monitoring of, and dialogue with, those customers. This in turn requires a clear understanding of who they are and how to access them. The clearer the focus of the firm's activities on one or a few market targets, the more likely it is to serve those targets successfully. In the increasingly segmented and fragmented markets of the 2000s the companies that fail to focus their activities are less likely to respond to changing opportunities and threats.

11.5.3 Enhanced customer linkages

Creating closer bonds with customers through enhanced service can help establish a more defensible position in the market (see Chapter 14). As suggested above, a major advantage of JIT manufacturing systems is that they require closer links between supplier and buyer. As buyers and suppliers become more enmeshed, so it becomes more difficult for newcomers to enter.

Creating switching costs, the costs associated with moving from one supplier to another, is a further way in which customer linkages can be enhanced. Loomis, writing in *Fortune* (30 April 1984), pointed to the success of Nalco in using its specialist expertise in the chemicals it markets to counsel and problem solve for its customers. This enhancement of the linkages with its customers makes it less likely they will shop around for other sources of supply.

11.5.4 Established brand and company credibility

Brand and company reputation are among the most defensible assets the company has, provided they are managed well and protected.

> *Worthington Steel in the US have an enviable reputation for superior quality workman-ship. The company also has a high reputation for customer service. Combined they make it hard for customers to go elsewhere.*

(Peters, 1987)

The rate of technological and market change is now so fast, and products so transient, that customers find security and continuity in the least tangible of a company's assets: the reputation of its brands and company name. Brand, styles and products change year on year, but people the world over desire Nike, Sony, Mercedes, Levi's and Rolex. They 'buy the maker', not the product (Sorrell, 1989).

11.6 Offensive and defensive competitive strategies

Successful competitive strategy amounts to combining attacking and defensive moves to build a stronger position in the chosen marketplace. A number of writers, most notably Kotler and Singh (1981), James (1984) and Ries and Trout (1986), have drawn an analogy between military warfare and competitive battles in the market-place. Their basic contention is that lessons for the conduct of business strategy can be learned by a study of warfare and the principles developed by military strategists. Indeed, the bookshelves of corporate strategists around the world now often contain the works of Sun Tzu (Trai, 1991; Khoo, 1992) and von Clausewitz (1908).

Similarly, much can be learned from the approaches used in competitive sports, pastimes and team games, where brains as well as (or instead of) brawn are important for success. Successful sportsmen and women, such as previous England cricket captain

Mike Brearley, and rugby captain Will Carling, have made successful second careers through speaking about strategy and motivation at corporate development seminars.

There are five basic competitive strategies pursued by organisations. These include build (or growth) strategies, hold (or maintenance) strategies, niche (or focus) strategies, harvest (or reaping) strategies and deletion (divestment) strategies. The structure of the discussion draws from both Kotler (1997) and James (1984).

11.6.1 Build strategies

A build strategy seeks to improve on organisational performance through expansion of activities. This expansion may come through expanding the market for the organisation's offerings or through winning market share from competitors.

Build strategies are most suited to growth markets. In such markets it is generally considered easier to expand, as this need not be at the expense of the competition and does not necessarily provoke strong competitive retaliation. During the growth phase of markets companies should aim to grow at least as fast as the market itself.

Build strategies can also make sense in non-growth markets where there are exploitable competitor weaknesses or where there are marketing assets that can be usefully deployed.

Build strategies are often costly, particularly where they involve a direct confrontation with a major competitor. Before embarking on such strategies the potential costs must be weighed against the expected gains.

Market expansion

Build strategies are achieved through market expansion or taking sales and customers from competitors (confrontation). Market expansion, in turn, comes through three main routes: **new users** (attracted as products progress through their life cycles from innovators of to laggards via a trickle-down effect), **new uses** (introduced to existing or new users), and/or **increased frequency of use** (by encouraging existing users to use more of the product).

For products that have reached the mature phase of the life cycle a major task is to find new markets for the product. This could involve geographic expansion of the companies' activities domestically and/or internationally. Companies seeking growth but believing their established market to be incapable of providing it roll out into new markets.

Market share gain through competitor confrontation

When a build objective is pursued in a market that cannot, for one reason or another, be expanded, success must, by definition, be at the expense of competitors. This will inevitably lead to some degree of confrontation between the protagonists for customers. Kotler and Singh (1981) have identified five main confrontation strategies (see Figure 11.9).

Frontal attack

The frontal attack is characterised by an all-out attack on the opponent's territory. It is often countered by a fortification, or position, defence (see below). The outcome of the confrontation will depend on strength and endurance (see Figure 11.10).

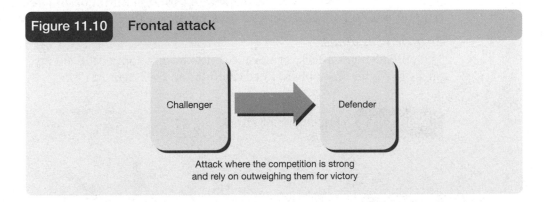

Figure 11.9 — Market challenger strategies

- Frontal attack
- Flanking attack
- Encirclement attack
- Bypass strategy
- Guerrilla tactics

Figure 11.10 — Frontal attack

Challenger → Defender

Attack where the competition is strong
and rely on outweighing them for victory

The requirement of a similar 3 to 1 advantage to ensure success in a commercial frontal attack has been suggested (Kotler and Singh, 1981), further calibrated (Cook, 1983) and questioned (Chattopadhyay *et al.*, 1985). All agree, however, that to defeat a well-entrenched competitor, which has built a solid market position, requires substantial superiority in at least one key area of the marketing programme. For a frontal attack to succeed requires sufficient resources, a strength advantage over the competitors being attacked, and that losses can be both predicted and sustained.

Flanking attack

In contrast to the frontal attack, the flanking attack seeks to concentrate the aggressor's strengths against the competitor's weaknesses (see Figure 11.11).

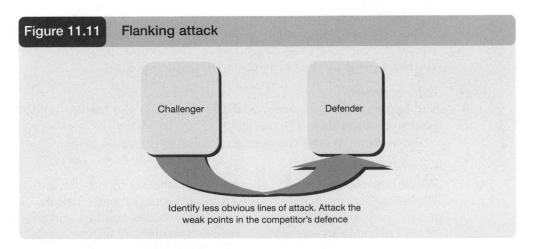

Figure 11.11 — Flanking attack

Challenger   Defender

Identify less obvious lines of attack. Attack the
weak points in the competitor's defence

A flanking attack is achieved either through attacking geographic regions where the defender is underrepresented or through attacking underserved competitor segments. The principle is to direct the attack at competitors' weaknesses, not their strengths.

Segmental flanking involves serving distinct segments that have not been adequately served by existing companies. Crucial to a successful flanking strategy can be timing. The Japanese entry into the US sub-compact car market was timed to take advantage of the economic recession and concerns over energy supply. The strategy requires the identification of competitor weaknesses, and inability or unwillingness to serve particular sectors of the market. In turn, identification of market gaps often requires a fresh look at the market and a more creative approach to segmenting it.

Encirclement attack

The encirclement attack, or siege, consists of enveloping the enemy, cutting them off from routes of supply to force capitulation (see Figure 11.12).

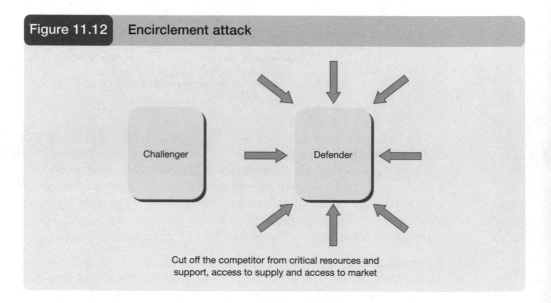

Figure 11.12   Encirclement attack

Cut off the competitor from critical resources and
support, access to supply and access to market

There are two approaches to the encirclement attack. The first is to attempt to isolate the competitor from the supply of raw materials on which they depend and/or the customers they seek to serve. The second approach is to seek to offer an all-round better product or service than the competitor.

Bypass strategy

The bypass strategy is characterised by changing the battleground to avoid competitor strongholds (see Figure 11.13).

Bypass is often achieved through technological leapfrogging.

Guerrilla tactics

Where conventional attacks fail or are not feasible guerrilla tactics are often employed. During the Second World War the French Resistance harassed the occupying German forces to weaken them in preparation for the Allied landings and counter-attack. In chess a player in an apparently hopeless situation may sacrifice a piece unexpectedly

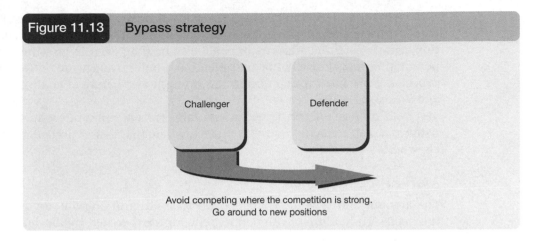

Figure 11.13   **Bypass strategy**

Challenger

Defender

Avoid competing where the competition is strong.
Go around to new positions

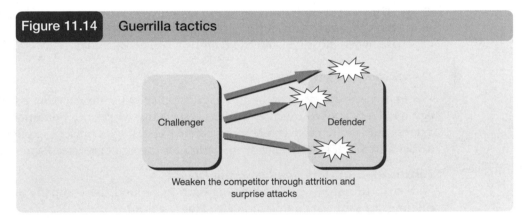

Figure 11.14   **Guerrilla tactics**

Challenger

Defender

Weaken the competitor through attrition and
surprise attacks

if it disrupts the opponent's line of attack (see Figure 11.14). In boxing it has been known for a contender on the ropes to bite the ear of his opponent to disrupt the onslaught!

Unconventional or guerrilla tactics are in business employed primarily as 'spoiling' activities to weaken the competition. They are often used by a weaker attacker on a stronger defender. Selective price cuts, especially during a competitor's new product testing or launch, depositioning advertising (as attempted by the Butter Information Council Ltd in its campaign against Krona margarine), alliances (as used against Laker Airways), executive raids and legal manoeuvres can all be used in this regard. Guerrilla tactics are used by companies of all sizes in attempts to soften up their competitors, often before moving in for the kill. Their effectiveness lies in the difficulty the attacked has in adequately defending against the tactics due to their unpredictability.

11.6.2   Holding and defensive strategies

In contrast to build strategies, firms already in strong positions in their markets may pursue essentially defensive strategies to enable them to hold the ground they have already won.

For market leaders, for example, especially those operating in mature or declining markets, the major objective may not be to build but to maintain the current position against potential attackers. It could also be that, even in growing markets, the potential rewards judged to be possible from a build strategy are outweighed by the expected costs due, for example, to the strength and nature of competition (Treacy and Wiersema, 1995).

A hold strategy may be particularly suitable for a business or product group designated as a cash generator for the company, where that cash is needed for investment elsewhere.

Market maintenance

The amount and type of effort required to hold position will vary depending on the degree and nature of competition encountered. When the business dominates its market it may have cost advantages through economies of scale or experience effects that can be used as a basis for defending through selective price cutting. Alternatively, barriers to entry can be erected by the guarding of technological expertise, where possible, and the retention of key executive skills.

Defensive strategies

While in some markets competitor aggression may be low, making a holding strategy relatively easy to execute, in most, especially where the potential gains for an aggressor are high, more constructive defensive strategies must be explicitly pursued. Kotler and Singh (1981) suggest six basic holding strategies (see Figure 11.15).

Fortification strategies and position defence

Market fortification involves erecting barriers around the company and its market offerings to shut out competition (see Figure 11.16).

In business a position defence is created through erecting barriers to copy and/or entry. This is most effectively achieved through differentiating the company's offerings from those of competitors and potential competitors. Where differentiation can be created on non-copyable grounds (e.g. by using the company's distinctive skills, competencies and marketing assets) that are of value to the customers, aggressors will find it more difficult to overrun the position defended.

For established market leaders, brand name and reputation are often used as the principal way of holding position. In addition, maintaining higher quality, better delivery and service, better (more appealing or heavier) promotions or lower prices based on a cost advantage can all be used to fortify the position held against a frontal attack.

Figure 11.15	Defensive strategies

- Position defence
- Flanking defence
- Pre-emptive strike
- Counter-offensive
- Mobile defence
- Contraction defence

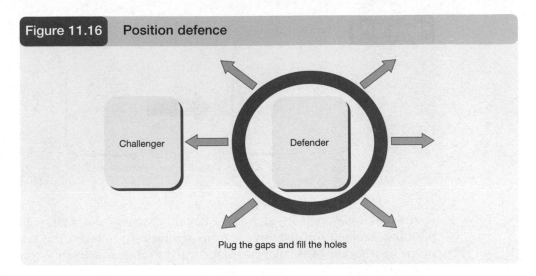

Figure 11.16   Position defence

Challenger

Defender

Plug the gaps and fill the holes

A fortification defence may also involve plugging the gaps in provision to shut out competitor attacks.

Flanking defence

The flanking defence is a suitable rejoinder to a flanking attack. Under the attack strategy (see above), the aggressor seeks to concentrate strength against the weaknesses of the defender, often using the element of surprise to gain the upper hand (see Figure 11.17).

A flanking defence requires the company to strengthen the flanks, without providing a weaker and more vulnerable target elsewhere. It requires the prediction of competitor strategy and likely strike positions. In food marketing, for example, several leading manufacturers of branded goods, seeing the increasing threat posed by retailer own-label and generic brands, have entered into contracts to provide own-label products themselves rather than let their competitors get into their markets.

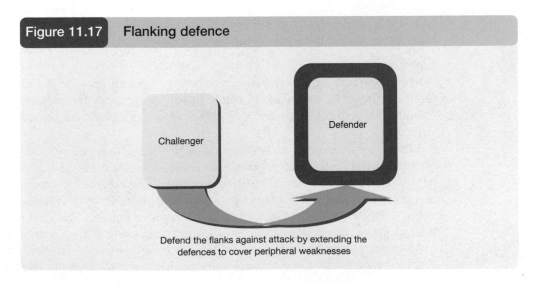

Figure 11.17   Flanking defence

Defender

Challenger

Defend the flanks against attack by extending the defences to cover peripheral weaknesses

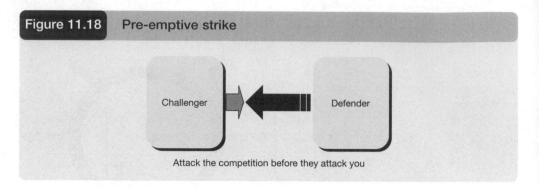

Figure 11.18   Pre-emptive strike

Attack the competition before they attack you

The major concerns in adopting a flanking strategy are, first, whether the new positions adopted for defensive reasons significantly weaken the main, core positions. In the case of retailer own labels, for example, actively cooperating could increase the trend towards own label and lead to the eventual death of the brand. As a consequence many leading brand manufacturers will not supply own label and rely on the strength of their brands to see off competition (effectively a position, or fortification, defence).

The second concern is whether the new position is actually tenable. Where it is not based on corporate strengths or marketing assets it may be less defensible than the previously held positions.

Pre-emptive defence

A pre-emptive defence involves striking at the potential aggressor before they can mount their attack (see Figure 11.18).

The pre-emptive defensive can involve an actual attack on the competition (as occurs in the disruption of competitor test marketing activity) or merely signal an intention to fight on a particular front and a willingness to commit the necessary resources to defend against aggression.

Sun Tzu (Khoo, 1992) summed up the philosophy behind the pre-emptive defence: 'The supreme art of war is to subdue the enemy without fighting.' Unfortunately it is not always possible to deter aggression. The second-best option is to strike back quickly before the attack gains momentum, through a counter-offensive.

Counter-offensive

Where deterrence of a potential attack before it occurs may be the ideal defence, a rapid counter-attack to 'stifle at birth' the aggression can be equally effective. The essence of a counter-offensive is to identify the aggressor's vulnerable spots and to strike hard.

When Xerox attempted to break into the mainframe computer market head-on against the established market leader, IBM launched a classic counter-offensive in Xerox's bread-and-butter business (copiers). The middle-range copiers were the major cash generators of Xerox operations and were, indeed, creating the funds to allow Xerox to attack in the mainframe computer market. The IBM counter was a limited range of low-priced copiers directly competing with Xerox's middle-range products, with leasing options that were particularly attractive to smaller customers. The counter-offensive had the effect of causing Xerox to abandon the attack on the

Figure 11.19	Mobile defence

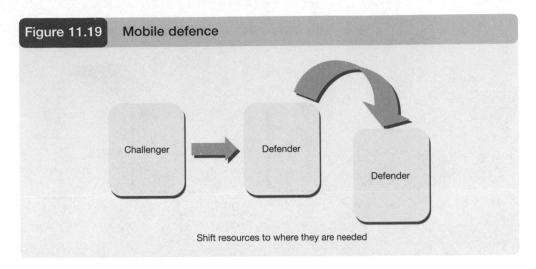

Shift resources to where they are needed

computer market (it sold its interests to Honeywell) to concentrate on defending its copiers (James, 1984).

The counter-offensive defence is most effective where the aggressor is vulnerable through overstretching resources. The result is a weak underbelly that can be exploited for defensive purposes.

Mobile defence

The mobile defence was much in vogue as a military strategy in the 1980s and 1990s. It involves creating a 'flexible response capability' to enable the defender to shift the ground that is being defended in response to environmental or competitive threats and opportunities (see Figure 11.19).

A mobile defence is achieved through a willingness continuously to update and improve the company's offerings to the marketplace. Much of the success of Persil in the UK soap powder market has been due to the constant attempts to keep the product in line with changing customer requirements. The brand, a market leader for nearly half a century, has gone through many reformulations as washing habits have changed and evolved. Reformulations for top-loading washing machines, front loaders, automatics, and more recently colder washes, have ensured that the brand has stayed well placed compared with its rivals.

Interestingly, however, Persil went too far twice in recent years: first, when it was modified to a 'biological' formula. Most other washing powders had taken this route to improve the washing ability of the powder. For a substantial segment of the population, however, a biological product was a disadvantage (these powders can cause skin irritation to some sensitive skins). The customer outcry resulted in an 'Original Persil' being reintroduced. A few years later Persil came back again with even more disastrous Persil Power with its magnesium accelerator. Initially Unilever denied its competitor Procter & Gamble's claim that Persil Power damaged clothes in many washing conditions. However, within months 'Original Persil' was back again.

The mobile defence is an essential strategic weapon in markets where technology and/or customer wants and needs are changing rapidly. Failure to move with these changes can result in opening the company to a flanking or bypass attack.

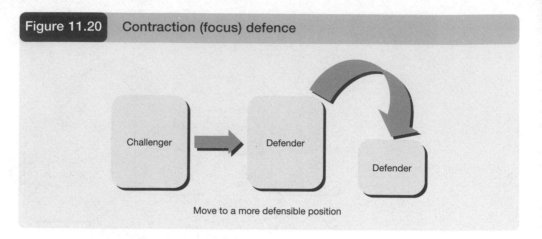

Figure 11.20 Contraction (focus) defence

Challenger → *Defender* ↷ *Defender*

Move to a more defensible position

Contraction defence

A contraction defence, or strategic withdrawal, requires giving up untenable ground to reduce overstretching and allow concentration on the core business that can be defended against attack (see Figure 11.20).

In the 1980s, in response to both competitive pressures and an adverse economic environment, Tunnel Cement rationalised its operations. Capacity was halved and the workforce substantially reduced. Operations were then concentrated in two core activities where the company had specialised and defensible capabilities: chemicals and waste disposal.

Strategic withdrawal is usually necessary where the company has diversified too far away from the core skills and distinctive competencies that gave it a competitive edge.

11.6.3 Market niche strategies

Market niche strategies, focusing on a limited sector of the total market, make particular sense for small and medium-sized companies operating in markets that are dominated by larger operators. The strategies are especially suitable where there are distinct, profitable, but underserved pockets within the total market, and where the company has an existing, or can create a new, differential advantage in serving that pocket.

The two main aspects to the niche strategy are, first, choosing the pockets, segments or markets on which to concentrate and, second, focusing effort exclusively on serving those targets (see Figure 11.21).

Choosing the battleground

An important characteristic of the successful nicher is an ability to segment the market creatively to identify new and potential niches not yet exploited by major competitors. The battleground, or niches on which to concentrate, should be chosen by consideration of both market (or niche) attractiveness and current or potential strength of the company in serving that market.

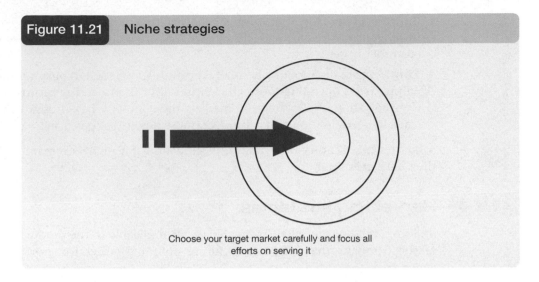

Figure 11.21   Niche strategies

Choose your target market carefully and focus all
efforts on serving it

For the nicher the second of these two considerations is often more important than the first. The major automobile manufacturers, for example, have concentrated their attentions on the large-scale segments of the car market in attempts to keep costs down, through volume production of standardised parts and components and assembly-line economies of scale.

This has left many smaller, customised segments of the market open to nichers where the major manufacturers are not prepared to compete. In terms of the overall car market these segments (such as for small sports cars) would be rated as relatively unattractive, but to a small operator such as Morgan Cars, with modest growth and return objectives, they offer an ideal niche where its skills can be exploited to the full. The Morgan order book is full, there is a high level of job security and a high degree of job satisfaction in manufacturing a high-quality, hand-crafted car.

Focusing effort

The essence of the niche strategy is to focus activity on the selected targets and not allow the company blindly to pursue any potential customer. Pursuing a niche strategy requires discipline to concentrate effort on the selected targets.

Hammermesh *et al.* (1978) examined a number of companies that had successfully adopted a niche strategy and concluded that they showed three main characteristics:

1 **An ability to segment the market** creatively, focusing their activities only in areas where they had particular strengths that were especially valued. In the metal container industry (which faces competition from glass, aluminium, fibrefoil and plastic containers) Crown Cork and Seal has focused on two segments: metal cans for hard-to-hold products such as beer and soft drinks, and aerosol cans. In both these segments the company has built considerable marketing assets through its specialised use of technology and its superior customer service.

2 **Efficient use of R&D resources.** Where R&D resources are necessarily more limited than among major competitors they should be used where they can be

most effective. This often means concentrating not on pioneering work but on improvements to existing technologies that are seen to provide more immediate customer benefits.

3 **Thinking small**. Adopting a 'small is beautiful' approach to business increases the emphasis on operating more efficiently rather than chasing growth at all costs. Concentration of effort on the markets the company has chosen to compete in leads to specialisation and a stronger, more defensible position.

A quarter of a century on, these three guidelines for nichers remain as relevant as they have ever been.

11.6.4 Harvesting strategies

Building, holding and niche strategies are all applicable to the products and services of the company that offers some future potential either for growth or revenue generation.

At some stage in the life of most products and services it can become clear that there is no long-term future for them. This may be because of major changes in customer requirements, which the offering as currently designed cannot keep pace with, or it may be due to technological changes that are making the offer obsolete. In these circumstances a harvesting (or 'milking') strategy may be pursued to obtain maximum returns from the product before its eventual death or withdrawal from the market (see Figure 11.22).

Kotler (1997) defines harvesting as:

a strategic management decision to reduce the investment in a business entity in the hope of cutting costs and/or improving cash flow. The company anticipates sales volume and/or market share declines but hopes that the lost revenue will be more than offset by lowered costs. Management sees sales falling eventually to a core level of demand. The business will be divested if money cannot be made at this core level of demand or if the company's resources can produce a higher yield by being shifted elsewhere.

Candidate businesses or individual products for harvesting may be those that are losing money despite managerial and financial resources being invested in them,

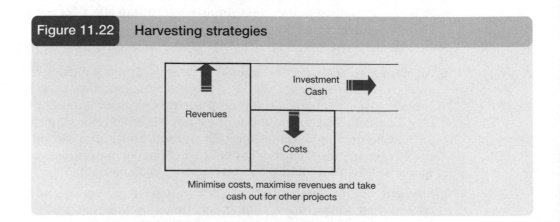

Figure 11.22 Harvesting strategies

Minimise costs, maximise revenues and take cash out for other projects

or they may be those which are about to be made obsolete due to company or competitor innovation.

Implementing a harvesting strategy calls for a reduction in marketing support to a minimum, to cut expenditure on advertising, sales support and further R&D. There will typically be a rationalisation of the product line to reduce production and other direct costs. In addition, prices may be increased somewhat to improve margins while anticipating a reduction in volume.

11.6.5 Divestment/deletion

Where the company decides that a policy of harvesting is not possible, for example when, despite every effort, the business or product continues to lose money, attention may turn to divestment, or deletion from the corporate portfolio (see Figure 11.23).

Divestment – the decision to get out of a particular market or business – is never taken lightly by a company. It is crucial when considering a particular business or product for deletion to question the role of the business in the company's overall portfolio.

One company, operating both in consumer and industrial markets, examined its business portfolio and found that its industrial operations were at best breaking even, depending on how costs were allocated. Further analysis, however, showed that the industrial operation was a crucial spur to technological developments within the company that were exploited in the consumer markets in which it operated. The greater immediate technical demands of the company's industrial customers acted as the impetus for the R&D department to improve on the basic technologies used by the company. These had fed through to the consumer side of the business and resulted in the current strength in those markets. Without the industrial operations it is doubtful whether the company would have been so successful in its consumer markets. Clearly, in this case, the industrial operations had a non-economic role to play and divestment on economic grounds could have been disastrous.

Once a divestment decision has been taken, and all the ramifications on the company's other businesses have been carefully assessed, implementation involves getting out as quickly and cheaply as possible.

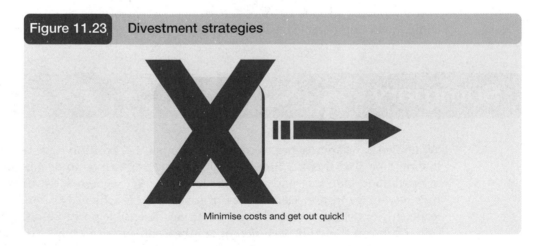

Figure 11.23 Divestment strategies

Minimise costs and get out quick!

11.6.6 Matching managerial skills to strategic tasks

The above alternative strategies require quite different managerial skills to bring them to fruition. It should be apparent that a manager well suited to building a stronger position for a new product is likely to have different strengths from those of a manager suited to harvesting an ageing product. Wissema *et al.* (1980) have suggested the following types of manager for each of the jobs outlined above.

Pioneers and conquerors for build strategies

The pioneer is particularly suited to the truly innovative new product that is attempting to revolutionise the markets in which it operates. A pioneer is a divergent thinker who is flexible, creative and probably hyperactive. Many entrepreneurs, such as Jeff Bezos at Amazon.com and James Dyson of vacuum cleaner fame, would fall into this category.

A conqueror, on the other hand, would be most suited to building in an established market. The conqueror's main characteristics are a creative but structured approach, someone who is a systematic team builder who can develop a coherent and rational strategy in the face of potentially stiff competition.

Administrators to hold position

The administrator is stable, good at routine work, probably an introverted conformist. These traits are particularly suited to holding/maintaining position. The administrator keeps a steady hand on the helm.

Focused creators to niche

This manager is in many ways similar to the conqueror but in need, especially initially, of more creative flair in identifying the area for focus. Once that area has been defined, however, a highly focused approach is necessary at the expense of all other distractions.

Economisers for divestment

The diplomatic negotiator (receiver, or hatchet man!) is required to divest the company of unprofitable businesses, often in the face of internal opposition.

Summary

While two basic approaches to creating a competitive position have been discussed it should be clear that the first priority in marketing will be to decide on the focus of operations: industry wide or specific target market segments. Creating a competitive advantage in the selected area of focus can be achieved through either cost leadership or differentiation. To build a strong, defensible position in the market the initial concern should be to differentiate the company's offerings from those of its competitors on some basis of value to the customer. The second concern should then be to achieve this at the lowest possible delivered cost.

A variety of strategies might be pursued once the overall objectives have been set. The strategies can be summarised under five main types: build; hold; harvest; niche; divest. To implement each type of strategy different managerial skills are required. An important task of senior management is to ensure that the managers assigned to each task have the necessary skills and characteristics.

Nokia Case study

Getty Images News

Nokia is a company that has got its timing spectacularly right in the last decade, but the optimism it expressed last December about prospects for the mobile phone industry seems to have been one of its less successful calls.

Jorma Ollila, the company's chairman and chief executive, rounded off an upbeat presentation to analysts by stating that 'in the mobile world, the best is yet to come'.

He may yet be right in the long term, but in the short term at least the prediction has proved wide of the mark.

Nokia has been forced to cut its projections about worldwide handsets growth and its own sales growth at least three times this year.

The latest occasion was last month when the group slashed earnings and sales forecasts and suggested the current industry slowdown would continue into the second half.

The result was that its share price fell by 20 per cent in a single day. Analysts say the company's credibility has been damaged, because it has generally been much more optimistic about the outlook for the mobile phone business than rival handset makers or leading telecom operators.

The shock profit warning shows that even Nokia, the world's leading maker of mobile phones, is not immune to what is going on around it, even though it is still looking stronger than many of its rivals.

Nor can it necessarily predict likely market trends better than its competitors. Mobile phone makers are being hit by the economic slowdown that started in the US but which is now spreading to other parts of the world, including Europe. But they are also being hit by clear signs of market saturation, with replacement phone sales not developing as well as originally hoped.

This means the market environment has changed dramatically. Whereas last December Nokia was forecasting that 550m handsets would be sold worldwide in 2001, it is now predicting sales only modestly higher than last year's 405m. Some analysts predict sales will actually be lower than 405m.

In any case, handset makers' revenues will almost certainly be down from last year because of a drop in the products' average selling prices.

It is an abrupt change for an industry that had almost stopped thinking of itself as cyclical. In 1999 the industry grew by 67 per cent, last year it grew 42 per cent. Per Lindberg, analyst with Dresdner Kleinwort Wasserstein in London says: 'The handset industry will be turning ex-growth for the first time in its 20-year history in 2001.'

Nokia is perhaps the only handset maker anywhere to be making money. Its margins at around

20 per cent are still remarkably healthy – the result of the extraordinary economies of scale which the company enjoys due to its leadership position and mastery of logistics.

It is also taking full advantage of the problems being experienced by rivals such as Ericsson of Sweden and Motorola of the US to drive its market share higher. It already has about 35 per cent of the global handsets market – about three times that of Motorola, its nearest rival – and is aiming to move still higher to around 40 per cent.

But how much further can it go? Analysts suggest some operators already feel they are too dependent on Nokia, although there may be little they (the operators) can do about it, if Nokia phones are what their end customers – ordinary consumers – want.

But what about those end customers? Petri Korpineva, analyst at Evli Securities in Finland, says: 'If Nokia continues to increase its share towards 50 per cent, it could well be that some consumers want to differentiate themselves by not choosing the Nokia brand.'

Nokia seems already to be sensing that it is too reliant on handsets, which account for around 70 per cent of its sales. It is making a significant push to increase sales of mobile phone infrastructure in an implicit challenge to Ericsson, the world leader in this business.

Nokia has set an aggressive target of winning a 35 per cent market share in the W-CDMA, the third generation mobile telephony standard.

The group is also looking to build up other sources of revenue. One source that could eventually prove fruitful is Club Nokia, a virtual club that allows Nokia handset owners to download games, ring tones and other material on to their handsets from a website.

This facility is currently free, but Nokia is hoping it could prove a revenue generator in its own right, particularly when 3G takes off. This initiative takes Nokia more into the software business and analysts warn it could cause conflicts with operators who are concerned about Nokia straying on to their territory.

Many analysts believe that Nokia will struggle to maintain its margins in the long term, because they argue that mobile phones will become a commodity like personal computers and other high-tech products. Nokia insists that this will not happen, partly because the complexities involved in making ever more sophisticated handsets are a formidable deterrent to new entrants. But not even Nokia would dispute the view that its fortunes may depend on the development of the mobile Internet.

Already delayed, it is still far from certain when 3G will take off, with continuing concerns about consumer demand and technical issues like interoperability. Nokia talks of the 3G breakthrough coming towards the end of next year, with intermediate GPRS services beginning the transition to 3G already later this year.

If it is right, the current slump in market growth may indeed be as temporary as Nokia is hoping.

Source: Christopher Brown-Humes, 'Behemoth maintains growth prospects while rivals begin to feel the chill', *Financial Times*, 5 July 2001, p. V.

Discussion questions

1 What has allowed Nokia to grow to its strong position in the marketplace?

2 What advantages and dangers does Nokia's market share relative to its competitors bestow?

3 Suggest strategies for Nokia that build upon its unique strengths. Suggest strategies for Nokia's competitors that Nokia could find hard to follow.

chapter twelve

Competing through the new marketing mix

12

[An executive is] a mixer of ingredients, who sometimes follows a recipe as he goes along, sometimes adapts a recipe to the ingredients immediately available, and sometimes experiments with or invents ingredients no one else has tried.

(Culliton, J., 1948)

When building a marketing program to fit the needs of his firm, the marketing manager has to weigh the behavioural forces and then juggle marketing elements in his mix with a keen eye on the resources with which he has to work.

(Borden, 1964)

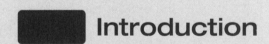 **Introduction**

In the early 1960s one of the leading US marketing writers, Neil Borden (1964), coined the term 'marketing mix' to cover the main activities of firms that were then thought to contribute to the marketability of their products and services. These were classified under the famous '4Ps' of marketing: product, price, promotion and place.

Recent thinking, spurred on through the development of relationship marketing (see Chapter 14), has extended the four Ps to include people, processes and physical evidence. In addition, as the service sector has grown in many developed economies, a new 'dominant logic' is emerging in marketing (see Vargo and Lusch, 2004; Lusch, Vargo and Malter, 2006), in which service provision rather than the exchange of goods has centre stage. This has further encouraged a re-think of the traditional elements of the marketing mix and their relevance to twenty-first century marketing.

Particularly significant has been the increasing use of the Internet for marketing purposes. The advent of the Internet as a major marketing medium has had impacts right across the spectrum of activities of the marketing mix. Initially seen primarily as a communications tool for reaching prospective customers, it is clear that the impact of the Internet has been far more pervasive, affecting the ways in which customers shop, how they gather and use information, and also their expectations of the type and level of service they should receive. Not least, the Internet has resulted in new forms of product. The music retailer i-Tunes, for example, now sells more tracks for download electronically than its largest high-street competitor sells tracks on conventional CDs. New 'bit-based' products, immediately and cheaply downloadable, are affecting many markets.

In this chapter we summarise the main ingredients of the new marketing mix and examine the changes brought about by Internet technology.

12.1 The market offer

Most market offers are combinations of physical, tangible product and intangible service (see Chapter 14). For ease of presentation here we refer to 'product' as the mix of physical, emotional, tangible and intangible elements that go to make up the overall market offer. It is important to always bear in mind that the product is what it does for the customer. Customers do not buy products; they buy what the product can do for them.

12.1.1 Key product/service concepts

Products are best viewed as solutions to customers' problems or ways of satisfying customer needs. American Marketing guru Philip Kotler (1997) put this neatly when he said that customers do not buy a quarter-inch drill bit – they buy the hole that the drill bit can create. In other words customers buy the benefits a product can bring to them, rather than the product itself.

That has two particularly important implications for marketing. First, it follows that customer perceptions of the product – what they believe about it – can be as, or even more, important to them than objective reality. If customers believe that a product gives them a particular benefit (for example enhanced attractiveness from using a particular cosmetic), that is what is likely to motivate them to purchase. Second, most if not all products are likely to have limited lives; they will only exist as solutions to customer problems until a better solution comes along. There is some evidence that product life cycles are shortening, with new offers coming to market more rapidly than in the past, and existing products becoming obsolete more quickly. That has implications for new product development (Chapter 13).

12.1.2 Product/service choice criteria

The reasons why customers choose one product over another can be simple ('it's cheaper') or far more complex ('it feels right for me'). In seeking to understand

Figure 12.1	Product choice criteria

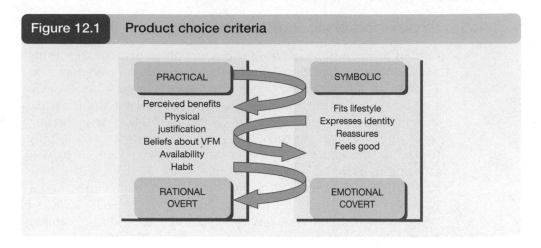

choice criteria it is useful to distinguish two main sets, the rational and overt; and the emotional and covert (Figure 12.1).

When questioned about their purchase decisions in market research surveys most customers will rationalise their choices. They will articulate objective reasons for their actions that they feel can be logically justified. These might include the practical benefits of the product, belief about value for money, the availability of the product and perhaps habit. These are reasons customers can give without loss of self-esteem, demonstrating that they are in control of the buying situation.

For many products, however, emotional reasons may play as big a, or even a bigger role. The purchase of branded goods, for example, may be prompted by the reassurance that a well-known and respected brand can bring. The physical product may be no better, a 'rational' comparison may show no differences, but customers will pay more to have the reassurance of the brand. Similarly, products may be chosen because they are believed to fit the lifestyle of the customer more closely, or make a statement about the purchaser (why else would someone pay thousands of pounds for a watch, such as a Rolex, when a cheap alternative can be as accurate in delivering the overt, rational benefit of telling the time?).

While conventional quantitative market research may uncover the rational and overt motivations of customers, more in-depth, qualitative and often projective research is needed to uncover emotional and covert motivations. Famously, researchers in the USA trying to understand why more people did not fly between major cities rather than driving found through direct questions that reasons given were rational (cost of flying, greater convenience of driving) but when projective techniques were used (asking respondents why others did not fly more) fears of flying and concerns for safety began to emerge.

Most purchases are a combination of the rational and the emotional. The balance between the two, however, will vary significantly across brands and it is an important task for marketers to understand the balance for their particular market offering.

12.1.3 Product/service differentiation

Central to successful marketing is product differentiation – ensuring that the total market offer is different and distinct from competitor offerings in ways that are of value to the target customer. This was discussed in more detail in Chapter 11.

With the convergence of manufacturing technology, and the widespread application of total quality management (TQM) methods, it is increasingly difficult for firms to differentiate on their core products. Differentiation in most markets now focuses on the augmented product (see Chapter 11), and in particular on ways of tailoring to individual customer requirements. In automobiles, for example, using basic building blocks of sub-frames, engines, body panels and interior options, there is now the opportunity for new car buyers to create near unique cars, matching their requirements or tastes very closely. Indeed, the industry's quest in the 3DayCar Programme is to find ways to customise the vehicle to the buyer's exact preferences and to deliver it three or four days after it is specified and ordered.

12.1.4 Diffusion of innovation

New products (those new to the market) require careful management as they enter the product life cycle. A theory of the diffusion of innovations (of which new products are one type) was proposed by Rogers (1962) (see Chapter 3). He suggested that the rate of diffusion of any innovation depends on a number of factors including:

- the relative advantage of the innovation over previous solutions;
- the compatibility of the innovation with existing values and norms;
- a lack of complexity in using the innovation;
- the divisibility of the innovation facilitating low-risk trial; and
- the communicability of the advantages of the innovation (see Chapter 13 and Figure 13.3).

In considering these factors with regard to the adoption of the Internet and e-business techniques, for example, it can be seen that some of those techniques are likely to diffuse more rapidly than others.

Recently, Parasuraman and Colby (2001) have introduced the concept of 'technology readiness' as a measure of customers' predispositions to adopt new technologies – based on their fears, hopes, desires and frustrations about technology. They identify five types of technology customers:

1 **Explorers** – highly optimistic and innovative.

2 **Pioneers** – the innovative but cautious.

3 **Sceptics** – who need to have the benefits of the technology proven to them.

4 **Paranoids** – those who are insecure about the technology.

5 **Laggards** – those who resist the technology.

Rogers identified five adopter groups, namely innovators, early adopters, early majority, late majority and laggards which were further developed by Moore (1991,

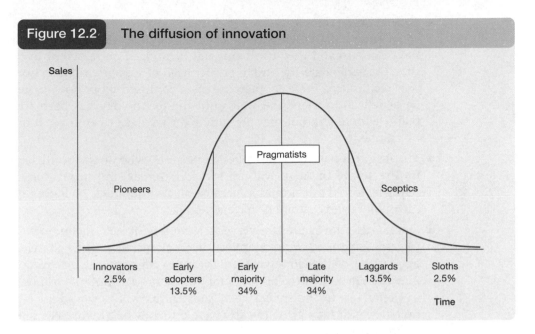

Figure 12.2 The diffusion of innovation

2004, 2006) in his discussion of the adoption of high-technology products and services. We add a sixth and final adopter group, the sloths (see Figure 12.2).

- **Innovators** are the first to adopt a new technology or product. Often they are technology enthusiasts and adopt because the technology is new and they wish to be, and be seen to be, up to date. It is often the novelty value of the technology that drives their adoption. Many innovations fail as they are technology driven rather than meeting the real needs of customers and once the novelty value has worn off, and newer technologies have been substituted by the innovators, the product dies a natural death.

- **Early adopters** are similar to the innovators, but often demonstrate a more visionary reason for adopting the new technology. In business markets, for example, early adopters often see significant advantages from adoption and ways in which the new technology can enable them to change the way a market works, to the benefit both of themselves and of customers. Early adopters of e-business approaches, for example, include Jeff Bezos at Amazon.com who saw in the use of the Internet a whole new way of retailing books and other products that could add value for customers. Vision such as this can lead to spectacular success, as well as spectacular failure.

- **Early majority** adopters are even more pragmatic than the early adopters. Typically they are less likely to see ways of revolutionising their markets, more likely to see incremental possibilities for improvement. They may, for example, take a particular aspect of the supply chain, such as purchasing, and use Internet technologies to improve the efficiency of this activity. Early majority adopters are often efficiency driven while the early adopters had seen opportunities to improve effectiveness.

- **Late majority** adopters have been described as 'conservatives' (Moore 1991) who often enter a market or adopt a technology largely because others in the market have done so and they fear being left behind. More reluctant in their adoption than the early majority, and in greater need of support and direction in use of the new technology, these adopters are often confused about how the technology can be beneficial to them and wait until the technology has been tried and tested before adopting it. But they are sure that they need to embrace it or be overtaken by competitors.

- The **laggards** have been described as 'sceptics' who do not really see the potential for the new technology, will resist its adoption as long as possible, but may eventually be forced into adoption because all around them, including their suppliers, distributors and customers, have adopted.

- Finally, the **sloths** are the very last adopters of new technologies, often going to great lengths to avoid adoption. In some instances they change the way they operate to isolate themselves from the innovations taking place around them, and may even make a virtue of non-adoption. Some accountants still use the quill pen in preference to the spreadsheet! Some firms will never adopt e-business technologies, and may actually carve viable niches for themselves serving similarly minded customers.

Moore (1991) argued that, in the adoption of new high-technology products, there existed a gulf between the early adopters and the early majority that he referred to as the new product chasm, into which many fall (Figure 12.3). This is essentially the transition from a technology for enthusiasts and visionaries to a technology for the pragmatists. While the enthusiasm of the innovators and early adopters is often sufficient to carry an innovation forward, its ultimate success depends on its ability to convince the pragmatists of the productivity and process enhancements it can deliver.

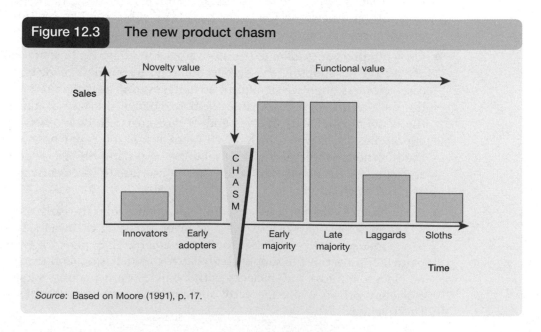

Figure 12.3   The new product chasm

Source: Based on Moore (1991), p. 17.

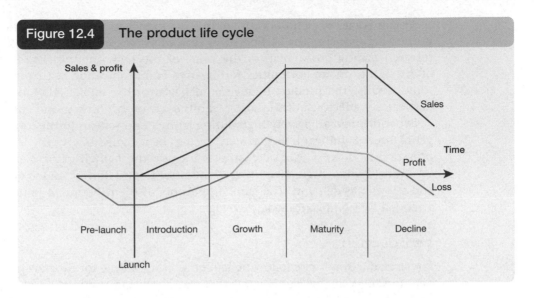

Figure 12.4   The product life cycle

12.1.5 Managing the product over its life cycle

The concept of the product life cycle was introduced in Chapter 3 (see Figure 12.4). With changing market conditions over the life cycle it is important that product and service strategies are designed to match. It will also be apparent that different adopter groups (see above) are likely to form key target markets at different stages of the product life cycle.

Pre-launch

In the pre-launch phase, before the product has appeared on the market, the main emphasis of the organisation will be on research and development, as well as gearing up production capacity for launch. High levels of expenditure may be incurred before any returns are seen through sales receipts. Also important at this stage is market research to identify likely early adopters of the product (see Chapter 13) and to develop key sales messages demonstrating the benefits of the new offering relative to the current solutions to customers' problems.

Market research into wholly new products can be notoriously inaccurate. Sony's formal market research into the Walkman concept showed that there was little potential demand for a mobile music player, but the Chairman, Akio Morita, went ahead anyway and created a whole new market now dominated by Apple's iPod. The lesson is that customers may not know what they want, or what they could find useful, before they see it.

Launch

The launch phase of the life cycle is the major opportunity for the organisation to shout loudly about the benefits the new product can offer. This will often take the form of explaining to customers the new benefits over and above those enjoyed from the products they currently use to satisfy their needs.

At this stage, by definition, there is one product in the market and the real task is one of convincing the best prospect customers (the innovators identified through research during pre-launch) of the value of the new offering. The launch period offers significant opportunities for creative communication with prospective customers while the product is novel and newsworthy. Public relations (PR) can be particularly effective at this stage as can the use of exhibitions and conventions.

Expenditures can be very high during launch and returns in the form of sales not yet realised. Significant budgets may need to be assigned to give the launch the best prospects of success. Classic examples include the launch of new movies or new car models where high advertising spend prior to and during launch excites interest and stimulates demand. The launch by Apple of their iPhone in January 2007 was attended by significant media coverage.

Introduction

The introduction phase following launch is crunch time for the new product. Many new products do not get beyond this phase. During the introductory phase sales begin to take off but expenditures on marketing remain high to establish the new product as a superior alternative to previous offerings.

It is at this stage that competitors are likely to take increasing interest in the new product, attempting to gauge whether it will be a success, and hence present opportunities for copy or further improvement, or a costly failure. As the success of the new product becomes more certain, so competitive products will begin to appear as 'me too' products or improvements on the market pioneer. In digital portable music the pioneering iPod was soon joined in the market by rival products from iRiver, Sony, Phillips and others.

Growth

The growth phase of the PLC is often considered the most exciting. Most brand and marketing managers prefer to operate in growth markets. At this stage the product is becoming rapidly accepted on the market, sales are growing rapidly and returns begin to outstrip expenditures. Other things also happen during this phase that significantly affect marketing strategies. First, the success and growth are likely to attract more competitors into the market, especially those that have adopted a 'wait and see' attitude during launch and introduction. Now that the market is proven, risks are lowered and potential returns beckon.

With further competitor entry comes greater product differentiation among offerings, and typically greater segmentation of the market. The early majority, the new macro-target, are likely to be diverse in their exact wants and needs, offering greater opportunities for micro-targeting. Expenditures continue to be high in researching market opportunities and product improvements, second generation and so on. In the MP3 player market, for example, by Christmas 2006 there were several different versions of the iPod available (from Shuffle to Nano to Video). For Apple a problem began to emerge as the innovators, primarily younger and more fashion-conscious purchasers, saw their parents' generation buying the bigger, 60GB iPod Videos. In response Apple launched coloured versions of the iPod Nano, with additional add-on features and skins, to retain the younger market.

iPod range in January 2007

Corbis/Ruaridh Stewart/ZUMA

It is at this stage that returns peak and surplus cash can be diverted into developing and launching the new generation of new products (see portfolio theory section).

Maturity

The mature phase is reached when growth slows and the bulk of the market (late majority) have entered. This phase can be characterised by particularly fierce competition as those who entered the market during the growth phase fight for market share rather than market expansion to improve performance. Price wars are common, profit margins are squeezed, and expenditures on marketing and research and development scrutinised more critically. Mobile phones are a case in point, where prices have tumbled as excess supply has left manufacturers with unsaleable stocks.

Decline

The decline, and eventual death, phase sees profits squeezed even more as the next generation of products takes over the market. Figure 12.5 shows the sales of cameras

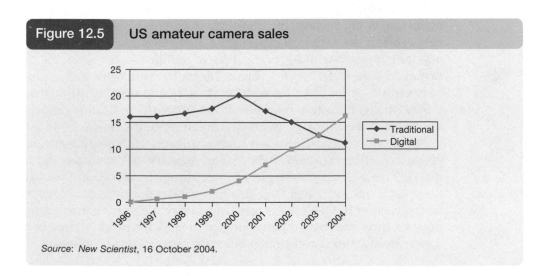

Figure 12.5   US amateur camera sales

Source: *New Scientist*, 16 October 2004.

Figure 12.6   US amateur camera market

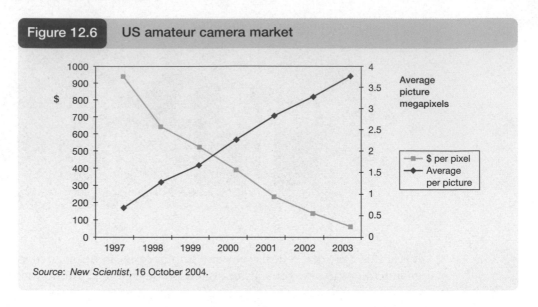

Source: New Scientist, 16 October 2004.

in the USA. The sales of traditional, film-based cameras peaked around 2000 but since then have been in steep decline due to the growth of digital versions. Surprisingly, the market downturn for film-based cameras has been even more dramatic in countries like China. This switch in market has been fuelled by technological advances (Figure 12.6) where the cost of sharper definition in digital pictures (as measured by the number of megapixels) has plummeted, allowing the quality of digital pictures to rapidly challenge that of film.

Turning points

The phases of the product life cycle are notoriously difficult to predict, and especially difficult to identify are transitions between stages (Figure 12.7). First, the transition from introductory phase to growth. Here the danger is being left behind as the market takes off. Second, the transition from growth to maturity. The clear danger here is being left with over-capacity, or high stock levels, of difficult to move products (as happened with the over-supply of mobile phones when the market became mature in the early 2000s). This is another reason why the mature phase is so competitive – firms often have excess capacity and stock available that they need to move. Finally, transition from steady state maturity to decline can leave some firms wedded to old technology and unable to embrace the new.

The product life cycle concept has also been criticised for encouraging tunnel vision in marketers (Moon, 2005). Moon suggests that managers slavishly following the PLC see only an inexorable advance along the curve, and because they all see the cycle in the same way they all adopt similar positions for products and services during each of the life cycle stages. To counter this convergence of strategies Moon suggests three alternative positioning strategies for breaking free of the life cycle: reverse positioning; breakaway positioning; and stealth positioning.

Figure 12.7	The product life cycle

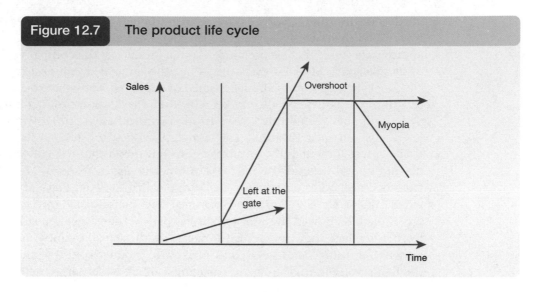

- **Reverse positioning** involves stripping down the augmented product to its core, and then seeking new ways to differentiate. This strategy recognises that in the quest to augment core products firms may have added so many additional features that they become the expected, rather than the exception that differentiates. The example of toothpaste is cited where the core product has been augmented with whitener, fluoride, plaque preventative, breath freshener etc. to the extent that all these now feature in leading brands and no longer serve to differentiate. Ikea have adopted this approach in their successful self-assembly furniture stores. Rather than adopt the strategy of other furniture retailers of carrying enormous product lines, varied inventories, high-pressure sales operations and seemingly permanent 'sales' and 'special offers', Ikea offers stores with play areas for children, Scandinavian restaurants, no high-pressure sales staff, very little in-store support or service, self-collection (rather than delivery weeks or months after order) and self-assembly.

- **Breakaway positioning** is where a product is deliberately moved from one product category to another. The category a product occupies is determined by the way customers perceive that product – the competing products they associate it with, the messages that are employed to promote it, the price charged, the channels through which it is distributed – in short, the entire marketing mix employed. By switching categories products can gain a new lease of life beyond the existing PLC. Swatch, for example, is an example of breakaway positioning. Before its launch in 1983 Swiss watches were sold as jewellery and most customers rarely bought more than one model. Swatch changed that by defining its watches as playful fashion accessories, fun, ephemeral, inexpensive and showy. Impulse buying was encouraged and customers typically bought several watches for different outfits.

● **Stealth positioning** involves shifting to a different product category in a covert way, rather than overtly as practised through breakaway positioning. This may be appropriate where there is prejudice about a product or the company which needs to be overcome. Moon stresses this is not the same as deceit and can backfire if customers believe they are being cheated or exploited. Sony have been highly successful in the games console market with their PlayStation product but its market penetration has been limited to a narrow customer base – primarily males in their late teens and early twenties. The company wished to broaden its platform for home entertainment and communications but found that the PlayStation format did not appeal beyond the narrow customer focus. In response, in July 2003 it launched a PlayStation product in Europe called EyeToy: Play. This included a video camera (EyeToy) and game software (Play) that plugged into the PlayStation 2 console but allowed the user to become part of the game, appearing inside the television where they interact with objects on the screen by moving their bodies, rather than using hand-held controllers. The product sold 2.5 million units in the first seven months, crucially engaging a much wider target market including parents and even grandparents (Moon, 2005).

12.1.6 The impact of the Internet on market offerings

With the advent of marketing over the Internet, two types of market offering became apparent: the so-called 'atom-based' and 'bit-based' products.

Atom-based products are physical offerings that have a separate presence and form for the customer. While they may be promoted over the Internet they need to be physically shipped to the customer, are subject to returns where they are not satisfactory and can be resold by customers. Typical examples include books and videos (Amazon.com), clothes and appliances. For the customer the product at the end of the day is the same as that purchased through a bricks-and-mortar retailer, but the experience may be enhanced through the additional services, convenience and low price available through Internet purchase. For the retailer the logistics of delivery represent significant challenges.

Bit-based products, on the other hand, do not have a physical presence. They can be represented as digital data in electronic form. They are typically non-returnable but do not require separate shipping and can be transferred online. Bit-based products include music, news, information services, movies and TV programmes. These products are ideally suited to marketing over the Internet as the complete supply chain, from procurement, through sales and marketing, to delivery can be conducted online. This synergy provided the logic for the global merger in 2000 of AOL (a leading Internet Service Provider) with Time Warner (an entertainment and news conglomerate) as a foundation for online provision of enhanced information and entertainment products (though integration of the two business cultures proved more problematic).

For both atom- and bit-based products sold over the Internet, the power of the customer is significantly greater than in purchases from bricks-and-mortar suppliers. Put simply, the information available to the customer is far greater, enabling wider search of competitor offerings, online recommendations, and greater price comparisons. The online customer can decide at the click of a mouse to buy or bypass a firm's offerings, whereas in a face-to-face situation a vendor may rely more on personal selling and persuasion. For offerings to be consistently chosen over competing offerings they need to offer greater value to customers, through lower prices, greater convenience, additional valued features, speed, or whatever. Hence the driver of web-based marketing is increasingly to look to the augmented product for differentiation (see Chapter 14).

The Internet has also facilitated integrated marketing of bit-based and atom-based products. In December 2001 New Line Cinema launched their epic movie *The Lord of the Rings: The Fellowship of the Ring* (LOTR) based on the bestseller books by J.R.R. Tolkien. More than 100 million copies of the books have been sold in 45 languages prior to the movie launch. To heighten interest in the movie New Line created a website in May 1999 (www.lordoftherings.com). A trailer for the movie became available on the website in April 2000 and was downloaded more than 1.7 million times. The site was updated three to four times per week as part of a four-year editorial schedule spanning the life of the three films in the trilogy (the second was released in December 2002, the third in December 2003). The aim was to create an online community as a hub for the 400 fan sites devoted to LOTR.

Merchandising associated with the movie is extensive with toys and 'collectibles' based on the film sculpted by WETA, the New Zealand-based firm that created the creatures and special effects of the film. There have also been marketing partnerships with restaurants (Burger King), consumer products manufacturers (JVC, General Mills), book sellers (Barnes and Noble, Amazon – sales of the books are up 500 per cent since the launch of the film) and even the New Zealand Post Office (in December 2001 a set of New Zealand stamps was issued with images from LOTR on them – see http://www.newzeal.com/Stamps/NZ/LOTR/Rings.htm). In addition, AOL Time Warner launched a new version of AOL (version 7) with an LOTR sweepstake which generated 800,000 entries in its first two weeks.

Customer service and support

Potentially the Internet offers many opportunities for customising and tailoring the service offered to the needs and requirements of individual customers. Jeff Bezos, CEO and founder of Amazon.com, is reported as saying that if Amazon has 4.5 million customers it should have 4.5 million stores, each one customised for the person who visits (Janal, 2000). When customers make initial purchases from Amazon they are invited to give information, such as billing details and address shipping address, which will be stored and used for future transactions. On logging into Amazon the customer is greeted by a 'personalised' greeting, recommendations for books based on previous purchases, and one-click ordering for new books. The system is automated for efficiency, but, from the perspective of the customer, tailored to their individual needs and requirements.

The interactivity of the Internet makes it possible to establish two-way relationships with customers so that feedback on product performance or operational problems can be received, as well as advice for solving problems provided. Firms offering bit-based products, such as software, often use the Internet as a way of providing product upgrades and patches. Norton Antivirus, for example, post on their web pages new files to update their virus-checking software each month. These are downloadable files that subscribers can access to update their Norton software.

Some firms offer added value services by encouraging chat rooms and online communities through their sites. Reebok, for example, established an online community where potential customers could 'chat' with famous sports personalities. They regularly post articles and news items of interest to their target customers. All these activities are designed to help build the brand and establish its credentials with the target market (Janal, 2000).

Deise *et al.* (2000) identify five types of website that allow or encourage customers to interact with the company. Content sites provide customers with basic information about the company, its products and its services. FAQ sites answer frequently asked questions and can help customers with common queries. Knowledge-based sites have knowledge bases, or databases, that can be searched by customers. These require a greater degree of involvement from the customer but may be more convenient than making a service call. Trouble ticket sites allow customers to post queries or problems and then receive personalised feedback or problem solving. Interactive sites facilitate interaction between the firm and its customers. Often these are part of an extranet where customers are given access to proprietary information.

Again, however, it should be noted that the power lies with the customer. Online, as in the physical world, customers are only likely to be attracted by services that provide value for them. The key to successful service online will remain identifying what gives customers value, and what can be uniquely offered through the Internet. Because of the ease of competitor copying, however, service benefits need to be constantly upgraded.

A related issue which may complicate matters is broader concerns for issues like customer privacy, which may hold some back from Internet relationships with companies, as well as the enormous potential for dissatisfied customers to quickly spread news of their dissatisfaction through the Internet, e.g. the companyXsucks.com website may be just a start.

12.2 Pricing strategies

Setting prices can be one of the most difficult decisions in marketing. Price too high and customers may not buy, price too low and the organisation may not achieve the profit levels necessary to continue trading. In the 1960s British Leyland had major product success with the Mini, a small car aimed at a growing market of increasingly affluent consumers. Part of the market success was down to relatively low prices being charged. Unfortunately, however, the margins achieved were very thin and the company did not generate enough profits from the Mini to put back into R&D to develop the next generation of cars, and cars for other market segments. The company was financially crippled in 1975 by falling sales (brought about by strong competition from Japan and elsewhere), the first OPEC oil crisis, and high levels of UK inflation.

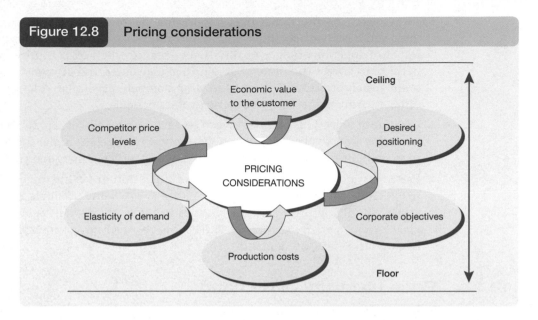

Figure 12.8   Pricing considerations

12.2.1   Pricing considerations

A number of factors need to be taken into account when setting price levels
(Figure 12.8).

- **Production costs**. The simplest, and most often used, pricing method is to set
  price at cost plus a percentage mark-up (e.g. cost plus 20 per cent). Provided the
  product sells in sufficient quantities at this price, this strategy ensures a given
  level of profitability. It also ensures that products are not sold at below cost – a
  strategy that is not sustainable in the long term without subsidy. In practice costs
  should be seen as a floor below which prices should not be allowed to fall.

- **Economic value to the customer**. The value of the product to the customer over
  its lifetime gives a ceiling above which prices would be unacceptable to customers.
  Doyle and Stern (2006) explain how EVC can be calculated with an example from
  B2B marketing (see below).

- **Competitor price levels**. Also important to consider are the prices set by competitors. Where two or more product offerings are similar on other characteristics,
  price can become the final determinant of choice. Firms may decide to price
  higher than competitors (as a signal of superior quality), at similar prices (and
  compete on other features), or lower prices (and compete primarily on price). In
  the UK market for petrol (gas) there is very little price differentiation between
  competitors. This is in part due to the high level of taxation (VAT and duty) on
  petrol, at 72 per cent in 2000, leaving little margin for price differences.

- **Desired competitive positioning**. The price charged can be a powerful signal
  to the market of the quality and reliability of the product. Too low a price may

349

suggest poor quality rather than good value for money. In the hi-fi market Bose have deliberately priced their offerings significantly higher than competitors as a signal of superior product quality. Other brands, such as LG, price below competition to attract the more price-sensitive consumer. In between these extremes brands such as Sony, JVC and Samsung compete at similar prices but offering different features, styles and other customer benefits.

- **Corporate objectives**. Are the objectives to grow the market rapidly (which might argue for a relatively low price), to harvest (which might argue for prices at the high end), or to maximise profit (which would indicate marginal cost pricing)?
- **Price elasticity of demand**. A further consideration in setting prices is the extent to which demand will vary at different price levels. Some products, such as luxury goods, are highly price elastic – changes in price affect quantity demanded to a great extent. Others, such as essentials, are relatively price inelastic, with price having little effect on demand.

12.2.2 Price elasticity of demand

The price elasticity of demand is the effect of changes in price on demand for the product. Most demand curves slope downwards from top left to bottom right (see Figure 12.9). In other words, the lower the price, the more of a product is purchased, and conversely, as prices rise, less is demanded. Price elasticity is defined as:

Price elasticity = (% change in demand) ÷ (% change in price)

Where price elasticity >1 we term this 'elastic demand' (a change in price generates a greater change in quantity demanded); where price elasticity <1 we term this 'inelastic demand' (a change in price generates a smaller change in quantity demanded).

The extent to which quantity demanded is affected by differences in price varies from market to market. Where there is a steep slope to the demand curve (a in Figure 12.9) a change in price has relatively little effect on quantity demanded; demand

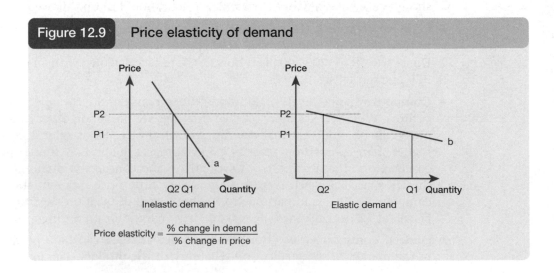

Figure 12.9 **Price elasticity of demand**

is 'inelastic'. A price rise from P1 to P2 results in a reduction in quantity demanded from Q1 to Q2. By multiplying price by quantity we can see that revenue changes from P1 × Q1 to P2 × Q2. The loss of quantity demanded is offset by the higher prices and revenues will increase. Markets which enjoy inelastic demand are often monopoly or near monopoly supply where customers have little or no choice about how much of a product they use and where switching costs are high.

A shallow demand curve (b in Figure 12.9) occurs where a relatively small change in price stimulates a more significant change in demand; demand is 'elastic'. An increase of price from P1 to P2 results in a much more significant reduction of demand from Q1 to Q2. Similarly, price reductions are likely to have a more significant effect on stimulating demand. Markets where demand is more price elastic are generally characterised by greater levels of competition, more customer choice and the easy ability of customers to switch from one supplier to another.

12.2.3 Assessing value to the customer

Economic value to the customer (Forbis and Mehta, 1981) and customer value propositions (Anderson *et al.*, 2006) are central concepts in pricing of industrial products such as plant and equipment. This approach entails attempting to identify the lifetime value to the customer of the purchase, taking into account all costs (e.g. purchase price, running costs, maintenance etc.) and all benefits.

Doyle and Stern (2006) show the example of a market-leading machine tool selling at €30,000. In addition to the purchase price the customer will incur €20,000 start-up costs (including installation, training of operatives etc.), and post-purchase running costs over the life of the machine of €50,000. In total, the lifetime cost is €100,000. Of this the initial purchase price is less than one-third. A new competitor coming into the market might be tempted to charge less for the product, but the effect of that lower price over the life will be considerably less. A 20 per cent reduction in initial price, for example, of €6,000 is in effect only a 6 per cent reduction in lifetime costs.

A more productive approach might be to estimate the total output value to the customer over the life of the machine. This could be done by estimating the number of outputs from the machine tool over its life together with an assessment of likely defects. If the new machine is an improvement on the existing one, with say 20 per cent greater efficiency, it can be expected to save 20 per cent of total costs or produce 20 per cent more output (both equivalent to €20,000 added value for the customer). Hence there is scope to actually increase the initial purchase price to, say, €40,000 while still offering an overall saving of €10,000 to the customer. In this case a higher price might also be needed to signal a higher quality product that can deliver the 20 per cent savings claimed. A lower price might raise doubts on ability to deliver the savings.

In markets where lifetime value may be less easy to demonstrate (e.g. consumer markets for appliances) the perceived value of the product can be used as an alternative to EVC. Using techniques such as Vickrey auctions value to the customer can be estimated. In normal auctions the item will go to the highest bidder. There can be times, however, where bidders will bid below the perceived value of the item in an attempt to get a bargain (this happens regularly on eBay!). Vickrey auctions are a technique to get to the true value the bidder places on the item. They are sealed bids to purchase where bidders submit written bids without knowledge of who else is bidding for the same item. While the highest bidder wins, they pay the price bid by the second highest, not the price they bid. This creates a powerful incentive for bidders to bid the real value they place on an item rather than gamble on getting it for a bargain, lower price (see www.wikipedia.org).

Trade-off analysis (also called conjoint analysis) can also be used to estimate the 'utility' of different price levels, and how customers will trade-off between alternative configurations of benefits (features) at different prices (see Green, Carroll and Goldberg, 1981).

12.2.4 Pricing methods

A number of alternative pricing methods are used by organisations, sometimes in combination.

- **Cost plus pricing.** This the simplest approach to setting prices and employs little understanding of customers and their needs. Prices are set at cost plus a percentage mark-up. Prices therefore reflect directly the costs of creating and delivering the product. The disadvantage of this method, of course, is that it takes no account of the value of the product to the customer. If the value to the customer is greater than cost plus mark-up, the product will be attractive, but if the value to the customer is lower, sales are likely to suffer.

- **Going rate pricing.** In some markets, such as petrol and diesel, prices are typically set on a 'going rate' basis – at what others set – and there is little price competition between suppliers. Competition takes place on other factors such as availability, location, convenience.

- **Perceived value pricing.** Pricing products at their perceived value to customers requires sophisticated research methods to identify value. When customers are asked direct questions about value (e.g. 'how much would you pay for . . .') few would vote for high prices! Projective techniques and other approaches such as trade-off, or conjoint, analysis (see above) can be more useful. Under these approaches customers are put into simulated purchasing situations and their behaviour is observed to gauge the value they perceive in the market offer.

- **Sealed bids.** In many industrial purchasing situations, especially in capital projects, a number of potential suppliers may be invited to bid to supply. Normally at least two stages will be employed. First, a specification stage where suppliers need to demonstrate their ability to supply to specification and on time. This stage will reduce the number of potential suppliers to a manageable number. Second, a sealed bid which indicates the price each selected supplier would charge. Deciding how to bid under competitive situations can be highly sophisticated. Typically firms will take into account not only their own costs but also their predictions of the prices competitors will bid at (based on their costs and expectations of competitors). Game theory may be useful in this context. Game theory refers to a set of techniques and approaches that studies situations where players choose different actions in an attempt to maximise their returns. It provides a formal modelling approach to situations in which decisions are not made in isolation, and where the decisions of one party can be influenced by the decisions of others. Hence the need to model and predict the intentions of others (see www.Wikipedia.org). The growing use of Internet auctions that ask suppliers to bid prices online to a purchaser's product specification is the newest approach to this situation.

12.2.5 Promotional pricing

- **Loss leaders.** Used extensively by retailers and other suppliers as a means of attracting customers into their stores, or on to their websites, loss leaders are products sold below cost for promotional purposes. Once customers have been attracted in by the loss leader the retailer will attempt to sell other market offerings at a profit. Manufacturers also use this tactic where the lifetime cost of a product is considerably greater than the initial purchase price. Home photograph printers, for example, are sold at very low prices with little margin because the manufactures and retailers can make their profits through selling ink cartridges, photo quality paper and other consumables.

- **Special events.** Seasonal sales, special price promotions and 'once-in-a-lifetime' deals are ways in which price is used to gain customers. Sales originated as a means of moving old stock to make way for new season offerings. Some organisations now appear to have near permanent sales, suggesting that really they are offering products at prices lower than the 'ticket price' but, because they do not want the product to appear low quality, justify this through discount.

- **Cash rebates.** Money back offers and coupons are popular among marketers of fast moving consumer goods. Coupons can be most cost effective as not all are cashed in, and only when another purchase is made. Money back can be more expensive as claims are more likely to be made.

- **Low interest finance.** For the purchase of significant goods such as furniture and automobiles, some suppliers will offer low, or 'zero' interest on hire purchase deals. In effect this gives a discount on price when net present values are calculated and can be powerful inducements to customers to move to higher price points.

- **Psychological pricing.** Pricing just beneath psychological barriers (e.g. €2.99 rather than €3 or at €9,995 rather than €10,000) is common practice. The assumption (rarely tested) is that customers have a psychological price threshold and will group prices in broad bands for comparison purposes. A car priced at €19,995 is seen in a lower price band than one priced at €20,000.

12.2.6 The effects of the Internet on pricing decisions

The Internet makes it far easier for customers to compare prices than in the past. Not only can prices be compared between manufacturers (for example, the price of a BMW compared with the price of an equivalent model Mercedes) but also the prices of alternative suppliers of the same product or model. And the latter is no longer confined to the immediate geographic vicinity – comparisons can be made nationwide and even globally. The advent of a single currency in some parts of the EU has made price comparisons across the Euro Zone even easier.

Kerrigan *et al.* (2001) report that in B2B markets customers experience price savings of around 10 per cent for commodity products and up to 25 per cent for custom purchases. These result from the increased choice customers enjoy, coupled with increased price competition between suppliers. P&G, for example, is reducing its supply costs by conducting 'reverse auctions' with suppliers and estimates annual savings in the order of 20 per cent on supplies of around $700 million.

In addition, the advent of C2C communications or chat lines between customers help to spread information about competitive prices, as well as product and service recommendations or warnings. Through C2B communications reverse auctions are now taking place where buyers post what they are looking for and invite suppliers to bid to supply them.

Overall, it is likely that the Internet will make customers more, rather than less, price sensitive in future as they will have access to greater amounts of information, easily searched, and not controlled by the sellers.

12.3 Communications strategies

For many people advertising is synonymous with marketing. In practice, advertising is one (albeit an important one) of the ways in which firms communicate with their customers and prospective customers. The range of communications tools available is increasing as new technologies present new opportunities. At the time of writing podcasting is becoming a new and popular communications tool. Very soon that will become a standard tool in the communications tool box, and other approaches will be developed.

12.3.1 The communications process

Communications are about two-way exchanges between sender and recipient (see Figure 12.10).

All marketing communications take place under 'noisy' conditions. Other communicators, both direct competitors and others with different market offerings to communicate, are also bombarding the same audience with messages. It has been estimated, for example, that US consumers are subjected to some 3,000 advertising messages each day (*The Economist*, 26 June 2004). It is therefore important to ensure that the message is clear as well as effectively communicated. A starting point is to be clear about what the communications objectives are. These are best viewed using a simple model of marketing communications.

12.3.2 A basic communications model

A number of models of how communications work have been developed. Most, however, come back to a basic model termed AIDA – Awareness→Interest→Desire→ Action.

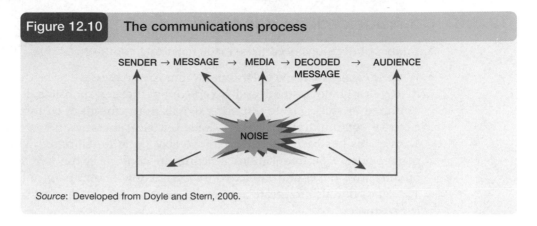

Figure 12.10 **The communications process**

SENDER → MESSAGE → MEDIA → DECODED → AUDIENCE
MESSAGE

NOISE

Source: Developed from Doyle and Stern, 2006.

● **Awareness.** At a very basic level marketing communications set out to create or raise awareness of the market offering among the selected target market. If customers are not aware of the existence of the offer they are very unlikely to purchase! Awareness raising is particularly important at the launch and introductory stages of the product life cycle. In the early stages of the MP3 player market, for example, the communications task was to explain to the market what an MP3 player was and what it did.

● **Interest.** Once awareness has been created the communication goal changes to creating interest in the market offer. Customers are bombarded by many messages every hour of every day and may have an awareness of many products and services. Relatively few will interest them, however. Key to creating interest is demonstrating how the offer is relevant to the wants and needs of the customer. In the case of the MP3 player, the advantages of music on the move beyond the personal cassette player (Walkman) and personal CD player were stressed (e.g. does not skip tracks or mangle the tape, is smaller and more convenient, batteries last longer, there is no need to carry libraries of cassettes or discs as they are already loaded etc.).

● **Desire.** Once interest has been stimulated, communications seek to create desire for the offer ahead of other offers in the market. Rather than demonstrating the benefits of the generic product group the emphasis is now on creating a desire for this particular brand or offering. Much of Apple's promotion of the iPod MP3 player centres on creating a cool image for iPod as the only MP3 player to own. So successful has this been that iPod has now moved from its original target market of 15 to 30-year-olds to a more mature market. This is in danger of weakening its position among the original market (see above).

● **Action.** Awareness, interest and desire are of little value to a supplier unless they result in purchases or other forms of support. Communications aimed at taking the customer to the next stage, creating action, include offers, promotions and deals to stimulate purchase, as well as the use of personal selling.

12.3.3 Communications decisions

A number of decisions need to be made regarding communications.

- **What message to convey.** First and foremost the message to be conveyed needs to be clearly understood and accepted by those responsible for sending it. Confused messages create confusing signals in the minds of customers. The most effective communications have a single but clear message they are trying to get across. This has been referred to as the USP (unique selling proposition) of the market offer. Communications centring on conveying the key benefits of the product in a novel and attractive way (see copy below) help not only to raise awareness but also to create a powerful position for the product in the mind of the customer.

- **What communications tools to use.** There are many different communications tools available. These include advertising, public relations, sales promotions, personal selling (see Chapter 15), direct marketing and sponsorship. Each has advantages and disadvantages (discussed below). Some are better at creating awareness (e.g. advertising) while others focus more on creating desired actions (personal selling). The various tools are used in combination at different stages in the communications process.

- **How to translate the message in copy.** Not only is it important for the communicator to known what message they are trying to convey, they must also translate it into effective words and symbols that the recipient of the message can understand and decode. Too subtle, or complicated, translations can result in a confused message being received, or even the wrong message being received. Early anti-drug use advertisements in the UK were criticised for actually making drug taking look glamorous, rather than getting across the message that drugs can seriously damage your health.

- **Which media to use.** The media available for marketing communications vary across different countries, as do their effectiveness. Relevant media include press, television, cinema, posters, Internet, radio, post box (e-mail inbox as well as the physical letterbox still used for direct mail), point of sale, fax machines, WAP phones.

- **How much to spend on communications.** Setting communications budgets is notoriously difficult. Years ago a marketing executive said, 'half my advertising budget is wasted – the trouble is, I don't know which half!' Advertising effectiveness modelling by leading firms such as Millward Brown can assess the levels of awareness created through promotional campaigns (see Maunder, Harris, Bamford, Cook and Cox (2005)) by surveying the target audience regularly and modelling the relationship with advertising activity.

12.3.4 Communications tools

- **Advertising.** Advertising is particularly effective at creating awareness. It can have high visual impact, wide reach and is easily repeated to reinforce messages. Its disadvantages are that it is impersonal, lacks flexibility, is generally not interactive

| Figure 12.11 | UK advertising expenditure by media |

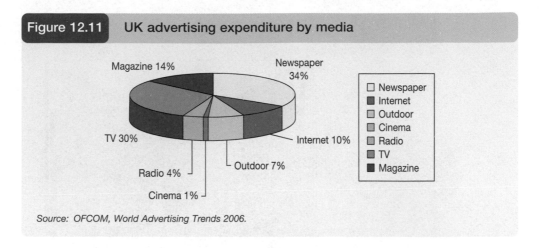

Source: OFCOM, World Advertising Trends 2006.

with the customer (questions cannot be answered, objections cannot be overcome) and has a limited ability to close the sale on its own. Figure 12.11 shows the proportion of advertising expenditure in each of the main media in the UK in 2006.

● **Public relations.** PR can be more credible than advertising at is uses a third party, the reporter and the medium used, to convey the message – the final message to the customer does not come directly from the marketer. As such it can have a higher impact than advertising for a fraction of the cost, and may also reach audiences that would be difficult or impossible to reach otherwise. The major disadvantage, however, is the loss of control. Once a press release has been issued there is no guarantee that it will be taken up and acted on by the media, and it is quite possible that the message will be distorted so that it does not get across as intended. It may also reach the wrong audience.

● **Sales promotions.** Sales promotions include money off, bonus packs, three for the price of two, free samples, coupons, loyalty cards, prizes, bulk discounts, competitions, allowances and any other creative 'deal' that firms can dream up. Their advantages are that they can have a very direct effect on behaviour and those effects can generally be directly monitored and evaluated. The disadvantages are that their effects may be short-lived and hence they could be a costly way of achieving sales. Excessive use of promotions may also weaken the image of a brand ('it can't be very good if they are always giving it away!').

● **Personal selling.** One of the most effective tools for closing a sale is personal selling (see Chapter 14). It is flexible, can be adjusted to individual situations, can be used to build relationships with customers, and can be used to understand, address and overcome barriers and objections to purchase. It can, however, be costly, is highly dependent on the skills of individual salespeople, and in some markets may incur customer resistance.

● **Direct marketing.** At its best direct marketing can offer a highly personalised service, tightly targeted to those customers who are prime targets for the offers made. Thus there is less wastage of the promotional budget. At its worst, however, direct mail can be indiscriminate, can generate high levels of scepticism among customers and result in message and material overload. As with all communications

> ### Figure 12.12   Communications effectiveness
>
>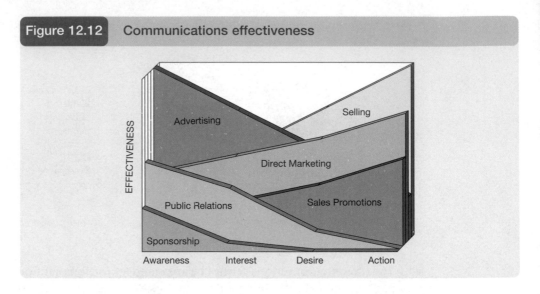

tools, effective targeting is the key to ensure the messages are effectively directed to the target market.

● **Sponsorship.** Sponsorship of sporting, social, cultural and other events, or of teams, causes or facilities, can be an effective way of targeting potential customer groups through their wider interests and concerns. This can help with credibility building and reputation enhancement. It is perhaps the most difficult communications tool to measure the impact of, however. It can be expensive, and may not be particularly effective in achieving awareness goals. Sponsorship of the Sydney Olympics achieved very low levels of recall among target audiences. It can also be subject to 'ambush' – competitor products achieving placement in sponsored events.

Communications tools effectiveness

Figure 12.12 shows the effectiveness of each of the above across the four stages of the communications model. In general, advertising, PR and sponsorship are better at raising levels of awareness and interest than creating desire or action. Personal selling, direct marketing and sales promotions are more effective at inducing action. An effective communications campaign will determine first what the objectives are, then select an appropriate mix of tools to achieve that objective.

12.3.5 The use of the Internet for marketing communications

In 2001 it was estimated that advertising over the Internet totalled $9.6 billion. By 2006 that had risen to $27 billion. In 2006 that represented approximately 5 per cent of worldwide advertising expenditure, but is expected to rise to around 20 per cent over the next few years (*The Economist*, 25 November 2006). By 2010 it is expected to rise to over $60 billion.

In the UK over £2 billion was spent on Internet advertising in 2006 (up 41 per cent on 2005), accounting for 11.4 per cent of all advertising spend. For the first time Internet advertising overtook newspaper advertising (10.9 per cent of all spend). Of that the biggest sectors were recruitment ads (25 per cent), finance and banking (14 per cent), technology (13 per cent) and motors (13 per cent) (*The Observer*, 1 April 2007, quoting PriceWaterhouseCoopers).

As noted above, a significant feature of the Internet is the shift in power away from manufacturers and retailers towards customers. While the period to the middle of the twentieth century saw power concentrated in the hands of manufacturers and suppliers (due to demand typically outstripping supply in many industries), a major feature of the last quarter of that century was the shift in power to retailers. It was the retailers who controlled the connection between manufacturers and customers, and crucially managed the information flows to customers. Customers who wanted to gather information about competing products could do so, but the process was often time consuming and cumbersome, resulting in choices being made with limited, imperfect information. A major characteristic of the Internet-based marketplace of the twenty-first century is the 'information superhighway' that makes comparative information far more easily available to customers. Indeed, the customer now typically initiates information search, whereas in the past the manufacturer or the retailer initiated and controlled this.

For example, powerful retailers like Tesco and Wal-Mart participate in global online exchanges based on the web. They can source products from the cheapest suppliers anywhere in the world. They can also pressure their suppliers to switch sources for raw materials and components to cheaper alternatives located on the exchange (though not obliged to adopt such suggestions, suppliers find that their prices are adjusted down as though they had). This represents a significant change in the marketing communications process, and shift in power from seller to buyer. Information search is more likely to be triggered by customers than by marketers, despite the large sums being spent on online advertising.

Customers are becoming information seekers rather than passive recipients as evidenced by the extensive use of search engines such as Google and Yahoo. Coupled with this are changes in media viewing habits brought about by the explosion in channel availability through cable and satellite and media merging as the boundaries between phones, television and Internet technologies become blurred.

One of the potential benefits of communicating over the Internet is the possibility to more accurately relate sales to promotions. These are reflected in a number of new marketing communication methods emerging to take advantage of the particular characteristics of the Internet. Among these are banner advertising and viral marketing.

Banner advertising and pay-per-click

Banner advertising is the use of advertisements on web pages that have click-through options to take browsers through to company websites. They are currently the main form of advertising on the Internet. Advertisers bid on key words they believe potential customers will use in their searches (using Google, Yahoo or other Internet search engines). The search engines then display advertisements next to the results of the Internet search. While irritating to some customers they have proven very successful when linked to the page content being viewed. For example, search engines such as Yahoo and Lycos will flash links to commercial sites offering goods and services related to the items that are the subject of searches. Much of the early success of Amazon was attributed to the banner advertising it enjoyed on the AOL website which directed purchasers to books on the topics of interest. The effectiveness of banner advertisements in general, however, is questionable, with Timmers (1999) reporting that click-throughs (visitors clicking on banner ads to link through to the corresponding website) can be as low as 0.5 per cent (one in two hundred). As users of the Internet become more sophisticated and experienced it is likely that the click-through rate will fall rather than increase. To be effective a banner advertisement must make an immediate impact on an often crowded computer screen, as well as conveying in a few words reasons to click through.

Most rapidly growing, and predicted to account for more than half of Internet-based advertising by 2010, is pay-per-click advertising. The advertiser only pays when a customer clicks on their advertisement and is taken to their website. As only interested customers are likely to click through, the quality of the leads generated is very high and can therefore cost between $0.10 and $30 (average in 2006 was $0.50) depending on the keyword (*The Economist*, 25 November 2006).

Viral marketing

Viral marketing involves creating a marketing message with the intention that people will forward it to friends. This has a significant advantage over 'spam' messaging in that the friend will have some level of credibility which may cause the messageto be viewed more sympathetically. While not unique to the web, Internet-based technologies have greatly facilitated easy use of this type of marketing.

The paint marketer Dulux, for example, wanted to sell more paint to British women. Rather than indiscriminately bombarding women with e-mail messages to 'buy more paint' the company created a website featuring a 'belly fluff' game and e-mailed 10,000 women invitations to play. In the event, 13,000 did play. The company estimates that one-third of the people entering the competition received the e-mail forwarded from a friend (*The Guardian*, February 2002).

Forrester Research (www.forrester.com) estimates that a high-quality e-mail distribution list should generate a response rate (purchase) of around 6 per cent. A list created through panning will generate 1 per cent. Viral marketing, on the other hand, has achieved response rates of between 25 and 50 per cent (Forrester Research, quoted in the *The Guardian*, February 2002).

Nestlé uses viral marketing for its Nescafé products including Blend 37. In one campaign 20,000 Nescafé drinkers were e-mailed invitations to click onto www.b37.challenge.com to enter a prize draw for tickets to the Silver Historic Festival in August 2001. The top 36 scores won VIP passes to an event at the Silverstone racing circuit (*Precision Marketing*, 29 June 2001).

Pre-launch promotion

The Internet can be an ideal vehicle for 'teaser' ads prior to new product launches (see for example *The Lord of the Rings* movie above). Before launching its new Crest

Whitener into the US market P&G set up a pre-retail launch website which attracted 1.2 million visitors and actually sold 140,000 units (worth over $6 million retail). The company estimated that the initiative created around 500,000 buyers before the launch advertising and retail distribution began (*Marketing Business*, July/August 2001).

Advertising audience measurement

In order to standardise the ways in which measurements of advertising reach and effectiveness are made the UK advertising industry has established a Joint Industry Committee for Web Standards (JICWEB). The committee has now agreed definitions of 'users', 'page impressions', 'visits' and 'sessions'. JICWEB is addressing circulation issues, but there has been little attention to date to audience profiling through panels and surveys, as exists for other media such as television (BARB) and the press (JICNAR). A newly formed industry committee for Internet Advertising Research (JICNET) is putting forward proposals for one survey-based audience measure for the UK advertising industry to use with confidence (*Marketing Business*, July/August 2001).

12.4 Distribution strategies

Distribution strategy focuses on how products and services will be physically delivered to the customer. The distribution network used or created will depend on a number of factors including whether the final customers are consumers or other businesses.

12.4.1 Channels of distribution

The main choice facing most marketers is whether to sell through intermediaries or direct to customers. Intermediaries, such as wholesalers and retailers, can have a number of advantages. The most significant advantage is that they have direct relationships with customers that may be helpful.

In UK consumer grocery markets, for example, retailers such as Tesco, Sainsbury, Asda, Morrisons and Waitrose have loyal customers who regularly shop in their stores. Products sold through the stores gain credibility in the eyes of the customer because of where they are sold. The disadvantage, however, is that the retailer has many competing products on their shelves, and has little incentive to promote one brand over another. Suppliers attempt to counter this through either a 'push' or a 'pull' strategy. A push strategy is one where the retailer is given incentives to stock the product (for example, bulk discounts or additional promotional offers that might encourage additional shoppers into the store). A pull strategy, on the other hand, is where the supplier encourages customers to go into the store demanding the product. In this way the product is 'pulled' through the distribution channel rather than being 'pushed'.

In business markets intermediaries may also be used (usually trade wholesalers) but it is more common to find direct sales through the firm's salesforce. The advantages of direct selling through a salesforce are discussed above. The obvious disadvantage is the cost incurred, though this is generally offset by the higher prices that can be charged. In addition many firms may hire a contract salesforce to help with special activities, such as the launch of a new product, or peak demand periods.

12.4.2 Effects of the Internet on distribution strategies

The Internet has greatly facilitated the distribution of bit-based products such as information, music and video. Indeed, in the recorded music industry, many now suggest that physical products like the CD are on the point of obsolescence because of the attractiveness of downloading music from the web. In 2005 there were more sales of albums as music downloads in the UK from iTunes than through the leading high-street CD retailer. The challenge for the music companies is to find ways of generating income from music downloads in the face of competition from pirate sites providing the music free.

With atom-based products the key to success has often rested with efficient and effective distribution systems and logistics. Every book sold by Amazon online must be delivered to the customer, and customers increasingly accustomed to rapid access via the Internet also expect rapid physical delivery once they have made purchases. The traditional '28-day delivery' period is no longer acceptable to many customers. Failures in distribution destroyed many of the dot.coms – eToys found, for example, that the 'virtual business' is an illusion, when you have to operate warehouses full of toys. The fulfilment strength of Amazon.com is proving a core competence, driving many of its alliances, for example with Toys 'R' Us.

Increasingly, the distribution issue becomes one of multi-channels – numerous ways in which the same products and services reach the customer. For example, one major strength of the Tesco.com Internet grocery offering was that it recognised that Internet grocery purchasing is not a substitute for store visits; it is a supplement. Managing complex multi-channel systems will be a substantial challenge for many companies. The critical tension will be between what companies want from multi-channel strategies and how customers react to them.

For example, PC market leader Dell Computers aims to get the majority of sales onto the web because of the huge economies this achieves. However, the company also has internal and external salesforces to promote new products with corporate customers and to win business from the competition. Their view is that, if you want to buy a few PCs, then you buy on the web or go elsewhere. If you want to buy for a whole company, then you buy through the direct salesforce. If you are another Boeing with a potential installed base of 100,000 PCs, then the founder Michael Dell will come and see you. To make this multi-channel work, Dell has grasped the nettle of paying salespeople commission for sales through the web, and even offering salespeople additional bonuses for moving smaller buyers on to the web.

However logical multi-channel models may be, they can be re-interpreted by customers in other ways. One leading financial services company in the UK designed its channel system with three main options: the Internet, the branch network, and postal/telephone banking. They saw customers as either Internet customers or branch customers. Customers, on the other hand, tended to redefine the model in their own terms: why not go to the branch to open a deposit account and get a passbook, then do all the transactions through the post or on the telephone, and then operate the current account on the Internet? The company's multi-channel strategy was wrong-footed (along with all the cross-selling and promotional plans in each channel), but they are learning to cope with the fact that this is how their customers want to use different channels.

12.5 The extended marketing mix – people, processes and physical evidence

12.5.1 People

While important in any business, the quality, training and enthusiasm of the people employed in the organisation are absolutely critical to service businesses. Happy, skilled and motivated staff are much more likely to serve customers well and effectively, and establish an ongoing relationship that can be mutually beneficial. A number of factors are important in designing the staffing strategy:

- **Job design and description.** The starting point is to have a clear idea of the job roles and tasks that staff will be required to carry out. This will include identifying the level of technical competence required, as well as the softer skills of dealing with people in a manner that will leave them satisfied (or better still, delighted). In service firms, however, jobs rarely conform to exact specifications. There is a need for flexibility to adapt the job as conditions change and as customer requirements also change.

- **Selection.** Choice of which staff to employ is largely driven by the job specification. If a 'bouncer' is being hired for a nightclub, the job specification will include an ability to physically defend himself and others. In hiring an accountant, however, other technical qualifications will be more important.

- **Training.** While staff may be highly skilled on appointment, ongoing training is essential to ensure that skills are maintained and enhanced in the light of changing circumstances. Much training may occur 'on the job' but it can also be important to allow time out for reflection and to sharpen specific skills.

- **Appraisal.** Also important is regular appraisal and feedback to staff on their performance. Provided this is done in a constructive manner most staff welcome feedback on their performance and suggestions as to how it can be improved. Also part of the appraisal process is revisiting the job description and updating it in the light of experience.

Because the people employed have the direct contact with customers it can be problematic when staff leave. In some instances they make take the customers with them if they move to a rival organisation (e.g. account executives being poached from one advertising agency to another). The human resource management strategy needs to ensure the firm is not over-vulnerable to changes in personnel. This may be through rotation of customer contact staff, or through team approaches to serving particularly valuable customers or clients. In some instances 'golden handcuffs' might be appropriate to stop particular staff leaving and taking key clients with them.

12.5.2 Processes

The systems and processes involved in delivering the product or service to customers will not only impact on the ability of staff to effectively serve customers, they will also affect how customers judge the level of service they have received. Staff need to be given the tools to do the job. This may include ICT tools such as customer relationship management (CRM) packages (see http://en.wikipedia.org/wiki/Customer_ relationship_management), as well as more basic order processing and delivery techniques.

CRM covers all the methods and technologies used by companies to manage their relationships with customers and clients. Information held on existing customers (and potential customers) is analysed and used to create a stronger and hopefully mutually beneficial relationship. Amazon.com use automated CRM processes to generate automatic personalised marketing (such as book and CD suggestions or recommendations) based on the customer information, including recent purchases, stored in the system. Using this technology advantage, Amazon is becoming a general trading platform for diverse products and services beyond books and CDs.

An effective CRM system helps organisations to acquire customers, build closer relationships with them, provide better customer services and hence retain valued customers. By tracking customer contacts through the CRM the organisation is able to ensure appropriate levels of contact are maintained, and to monitor the effectiveness of specific interactions.

In the public sector, universities are increasingly using CRM packages to track contacts with students through initial enquiry, decision to study, course performance and progress, on to graduation, career progress and alumni status. In this way additional opportunities can be pursued for improving the overall student experience through a complete life cycle, and hopefully maximise the return to the university by way of repeat business, donations and endowments from the student as well!

CRM applications often track customer interests and requirements, as well as their buying habits. This information can be used to target customers more selectively. In addition, the products a customer has purchased can be tracked throughout the product's life cycle, allowing customers to receive information concerning a product or to target customers with information on alternative products once a product begins to be phased out. Baby products companies now have sophisticated CRM packages that alert them to stages in the baby's development when, for example, there is a need to change from one type of nappy to another, or from baby food to toddler food. In some cases they even trigger automatic birthday cards.

12.5.3 Physical evidence

As discussed in Chapter 14, a key aspect of service delivery evaluation is tangibles, or the physical evidence that accompanies the offer. In the marketing of physical, atom-based, products the appearance of the product itself and its packaging, together with the surroundings in which it is marketed, can have an impact on the overall attractiveness to customers. For example, sophisticated retail facility design pays detailed attention to the smells and sounds that comprise part of the retail experience, as well as the sound and feel of the floor underfoot, and the space allowed to avoid the 'butt brush' (when one shopper brushes against another and disturbs their purchase consideration), and the effect of lighting on mood and ambience. In service encounters the appearance and demeanour of staff can be equally important.

Customers take many cues to the quality of the product or service they are purchasing from the physical evidence that surrounds it. When lecturing to MBA students or executives on management development programmes, most faculty members will dress in a more 'businesslike' fashion than when teaching undergraduates. The formalities of dress code are used to establish rapport with the audience and are varied depending on the particular audience. Packaging for products may also vary to give cues as to quality. For example, the Sunday Times Wine Club distributes to members some of its fine wines in wooden crates while more everyday wines are despatched in cardboard boxes.

12.6   New businesses and business models

In the wake of the uncertainty and undoubted opportunities generated by the Internet, two distinct types of firms are emerging: Internet pioneers and Internet pragmatists.

12.6.1   Internet pioneers

The Internet pioneers have set up radically new types of business to exploit the benefits of the new technology to do business in very different ways. Straub and Klein (2001) refer to these as 'Omega' level firms and note that the successful ones have harnessed the power of the new technology to gather information about customer preferences and to tailor products and services specifically to the needs of individual customers. These firms, however, are relatively rare but do include the likes of Amazon.com in consumer goods retailing, e-Bay in online auctions and Monster.com in the jobs market.

eBay is a prime example of an Internet pioneer. In the late 1990s it became the preferred place on the web to trade collectibles, building its position largely through word of mouth rather than media advertising, and creating a virtuous circle whereby more buyers attracted more sellers, who in turn attracted more buyers. In 2001 eBay had 38 million users worldwide. In the third quarter of 2001 they listed 109 million items and spent US$2.4 billion between them. eBay received $194 million in revenue from the sales, 71 per cent up on the same period in 2000 (*Fortune*, 21 January 2002).

A further example of an Internet pioneer is Egg, the UK's first Internet bank. The bank was launched with a positioning as both innovative and tailored to customer needs (the brand statement was 'Egg is your ground breaking partner, who is always there for you offering simple, smart financial solutions'). Within a week of its launch it had received 1.75 million visits to its website. By the end of 2001 it had gained 9 per cent of the UK credit card market and brand awareness has risen to a staggering 88 per cent. By then it had 1.58 million customers, on a par with many of the high-street banks. This was all achieved through the use of innovative technologies, which effectively lowered the entry barriers to a once well entrenched market (*Marketing Business*, September 2001).

12.6.2 Internet pragmatists

The second type of firm to emerge has been termed 'Internet pragmatists' (Fahy and Hooley, 2002). These firms have embraced the opportunities of the Internet to enhance their existing business models. Dell, for example, uses online ordering to enhance its direct marketing operations, FedEx uses the technology to enable personalised tracking of customer packages during transit (3.1 million packages per day with 99 per cent on-time, accurate delivery), and Cisco saves US$700 million annually through offering customer support over the web. These pragmatists have used the Internet to enhance the services they already offered to their customers, and also to reduce costs, but have not completely thrown out their existing business models. Rather, these have been adapted to the new environment.

The national roll-out of Tesco's Internet grocery service in 2000 followed almost five years of preparation and piloting, and that preparation means Tesco.com leads the Internet quality measurements published by the Chicago-based Gomez company, and is regarded by many US companies in this field as a world leader. Certainly, Tesco.com is now the world's largest e-grocery business, and plans expansion into the USA. The formulation of Tesco Direct's value proposition and business model was based on close study of what customers wanted from Internet grocery shopping. Contrary to expectations that online shoppers would want to abandon traditional stores, they found customers liked to visit stores to examine fresh produce personally and to see what new products were available, and trusted their local stores to provide quality goods at fair prices. Most customers did not see online shopping as a substitute for traditional shopping, but as a complement. For this reason the online shopper uses the same store that they visit in person, choosing from the same regional product selection and buying at the same prices. The proposition was to 'shop online from my store'. The Tesco model integrates online and offline business – online sales are part of branch sales and feed into store-based replenishment. The value proposition is convenience and time-saving, but also greater personalisation – the software remembers previous purchasing and gives 'reminders', and can also warn those vulnerable about things like nut allergies and food choices. The relatively low start-up costs (£35 million) and fast national coverage reflect use of the conventional stores as 'mini-depots' where pickers can make up six online orders a time using a special trolley. Company estimates are that the average online shopping order is 2 or 3 per cent more profitable than the average in-store order, because Internet shoppers tend to select the higher margin products on offer.

The difference between the pioneers and the pragmatists can clearly be seen by the stage of diffusion at which they adopted the newer technologies. It seems that we are now firmly in the majority phase of diffusion of the Internet as an enabling technology (possibly even late majority stage) where the majority of adopters are pragmatists, using the new technology to enhance and improve existing business models, rather than to revolutionise them.

Many of the pragmatists represent the much-maligned 'old economy'. These are companies that, in some instances, were slow to join the information technology revolution and also includes those firms that are selective in their use of the Internet. For example, firms like IBM and Cisco Systems have moved most of their customer service online and customers now serve themselves from the menus of options available on their websites. These companies claim cost savings of the order of $500–700 million per annum through providing service online. Some of the kinds of online customer service currently available include customised web pages, targeted information, customer-service provider interaction, customer-to-customer interaction, customised products and rewards and incentives (Walsh and Godfrey, 2000).

Similarly, right through the business system, pragmatists are using the Internet to enhance what they are currently doing (Porter, 2001). For example, Compaq Computer Corporation is increasingly distributing software online rather than on CD and floppy disk. They have pioneered a 'try it and buy it' distribution system where customers use the software for a trial period and then the licence is extended should a customer wish to purchase. Sales conversion rates have increased significantly using this system. Many of the basic organisational activities are now being outsourced electronically. Mobile phone companies like Vodafone offer fleet management services for corporate clients while corporate health plans can be managed off-site by companies like BUPA. Corporate training services can be managed remotely by e-learning companies like Smartforce and even basic corporate R&D activity is enhanced by vast stores of information now available electronically. In summary, Internet pragmatists are those that have adopted the Internet to enhance existing products and processes. These are frequently labelled 'bricks and clicks' operations, meaning that the company sees the Internet as an additional channel which complements existing activities. Dell Computer Corporation found that its make-to-order model was very well suited to the Internet and consequently more than 50 per cent of its business is now being conducted through this medium. Allied Irish Banks examined the option of setting up an Internet-only bank to compete with the likes of First-e but dropped the idea in favour of improving its Internet banking facilities for existing customers.

While the Internet pioneers have grabbed the headlines, it is likely to be Internet pragmatists who eventually dominate the use of the Internet as a business channel.

Summary

The 'new' marketing mix is constantly changing. New ingredients are being added all the time by creative marketers. The most significant development over the last decade, however, has been the advent of the Internet. This has significantly impacted on all aspects of the marketing mix, from product and price through to promotions and distribution. A number of conclusions (and possible warnings) emerge:

1 Don't assume that the Internet will cure all your marketing ills. Firms that are poor at marketing in the bricks-and-mortar world are unlikely to suddenly succeed in the virtual world of the Internet. For creative, Internet-savvy firms, however, the new technologies may offer ways of leapfrogging more conventional competitors and adding value for customers in innovative ways.

2 Remember that atom-based products will still need efficient and effective distribution systems to physically get them to customers. Indeed, the logistics and distribution systems of online retailers may need to be even more effective than

those of bricks and mortar firms as expectations of speed are greater for Internet-based firms.

3 Beware of assuming that today's atom-based products will be tomorrow's atom-based products. Increasingly, physical products (such as music CDs, videos, newspapers, magazines) are being turned into bit-based products. Because of the Internet the market for TVs and PC monitors is blurring; PDAs and mobile telephones can now access broadcast material.

4 Continue to base your competitive advantage on the marketing resources you possess that can be protected from competitor imitation. Actively develop the new resources, skills and competencies necessary to take advantage of the new technologies.

Tyrrells   FT   Case study

Courtesy of Tyrrells Crisps

William Chase is not 'a corporate person'. The farmer turned creator of Tyrrells Potato Chips – an entrepreneurial Herefordshire business producing 'artisan' crisps – is blunt and outspoken. He eschews 'management jargon' in favour of home-grown opinions. 'It's not turnover, it's left-over [profits] that matters,' Mr Chase declares repeatedly.

So far Tyrrells Potato Chips is living up to his maxim. Sales grew more than 80 per cent in its second year. The fledgling company is already producing tasty 'leftovers', as Mr Chase puts it, with pre-tax profits of £1.2m in the last financial year, yielding a 35 per cent margin.

Recent success at Tyrrells Potato Chips shows how niche marketing can help a small player hold its own against the distribution power of large supermarkets.

Mr Chase bought Tyrrells Court, the farm where he grew up, from his father in 1982, at the age of 20. By the mid-1990s the farm was producing reasonable profits, but the one fly in the ointment was dealing with large supermarkets.

They were 'constantly pressing for discounts' and prone to cutting off suppliers at short notice, he says. 'We could see the cracks appearing on the wall. We had no bargaining power plus we were producing a commodity, which is no fun at all.'

To get off the treadmill of selling a low-margin commodity to price-conscious buyers, Mr Chase began looking for branded products that would make use of the farm's potatoes and move the business up the value chain.

After toying with various possibilities, such as potato wedges, he hit on the idea of making premium-priced 'artisan'-style potato crisps, or 'chips'.

He set up Tyrrells Potato Chips in 2002 with start-up capital of £2.5m, raised from personal finance and bank loans. The company generated sales of nearly £2m in fiscal year 2004, followed by £3.6m the next year. By March 2006 revenues are forecast to reach about £6m.

As he speaks, Mr Chase cranes his neck towards the yard where big agricultural vehicles carry loads of potatoes harvested from his fields. They are on their way to the factory, which sits below his office.

The premises are cramped, which is not surprising given the rate at which Tyrrells – a finalist in the current National Business Awards Entrepreneur of the Year contest – is growing.

Changes in eating habits combined with rising levels of disposable income have helped the brand grow quickly. Consumers, once content with mass-produced crisps, have proved willing to pay extra for traditionally made products containing only natural ingredients.

Tyrrells' packaging, which Mr Chase designed himself, highlights the fact that his potatoes are home-grown and cooked on the Herefordshire farm.

This helps differentiate Tyrrells from competitors such as Walkers Sensations (the premium sub-brand of Walkers Crisps) and niche producers of 'hand-fried' chips, such as Burts and Kettle Chips, which pioneered the market.

Where possible, Mr Chase prefers to sell directly to retailers, maintaining that distributors 'lack the passion and commitment' to get an unknown brand into the best shops.

Working from the premise that it is easier to trade down than trade up, Tyrrells has made a point of targeting the most exclusive shops first, using the cachet of being seen on the shelves of famous stores – such as Harrods, Fortnum & Mason and Harvey Nichols – to spark interest in Tyrrells and persuade other fine-food retailers to stock its products.

Making up the bulk of Tyrrells' customers are several thousand independent retailers – delicatessens, sandwich shops, tea-rooms and gastro-pubs, plus some chains such as Costa Coffee, as well as Pret A Manger, for which Tyrrells manufactures under contract.

The UK's largest supermarkets are notably absent. Mr Chase says he was approached two years ago by J. Sainsbury, which wanted to sell his products nationally. He turned down the opportunity. 'If you go in too early with the largest supermarkets they dictate the terms on which you sell your brand.'

One supermarket that Mr Chase has no reservations about supplying is Waitrose, which he praises for 'respecting its suppliers'.

Tyrrells is also to be found in smaller community-based stores, such as Budgens and some local co-operatives, because, Mr Chase claims, they – like Waitrose – treat their suppliers well and allow them a reasonable margin.

The rationale for selling through such stores is that they serve a cross-section of consumers, including the less price-sensitive ones, who use them for 'top-up' purchases of smaller snack items.

With this strategy, Mr Chase aims to double sales each year. Yet he faces the challenge of expanding rapidly without devaluing his brand. One line of attack is to expand overseas, again targeting the best stores first.

So far the approach has paid off. Around 20 per cent of Tyrrells' sales now come from exports, predominantly to France, where the brand is sold in a number of top food halls, such as La Grande Epicerie de Paris.

Other countries where Tyrrells has made headway include Ireland, Denmark, Italy and Norway, where the brand is stocked by leading delicatessens Smør-Petersen and the upmarket convenience chain, Deli de Luca.

Developing new flavours and higher value products creates further opportunities for growth. Tyrrells' apple and root vegetable chips retail at

99p for 40g, or almost twice the price of its potato crisps. Mr Chase also intends to diversify into related categories, such as cereal bars, biscuits and muesli.

But in some ways Tyrrells' home-grown nature is in danger of being compromised by expansion. Tyrrells has the capacity to supply all of the potatoes that it needs for several more years, but a number of the other vegetable ingredients used in its other products have had to be bought in until the home farm can become 'self-sufficient'.

Exporting has also forced the company to depend more heavily on distributors. In addition, it has modified its packaging and pricing for overseas markets. To meet the expectations of French consumers, Tyrrells has recently added a smaller 35g pack to the range, which is priced below the psychologically significant threshold of €1.

If he is to fulfil his growth plans for Tyrrells, Mr Chase may have to revisit the thorny question of whether to work with the major supermarkets. But he admits not relishing the prospect and hints at seeking a buyer, or taking a back seat in the business to avoid having to deal with the largest supermarkets personally.

'Supplying the big stores involves you in a huge number of meetings; it's not how I want to live my life,' he says simply.

Whether Mr Chase lives up to that maxim remains to be seen.

How to create cachet and reap profits

The public's appetite for premium and 'hand-fried' chips has lightened the gloom of crisp manufacturers in a market that Mintel, the researchers, term 'otherwise disappointing'. A relative latecomer, Tyrrells has worked to capture a share of this growth through:

- Branding. Tyrrells' marketing taps into the public's enthusiasm for 'authenticity' and 'provenance'. Its crisp packets tell the story of Tyrrells. Pictures of employees growing potatoes on the Herefordshire farm and then cooking them illustrate the journey from 'seed to chip'.

- Quality. Tyrrells chips are made from traditional varieties of potato and 'hand-fried' in small batches.

- Distribution. Tyrrells sells directly to 80 per cent of its retail stockists. Students from a local agricultural college are employed to trawl through directories and identify fine-food shops to target with samples. After winning their business, Tyrrells develops the relationship through personal contact.

- Diffusion strategy. Selling to the most exclusive shops creates a showcase for Tyrrells to target consumers who are not sensitive to price, allowing it to grow profitably.

- New product development. Tyrrells is constantly bringing out new flavours and products. Experimental recipes are produced in sample runs and given free to shops to test with customers. Recent introductions include apple chips, honey glazed parsnips and Ludlow sausage with wholegrain mustard.

- Exporting. This has created a further sales channel through fine-food stores. Yet it has also forced greater dependence on distributors, introducing an unwelcome layer between itself and its customers.

Source: Alicia Clegg, 'Crisp profits at the potato farm', *The Financial Times*, 11 October 2005.

Discussion questions

1 Tyrrells have successfully moved away from selling a commodity to producing an added value product. What are the reasons for this success?

2 How can Tyrrells use the PLC and diffusion of innovation theories to further grow sales?

3 Personal selling is a key part of Tyrrells' communications strategy. With what tools and media should this be supplemented, bearing in mind that the communications mix should be fully integrated and in line with the rest of the marketing mix?

chapter thirteen

Competing through innovation

The key to long-term success in business is what it always has been: to invest, to lead, to create value where none existed before.

Robert Hayes and William Abernathy (1980)

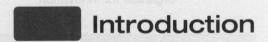

■ Introduction

Innovation may emerge on many fronts: an innovation in customer service experience and store atmospherics to reinvent a business by a firm such as Jordan's Furniture with two of their stores boasting IMAX theatres and restaurant facilities, a brand extension strategy by Virgin, or a new access method for conventional products by First Direct in financial services. However, the nature of innovation in marketing strategy is best understood by examining the new product development process. The lessons here may be applied more generally to understanding innovation in the services and brand elements of marketing strategy.

There are many factors that may spur an organisation to innovate (see Figure 13.1). These include internal pressures to exploit existing and new technologies to the full, together with the desire to use the organisation's resources, its assets and capabilities, as effectively as possible. External pressures include the push from intense

Besides the price and performance advantage, successful new products often provide benefits that are dramatically different from current offerings. Examples include Linx printing technologies (Doyle and Bridgewater, 1998), Innocent smoothies (which contain nothing else but fruit) and the Toyota Prius with its hybrid technology. New products need to have a significant advantage over existing products. That may mean going against industry trends: Motorola, when competitors were including more and more features into their phones, decided to do the opposite and focus on form and developed the smallest and thinnest handset on the market – the Razr. It exceeded Motorola's total lifetime projections within its first three months of commercialisation (see Anthony *et al.*, 2006).

Even though companies such as Spring Ram Corporation in kitchen and bathroom products, Honda in motorcycles and Amstrad in PCs have succeeded despite their late market entry, it is almost always better to be first.

Despite the inevitable risk of being a pioneer, first to market is often best for several reasons. The news value of an innovation peaks in the early stages, and this offers maximum communication impact and a chance for widespread consumer trial. The innovator catches consumers first; this means that competitors who follow must improve their market positioning and produce better and/or cheaper products to make consumers switch. This is not so easy to achieve once the pioneer has secured strong consumer loyalty and a reputation for innovation in the marketplace.

13.1.2 Business product success

Studies of new business-to-business product successes and failures make the following distinctions between successes and failures (Cooper and Kleinschmidt, 1993):

- product uniqueness (innovativeness) or superiority;
- management's possession of market knowledge and marketing proficiency;
- presence of technical and production synergies and proficiency.

The first dimension – industrial product uniqueness/superiority – is very close to that for consumer products. In this respect industrial and consumer products are similar. It is likely that industrial and consumer products are similar in other ways too. Successful industrial innovators study their customers and market well. They carry out market research to gain knowledge of customer's requirements/needs; they are sensitive to price as well as to the intricacies of buyer behaviour. Before the launch of the Land-Rover Discovery, for example, extensive and sophisticated marketing research was conducted to reveal customer requirements and the deficiencies in competing offerings.

Successful innovators acquire as much of the required information as possible to enable them to forecast market size and determine potential demand for their new product. They test the market prior to product launch. There is strong and often well-targeted sales support, which recognises the need for forceful communications to stimulate primary demand and to prise open new markets. Glaxo's forceful and focused marketing efforts were significant factors contributing to the astounding market success of their anti-ulcer drug, Zantac, while Wellcome's failure to maximise new drugs sales has been attributed to the company's poor marketing skills.

Successful industrial innovations are clearly not the result of sophisticated technology alone. Mismanagement of technical and technological resources can have a detrimental effect on new product performance. Successful industrial innovators ensure there is synergy between the firm's engineering and production capabilities and the new product project. They also undertake a range of technical activities and do these proficiently – preliminary technical assessment, product development, prototype testing with customers, production start-up, with facilities well geared for launch. Their technical staff know the product technology well. They are familiar with the product design.

13.1.3 Types of new product failure

In what way do new products fail? Answering this question helps us appreciate what actions the firm should take to avoid different types of product failure. There are six classes of product failures (Cooper and Kleinschmidt, 1990): the better mousetrap no one wanted, the me-too meeting a competitive brick wall, competitive one-upmanship, environmental ignorance, the technical dog product and the price crunch (see Figure 13.4):

1 **The better mousetrap no one wanted** is the classic 'technology-push' type innovation for which little or insufficient market demand exists. Customers do not perceive they have a real need for the technology and, consequently, are not prepared to buy the innovation. Sinclair's C5 electric car falls firmly into this category – an innovation without an obvious market.

2 **The me-too meeting a competitive brick wall** is the result of followers failing to reconcile with the market leader's or established competitors' strengths (e.g. Lidl's attack on the UK grocery market against Asda, Sainsbury's and Tesco).

3 **Competitors** can spring surprises and come up with a better product that is preferred by customers. 'Competitive one-upmanship' is not easy to predict but can be seen in the case of decaffeinated Nescafé Gold Blend upstaging innovative Café Hag in the coffee market. Innovations may achieve great short-term advantage, but if competitors can easily and simply imitate the innovation (and have other advantages as well), then the innovator is likely to achieve little long-term value. For example, Direct Line had a major impact on the financial services market by offering simple products and fast telephone access for customers. This was a major success story in the early 1990s. By 1997 Direct Line was close to a loss-making position. Direct telephone marketing is easily copied by established firms and this is exactly what they have done.

Figure 13.4	Causes of new product failures

- The better mousetrap no one wants
- The me-too meeting a competitive brick wall
- Competitive one-upmanship
- Environmental or market ignorance
- The technical dog
- The price crunch

4 **Environmental or market ignorance** occurs when the innovating firm fails to study market or customer requirements or to monitor and scan its external environment for signals of change. Socio-economic, technological, political and/or legislative conditions and/or changes are ignored, overlooked or misunderstood, resulting in poor sales after launch. In the case of Concorde, society's resistance to the noise it makes was grossly underestimated – this resistance was a major barrier to rapid adoption of supersonic aircraft by other airlines.

5 **The technical dog** product does not work or users are dogged by technical problems (e.g. Amstrad's PC2000 business computer, or first the Rover SD1 and then the Rover Stirling in the US market).

6 **The price crunch** comes when the innovating firm sets too high a price for a new product whose value is not perceived by target customers to be better or greater than existing products. Often if competition offers a lower-cost product the innovating firm has to cut its price so fails to obtain the required return on investment from the innovation. Despite repeated relaunches, Sony's mini-disc seems to be falling into this category, as did video discs.

Sinclair C5

Alamy/Motoring Picture Library

13.2 Planned innovation

Since innovation is so uncertain, can innovation be managed? Using formalised new product development processes achieves greater new product success than does an ad hoc approach to product innovation. There is, however, a distinction between invention and innovation. The former is the discovery of a new device or a new process. It is fair to say that managers cannot specify deadlines for the discovery of new ideas or predict when a particular invention will occur or, indeed, when exactly a scientific discovery will be made. Invention cannot be planned for. Often it is left to chance, or the perseverance and ingenuity of the scientist/inventor. Innovation is different. Once the new scientific or technical discovery is made, or a novel product idea has been conceived, its chances of being successfully commercialised rest predominantly on the astuteness of the firm's management in new product planning and strategy determination as well as the proficiency with which certain new product developments and launch activities are undertaken. From discovery/conception of the idea to marketplace, management and employees of the firm have direct control and influence over the fate of the discovery/idea.

Businesses can reduce the risk of product innovation while improving the likelihood of success by adopting a planning orientation and sophisticated new product development process (Wong *et al.*, 1992). There was nothing accidental or ad hoc about the results achieved by Glaxo for Zantac in the anti-ulcer drugs market, or McDonald's in fast foods – they succeeded through careful preparation of the strategies for product development and market entry.

13.2.1 The new product planning process

Most successful innovating companies develop a new product process, such as that shown in Figure 13.5, which is linked to their company's overall longer-term planning process.

First, companies should define their business mission by asking: What business are we in? And what business do we want to be in? By considering the growth potential of the sales and market share and profitability of the company's current range of products, and the extent to which growth objectives will be fulfilled, management can begin to identify gaps in achievable and desired growth. The role of new products and how the firm's portfolio of businesses might be changed to achieve planned growth can be determined.

Firms also have to decide on the types of new product that are to be developed. It is usual to classify new products according to the degree of newness to the company and to the customers (Figure 13.6).

| Figure 13.5 | New product development stages and time lapse |

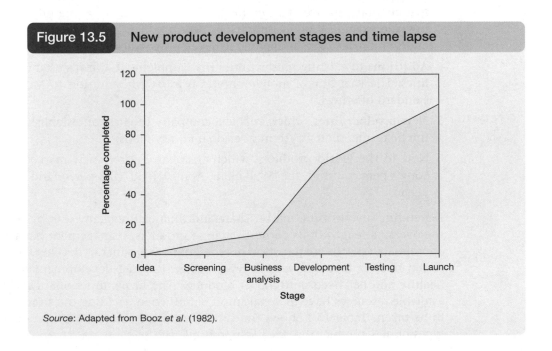

Source: Adapted from Booz *et al.* (1982).

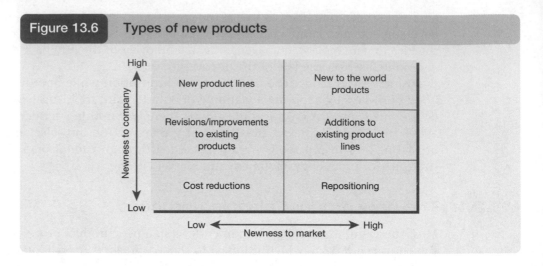

Figure 13.6 **Types of new products**

Six categories of new products emerge, each one taking the company further and further away from its current activities and, therefore, being more risky.

1 **Cost reductions**, which provide similar performance at lower cost, as Mercedes achieved with their new C series saloon.

2 **Repositionings**, which are current products targeted at new customer segments or new markets. For example, Lucozade, a soft drink, traditionally aimed at the 'convalescent', is now targeting the youth and sporty user segment.

3 **Improvements** or revisions to existing products, which enhance performance or perceived value and replace existing products. For example, Intel Pentium IV is an incremental improvement on the Pentium III. Japanese car manufacturers tend to upgrade existing models, supplying 'new products' with improved performance and/or more features, as opposed to developing radically new models from scratch.

4 **Additions** to existing product lines that supplement a firm's established product lines. The Razr line of mobile phones is a 'stylish' addition to Motorola's more standard offerings.

5 **New product lines**, which enable a company to enter an established market for the first time, such as Virgin's Personal Equity Plans.

6 **New to the world products**, which create an entirely new market, for example Sony's personal hi-fi, the 'Walkman', Apple's iPod MP3 player and JCB's original digger.

Depending on the sales, market share and financial objectives set by the firm, and the overall strength of its current range of products, management has to select the appropriate type, or combination of types, of new product to develop. Usually a firm would have to invest in various types of new product development to maintain a healthy and balanced portfolio of products. The firm's functional capabilities and available resources have to be taken on board when deciding the strategic direction to be taken. Table 13.1 shows the various strategic roles for new products and the types of new product that are likely to fulfil each of these roles.

Table 13.1 The strategic role of new product types

Strategic role	New product type
Maintain technological leadership	New to the world New product line
Enter future/new markets	New to the world
Pre-empt competition or segment of the market	New to the world New product line Repositioning
Maintain market share	New product line Repositioning Additions to existing product line
Defend market share position/prevent decline	Repositioning Cost reduction Revisions/improvements to existing product lines
Exploit technology in a new/novel way	New to the world New product line
Capitalise on distribution strengths	Additions to existing product line

Source: Based on Wong (1993).

The magnitude of the risk attached to innovation alters with the type of new product being developed. Planning can help; failure to do so increases the risks, while decreasing the chances of new product success.

13.3 The new product development process

Figure 13.7 presents the key stages in the new product development process that show the mortality rate on new product ideas. It shows two rates of decay: the first shows average performance; the second contrasts the achievements of best performing companies.

13.3.1 Idea generation

For new products, a firm has to find novel ideas, do new things and do things differently. This is the essence of product innovation. New ideas trigger the innovation process and the development of new products. Ideas are where all new products start. Both the creativity of individuals and the methods of idea generation can be employed to obtain novel ideas.

Creativity and productive ideation

Really innovative ideas come out of inspiration and use appropriate techniques. Because of the high mortality rate of new ideas it is desirable to generate and consider a large number of ideas. The use of appropriate methods to generate new

13.3.2 Screening

Take ten new product ideas. The chances are that two will pay, seven will fail, and only one will be a big winner. New product idea screening and selection is not about dropping bad ideas but catching the winner. Picking a potential 'winner' is not an easy task. What should managers take into account when evaluating new product ideas? What are the critical screening criteria? How do managers choose the best from among a pool of apparently viable ideas?

Systematic screening

If resources are committed to the development of a new product idea, management should assess the commercial potential and technical (including production) feasibility of the idea. If there are alternative ideas or projects competing for development funds and management time, these have to be screened and the more viable and attractive ideas selected.

Ideas screening is, therefore, an important component of the product innovation process. Screening can take up management's time. It is often tempting for the management team to devote a minimum amount of time and effort to it, and even to skip the exercise, in the rush to get idea development started and new products out to market quickly. An idea coming from a senior manager in the firm may sometimes also escape thorough screening and evaluation because of the assumed credibility of the source – which could turn out to be a costly error of misplaced confidence! Or ideas may not be systematically evaluated because management regards screening as a superfluous exercise given the lack of concrete data, in the early stages, on what are still apparently vague and ill-formed ideas.

Whatever the barriers, it pays to give serious attention to screening. There are good reasons for doing this. Screening helps avoids potentially heavy losses by reducing the possibility of bad ideas being accepted, and raises the chances of good ideas being developed. It encourages more efficient resource allocation by directing the firm's attention to the 'best' ideas and encourages firms to pursue those ideas that build on its core strengths. Also, as screening experience accumulates, it improves the managers' precision in ideas selection, so increasing the chances of success.

Initial screen

Screening can be conducted at different levels of detail. The preliminary screening may be treated as a coarse filter, enabling managers quickly to separate out useful ideas for further investigation. Figure 13.8 shows the key screening questions. Remember that the initial screen is only a crude filtering device. Sometimes a new product idea might hit a legal, technical or marketing barrier which might not be particularly insurmountable. It is therefore important for the management team to use the tool cautiously, taking on board internal company, as well as market and technological, developments that could be exploited to avoid premature closure of new product opportunities.

Formalised screening system

Potentially viable ideas should be evaluated more thoroughly for selection purposes. It is important for management to appreciate that full screening requires

Figure 13.8	Initial screening of new product ideas

1. Is idea compatible with company objectives?	Yes – Go on No – terminate
2. Is idea legally acceptable?	Yes – Go on No – terminate
3. Can idea be technically developed within desired time and budget constraints?	Yes – Go on No – terminate
4. Is there a demand for the proposed product?	Yes – Go on No – terminate
5. Does the idea fit the firm's current and desired marketing objectives and resources?	Yes – Go on No – terminate
6. Are the commitments and risks involved acceptable?	Yes – proceed to further investigation and development No – terminate

identification of specific information and the investment of resources to obtain these data. Formalised screening means that new product ideas are evaluated logically and within a systematic structure. It is less impressionistic than initial screening and attempts to increase the objectivity of idea selection.

When actual data are unobtainable the management team doing the screening must exercise subjective, qualitative judgements. It is important to record all major assumptions and quantitative estimates so that they can be used as control standards for future reference.

The screening devices are not a panacea for a poor innovation record. The analyses rely on the ability of the firm's management team to combine high-quality subjective judgements with good objective data. The tools do not absolve management using them from exercising creativity, nor are these techniques a substitute for management vision.

The analyses are time- and resource-consuming. The many uncertainties at the early stage of ideas selection make detailed and sophisticated evaluation somewhat meaningless. This encourages rejection of screening. But it is certainly misguided to make no attempt to consider the determinants of project success and failure, or the attendant risk and uncertainty when committing resources to major product innovation programmes.

The output of screening and evaluation is only as good as the input data. This means that, to benefit from utilising screening systems, management must commit time and resources to building an information system geared to supporting ideas screening, evaluation and selection decisions. As with building any management information system, this takes time but, if implemented properly, yields a lasting and positive effect.

Screening based on the opinions and judgements of staff within the firm can be highly biased. Judgements can be distorted because of undue pressure applied on

13.3.6   Commercialisation

Commercialisation is often the 'graveyard' of product innovation, not because new products die here but because real innovation often stumbles at this point of the process. By this we mean that things are going wrong and the product concept that seemed so feasible in the beginning is now tarnished and facing considerable pressure of compromise because of time, cost and other resources. Managers who are impatient to get the product to market fail to allocate sufficient time and resources to developing an effective launch campaign. Surprisingly, after all that has gone into development, products often fail because they are launched with insufficient marketing support. Most new products fail, not because of any inherent deficiency, but because the market launch strategy and tasks were poorly conceived and executed.

The launch managers should work closely with sales and other operating staff to achieve good coordination of the timing and scheduling of all these activities. Every effort must be made to ensure that critical activities (e.g. salesforce training, sales and promotions materials) are completed proficiently to secure launch success. In conjunction with key operating personnel, the launch manager has also to put together a launch plan, which consists of a programme outlining the sequence of tasks to be performed, a schedule that relates the programme to a time sequence, and budgets for the programme and schedule.

Launch programmes easily turn into a complicated and unwieldy task. There is little point in turning out project control or milestone events charts hundreds of pages long because this is bound to break down, providing hardly any basis for effective project control. Except for the most complex technological developments, as found in car, aerospace and defence projects, complex, computer-based systems for project control are usually not necessary. For the small to medium-sized company simple 'checklists' may suffice. Remember, there is also 'eyeball control', which relies on managers being constantly on the go, visiting every area of the firm (daily, if possible), gathering their own information, and becoming 'expert' enough to exercise sound judgement and keep launch tasks under control.

13.4   Speeding new product development

Managers must appreciate the value of being fast at innovation. A company that takes less time to develop and commercialise a new product can be expected to be more competitive than a slower competitor. The firm would be able to launch more new products in a given period of time, therefore building a strong innovation leadership image. Speedy companies are also able to respond faster to changing customer requirements, thereby securing sales and building customer loyalty. Also, by increasing the frequency with which it introduces new products into the market, the firm could pre-empt competition, thereby creating and maintaining a market leadership position.

The cost of new product development could be reduced by undertaking innovation of an incremental, as opposed to radical, nature, with substantial reduction in the risks of innovation. Companies should, however, ascertain if they have the capabilities for accelerating new product development. Also, management should ensure that the firm supports a balanced innovation programme such that opportunities are not forgone because of failure to fund more radical (and longer-term) product innovation programmes in view of the obsession with speed.

Speeding the new product development process needs action at all stages of the process. At the start, avoid delays in approving budget for developing product idea and pay early attention to 'snagging' at the end of the process. Overlapping product and process design and development phases has two benefits. It means that processes take place in parallel and forces the formation of multi-functional project teams (design, engineering, production, sales, marketing, etc.). Big technological breakthroughs are not necessary to make big commercial gains, so take an incremental approach to product improvement and development, making many small steps rather than attempting giant leaps forward. New product innovation often clashes with the systems and controls designed to make firms 'well managed'. To overcome this, successful businesses adapt operational and organisational procedures to give the flexibility and freedom that new product innovation needs.

13.5 Organising for new product development

'Mental walls . . . block the problem solver from correctly perceiving a problem or conceiving its solution' (Adams, 1987). The nature and intensity of these blocks vary from individual to individual, but organisations that innovate recognise and avoid them (see Figure 13.9).

13.5.1 Blocks and bugs

- **Perceptual blocks** prevent the person from perceiving clearly either the problem itself or the information needed to solve the problem (e.g. problem isolation difficulty; narrow definition of problem; limited viewpoints examined).

Figure 13.9	Roadblocks and barriers to innovation

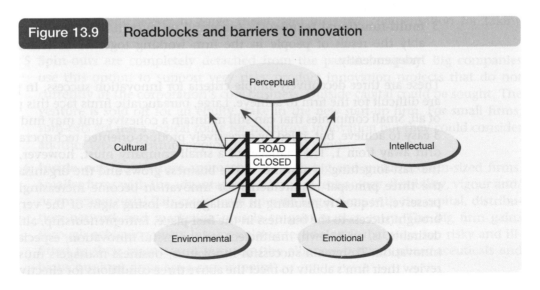

The more radical the new product project (which means higher risk), the greater the need for project focus and its protection from current departmental and operational influences and constraints. The functional and taskforce options are therefore appropriate for low risk, incremental product innovations (e.g. improvements, repositionings, new sizes, etc., involving present product lines).

A project team–functional matrix is most suitable for marginally riskier projects, involving expansion in the number of product lines. Venture teams, spin-outs and inside–outside venture options are for radical, high risk projects where internal constraints and opposition are expected to be very high (e.g. the IBM PC project and GM's Saturn car).

The proposed radical structures help large firms capture the benefits of a small firm. Ironically, the idea that 'small is good' stems from the observations that large, innovative firms work in non-bureaucratic, smaller settings. They try to gain the advantages of being small (Quinn, 1985). But, of course, size is not a determinant of innovation success. Many new products introduced by small firms fail because they should never have come about – it may be that they were badly conceived, they failed to meet market needs, or that the company lacked the marketing skills required to prise open new markets.

Summary

Product innovation is not a one-off activity. A successful, profitable innovation can see a firm through for a while, but long-run survival depends on new products to balance its future portfolio (Chapter 2), replace declining products and cater for new customer needs. Glaxo cannot thrive on the back of its blockbuster drug Zantac alone.

Many businesses are caught out because management has failed to use the profits from current innovations to develop more innovations for future markets. Today's breadwinners will eventually dry up as competitive forces intensify over the product's life cycle. New products – tomorrow's breadwinners – are necessary to maintain the firm's position in the marketplace. One win is insufficient; multiple wins are necessary for corporate longevity!

The more the firm innovates, the greater the experience accumulated; the greater the experience gained, the better it gets at innovation; the better the firm becomes at this daunting activity, the greater its chances of competitive survival. A virtuous cycle of innovation is established.

Increasingly, a multidisciplinary, team-based approach to product innovation is required. Team work is important and has been one of the most significant organisational factors behind Japanese companies' ability to accelerate new product development in the drive to achieve lasting competitive advantage, as observed, for example, in the consumer electronics, computer and motor vehicle markets.

There are many factors that affect new product performance. Neglect of one factor alone can bring about failure. Management should check that their firm is pursuing a balanced and realistic new product development strategy, that customer/market needs are clearly identified and well understood and that requisite technical and technological skills are married with a market orientation to ensure success.

Gillette Case study

Alamy/David Crausby

Gillette on Wednesday set out to prove that men who shave are ready for a five-bladed razor and are willing to pay a premium for it by unveiling two razors featuring battery power, microchips and a goatee-trimmer.

The launch of the Fusion and Fusion Power razors, billed by Gillette as its most ambitious product launch, is the most striking sign this year that consumer goods companies are betting on innovation to drive margin growth.

This comes at a time of competition from own-label rivals, rising commodity costs and a scramble to gain shelf space with the strongest retailers.

Gillette's razor trumps a four-bladed version from the Schick brand of rival Wilkinson Sword, confounding sceptics who believed the industry had reached the limit on the number of blades that could be accommodated on a standard razor. Not to be outdone, Schick plans to offer a battery-powered version of its four-bladed razor this year.

Peter Hoffman, president of Gillette's razor and blades unit, said that the two Fusion blades, one a manual version and the other battery-powered, would command a 30 per cent price premium compared with Gillette's three-blade Mach3 razors.

'Pricing research confirms that at these prices consumers in significant numbers will trade to our newest flagship brands,' he said. A pack of four Fusion razors would sell for $12–$13.

Mr Hoffman said Gillette had spent less developing the razors than on the Mach3 products, which were launched in 1998.

Yet the company expected the new razors to have sales of $1bn within three years, outstripping the $500m Mach3 business, itself bigger than the combined shaving businesses of Gillette's rivals.

The launch of the Fusion razors comes as Gillette is preparing to be integrated into Procter & Gamble, which agreed to buy its Boston-based rival for $57bn in January.

It will provide a test of the rationale for the merger, which was partly to use P&G's global distribution to boost sales of Gillette's premium-priced products.

'We will take full advantage of P&G's ability to execute initiatives around the world,' said Jim Kilts, Gillette chief executive.

Gary Stibel, chief executive of The New England Consulting Group, said: 'This is going to prove that P&G got Gillette for a steal, despite what they paid.'

A microchip in the Fusion Power regulates voltage, providing consistent power over the life of the blade. Gillette claims the razor brings 'advanced electronics to wet shaving'. The products will be launched in North America in the first quarter of next year, before being introduced abroad.

Source: Jeremy Grant, 'Gillette sharpens innovation edge', *The Financial Times*, 14 September 2005.

Discussion questions

1 What type of innovation is Gillette's Fusion, and how likely is it to be a success in the marketplace?

2 Are Gillette's sales expectations justified in view of what is happening in the marketplace, and why do you think new products often have to succeed against resistance both within the company developing them and in the marketplace?

3 What are the organisational alternatives that Gillette could use to manage innovation? Which alternative is best suited to a product like 'Fusion'?

Competing through superior service and customer relationships

14

Thank you for your call . . . (The Four Seasons) . . . all our operators are busy at present . . . (The Blue Danube) . . . your call is valuable to us . . . (Dvořák's New World Symphony) . . . please hold while I try to connect you to an operator . . . (Vivaldi's Flute Concerti) . . . we value your call, please hold . . . (Scott Joplin's The Entertainer) . . . your call is next on the list and will be answered shortly . . . (John Williams plays Cavatina) . . . please hold while I try to connect you . . . (The Thorn Birds) . . . thank you for your understanding . . . (Chariots of Fire) . . . we will answer your call shortly . . . (The Flight of the Valkyrie) . . .

 **Introduction**

One of the most significant trends in marketing thinking and practice during the last few years has been the shift in focus from achieving single transactions to establishing longer-term relationships with customers (see, for example, Gummesson, 1987; Webster, 1992; Grönroos, 1994; Morgan and Hunt, 1994; Payne; Zielke and Pohl, 1996; Vargo and Lusch, 2004). While transactional marketing is concerned with making a single sale, relationship marketing is more concerned with establishing a rapport with the customer that will result in repeat business and opportunities for further business development.

Many markets in developed countries are now mature, or at best growing only slowly, and there are fewer new customers to compete for. Competition is intense, and the costs of attracting new customers are high. It has been estimated that the costs of attracting new customers can be up to five times as much as the costs of adequately serving existing ones to ensure that they stay with you. As the RSA (1994) put it: 'The fundamental strategic battle is for the customer: only those companies which have as their goal the winning and retention of customers will succeed.'

Customer retention is becoming a key predictor of profitability. Reichheld and Sasser (1990) showed the value to companies operating in a variety of markets of cutting customer defections (lost customers) by as little as 5 per cent. For an auto-mobile service chain a 5 per cent cut in customer defections resulted in a 30 per cent increase in profits, for an industrial laundry a 47 per cent increase in profits, for an insurance brokerage a 51 per cent increase and for a bank branch a staggering 84 per cent increase. Customers that have been with a company longer tend, on average, to spend more on each transaction, offer more opportunities for cross-selling (selling them other products and services), and give better recommendations to their friends and colleagues. In the bank, customer relationships of ten years or more accounted for 29 per cent of the account base but 71 per cent of the profits. Lancôme, for example, a premium beauty brand, created an exclusive loyalty card called 'Rendez-vous' and found that members now spend 13.5 per cent more than before they were members.

A recent survey of 500 marketing practitioners for *Marketing Business* (Wells, 1994/5) showed the most important driver of success to be customer loyalty. Forty-nine per cent of respondents placed this as the single most important success driver in their business, compared with only 13 per cent for second-placed new product development.

However, in all this it is important that we distinguish between customer retention and customer loyalty, together with the relationship each of these has with customer satisfaction. There is a danger, in practice, that these concepts become confused. Customer retention is essentially a measure of repeat purchase behaviour and there are many reasons why customers may come back even if we have failed to provide them with a high level of satisfaction – they may have no choice or they may not know any better. Customer loyalty, however, is more to do with how customers feel about us: Do they trust us? Do they actively want to do business with us? Will they recommend us to others? Customer loyalty in this sense is more closely related to customer satisfaction.

To confuse retention and loyalty can be dangerous. Retention may be achieved through a 'bribe' – discounts for repeat purchase, and so on. Achieving high customer loyalty is likely to be far more difficult and requires greater long-term investment. The practical difference is great. Elements of the 'customer loyalty' card schemes at House of Fraser's and Sainsbury's are more about customer retention than loyalty and satisfaction, and it is likely that their effects will last only until there is a better offer available. On the other hand, the John Lewis Partnership achieves high customer loyalty through satisfaction building above and beyond such 'loyalty cards'. This is expressed in their strategic statement: 'The Partnership should recruit and retain loyal customers through their continued trust and con-fidence in our reputation for value, choice, service and honesty and for behaving as good citizens' (www.johnlewispartnership.com). As airlines have discovered, for example, if all competitors offer the same thing, then customer 'loyalty' programmes such as frequent flyer awards become a cost of being in business rather than a differentiator. Many frequent fliers will have loyalty cards with both Star Alliance and One World networks.

To build customer retention for the major financial benefits it brings, let alone longer-term customer loyalty, requires companies to invest in strategies focused on these goals, not just on sales volume. It is suggested that retention is not enough as an absolute concept and that these strategies should also be about correcting any downward migration in customers' spending habit long before they defect. A recent two-year study of attitudes of US households about companies in 16 diverse industries shows that 'improving the management of migration as a whole by focusing not only on defections, but also on smaller changes in customer spending can have as much as ten times more value than preventing defections alone' (Coyles, S. and Gokey, T.C., 2005).

This may involve brand building (of the type practised at Virgin) or specific programmes (such as the retailer 'loyalty' card schemes or product innovation), but increasingly it involves emphasis on achieving excellence in the service activities that augment the basic product offering.

This chapter explores the concept of 'service' and examines methods for competing through providing superior service.

14.1 The goods and services spectrum

Most offerings in the marketplace are some combination of tangible and intangible elements. This is shown diagrammatically in Figure 14.1.

Tangible elements can be seen, touched, smelled, heard or tasted. They constitute the physical aspects of the offer, such as the product itself and the surroundings in which it is bought or consumed. The intangible elements are often more elusive. They comprise the level of service offered in support of the tangible and the image or beliefs that surround the product.

At the left-hand end of the spectrum the offer to customers is primarily physical and hence tangible. Examples include packaged goods such as baked beans and batteries, and consumer durables such as stereos and televisions. From the customers' perspective, however, the benefits derived from purchase and consumption may well be less tangible – baked beans defeat hunger, batteries provide portable light, stereos provide entertainment and televisions are the 'opiate of the people'! The distinguishing factor is that these benefits are primarily delivered by the physical features and characteristics of the product. There are also, of course, even less tangible elements to these purchases. Physical products are sold through retail outlets where sales staff may provide advice and demonstrations. Individual brands, through their media advertising and other promotional activities, will have established images and reputations in the minds of customers that may enhance value to them.

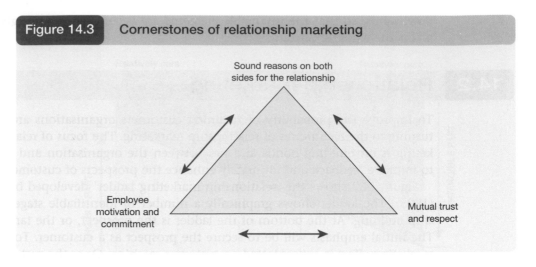

Figure 14.3 Cornerstones of relationship marketing

Sound reasons on both
sides for the relationship

Employee
motivation and
commitment

Mutual trust
and respect

Not all customers will be equally worth the effort needed to move them up the ladder, however. Critical to a successful relationship marketing strategy is the targeting of customers of sufficient value (current or potential) to warrant the investment in creating a relationship with them. IBM, for example, has identified its top 1,000 customers and puts great effort into identifying their current and future needs. The firm has combined its customer relationship management processes with its opportunity management system and ranked these customers according to their estimated lifetime value to IBM. When a high-ranking customer launches a big project with opportunities for IBM to tender it is given highest priority across the organisation (Eisenstat *et al.*, 2001).

For relationship marketing to be effective requires sound reasons on both sides for the relationship (Figure 14.3). In some markets, such as rail travel, customers may not see advantages in becoming 'partners' and may prefer to stay at arm's length from the supplier. One respondent filling in a customer satisfaction questionnaire on a train was overheard to say: 'I wish I could go back to being just a passenger rather than a customer!'

One recent commentary suggests that there is an element of spuriousness about the relationship offering made by some companies. From the customers' perspective, the British Airways relationship does not offer more seat room, and the Sainsbury's relationship does not offer much more than a bribe to come back next time. The only tangible aspect of the customers' relationship with these companies seems to be becoming the target of large quantities of junk mail selling financial services (Piercy, 1997). These can be the result of poorly designed loyalty programmes based on weak value propositions (see Capizzi and Ferguson, 2005). In fact, a recent survey conducted by IBM of about 1,000 customers of 10 major retailers uncovered that factors relating to overall customer experience were far more relevant to customer satisfaction than price and value (Chu, 2002).

In other markets firms may misjudge the value customers would put on a relationship. In financial services, for example, attempts to create closer relationships with individual clients may have been naive in assuming the client will automatically see a value in having a 'personal banking manager'. Fundamental to establishing a relationship is to determine what each party gets, or could get, from that relationship. Too many organisations still look primarily from their own perspective, recognising the value to them of customer retention or loyalty, but not thinking through clearly what the customer will get from the deal.

In contrast, other firms are now coming to realise that the type of relationship customers want with a supplier can in itself be an effective way of segmenting markets around fundamental customer needs. This can lead to focusing relationship-building resources on those customer groups where this is mutually advantageous, and significantly cut the cost and the ill-will created through more scatter-gun approaches. In business markets, for example, Narayandas (2005) suggests four types of customers depending on their location on the loyalty ladder and the sellers' costs of serving them.

- **Commodity buyers** are only interested in obtaining the lowest price and are unlikely to be worthy of education to go up the relationship ladder.
- **Underperformers** should not be allowed to remain in that position as they have low loyalty and are expensive to service.
- **Partners** are expensive to run but high on the ladder and normally rewarding financially. Their management requires ongoing care to prevent them from becoming underperformers.
- **Most valuable customers** (normally accounting for less then 10 per cent of revenues) are as loyal as partners but cheaper to service.

Essential for more advanced relationships such as partnering, or awarding most valuable customer status, is the establishment of mutual trust and respect between the parties (Crosby *et al.*, 1990). This involves being prepared to share sometimes commercially sensitive information.

Recent research in the United States suggests that the challenge to companies in business-to-business markets is no longer simply to sell, but to become the 'out-source of preference' through a collaborative relationship between vendor and customer, where the customer expects the vendor to know the customer's business well enough to create products and services that the customer could not have designed and created, and to give proof in hard evidence that the supplier has added value in excess of price. The excellent suppliers are those which add value to the customer's business by being close enough to measure the customer's needs, develop added services to improve the customer's business performance, and prove to the customer that this has been done. This is a long way removed from simple, transaction-based business (H.R. Chally Group, 1996).

The third cornerstone of relationship marketing stems from employee involvement and commitment to the relationship building and maintaining process. While companies may set strategies in the boardroom for relationship marketing, the success of those strategies ultimately rests with the employees who are charged with putting them into practice. Employees, from front-line sales staff through accounts personnel to car park attendants, need to understand their role in relationship building, be committed to it and be motivated to achieve it. In many situations, as far as the customer is concerned, the employee they meet at the point of sales or service delivery *is* the company and its brand. We shall consider the importance of this relationship in examining the growing importance of internal marketing in Chapter 17.

or delighted customers retention rates are significantly higher, and they are more likely to become 'apostles', or advocates, telling others of their good experiences.

Creating delighted customers demands that a high priority be given to customer service, both in the strategies the organisation designs and the actions it takes in the marketplace.

14.3　The three *Ss* of customer service

There are three critical ingredients to successful service provision. These have been called the 'three *Ss* of service': strategy, systems and staff.

First, there is a need to have a clear service strategy that is communicated throughout the organisation so that everyone knows their role in providing service to customers and clients. The strategy needs to demonstrate the company's commitment to service and its role in overall corporate strategy. Increasingly companies are using customer satisfaction measures alongside financial and other criteria for measuring overall performance, signalling the higher priority they now give to creating customer satisfaction. Indeed, some of these companies now promote and reward staff on the basis of customer satisfaction ratings achieved.

Not only do firms need to be committed to superior service in their strategies, but they need to put in place the systems to enable their staff to deliver service to their clients (Payne, 1993). This may entail computer systems to share information rapidly and easily throughout the firm, or more mundane but no less critical queuing practices. A hallmark of good service providers in the 1990s has been their ability to embrace and use (rather than be swamped by) new technologies to improve service to customers.

Third, and perhaps most important of all, the staff must recognise the importance of customer service and be committed to providing it. That means recruiting, training and empowering employees to provide the levels of service that will create customer delight and then rewarding them appropriately. Bowen and Lawler (1992) suggest a number of factors in empowering employees to deliver excellent service. Central is the provision of information, both on what customers require and how well the organisation is doing in providing that level of service. Also important is the power to make decisions that will affect the level of service provided.

14.4　Providing superior service

There has now been a great deal of research published in the United States (e.g. Berry and Parasuraman, 1991) and in Europe (e.g. Gummesson, 1987; Grönroos, 1994; Payne *et al.*, 1995) looking at the nature of 'service' and what constitutes excellent or superior service in the eyes of customers.

Much of the literature on customer satisfaction measurement (e.g. Berry and Parasuraman, 1991) concludes that customers measure their experiences against a benchmark of the service they expect to receive. The quality of a service provision, and subsequently the level of satisfaction of the customer, is directly related to the difference (or 'gap') between expectations and experiences (see Figure 14.4).

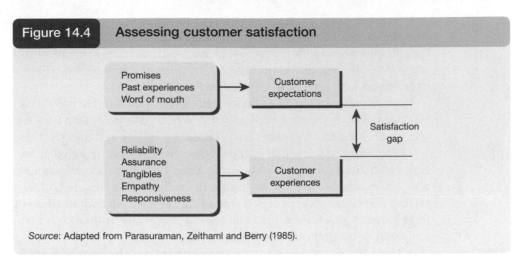

Figure 14.4 Assessing customer satisfaction

Source: Adapted from Parasuraman, Zeithaml and Berry (1985).

14.4.1 Expectations

Berry and Parasuraman (1991) discuss two different ways in which expectations may be used as comparison standards. First are expectations of what customers believe will occur in a service encounter. These they call predictive expectations. Second are what customers want from the service encounter, their desires. These two levels constitute adequate and desired levels of service. Between these two levels Berry and Parasuraman (1991) suggest lies a 'zone of tolerance'. A performance level above the zone of tolerance will pleasantly surprise the customer and strengthen loyalty, while performance below the zone of tolerance will create customer dissatisfaction, frustration and may ultimately lead to decreased customer loyalty (see Figure 14.5). Their research showed that both types of expectations are dynamic – over time expectations generally increase. There was some suggestion, however, that desired levels change more slowly than adequate levels.

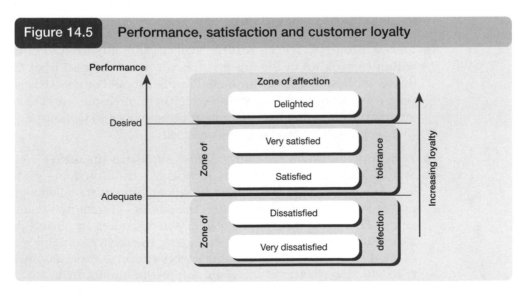

Figure 14.5 Performance, satisfaction and customer loyalty

A number of factors have been found to influence expectations, ranging from the personal needs of the customer, through the alternative services considered, to the specific promises made by service providers in their bid to win business in the first place. Word-of-mouth communications with influencers and the customers' past experiences also affect the service level expectations.

Prior experiences of the service provider, or of similar providers, are often the starting point in creating expectations. When customers step into a restaurant they are often judging the experience based on other restaurants they have visited. They typically make verbal comparisons: 'It was more relaxed than . . .' 'The food was better than at . . .' In addition to their own prior experiences expectations are also often affected by the opinions of friends, relatives or colleagues, who have related their own experiences. Depending on the standing of these opinion makers in the customer's esteem they can have a significant influence on what is expected, and even deter trial of a particular service.

A third major determinant of expectations are the promises the company itself makes prior to customers using it. These promises, by way of advertising messages, sales pitches and general image created through pricing strategies and so on, set standards that the company is expected to live up to. Pitching them can be difficult. Promising too little may result in failing to attract the customers in the first place (they may be seduced by more attractive competitor promises); promising more than can be delivered may result in dissatisfied customers. The smarter companies manage their customers' expectations at each of the steps of the service encounter so that they expect what the firm can actually deliver (Coye, R.W., 2004)

Managing and exceeding customer expectations

From Figure 14.5 it can be seen that, in order to create delighted customers, organisations need to exceed customer expectations. There are two main ways to achieve this: provide an excellent service or manage customer expectations downwards so that they *can* be exceeded. They are not, of course, mutually exclusive but should be used together. Berry and Parasuraman (1991) offer a number of suggestions for managing customer expectations.

- **Ensure promises reflect reality**: Explicit and implicit promises are directly within the control of the organisation yet many promise what they can never deliver in the desire to win business. Promises should be checked beforehand with the personnel responsible for delivering them to ensure they are achievable and attention paid to methods that might be employed to demonstrate to customers that promises have been kept (or exceeded).

- **Place a premium on reliability**: Below we discuss the main elements of service evaluation. A key aspect of most services is reliability: doing what you say you will do when you say you will do it. Where services are reliably performed they may fall down on other criteria (e.g. the manner of their performance), but overall evaluation is likely to be acceptable. Where services are reliably performed they also reduce the need for rework, or redoing the service, a highly visible indicator of poorly performed service. During rework customer expectations are likely to be raised and the chances of successful completion diminished.

- **Communicate with customers:** Keeping in touch with customers to understand their expectations and explain the limits of service possibilities can be a powerful way of managing their expectations. Communication can encourage tolerance, demonstrate concern for the customer and may serve to widen the tolerance zone. Phoning ahead to warn a customer of being late for an appointment is a simple example of communication being used to reduce the probability of customer frustration (though not a guarantee it will be eliminated altogether!).

16.4.2 Evaluations

Against expectations customers evaluate the performance of a service provider. Again, there are a number of factors that customers typically take into account when evaluating the service they have received. The most enduring classification is the five-dimensional model proposed by Parasuraman *et al.* (1988) and easily remembered by the acronym RATER: **R**eliability, **A**ssurance, **T**angibles, **E**mpathy and **R**esponsiveness.

- **Reliability** is the ability of the provider to perform the promised service dependably and accurately. In other words it is conformance to specification – doing what you said you would do when you said you would do it. In many service situations reliability has been shown to be the single most important aspect to many customers. Besides contributing to customer satisfaction or delight reliable service reduces the costs of redoing the service and can contribute to employee morale and enthusiasm (Berry and Parasuraman, 1991).

- **Assurance** stems from the knowledge and courtesy of employees and their facility to convey trust and confidence in their technical abilities. Customers want to be assured that the chef in the restaurant can cook without endangering their life, that the garage mechanic can fix the car, and that their accountant will not have them convicted for tax evasion. Assurance stems from professional competence. It is not enough, however, merely to have a high level of competence. It must also be demonstrated to the customers, often through the use of tangible cues.

- **Tangibles** are the appearance of physical features: equipment, personnel, reports, communications materials, and so on. Chartered accountants, for example, are critically aware of the impression their physical appearance creates with their clients. Care and attention is exercised when choosing company cars for partners and managers. Too expensive or luxurious a car might signal to clients that they are paying too high a fee for the services they are getting, while too cheap a car might signal that the firm is not particularly successful. Tangibles can be used in this way as indicators of professional competence.

- **Empathy** is the provision of caring, individualised attention to customers. It is the quality good doctors have of being able to convince patients that they really care about their welfare beyond addressing the current ailment. Empathy implies treating customers as individual clients and being concerned with their longer-term interests.

- **Responsiveness** is the ability of the organisation to react positively and in time to customer requests and requirements. Some businesses, such as Richardson

Sheffield Ltd which makes kitchen knives under the Laser brand, have built their positions on being more responsive to the customer than their competitors. The company claims to respond to written enquiries within the day, faxed enquiries within minutes, and telephone enquiries instantly. They can also provide samples of products the next working day, even to new specifications. In some markets instantaneous, or near-instantaneous, responsiveness is critical. In Japan, for example, a key factor for success in the elevator business is the speed with which faults are fixed as the Japanese hate to get stuck in a faulty lift! Responsiveness typically requires flexibility. Customer requests can often be off-beat, unexpected. The highly responsive organisation will need to predict where possible, but build into its systems and operations capacity to respond to the unpredictable.

These five main dimensions of service quality have been found in many different service situations, from banking to restaurants, construction to professional services (Parasuraman *et al.*, 1988). The relative importance of each might vary, and the way in which each is manifest in any situation will be different, but time and again these factors have been shown to be relevant to customers in their evaluation of the services they receive.

14.5 Measuring and monitoring customer satisfaction

A start to measuring customer satisfaction can be made through complaint and suggestion systems. These catch those highly dissatisfied customers who bother to complain. The problem, of course, is that it may be too late to retrieve the situation, though swift attention to customer problems has actually been shown to help bond closer relationships – what Berry and Parasuraman (1991) refer to as 'doing the service *very* right the second time' (see also Hart *et al.*, 1990).

For every dissatisfied customer who complains, however, it is estimated that around 12 others will be equally dissatisfied but not bother to complain. They will simply take their business elsewhere and may even tell others about their bad experiences (the 'well poisoners'). There is, therefore, a need for a more systematic assessment of customer satisfaction rather than sitting back and waiting for problems to emerge.

A more systematic approach is the use of regular customer satisfaction surveys, as now used by many service providers from railway companies to the leading international accounting firms. A four-step approach is typically adopted (Figure 14.6).

1 Identify the factors that are important to customers. These are not necessarily the same as the factors that managers think are important. Qualitative research techniques such as group discussions and depth interviews can be useful here. Depth interviews with the clients of a large accountancy firm showed that partners demonstrating that they really cared about the development of the client's business (showing empathy) was critical to building a long-term relationship.

2 Assess the relative importance of the factors identified and measure customer expectations on those factors. While some clients may expect their problems to

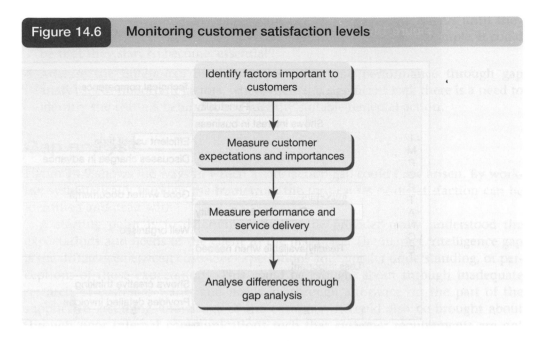

Figure 14.6   Monitoring customer satisfaction levels

Identify factors important to customers

↓

Measure customer expectations and importances

↓

Measure performance and service delivery

↓

Analyse differences through gap analysis

be dealt with immediately, others may have more relaxed expectations. While for some reliability may be paramount, for others cost could be more critical.

3 Assess performance of the service provider on the factors important to the clients. Here it can be useful to assess performance relative to expectations directly (Parasuraman *et al.*, 1994). Did performance live up to, fall short of, or exceed expectations? At this stage a useful summary can be made of the factors under consideration in a performance–importance matrix (Figure 14.7). Here the factors are plotted in terms of their importance to customers and the performance of the firm on them.

A typical example is shown in Figure 14.8 for a firm of chartered accountants (disguised data). The evaluations were made by a client, a finance director of a

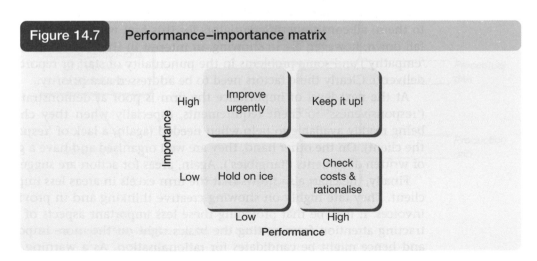

Figure 14.7   Performance–importance matrix

	Low Performance	High Performance
High Importance	Improve urgently	Keep it up!
Low Importance	Hold on ice	Check costs & rationalise

could typically be caused by resource constraints, where a service provider is too stretched to provide the service he or she knows the customer expects. Rather than increase the resource, or admit that the expected service cannot be provided, the service provider attempts to get as close as possible to customer expectations.

Even where the service specification is closely aligned to customer expectations there is a possibility that the actual service delivered falls short. The production gap is the difference between the service specification and the service that is actually delivered to the customer. There are a number of reasons why there may be a gap here. First, the service design might be so complex as to make accurate delivery unlikely. Service promises may be unrealistic given the resources put into them. Response times planned for telephone enquiries, for example, may be unrealistic given the number of staff available to answer the phone or the number of lines available to take the calls. Second, staff may not have the skills or the systems back-up to deliver the service as specified. Poor employee training, poor technology provision or even inadequate internal communications can result in frustrated employees unable to deliver the service as specified to the customer. Third, a major problem in service provision is the very heterogeneity of services. The quality of service can vary from employee to employee, and from time to time for the same employee. Quality control systems are more difficult to implement in services than in manufacturing; they can be no less important, however.

The final gap that can lead to a satisfaction gap is the perceptual gap. Here it may be that the service has been delivered to specification and that the specification was in tune with customer expectations, but that the client, for one reason or another, does not believe the service has been delivered as expected. This could be brought about through poor use of tangible cues, lack of reinforcement of delivery, poor delivery manner or through the intercession of external influencers. In many ways a perceptual gap is the easiest to rectify. It requires the service provider to demonstrate to the client that the service really has been delivered to original expectations.

Summary

This chapter has examined the recent recognition by many companies that successful positioning is increasingly about creating ongoing relationships with selected target customers rather than relying on more sporadic transactions. Relationship marketing seeks to build longer-term relationships with selected customers, moving them up the relationship marketing ladder from customers to clients to supporters to advocates and ultimately, where applicable, to partners. A major factor in creating longer-term relationships is the provision of superior service, beyond original customer expectations.

Customer satisfaction monitoring is suggested as a means of assessing the quality of the service offered. Where there is a gap between expectations and customer evaluations of the service provided, a systematic gap analysis can be used to identify and eliminate the causes.

Pret a Manger Case Study

Getty Images News

Julian Metcalfe asks how often I 'go to eat in the fast food industry'. He makes it sound like a slightly seedy activity, which is odd coming from the co-founder of Pret a Manger, which, for all its classy, freshly prepared sandwiches, is indisputably a fast food chain – one, moreover, part-owned by McDonald's.

I eat fast food almost every day, I tell him – lunch for me usually being a sandwich at my desk. He probes a little further. 'But would you go to the very inexpensive Mexican places or Burger King? No.' It is time to get the awkwardness over. I think Pret is very good and its staff are unfailingly friendly but the nearest branch is a fair walk from the office. So, I tell him, I buy my lunch from Eat, Pret's fierce rival, which is just next to the FT.

Metcalfe looks downcast. 'Right. The fundamental difference between Eat and us is that their food is made in a big depot, a factory, and then it's shipped around the country. It's quite an efficient system, I should think.' Efficient? 'Quite efficient, yeah. I'm sure accountants would like it.'

Pret's food is all made on the premises, each branch putting together its own sandwiches, sushi boxes and salads. I concede that Pret probably has the edge over Eat – although I doubt I would be able to tell the difference in a blind tasting. Metcalfe sharply assures me that I would. His management team have no problem picking out their own food in blind tastings. So they bring in their competitor's food to compare? 'All the time. If we don't win hands-down, we'll freak out.

We'd have people practically commit hara-kiri.' The last time they did a blind tasting, he says, 'our brownie won five stars. Eat's brownie got no star.'

We are talking in a windowless room at Pret's head office at the side of Victoria Station, just near where Metcalfe and Sinclair Beecham, a fellow chartered surveyor, launched their first branch of Pret 21 years ago – spurred on by their frustration at not being able to buy a decent sandwich in London. It took them five years to get the formula right. Today there are 163 Pret branches in the UK and 11 in New York. Pret also has 11 restaurants in Hong Kong and one in Singapore. The business generated total sales of £193m last year. Beecham remains a non-executive director and he and Metcalfe jointly own the majority of shares in the company. But Beecham, who has gone into the hotel business, is no longer involved in day-to-day management, whereas Metcalfe is there every day, as creative director.

Creative director sounds like an advertising agency job rather than a food industry one. In fact, the 47-year-old Metcalfe, with his dark suit, white open-necked shirt and fashionably boxy glasses, could pass for an ad man. What does Pret's creative director actually do? 'The creative director title was given to me, or I took it on, about four or five years ago. I believe that creativity plays a huge role in what we do at Pret – creativity with regard to the food, the packaging, the design of the stores, the way people are hired and motivated and trained.' He is also there, he says, 'to stand back and try and help the CEO and other directors'.

On cue, the door opens and Clive Schlee, Pret's chief executive, peers in. 'Are you in full flow?' he asks. 'Come in, join us,' Metcalfe says. We are talking about how Metcalfe interacts with you, I tell Schlee, who is wearing the same dark suit–white shirt combination as his creative director.

What appears to excite Metcalfe most, though, is the nitty-gritty of food making. 'I like the detail of Pret,' he says. 'You have to enjoy redoing the carrot cake 50 times.' Once a year, Pret head office closes for three or four days and everyone heads off to work in one of the restaurants. Metcalfe's last stint was in London's Fleet Street. 'I was in my jeans, in my cap, in my white shirt, getting to grips with the difficulty of putting a warm chocolate croissant on the tray. Anyone can put a bad chocolate croissant from the oven on to a tray, but our chocolate croissants, we bake them in the shop, they are warm, and I can assure you they're kept warm. The only way you really get to grips with that is by doing it yourself, reminding yourself how difficult it is to bake a croissant perfectly, how easy the instructions are, how easy it is to open the box.'

If customers are unhappy, Metcalfe says, he hears about it. 'We have a customer service department, and if you were to ring up today saying I've just bought an avocado wrap and there's too much salt and I'm very angry and I want to speak to Julian Metcalfe, I guarantee you'll be put through to me without a quibble. You try and do that now to British Airways on a £4,000 ticket. Go on. Say there was some chewing gum on my seat and I want to speak to the managing director of British Airways. You'll never get through.'

Metcalfe says Pret does no customer service training. So how does he persuade his staff to be so friendly? Potential recruits are assessed for the quality of their English, their warmth, their right to work in the UK and what Metcalfe calls their 'Pretability'. Those who get past those barriers do a day's paid work in a Pret branch, after which the staff are asked what they think of them. If the staff like them, they will get a job offer. (Schlee proudly tells me that his nephew tried out for a job, incognito, and the staff turned him down.)

There is not much to the Pret corporate structure apart from customer service and recruitment. There is no marketing department. Pret does no advertising. It also has no public relations department to prepare Metcalfe for interviews, which is why he is fretting about a book he was supposed to mention to me. What book? 'The Pret book,' Metcalfe says. What Pret book? 'The recipe book.' Fortunately, I have seen the book of Pret recipes on display in the restaurant I popped into that morning for research purposes.

The publisher, Murdoch Books, had told him he would be speaking to a journalist about the book. Metcalfe thought that was me. And it wasn't, I tell him. 'No, but I don't mind,' he says. 'I mean, after my gaffe the other day.' The 'gaffe' was telling a journalist that Pret was considering a stock exchange listing. It all happened by accident, Metcalfe explains. The journalist, who was there to talk about the book, said how good it would be to able to buy shares in Pret and Metcalfe recalls saying: 'Oh, one day, maybe.' After which, all the papers excitedly reported that Pret was considering a listing and speculated on how much money Metcalfe might make out of it. He is philosophical about the fuss he caused. 'Suddenly, this thing: Pret floats. It doesn't really matter.'

But it might matter. He seems to be considering it. 'It's being considered. It may take some time. I don't know.' The company will talk about it next month and then in July. Why do it? Well, Pret might want to expand more quickly, he says. 'In our three-year plan, we're talking about going into Boston in 2009 or 2010. There's no doubt we could have three or four stores built in Boston and they would work, but this takes money.' Also, he is not averse to realising some of his 21-year investment. 'I don't want to die with all my shares wrapped up in Pret.'

Wouldn't a listing change the way Pret operated? Wouldn't investors think it more efficient and profitable to make food centrally rather than in each restaurant? 'As long as we go on pleasing our customers, the financial industry is not silly. They're very smart. All we need are customers who care about what they eat and if we look after our customers, we'll be fine,' Metcalfe says.

The last time people speculated about Pret floating, in 2001, it sold a one-third stake to McDonald's for £50m instead. 'We got them in to learn how on earth you build an infrastructure which works internationally. At the time we did the deal with McDonald's, we'd just opened a shop in New York but we were pretty scared. It's all very well two young entrepreneurs thinking they can make a difference to food in New York but, let's face it, Sinclair and I knew perfectly well it was going to be hard. McDonald's at that stage had 30,000 places, I think, worldwide, so they had an infrastructure. In Asia, they really helped us legally: property, law, building, everything. We couldn't have done it without them.'

How did he feel when people accused Pret of selling its soul? 'From a PR point of view, it probably wasn't the smartest move but we knew we were in charge of our recipes. We knew we were in charge of the destiny of the food and our staff.'

Pret is not Metcalfe's only business. Together with Schlee, he owns Itsu, a small chain of Japanese restaurants, run along similar lines to Pret. When the FT asked Metcalfe about Itsu last September, he refused to talk about it, saying: 'The higher the monkey climbs the tree, the more you see of its arse.'

But Itsu soon got more publicity than Metcalfe ever wanted, and it happened in the cruellest way. When Alexander Litvinenko, the former Russian spy, was poisoned last November, police initially thought – incorrectly, as it turned out – that he had swallowed his fatal dose of polonium-210 at Itsu in London's Piccadilly. 'We were rung up by the police in the middle of the night and told to be there,' Metcalfe says. 'It was horrible for the staff because they had to endure a week of not knowing whether they were ill or not. As it turned out . . . they were given the all-clear.'

Metcalfe is disappointed that I have never eaten at Itsu and Schlee is deputed to take me there for lunch. We walk through Pret's vast open-plan office, where the windows overlook the Victoria Station platforms and where staff work under large banners decorated with the Pret logo and improving exhortations from the likes of Abraham Lincoln, Martin Luther King and Andy Warhol. (Andy Warhol? Yes, he apparently said: 'They always say that time changes things, but you actually have to change them yourself.')

As Schlee and I stroll past Buckingham Palace and through Green Park, he says what I had already been thinking: how un-English the old Harrovian Metcalfe seems. Schlee is talking about Metcalfe's directness. I was thinking about the unembarrassed way Metcalfe says things such as, 'It's about being inclusive and about hope,' or, 'I think as human beings we need to be able to know we're making a difference.'

Itsu Piccadilly is heaving with customers. Schlee takes me and my sushi box to a quieter table downstairs. The food is excellent. As we re-emerge on to Piccadilly, Schlee informs me that we had just sat at Litvinenko's table. I suppress my momentary queasiness by telling myself the place would not be open if the authorities hadn't declared it safe, that the staff who were there six months ago hadn't been affected, and that Schlee would hardly have sat at the same table if he thought there was the slightest danger. No, I persuade myself, this was just Metcalfe and Schlee wanting to show off their food and not some devilish punishment devised for people who eat at Eat.

Source: Michael Skapinker, 'Thinking outside the sandwich box', *The Financial Times*, 19 May 2007.

Discussion questions

1 How can 'customer service' be a differentiator in the service industry?

2 How does Pret use the three Ss of customer service to improve customer satisfaction? What else could they do?

3 If the company does expand more quickly, how can the managers ensure they maintain customer service? Should they reconsider having a marketing department?

part five

Implementing the Strategy

Part 5 looks at several of the topical and relevant issues which are emerging in marketing practice concerned with the challenges of implementing or executing marketing strategies. We have featured here two areas not extensively covered in earlier editions of the book: the management of strategic customer relationships through sales and account management methods (Chapter 15), and the topical question of corporate social responsibility and its link to competitive positioning and advantage (Chapter 18). The logic for these additional points of focus is that these are topics proving of substantial and growing significance to the shaping and implementation of marketing strategy.

In the earlier parts of the book, we have provided extensive coverage of the analytical and theoretical underpinning of marketing strategy: planning market-led strategy; analysis of the competitive marketplace and organisational capabilities; and market segmentation and competitive positioning. However, the focus now changes from the *content* of strategy to the *context* – the organisational and environmental realities in which marketing strategy must be put into effect. Nonetheless, the conventional dichotomising of strategy and implementation is largely unproductive. Both issues are interdependent parts of the same process of strategic development and market performance. It is also intriguing that, in each area of strategy context that we examine, there are both challenges and obstacles for executives to meet, and also, importantly, new opportunities to compete more effectively and develop new types of competitive advantage.

Chapter 15 is concerned with strategic customer management. The focus here is the strategic role of the sales organisation and the development of strategic account management approaches to handle relationships with large, powerful, dominant business-to-business customers. We examine the role of strategic sales capabilities in managing business-to-business customer relationships and the evolution of the strategic sales organisation to enhance and apply these new types of capabilities. Strategic customer management is concerned both with the strategic management of investment of resources in different parts of the customer portfolio and, relatedly, with the management of relationships with strategic customers. Very large (or, more strictly, very important) customers provide the domain of strategic account management – moving from transactional and relationship marketing approaches to major accounts towards the partnering with a small number of key accounts. This strategy has potential gains in locking in relationships with the most dominant customers in the portfolio, but also carries substantial risks from dependence and customer opportunism, which should be carefully weighed. Nonetheless, strategic account management approaches are highly topical and a balanced case should be established prior to making decisions and commitments.

Our concern with key external dependencies continues in Chapter 16, which examines the role of alliances and networks in marketing strategy as the organisational forms developed by many organisations to take their strategies to market. Environment change and complexity has heralded for many organisations an era of strategic collaboration. We examine the drivers of collaboration strategies and the types of networks, alliances and partnerships which result. Our emphasis is on the emergence in many sectors of alliances as the way in which we compete, but we also underline the risks in strategic alliances. Competing through strategic alliances offers many potential benefits, but requires that attention be given to the underlying rationale and priorities for collaboration and investment of effort in managing and appraising alliances, which pose quite different challenges to conventional organisational structures.

Chapter 17 turns explicit attention to strategy implementation and internal marketing, where our focus is more on key internal dependencies than external ones. We review the sources of the continuing implementation or execution challenges in marketing, and examine internal marketing as a set of tools, or a template, for structuring and managing the implementation process. The development and scope of internal marketing has been associated with enhancing service quality, improving internal communications, innovation management, and internal markets, but our focus is on internal marketing as a parallel to external marketing, which focuses on the organisational and behavioural changes required to effectively implement strategy. A particularly vital purpose of strategic internal marketing is achieving cross-functional collaboration and seamlessness in delivering value to customers.

Chapter 18 focuses on the rapidly emerging area of corporate social responsibility, and its impact on the ways organisations must adapt to new societal demands, but also how it is creating new areas to consider in developing different kinds of competitive strength. This chapter is concerned with an important linkage between external and internal dependencies. At one level, attention to corporate social responsibility concerns is mandated by customer pressures, both in consumer and business-to-business markets. However, a fuller consideration of the scope of corporate citizenship suggests that the drivers of social responsibility go much further than moral obligation and are linked to the ability of companies to compete effectively. We look at defensive social responsibility initiatives in responding to competitor and customer pressures. However, what emerges is a view of corporate social responsibility as a route to competitive advantage. This view emphasises a strategic perspective on social responsibilities, where a social dimension becomes part of the company's value proposition to its customers. The goal becomes not altruism for its own importance, but the combination of business and social benefits. It is likely that this challenge will be extremely important to management thinking in the current business environment.

Strategic customer management

15

Irresistible new forces are reshaping the world of selling. Sales functions everywhere are in the early stages of radical and profound changes comparable to those that began to transform manufacturing 20 years ago. . . . The meaning of selling itself is changing. The very purpose of sales is being rapidly redefined.

Rackham and DeVincentis (1999)

Today's competitive environment demands a radically different approach. Specifically, the ability of firms to exploit the true potential of the sales organization requires that company executives adopt a new mindset about the role of the selling function within the firm, how the sales force is managed, and what salespeople are expected to produce. The sales function must serve as a dynamic source of value creation and innovation within the firm.

The Sales Educators (2006)

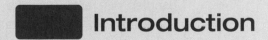 **Introduction**

This chapter is an innovation for the current edition of this book. Interestingly, it is relatively rare for books concerned with marketing strategy to pay much attention to issues concerning the salesforce or strategic account management structures. The view has generally been that marketing executives and business planners make strategic decisions, and create value through product and brand innovation, while sales and account management are really concerned only with the implementation of the plans created by strategic decision-makers. However, this oversimplified view of the world does not stand up to the scrutiny of managers who have to develop and implement strategy in the complex and highly competitive conditions that characterise most business-to-business situations. It is illustrative that a growing number of companies are making appointments such as director of strategic customer management, or strategic customer manager.

The ability of organisations to achieve superiority in how they manage customer relationships to create value and to sustain profitable relationships is increasingly recognised as a core capability – a capability which has been largely ignored in the literature of marketing strategy (Piercy, 2006). This chapter seeks to explain why the sales organisation and related account management activities should form an important element in considering the development of marketing strategy – and they certainly define important implementation capabilities (see Chapter 17). Many marketing strategy implementation failures are explained by the poor alignment of strategy with sales capabilities. Sales capabilities provide a critical resource which differentiates suppliers from each other in the eyes of professional purchasers.

First, we examine the factors which should encourage executives to re-examine the salesforce as a strategic capability, and the marketplace demands which are reinforcing these efforts. Then we examine the notion of the strategic sales organisation – the new forms of organising the front-line resources that impact on customer relationships and deliver superiority in customer value.

This brings us to the issue of 'strategic customer management'. Our logic is that in the same way that companies have come to recognise the strategic aspects of operations management (for example, in total quality deployment, and business process re-engineering initiatives), and in supply chain management (rather than simpler notions of transportation and warehousing), then there is now an increasing priority for a strategic perspective on the management of customer relationships.

There are two aspects of strategic customer management. The first relates to the strategic management of the customer portfolio – making investment choices between different types of customer to deliver the goals of marketing strategy, but also to shape that strategy. The second aspect relates to the management of strategic customers – building relationships with the dominant customers in the company's portfolio, some of which may be classified as strategic accounts and handled differently from the rest. These are important strategic decisions which impact directly on the profitability and risk profile of the company's business.

15.1 Priorities for identifying strategic sales capabilities

To begin, we examine the factors that are encouraging executives in many major organisations to re-examine the role of salesforce capabilities in the context of developing and implementing marketing strategy. This is an important starting point in understanding the potential role of strategic customer management approaches to enhancing the development and implementation of strategy.

Traditional views were that marketing and sales should be considered separate entities in the organisation because, according to Levitt, 'Selling focuses on the needs of the seller; marketing on the needs of the buyer' (Levitt, 1960). The conventional subordination of marketing (strategic) from sales (tactical) was elaborated by statements like Drucker's view that 'the aim of marketing is to make selling superfluous' (Drucker, 1973). However, it should be noted that Levitt was writing almost 50 years ago, and Drucker more than 30 years, underlining the risk that their views may have dated somewhat. It is worth considering the following issues in reaching a view about the strategic significance of sales capabilities in a particular company situation.

15.1.1   Customer relationships

Clearly, in many companies channels development has included the establishment of direct channels, such as those based around Internet websites – even in consumer marketing, by 2007 10 per cent of all retail spending took place on the Internet (Rigby, 2007), and this figure is much higher for many business-to-business sellers. At the same time, there is a growing trend towards the outsourcing to third parties of routine sales operations (Anderson and Trinkle, 2005) – while in the US Procter & Gamble has a 200-person team wholly dedicated to Wal-Mart (the single customer that constitutes 20 per cent of P&G's business), it is relatively easy for P&G to outsource routine sales visits to stores to a third-party sales organisation. Similarly, global corporate expenditure on customer relationship management (CRM) technology is measured each year in billions of dollars, and individual spends by companies can be in tens of millions of dollars. CRM explicitly aims to automate many of the functions traditionally associated with the salesforce.

However, this leaves the vital issue of whether a company's most important business-to-business customer relationships can really be managed to full advantage through a website, a third-party seller, or a call centre. Consider, for example, that Home Depot in the USA has asked many suppliers, including Black & Decker, to pull back from their more extreme Internet strategies, or risk losing the Home Depot business (Friedman, 2002). Answering this question is important to understanding the strategic role of sales for a company, rather than considering only the routine activities involved in taking and processing orders, For instance, Dell Computers is an Internet-based company – the majority of sales and service provisions are on the web. Nonetheless, Dell maintains both account executives in the field and internal salespeople in branches, because the view is that the technology exists to free salespeople to sell and develop customer relationships, not to process orders (which the technology generally does better and more cheaply).

There is a substantial business and competitive risk in underestimating the role of the salesforce in defending and sustaining a competitive position. Consider the case of a $210 million manufacturer of specialty industrial lubricants, based in Atlanta. Expecting in an Internet-enabled world that the 400-person salesforce would be increasingly irrelevant, the company spent $16 million on its website, e-portals, call centres and an integrated CRM system. When the new sales model went live, the anticipated 35 per cent sales increase in sales turned out to be an 18 per cent decline, with falling margins (largely because of the cost of the new Internet infrastructure). In addition, nearly a third of the salesforce resigned in just over a year (including 17 of the top 20 salespeople), because there was a general feeling that there was no point in staying to compete with the new website, after spending years developing personal relationships with their customers. There had been no customer involvement in developing the new sales model – the company had not bothered to ask customers how they wanted to do business. When asked, customers identified this company's only real competitive advantage as the expertise of the salesforce and their ability to design solutions to solve technical problems for customers. The new sales model deploys salesperson expertise in the specification and design phases, and in negotiating prices and terms, and uses the web for routine repeat purchases and order tracking, and the competitive situation is being retrieved (Friedman, 2002).

Understanding and enhancing the ways in which sales resources add value and protect customer relationships is becoming of strategic importance in markets being driven towards commoditisation (see below). To the extent that a marketing strategy depends upon strong and sustained customer relationships, there is an implicit reliance on sales capabilities. To the extent that a salesforce has built and sustains strong customer relationships by creating value for customers, this provides a strategic resource for the company, which should impact on strategic choices.

15.1.2 Customer sophistication and complexity

The growing sophistication and aggressiveness of purchasers in business-to-business markets has escalated the strategic importance of effectively managing buyer–seller relationships (Jones *et al.*, 2005). The challenge to the seller is to implement effective marketing strategy in a dramatically changed world of sophisticated buyers (Shapiro *et al.*, 1998). This change is underlined by the shift in the traditional role played by purchasing functions in customer organisations. Increasingly, purchasing has become a strategic function linked to the customer's strategic plans, with a major level of responsibility for profitability, cost control and enhanced shareholder value (Janda and Sheshandri, 2001).

When professional purchasing managers use complex sourcing metrics to select the 'right' suppliers, and to dictate terms on how they will be supplied, more than ever before supplier profitability is determined at the point of sale, where the sales organisation meets the customer (De Boer *et al.*, 2001; Talluri and Narasimhan, 2004). Correspondingly, the sales task has become much more complex and the stakes have become much higher.

Sellers in business-to-business markets increasingly face much more complex decisions about their marketing and sales investments in customer relationships. Historically, seller profits were generally in line with account size, because prices tended to be cost-based, sales costs were relatively low, and the size of accounts did not vary dramatically. However, consolidation by merger and acquisition and attrition has changed this situation in many markets. In industrial markets, sales situations are increasingly characterised by fewer, larger and more complex purchasing organisations, and in consumer markets there has been a massive shift in power to retailers (Shapiro *et al.*, 1998). Unsurprisingly, very large customers are powerful and demand customised sales and account management, and are challenging in terms of profitability for the supplier. Other customers also demand special treatment, but it is likely to be different. Small and medium-sized accounts require yet more different approaches, mainly because of the cost of serving them. The strategic challenge is to match sales efforts and approaches to different parts of a complex portfolio of customers, to balance revenue and profitability with business risk. These choices impact substantially on corporate performance.

These market trends have elevated the importance of the effective deployment of sales capabilities to a strategic issue. In particular, we will develop the themes of the customer portfolio and the impact of dominant customers as the chapter develops.

15.1.3 Commoditisation

One impact of the revolutions that have taken place in operations management and supply chain design has been to reduce product and service differentiation in many sectors. Competing products are frequently built to near-identical modularised platforms, and supply chains are designed for maximum speed and lowest cost. Benchmarking systems encourage suppliers to achieve similar performance against the same metrics. It is unsurprising that the result is growth in product similarity rather than differentiation.

In parallel, customer organisations increasingly pursue aggressive commoditisation strategies with their suppliers – if all competitive offerings are essentially similar, then differentiation can only be achieved through price, because that is how commodities are sold. This is a preferred situation for the purchaser, but not usually for the seller. The chief purchasing officer's modern armoury includes: RFPs (request for proposal or an invitation to suppliers to bid for business on a specific product or service); internet auctions; purchasing consultants; and buying consortiums. These mechanisms all seek to reduce purchasing to a comparison of prices and specificiations. The challenge to sellers is to constantly expand the scope and value of the offering to the customer, and the impact of the offering on the customer's business performance. Achieving differentiation with strategic customers requires new types of buyer–seller relationships that assist customers in implementing their own strategies. This underlines the need for the sales organisation to take a more strategic and less tactical role in developing and implementing business and marketing strategy.

It may be that the sales/customer interface is the place where competitive differentiation is actually achieved. Indeed, research by the US consultancy H.R. Chally suggests that salesperson effectiveness accounts for as much as 40 per cent of business-to-business customer choice of supplier, because technology has made products increasingly substitutable (Stephens, 2003).

15.1.4 Corporate expenditure

It is worth recalling also that corporate expenditure on sales operations exceeds that on higher profile advertising and sales promotion activities. Figures can only be estimated, but 2000 levels of UK expenditure on personal selling by British companies is estimated at £20 billion, compared with £13 billion on advertising and £14 billion on sales promotion (Doyle, 2002). Indeed, it is also clear that sales activities are frequently among the most expensive in the marketing budget. US survey data suggest that in 2005 the average salary for salespeople was approximately $130,000, while high performers averaged almost $160,000. Survey participants expected sales salaries to continue to increase (Galea, 2006). Research in the US finds that, while in some sectors companies spend as little as 1 per cent of sales on their salesforce (e.g. banking, hotels), the average company spends 10 per cent of sales revenue on the salesforce, and some spend as much as 22 per cent (e.g. printing and publishing) (Dartnell, 1999). Indeed, it is not uncommon for sustained salesforce costs to be as high as 50 per cent of sales (Zoltners *et al.*, 2004).

In addition, the sales function employs more people and in many companies is a much larger function than marketing. Interestingly, estimates in both the UK and the USA suggest that sales employment is expected to increase up to 2010. The 'death of the salesman' forecast as a result of the expansion in Internet marketing and other direct channels appears to have been somewhat exaggerated.

The expenditure levels and the growth in employment suggest that managers are likely to continue asking questions about the full utilisation of these resources to add value to the company. Indeed, evidence in the US suggests that many senior managers are dissatisfied with the productivity of their sales organisations, and many see salesforce costs poorly aligned with strategic goals (Deloitte Touche, 2005). These indications support the view that the sales organisation will become a substantially higher priority issue for strategic decision-makers. However, notwithstanding the cost of the salesforce, the changing role of the sales organisation is driven by more than cost, and reflects the power of salesforce capabilities to change a company's competitive position for the better or for the worse.

15.2 The new and emerging competitive role for sales

This section draws on Piercy, 2006.

Writing in *Harvard Business Review*, Thomas Stewart summarises the new and emerging role for the sales organisation in the following terms:

> . . . *Selling is changing fast and in such a way that sales teams have become strategic resources. When corporations strive to become customer focused, salespeople move to the foreground; engineers recede. As companies go to market with increasingly complex bundles of products and services, their representatives cease to be mere order takers (most orders are placed online, anyway) and become relationship managers.*
>
> (Stewart, 2006b)

Understanding the evolution of the sales organisation, and the strategic capability it represents, and the forces shaping this capability, has become an important issue for strategic decision-makers.

15.2.1 The evolution of the sales organisation to strategic importance

There is little doubt that the role of the sales organisation has gone through major changes in many companies in recent years, and it is likely that this change process will continue and escalate. However, what should not be underestimated is the extent to which such changes are increasingly radical and disruptive to traditional business models and theories (Shapiro *et al.*, 1998).

For example, in identifying priorities for sales in 2001, Thomas Leigh and Greg Marshall wrote that 'The sales function is undergoing an unparalleled metamorphosis, driven by the plethora of changing conditions' (Leigh and Marshall, 2001). They suggested that this metamorphosis was seeing the selling function shift its role from selling products and services to one emphasising 'increased customer productivity' through enhanced revenues or cost advantage. They support the transformation of the traditional sales function to a pan-company activity or process, driven by market pressures: 'customers indicate that the seller's organisation must embrace a customer-driven culture that wholeheartedly supports the sales force.' Interestingly, they also underline the parallel between the transformation of the sales organisation and other company-wide marketing developments, such as: market orientation (Jaworski *et al.*, 1993), market-oriented organisational culture (Homburg and Plesser, 2000), and marketing as a cross-functional process rather than a functional department (Workman *et al.*, 1998).

A further analysis suggests that 'the sales function is in the midst of a renaissance – a genuine rebirth and revival. Progressive firms are becoming more strategic in their approaches to the sales function . . . Enlightened firms view their customers as assets, and are entrusting their salespeople to management of these assets' (Ingram *et al.*, 2002). These authors call for joint action by sales managers, educators, trainers, consultants and professional organisations to improve the conceptualisation and practice of sales management. Certainly, there appears growing consensus that traditional approaches will fail, and that 'The shaping of the selling function has become a strategic corporate issue', requiring clarity about the new sales role, new structures and new management approaches (Shapiro *et al.*, 1998).

Many suggest that the revolution has already arrived, even if marketing executives (and educators) have yet to notice. One British commentator has suggested that 'sales functions are in the early stages of a transformation comparable to that which reshaped manufacturing 20 years ago (Mazur, 2000). The evolution of the sales organisation is already becoming apparent in studies of marketing organisations and there is growing evidence of the expanding influence of sales over strategic decisions. For example, there are research findings that the sales department has more influence than the marketing department on many so-called 'marketing' decisions (Krohmer *et al.*, 2002), and that 'primary marketing coordinators increasingly reside in sales rather than the marketing organization' (Homburg *et al.*, 2000), while sales plays a growing role in formulating as well as executing marketing strategies (Cross *et al.*, 2001). In fact, even the success of marketing initiatives like market orientation may depend in large part on the sales organisation – for example, one study shows the impact of market orientation on performance to be fully mediated by the adoption of customer-oriented selling by the salesforce (Langerak, 2001). Similarly, the sales organisation may have a decisive influence on shaping the direction of new product innovation through the intelligence they collect and interpret (Lambert *et al.*, 1990), and on assessing and accessing targeted key market segments (Maier and Saunders, 1990).

These arguments suggest that there is an urgent need in many companies to consider the transformation of the traditional sales organisation and its more strategic role.

15.2.2 Shaping forces for the new sales organisation

The sales organisation has for some time been under powerful company and customer forces that have reshaped its role and operation (Jones *et al.*, 2005). The forces acting to reshape the sales function in organisations are summarised in Figure 15.1. As we have already seen, the implementation of new types of marketing strategy requires the realignment of sales processes with the strategy. At the same time, multi-channelling and the growth in Internet-based direct channels are substituting for many traditional sales activities.

Perhaps most telling in business-to-business marketing has been the dramatic escalation in the demands for enhanced service and added value by customers. For example, the H.R. Challey consultancy's *World Class Sales Excellent Research Report* (2006) reports the views of corporate purchasers and their expectations for the relationship with the salesperson from a supplier as follows:

1 **Be personally accountable for our desired results** – the sales contact with the supplier is expected to be committed to the customer and accountable for achievement.

2 **Understand our business** – to be able to add value, the supplier must understand the customer's competencies, strategies, challenges and organisational culture.

3 **Be on our side** – the salesperson must be the customer's advocate in his/her own organisation, and operate through the policies and politics to focus on the customer's needs.

4 **Design the right applications** – the salesperson is expected to think beyond technical features and functions to the implementation of the product or service in the customer's environment, thinking beyond the transaction to the customer's end state.

5 **Be easily accessible** – customers expect salespeople to be constantly connected and within reach.

Figure 15.1   Forces acting on the sales organisation

6 **Solve our problems** – customers no longer buy products or services; they buy solutions to their business problems, and expect salespeople to diagnose, prescribe, and resolve their issues, not just sell them products.

7 **Be creative in responding to our needs** – buyers expect salespeople to be innovators, who bring them new ideas to solve problems, so creativity is a major source of added value.

These qualities characterise how world-class salesforces are distinguished in the eyes of their customers. They describe a customer environment which is radically different from the transactional approaches of the past, and which poses substantially different management challenges in managing business-to-business customer relationships. However, at the same time, business constraints in seller organisations suggest that in most companies there is considerable pressure to reduce costs and enhance productivity in the salesforce.

While the ways in which traditional sales organisations are likely to transform to meet these contrasting forces to reshape will vary considerably between different industrial and commercial sectors, one way of integrating the outcomes in general terms is in a model of the strategic sales organisation.

15.3 The strategic sales organisation

The importance of strategic customer relationships mandates a strategic response from sales and account management. The strategic sales organisation is an attempt to capture the range of changes which may transform the traditional sales organisation into a strategic force, impacting on the ability to implement marketing strategy, but also providing leadership in the shaping of that strategy.

The bulk of attention given to the sales and account management area in the past has been largely concerned with tactical and operational issues, and has failed to adopt a strategic perspective on the management of customer relationships. Interestingly, similar comments would have applied in the operations and supply chain strategies prior to the revolutions in thinking and practice experienced by those disciplines in the 1990s and early 2000s. We suggest that the sales and account management field is in the early stage of a similar and related revolution, characterised by a shift in approach from tactical to strategic. There can be little further doubt that, as Shapiro and his colleagues at Harvard have asserted, once again 'Sales is a boardroom topic' (1998), and that the strategic sales organisation is positioned on the top management agenda in many organisations.

However, the new processes and structures needed to enhance and sustain value delivery to customers through the sales organisation are likely to require careful evaluation and appraisal that extends to domains far beyond those traditionally associated with selling activities (Ogbuchi and Sharma, 1999). To support this analysis and to provide a framework for management action, we propose the framework shown in Figure 15.2 and identify several tools for practical application.

The framework we propose suggests the following imperatives for management focus:

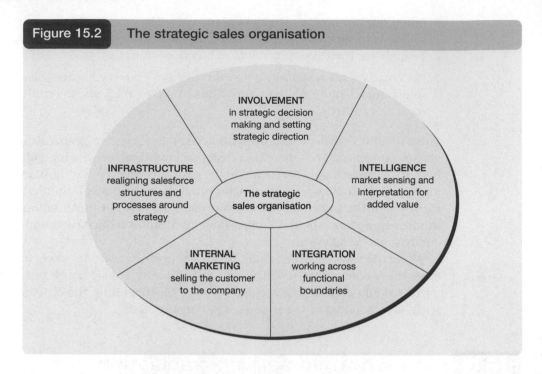

Figure 15.2   The strategic sales organisation

- **Involvement** – placing the sales organisation in the centre of the business and marketing strategy debate in companies, and aligning sales operations with strategic direction.

- **Intelligence** – building customer knowledge as a strategic resource critical both to strategy formulation and to building added-value strategies with major customers.

- **Integration** – establishing cross-functional relationships necessary to lead the processes which define, develop and deliver superior value propositions to customers, and managing the interfaces between functions and business units impacting on service and value as it is perceived by customers.

- **Internal marketing** – using sales resources to 'sell' the customer across functional and divisional boundaries within the company and across organisational boundaries with partner companies, to achieve seamless value delivery.

- **Infrastructure** – developing the structure and processes needed to manage sales and account management organisations to match customer relationship requirements and to build competitive advantage.

15.3.1   Involvement in strategic decision making

As customer demands for superior seller relationships continue to evolve and escalate, a distinct new role is becoming critical in selling organisations – the strategic management of the relationship with the customer. While harsh economic conditions and the search for competitive edge mandate cost reductions to increase margins, sales revenues and profits are derived not only from finding new customers and sales channels, but also from growing relationships with existing customers and sales channels. However, conventionally, sales organisations manage customers for short-term revenues, which in highly competitive markets often results in declining margins and commoditisation (Lombardi, 2005). Underpinning a strategic response to radical market change is the challenge of repositioning sales as a core part of the company's competitiveness, where the sales organisation is closely integrated into marketing strategy (Stephens, 2003).

Involvement of the sales organisation in strategy has two aspects. The first strategic sales issue is concerned with developing a perspective on the sales organisation which does not focus simply on the tactical management of transactional sales processes, but examines the relationships formed with different types of customers as the basis for long-term business development (Olson *et al.*, 2001). This implies a new appraisal of the activities and processes required to enhance and sustain value delivery to customers through the sales organisation. It is also increasingly the case that major customers require a highly specific value proposition built around 'unique value' for the customer. Nonetheless, different customers have different value requirements, for example: intrinsic value buyers, who require transactional selling; extrinsic value buyers, who require consultative selling; and strategic value buyers, who require enterprise selling (Rackham and Vincentis, 1999).

The second strategic sales issue is concerned with the role of sales and account management in interpreting the customer environment as a basis for strategic decisions. As the costs of dealing with major customers continue to increase, companies face major choices in where they choose to invest resources in developing a customer relationship, and where they choose not to invest. With large customers in particular, the risks in investment or disinvestment are high, and it likely that the intelligence-gathering and market sensing capabilities of the sales and account organisation will play a growing role in influencing strategic decisions about resource allocation in the customer portfolio. The shift in thinking required is from the tactical management of sales transactions to focus on the relationships formed in different ways with different types of customers as the basis for long-term business development (Olson *et al.*, 2001). We will consider below the customer portfolio as a tool for surfacing these issues.

15.3.2 Intelligence to add value

One clear and repeated demand by corporate buyers is that salespeople should demonstrate deep knowledge of the customer's business, such that they can identify needs and opportunities before the buyer does (H.R. Chally, 2006). The deployment of such superior knowledge and expertise is a defining characteristic of the world-class sales organisation, in the buyer's eyes. The buyer logic is straightforward: if the seller cannot bring added value to the relationship by identifying new opportunities for the buyer to gain competitive advantage in the end-use marketplace, then the seller is no more than a commodity supplier, and can be treated as such (the product is bought on price and technical specification).

This represents a challenging change in focus in the way sales organisations interact with major customers. While traditional selling activities focus primarily on the need to convert product and service into cash flow, conventional marketing shifts

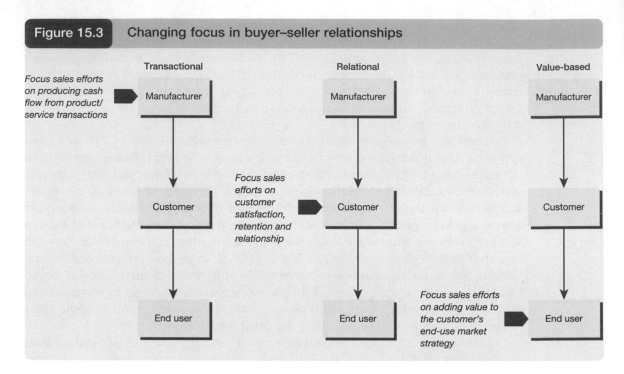

Figure 15.3   Changing focus in buyer–seller relationships

the focus from seller need to buyer need and developing the customer relationship. However, in many situations now faced by suppliers, strategic customers demand that the seller displays not simply a superior understanding of the customer's own organisation, but detailed and insightful knowledge of the customer's end-use markets. The strategic sales role is becoming one of deploying end-use market knowledge to enhance the customer's competitive position and cost efficiency. This is summarised in Figure 15.3, which provides a framework for evaluating where a company's salesforce is currently focusing efforts and how this compares with customer demands.

Even in the consumer goods sector, retailers still report that their suppliers perform inadequately in key areas which help differentiate them to the consumer, such as consumer insight development. Major retailers emphasise that trade relationships are no longer based on buyer–seller roles, and characterise the best-in-class supplier as one that has a firm understanding of the retailer's position, strategy and ambitions in the marketplace – they require consumer insight from their suppliers (IBM, 2005).

Successful business models like those at companies as diverse as Dell Inc. in computers, Johnsons Controls in automotive controls, and Kraft in groceries display this type of end-use market perspective in strategic sales relationships. Major customers evaluate their suppliers on the seller's success in enhancing the customer's competitive position, and increasingly expect proof of this achievement.

The challenge to suppliers from an increasing proportion of their major customers is to understand the customer's business and the customer's end-use markets, to leverage that knowledge to create competitive advantage for the customer. The alternative is to face growing commoditisation and declining margins. Meeting this challenge with major accounts and strategic accounts is a central element of strategic sales choices. The corresponding challenge for the reformed sales organisation is to develop, deploy and sustain new skills and capabilities in market sensing.

15.3.3 Integration across functional boundaries

Turbulent and demanding markets create new challenges for managers in supplier organisations. Powerful customers increasingly demand problem-solving and creative thinking about their business, requiring the commitment of, and access to, the supplier's total operation. One European executive describes this as 'the convergence of strategic management, change management and process management, all critical elements of transforming the sales function to meet today's customer requirements.' (Seidenschwartz, 2005) Certainly, in some cases programmes of value creation around major customers have been plagued by problems of 'organisational drag' – the seller's organisational functions are not aligned around processes of creating and delivering customer value (Koerner, 2005). Similarly, retailers emphasise supplier organisational structure and culture as key obstacles to improving customer management effectiveness (IBM, 2005).

Success in the new marketplace increasingly demands the integration of a company's entire set of capabilities into a seamless system that delivers superior customer value – what has been called elsewhere 'total integrated marketing' (Hulbert *et al.*, 2003). This logic is based on the observation that superior performing companies share a simple characteristic: they get their act together around the things that matter most to their customers, and they make a totally integrated offer of superior value in customer terms. Management attention must focus on the actual and potential contributions of functional units and departments, and third-party suppliers in alliances and networks, in delivering superior value to customers, and how to improve the integration of these activities.

One of the developing roles of the sales organisation will be in managing processes of value definition, development and delivery that cut across functional interfaces to build real customer focus. Many of the barriers to developing and delivering superior customer value come from the characteristics of supplier organisations. One challenge of strategic customer management mandates effective approaches to cross-functional integration around value processes. Rather than managing only the interface with the customer, the reformed salesforce must cope with a range of interfaces with internal functions and departments and, increasingly, partner organisations to deliver value seamlessly to customers. We discuss the issue of cross-functional partnership further in Chapter 17.

15.3.4 Internal marketing of the customer

It seems inevitable that a strategic approach to the role of sales in managing customer value will simultaneously impose the problem of positioning and 'selling' the customer value strategy inside the organisation.

For example, consider the issue of service quality, which has proved to be a decisive competitive weapon in many industries. Service quality is normally evaluated in the customer marketplace in terms of the perceived delivery of the product or service confirming or disconfirming customer expectations to create satisfaction or dissatisfaction (Berry and Parasuraman, 1991). However, those same dimensions of attitudes and beliefs are mirrored in the internal marketplace of company employees and managers.

In the internal marketplace, expectations are concerned with anticipations by people inside the company of external customer preferences and behaviour, and perceived delivery is about differences between internal and external criteria of what 'matters' – priorities of people in the 'back office' or the factory may conflict with those of the external customer. Confirmation/disconfirmation relates not to consumption of the product, but to judgements people inside the company make about the external customer. When external customers 'disappoint' employees by their adverse reaction or complaints, this may easily have a negative effect on the future behaviour of employees in dealing with customers (Piercy, 1995; Bell *et al.*, 2004).

The risk of undermining the competitive position with a major customer as a result of such internal market factors is too serious to be ignored. One role of the reformed sales organisation is likely to be 'selling' the customer to employees and managers, as a basis for understanding customer priorities and the importance of meeting them, as an activity that parallels conventional sales and marketing efforts, as suggested in Figure 15.4.

Internal marketing is discussed further in Chapter 17.

15.3.5   Infrastructure for the new sales organisation

The role of the transforming sales organisation is unlikely to be implemented effectively through traditional salesforce structures and processes. Shapiro and his colleagues suggest that 'most established sales forces are in deep trouble. They were designed for a much simpler, more pleasant era . . . The old sales force must be redesigned to meet the new needs' (1998). New definitions of the sales task will require

Figure 15.4   **The internal marketing challenge for sales**

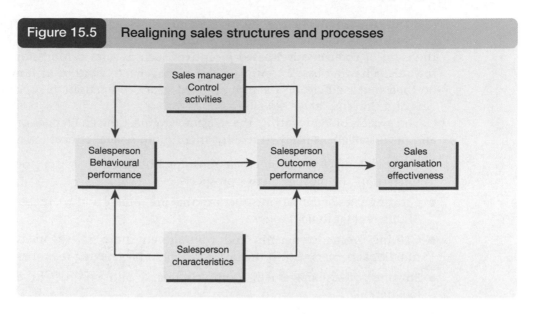

| Figure 15.5 | Realigning sales structures and processes |

substantial shifts in the way that the sales organisation is managed. Turbulent markets mandate constant attention to alignment between sales processes and the goals of market and business strategy (Strelsin and Mlot, 1992). Certainly, research suggests that the move from transactional relationships with customers (selling on the basis of price and product advantages) to value-added relationships is proving extremely challenging for many organisations striving to pursue this strategy (*American Salesman*, November 2002).

Change in the infrastructure supporting the strategic sales organisation is likely to span organisation structure, performance measurement systems, competency creation systems, and motivation systems – all driven by the definition of the new task and role of the sales operation (Shapiro *et al.*, 1998).

Figure 15.5 suggests some of the areas where particular attention is required, and where new research into sales organisation effectiveness indicates some of the productive approaches to be explored. The logic is that the overall result on which attention should focus is the effectiveness of the sales organisation in implementing business strategy and meeting organisational goals. Traditionally, management attention has focused on outcome performance as the main indicator of effectiveness (i.e. meeting sales volume and revenue targets). However, if strategy requires the development of closer customer relationships and the implementation of a value-based strategy, then salesperson behaviour performance may be a more productive point of focus (i.e. not simply what salespeople sell, but the behaviours they undertake to achieve their goals and to build customer relationships).

If salesperson behaviour performance is key to delivering the outcomes and overall effectiveness required as marketing strategy moves towards a relationship focus, then this has several important implications for the competencies and behaviours to be developed in salespeople, and against which to evaluate their performance. This, in turn, has major implications for the type of people to be recruited to sales and account management roles, as well as for the way in which they are managed

(Baldauf, Cravens and Piercy, 2001; Baldauf, Piercy and Cravens, 2001). Particular controversy is reserved for the move from outcome-based control (primarily in the form of compensation-based incentives such as sales commission and bonus) towards behaviour-based control (direct manager intervention in how salespeople do their jobs, and greater reliance on fixed salary compensation packages) (Piercy, Low and Cravens, 2004a, 2004b).

The process of 'reinventing' the salesforce to meet the challenges of new markets and new strategies is likely to require attention to several critical issues:

● Focus on long-term customer relationships, but also assessing customer value and prioritising the most attractive prospects.

● Creating sales organisation structures that are nimble and adaptable to the needs of different customer groups.

● Gaining greater ownership and commitment from salespeople by removing functional barriers within the organisation and leveraging team-based working.

● Shifting sales management from 'command and control' to coaching and facilitation.

● Applying new technologies appropriately.

● Designing salesperson evaluation to incorporate the full range of activities and outcomes relevant to new types of sales and account management jobs (Cravens, 1995).

While beyond the scope of this present review, a study of the antecedents and consequences of sales management control strategy is revealing of several issues, which are commonly neglected in leveraging change and superior performance in the salesforce in aligning sales efforts with strategic direction (Baldauf *et al.*, 2005). It should be quite apparent, however, that new business and marketing strategies and an evolving role for the sales organisation in leading strategic customer management will inevitably require considerable re-evaluation of the management of the sales organisation.

15.4 Strategic customer management tasks

The transformation of the traditional sales organisation into a strategic force that should feature centrally in the analysis that underpins strategic choices by marketing executives may be achieved by moves towards at least some of the characteristics of the strategic sales organisation. However, the larger goal we pursue is a strategic customer management perspective, which may be achieved through the strategising of sales processes and structures. The key distinguishing features of a strategic customer management (SCM) approach are summarised below and developed further in the sections that follow.

15.4.1 Alignment of sales processes with strategy

At one level, the SCM mandate is concerned with the issue of marketing strategy implementation. To many business-to-business customers, the salesperson who visits *is* the supplier company, and has far more impact on customer perceptions of the supplier than promotional and other communications approaches. The interface between the customer and the supplier managed by the salesforce has long been recognised as a major source of implementation failures. We consider implementation issues in Chapter 17, but particular problems relating to the sales/marketing strategy interface which are frequently encountered include:

- Marketing strategies which aim to build strong competitive positions through superior customer relationships fall foul of sales organisations where salespeople are rewarded by volume-based commission paid for sales transactions – traditional evaluation and reward systems often value most sales activities that run counter to strategic goals of customer orientation and relationship building and favour short-term volume.

- Strategies are built around vertical markets and customer focus, but salespeople struggle to implement these approaches because they are organised into geographical areas or product divisions.

- Sales managers do not 'buy in' to marketing strategies, and cling to traditional leadership behaviours and performance management in controlling sales operations.

- Traditional conflicts of interest between marketing and sales executives (they are frequently rewarded for different achievements and evaluated against different measures) spill over into lack of cooperation and coordination.

- Marketing strategies are developed in isolation from the customer and competitor insights provided by salespeople and account managers, and without any understanding of the company's sales capabilities compared with competitors.

- Salespeople and sales executives experience job ambiguity and conflict in attempting to implement strategies that fit poorly with the systems and structures in the sales organisation, experiencing lower motivation, lower job satisfaction and perhaps higher levels of stress and burnout (Baldauf *et al.*, 2005).

Poor alignment of the realities of existing sales processes and structures and the intent of marketing strategy is likely to make effective implementation difficult to achieve. Nonetheless, it must be recognised that changing issues like evaluation and reward systems, leadership and control strategies, and organisational structures in the salesforce is usually not a minor undertaking.

15.4.2 Providing the customer perspective to marketing strategy

However, the importance of understanding the sales/customer interface is important to strategy analysts and decision-makers for another reason as well. In most business-to-business situations, the salesforce represents an important market sensing capability, or source of intelligence. However, research evidence suggests that this resource is generally poorly used and applied by marketing decision-makers (Fitzhugh and Piercy, 2006). A high priority is emerging for the better management of market sensing processes which involve the salesforce and account management teams as primary sources of intelligence.

15.4.3 Managing the customer portfolio

Our earlier comments on changing customer relationship requirements and demands for service enhancement suggest that different customer groups should be evaluated very differently in terms of their potential attractiveness and the supplier's cost to serve them. Choices regarding the customers in which to make investments of selling efforts of different types, and where not to make such investments, will shape the future of a business and merit senior management attention. We will consider the customer portfolio in the next section of this chapter.

15.4.4 Developing effective positioning with dominant customers

Currently, one of the most troublesome issue for developing effective strategy in business-to-business companies is the impact of powerful customers and the demands that they can make on their suppliers – whether the consumer goods manufacturer dealing with very large retailers like Tesco and Wal-Mart, or the components manufacturer dealing with automotive companies. One response to this has been the growth in strategic (or key) account management approaches to 'partner' with the most important customers. However, it is clear that some customers do not provide good partnership prospects – while they may be large, they are transactional customers, not collaborators. The last major section of this chapter turns to the issue of dominant customers.

15.5 Managing the customer portfolio

In much the same way that we can examine a portfolio of products or brands, the importance of customers as assets and investment centres mandates a similar portfolio analysis. Figure 15.6 shows an approach to mapping the number of customer accounts held by a company or business unit, by their sales level and potential, and their service and relationship requirements from the supplier. This categorisation can be initially made simply by the number of accounts, but can be subsequently enhanced by examining the profitability and stability of business in the different account categories. Identifying the categories is the important first step.

The *direct channel* is typically the route to market for smaller accounts with low relationship/service requirements, e.g. the Internet, telemarketing. Importantly, customer development strategy may also involve moving some accounts towards the direct channel, because they are consuming more service/relationship resources than they merit, but also moving some out of the direct channel, based on changing prospects and the costs of serving the account. Such considerations illustrate the potential importance of shifting some salesforce resources from a short-term transactional focus to longer-term business development issues in line with business strategy.

The *middle market* contains customers with varying prospects, but generally with moderate relationship/service requirements. These are the most conventional buyer–seller relationships. Those with promising potential may be moved into the

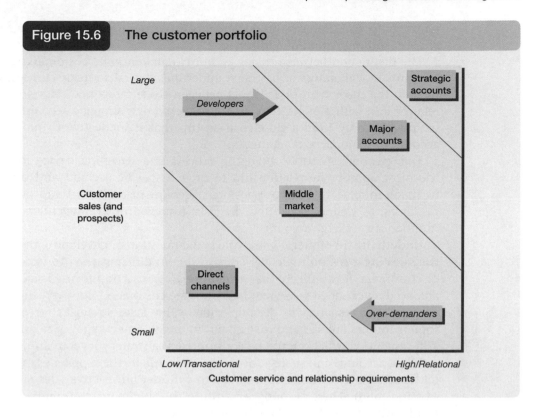

Figure 15.6   The customer portfolio

major account area over time, while those with relationship/service requirements which are excessive compared with their potential may be moved towards the direct channel.

Major accounts are usually large in the supplier's terms and have high relationship/service requirements, but they are customers in a conventional buyer–seller relationship. While major accounts are important to the supplier, it is quite possible that the supplier is of far less importance to the customer (if accounting for a relatively small part of the customer's expenditure, or capable of being replaced reasonably easily). However, major account size and prospects identifies the need to develop appropriate salesforce approaches to deliver added value to these customers. Nonetheless, it is likely that appropriate salesforce strategies will be, and should be, substantially different between major accounts and strategic accounts.

Strategic accounts are those where collaborative and joint problem-solving approaches are appropriate to win strategic supplier status. Strategic account management strategies and structures have developed in many companies as a way of developing close, long-term and collaborative relationships with the most important customers and meeting their needs in ways which the traditional salesforce did not (Homburg *et al.*, 2002). Important questions surround the selection and management of relationships with strategic accounts, which may be the most expensive customers to serve. Growing buyer concentration in many markets mandates collaborative relationships with these accounts as strategic suppliers, but the costs of partnership and the growing dependence involved underline the need for careful choices and evaluation of performance.

The distinction between major accounts (conventional customers) and strategic accounts (collaborators or partners) underlines several strategic choices. Plans may include the movement of accounts between these categories – developing a closer relationship with a major account to develop a new strategic account relationship, or moving away from a close relationship that is ineffective to move a strategic account to major account status.

This customer portfolio mapping process is a screening device for identifying the most appropriate relationship to offer a specific account and the choices to be made in allocating scarce salesforce, account management and other company resources, as well as evaluating the risks involved in overdependence on a small number of very large accounts.

Underlying the strategic sales issue is the question of developing the capability of the sales organisation to deliver added value in different ways to various categories of customers. It is unlikely that a traditional, transaction-focused salesforce will be able to deliver added value required by some customers. However, the deployment of expensive resources to develop added-value sales strategies for particular customers implies choices and investment in creating new types of salesforce resource and capability, which should be confronted at a strategy level in an organisation.

Major accounts and strategic accounts are normally the supplier's largest customers (although it may be more appropriate to consider prospective sales rather than just existing sales). These accounts constitute the dominant customers whose impact can be massive on the supplier's performance and ability to implement marketing strategies. We now turn more detailed attention to the dominant customer issue.

15.6 Dealing with dominant customers

This section draws on Piercy and Lane, 2006a, 2006b, 2007.

15.6.1 Differences between customers, major accounts and strategic partners

One important insight from the customer portfolio analysis is the recognition of the different types of customer in the company's portfolio, and their differing demands for value and relationship. Particular questions are raised about the largest and most influential customers – perhaps the 20 per cent of customers who may account for 80 per cent (or more) of the supplier's business.

It is important for strategic decision-makers to understand the basis for the different types of customer relationship which exist in the portfolio, and particularly the idea of a transition from traditional transactional relationships to much closer links between the seller and the most dominant buyers. Figure 15.7 summarises some of the commonest business-to-business buyer–seller relationships, and the critical differences between them.

The *conventional buyer–seller relationship* is the most familiar – it typifies the middle market. Links are between salespeople and purchasers, and the relationship

Figure 15.7   The transition from customer to strategic partner

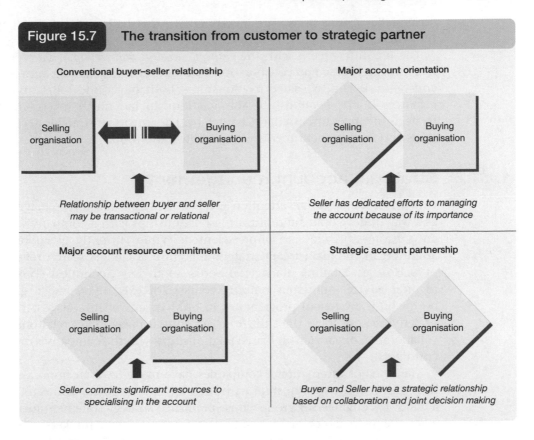

Conventional buyer–seller relationship

Selling organisation ◄▌▌► Buying organisation

Relationship between buyer and seller may be transactional or relational

Major account orientation

Selling organisation   Buying organisation

Seller has dedicated efforts to managing the account because of its importance

Major account resource commitment

Selling organisation   Buying organisation

Seller commits significant resources to specialising in the account

Strategic account partnership

Selling organisation   Buying organisation

Buyer and Seller have a strategic relationship based on collaboration and joint decision making

may be purely transactional (depending largely on the importance of the purchase to the customer, or the way in which the customer chooses to do business), or it may involve a higher level or closer relationship being built between buyer and seller. This is the type of relationship which most traditional salesforces were created to manage.

However, the existence of larger, more dominant customers requires different approaches. The *major account orientation* case is where the size and impact of a customer requires that sales and management efforts should be refocused to provide a dedicated approach to a particular customer. This may involve the appointment of an account manager, or a national account specialist, and the development of plans around this customer's specific needs. Nonetheless, the relationship remains largely a conventional buyer–seller format.

The *major account resource commitment* situation takes things substantially further in terms of dedicated efforts around the major account. Substantial teams of people may now work around the single account and offerings may be substantially different for this customer. Nonetheless, the resource commitment remains essentially one-sided. Procter & Gamble's 200-person team for the Wal-Mart account is P&G's investment in that customer. Correspondingly, while Dell Computers has a dedicated team for its major customer, Boeing, this does not suggest that Boeing makes decisions about Dell's business. At the end of the day, these relationships remain buyer–seller transactions. The investment is essentially one-sided – it is made by the seller.

The big difference is with the *strategic account partnership*. This type of account relationship is based on collaboration and joint decision making between the buyer and seller. It is a two-sided relationship – both buyer and seller invest time and resources in the relationship. This relationship has much in common with the strategic alliances discussed in Chapter 16. The impact of strategic account relationships and management merits more detailed attention.

15.6.2 Strategic account management

Growth in management attention given to strategic account management (SAM)* as a way of developing and nurturing relationships with a company's most important customers is close to unprecedented. While currently given relatively little attention in the mainstream strategy literature, a Google search reveals hundreds of web pages detailing managerial books about SAM, countless consultants eager to offer advice, numerous training courses for executives, and a growing number of business school programmes in SAM in universities across the world. The underlying concept is the shift from adversarial buyer–seller relationships towards collaborative or partnership-based relationships with the company's most important customers.

Many major international companies have made SAM an important element of how they manage relationships with their largest customers. For example, IMI plc is a major UK engineering group whose published strategy statement identifies SAM as a key theme in achieving its goal of 'leading global niche markets'. The company is investing heavily 'to enhance our ability to create and manage close customer relationships with our clients [and] provide IMI business managers with the skills to create and develop close and successful relationships with major customers . . . which places key account management among the central elements of IMI's business approach' (www.imi.plc.uk). For a growing number of companies, SAM is a deep-seated strategy for customer partnering, often on a global basis.

Norgren, a brand of IMI PLC

Courtesy of Norgren/IMI plc

---

* For purposes of discussion we regard the terms strategic account management and key account management as interchangeable, and our commentary generally applies to what some designate as national account management and global account management.

At the same time, many major buyers have adopted radical strategic supplier strategies. In 2005, Ford Motor Company announced it was consolidating its supply base for its $90 billion components purchases from 2,000 suppliers to 1,000 globally. Moreover, the first seven 'key suppliers' constitute some 50 per cent of Ford's parts purchases, and will enjoy superior access to Ford's engineering resources and product planning. Ford will work closely with its key suppliers, giving them access to key business plans for new vehicles and committing to give them business (Mackintosh and Simon, 2005).

On one hand, a compelling case can be made for the attractiveness of SAM as a strategy of collaboration and partnership with major customers. However, there are several assumptions and propositions underpinning the case for SAM, which appear to have been largely ignored by its adopters and advocates. Balancing these issues is an important challenge for strategic decision-makers in marketing.

15.6.3 The case for strategic account management

A recent study suggests that strategic/key account management is one of the most fundamental changes in marketing organisation (Homburg *et al.*, 2000), and yet one in which a sound research foundation to guide management's strategic decisions remains almost completely lacking (Homburg *et al.*, 2002). Indeed, while there is a long stream of research in the areas of national and key account selling starting in the 1960s, this research has been largely descriptive and conceptual and has not addressed the long-term impact of SAM on buyer–seller performance (Workman *et al.*, 2003).

The rationale for SAM is that demands from large customers have caused suppliers to respond with dedicated organisational resources to concentrate on these 'key' or 'strategic' accounts and to incorporate special value-adding activities (e.g. joint product development, business planning, consulting services) into their offering to the customer (Dorsch *et al.*, 1998). Fundamental to the logic of SAM is the suggestion of an inevitable concentration effect whereby a small number of customers provide a disproportionately large share of a seller's sales and profits (the so-called '20:80 rule'). Almost as a natural consequence, suppliers frequently dedicate most of their resources to the core portfolio of buyers who represent the highest stakes and are identified as 'strategic accounts' or 'key accounts' (Pardo, 1997).

SAM is a strategic development which has become increasingly widespread in response to a variety of customer and market pressures, which may be summarised as:

● escalating levels of competition in most markets and consequently higher selling costs for suppliers;

● increased customer concentration resulting from merger and acquisition activity, as well as competitive attrition in many markets;

● growing customer emphasis on centralised strategic purchasing as a major contributor to enhancing the buyer's cost structure and building competitive success in their end-user markets;

● active strategies of supplier-base reduction by larger buyers to reduce purchasing costs; and

- increasing exploitation by large customers of their position of strategic importance to their suppliers to gain lower prices and enhanced terms of trade (Capon, 2001).

Importantly, however, SAM is not seen simply as an organisational response that focuses on meeting growing demands from dominant customers; it is seen as progression towards a form of 'partnership' with those customers, characterised by joint decision making and problem solving, integrated business processes and collaborative working across buyer–seller boundaries, described as a process of 'relational development' (Millman and Wilson, 1989). However, while we have discussed the strengths in effective strategic account relationships, decision-makers should also recognise the growing evidence that ineffective strategic account relationships may create a range of strategic vulnerabilities for sellers.

15.6.4 Vulnerabilities in strategic account relationships

There are a number of potential flaws in the underlying logic for SAM, which may make it unattractive for sellers in some situations, and which should be explicit in making strategic customer management choices.

Investing in strategic weakness

There is a case that SAM involves the seller investing in strategic weakness, in the sense that it may be unattractive to institutionalise dependency on major customers as a way of doing business. The SAM approach rests on the notion that the 20:80 rule produces a situation for the seller which is attractive, or at least inevitable. Conversely, it can be argued that any company which has reached a situation where a 20:80 position exists – i.e. 80 per cent or more of profits and/or revenue come from 20 per cent or less of the customer base – has already witnessed the failure of its business model. The business model has failed because it has led to such a high degree of dependence on a small number of customers that the company's strategic freedom of manoeuvre has been undermined, and much control of the supplier's business has effectively been ceded to its major customers. The eventual outcome for selling companies in this situation is likely to be falling prices, commoditisation of their products, and progressively lower profits as major customers exert their market power.

Clearly, many practitioners would dismiss this line of argument as pointless. They argue that in businesses like grocery there is no choice other than to deal with the major retailers who dominate the consumer marketplace, because there is no other route to market, and little choice other than to accept the terms they offer. Similarly, suppliers of automotive components would point to the limited number of automobile manufacturers in the world, and producers of computer components would argue that, if you want Dell's business, then you do business on Dell's terms, robust though those terms may be. Such responses at least clarify that in many 'strategic account' situations the real issue is less partnership and more about one party dictating terms to the other, which is not the concept of 'collaboration' normally advanced to justify SAM investments by suppliers.

If it is conceded that powerful customers will ultimately exploit that power to their own advantage, then their business carries a disproportionately higher risk than that of less powerful, less dominant customers, and it is less attractive as a result. If it is inevitable that major customers will demand more concessions and pay less, then it is likely they will also be substantially less profitable than other customers. There is little consistent empirical evidence, but there are suggestions that for many sellers strategic or key accounts are the least profitable part of their business.

The importance of understanding the balance of power

Notwithstanding the importance of strategic buyer–seller relationships, there seems a strong case that the party in the supply chain enjoying the balance of power will use that to their advantage. For example, in spite of surging raw material costs in 2005, the pricing power of manufacturers continued to deteriorate. Producers were absorbing most cost increases and were unable to pass them fully through the supply chain, simply because powerful buyers would not permit it (Cave, 2005). It is further illustrative that in the automotive components market, notwithstanding escalating steel and oil prices faced by producers, Volkswagen told its parts suppliers in 2005 it wanted 10 per cent cost savings over the following two years. At Chrysler, the CEO demanded an immediate 5 per cent price cut by suppliers, with a further 10 per cent over the following three years (Mackintosh, 2005).

For such reasons, in sectors like automotive components, suppliers are actively seeking to diversify their customer bases and to change product portfolios to reduce dependence on a small number of powerful accounts (Simon, 2005). The issue is becoming one of staying close to key customers, but reaching out to other customer groups as a route to reduced dependency on a few and enhanced profits (Witzel, 2005). Indeed, this shift in dependency may be one of the highest strategic priorities impacting on survival.

The real buyer–seller relationship

The critical issue is interdependence between buyer and seller, or perhaps more aptly the balance of dependence, since it is rarely symmetrical. The question is, who is dependent on whom in the buyer–seller relationship? Failure to grasp the simple issue of the direction of dependency is likely to blind the seller to a critical vulnerability of SAM, while simultaneously souring relationships with the account in question – professional purchasers find it difficult to work with suppliers who misunderstand the nature of the relationship they really have with the buyer. Sellers with an exaggerated view of their strategic importance to a buyer have unrealistic expectations of the customer, with the potential for growing frustration because the customer does not behave in the way expected, and ultimately leading to conflict between buyer and seller.

Figure 15.8 illustrates a buyer perspective on supplier types – the professional purchaser distinguishes on the basis of risk (substitutability) and impact (reduced costs or improved competitive advantage) in the end-use marketplace. From a purchaser perspective, suppliers with significant impact on the buyer's business, but who can easily be replaced, are mainly targets for pressure on price and terms, while

---

Figure 15.9   Buying and selling relationship strategies

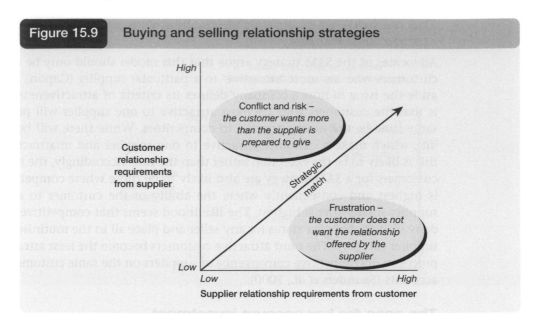

---

them. However, most times all I really do is to get concessions on price and terms. I almost feel guilty, it is so easy, but it's my job' (Piercy and Lane, 2006a). Underpinning the weakness of SAM strategy in potentially mismanaging critical inter-organisational dependencies is the observation that suppliers frequently tend to have exaggerated views about the relationship that major customers want to have with their suppliers.

It is likely that SAM can only be an effective strategy from a supplier perspective where there is a close match between seller and buyer relationship requirements. Consider the scenario in Figure 15.9. Frustration results for the supplier attempting to build closer relationships with customers who mainly want efficient transactions – from the buyer perspective the supplier is not important enough to justify strategic supplier status, or this may simply not be how this company does business with its suppliers. On the other hand, conflict arises when a customer looks for a close relationship with a supplier prepared only to offer more limited engagement – this customer does not warrant a larger relationship investment by the supplier. Only where there is continuous alignment between buyer and seller relationship requirements is there potential for effective SAM. The problem facing suppliers seems to be recognising how rare alignment may be in practice, as well as how transitory.

Distinguishing large (major) customers from strategic accounts

The tendency among sellers is to equate large customers with strategic accounts. We commented earlier on the importance of distinguishing major accounts from strategic accounts in the customer portfolio. The danger of not distinguishing these types of customer is threefold: first, confusing the major account with the real strategic account prospect, leading to unproductive investments in the relationship;

second, diverting attention from developing new and profitable major accounts growing out of the traditional middle market; and, third, neglecting the productivity enhancements available by moving over-demanding customers from the traditional middle market to the direct channel. Identifying major customers wrongly as strategic accounts is capable of undermining the management of the whole portfolio of accounts being serviced by the seller, with likely further negative effects on overall performance and profitability.

Furthermore, some major customers may be relatively unattractive because they offer little profit or future growth. The fact that such customers may presently be large buyers does not alter this fact. On these grounds, simply being a large customer does not justify supplier relationship investments like SAM. There is no logic in building stronger relationships with unattractive customers, particularly if this reduces opportunities to invest more productively elsewhere. As noted earlier, in many ways the large low-profit customer should encourage ring-fencing to minimise additional investment to the lowest level that retains the business, and the diversion of resources to more profitable applications elsewhere in the business.

Understanding the reality of customer loyalty

Much of the attraction of SAM lies in the promise that collaborative relationships with key customers will enhance the retention of that business – i.e. strategic accounts will reciprocate by offering loyalty to their long-term strategic suppliers. This promise may not be fulfilled.

Consider the long-term textile and clothing suppliers who believed their relationship with Marks & Spencer was secure, only to discover that, when their customer was under pressure, purchasing transferred to cheaper offshore sources. Examine the current US situation for clothing manufacturers for whom Wal-Mart is a 'key account' – Wal-Mart is now the eighth largest purchaser of Chinese products at incredibly low prices, which matters more than long-term relationships with domestic suppliers. Alternatively, view the Dell Inc. situation – a company renowned for its strategic account strategy, acting almost as an outsourced IT department for major customers. Dell Inc. does not extend the same philosophy to its suppliers – a company remains a Dell supplier only as long as it has better technology than the rest.

Recent research suggests that relational exchanges between suppliers and customers frequently benefit customers in performance improvements, but that generally the customers concerned do not reward suppliers with a higher share of their expenditure or long-term contractual commitments (Fink *et al.*, 2007). The mutual benefit and long-term relationship building implicit in strategic account management approaches may have been exaggerated.

If SAM is seen as a model of collaboration that has many similarities with strategic alliances (both involve agreement for partnership and joint decision making, with no transfer of ownership), then it is perhaps worth considering the evidence that the majority of strategic alliances fail, and in the view of many executives do not deliver the benefits they promised. The success of alliances seems to depend on conditions of mutuality and symmetry between partners. Those conditions do not appear to exist in many SAM situations.

Underestimating the rate of change

Even if a customer is willing and eager to offer a seller the status of a strategic supplier and is treated as a strategic account, with all the additional investment that this is likely to require, some sellers believe that strategic relationships with these accounts will be stable and long term.

The more likely truth is that, as a seller's own strategy changes, the importance of a particular supplier will change – possibly dramatically and quickly. As the recorded music business transforms to one based on Internet downloads instead of physical products, strategic suppliers will be those with expertise in the new technology, not those offering CDs and support for the old technology. Indeed, supplier switching may increasingly be an explicit element of a company's business strategy. In 2005, Apple announced it was teaming up with Intel to provide the components suitable for new generations of Apple products, effectively bringing an unexpected end to long-term supplier relationships with IBM and Freescale (formerly Motorola) (Morrison and Waters, 2005; Witzel, 2005). Apple's goal is to build on the momentum created by its iPod digital music player and to meet the lower prices demanded in the mass consumer market. Also in the consumer marketplace, Dixons, the electrical retailer, ceased selling video recorders in favour of DVD players at the end of 2004 and film-based cameras in favour of digital cameras in 2005. Dixon's strategy follows trends in the consumer marketplace notwithstanding disruption to established supplier relationships (Rigby and Wiggins, 2003). Supplier switching may be an inevitable consequence of strategic change.

The reality is that the strategic supplier relationship for many suppliers will be temporary and transitory, as customers develop their own market strategies and adopt new technologies. This leaves the supplier investing heavily in the strategic account relationship, only to see that relationship disappear as the customer moves on. Customers rarely offer recompense to a supplier to cover the costs of dismantling a redundant SAM system.

Even more traumatic is the sudden collapse of a key account/strategic supplier relationship. Changes in customer businesses may end relationships that had taken years to build – the key account is taken over and the acquiring company imposes its own supplier arrangements on the acquired business; there is a change in supply strategy from the top of the customer organisation, for example the move from single sourcing to multiple sourcing; the customer learns technology and process from its strategic supplier, enabling it to undertake production of the product in-house; or customer personnel move on and their replacements do not have a close relationship with the supplier and maybe do not want one. The collapse of a strategic account relationship will have a major negative impact on sales volume, which may not have been predicted. The end of a SAM relationship may impose additional and substantial costs – adjusting operations capacity to allow for short-term volume reduction, disentangling integrated systems, rebuilding processes previously shared with the key account, reallocating or removing personnel previously dedicated to the key account, putting in place new arrangements to retain whatever residual business there may be in the account.

The failure of a strategic account relationship may be very public and create additional vulnerability. If a company's shares are written down because of the collapse of business with a strategic account, then the supplier becomes vulnerable to a predator – perhaps even the customer in question, who has the opportunity to in-source the product by buying the supplier; possibly a competitor; or possibly a stalker from outside the sector. The point is that the cost of a failed key account relationship may not simply be losing the customer, it may be losing the company as well.

Consider the experiences of Marconi in its strategic relationship with British Telecom. Marconi is the rump of the former GEC and through the 1990s focused investment heavily on the telecommunications sector. Marconi was one of British Telecom's largest suppliers of network equipment for several decades. By 2004 BT represented a quarter of Marconi's total sales – as much as the next nine customers put together. Notwithstanding being described as a 'terrific partner' by the chief executive of BT Wholesale, in 2005 Marconi was shut out of BT's £10 billion '21st Century Network' project. BT's decision was based on price, not technology or relationships, and Marconi could not equal the prices of overseas competitors from eight countries ranging from France to China. Under BT pressure, Marconi had even lowered prices to a level that would have represented substantial losses in its UK operation, but not enough to satisfy BT. With the loss of a quarter of its sales base, shares falling 60 per cent in value, and substantial job losses in prospect, Marconi's experience underlines the risks of over-reliance on one customer, and the critical error of believing that BT would be a loyal partner. The loss of the BT business fundamentally weakens Marconi's ability to compete globally in new areas like Internet protocol networks. Within months of the BT decision, it was clear that investors were looking for Marconi to sell the business or merge to survive. Marconi's Chinese joint venture partner, Huawei, gained two parts of the BT contract, and ironically Marconi's technology may be available to BT through this low-price channel. In 2006 the main Marconi business was sold to Ericsson, leaving Marconi only a smaller services business working on maintenance of legacy systems (Ashton, 2005; Brummer, 2005; Durman and Box, 2005; Grande, 2005).

Challenging the regulator

SAM strategy is akin to a full-blown merger between buying and selling organisations – in buyer and seller making joint investment decisions, the exchange of proprietary information, the exclusion of third parties, and so on. SAM strategy creates a potential for anti-trust violation. Competition regulators are increasingly taking the view that close collaboration between buyer and seller is potentially anti-competitive.

Believing that SAM is easily implemented

Lastly, there appears inadequate recognition of the implementation barriers and organisational issues faced in SAM strategy. To assume that this is a strategy that can be made effective easily underestimates the degree to which this is a quite radical new business model. Even if a SAM strategy is appropriate for a supplier to manage strategic relationships with certain critical customers, there remains the issue of whether the supplier has the capabilities and resources to make the strategy real, in ways which matter to the customer.

5.3.7 Balancing the case for strategic account management

We have attempted to contrast the apparently compelling case for strategic account management (SAM) models that develop collaborative and integrative relationships with major or dominant customers, with the serious flaws in the underlying assumptions of those models and the potentially damaging traps for the unwary. In many situations, it appears that the adoption of SAM models is based on the suspect logic that the best use of a company's resources is to invest heavily in that part of the business (the largest most dominant customers) which has the lowest margins and the highest business risk.

Defenders of the SAM model would argue that this scenario reflects not the weakness of the model, but poor choice of key accounts by companies. There is some merit in such a response. However, since the apparent reality is that companies choose as strategic accounts those customers to which they sell most, or respond to the demands of large customers for special treatment, then suggesting that the weaknesses inherent in the SAM model can be overcome by better choice of strategic accounts seems somewhat unrealistic.

One logic is that the search should be for alternative strategies that avoid the trap of high dependence on a small number of powerful dominant accounts. Some would probably suggest that this is a search doomed to failure – the most powerful customers control markets and are unlikely to surrender this control willingly. Yet, on the other hand, consider the potential disruption of the *status quo* in a market by the introduction of a new business model. For example, consumer and business computer users have voiced numerous complaints over the years about the product functionality of Microsoft offerings, and struggled in vain against the massive Microsoft market share in areas like operating systems and server software. In 2005, we saw the dramatic impact of Linux software – available free or cheaply – developed through a peer-to-peer network, in a business model that appears uninvolved with concerns like profitability. Microsoft increasingly looks like a company with a mid-life crisis, that has no effective response to Linux. However, more interesting yet is the fact that much of the Linux revolution has been driven and facilitated by IBM, Sun Microsystems and Dell, which are dramatically reducing their dependence on the old adversaries at Microsoft. Actively managing dependence between buyer and seller may be one way out of the trap.

It is illustrative that 2006 saw the Procter & Gamble/Gillette merger to create the world's largest consumer brands group. The combined portfolio of brands provides a much stronger hand in dealing with major retailers (Quinn, 2005). However, the merger also represents a fundamental change to P&G's business model. The goal is to serve not only the world's most affluent 1 billion consumers in developed countries, but to serve the world's 6 billion consumers, with a new focus on lower-income consumers in such markets as China and India. In developing these emerging markets, P&G is not deliberately partnering with global retailers like Wal-Mart and Carrefour. Instead, in China P&G will offer Gillette access to a huge distribution system staffed by an army of individual Chinese entrepreneurs – what P&G calls a 'down the trade' system ending up with a one-person kiosk in a small village selling shampoo and toothpaste. The effect should be that stable growth in Asian markets will reduce the combined company's dependence on mature markets dominated by powerful retailers (Grant, 2005).

New business models that will be effective in avoiding the dominant customer trap will probably share some of the following characteristics:

- reducing critical dependencies and risks by developing alternative routes to market – consider the example of the automotive manufacturers developing direct channel strategies to take back control of the value chain and reduce dependencies on independent distributors;

- developing alternative product offerings to rebuild brand strength as a counter to the power of the largest customers;

- emphasising the need for high returns to justify taking on high-risk business, not the other way around;

- reducing strategic vulnerabilities created by excessive levels of dependence on a small number of customers or distributors;

- clarifying the difference between major accounts and key accounts and developing appropriate ways of managing these different types of relationship profitably;

- actively rejecting business from some sources because the customer is unattractive in terms of profitability and risk, even if the business on offer is large;

- managing customer accounts as a portfolio (see Figure 15.3), using criteria of attractiveness and prospective performance, not simply customer size.

There are situations when SAM is an effective strategy to manage relationships with major buyers and to develop collaboration and partnership rather than adversarial transactions. However, what requires careful management consideration is under what conditions this is true, and whether these are truly the conditions they face. There is potential insight in evaluating the customer portfolio and its changing composition, and to consider not simply the quantity of business offered by the largest accounts, but also the quality of that business. The quality of business with major accounts includes the profitability of the business, but also the business risk involved, the impact of increased dependence on a small number of customers, and the opportunities given up. A balanced evaluation of this kind provides the basis for a more informed decision, but may also be the trigger for the search for strategic alternatives that may avoid the downside of dependence on powerful key accounts. This balanced evaluation and search for new business models appears urgently needed in many organisations.

15.7   SUMMARY

Strategic sales capabilities are an increasingly vital resource in adding value and sustaining effective customer relationships. Strategic customer management is a broad term describing the sales and account management relationships that link buyers and sellers in business-to-business markets. In particular, it focuses on the choices companies face in how they allocate selling and marketing resources between different customer types and the approaches taken to implementing effective relationships with powerful, dominant customers. The growing attention given to these issues reflects both internal company pressures to reform and reshape the traditional sales organisation so that it can deliver the value and the customer relationship upon which marketing strategy implementation rests. However, the strategic sales organisation elevates attention from the salesforce as the route to implementing strategy, to a force that participates in shaping strategy around the realities of the marketplace. Analysis of the customer portfolio provides the basis for distinguishing between customers in a direct channel and in the traditional middle market, but importantly major account and strategic accounts. Strategic account management represents a new business model based on collaboration and joint decision making between buyer and seller. It provides a mechanism for managing some dominant customer relationships. Nonetheless, while there is a compelling case for strategic account management, there is a balancing case of the vulnerabilities and risks in this model. Managers need to balance these factors carefully in deciding whether to implement strategic account management models. The analysis of choices in marketing is closely related to strategic sales capabilities in the business-to-business marketing company.

Xerox

 Case study

Punchstock/Corbis

In the four years since she was appointed chief executive of Xerox, Anne Mulcahy has cut costs, closed business units, repaired the balance sheet, settled an accounting investigation, outsourced operations, refreshed product lines and rethought strategy. Now comes the hard part.

'They can't ease up on the cost cutting, but what they have really got to do now is grow the top line,' says Jack Kelly, analyst at Goldman Sachs in New York.

It is a measure of Ms Mulcahy's achievement so far that growth is even on the agenda. In 2001 and 2002, against a background of mounting debt, falling sales and an investigation by the Securities and Exchange Commission, the question was whether Xerox would survive.

It is also a measure of her down-to-earth directness that the growth question is tackled head-on: 'We've got to show that we can deliver on the top line as well as the bottom line,' she says. 'This is a defining moment for the company.'

The consensus among Wall Street analysts is that strategy mapped out by Ms Mulcahy and her team could, in principle, deliver all the growth required. This three-pronged approach involves speeding up the shift from black and white to colour copying; pushing hard into the graphics and printing industries with a new breed of high-end digital presses; and persuading big corporate customers to buy not only copiers and printers but also software and services.

The unanswered question is whether Xerox can pull it off. The crisis of 2001 and 2002 was in many ways the culmination of a comedy of errors. Investors still wince at the memory of the botched sales force reorganisation that hastened the exit of then-CEO Rick Thoman. Don't even mention the dysfunctional billing and debt collection system that, in late 2001, exacerbated an already precarious financial position.

The good news is that Ms Mulcahy knows the troubled history as well as anyone. She joined Xerox in 1975 as a sales rep and worked her way up through the managerial ranks. Her husband is a retired Xerox employee; her older brother is part of the senior executive team.

She also knows – and has set out to change – the bureaucratic corporate culture that allowed problems to fester until it was too late for anything but drastic action.

Ms Mulcahy's direct personal style is itself a force for change. Her elevation to the top job was a signal that Xerox would have to shed its lingering stuffiness if it was to survive. The new CEO soon found a weapon that would ram the point home: Six Sigma, the process improvement technique pioneered by Motorola and popularised by General Electric (see below).

She explains: 'I went after Six Sigma because I wanted to embed productivity improvement in the company in a way that would prevent problems building up over time. If you really get it going in your company it massively reduces the chance that you will discover problems that require dramatic restructuring.'

So far, it appears to be working. Thanks in part to productivity improvements yielded by Six Sigma, Xerox has been able to regain market share while also maintaining its investment in research and keeping earnings on a rising trend. Neither has the company slipped on any serious operational banana skins.

But Ms Mulcahy and her team know they are entering a crucial – and potentially dangerous – phase. The growth strategy demands organisational changes of the type that Xerox has stumbled upon in the past. Importantly, the services strategy will make new demands on a sales force that, until now, has focused on selling mostly hardware.

Xerox is hardly the first big company to make the transition from products to 'solutions'. General Electric and International Business Machines, its near neighbours north of New York, made similar journeys in the 1990s. More than half of IBM's revenue comes from IT-related services.

But the fact that it has been done before does not make it any easier. The immediate task of making it happen at Xerox falls to Jim Firestone, former strategy chief and now head of the North American business.

'We need to integrate services into the discussion from day one with our biggest clients,' he says.

At first glance, the management issue seems trivial. Xerox's small services sales team, numbering 200–300, must be integrated into the 2,500-strong army of account managers and product specialists. Crucial to this process are the 'major account managers' who look after relationships with Xerox's 300 largest corporate customers. They must be educated in the art and science of selling services: everything from analysis of document flow through organisations to outsourcing of document imaging, archiving and retrieval. This is a very different proposition to selling copiers and printers.

But while the number of people is tiny as a proportion of the total workforce (Xerox employs 58,000 worldwide), on their shoulders rest many of the company's most important client relationships. Ineffective – or disaffected – account managers could cause more than a blip in quarterly revenues and earnings.

'When we did this in the past we did this in a way that caused a lot of disruption for the customer. This time we don't anticipate that many account managers will change roles. The emphasis is on stable account relationships,' says Mr Firestone, whose style is as measured as Ms Mulcahy's is direct.

Judging the pace of change correctly is crucial. Move too quickly and relationships are jeopardised. Proceed too slowly and competitors move in. Hewlett-Packard is counting on its printing and imaging division to drive growth and already boasts a large services division. Ikon Office Systems, which distributes Canon, Ricoh and HP equipment, is another formidable competitor – and, incidentally, another proponent of Six Sigma.

'The services-solutions arena is getting more crowded,' observes Mr Kelly at Goldman Sachs.

Against this background, Xerox has reached the point where it must press ahead with organisational changes and trust to careful planning. Even the cautious Mr Firestone concedes: 'This set of changes is in many ways the most fundamental we have made in changing the nature of Xerox.'

Adventures in Six Sigma: how the technique helped Xerox

Like many other US companies, Xerox was introduced to Six Sigma through its interactions with General Electric. The financial services to biotechnology conglomerate adopted the metrics-mad process improvement technique in the mid-1990s. Thanks to its size and influence, it has served as an effective missionary.

Anne Mulcahy's conversion came as she was negotiating the outsourcing of Xerox's troubled billing and collections operation to GE Capital. She recalls: 'I remember sitting there and watching the discipline with which [the GE team] defined the problem, scoped the problem and attacked it from a Six Sigma perspective. I remember feeling for the first time that the problem would be fixed.'

The precise definition of Six Sigma quality is an error rate of 3.4 per million. More important than the exact number, however, is an approach to problem solving that emphasises small teams, measurement and economic return.

Quality improvement techniques were by no means new to Xerox. In the 1980s, it was one of the first US companies to adopt Total Quality Management (TQM) as it fought to turn back the tide of Japanese competition.

As an up-and-coming manager, Ms Mulcahy experienced TQM first hand. 'The financial metrics were not as precise with TQM,' she recalls. 'Six Sigma is very rigid and very disciplined by comparison. Every project is managed with economic profit metrics. There is none of the squishy stuff.'

The 'squishy stuff' is the emphasis in TQM on consensus building that, while part of an earnest desire to replicate the best of Japanese management, did not always play well at US companies.

Ms Mulcahy is also at pains to point out that Xerox practises Lean Six Sigma, a variation that asks managers to think not only how processes can be improved but also how waste can be reduced: 'Lean is an important nuance. The leaning process begins with taking out waste, working out where value gets added and where it does not. For big companies, this is very important.'

While companies generally adopt Six Sigma to improve efficiency, converts insist that there are other benefits. The introduction of a company-wide approach to project management is reckoned to break down barriers between departments, and make it easier to work with suppliers and customers. Ms Mulcahy says: 'The reality of our business is that in order to compete you have to find ways to deliver 8, 9, 10 per cent productivity improvements every single year. You only get there if you have a systemic approach.'

Source: Simon London, 'Xerox runs off a new blueprint', *The Financial Times*, 22 September 2005.

Discussion questions

1 How does strategic customer management differ from selling? How is it strategic?

2 Xerox aims 'to show that [they] can deliver on the top line as well as the bottom line'. How can strategic customer management help the company achieve this aim?

3 How can Xerox implement an SCM programme? What challenges is it likely to face?

chapter sixteen

Strategic alliances and networks

The competitive realities of surviving and prospering in the complex and rapidly changing business environment encourage teaming up with other companies. Co-operative strategic relationships among independent companies are escalating in importance.

David W. Cravens (1997)

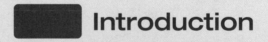 **Introduction**

The environment in which businesses must go to market has changed radically in most sectors. We will consider the nature of this revolution and its profound implications further in Chapter 19. For the moment we note that the new environment for business is increasingly characterised by:

● **scarcer resources**, literally, in the physical environment, and also in terms of the down-sized, leaner, strategically focused corporation;

● **increased competition**, frequently from new sources, new types of competitor and new technologies, at home and overseas;

● **higher customer expectations** for service and quality from more sophisticated and better informed customers, requiring high levels of expertise at the market level;

455

- **pressures from strong distributors,** like retailers in consumer goods marketing, to achieve ever-greater economies in supply-chain costs;

- **high levels of customer concentration** in many business-to-business markets, shifting power from seller to buyer;

- the onslaught of **internationalisation of markets and competition**, driven by such technological forces as the Internet;

- **faster rates of change in markets and technologies**, demanding higher levels and more rapid responsiveness in organisations; and

- **more turbulent, unpredictable markets**, where change is great in magnitude and very difficult to anticipate with any high degree of certainty.

Importantly, business environment changes of this kind, and the new business models they demand, have been associated with the evolution and growth of new organisational forms. Often these new types of organisational arrangements reverse the historical trends of aggregation and integration into large conventional structures, in favour of disaggregation and devolution of functions:

> *Organizations of the future are likely to be vertically disaggregated: functions typically encompassed within a single organization will instead be performed in independent organizations. The functions of product design and development, manufacturing, and distribution . . . will be brought together and held in temporary alignment by a variety of market mechanisms.*

(Miles and Snow, 1984)

The realignment of company resources with the demands of a new and more challenging business environment – characterising the 1990s and 2000s – has seen the widespread emergence of strategies of collaboration and partnership with other organisations as a key element of the process of going to market. While precise terminology does not exist, these new organisational forms and network arrangements have been variously termed marketing partnerships, strategic alliances and marketing networks (Cravens and Piercy, 2006).

In some interesting ways, the trend towards interorganisational collaboration in the route to market provides the other face of relationship marketing. While the priority of managing better the relationship with the customer remains, for a growing number of companies this is accompanied by the need for efforts to be made in managing the relationship with the collaborator as well. These new collaborative and networked organisations are distinctive and different from conventional structures. They are, for example:

> *characterized by flexibility, specialization, and an emphasis on relationship management instead of market transactions . . . to respond quickly and flexibly to accelerating change in technology, competition and customer preferences.*

(Webster, 1992)

It is important to recognise that in many industries the emergence of networks of collaborating organisations, linked by various forms of alliance, has become a dominant platform for strategic development. For example:

- It was estimated that by 2001 the top 500 global businesses had an average of 60 major strategic alliances each.

- At the end of the 1990s, it was reported that the number of US company alliances had grown by more than 25 per cent annually for the previous five years.

- In 1993, when Lou Gerstner took over as CEO, only 5 per cent of IBM's sales outside personal computers were derived from alliances. By 2001, IBM was managing almost 100,000 alliances, which account for more than one-third of its income.

- A Vantage Partners survey of the top 1,000 US companies in 2003 found that nearly 20 per cent of their income resulted from alliances, with forecasts this would reach 30 per cent by 2004, and continue to grow. Reliance on alliances was even higher in European companies.

- Outsourcing and networking has become a major strategy at marketing research agencies like A.C. Nielsen (Cravens and Piercy, 2006).

In the light of such evidence of the growing importance of alliance and inter-organisational collaborative forms, it is important that our thinking about the implementation of our own strategies, and also our understanding of the emerging forms of competition we face in the market, should embrace the strategic alliance and the resulting growth of networks of organisations linked by various forms of partnered relationship. However, it is also important to emphasise that some of the strategic issues faced in alliances and networks go far beyond simple inter-organisational cooperation, but are leading to new ways of doing business with the customer.

This chapter examines the following issues as a framework for competing through strategic alliances and networks:

- the implications of an era of strategic collaboration for our strategic choices;

- the types of partnership, collaboration and strategic alliance which are emerging in the marketplace, as important ways of building networks;

- the forms which networks of collaborating organisations take, and the development of new organisational forms for marketing based on networks;

- the importance of strategic alliances as a competitive force in global markets;

- the risks involved in strategies of collaboration and alliance;

- a management agenda which details the issues that should be addressed in evaluating alliance-based strategies as a way for us to go to market.

16.1 The era of strategic collaboration

Cravens and Piercy (1994) argued that factors like rapidly changing markets, a complex array of technologies, shortages of important skills and resources, and more demanding customers present organisations with an unprecedented set of challenges (e.g. Tapscott and Castor, 1993; Gummesson, 1994). One central feature of effective response to these challenges has been the recognition by many business executives that building relationships with other companies is essential to compete effectively in the turbulent and rapidly changing post-industrial era confronting the developed world economies, and in working with the rapidly growing opportunities in the Asian and Chinese markets. In effect, we are experiencing an important change from an era of competition to an era of strategic collaboration.

There are a variety of interorganisational relationships which we have increasingly to consider in building effective marketing strategies: vertical channel relationships and supplier/manufacturer collaborations, and horizontal relationships in the form of strategic alliances and joint ventures – all share a growing emphasis on collaboration and partnership rather than simple contractual obligations.

These new collaboration-based relationships with customers, suppliers, distributors and even competitors are resulting in a variety of new organisational forms, which are commonly grouped together and classified as 'networks', where members may constitute 'virtual corporations' (Achrol, 1991; Quinn, 1992; Ring and Van de Ven, 1992; Webster, 1992). As we shall see, many of the pioneers have been in the services sector, but networks spanning complexes of supply chains are becoming more usual. In fact, the network paradigm may become the dominant organisation form of the twenty-first century – the revolutionary nature of the changes occurring in the traditional hierarchical forms of organisations and the adjustment of their traditional adversarial relationships with suppliers and competitors is underlined by the comment of John Sculley, then the Chairman of Apple Computer: 'the network is *the* paradigm, not the Catholic Church or the military' (Sculley, 1992).

The reality we face may be a complex mix of collaborative organisational forms with conventional structures. For example, formed in 1969 by the merger of the Standard Bank of British South Africa and the Chartered Bank of India, Australia and China, Standard Chartered is one of the world's most international banks with an extensive global network of over 1,400 branches – many in the fast-growing markets in Asia, Africa and the Middle East (which regions provide 90 per cent of the company's profits). Standard Chartered's impressive international performance is based on a complex network of subsidiaries, acquisitions, strategic alliances, associates and joint ventures, to achieve deep local market knowledge alongside global capabilities. A simple, single channel route to market and conventional organisational structure could not sustain this level of performance (*Al Bawaba*, 2006b).

We shall examine a variety of examples of network organisations below, but the characteristics of network organisations can be discussed in the following terms. A defining characteristic of the network organisation is the performance of marketing and other business functions by different independent organisations and individuals – the process of 'vertical disaggregation' (Cravens *et al.*, 1994). The network is a flat organisational form, involving interaction between network partners rather than the multi-layered functions of the traditional hierarchical organisation.

In fact, dramatic changes are taking place in the traditional hierarchical forms of organisations as a result of alliance and network strategies. Although in some ways similar to channel of distribution networks (e.g. suppliers/producers, marketing intermediaries and end users), network organisations may display both horizontal and vertical structures (e.g. collaborations between suppliers as well as supply chain linkages). Moreover, networks are frequently complex and liable to change more frequently than traditional distribution channels. Interestingly, recently network concepts have fed back into traditional channel structures, in the form of collaborative 'channel partnerships' which go far beyond conventional channel relationships (Buzzell and Ortmeyer, 1994).

Typically, network operations are guided by sophisticated information and decision support systems, often global in their scope, which perform many of the command and control functions of the traditional hierarchical organisation (Tapscott and Castor, 1993). The resulting network is flexible and adaptable to change, and the more successful network designs are customer driven – guided by the needs and preferences of buyers (Powell, 1990). Quinn (1992) characterises networks as 'intelligent enterprises', and outlines various structural concepts such as infinitely flat, spider's web, starburst and inverted organisations. As we shall see below, the resulting networks may be complex and unfamiliar.

The interorganisational ties in a network may span organisations from suppliers to end users, and/or actual or potential competitors. The network may also include service agencies, such as advertising, research, consulting services and distribution specialists. The relationships among the firms in a network may include simple transactional contracts of the conventional buyer–seller type, supplier–producer collaborative agreements, strategic alliances or partnerships, consortia, franchising and distribution linkages, joint ventures or vertical integration (Doz, 1988; Achrol, 1991; Anderson and Narus, 1993; Bucklin and Sengupta, 1993; Cravens et al., 1993). We shall examine these relationships in more depth below.

Developing from these general points about networks, we shall attempt in this chapter to build a framework for evaluating, designing and managing network organisations as part of the implementation of marketing strategy and as a fundamental change in the competitive scenario. However, it is important to recognise that our understanding of the network paradigm is still relatively limited, although we certainly know that it is different: 'These relationships vary in significant ways from those governed by markets or hierarchies, and pose very different issues for researchers and managers' (Ring and Van de Ven, 1992). Our lack of developed knowledge and effective management capabilities for managing in these new organisational forms is illustrated by the continued high failure rate of strategic alliances.

16.2 The drivers of collaboration strategies

A starting point is to identify the potential drivers or motivating factors that lead organisations towards collaboration in delivering their strategies to market. Such driving forces include factors like the following.

16.2.1 Market complexity and risk

Modern markets are frequently characterised by complexity and high degrees of risk. One way of coping with that complexity and reducing (or sharing) risk is through collaboration. For example, Microsoft invested some $150 million in developing Windows NT, but this product was pre-sold to PC manufacturers prior to production; when the PC partners could offer 5 million unit sales, then the product was manufactured. This type of complexity and risk may be exhibited in various situations:

- **Blurring of market boundaries** – conventional market definitions may become outdated and expose a company to new types of customer demand and new types of competition. The information industry is a prime example, where we see the telecommunications, consumer electronics, entertainment media, publishing and office equipment industries becoming intermingled. A converging industry greatly increases the complexity for a single firm trying to compete in the face of a widening range of customer requirements and technologies to satisfy customer needs. Many of the products required are likely to be beyond the design, manufacturing and marketing capabilities of a single company, thus driving companies to pool their skills. This pooling of capabilities may be very effective – Hewlett-Packard and Matsushita combined their relative capabilities in ink-jet and fax technologies to enter the market for an ink-jet fax machine far more rapidly than either could have done alone. Similarly, technological convergence making the mobile telephone both a camera and a music player have disruptive effects for the traditional photography and music businesses.

- **Escalating customer diversity** – in many markets buyers are demanding increasing value but also uniqueness in their purchases: one-to-one marketing, or micro-segmentation, is becoming a reality. To respond positively to this demand may be beyond the scope of a single company in terms of expertise and economy, and may require new ways of doing business. For example, Calyx & Corolla (C&C) reinvented the US market for fresh flowers by developing a network organisation (see Figure 16.1). Traditionally, fresh flowers are a week old when purchased and displays are expensively made to order at a retail flower shop level, if a standard display is not what the customer wants (and if the shop has a wide enough range in stock). The C&C network markets fresh flowers by catalogue (print and online), offering more than 100 flower arrangements and designs. Customer orders are phoned/faxed/e-mailed to C&C, and the information is transmitted by computer link to one of the growers in the network and to Federal Express. The growers make up the chosen design, branded by its packaging as a C&C product, which is then collected by Federal Express and shipped to the customer. The customer has a far greater choice, the flowers received are up to nine days fresher, and three middlemen are avoided. This is a new way of going to market that reflects the need for 'mass customisation', but that offers superior value at the same time. It has only been achieved by developing an effective network organisation.

- **A borderless world** – Ohmae (1990) wrote about the interlinked economy of *The Borderless World*. Companies are increasingly driven to compete globally, and collaboration offers an attractive alternative to competing alone in a new

Figure 16.1	The Calyx & Corolla network organisation

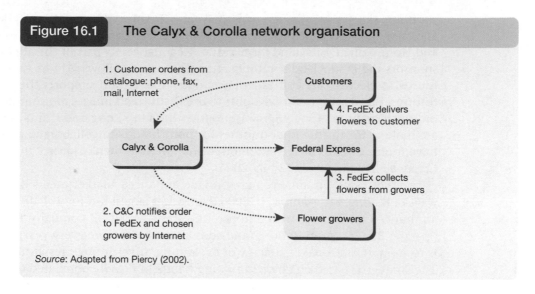

Source: Adapted from Piercy (2002).

environment. For example, British Airways' globalisation strategy is driven by international partnerships with other carriers – a partnership with USAir offered access to the US internal market, although this partnership collapsed and BA entered an alliance with the stronger American Airlines to control more than 60 per cent of transatlantic traffic. The competitive importance of this alignment is demonstrated by the outraged opposition provided by the other international airlines, led by Richard Branson of Virgin, and the continued hostility of the European competition regulators.

16.2.2 Skills and resource gaps

It follows that there are growing pressures on firms to collaborate to compete effectively in globalised, technology-driven markets. The costs of developing internally the full range of skills and capabilities needed to compete effectively may be beyond the resources of a single company, or simply more cheaply available through alliances with specialised partners – where each partner can concentrate on applying its own core competencies, i.e. what it does best.

This may be of most importance with strategic accounts – the powerful major customers upon whom we have greatest dependence as a seller (see Chapter 15). Strategic customers generally seek 'solutions-oriented' packages that relate to their business problems and opportunities, and will accept nothing less from their strategic suppliers. Selling products or services is not acceptable. The problem faced is that constructing the appropriate 'solution' for the strategic customer may involve expertise and technology that forces the seller to partner with others. Johnson Controls, for example, is the highly successful seller of automotive seating and electrical switching. While Johnson manufactures seats and switches, it has had to partner with others to provide the simple 'bolt-on', modularised seating and electronics components systems required by modern car assembly plants.

Filling skills and resource gaps may also involve the creation of new brands and new business forms in surprising ways. For example, 2006 saw Honda Motor and Hong Kong Disneyland form a strategic alliance. As part of the alliance, Honda sponsors the Disneyland's Autopia attraction, which allows visitors to 'drive to the future' in electric cars and experience 'outer space', and supports the park's safety features. Honda gets exclusive rights to use Disneyland images to promote their cars, motorcycle and power equipment products in Hong Kong and China. The partners are looking for further opportunities for both brands to collaborate, and appear to have found ways to merge automotive and entertainment industry interests (*Japan Corporate News Network*, 12 July 2006).

In other cases, an alliance may provide enhanced market access and open new ways of trading. For example, in 2006 the world's largest fast-food chain, McDonald's, announced an alliance with Sinopec, the state-owned oil company in China that operates 30,000 petrol stations (and adds around 500 more every year). The alliance is to support McDonald's strategy of expanding drive-through restaurants in China. The strategy is based on changing eating habits in heavily populated Chinese cities, which are becoming more Westernised, with more widespread car ownership and mobile lifestyles among the young, which favour purchases directly from vehicles. McDonald's believes that Sinopec will provide a platform to build its China business around drive-through restaurants (Yeh, 2006).

16.2.3 Supply chain management

One manifestation of the pressure to collaborate has come through the proposal for the 'lean enterprise' (Womack and Jones, 1996), and perhaps most clearly in the related efficient consumer response (ECR) programme in the grocery business.

One powerful example of lean thinking is ECR, which is advanced in the US and starting to impact in Europe. ECR is based on 'cooperative partnerships' between retailers and manufacturers who commit to collaborate in reducing costs in the supply chain. Three years after launch in the US, 90 per cent of firms in the grocery business were participants in ECR. Launched in 1996 in the UK, participants included the six major retailers and the leading manufacturers of packaged goods. The key elements of ECR are: category management instead of the traditional product and brand approach, and the elimination of weak brands; more efficient promotion by substituting value pricing for special offers; continuous replenishment systems and cross-docking to reduce and possibly eliminate stocks in the channel; electronic data interchange for automated ordering and information flow; and organisational change – Procter & Gamble in the US has replaced its sales organisation with its new customer business development organisation. ECR is a powerful weapon which demonstrably reduces supply chain costs, but has been criticised for reducing consumer choice and competition and restricting manufacturer strategic development (Piercy, 2002).

These developments are dangerous to ignore as they provide powerful pressures towards collaboration between companies conventionally viewed as having only a buyer–seller relationship, or which were traditionally competitors. It is important that in evaluating our markets and our strategies for the future we should carefully and systematically consider the emergence of factors like those listed above, which may drive our competitors' and our own strategies into collaborative network forms.

The next questions to consider are the types of networks which can be identified and the nature of the links which hold them together. As strategic alliances have become one of the most important organisational forms in modern business, managers are constantly faced with decision choices in terms of which type and form of alliance should be adopted (Pansiri, 2005).

16.3 Types of network

There is no broadly accepted typology of network organisational forms. However, two approaches are useful in clarifying our ideas about the types of network which exist and may emerge in our markets.

First, Cravens *et al.* (1996) integrated the perspectives offered by Achrol (1991), Powell (1990), Quinn (1992) and Webster (1992) to propose the model of network organisation types shown in Figure 16.2. They argued that networks differed and could be classified in two important respects:

1 **The type of network relationship**, which can vary from the highly collaborative (involving various forms of interorganisational cooperation and partnership), to the mainly transactional (the traditional buyer–seller transaction, for example).

2 **The volatility of environmental change** – the argument that, in highly volatile environments, external relationships with other organisations must be flexible enough to allow for alteration – and possibly termination – in a short time period. On the other hand, when the environment is more stable, more enduring forms of collaboration are more attractive.

Using these dimensions to classify networks produces the model in Figure 16.3, suggesting that there are at least four types of network prototype:

1 **The hollow network** – a transaction-based organisational form, associated with highly volatile environments. The term 'hollow' emphasises that the core organisation draws heavily on other organisations to satisfy customer needs. For example, organisations that compete in this way are often specialists that coordinate an

Figure 16.2 Types of network organisation

		Environmental volatility	
		Low	High
Type of network relationships	Collaborative	Virtual network	Flexible network
	Transactional	Value-added network	Hollow network

Source: Adapted from Cravens *et al.* (1996).

Figure 16.3	The marketing exchange company

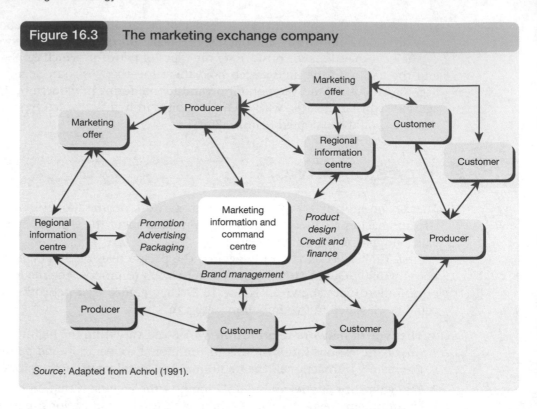

Source: Adapted from Achrol (1991).

extensive network of suppliers and buyers. One example of this type of network is Monster.com, the online recruitment and careers company. Monster connects job seekers with employers, as well as providing them with careers advice online. Some 75 million individuals have established personalised accounts with Monster, which operates in 36 countries with 4,200 employees. The hollow organisation offers a buffer against the risks in a frequently changing environment (Achrol, 1991).

2 **The flexible network** – associated with conditions of high environmental volatility but characterised by interorganisational links which tend to be collaborative and long term in duration, where the network coordinator manages an internal team that identifies customer needs and establishes sources of supply to satisfy customer requirements. For example, many of the multinational pharmaceutical firms are tied to core competencies in organic and inorganic chemistry and are seeking to establish alliances with entrepreneurial biotechnology firms. The larger firms have too much invested in their current technology to switch completely to biotechnology, but want to exploit partnerships to ensure they have a source of biotechnology-based products. The Calyx and Corolla (C&C) example discussed earlier also provides a model of a flexible network, where C&C acts as a hub performing internally product design, packaging design, promotion and pricing, but using a network of external partners to provide the flowers and deliver them to the customer. It is notable, for example, that ICL, once the 'British' computer

company (renamed Fujitsu Services in 2002 to reflect its changed ownership), no longer owns factories to manufacture computers; it focuses on service and design and sources hardware from partner organisations.

3 **The value-added network** – associated with less volatile environments and based mainly on transactional relationships between network members. For example, the network coordinator may use a global network of suppliers, but still maintain substantial internal operations – the core organisation may contract for many added-value functions such as production, but retain responsibility for innovation and product design. The Bombay Company, a successful speciality furniture retailer in the USA, is an example of this network form. The Bombay Company has transactional (buyer–seller) links with speciality producers throughout the world – the company buys from 27 countries, with focus on suppliers in China, Malaysia, Vietnam, Taiwan, India and Indonesia. The Bombay role in the network is to design, source and market products in home furnishings and décor. Suppliers provide 90 per cent of Bombay's purchases to design. A particular supplier may produce only a contracted quantity of table tops, which are assembled by another company along with other items produced by other suppliers to produce tables. The transactional relationship is appropriate because the supplier is simply filling a contract for one of their standard products. Members of the network are specialists in performing certain value-adding functions at low cost. The Bombay Company's ability to construct and market a unique product selection through its network has achieved substantial success in the US marketplace, with licensed stores now opening in the Middle East and Caribbean areas. Other industries using this type of network are clothing manufacture, furniture, eye-glasses and some services – the link is that the value-added network fits situations where complex technologies and customised product offerings are not required.

4 **The virtual network** is associated with situations where environmental volatility is relatively low, and the core organisation seeks to establish collaborative relationships with other organisations. This is similar to what has been called the 'virtual corporation' (*Business Week*, 1993), which seeks to achieve adaptability to meet the needs of segmented markets through long-term partnerships rather than internal investment. Examples of companies forming virtual networks include GE, Hewlett-Packard and Motorola. In these cases market access and technology access are the key drivers and, as with the flexible network, formal strategic alliances are the most common method for collaborating. The virtual network provides a buffer against market risks and access to new technology.

A broader and more complex view of network types has been provided by Achrol (1997), who has attempted to reflect three important characteristics that may differentiate different types of network: whether they are single-firm or multi-firm; whether they are single-industry or multi-industry; and whether they are stable or temporary. Achrol's (1997) view of networks identifies the following types:

● **Internal market networks** – this describes the re-formation of major companies to break free of the restrictions of traditional hierarchies and multi-divisional forms, by organising into internal enterprise units that operate as independent profit centres. For example, General Motors has reorganised its rigid and inefficient component manufacturing units into eight internal market units, each specialised in an automotive system area and able to sell its products on the open market as well as to GM, including GM's competitors in automotive manufacture.

- **Vertical market networks**, or **marketing channel networks**, reflect the traditional view of vertical channel relationships, but go further to recognise the focal firm that coordinates upstream supplier firms and downstream distributor firms. Often the integrator specialises in marketing functions and uses specialists for manufacture and distribution. Early forms included the 'hollow corporation', for example Casio, Nike, Liz Claiborne. In such networks, the typical pattern is that the integrator is the firm which owns the brand and which specialises in the marketing function, while alliance partners are specialised resource centres providing some aspect of product or production technology. Another example is provided by IKEA, the retailer of Swedish furniture, which successfully operates a global sourcing network of 2,300 suppliers in 67 countries, to get 10,000 products on the shelf at prices up to 30 per cent cheaper than traditional rivals. On the other hand, in technology-based markets the integrator may well be a technology specialist – Sun Microsystems has subcontracted chip manufacturing, distribution and service functions to specialise in designing advanced computers. Achrol suggests this is not so much a strategic alliance as a functional alliance.

IKEA

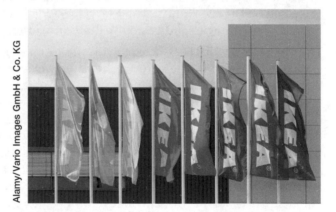

Alamy/Vario Images GmbH & Co. KG

- **Intermarket or concentric nFetworks** – this is largely the province of the Japanese and Korean economies – the well-known *keiretsu* and *chaebol* 'enterprise groups' representing alliances among firms operating in a variety of unrelated industries. The intermarket network involves institutionalised affiliations among firms operating in different industries and the firms linked in vertical exchange relationships with them. They are characterised by dense interconnections in resource sharing, strategic decision making and culture and identity. The centre may be a trading company – possibly functioning as the marketing arm of the network – associated with manufacturing affiliates, which in turn have large vertical clusters of subcontractors, distributors and satellite companies, and are often involved in technology alliances with competitors. For example, Toshiba has around 200 companies in a direct exchange relationship, and another 600 'grand-child companies' below them. While the Japanese and Korean networks may appear impenetrable, it is interesting to note that recent commentators have attempted to explain the operation of Virgin as a *keiretsu*, to explain the growth of the business through music and entertainment, transportation, financial services and diverse branded goods linked primarily by the Virgin brand and mainly funded by partner organisations.

- **Opportunity networks** – this is represented as a set of firms specialising in various products, technologies or services that form temporary alignments around specific projects or problems. Characteristically, the hub of the network is a marketing organisation specialising in collecting and disseminating market information, negotiating, coordinating projects for customers and suppliers, and regulating the network. Achrol (1991) has described this as the 'marketing exchange company', as we saw earlier (see Figure 16.3). One prototype is the direct marketing company using media like the Internet to market a wide variety of consumer products and novelties.

This review illustrates the diversity and potential complexity of network organisational forms as they are emerging and as we are trying to classify and understand them. However, it remains true that our general understanding is not well developed: 'network and virtual organizations have been here for a long time, although our ability to define them and communicate their true content is still limited' (Gummesson, 1994).

We may be able to improve that understanding if we turn our attention next to the nature of the links which tie organisations together in these various forms of collaboration.

16.4 Alliances and partnerships

Achrol (1997) underlines the importance of thinking of networks in the terms of relationship marketing, where the relationships between network partners go beyond those that would be defined by contract or written agreement or buyer–seller exchanges in the channel of distribution. He argues that 'the mere presence of a network of ties is not the distinguishing feature of the network organization', but that 'the quality of the relationships and the shared values that govern them differentiate and define the boundaries of the network organization' (Achrol, 1997).

This said, a starting point in understanding the dynamics of the network organisation, and its attractiveness or otherwise in developing a specific marketing strategy lies in analysing partnership. It is important that we do not see strategic alliances and network formation as ends in their own right, but as a means to an end – the implementation and regeneration of our marketing strategy and the enhancement

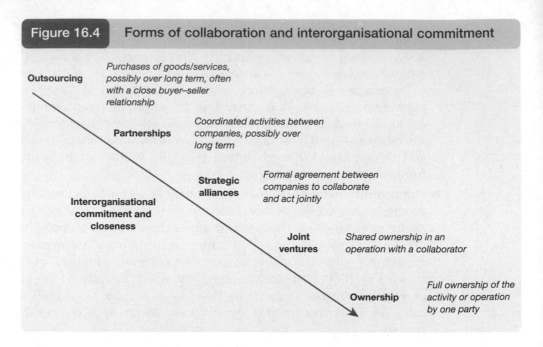

Figure 16.4 Forms of collaboration and interorganisational commitment

Outsourcing — *Purchases of goods/services, possibly over long term, often with a close buyer–seller relationship*

Partnerships — *Coordinated activities between companies, possibly over long term*

Strategic alliances — *Formal agreement between companies to collaborate and act jointly*

Interorganisational commitment and closeness

Joint ventures — *Shared ownership in an operation with a collaborator*

Ownership — *Full ownership of the activity or operation by one party*

of our process of going to market – to be used selectively and appropriately based on our objectives and our capabilities for managing collaborations with other organisations.

One way of categorising collaborative relationships is shown in Figure 16.4. These relationships form a spectrum running from a largely traditional, transactional relationship to full-scale vertical integration. The relationships shown have the following characteristics.

16.4.1 Outsourcing

At one extreme is an 'arm's length' relationship, where we may simply buy in goods and services from outside, as the alternative to producing them internally. This might involve outsourcing for services like advertising, market research, the sales-force, and direct marketing expertise. It may also describe how we buy in goods for resale, or handle relationships with our distributors. However, increasingly even at this end of the spectrum people may see suppliers and distributors as partners and use terms like 'strategic alliance' to describe what appear to be no more than conventional, though close, buyer–seller relationships. This may be inaccurate, but underlines Achrol's point above that networks are about more than the nature of the legal ties between partners. Transactional relationships of this kind also characterise what Cravens *et al.* (1996) described as value-added and hollow networks (see above). It is also true that in many situations arm's length relationships are reshaping into closer collaborative relationships – for example, in the efficient consumer response programme (see above), and in the customer pressure in business-to-business marketing for suppliers to build closer relationships between all their resource departments and the equivalents in customer organisations (see Chapter 15). In such cases, what starts as outsourcing may acquire many of the collaborative characteristics of a formal strategic alliance.

For example, British Airways is outsourcing significant sections of its business, as part of an array of franchising, alliance and partnership relationships with other companies, in moving towards the concept of a 'virtual airline'.

For quite other reasons, 2006 saw Gap Inc. opening its first franchised stores. Faced with falling sales in North America and Europe in its owned stores, Gap has partnered with Singapore retailer F.J. Benjamin Holdings to open franchised Gap stores in Singapore and Malaysia. These are to be followed by Banana Republic franchises (Gap's upmarket brand). Faced with problems in its established markets, Gap has turned to franchising to gain rapid entry to new markets, where its brand is known to consumers who travel to the US and Europe and buy in Gap stores (Lim, 2006).

GAP

Alamy/PSL Images

16.4.2 Partnerships

These are collaborations that involve a closer relationship between organisations, but stopping short of a formal strategic alliance agreement, shared ownership in a joint venture or vertical integration. Lambert *et al.* (1996) suggest that partnerships vary in the degree and type of integration. They suggested that: (1) some partnerships are short term in focus and involve limited coordination; (2) other partnerships have a longer-term focus and move beyond coordination to integration of activities; and (3) the closest partnerships are viewed as 'permanent' and each party views the other as an extension of its own firm.

For example, in a strategic alliance extending to 2011, Dell Inc. and EMC have a partnership relationship in the data storage business, providing advanced networked storage solutions for organisations of all sizes. The partnership has made Dell the fastest growing disk storage systems seller, and EMC the mod-tier market share leader in revenue. The combined capabilities of Dell and EMC have made a major impact on the data storage business; Dell and EMC have leveraged a unique model of sales, marketing, engineering and manufacturing collaboration to exploit each other's strengths and deliver superior value to customers (*Al Bawaba*, 2006a).

A different form of marketing alliance is shown by the Jigsaw Consortium formed by Cadbury Trebor Bassett, Unilever and Kimberley-Clark. The consortium is managed for the members by direct marketing agency OgilvyOne. The members of the consortium own brands like Persil, Flora, Lynx, Huggies, Cadbury Creme Egg and Flake. The alliance has created a consumer database covering the purchasing behaviour and brand attitudes of 9 million consumers. Importantly, while retailers like Tesco and Sainsbury's have the strength of consumer purchase data through point-of-sale scanning, the consortium database includes attitudinal data for additional insight and predictive power.

16.4.3 Strategic alliances

Strategic alliances are more formal arrangements, sometimes under contract, for companies to collaborate and act jointly. The defining characteristics of strategic alliances are that (1) two or more companies unite to pursue a set of agreed goals, but remain independent even though in an alliance; (2) the alliance members share the benefits of the alliance and control over the assigned tasks; and (3) the firms in the alliance contribute on a continuing basis to one or more strategic areas (e.g. technology sharing, product development or marketing) (Taylor, 2005; Todeva and Knoke, 2005).

For example, AT&T (the leading US high-speed DSL, Internet and consumer voice services company) and Yahoo (the global Internet destination company) have operated a successful strategic alliance since 2001, to bring broadband Internet services to a wide range of consumer and small business customers. Together the companies provide a fully integrated, co-branded broadband experience serving the majority of AT&T's 8 million high-speed DSL Internet customers (*FinancialWire*, 2006).

16.4.4 Joint ventures

These are alliances where the ownership of a project or operation is shared between the parties concerned. For example, Mercedes, the German car company, and Swatch, the Swiss watch company, entered into a short-lived joint venture to produce the smart minicar, supported by partnership sourcing by its ten key suppliers, which relocated their operations to a 'smart ville' in France. This relationship focused on partners from different industries sharing innovative design abilities, technological expertise and marketing capabilities to innovate. The concept was that the partners were selling 'mobility' as a total product, not just a car – the overall market offer included the ability to borrow larger cars when needed for particular mobility needs. The joint venture became a wholly owned subsidiary of DaimlerChrysler (it is now part of Mercedes Car Group).

16.4.5 Vertical integration

An activity in another part of the value chain is fully owned by the core organisation, although the relationship may still be seen as a strategic alliance, even though strictly one company owns another. Apple Inc. provides an interesting example of a company which is vertically integrated using both outsourcing and direct financial ownership. Apple designs the computer hardware, accessories, operating system and much of the software itself, but does not manufacture. Production is outsourced to specialist suppliers like Foxconn. Apple has recently established a chain of high-profile, upmarket retail outlets to protect its consumer market position, using forward vertical integration to retain control over its product presentation in the marketplace.

It is important that we consider the strengths and weaknesses of these different degrees and types of partnership in developing appropriate alliance strategies, and that we recognise that in reality networks may contain a mix of different partnership styles. It should also not be assumed that interorganisational relationships are static – collaborative forms may change or be removed during the course of a project, for example if one partner is gaining benefits while the other(s) is/are not. For example, BMW and Rolls-Royce operated an alliance in the form of a joint venture – BMW Rolls-Royce GmbH – for some ten years in the aerospace industry, focused on advanced aero engine development. The partners succeeded in producing a commercially successful family of advanced engines. The alliance provided Rolls-Royce with a stronger product strategy, but after ten years BMW withdrew to concentrate on the automotive industry and the business became wholly owned by Rolls-Royce as Rolls-Royce Deutschland (Smith, 2003).

16.5 Strategic alliances as a competitive force

It is important that we recognise in our marketing strategy development that, in some markets, competition is increasingly based on the relationship between alliances and the networks they create and no longer between individual companies. This is particularly true in global businesses:

● 2007 saw German car manufacturer Volkswagen establishing a strategic alliance – half-ownership but with management control – with Proton in Malaysia. While struggling Proton was looking for an established global player to bring greater economies of scale in operations, purchasing and R&D, the attraction for VW was gaining better access to the south-east Asia passenger car market and its expected growth. The Proton alliance offers VW a filler for a gap in its coverage of the south-east Asia region, but also complementary capacity to its plants in China and its Skoda factory in India (Shameen, 2007). Increasingly, the global automotive business is characterised by global networks, rather than free-standing manufacturers. As part of its massive restructuring and downsizing strategy, Ford Motor Co. is not merely willing to cut some of its brands, but is looking for strategic alliances with other carmakers (industry rumours suggest that Renault-Nissan may be a target) (*Business Week*, 2006).

- In the aerospace industry, 2007 saw a strategic alliance between Boeing and Lockheed-Martin. By working together the companies can leverage their expertise in air traffic management and aircraft-focused solutions to transform air traffic control system products. Lockheed-Martin brings air traffic route management experience, while Boeing contributes expertise in aircraft systems, avionics and airspace simulation and modelling (*Airline Industry Information*, 2007).

- The international airline business is dominated by alliances, each anchored by a small number of major airlines, and built through relationships with a cluster of smaller companies offering additional geographical coverage and links. The main alliances and their anchors are: Star Alliance (Lufthansa and United); Oneworld (BA and American); SkyTeam (Air France/KLM, Delta). Moves towards more extensive partnering around China and the Far East are under way. The airline alliances have pioneered the establishment of alliances as brands in their own right (He and Balmer, 2006).

At the very least, our analysis of competitive structures would be potentially misleading if we did not account for the potential impact of strategic alliances.

16.6   The risks in strategic alliances

We stressed earlier that strategic alliances are no panacea. They may be an important way to achieve the things we need, but there are significant risks also. To begin with, we should be aware that, for one reason or another, strategic alliances sometimes simply do not work, and they may crash spectacularly:

- IBM and Microsoft were partners in the 1980s, and Microsoft provided the DOS operating system that drove IBM's PCs. However, IBM did not have exclusive rights to DOS and it was adopted by their competitors in clones of the IBM PC. IBM lost much market share and profit, while Microsoft benefited from the additional sales of DOS under licence. In 1985 IBM signed a formal joint development agreement with Microsoft to create the next generation operating system – OS/2. The development of OS/2 proceeded slowly. Meanwhile, Microsoft developed Windows, which was quickly taken up by the market – the same market IBM wanted for OS/2. The alliance exploded in an acrimonious press conference in Las Vegas in 1989. The partners finally parted company in 1991. As a partnership, the alliance had been a total failure. However, as in many 'divorces' the division of costs and benefits was far from equal: Microsoft got the time and space to develop the worldwide success of Windows, while IBM was left with the unpopular OS/2 system in a market now dominated by Microsoft. Perhaps unsurprisingly, Microsoft and IBM are now deadly rivals.

- A key component of British Airways' globalisation strategy was its partnership with USAir, to gain access to the critical internal US market. By 1996 the two companies were in court because BA had announced a new alliance with American Air. The first that the chairman of USAir knew of this was when he read the news in the *Wall Street Journal*. The USAir/BA alliance crumbled immediately. However, competitors including Virgin and a new alliance of US airlines is doing its utmost to prevent the BA/AA alliance.

- Rover and Honda formed an early R&D and marketing partnership in the UK automotive industry. Some fifteen years into that partnership, in secret negotiations, Rover was sold to BMW, the German car company. Rover appeared to believe that the Honda partnership was part of the deal. The acquisition came as a surprise to Honda which, on considering its options, withdrew from the partnership to avoid allowing BMW access to Honda technology.

- We described above how the strategic alliance has become the dominant competitive form in the global airline business. Nonetheless, airline alliances have proved unstable with sometimes dramatic membership shifts and withdrawals. Indeed, some passenger groups are critical of the code-sharing that results in a passenger buying a ticket with Airline A, only to find themselves sitting in a seat on an aircraft owned by Airline B (which was by definition not their chosen carrier). In addition, there are growing concerns that the strength of the alliance brand may undermine the brands of the partner organisations (Kalligianis *et al.*, 2006).

- A study by Cravens *et al.* (1993) found that in 82 large multinational corporations fewer than half the companies operating strategic alliances were satisfied with the effectiveness of those alliances.

It is perhaps wise not to overestimate the strength and durability of strategic alliances. Quinn noted some time ago:

Like earlier decentralization and SBU concepts, some of these newer organizational modes have been touted as cures for almost any managerial ill. They are not. Each form is useful in certain situations, and not in others. But more importantly, each requires a carefully developed infrastructure of culture, measurements, style and rewards to support it. When properly installed, these disaggregated organizations can be awesomely effective in harnessing intellectual resources for certain purposes. When improperly supported or adapted, they can be less effective than old-fashioned hierarchies. (Quinn, 1992)

Indeed, as well as the outright failure of an alliance and the crash of the network involved, there are a number of other important issues to bear in mind as potential limitations to the application of strategies of collaboration.

Achrol (1997) argues that we should consider the following factors as key elements of designing and operating network organisations (see Figure 16.5).

- **Power**: we need to take a careful look at the relative dependence and power within a network, both in terms of whether the relative position we take is acceptable to us and if we are going to be able to cope with the way power is likely to be exercised in the network, and how vulnerable this may make us.

- **Commitment and interdependence**: at its simplest, are the people in the partnering companies going to be behind the alliance, and what mechanisms may be needed like interlocking directorships and exchange of personnel or other liaison mechanisms? In the *keiretsu*, the Japanese refer to what is necessary to 'keep each other warm' (Gerlach, 1992); their example suggests we should not underestimate the importance of people's commitment, or lack of it, in an effective network organisation.

- **Trust**: the network organisation requires that each partner give up some influence or control over important issues and become vulnerable to ineffective or

Figure 16.5	The jigsaw of network organisations

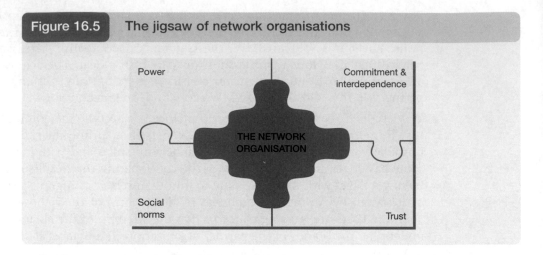

hostile actions by other network members. This is a key aspect of relationship management in a network. The cases of network failure cited above illustrate the vulnerability involved. Compare this with the risk of lack of commitment to a collaboration through an unjustified lack of trust in the partner organisation, and the significance of the issue becomes clearer. This point is underlined in Morgan and Hunt (1994).

● **Social norms**: it is suggested that network organisations should be considered in terms of behavioural issues like (a) solidarity – the unity of action among network members, (b) mutuality – network partners acting in the common good and receiving a pay-off in terms of benefits from the collaboration, (c) flexibility – the willingness of partners to change the joint arrangements as conditions change, (d) role integrity – clarity in what each partner organisation is to do, (e) conflict handling – agreement on how conflicts will be handled in the network. The important point to bear in mind is that, while organisations are familiar with how to handle these questions in conventional, independent, hierarchical structures, we are still learning how best to manage them in the very different setting of the collaborative network of organisations.

We need to consider the attractiveness of a collaborative or alliance-based strategy in terms not simply of the pressures of factors like resource gaps and market access, but also in the light of whether we can design and implement an effective network, and whether we have the skills and capabilities to manage through a network of relationships with other companies.

We shall consider these points in more detail in the managerial agenda in the next section. Issues like trust, commitment and power may hold the key to identifying the large business risks involved in reliance on strategic alliances. For example, we discussed earlier the successful partnership between AT&T and Yahoo to provide integrated broadband services to AT&T customers. Notwithstanding the success of the relationship, in 2007 AT&T placed a story with the *Wall Street Journal* indicating that its DSL partnership with Yahoo was in jeopardy. The story led to a 5 per cent drop in Yahoo's share value and removed $2.2 billion in Yahoo's market value. In fact, Yahoo obtains $250 million a year in high margin revenue from monthly fees for AT&T's subscribers to the broadband service. AT&T wants to retain more of the customer revenue and to pay Yahoo only a percent of revenue for the sale of the products Yahoo provides (music, photo services, etc.). One reason AT&T now believes it should not have to share its broadband subscription revenue is approaches from other Internet companies prepared to pay to reach its broadband customers – rumours suggest the most significant approach has been from Google (Arrington, 2007). As situations change, so may the commitment of a partner to an alliance. The risk of opportunistic behaviour by a partner is an important issue to be monitored (Kale *et al.*, 2000).

16.7 Competing through strategic alliances

The discussion above and the examples examined in this chapter suggest that the managerial issues that should be addressed carefully and systematically in evaluating the strategy of collaboration and alliance as a route to market are the following.

16.7.1 Core competencies

One of the fundamental attractions of collaboration and partnership with other organisations is that it allows each organisation to focus on its own core competencies and to benefit from the specialisation of other organisations in their own areas of expertise (Achrol, 1991; Webster, 1992). Quinn (1992) notes: 'If one is not "best in world" at a critical activity, the company is sacrificing competitive advantage by performing that activity internally or with its existing techniques.' Certainly, research by Buffington and Frabelli (1991) in the telecommunications industry suggests that, when partners in a collaboration do not contribute their core competencies, then the probability of success for the alliance is substantially reduced. This suggests that clarity in defining those core competencies may be critical to negotiating and sustaining effective interorganisational relationships of this type.

However, there are two problems. First, it is clear that the identification of core competencies may be far from straightforward within an organisation or between partners (e.g. see Piercy and Cravens, 1996). Second, we have to factor in not just existing and recognised core competencies, but issues of complementarity and 'fit' between potential partners, and the potential for synergy through collaboration (Sengupta and Bucklin, 1994).

16.7.2 Strategic priorities

The issue of core competencies also raises important questions about competitive strategy and the choices faced in when, where and how to compete (Prahalad and Hamel, 1990). While networking offers a company the opportunity to focus on and exploit its core competencies, it will rarely create such capabilities for a company.

However, this focus and concentration may create vulnerabilities. We saw earlier that the British Airways alliance with USAir collapsed before the new alliance with American Airlines was approved. This left BA potentially with no US-based collaborator and highly exposed to competitive attack by other alliances. While there is much current favour in corporate thinking for strategic focus and concentration, using collaborations as a vehicle, we should be aware of the risks involved in this prioritising. Reliance on partners to perform critical activities involves risks if the partnership fails or underperforms, and may leave us without the capacity to develop new competencies.

16.7.3 Managing network organisations

It is apparent from the case examples above that organisations differ markedly in their ability to manage effectively in networks. Forming and managing networks calls for a different set of management skills and issues compared with the conventional organisation. *Business Week* (1993) concluded that for managers in the 'virtual corporation':

> They'll have to build relationships, negotiate 'win-win' deals, find the right partners with compatible goals and values, and provide the temporary organization with the right balance of freedom and control.

Research suggests that lack of success in business partnerships and alliances is frequently because companies pay inadequate attention to planning. Lack of careful planning leads to conflicts about strategy, problems with governance and missed opportunities (Bamford *et al.*, 2004). Bamford *et al.* (2004) suggest forming a team dedicated to exposing tensions as early as possible, and to deal with four challenges: (1) to build and maintain strategic alignment across the partner companies; (2) to create a shared governance system; (3) to manage the economic interdependencies between the partner organisations; and (4) to build a cohesive organisation.

Indeed, many of the problems which have emerged in the management of alliance-based organisations were captured in Bensimon's (1999) executive guidelines.

● Assimilate the competencies of your partner.

● Think of your partner as today's ally and tomorrow's competitor.

● Share power and resources, but share information wisely.

● Structure your alliance carefully.

Before making the commitment to enter an alliance, we should consider the following factors:

● **Drivers** – which of the drivers of collaboration strategies apply in this case? What does a collaboration strategy offer us in terms of: asset/cost efficiencies; customer service improvements; marketplace advantage over the competition, profit stability/growth (Lambert *et al.*, 1996)?

● **Choice of partners** – which potential partners are available, and what basis do we have for believing that we could create an environment of trust, commitment and cooperation between the members of the alliance (Cravens *et al.*, 1997)?

● **Facilitators** – are the circumstances and environment favourable for a partnership? Lambert *et al.* (1996) suggest that partnerships are more likely to be successful if the following conditions prevail:

- *corporate compatibility*: the cultures and business objectives of the partners must mesh;

- *managerial philosophy and techniques*: are the partners' organisational structures, attitudes towards employees and method of working compatible?

- *mutuality*: are there equally important benefits for both partners?

- *symmetry*: are the partners similar types of company that understand each other?

- *exclusivity*: are partner organisations willing to shut out others who are not part of the network?

- *shared competitors*: partnerships work best as an alliance against a common foe;

- *prior history*: experience in successful collaboration is a plus;

- *shared end user*: when partners serve the same customer, collaboration is likely to be more successful.

● **Components** – these are the activities and processes that management establishes and controls throughout the life of the partnership, and effective partnerships understand these from the outset (Lambert *et al.*, 1996). This includes arrangements for joint planning, joint operating controls, communications between partners, equitable risk/reward sharing, facilitating trust and commitment between partner organisations, a contract acceptable to both sides, the definition of the scope of the partnership and clarity about the financial investments to be made by partners.

● **Network effectiveness** – we saw earlier that Cravens *et al.* (1993) found that many companies pursuing alliance-based strategies were dissatisfied with the results. Defining realistic expectations at the outset and evaluating progress against them is required. We may have to think in terms of somewhat different measures to the conventional evaluation of effectiveness – network stability and sustainability, relationship strength, network synergy, and the like. If we cannot offer convincing evidence that the network provides a superior way of going to market, it is unlikely to endure. We consider the evaluation and appraisal process in more detail below.

● **Organisational change** – it is highly likely that the formation of network organisations will be stimulated by, and in turn lead to further changes in, alliance companies' internal organisational structures and processes. The requirements for effectiveness here may be complex and currently outside the experience of many senior managers in traditional organisations (Cravens *et al.*, 1996). The complexity of this issue is underlined by Gummesson (1994): 'organizing a network business requires continuous creation, transformation and maintenance of amoeba-like, dynamic processes and organizational structures.'

● **Market orientation and customer service** – a particular point of concern for the marketing strategist is the impact of networked operations on the market orientation of the new type of organisation and its ability to deliver the required levels of customer service and superior customer value. Where the primary motivation for collaboration is technological or supply-chain efficiency, this may be a particularly significant concern. For example, we reported elsewhere that some companies in the airline business are moving towards the concept of the 'virtual airline' which owns no aircraft or facilities and exists primarily as a brand and information system with a small core staff. Some executives suggest that, while the core organisation is highly market-oriented and committed to high-quality service, in a networked organisation they lack the means to share these imperatives with their partners. Quite simply, we may believe in service quality at the core airline, but is this shared by the people who run the operation the customer experiences at check-in (Piercy and Cravens, 1996)? This suggests that one of the major questions we need to consider is what mechanisms we may need to create to drive goals like service and quality through a network to the end user.

- **The role of marketing in network organisations** – there is some lack of clarity about how marketing is located and operated in a network organisation. In some models, like the 'marketing exchange company', the hub of the network is the marketing facility (Achrol, 1991). Others suggest that the critical role for marketing in the alliance-based network is applying relationship marketing skills to managing the links between partners in the network (see Chapter 17 and our discussion of internal marketing as an implementation approach in partnerships). Certainly, there is a compelling argument that the concepts and processes of relationship marketing are pivotal to the management of networks. Relationship marketing involves the creation and distribution of value through mutual co-operation and interdependence (Sheth, 1994), and we have seen that cooperation and interdependence are central features of network organisations. It is too early to reach conclusions about the role that marketing can and will take generally in these new organisational forms, although it is highly likely that there will be some redefinition of its role which may be radical.

16.7.4 Staying vigilant

As experience grows in the advantages and pitfalls of going to market or operating key processes through strategic alliances, it is apparent that there may be temptations to persist with alliance relationships way past the point where this makes sense. The benefits of some interorganisational relationships may be transitory, and the relationship may need to be reconsidered on a regular basis. Indeed, one of the attractions of networked organisations is that they may be designed to be temporary and to exploit a given opportunity, and then be dissolved. However, there is evidence that recognising the point when the alliance should end and managing the dissolution or disengagement process may pose some problems.

For example, there is some evidence that managers may be reluctant to end alliance relationships, even though they have evidence that the alliance is failing to meet its purposes and there is little chance that things will improve. This appears to be most likely with large joint ventures when closing costs may be high, sunk costs may have escalated, and where the alliance has high visibility – terminating large expensive partnerships may impact negatively on management careers and prospects (Delios *et al.*, 2004).

While an early concern about strategic alliances was that they could be unstable and unreliable because of the nature of interorganisational, non-ownership relationships, it has been suggested, for example, that alliances may be too stable. Companies are urged now to routinely review and rethink their alliance arrangements. Rather than waiting for a crisis to emerge, a company should scan its major alliances to see which need restructuring, to understand the root causes of the venture's problems, and to estimate how much each problem is costing the company (Ernst and Bamford, 2005).

Indeed, there may be greater risks that emerge in some situations which are even more threatening than inertia allowing underperforming alliances to stay in place. The outsourcing or contract manufacturing area provides an illustrative example of the risks to be considered. Contract manufacturing is attractive to an original equipment manufacturer (OEM), the traditional brand owner, because it reduces labour costs and frees up capital to outsource manufacturing, leaving the OEM free to focus on product research, design and marketing. This practice started in the computer business, and has spread to areas as diverse as toys, clothing, footwear, beer and pharmaceuticals. Even in the automotive sector, Finland's Valmet Automotive assembles the Porsche Boxer, and Austria's Magna Steyr assembles cars for Mercedes, BMW and Saab. However, research suggests that the outsource relationship may develop in threatening ways, where the contract manufacturer displays:

- **Promiscuity** – the contract manufacturer seeks business with OEM's competitors.
- **Infidelity** – the CM becomes a competitor by selling to the OEM's retailers and distributors.
- **Betrayal** – the CM shares the OEM's intellectual property with competitors or retains it for its own exploitation.

Meanwhile, the OEM cannot terminate the outsourcing because there are no alternative sources of product. Considerable care is required in making outsourcing decisions and deciding when they should end (Arruñada and Vázquez, 2006).

It is likely that reliance on strategic alliances will continue to increase but, as situations change, companies will need to consider what is involved in effective disengagement from an alliance.

16.7.5 Asessing the performance of strategic alliances

It is perhaps symptomatic of the relative lack of maturity of the strategic alliance organisational model that it is claimed that a major reason for the high failure rate of alliances is that relatively few have developed and implemented formal performance measures (Cravens *et al.*, 2000). Appropriate control mechanisms will depend upon the underlying rationale for the alliance relationship, i.e. the strategic intent of the partners; the form of the alliance relationship; and the strategic objectives of the relationship. This context provides the basis for selecting evaluation criteria and methods of evaluation and implementing an alliance evaluation plan. For example, the evaluation criteria for a global airline alliance, reflecting the 'Balanced Scorecard' approach (Kaplan and Norton, 1996), and the several stages of management control activity are shown in Table 16.1.

This provides a generic template, but one that should be adapted and refined for specific application. The goal of establishing and clarifying the performance criteria for an alliance and evaluating performance against those criteria is, however, a general requirement.

Table 16.1 **Selecting the evaluation criteria for a global airline alliance**

Management control activities	Balanced Scorecard dimensions			
	Financial	*Customer focus*	*Internal business process*	*Learning and growth*
Planning	Profit by route and coverage of destinations	Identify potential customer groups not served by existing routes	Identify partner responsibilities	New ideas for the extension of the collaboration
Coordinating	Potential income from network	Use of airline lounges by partners' passengers	Savings from shared services	Increase in market share from collaborative routes
Communicating	Detailed financial reports by segment for passengers using alliance network	Potential increase in load factors from partners' customers	Process improvements initiated by partners relative to the alliance	Employee satisfaction regarding alliance
Evaluating	Revenue per seat mile from collaboration relative to potential	Repeat and new customer passenger miles by customer type and route	Provision of comparable service for customers on collaborative routes	Employee productivity by function and general service activity for collaborative routes
Deciding	Operating profit per seat mile from collaboration	Market share on collaborative routes	On-time performance on collaborative routes	Demand information by segment on collaborative routes
Implementing	Percentage contribution of collaboration load factor	Customer complaints from collaborative routes	Performance improvement and complaints reduction on collaborative routes	Staff turnover relative to collaborative routes

Source: Adapted from Cravens *et al.*, 2000.

16.7.6 Disengaging from alliances and networks

Vigilance and more thorough appraisal are likely to identify situations where it is desirable to end an alliance relationship. Research suggests that companies face important challenges in withdrawing or disengaging from alliances that are under-performing or have outlived their usefulness. For a start, companies may not recognise the life cycle underlying the alliance relationship, and treat alliances as though they were permanent organisational arrangements (Taylor, 2005). The problem is compounded because typically disengagement is not agreed at the outset of the alliance. It is highly desirable to negotiate exit options while still at the alliance formation stage, with clarity about the events or contingencies which will trigger the termination of the alliance.

It appears that part of the problem is that without clear agreement on how to withdraw from an alliance relationship, when tensions arise between partners, managers may be reluctant to report problems, fearing they will be blamed for the alliance's failure. Instead, they tend to blame their alliance counterparts. The typical outcome is likely to be a dysfunctional strategic alliance characterised by deep animosity between alliance managers, making negotiation of alliance termination highly problematic. It may be more effective to handle alliance disengagement with a core team of senior managers, chosen in part because they were not involved in the original alliance. A strong communications plan also assists in avoiding damage to the company's reputation during the break-up (Gulati *et al.*, 2007).

Summary

We have argued in this chapter that there are many factors compelling organisations to collaborate and form alliances with others, rather than to compete independently – we may be in an era of collaboration rather than competition. The network paradigm is impossible to ignore for two reasons: it may be how we take our strategy to market; and it may be how our competitors build their market power. The factors driving this process include market complexity and risk, skills and resource gaps, supply chain management imperatives, and the strategic priority of focusing on core competencies and outsourcing to partners for other activities and resources.

We attempted to identify the types of networks which are emerging in the modern marketplace. One approach looks at the type of relationship on which alliance is based and market volatility in order to identify the hollow network, the flexible network, the value-added and the virtual network (Cravens *et al.*, 1996). A broader view suggests that there are internal market networks, vertical market networks, inter-market or concentric networks and opportunity networks (Achrol, 1997). Related issues concerned the type of relationship ties between network members, ranging from outsourcing, through partnership, to joint venture and vertical integration.

The conclusion we reached at this point was that strategic alliances are a major competitive force, which in some industries like the airlines, computing and telecommunications is replacing conventional competition between individual companies. However, the cases and studies available to date suggest that, while the potential gains may be great, strategic alliances and networks carry major risks.

This led us to an important management agenda to be considered in evaluating the importance of strategic alliances and networks as part of marketing strategy. We suggest that, in considering a strategy of alliance, managers should focus on the issue of core competencies brought to the alliance by each partner, and the benefits and vulnerabilities associated with focus and outsourcing, and the capabilities that a company has to manage its strategy through a very different organisational environment. Questions to raise regarding those managerial capabilities include: understanding the underlying drivers favouring collaboration strategies, the choice of partners, the facilitators and components important to effective collaboration, the ability to define and evaluate network effectiveness in achieving marketing goals, and the capacity of a network to deliver the customer value on which our marketing strategy is based. The redefinition of the role of marketing also falls into this area. Maintaining vigilance regarding changing circumstances and an effective alliance appraisal approach are priorities for managing in networked strategies. Managing disengagement or withdrawal from ineffective or damaging alliances may be a necessary consequence of improved appraisal and control.

Strategic alliances and networks are not a panacea for strategic problems. They are an important development with many potential benefits. They also carry major strategic risks and vulnerabilities, and demand new managerial skills. This is an issue requiring particularly careful and detailed analysis.

Yahoo and eBay Case study

Courtesy of Ebay UK

A new web of strategic alliances between the US internet giants started to take shape yesterday as Yahoo the biggest online portal, and Ebay, the world's leading e-commerce company, announced plans to tap into each other's large online audiences.

For now, it seems, full mergers are not on the cards. But as the internet companies grapple with tying their services more closely together and learning more about each others' user bases, the impetus towards deeper links could accelerate, according to analysts.

In the early days of the internet, alliances between big online firms took the form of traffic deals with e-commerce or media companies typically paying portals like AOL for the privilege of advertising their brands and linking to their sites.

Those links generally proved ineffective in driving traffic. AOL's inability to renew the partnerships was a big reason for the drop-off in its revenues after the dotcom bust. Now a new network of more coherent commercial relationships has started to form, as the internet companies look to profit from each others' traffic without the disruption and potential loss of momentum big mergers would entail.

The most fundamental driving force has been the rise of search advertising, a form of advertising that is expected to generate $10bn for Google alone this year.

As the largest supplier of graphical, or 'branded', advertising, Yahoo is also looking to extend the reach of its advertising network more broadly across the web. Along with Microsoft, which has just entered the business, Google and Yahoo are rushing to sign up the remaining big untapped audiences on the web while forging ties to new users coming online.

Ebay's audience remains one of the most attractive under-utilised communities on the internet.

To power its sites, which let buyers trawl for goods to buy from millions of different sellers, it has built a search engine to compare with those of the big web search firms, at least in terms of scale.

According to Ebay executives, the 350m searches a day carried out on its sites rivals the number of searches on Google.

However, for Ebay, 'monetising' those searches by placing ads in front of shoppers raises some difficult questions.

Sellers pay listing fees for the privilege of having their goods displayed on Ebay and included in its internal search results. Putting ads on these pages could frighten buyers away, creating a form of competition that would weaken the value of an Ebay listing.

Executives of both Ebay and AOL made clear yesterday that they would tread carefully. While Yahoo will supply graphical, or 'branded', advertising to all Ebay sites, the search ads will be limited.

Meanwhile, new audiences are quickly emerging online, such as those created by MySpace and other social networking sites.

It will not be easy to build an advertising business around these new audiences, which are converging around communications services like e-mail and instant messaging, as well as user-generated content like personal blogs and photographs.

As Steve Ballmer, chief executive officer of Microsoft, pointed out this month, MSN has one of the biggest user bases online, thanks largely to its role as the world's largest instant messaging service.

Yet it has yet to find a way to serve up ads to these people.

Also, many advertisers may hesitate before linking their brands to the burgeoning user-generated content on the web – a point made by Yahoo, which questions how much of the traffic on a site like MySpace is susceptible to advertising.

While search advertising has been the most significant factor, other chances to cash in on their mutual audiences are also driving the new online alliances.

Through its ownership of the PayPal online payments system and the Skype internet voice service, Ebay owns two of the Web's best-known brands. Linking with Yahoo may give it the chance to extend the reach of those services to a community of users that now numbers more than 400m people.

Wall Street has turned a sceptical eye of late on Ebay's claims for the broader potential in these services, making the Yahoo alliance the first potential validation of its strategy.

Source: Richard Waters, '400 m Internet users. But how to reach them?' *The Financial Times*, 26 May 2006.

Discussion questions

1 What factors are compelling Yahoo and Ebay, already 'internet giants', to collaborate and tap into each other's online audiences?

2 What are the potential risks associated with such an alliance?

3 What types of networks are potentially emerging across the web?

17

Strategy implementation and internal marketing

You want to create the same buy-in to the products, services, and philosophy of your organization among your employees as you would hope for among customers.

Susan Drake *et al.* (2005)

A company is either customer-focused from top to bottom, or it simply is not customer-focused . . . To become genuinely customer-focused you have to be prepared to change your culture, processes, systems and organization.

George Cox, Chief Executive, Unisys Ltd, June 1995

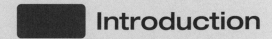 **Introduction**

This chapter continues our consideration of marketing strategy, by evaluating the issue of implementation and particularly the role of internal marketing in enhancing and sustaining a company's ability to compete. There are several different models of internal marketing which overlap to a degree and require clarification (since as a consequence there are a number of different roles that internal marketing can play in a company's strategic development in different situations). Linkages between internal marketing and certain of the issues we have examined earlier include the following:

● Much new thinking and practice in strategic marketing is concerned with *managing relationships*: with the customer (see Chapter 14), and with partners in strategic alliances (see Chapter 16). However, a further aspect of relationship management and relationship marketing is the relationship with the employees and managers, upon whose skills, commitment and performance the success of a marketing strategy unavoidably relies. This is the internal market inside the company. The logic being followed by an increasing number of companies is that building effective relationships with customers and alliance partners will depend in part (and possibly in large part), on the strengths and types of relationships built with employees and managers inside the organisation. The goal may be for all employees to become 'brand ambassadors' – brand owners such as Unilever, SABMiller, Cadbury Schweppes and BT are among those with established internal marketing excellence programmes to pursue this goal (*Brand Strategy*, 2006). At Honda, for example, all new staff receive the 'Book of Everything' containing the normal employee handbook information but also extensive explanation of the Honda brand philosophy – 'spreading "Honda-ness" and turning people into brand ambassadors' (Croft, 2007). In some companies, the emphasis has turned from internal communications to internal branding to build employee understanding and buy-in to corporate brand values – British Petroleum uses a behaviour reward scheme, based on its 'new spirit of radical openness', and a 'discuss, discover, and define' programme to show employees how to turn its brand values into actions that improve performance (Dowdy, 2005).

- We have emphasised the importance of *competitive differentiation* to build market position. Yet truly exploiting a company's potential competitiveness and its capabilities in reality is often in the hands of what Evert Gummesson (1990) has called the 'part-time marketers', i.e. the people who run the business and provide the real scope for competitive differentiation. Indeed, in some situations, the employees of a company may be the most important resource that provides differentiation. Certainly, research at Northwestern University found internal marketing to be one of the top three determinants of a company's financial performance – companies with better integration of internal and external marketing report better financial results (Chang, 2005).

- In a similar way, the growing emphasis on competing through superior *service quality* relies ultimately on the behaviour and effectiveness of the people who deliver the service, rather than the people who design the strategy. When the Hampton Inn hotel chain in the US was ready to roll out 122 changes to its products and services, its new marketing campaign was 'Make It Hampton', but was aimed at hotel managers and employees, not guests. Building internal brand enthusiasm and employee motivation involved a giant model of a hotel to showcase the improvements and allow employees to experience them, motivational conference calls, focus groups, targeted newsletters and training materials. The end of the first phase of 'Make It Hampton' saw a 5 per cent increase in market share, and a similar growth in the percentage of highly satisfied customers (Drake *et al.*, 2005).

485

- Indeed, increasingly it is recognised that one of the greatest barriers to effectiveness in strategic marketing lies not in a company's ability to conceive and design innovative marketing strategies or to produce sophisticated marketing plans, but in its ability to gain the effective and enduring *implementation* of those strategies. A route to planning and operationalising implementation in strategic marketing is 'strategic internal marketing' (Cespedes and Piercy, 1996).

These applications suggest that, depending on the particular circumstances, the internal marketing process might include the following types of activity and programme:

- Gaining the *support* of key decision-makers for our plans – but also all that those plans imply in terms of the need to acquire personnel and financial resources, possibly in conflict with established company 'policies', and to get what is needed from other functions like operations and finance departments to implement a marketing strategy effectively.

- Changing some of the *attitudes and behaviour* of employees and managers, who are working at the key interfaces with customers and distributors, to those required to make plans work effectively (but also reinforcing effective attitudes and behaviour as well).

- Winning *commitment* to making the plan work and 'ownership' of the key problem-solving tasks from those units and individuals in the firm whose working support is needed.

- Ultimately, managing incremental *changes in the culture* from 'the way we always do things' to 'the way we *need* to do things to be successful' and to make the marketing strategy work.

The potential importance of internal marketing to relationship marketing strategies, to strategic alliances, to competitive differentiation, to delivering superior service quality and above all to effective marketing implementation is underlined by the growing emphasis placed by companies on this issue. Nonetheless, studies suggest that many organisations reveal an 'inadequate' state of internal marketing – they cannot deliver their brand propositions, for example, because of lack of investment in the internal company marketplace (*Marketing Week*, 2003).

Certainly, it remains true that internal marketing means very different things in different companies and different situations. If we are to evaluate the potential contribution of internal marketing to building and implementing our competitive strategy and achieving our chosen position in the market, then we need to consider such issues as the following:

- the sources of internal marketing theory;
- the types of internal marketing practice in companies;
- how internal marketing can be planned as part of our competitive strategy; and

- the implication for other significant relationships such as the potential partnership between marketing and human resource management within organisations to achieve the effective implementation of marketing strategies.

However, first we place internal marketing in the context of strategy implementation, and the challenge that execution poses for marketing managers. Our view of internal marketing is that it provides a model to facilitate a company's effective execution of marketing strategies.

17.1 The strategy implementation challenge in marketing

Achieving more effective implementation or execution of marketing strategies remains a high priority for many organisations, because of the long history of strategy implementation failures which they may have experienced. For example, on the general front, Miller (2002) suggests that organisations fail to implement more than 70 per cent of their new strategic initiatives.

In fact, there are many pitfalls faced in moving from strategies and plans to effective implementation and the changes that are usually involved for an organisation, its people and its partners. One listing of implementation pitfalls likely to resonate with managers' experiences identifies the following issues:

- **Strategic inertia** – things never get started because executives resist change or fail to give it priority.
- **Lack of stakeholder commitment** – not having everyone on board, particularly at middle management levels, where progress can be blocked.
- **Strategic drift** – a lack of focus on where the strategy should end up, leading to failure to reach that destination.
- **Strategic 'dilution'** – an absence of strong drive behind the strategy means that managers give more priority to operational decisions than strategic goals.
- **Failure to understand progress** – not having the appropriate metrics to monitor progress towards strategic goals.
- **Initiative fatigue** – too many 'top priority' projects lead to cynicism and inadequate emphasis on the strategy.
- **Impatience** – expecting results too quickly, and giving up when the reality is slower.
- **No celebrating success** – failing to recognise and reward milestones that lead towards the strategic goal (Freedman, 2003).

In fact, there is a strong argument that much of the implementation problem comes down to the fact that generally managers are trained to plan, not to execute, and frequently are judged on their capabilities for managing day-to-day operations rather than strategic initiatives. The problem is likely to be worse when execution is seen as a low-level responsibility in the organisation (Hrebiniak, 2006). In fact, the reality is that strategy and implementation are interdependent – strategic choices should be linked to implementation capabilities, and implementation capabilities should be developed in line with strategic imperatives, and the dichotomy between strategy and implementation is false and unproductive (Cespedes and Piercy, 1996). Nonetheless, the tendency to separate strategy from implementation remains in organisations and creates obstacles and challenges in executing strategic initiatives.

Hrebiniak (2006) draws on a range of research studies and discussions with managers to identify the following factors as the top obstacles to effective strategy execution:

- **Inability to manage change effectively and overcome resistance to change** – managing change well is vital to effective strategy implementation. Nonetheless, where change impacts on corporate culture, then moving too fast may be dangerous.

- **Poor or vague strategy** – good implementation capabilities cannot compensate for a strategy which is weak or ambiguous. Strategy drives execution, and if strategy is unclear or weak then implementation is irrelevant.

- **Not having guidelines or a model to guide strategy implementation efforts** – managers want a logical model to guide implementation efforts and actions, particularly in translating strategic imperatives into practical actions.

- **Poor or inadequate information sharing among individuals/units responsible for strategy execution** – poor sharing of information or poor knowledge transfer and unclear responsibility and accountability make it unlikely strategy implementation will be effective.

- **Trying to execute a strategy that conflicts with the existing power structure** – working against the power structure presents a major obstacle to implementation effectiveness, and underlines the importance of gaining the support of the influential in the organisation and forming coalitions to share implementation responsibility.

- **Unclear responsibility or accountability for implementation decisions or actions** – lack of clarity in responsibility for implementation and the achievement of measurable progress presents another obstacle to effective implementation.

Similarly, it has been suggested that:

> *One key reason why implementation fails is that practicing* [sic] *executives, managers and supervisors do not have practical, yet theoretically sound, models to guide their actions during implementation. Without adequate models, they try to implement strategies without a good understanding of the multiple factors that must be addressed, often simultaneously, to make implementation work.*

(Alexander, 1991)

While it is not a complete answer to all these obstacles, internal marketing provides us with a set of tools to address some of the major barriers faced to the effective implementation of marketing strategies, and managing the associated organisational changes. It provides us with a model for structuring and managing the implementation process, defining responsibilities, evaluating progress, and managing the cross-functional relationships important to strategy execution.

17.2 The development of internal marketing

Conventional training and development of marketing executives, quite reasonably, focuses primarily on the *external* environment of customers, competitors and markets, and the matching of corporate resources to marketplace targets. The argument we now present is that, while analysing markets and developing strategies to exploit the external marketplace remains quite appropriately a central focus, it is frequently not enough on its own to achieve the effective implementation of marketing strategies. In addition to developing marketing programmes and strategies aimed at the external marketplace, in order to achieve the organisational change that is needed to make those strategies work, there is a need to carry out essentially the same process for the *internal marketplace* within companies.

That marketplace is made up of the people, the culture, the systems, the procedures, the structures and developments inside the company, whose skills, resources, participation, support and commitment are needed to implement marketing strategies. Indeed, the internal marketplace may increasingly extend to include our partners in alliances and network organisations.

It seems that the reality in many organisations is that often an implicit assumption is made by executives that marketing plans and strategies will 'sell' themselves to those in the company whose support and commitment are needed. When made explicit in this way, it is apparent that this is just as naive as making similar assumptions that, if they are good enough, products will 'sell themselves' to external customers. It is often surprising that those same executives who have been trained and developed to cope with behavioural problems – like 'irrational' behaviour by consumers and buyers, or the problems of managing power and conflict in the distribution channel, or the need to communicate to buyers through a mix of communications vehicles and media, or the problems of trying to outguess competitors – have taken so long to arrive at the conclusion that these same issues have to be coped with *inside* the company. Real commitment to strategic marketing must involve a managerial role of creating the conditions necessary to permit strategic change to happen.

What we are calling strategic internal marketing here has the goal of developing a marketing programme aimed at the internal marketplace in the company that *parallels* and *matches* the marketing programme aimed at the external marketplace of customers and competitors. This model comes from the simple observation that the implementation of external marketing strategies implies changes of various kinds within organisations – in the allocation of resources, in the culture of 'how we do things here', and even in the organisational structure needed to deliver marketing strategies to customer segments. In practical terms, those same techniques of analysis and communication, which are used for the external marketplace, can be adapted and used to market our plans and strategies to important targets within the company. The goals of the internal marketing plan are taken directly from the implementation requirements for the external marketing plan, and the objectives to be pursued.

This is not as radical as it may at first seem. The marketing literature traditionally displayed attempts to link the marketing concept to the 'human resource concept' (e.g. Cascino, 1969; Dawson, 1969) and attention has been given specifically to the interaction between the human and organisational context and the effectiveness of marketing (Arndt, 1983). Other evidence relating to the impact of the internal market on marketing effectiveness has focused on various aspects of the intervention of organisational issues as a determinant of marketing strategies rather than a result of them: Leppard and MacDonald (1987) attempted to relate the effectiveness and appropriateness of marketing planning to the different stages of organisational evolution; John and Martin (1984) have analysed the credibility and use of marketing plans in terms of characteristics of the surrounding organisational structure; Cunningham and Clarke (1976) studied product managers as self-serving manipulators of targets and marketing information; Deshpandé (1982) and Deshpandé and Zaltman (1984) attempted an analysis of the cultural context of marketing management and commented on the lack of a marketing theory of culture; while Bonoma (1985) commented on the problems of a lack of 'marketing culture' in the specific context of implementation obstacles. In a similar way, Ruekert and Walker (1987) studied the interaction between marketing and other functional units and the role of marketing in implementing business strategies.

While this focus on the significance of various dimensions of organisational context provides a foundation, the most specific attention given to acting on the organisational environment through internal marketing, to achieve marketing goals, is found in the services literature. One of the earlier conceptualisations of the employee as 'internal customer' was provided by Berry (1981) in the context of bank marketing, and this theme has been pursued by others, and it is heavily oriented towards the identification of employee training and development needs to improve quality in the delivery of services. Similarly, the interdependence of internal and external markets has been stressed by Flipo (1986), who emphasised the need to overcome conflict and challenges to marketing strategies from the internal market, implicitly following Arndt's (1983) conceptualisation of internal markets in a political economy model of marketing.

Perhaps the best-known conceptualisations of internal marketing come from the 'Nordic School of Services', where among other contributions Grönroos (1984, 1985) has written of the need for strategic and tactical internal marketing, and Gummesson (1987) has studied the use of internal marketing to achieve culture change in organisations. The practical application of these concepts is reflected in the literature of 'customer care' (e.g. Moores, 1986; Thomas, 1987; Lewis, 1989), which emphasises customer perceptions of quality, and the importance of fostering this perception through the training and development of personnel at the point of sale.

There is some established precedent for use of the terms 'internal marketing' and the 'internal customer'. We see these developments as important for two main reasons. First, the internal marketing paradigm provides an easily accessible mechanism for executives to analyse the organisational issues which may need to be addressed in implementing marketing strategies. Quite simply, concepts of marketing programmes and targets are familiar to marketing executives and they are 'comfortable' with them. The second point is that the internal marketing model provides a language which actually legitimises focusing attention on issues like power, culture and political behaviour which appear quite often to be avoided by executives as somehow 'improper'.

17.3 The scope of internal marketing

It follows from the emergence of the internal marketing paradigm from diverse conceptual sources that the practice of internal marketing and its potential contribution to marketing strategy are similarly varied. It is possible to consider the following 'types' of internal marketing, although they are probably not equal in importance:

- internal marketing that focuses on the development and delivery of high standards of *service quality* and customer satisfaction;
- internal marketing that is concerned primarily with development of *internal communications programmes* to provide employees with information and to win their support;
- internal marketing which is used as a systematic approach to managing the *adoption of innovations* within an organisation;
- internal marketing concerned with providing products and services to users *inside the organisation*; and
- internal marketing as the *implementation strategy* for our marketing plans.

17.3.1 Internal marketing and service quality

The original and most extensive use of internal marketing has been in efforts to improve the quality of service at the point of sale in services business like banking, leisure, retailing, and so on – the so-called 'moment of truth' for the services marketer. Some call this 'selling the staff', because the 'product' promoted is the person's job as a creator of customer service and value. This tends to be seen in customer care training programmes and similar initiatives. These types of internal marketing programme are, in practice, essentially tactical and often restricted to the operational level of the organisation.

The logic is that it is apparent and obvious that marketplace success is frequently largely dependent on employees who are far removed from the excitement of creating marketing strategies – service engineers, customer services departments, production and finance personnel dealing with customers, field sales personnel, and so on. As we noted earlier, these are all people Evert Gummesson (1990) called 'part-time marketers' – they impact directly and significantly on customer relationships, but are normally not part of any formal marketing organisation, nor are they typically within the marketing department's direct control.

Indeed, US research suggests we should think more carefully about the impact of the organisation's external communications on employees – as 'advertising's second audience' (Gilly and Wolfinbarger, 1996). The chances are that employees are more aware and more influenced by our advertising than are our customers, so the suggestion is that we should use that awareness productively to deliver messages to employees.

There are a growing number of cases of companies whose service quality excellence has been driven by explicit attention to internal marketing. Southwest Airlines is the much-admired originator of the 'no frills' airline model, and has achieved not only outstanding profit performance in a difficult sector, but has also regularly won industry awards for service quality and low levels of customer complaints. From the outset, Southwest's mission statement said, 'Above all, employees will be provided the same concern, respect and caring attitude within the organization that they are expected to share externally with every Southwest customer'. The company uses high employee morale and service quality to achieve excellent profitability. Tactics include offering employees a vision that provides purpose and meaning to the workplace, competing aggressively for the most talented people, providing skills and knowledge, but also emphasising teamwork and motivation, and ensuring that organisational management understands the internal customer. The effect is an integrated internal marketing approach that drives service quality. Southwest shows the positive impact of internal marketing on employees, external customers and performance. Southwest's success is based in large part on its employees' positive attitudes, high productivity and customer orientation. (Czaplewski *et al.*, 2001).

It can be argued that there is no one 'right' strategy in any given product market situation, but there are good and bad ways of *delivering* market strategies, which determine if they succeed or fail. The critical issue is becoming the consistency between strategies, tactics and implementation actions. This suggests that real culture change is a central part of the process of going to market effectively. At its simplest, the disgruntled employee produces the disgruntled customer. Bonoma (1990) summarises this point succinctly: 'treat your employees like customers, or your customers will get treated like employees'.

However, it is apparent that successfully exploiting the linkage between employee and customer satisfaction may not always be straightforward. Research into the way in which customer satisfaction is measured and managed in British companies is revealing (Piercy, 1995). Studies suggest that:

1 There is a need to create clarity for all employees regarding customer service quality policies and customer satisfaction targets. It is not enough to pay lip-service to these ideals and to expect success in attaining them. The starting point must be to identify what has to be achieved in customer satisfaction to implement specific market strategies, and to position the company against the competition in a specific market. It is unlikely that achieving what is needed will be free from cost. We need to take a realistic view of the time needed and the real costs of implementation in aligning the internal market with the external market.

2 Internal processes and barriers suggest the need to consider both the internal and external markets faced in implementing customer satisfaction measurement and management systems. To ignore the internal market is to risk actually damaging the company's capacity to achieve and improve customer satisfaction in the external market. If, for example, management uses customer feedback in a negative and coercive way, then it may reduce employee enthusiasm for customer service, or create 'game-playing' behaviour where people compete for 'Brownie points' in the system at the expense of both the company and the customer. This said, we have also to recognise not just the complementarity between internal and external markets, but the potential for conflict of interest. Achieving target levels of customer service and satisfaction may require managers and employees to change the way they do things and to make sacrifices they do not want to make. This may take more than simple advocacy or management threat.

| Figure 17.1 | Customer satisfaction – the internal market and the external market |

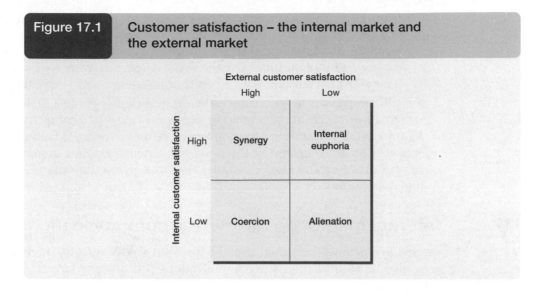

3 Related to the above argument, recognising the internal market suggests that there may be a need for a structured and planned internal marketing programme to achieve the effective implementation of customer satisfaction measurement and management. This has been described elsewhere as 'marketing our customers to our employees' (Piercy, 1995), and can be built into the implementation process to address the needs of the internal customer and to confront the types of internal processual barrier we have encountered.

4 Also related to the recognition of the internal market is the need to question the relationship between internal and external customer satisfaction. This can be discussed with executives using the structure shown in Figure 17.1. This suggests four possible scenarios that result when internal and external customer satisfaction are compared:

(a) **Synergy**, which is what we hope for, when internal and external customer satisfaction are high, and we see them as sustainable and self-regenerating. As one hotel manager explained it: 'I know that we are winning on customer service when my operational staff come to me and complain about how I am getting in their way in providing customer service, and tell me to get my act together!' This is the 'happy customers and happy employees' situation, assumed by many to be obvious and easily achieved.

(b) **Coercion** is where we achieve high levels of external customer satisfaction by changing the behaviour of employees through management direction and control systems. In the short term this may be the only option, but it may be very difficult and expensive to sustain this position in the longer term, and we give up flexibility for control.

(c) **Alienation** is where we have low levels of satisfaction internally and externally, and we are likely to be highly vulnerable to competitive attack on service quality, and to the instability in our competitive capabilities produced by low staff morale and high staff turnover.

(d) **Internal euphoria** is where we have high levels of satisfaction in the internal market, but this does not translate into external customer satisfaction – for example, if internal socialisation and group cohesiveness actually shut out the paying customer in the external market. These scenarios are exaggerated, but have provided a useful way of confronting these issues with executives.

5 A critical mistake is to ignore the real costs and challenges in sustaining high service quality levels and the limitation which may exist in a company's capabilities for improving customer satisfaction levels. While advocacy is widespread and the appeal is obvious, achieving the potential benefits requires more planning and attention to implementation realities than is suggested by the existing conventional literature.

17.3.2 Internal marketing as internal communications

As well as customer care training and a focus on service quality, internal marketing may also be seen as internal communications. In fact, the largest growth in this area has been investment by companies in broader internal communications programmes of various kinds – where 'communications' is understood as providing our employees with information and delivering messages which support the business strategy. Athough up-to-date figures are scarce, in 2001 one study found that the *Fortune* Top 200 'most admired' companies spent an average of $1.6 million (£1.1 million) each on internal communications (*Marketing Weekly*, 2001). The goal of internal communications is normally to build both understanding and commitment. Often, these activities tend to be a responsibility of the human resource department.

One industry study (Pounsford, 1994) suggested that managers saw the role of internal communications in the following terms and with the following advantages, as shown in Table 17.1.

The manifestations of this form of internal marketing include: company newsletters, employee conferences and training, video-conferencing, satellite TV transmissions, interactive video, e-mail, and so on. Increasingly, creating dialogue within an organisation and encouraging employee involvement can involve approaches like web-based internal blogs (Hathi, 2007). These delivery mechanisms are important, but are in danger of obscuring an important point. Instructing and informing people about strategic developments is not the same as winning their real involvement and participation. Communication is a two-way process – listening as well as informing. This may be why internal communications appear ineffective in some companies.

There is a risk that internal communications programmes become about telling and persuading, not listening. This may be said to be internal *selling* not internal *marketing*.

An interesting illustration of the gains from two-way communications comes from Dana Corp., the US car parts manufacturer. At that company, the 'suggestions box' is described by the CEO as 'a core part of our value system'. Employees contribute ideas to improve operations and service, and 70 per cent are actually used. Dana is an example of an organisation where employees have taken a share of the responsibility for keeping the company competitive. This underlines the important practical

Table 17.1 The role of internal communications

Perceived role	Illustrative comments
Team building	Educate employees about breadth and diversity of the organisation. Assist cooperation between divisions.
Damage control	Prevent managers getting communications wrong. Suppress bad news. Counter pessimism.
Morale builders	Build confidence. Increase motivation.
Involvement	Represent employee opinions upwards. Create channel to share problems/values. Increase people recognition.
Change management	Increase understanding of the need for change. Test new ideas. Help people relate to rapidly changing environment.
Goal-setting	Help organisation steer in a coordinated direction. Provide focus on corporate goals. Generate support for policies.

difference between producing company newsletters and taking internal communications seriously.

17.3.3 Internal marketing and innovation management

Somewhat different is the use of the internal marketing framework to place, and gain use of, innovations like computers and electronic communications in the IT field. These applications use tools of market analysis and planning to cope with and avoid resistance and to manage the process of change. This may be particularly important where the effectiveness of a marketing strategy relies on the adoption of new technologies and ways of working. The argument here is that people in an organisation are 'customers' for our ideas and innovations. This view encourages us to consider:

- **looking at customer needs** – even in hierarchical companies people are not robots waiting to be told what to do, so making the effort to understand their needs increases the likely effectiveness of innovation;
- **delivering the goods** – the needs of customers tell us what matters most to them;
- **raising unrealistic expectations** – is as dangerous with internal customers as it is with external customers (Divita, 1996).

An example of a company using this approach is OASIS, the IT consultancy firm, which has a well-developed system for the internal marketing of IT applications. The use of laptop computers by a geographically dispersed salesforce in one company was guided by the analysis of the 'internal market' using the classic diffusion of innovation model to identify opinion leaders as key influencers in the adoption process. Similarly, the BT problem of marketing its information systems and services to its internal customers was addressed through the same principles used to market solutions to the organisation's external customers: segmentation, targeting, and positioning IS solutions to the internal customer base (Morgan, 2004).

17.3.4 Internal markets instead of external markets for products and services

The terms 'internal market' and 'internal marketing' have been applied to internal relationships between different parts of the same organisation – making them suppliers and customers as a way of improving the focus on efficiency and value. This is common in total quality management programmes, and in wider applications like the reform of the UK National Health Service.

This can lead to some interesting issues. For example, work with the R&D division of a major brewery suggested that the internal customer issues were really about the type and degree of dependence between the internal supplier (in this case the provider of R&D solutions to process problems in the brewery) and the internal customer (here the production and sales units of the brewery), which in turn reflects the freedom of either internal supplier or customer to deal with third parties outside the company.

17.3.5 Strategic internal marketing

Lastly, we note the use of strategic internal marketing (SIM) as an approach to the structured planning of marketing strategy implementation, and analysis of underlying implementation problems in an organisation. This form of internal marketing is a direct parallel to our conventional external marketing strategy and marketing programme, which aims at winning the support, cooperation and commitment we need inside the company, if our external market strategies are to work. This is a somewhat different view of internal marketing compared with those discussed above, although it is informed by the other types of internal marketing which have a longer history. The key underlying issue here is the organisational and cultural change needed to make marketing strategies happen.

A structure for an internal marketing programme is shown in Figure 17.2. The underlying proposal is that the easiest way to make practical progress with this type of internal marketing, and to establish what it may achieve, is to use exactly the same structures that we use for planning *external* marketing. This suggests that we should think in terms of integrating the elements needed for an internal marketing mix or programme, based on our analysis of the opportunities and threats in the internal marketplace represented by the company with which we are working. This is shown in Figure 17.2 as a formal and legitimate part of the planning process.

In fact, in this model, we take the internal marketing programme not only as an *output* of the planning process and the external marketing programme, but also as an *input*, i.e. constraints and barriers in the internal marketplace should be considered and analysed as a part of the planning at both strategic and tactical levels. For the proposals to make sense in practice, we rely on this iterative relationship.

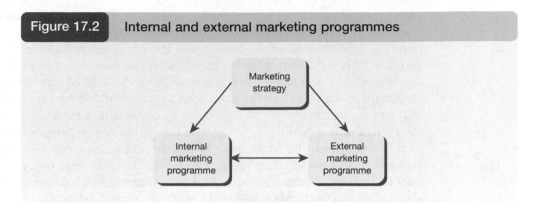

Figure 17.2 | **Internal and external marketing programmes**

The starting point for this approach is that the marketing strategy and the planning process may define an external marketing programme in the conventional way, and less conventionally the internal barriers suggest that some external strategies are not capable of being implemented in the timescale concerned, and we have to feed back into the planning process the message that some adjustments are needed while there is still time to make those adjustments to plans.

More positively, however, it is equally true that our analysis of the internal market may suggest new opportunities and neglected company resources which should be exploited, which in turn impact on our external marketing plan and thus on the planning process. What we are trying to make explicit for executives is the need to balance the impact of both internal and external market attributes on the strategic assumptions that they make in planning.

The structure of such an internal marketing programme can be presented in the following terms:

● **The product**: At the simplest level the 'product' consists of the marketing strategies and the marketing plan. Implied, however, is that the product to be 'sold' is those values, attitudes and behaviours which are needed to make the marketing plan work effectively. These hidden dimensions of the product may range from increased budgets and different resource allocations, to changed control systems and criteria used to evaluate performance, to changed ways of handling customers at the point of sale. At the extreme the product is the person's job – as it is redefined and reshaped by the market strategy so it will make people's working lives more enjoyable. There may also be negatives – changes people will not like, which brings us to price.

● **The price**: The price element of the internal marketing mix is not *our* costs; it is concerned with what we are asking our internal customers to 'pay' when they buy in to the product and the marketing plan. This may include the sacrifice of other projects which compete for resources with our plan, but more fundamentally the personal psychological cost of adopting different key values, and changing the way jobs are done, and asking managers to step outside their 'comfort zones' with new methods of operation. The price to be paid by different parts of the internal marketplace, if the marketing plan is to be implemented successfully, should not be ignored as a major source of barriers and obstacles of varying degrees of difficulty.

- **Communications**: The most tangible aspect of the internal marketing pro-gramme is the communications medium and the messages used to inform and to persuade, and to work on the attitudes of the key personnel in the internal mar-ketplace. This includes not only written communications, such as plan summaries and reports, but also face-to-face presentations to individuals and groups who are important to the success of the plan. Broadly, we should remember that to assume that simply 'telling' people will get them on our side is likely to be as naive inside the company as it is outside. We suggest it is important to consider the full range of communications possibilities and associated goals, as we would with external customers, and we should not forget to budget the time and financial costs that may be associated with these activities. At the simplest level, the purpose of our internal marketing communication may be served by a video presentation explaining things, or a roadshow taking the message out to the regions and the distributors. But real communication is two-way – we listen, we adapt, we focus on our audience's problems and needs.

- **Distribution**: The distribution channels element of the mix is concerned with the physical and socio-technical venues at which we have to deliver our product and its communications: meetings, committees, training sessions for managers and staff, seminars, workshops, written reports, informal communications, social occasions, and so on. Ultimately, however, the real distribution channel is human resource management, and in the lining up of recruitment, training, evaluation and reward systems behind marketing strategies, so that the culture of the com-pany becomes the real distribution channel for internal marketing strategies. In fact, as long ago as the 1990s, Ulrich (1992) made some radical points about this, which are worth confronting. He said that if we really want complete customer commitment from our external customers, through independent, shared values and shared strategies, then we should give our customers a major role in our:

  - staff recruitment and selection decisions;
  - staff promotion and development decisions;
  - staff appraisal, from setting the standards to measuring the performance;
  - staff reward systems, both financial and non-financial;
  - organisational design strategies; and
  - internal communications programmes.

  In effect this means using our human resource management systems as the inter-nal marketing channel, thus taking the internal and external customer issue to its logical conclusion (see Section 17.5.2 below). Companies developing such approaches in the US included General Electric, Marriott, Borg-Warner, DEC, Ford Motor Company, Hewlett-Packard and Honeywell.

For example, a simple internal marketing analysis for two companies is illustrated in Tables 17.2 and 17.3. These examples concern a key customer account strategy in a financial services organisation and a vertical marketing strategy in a computer com-pany. In both cases we can see a 'formal' level of internal marketing which concerns the marketing plan or strategy, but also levels of internal marketing concerned with the informal organisation and the processes of decision making and change inside the company. In the computer company, vertical marketing is not a simple strategy

Table 17.2 Internal marketing in a computer company

Internal market targets	(1) Business unit management
	(2) Product group management
	(3) Salesforce

Internal marketing programme	Internal marketing levels		
	Formal	Informal	Processual
Product	Marketing plan to attack a small industry as a special vertical market, rather than grouping it with many other industries as at present, with specialised products and advertising	Separation of resources and control of this market from the existing business unit	Change from technology-oriented management to recognition of differences in buyer needs in different industries – the clash between technology and customer orientation
Price	Costs of developing specialised 'badged' or branded products for this industry	Loss of control for existing business units	Fear of 'fragmentation' of markets leading to internal structural and status changes
Communications	Written plan Presentations to key groups	Support for plan by key board members gained by pre-presentation 'softening up' by planners	Action planning team formed, including original planners, but also key players from business unit and product group – rediscovering the wheel to gain 'ownership' Advertising the new strategy in trade press read by company technologists and managers
Distribution	Business unit board meeting Product group board meeting Main board meeting Salesforce conference	Informal meetings	Joint seminars in applying IT to this industry, involving business unit managers and key customers Joint charity events for the industry's benevolent fund

Alamy/Andre Jenny

Marriott, one of the best companies to work for, 2007

Table 17.3 Internal marketing in a financial services organisation

Internal market targets   *(1) Branch managers of retail banks and finance company offices*
(2) Divisional chief executives for the banks and the finance

Internal marketing programme	Internal marketing levels		
	Formal	*Informal*	*Processual*
Product	Integration of selling efforts around key customers, as a key marketing strategy	Head office group-based planning and resource allocation with greater central control	Change in the individual manager's role from independent branch entrepreneur to group-based collaborator
Price	Branch profit/commission from independent selling to smaller customers, to be sacrificed to build long-term relationships with key accounts	Loss of freedom/ independence of action in the marketplace Potential loss of commission-earning power	Time, effort and psychological 'pain' of collaborating with former 'competitors' with different ethnic/educational/professional backgrounds – the 'banker versus the hire purchase salesman' Fear that the other side would damage existing customer relationships
Distribution	Written strategic marketing plans Sales conferences	Written communications Informal discussion of chief executive's 'attitude' Redesign of commission and incentives systems in both companies	Joint planning/problem-solving teams for each region – built around central definition of target market segments Combining/integrating management information systems, and changing its structure to reflect new segments
Communications	Formal presentation by chief executive at conferences Written support from chief executive Redesign market information systems to be more up-to-date	Sponsorship by chief executive – 'the train is now leaving the station, you are either on it or . . .' (written memo sent to all branches)	Social events Joint training course Redefinition of markets and target segments

because it is linked to changing resource allocation and departmental responsibilities, and also to a change of management culture. In the financial services company, a key account strategy involves not simply a new marketing direction, but a change in line management freedom and ways of doing business. These cases are indicative of the types of implementation and change problem that can be addressed by internal marketing.

It also follows that we can use conventional market research techniques inside the company to get to grips with who has to change, in what way, how much and what the patterns are in our internal marketplace.

Finally, as with the external marketing programme, we should not neglect the importance of measuring results wherever possible. This may be in terms of such criteria as people's attitudes towards the market strategy and their commitment to putting it into practice, or customer perceptions of our success in delivering our promises to them – or, perhaps more appositely, our lack of success as presented by complaints, and so on.

Again, in exact parallel with the conventional external marketing plan, our internal marketing programmes should be directed at chosen targets or segments within the market. The choice of key targets for the internal marketing programme should be derived directly from the goals of the external marketing programme, and the types of organisational and human changes needed to implement marketing strategies. The internal marketplace may be segmented at the simplest level by the job roles and functions played by groups of people, e.g. top management, other departments and marketing and sales staff.

Alternatively, we might look beyond job characteristics to the key sources of support and resistance to the external marketing plan which are anticipated, to identify targets for reinforcement, or for persuasion and negotiation. Perhaps at the deepest level we might choose our targets on the basis of the individual's attitudes towards the external market and customers, and the key values that we need communicated to external customers, together with people's career goals.

It can be seen, therefore, that internal marketing can be used in different ways, and that the role may vary from developing customer care and service quality programmes to improve and maintain service standards and customer satisfaction at the point of sale, through to internal communications programmes, to providing a structured approach to planning the full implementation of marketing strategy. We noted also that internal marketing may be of particular importance in the alliance-based network organisation.

17.4 Planning for internal marketing

There are a variety of situations when strategic thinking about competitive strategy should address the possible role of internal marketing:

- where performance in critical areas of customer service are unsatisfactory and not sufficient to establish a strong competitive position;
- where customer satisfaction is consistently low and complaints suggest that the underlying causes are employee attitudes and behaviour, rather than poor product standards or inadequate support systems;
- when market conditions and customer requirements have shifted, so that continuing the standards and practices of the past will no longer bring success;
- when new marketing strategies require new skills and ways of behaving – a 'stretch' strategy;
- when bridging the gap between planning and implementation has proved problematic in the past.

In such situations, we may wish to consider an internal marketing strategy with the following components:

- **Internal market orientation** – recently attention has been given to internal market orientation as the foundation for success, in the same way that external market orientation has been linked to the effective implementation of external marketing strategies. The logic is that internal market orientation increases the responsiveness of a market-oriented company to external market conditions, because it allows management to better align external market objectives with internal capabilities. However, this symmetry relies on assessment of internal market orientation as a precursor to action (Gounaris, 2006). Lings and Greenley (2005) propose that assessing internal market orientation should encompass directly parallel measures to those associated with external market orientation, thus internal market orientation involves the generation and dissemination of intelligence pertaining to the wants and needs of employees, and the design and implementation of appropriate responses to meet those wants and needs.

- **Internal market strategy:** In broad terms what is needed to gain the successful implementation of an external market strategy. It is here that we need to confront the real implications of our external market strategy for the internal customer – the decision-makers, managers, operatives and others without whose support, cooperation and commitment the external strategy will fail. This is the most critical question in the whole internal marketing exercise. It may be worth consulting the people directly concerned – doing internal market research. It is certainly worth incorporating some diversity of opinion. As we learn more, we can come back and redraft and rethink our conclusions here. It is here that we should take a view of what it is likely to cost us to achieve these things and the deadline for achieving them to implement the external marketing strategy on time.

- **Internal market segmentation** is about identifying the targets in the internal marketplace around which we can build internal marketing programmes, which are different in what we have to achieve and how we are going to do it. This may not be straightforward, but is the route to real insights into the internal market problem and effectiveness in how we cope with that problem. The most obvious way of identifying internal segments may be by role or function, or location, and this may be sufficient. It might be more productive to think of who are the innovators and opinion leaders who will influence others. We might approach this more directly in terms of the role that different people will play in implementing the external strategy and the problems they may face in this, or simply how much different people will have to change to get the external strategy to work.

- **Internal marketing programmes** specify which internal marketing programmes will be needed in each internal market segment to achieve the objectives we have set. In each area we need to collect our thoughts about the rational issues but also the human and cultural issues. To us the product may be a new marketing plan that we need to inform people about (internal marketing communications) through formal presentations (internal marketing distribution), adjusting commission and evaluation systems as need be (internal marketing price). To the internal customer, the same plan may be about disruption and threat (product), loss of initiative and status (price), imposed without consultation by management (communication) and rigorously 'policed' through coercion (distribution). If internal marketing is about anything, it is about confronting and coping with this conflict. It is this confrontation which will drive us away from thinking about internal marketing as simply writing customer care brochures and doing great plan presentations, towards coping with the human and organisational realities of what strategic change involves and costs. This is also the stage to take a look at the cost implications of what we now see to be necessary in our internal marketing: does the internal marketing cost mean that the external market strategy is no longer attractive? Do we have to account for internal marketing cost which is more than we expected, but bearable? Do we have to change the external strategy to reduce the internal marketing cost? Are there cheaper ways of achieving the critical internal marketing goals?

● **Internal marketing evaluation** – what we can measure to see if we are getting there, ideally quantified and objective: reduced customer complaint rates or higher customer satisfaction scores. This may be ambitious and we should not abandon important objectives because they are difficult to evaluate – we may have to settle for a subjective or qualitative evaluation, which is better than nothing.

However, the possible problems to be anticipated in implementing internal marketing strategy programmes effectively should not be underestimated. For example, Don Schultz (2004) suggests that many, if not most, internal marketing approaches fail for the following reasons:

● **Lack of financial measures of internal marketing success** – the goal should be to link measurable behavioural changes to financial returns for the business.

● **Weak management cohesion** – the organisational location of responsibility for internal marketing is confused and those responsible have no authority or responsibility for the people whose behaviours they are trying to change.

● **Lack of senior management support** – internal marketing is not perceived as a senior management issue, but the concern of middle managers with all the inherent problems of turf wars and organisational politics.

● **No connection between internal stakeholders and external customers** – the difficulty for employees in non-customer-facing roles to understand how internal marketing affects them, or how they affect the external customer.

● **Lack of a management calculus** – there are no clear ideas about the value or return of internal marketing and an effective internal marketing planning system.

Schultz suggests that we should apply the lessons of integrated marketing communications in internal as well as external marketing. However, the issue of integration has yet further practical aspects, as we see in the next section of the chapter.

17.5 Cross-functional partnership as internal marketing

17.5.1 Rationale for cross-functional partnership

Perhaps the greatest contemporary challenge for internal marketing is the achievement of the effective cross-functional partnerships required to deliver superior customer value. Two things are increasingly apparent. First, delivering value results from a complex set of processes and activities inside the organisation and possibly

'strategic human resource management' approach, with a primary concern for aligning the skills and capabilities of employees and managers with the requirements of business strategy. The processes usually managed in HRM are extremely relevant to the goals of marketing strategy: recruitment and selection, evaluation and reward system, training and development, and other drivers of corporate culture. There is an opportunity for marketing to work with HRM in identifying the key elements of employee motivation, and the development of training and development programmes – but particularly in providing the research capabilities to evaluate the internal marketplace including employees, channel partners and customer service providers (Schultz, 2002).

Some companies are making large efforts to ensure that marketing and HRM work together to ensure that they communicate and deliver brand values to both internal and external audiences. The 'Everything is Possible' campaign at H-P Invest (formerly Hewlett-Packard) is aimed to be as inspirational for staff as it is for customers. Allied-Domecq sees its 'people brand' as one of its nine core brands. Some companies, such as Allied-Domecq and Sainsbury's, have appointed employer brand managers to bridge the gap between HR and marketing. Others have created jobs with titles like 'great place to work manager' (at B&Q), or 'head of great company' (at Microsoft) (Simms, 2003).

An internal marketing agenda concerned with the contribution of HRM to value processes might include the following issues:

● The better alignment of employee and manager training and development processes with customer priorities.

● Tracking and comparing employee satisfaction and customer satisfaction to understand the relationship between them.

● Working on the links between customer satisfaction and retention issues, and employee training, reward and evaluation processes.

● Looking at the way in which internal communications approaches support external market strategies. (Piercy, 2002)

The importance of the marketing/HRM link is such that in many situations major customers are increasingly playing a direct role in participating in the operation of suppliers' internal HRM processes, such as recruitment into sales and service jobs.

Indeed, more operational views of the interface between marketing and HRM issues focus on the link between HRM and relationship marketing strategies (Perrien *et al.*, 1993; Perrien and Ricard, 1995), and the need to direct HRM policies to focus on customer service and customer value (Cripe, 1994; Gubman, 1995). Conversely, Sheth and Mittal (1996) have examined the use of HRM skills in the management of customer expectations. Nonetheless, research suggests that the marketing/HRM relationship is frequently associated with conflict and poor interdepartmental conflicts with a detrimental impact on strategy implementation (Chimhanzi, 2004).

17.5.3 Marketing and finance and accounting

The conflict between marketing and finance/accounting in the past has reflected the goal of accounting to cut costs and to increase reported short-term profit, compared with the objective of marketing to gain long-term investment in brands and market share. Conflicts have also centred on different views of pricing – the accounting model of cost-plus pricing produces very different outcomes from a marketing model of price based on customer value. However, these disputes have been rendered largely obsolete by two important factors. The first factor is the overwhelming pressure that marketing is under in a growing number of companies to 'prove' its added value to the company and its shareholders (Ambler, 2003). Many of the metrics which marketing most needs to establish its shareholder value creation can only be achieved through collaboration with finance and accounting (Farris *et al.*, 2006). The second factor is the increasingly strategic view of business being taken by finance and accounting executives, which is likely to reduce the conflicts with marketing and sales. Moves towards internal alliances between marketing and finance/accounting are likely to be important in achieving the speed of change and market responsiveness required by modern customers.

17.5.4 Marketing and sales integration

In Chapter 15 we examined the growing role of the sales organisation in strategic customer management, and as a change agent inside the company. Nonetheless, for many companies the relationship between marketing and sales remains problematic. It has been noted: 'The relationship between sales and marketing functions has persisted as one of the major sources of organizational conflict' (Webster, 1997), and that 'The marketing–sales relationship, whilst strongly interdependent, is reported as neither collaborative nor harmonious' (Dewsnap and Jobber, 2000). For these reasons sales and marketing integration remains a high and very topical priority on the management agenda (Rouzies *et al.*, 2005). This question merits more detailed consideration, since it appears to be frequently one of the most critical obstacles to marketing strategy implementation.

The conventional literature often assumes that marketing departments and sales organisations are a single organisational unit, but they are frequently quite distinct functions in companies. For example, in their 1998 study, Workman *et al.* suggest that 'it is highly significant that more than thirty years after the call to integrate sales and marketing activities under a CME [Chief Marketing Executive], we find no firms that had adopted this recommendation.' In fact, part of the reason is that marketing and sales should not be the same because the functions they perform are different (Shapiro, 2002). However, the new market conditions and strategic sales role we described in Chapter 15 place considerable importance on cross-functional collaboration and cooperation, which may align poorly with the traditional need for functional separation based on task specialisation.

What is far from well understood is what conflicts or elements of conflict actually have negative consequences for business performance and which do not (Deshpande and Webster, 1989). While marketing and sales exist alongside each other as business functions, there are likely to be fundamental differences between them in perspective and priorities. However, in examining the coordination of these differentiated functions, Cespedes (1996) highlights an important paradox: 'the solution is *not* to eliminate differences among these groups', but that 'paradoxically, there is virtue in *separating* and distinguishing functional roles in order to improve the cross-functional coordination needed' (Cespedes, 1995). The suggestion is that differences between marketing and sales may actually provide a much-needed breadth of perspective and richness of market understanding *because* of the differences between the functions. As collaboration and cooperation between marketing and sales grow in importance, this paradox provides an important insight – teamwork and joint-working have to accommodate differences in perspective and understanding, and to focus on enhanced business performance not simply smooth team operation or harmonious interrelationships.

The marketing/sales interface

To other functions in the business, the marketing and sales functions look alike – they are both focused on the customer and the market – but aligning sales and marketing has proved difficult in practice and is likely to be even more difficult in the future. The importance of the issue is quite simply that poor cooperation between marketing and sales will lead to inconsistent and weak strategy, coupled with flawed and inefficient implementation (Shapiro, 2002).

When the customer base was homogeneous, simple and dominated by mid-sized accounts, marketing operated as a strategic function concentrating on product strategy, segmentation and competitive positioning, while sales executed the strategy in the field, selling to end users and distributors. The easy separation of sales and marketing has come to an end in markets dominated by very large accounts with sophisticated buying teams, and multi-channel strategies to reach medium and small accounts. With the largest accounts, marketing and sales need to make joint decisions to achieve an integrated offer that meets the standards required by purchasers who can dictate many terms to their suppliers. Marketing executives need to acquire new understanding of individual customers, key account needs, and the sales task – the reality is that 'As power shifted from the seller to the buyer, it also shifted from headquarters to the field' (Shapiro, 2002). With multi-channelling (e.g. an Internet channel, telesales, direct marketing and personal selling working alongside each other), effectiveness and profitability also require shared sales and marketing decisions on channel strategy and execution (Shapiro, 2002).

While relatively little empirical evidence is available, executive opinion and anecdote suggest the relationship between marketing and sales remains problematic in many companies, with conflict surrounding such issues as the division of responsibilities and demarcation lines, ownership of customer information, competition for resources, control of price, and the short-term orientation of sales versus the long-term orientation of marketing. Differences in reward systems (volume-based in sales and margin-based in marketing), information needs (geographically and customer-based in sales and product/brand oriented in marketing) and competencies underline the potential for conflict rather than collaboration between marketing and sales (Cespedes, 1993, 1994; Montgomery and Webster, 1997; Dewsnap and Jobber, 2000).

Underpinning the potential for marketing/sales conflict is what has been described as the existence of different 'mindsets' in marketing and sales – different perspectives on issues and approaches for addressing problems – which have been described as:

firmer links between R&D and marketing poses a greater challenge than simply providing new product pipelines.

In the other 'technical' functions, modern thinking is dominated by supply-chain strategy – in particular the promise of the 'lean' supply-chain to 'banish waste and create wealth' (Womack and Jones, 1996). The supply-chain model of identifying value streams for products and organising around flow and the demand pull of products has been enormously influential, because of the potential it offers for reducing storage and waste costs to a minimum. Nonetheless, from a marketing perspective, the weakness of the lean supply chain lies in its rigid definition of customer value in purely technical terms, and the desirability of reducing product choices to reduce supply-chain costs. However, the strategic link between supply-chain and marketing strategy lies in the relationship between supply-chain advantage and marketing/ brand advantage. Applying internal marketing efforts to enhancing the understanding and collaboration between supply-chain strategy and marketing strategy is a new mandate for marketing executives.

Certainly, at the supply-chain operations level, there is evidence that internal marketing efforts to stimulate the impact of front-line logistics workers on customer value creation can lead to higher job satisfaction and performance in distribution centre employees, and increased interdepartmental customer orientation (Keller *et al.*, 2006).

17.5.6 Marketing and external partners

It will very frequently be the case that the successful implementation of marketing strategy will rely on the efforts of partnered organisations operating externally – distributors at home and abroad, outsourced manufacturers, third-party suppliers of customer services, network members delivering the product or service for the supplier. We examined in Chapter 16 the growing role of alliances and networks, and the way in which in some sectors, such as global air travel, competition is between networks rather than individual airlines. The challenge of achieving effective delivery of strategic goals through partnered organisations remains considerable in many situations. Networks are characterised by dependencies. These increasingly common situations define a new and possibly critical function for internal marketing: the positioning of strategic imperatives with partner organisations in the networks which have been formed to reach the marketplace.

17.5.7 A processual role for internal marketing

The logic for this part of the chapter is based on the following premises: that increasingly the effective implementation of marketing strategies will rely on effectiveness in managing cross-functional relationships, and that the management of processes of collaboration and alliance building in organisations (and extended alliance-based networks) extends the internal marketing agenda from simply planning implementation strategy to a process design and management role. The Figure 17.3 model provides a basis for addressing the nature of the main value processes in an organisation and then identifying the actual or potential contributions of diverse functional specialisms to the effectiveness of the value processes. Once identified, the cross-functional integration and collaboration needs define the internal marketing role.

Summary

The focus of this chapter is strategy implementation – the transition from plans to execution. Strategy implementation faces a variety of obstacles and poses several important challenges for marketing executives. Part of the challenge is to avoid the separation of strategy and implementation and to recognise their interdependence. We take the increasingly widespread view that part of thinking about implementing competitive marketing strategy should be concerned with managing the internal market (of employees, functional specialists, managers, and so on), because this may enhance a company's ability to deliver its strategies to customers in the external market. In part, this view is based on the recognition of the importance of relationship management with partners, achieving competition differentiation through the skills of the 'part-time marketers' in the organisation, and the role of internal branding to parallel external branding.

We saw that internal marketing may be traced back to early views about the synergy between the marketing concept and the 'human relations' concept, and to have developed operationally in a variety of ways. The scope of internal marketing was seen to encompass service quality enhancement, internal communications programmes, managing the adoption of innovations inside an organisation, cross-functional and cross-divisional supply of products and services, and a framework for marketing implementation. Our interest here is primarily, though not exclusively, in strategic internal marketing as a framework for managing implementation.

In this area we saw that internal marketing offers a framework for evaluating the costs of change and for managing change that utilises the same concepts, terminology and techniques as planning external marketing. This provides a pragmatic model for guiding implementation choices and actions.

The last part of the chapter gave attention to the more process-based view of internal marketing, which focuses on integration of company efforts around customer value creation, and the challenges of forming cross-functional partnerships to deliver marketing strategy to the marketplace. We examined the potentials for internal marketing efforts to build closer ties and collaboration between marketing, human resource management, finance and accounting, sales, operations functions, and external partners. We suggested that perhaps one of the most important roles of internal marketing goes beyond aligning employees' values and behaviours with strategies, and confronts the need to achieve superior customer value through seamlessness in strategy delivery. This role emphasises internal marketing to achieve cross-functional partnerships within the organisation, and crossing organisational boundaries to align external partners with the imperatives of marketing strategy.

British Airways

 Case study

Getty Images News

British Airways has calculated that the economic damage from the Gate Gourmet dispute amounts to at least £30m.

No one has yet put a figure on the losses to the airline's brand image caused by cancellations and the travel chaos that ensued from this month's strike action. The final bill for that could be much higher. But experts suggest that a great deal depends on how BA handles its response. If there is any lasting damage to BA's image, the consequences could be significant.

This month, Mori, the polling group, reported a link between the reputation and share prices of listed companies. It tracked the 'favourability' rating of five companies and found changes in customer satisfaction led to corresponding moves in share performance, typically three to 12 months later.

Some fund managers have begun to commission research into customer perceptions of companies. Waheed Aslam, Mori development director, said: 'Investors believe in the link and increasingly want private data that add value to their investment decisions.'

The disruption faced by travellers in the holiday season, the scenes of low-paid workers protesting to get their jobs back, and a well-orchestrated union campaign have kept the dispute high up the news agenda. Tim Ambler, a senior fellow in the London Business School marketing faculty, believes that BA's brand risks hitting the low

points last seen in its days as a nationalised industry.

'It is now the third summer in a row that BA has made what looks from the outside like a serious managerial error,' he noted.

The unrest among BA's ground services staff at Heathrow showed that some of the biggest image problems lay in internal perceptions of the BA brand among the company's own staff.

'Colin Marshall [BA's former chairman and chief executive] took control of the internal branding of BA to the staff. That was lost when he left, and they never really got it back,' Mr Ambler said.

Internal marketing was not just a case of raising staff morale, which could be achieved by 'simply' paying people more and giving them longer holidays, according to Mr Ambler. 'It is actually motivating your staff to want what is best for BA.'

Jes Frampton, the chief executive of Interbrand, the branding consultancy, argued that BA had been pulled into a problem not of its making. 'When it is this important, it has a massive impact [on the brand].'

But BA had been able to limit the damage by acting quickly and being seen to be honest about the situation. 'Given the fact that they have had limited control over this [strike action], they have benefited by being very open and honest and straightforward.'

Companies that have been seen to respond effectively have limited the damage from difficult situations, one example being Shell's reversal of its decision to sink the Brent Spar oil platform, Mr Frampton said.

'The common thread that runs through the people that have done it well is speed of reaction and honesty.'

Source: Jonathan Moules, 'Damage limitation is vital to a brand under fire', *The Financial Times*, 24 August 2005.

Discussion questions

1 What is the link between internal marketing and service quality in the airline industry?

2 What internal marketing programmes could British Airways put into place to avoid further internal unrest? What potential is there to extend such programmes to external partners?

3 What challenges may BA face in implementing an internal marketing programme to deliver value to its customers?

chapter eighteen

Corporate social responsibility 18

If ... corporations were to analyze their prospects for social responsibility using the same frameworks that guide their core business choices, they would discover that CSR can be much more than a cost, a constraint, or a charitable deed – it can be a source of opportunity, innovation, and competitive advantage.

Porter and Kramer (2006)

The liberalization of markets is forcing executives and social activists to work together. They are developing new business models that will transform organizations and the lives of poor people everywhere.

Brugmann and Prahalad (2007)

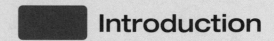 **Introduction**

The consideration of corporate social responsibility (CSR) as an element of, or a major influence on, marketing strategy is an innovation to this book. It may appear a surprising addition. It reflects the growing importance of CSR in how companies manage their key processes. However, the definition of corporate social responsibility is somewhat problematic, but in a Green Paper presented by the European Commission in July 2001, corporate social responsibility is identified as: 'a concept whereby companies integrate social and environmental concerns in their business operations and in their interaction with their stakeholders on a voluntary basis.' The Green Paper identifies four factors underpinning the growing attention by executives to issues of corporate social responsibility:

- The new concerns and expectations of consumers, public authorities and investors in the context of globalisation and industrial change.

- Social criteria increasingly influencing the investment decisions of individuals and institutions.

- Increased concern about the damage caused by economic and business activity to the physical environment.

- Transparency of business activities brought about by media and new information and communication technologies.

It is increasingly clear that business norms across the world are moving CSR into the mainsteam of business practice. Non-governmental organisations like the World Resources Institute (WRI), AccountAbility, Global Reporting Initiative (GRI), International Standards Organzation (ISO 14000) and the United Nations all have major initiatives aimed at improving the social involvement and performance of the world's business community (Godfrey and Hatch, 2007).

However, while CSR may be an important new element of the relationships between business, government and society, the case remains to be established that it is linked to marketing strategy in particular.

In fact, the twenty-first century is seeing issues of social responsibility and the morality and ethics of company practices become a key element of managing customer relationships and in how companies are perceived and understood by their customers. Recent research suggests that an integrated approach to CSR in marketing is largely missing in both theory and practice, and somewhat overdue (Maignan *et al.*, 2005). Certainly, some attention has been given to the operational role of marketing in managing corporate social responsibility initiatives within companies, by expanding focus beyond consumers to include other stakeholders and integrating social responsibility initiatives (Maignan and Ferrell, 2004). These developments have been particularly associated with the development of social marketing, concerned with the contribution of marketing activities to socially desirable behaviours and goals (Andreasen, 1994; Kotler and Levy, 1969), and 'cause-related' marketing (Varadarajan and Menon, 1988). However, while the impact of social marketing on the social duties attached to the marketing function has considerable managerial importance, our focus here is somewhat broader, and is concerned with the impact of the corporate social responsibility stance of the firm on its marketing and business strategy.

18.1 Marketing strategy and corporate social responsibility

From being considered primarily as a matter of 'corporate philanthropy' (Porter and Kramer, 2002), or entirely a question of moral obligation or pure altruism, corporate social responsibility (CSR) has been increasingly recognised as a potential source of competitive advantage, and thus a corporate resource, as well as an important part of how competitive relationships operate. This thinking extends beyond the view that good corporate citizenship is a marketing tool that can yield benefits in customer loyalty, employee commitment and business performance (Maignan *et al.*, 1999), to examine corporate social responsibility as a strategic resource. Strength in this resource, as in any other, may bring competitive advantages; weakness in this resource, as in any other, may bring vulnerability (Branco and Rodrigues, 2006). Consider, for example, the following situations.

In March 2007, Microsoft dropped one of its UK suppliers because that supplier failed to meet Microsoft's standards on employee diversity. Microsoft in the UK is one of an as yet small, but growing, number of British companies which monitor suppliers to ensure that they employ a representative mix of women and ethnic minorities. The decision resulted from Microsoft's diversity audit at its 250 largest British suppliers (Taylor, 2007). In the US, many large companies, including Microsoft, already insist on good diversity practices from suppliers, and are reducing or terminating the business they do with suppliers who fail to heed requests to diversify their workforces. Indeed, while many US-based multinationals have adopted voluntary corporate responsibility initiatives to self-regulate their overseas social and environmental practices, pressures mount for more active involvement of the US government in mandating such regulation (Aaronson, 2005). British-based companies that operate 'supplier diversity policies' include the bankers Morgan Stanley, BAA airports authority, and car rental group Avis Budget (Taylor, 2007). Suppliers unable or unwilling to meet the social responsibilities defined by major customers stand the considerable risk of losing those customers.

Also in 2007, the US retail giant Wal-Mart found itself in a bitter legal dispute with Ms Julie Roehm. Ms Roehm had previously overseen Wal-Mart's £300 million advertising account before she was dismissed amid accusations that she had an affair with her deputy, was entertained too lavishly by a potential client, solicited a job inappropriately, and wrongly accepted the gift of a case of vodka (Gapper, 2007). Aside from questions of ethics in executive behaviour, to which we will return, cases such as this are a compelling illustration of the costs of inappropriate behaviour in managing buyer–seller relationships. The accusations of corruption and bribery levelled against Volkswagen and Siemens executives in Germany – for example, the alleged Siemens 'slush fund' to pay bribes to win international contracts – have been damaging to both companies (Woodhead, 2007). Appositely, it should be noted that many practices regarded in the past as wholly acceptable – for example, 'corporate hospitality' – may now be enough to undermine or destroy buyer–seller relationships, not to mention the careers of individual executives. The impact is magnified by growing transparency and information availability, so dubious practices are more difficult to hide. A recent review of the 'integrity land mines' faced by companies concludes:

> *The changes in laws, regulations, stakeholder expectations, and media scrutiny that have taken place in the past decade can now make a major lapse in integrity catastrophic. Fines, penalties and settlements are counted in the hundreds of millions (or billions) of dollars . . . And worse, in some cases (as Enron and Arthur Andersen demonstrated) – a company can actually implode.*

(Heineman, 2007)

The management of business-to-business buyer–seller relationships has to be placed into this more demanding context.

Furthermore, at the level of the brand, questions of social responsibility and the ethics and morality of corporate behaviour are increasingly significant, posing both risks and opportunities. In 2007, the ethically minded coffee company Starbucks found itself in the midst of a damaging and intractable struggle over the legitimacy of coffee trademarking by the Ethiopian government. While the Ethiopian government – in one of the world's poorest countries – wants to trademark some of its most famous coffees, Starbucks objected to the trademarks as damaging to its own brand. The dispute was played out live on the video website YouTube. One commentator suggested that Starbucks was 'playing Russian roulette' with its brand (Rushe, 2007). Importantly, there may be an increasing number of trade-offs faced by companies between CSR and commercial goals.

The German car-makers were attacked in 2007 by Renate Künast, Green MP and former environment minister, who urged German consumers to buy the Toyota Prius instead of BMW and Volkswagen cars – because of the lower carbon dioxide emissions of the Toyota hybrid car. Porsche's chief executive responded with the claim that 'Toyota can hardly believe its luck.' In fact, Volkswagen and Mercedes-Benz produce cars with lower emissions than the Prius, which anyway accounts for only 3.5 per cent of Toyota's sales. In spite of the facts, public perceptions are that German car-makers are reluctant followers rather than leaders in building cleaner cars. The fear is that, if sales follow customer perceptions, then Toyota will win the race to provide the low-emission vehicles that people around the world will drive over the next decades. Weak defensive positioning on environmental concerns has created a major strategic weakness for the German car manufacturers, which they now have to overcome (Reed and Milne, 2007).

In the UK, 2007 saw another 'environmental arms race' between retailers, each claiming to be greener than the other. Marks & Spencer's announcement that it intended to be carbon neutral by 2012 led to claims from Tesco that it would carbon label all its products, and similar eco-promises from J. Sainsbury. Appositely, one analyst noted, 'Whether M&S wants to save the rainforest or save itself from Tesco is the question.' While cynics may suspect there is a degree of posturing and 'holier than thou' grandstanding in these environmental initiatives, there appears an underlying belief that in the current marketplace consumers are discriminating in favour of companies that can demonstrate they are trying to clean up their environmental act. The new retail mantra appears to be: 'Green pays. Green brings in customers' (Davey and Laurance, 2007). Mid-2007 saw the supermarkets attacking their own plastic carrier bags and attempting to persuade consumers to forgo this convenience in favour of other packaging – designer reusable cotton bags marked 'I'm Not A Plastic Bag' at Sainsbury's, vouchers for schools for consumers not using bags at Asda, and loyalty card points for reusing plastic bags at Tesco (Sherwood, 2007). Interestingly, the green competition between supermarkets quickly moved to public criticisms of suppliers' excessive product packaging policies, and promises to sanction suppliers who do not reduce packaging (and carry the additional costs incurred). While responding to competitors' CSR moves may not always be the best approach, the strategic significance of CSR to competitive positioning is growing.

'I'm not a plastic bag' by Anya Hindsmarch (Courtesy of Sainsburys plc)

The results of company manoeuvring on issues of corporate responsibility may be surprising. The fatal poisoning of seventeen cats and dogs in the USA in 2007 through contaminated petfood produced different responses from the companies affected. The big petfood brands and the supermarkets took the approach of announcing the product recall, clearing affected stock from stores, and then largely falling quiet. Petsmart and Petco took a considerably more aggressive approach than retail competitors like Wal-Mart, Krogers and Safeway, by using their response to the crisis to differentiate themselves from their competitors. Petsmart and Petco continued to actively publicise and flag the problem to consumers, in spite of the product recall. Continuing emphasis on the problem has undermined the position of the leading brands. Whether motivated by consumer interests and those of their pets, or purely commercial aims, Petsmart and Petco have apparently created competitive advantage through their actions in this crisis (Birchall, 2007).

However, CSR initiatives may not be effective in achieving either their social or business aims. While environmental politics sparked a 'green gold rush', with companies spending huge amounts on 'carbon credit' or carbon offsetting projects, the signs are that many such projects yield few if any environmental benefits. The primary beneficiaries appear to be those who sell carbon credit, rather than the environment or those who buy the credits (Harvey and Fidler, 2007).

However, there are signs that, while consumers do indeed appear to be discriminating between brands and companies on issues of societal impact and ethical

Table 18.1 The most ethically perceived brands in five countries*

France	Germany	Spain	UK	USA
1 Danone	1 Adidas	1 Nestlé	1 Co-op (including Bank)	1 Coca-Cola
2= Adidas	2= Nike	2 Body Shop	2 Body Shop	2 Kraft
2= Nike	2= Puma	3 Coca-Cola	3 Marks & Spencer	3 Procter & Gamble
4 Nestlé	4 BMW	4 Danone	4 Traidcraft	4= Johnson & Johnson
5 Renault	5= Demeter	5 El Corte Inglés	5= Cafédirect	4= Kellogg's
6 Peugeot	5= gepa	6= Adidas	5= Ecover	4= Nike
7 Philips	7 VW	6= Nike	7= Green & Black	4= Sony
8= Carrefour	8= Sony	6= Sony	7= Tesco	8= Ford
8= Coca-Cola	8= Trigema	9 L'Oréal	9 Oxfam	8= Toyota
10 L'Oréal	10= Bio Produkte; Body Shop; Hipp; Mercedes; Wrangler	10 Mercedes	10 Sainsbury's	10= Levi's; Starbucks

Note: * Based on a survey of 5,000 unprompted respondents.

Source: Adapted from Carlos Grande, 'Ethical Consumption Makes Mark on Branding', *Financial Times*, 20 February 2007, p. 24.

standards, they may be less impressed by corporate posturing than some companies may believe. A recent survey of the 'most ethically perceived brands' produced the findings shown in Table 18.1. The survey results contain some surprises both about which brands are believed to represent ethical behaviour, and in the similarities and differences across the countries studied.

The shift in attitudes towards consumption may be difficult to track – for example, while consumers claim they would pay a 5–10 per cent premium for many ethical products, in practice such brands usually have tiny market shares (Grande, 2007a). Moreover, a recent five-country survey conducted by market research group GfK NOP suggests that consumers in five of the world's leading economies believe that business ethics have worsened in the past five years, and they are turning to 'ethical consumerism' to make companies more accountable (Grande, 2007b). Respondents believe that brands with 'ethical' claims – on environmental policies or treatment of staff or suppliers – would make businesses more answerable to the public, and that companies should 'promote ethical credentials more strongly' (Grande, 2007a). Commentators on branding suggest that ethical consumption is one of the most significant branding issues in modern markets, and underlies change in the automotive sector, food, retailing, technology and health and beauty sectors. Its influence is behind the strong sales growth of hybrid cars, 'cruelty-free' beauty products, and dramatic growth in sales of organic food. The conclusion appears to be that ethical and environmental questions are being posed in growing numbers of consumers, but they are not always overly impressed by companies' responses. Nonetheless, the impact of 'ethical consumerism' is large and of escalating significance.

The growing frequency of situations of this kind suggests that issues relating to corporate social responsibility initiatives and the ethical standards evidenced by companies are increasingly relevant to the debate about marketing strategy and positioning relative to competitors, because:

● They represent a new kind of corporate resource which has implications for building a sustainable and defensible competitive position.

- The measurement and reporting of corporate social responsibility 'scores' (often computed with questionable methodologies) imposes new requirements for openness and transparency in company behaviour – of the world's 250 largest multinationals, 64 per cent published their own corporate social responsibility reports in 2005 (Chatterji and Levine, 2006).

- Reflecting the norms of behaviour determined by buyer organisations is increasingly mandatory in sustaining buyer–seller relationships in business-to-business markets (and is made yet more complex where those relationships are global in nature and span different cultures).

- Failure to conform to or exceed the standards of behaviour defined by a media-influenced and Internet-literate consumer may undermine conventional efforts to establish the credentials of a brand and to build a position in a market.

- Increasingly, employees and managers expect their companies to reflect emerging societal values as well as superior ethical standards, and the retention of critical talent in a company may be closely related to these perceptions and beliefs.

- Most telling of all, increasingly corporate social responsibility is not being viewed as purely altruistic, but as an element of competitive advantage (Porter and Kramer, 2006).

This chapter addresses the emergent question of the impact of corporate responsibility and ethical standards on marketing strategy and competitive positioning in the following way. The structure and logic of the approach we take is shown in Figure 18.1. First, we examine the scope of CSR and the corporate drivers of CSR strategies. This is followed by a review of CSR as a defensive strategy, and then as a source of sustainable competitive advantage.

Figure 18.1 Marketing strategy and corporate social responsibility

18.2 The scope of corporate social responsiblity and corporate citizenship

The modern era in which companies must operate is one which is increasingly characterised by a variety of anti-business sentiments and activism. Examples include the anti-globalisation movement, shareholder activism and corporate governance reforms – indeed, some suggest that we are experiencing a climate of 'defiance' towards business (Maignan and Ferrell, 2004). Certainly, global business scandals, such as the accounting abuses uncovered at Enron and Andersen's, and the bribery accusations at VW and Siemens, have done little to improve perceptions of business.

Even at a more trivial level, businesses of various kinds are under media-orchestrated attacks for their normal ways of doing business. Recent examples of these pressures include: public campaigns to complain and demand repayment of bank charges; close to hysterical protests about '4×4' (SUV) vehicles, inspired by the mythology of global warming; the siege-like conditions under which the tobacco and alcohol industries now operate; demands that airlines should reduce the number of flights they operate and that, like cigarette packs, holiday packages should carry 'health warnings' related to fears about carbon emissions; the anti-obesity campaign pressure on food retailers and restriction of the advertising of 'junk food' products to children. There is growing evidence that the way in which products are marketed in many sectors is changing because consumer groups believe business practices to be irresponsible.

Accordingly, the belief that consumers are more likely to buy from companies they perceive as socially responsible, and would switch brands to favour products and stores that show concern about the community has led to growing pressure on firms to behave as good 'corporate citizens' (Maignan *et al.*, 1999). In contrast to the traditional view that the only responsibility of the firm is to make a profit (Friedman, 1970), companies have been encouraged to undertake activities that provide benefits to various groups: supportive work–family policies, ethics compliance programmes, corporate volunteerism, green marketing. In this sense, 'corporate citizenship' is a term that describes the activities and processes adopted by businesses to meet their social responsibilities (Maignan *et al.*, 1999).

One link between these various trends and issues is the effect of inhibiting the ability of companies to develop effective marketing strategies or to establish and defend their desired competitive positions without making allowance for a societal dimension in their actions. Perhaps the most significant issue now in being a good 'corporate citizen' is not so much moral obligation as a business case for initiatives which protect and provide new business opportunities.

The growth in corporate attention to CSR has not always been voluntary, instead reflecting surprise at public reaction to issues not previously thought to be their responsibility – Nike faced consumer boycotts after media reporting of abusive labour practices in its Indonesian suppliers' factories; fast-food and packaged food companies are being held responsible for obesity problems and poor nutrition; pharmaceutical companies are expected to respond to the AIDS pandemic in Africa, though it is far removed from their main product lines and markets (Porter and Kramer, 2006).

More positively, CSR may be associated with important and measurable benefits to companies. For example, cause-related projects may impact directly on income: if firms that create social gains realise cash value in terms of increased purchases by morally conscious customers (or those customers are willing to pay higher prices), or in reduced costs. More broadly, CSR may have the impact of building long-term customer loyalty, legitimacy, trust or brand equity (Godfrey and Hatch, 2007). Indeed, some companies have made high-profile efforts to position as socially responsible, as part of their strategy, which may in part be a response to external critics, but also part of the underlying vision of what a business is about.

● British Petroleum attempted to underline its commitment to the natural environment by styling itself as 'Beyond Petroleum' (a move viewed with some cynicism by environmental campaigners).

● Nike advertises its commitment to adopting 'responsible business practices that contribute to profitable and sustainable growth', having come through a decade or more of vocal condemnation of employment practices in its overseas supplier workshops.

● The Body Shop was positioned from its outset as actively involved in social improvement projects throughout the world and opposed to practices such as animal-testing of cosmetics and toiletry products, which is thought to be one of the resources of the business which made it an attractive acquisition in 2006 for the more traditional cosmetics company L'Oréal.

Certainly, it has become increasingly important for strategic decision-makers to understand the scope of corporate social responsibility initiatives both in developing possible defences against attacks on their competitive position and ability to compete, and as potential sources of new types of competitive strength.

Scoping CSR possibilities involves initially considering the specific dimensions of CSR. Attention has been given to initiatives such as the support of charitable causes, and the advent of 'cause-related marketing' (Barone *et al.*, 2000), as well as the protection of the natural environment as an influence on purchasing behaviour and marketing strategy (Menon and Menon, 1997; Drumwright, 1989).

In developing an integrative framework to examine CSR, Maignan and Ferrell (2004) provide a useful overview of how CSR has been understood, and how that understanding is changing. They distinguish between CSR as social obligation, as stakeholder obligation, as ethics driven, and as managerial process. These distinctions are useful in understanding the case for CSR and providing a managerial framework for addressing the strategic implications of CSR.

CSR as social obligation

Since the 1950s onwards there has been a strong link between CSR and the alignment of corporate actions with the objectives and values of society. This ethos is still found in contemporary marketing studies, particularly regarding the potential for both positive and negative consumer reactions to CSR initiatives of this type (Sen and Bhattacharya, 2001). Classically, Carroll (1979) distinguishes social obligations as: *economic obligations* – to be productive and economically viable; *legal and ethical obligations* – to follow the law and accepted values and norms; and, *philanthropic obligations* – to actively give back to society.

CSR as stakeholder obligation

The 1990s saw the emergence of the view that CSR as social obligation was too broad to allow the effective management of CSR (Clarkson, 1995), and the argument that businesses are not responsible to society as a whole, but only to those who directly or indirectly affect, or are affected by, the firm's activities – i.e. the firm's stakeholders (Donaldson and Preston, 1995). Accordingly, stakeholders can be grouped into: *organisational* – employees, customers, shareholders, suppliers; *community* – local residents, special interest groups; *regulatory* – local authorities, legal controls; and *media* stakeholders (Henriques and Sadorsky, 1999).

CSR as ethics driven

Viewing CSR as either a social or stakeholder obligation suggests that CSR is motivated only by corporate self-interests, by enabling business to gain legitimacy with important external parties. It has been argued that such views fail to account for actions by companies which represent a positive commitment to society's interests that disregard self-interest and are genuinely altruistic (Swanson, 1995). Indeed, if CSR reflects only obligations, then it becomes difficult to evaluate whether business practices are or are not socially responsible, as opposed to simply reciprocal (Jones, 1995). An ethics-driven view of CSR is concerned with the rightness or wrongness of specific initiatives, independently of any social or stakeholder obligation. For example, justice-based ethics would lead a company to attempt to systematically favour decisions that stimulate equality and fairness for its partners and associates.

CSR as managerial process

The three perspectives above attempt to identify the factors that persuade businesses to undertake CSR initiatives. An additional view concerns CSR in terms of organisational processes (sometimes called 'corporate social responsiveness') (Ackerman, 1975). One view advocates that 'issues management' and 'environmental assessment' constitute managerial processes relevant to working towards a proactive responsibility stance (Wood, 1991). Others suggest the type of sequential management process useful to systematic development of CSR initiatives (Ackerman, 1975):

● monitoring and assessing environmental conditions;

● attending to stakeholder demands; and

● designing plans and policies aimed at enhancing the firm's impacts.

Carroll (1979) earlier described the managerial processes of response to social responsibility as involving planning and social forecasting, organising for social response, controlling social activities, and developing corporate social policy.

The importance of Maignan and Ferrell's integration of these disparate conceptualisations of CSR is that it provides us with an overview of the issues likely to be raised by CSR initiatives, and suggests the importance of developing appropriate organisational processes for managing CSR. Scoping the existing and likely future impacts of the diverse pressures towards CSR is becoming an important challenge for management. Porter and Kramer (2006) suggest that management attention should focus on:

● **Identifying the points of intersection between the company and society** – including the ways in which the business impacts on society in the normal course of business (e.g. transport emissions), but also the way in which social conditions impact on the business (e.g. regulatory standards). This involves mapping both the social impact of the value chain, and the social influences on the company's competitiveness.

● **Choosing which social issues to address** – selecting issues that intersect with the business which present an opportunity to create shared value, rather than trying to solve all society's problems.

● **Creating a corporate social agenda** – looking beyond external expectations to achieve both social and economic benefits.

Although the ways in which it can be addressed will differ greatly between company situations, the framework in this section provides an initial approach to making CSR issues explicit and integrating them into thinking about marketing strategy.

18.3 The drivers of corporate social responsibility initiatives

Notwithstanding the links we are building between corporate social responsibility and marketing strategy, it would be wrong to suggest that altruistic, corporate philanthropy is disappearing or diminishing in importance. Indeed, while traditional philanthropy has been criticised as ineffective, the birth of the 'social enterprise' movement represents a new model of addressing issues of social justice with approaches drawn from the business world. For example, Google.org is the philanthropic arm of the search engine company, established to invest in and support for-profit and not-for-profit groups that focus on energy, poverty and the environment. Achieving social goals through business means – social enterprise – represents a new type of business model, fuelled by individuals, like Microsoft's Bill Gates, who do not simply want to donate money to good causes but to bring their own philosophy and skills to managing it to achieve social return. Social enterprise aims to break down traditional barriers between business, government and charity in ventures that aim to combine innovation, market orientation and an objective to generate a public benefit (Jack, 2007). It is speculated by some that there may even be a move away from shareholder capitalism to a radically different enterprise model, in which social purpose is placed above profit or profit is harnessed to social purpose (Smith and Ward, 2007).

However, while social enterprise is an important extension of traditional concepts of corporate philanthropy, and it may enhance the reputations of companies and leaders who devote resources to these ventures, our present interests are in the drivers of more conventional corporate social responsibility initiatives, and the links to business and marketing strategy in existing companies rather than new hybrid business models.

Porter and Kramer (2006), in their recent review of CSR, suggest that, while CSR generally remains imbued with a strong moral imperative (as we saw in the last section of the chapter), modern supporters of the CSR movement rely on four arguments to justify attention and resources for these initiatives:

- **Moral obligation** – the duty for a company to be a good citizen and to do 'the right thing'. However, there are many dilemmas faced in such questions – Google's entry to the China market created a major conflict between Western dislike for censorship and the legal requirements imposed by the Chinese government.

- **Sustainability** – emphasis on the environmental and community impact of the business. To an extent this may reflect enlightened self-interest – changes to packaging at McDonalds have reduced its solid waste by 30 per cent.

- **License to operate** – the tacit or explicit permission a company needs from governments, communities and other stakeholders to do business.

- **Reputation** – CSR initiatives to enhance a company's image, strengthen its brand, improve morale, or even raise share prices. Some organisations have a distinctive position based on an extraordinary long-term commitment to social responsibility, for example, Ben & Jerry's, the Body Shop.

Perhaps to this list can be added the need to respond to the CSR-based positioning of competitors that are seeking advantage through an enhanced franchise with the customer, and coping with explicit customer demands for the standards they expect in, for example, their suppliers. Interestingly, Porter and Kramer note that 'All four schools of thought share the same weakness: They focus on the tension between business and society rather than their interdependence' (p. 83).

Thomas Stewart (2006a) underlines this point. He notes the contradiction between the classic argument that a company's only responsibility to society is to make as much money as it legally can, compared with the modern reality that a company that shunned society would be ostracised in turn, to its cost. The opposite problem for executives may be the conflict between social initiatives and business goals – is there perhaps hypocrisy in the brewer urging consumers not to drink, or the oil company promoting fuel conservation? Stewart's point is that such views share a logical flaw: they assume that companies and society have opposing interests. Thus, it follows that, starting from the premise that business and society are interdependent, CSR is identified as a strategic opportunity, which has far greater importance than moral duty alone.

Nonetheless, there is wide recognition that firms face choices in their responsiveness to social responsibility. For example, corporate social responsiveness may reflect one of the following modes or philosophies, ranging from 'do nothing' to 'do much' (Carroll, 1979):

- **Reaction** – firms that deny social responsibilities and do less than is required by society's standards.

- **Defence** – firms act through meeting social responsibilities only to defend their own business interests, but do only what is required.

- **Accommodation** – firms with a progressive stance to improving social responsiveness.

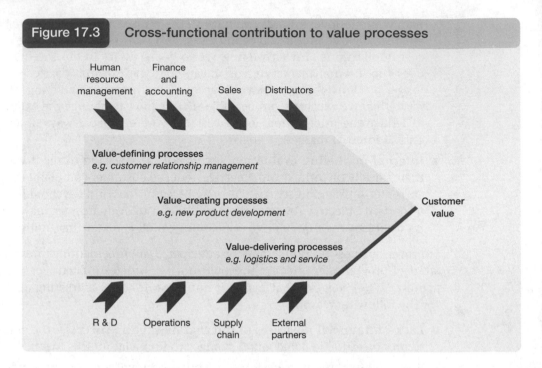

Figure 17.3   Cross-functional contribution to value processes

also in a network of organisations in a strategic alliance (see Chapter 16). Many of the processes of defining, creating and delivering value to customers are not 'owned' or directly managed by marketing or sales departments. Second, sophisticated customers will not accept anything less than seamless delivery of value in their terms – problems in the integration of processes in the seller's organisation are the seller's problem, not the buyer's (Hulbert *et al.*, 2003).

The integration of the whole organisation around the drivers of customer value has become an imperative – all activities must work together, fit together, and be seen to appear together by the customer. Nonetheless, many organisations appear to struggle with this imperative. The model in Figure 17.3 provides a framework for analysing the challenges in identifying and integrating the complex of functional specialisms and internal and external resource centres that impact on the operation of the value processes of value identification, creation and delivery (however these processes are labelled in a particular company).

We consider briefly the nature of each of the interfaces between marketing and other functional groups, which may provide internal marketing targets for internal alliance building.

17.5.2   Marketing and human resource management

It is now a considerable time since Glassman and McAfee (1992) called for the full-scale integration of marketing and human resource management departments. Their logic was that the two functions were both focused on 'people issues' (the one on customers and the other on employees), yet seemed unable to integrate their activities effectively. However, HRM in many organisations has moved towards a

● **Proaction** – firms that anticipate future responsibilities and act beyond minimal requirements, ensuring that they meet or even exceed their responsibilities.

Nonetheless, responsiveness alone may not be the same as good citizenship. For example, a responsive organisation may address social pressures by moving to a less demanding environment – consider the growing emphasis by tobacco companies on the relatively unregulated developing countries, where tobacco consumption remains socially acceptable. The simple prescription of responsiveness oversimplifies the complexity of the situations that companies face. The issue is how a company responds, and what its responses represent.

Indeed, the tobacco industry provides an interesting illustration of the limitations of CSR. Notwithstanding vehement criticism by anti-smoking groups, and opponents like the World Health Organization – which categorically questions the very possibility of social responsibility in the tobacco industry – recent years have seen tobacco companies starting to position themselves as good corporate citizens. These moves include corporate philanthropy – e.g. donations to universities for research and to environmental groups; CSR reporting – e.g. in annual reports and other publications; self-regulation – e.g. BAT, Philip Morris and Japan Tobacco launching an international voluntary code of marketing. However, research suggests that these moves are likely to be ineffective or even counter-productive – some scientific journals refuse to publish research sponsored by the tobacco industry, many stakeholder groups will not risk their own reputations by engaging with tobacco companies, and CSR claims are regarded by many as window-dressing at best. While the tobacco industry can defend its position by showing integrity in its supply chain (e.g. improving the working conditions of plantation employees), it is unable to demonstrate a contribution to the well-being of society (because of the addictive and lethal nature of its products) (Palazzo and Richter, 2005). While defensive CSR may offer some advantages to tobacco companies, a proactive stance is unlikely to be effective.

Certainly, there is a dilemma for some companies if their existing business model relies on resources and capabilities which become questionable in terms of social responsibilities and duty. One of the most successful British fashion retailers is Primark. The Primark business model relies on sourcing fashion items from low-cost manufacturing areas and turning catwalk trends into products within weeks at extremely low prices, which provides a major competitive advantage with the fashion consumer. Nonetheless, the result is that Primark buys from suppliers whose workers are paid as little as 9p an hour, working 90 hours a week in extremely poor conditions. The company's 'charm offensive' in the ethics and social responsibility field spans ethical initiatives for organic cotton tops promised to be Fairtrade, reduced environmental damage through fewer plastic bags, and signing up to the Ethical Trading Initiative, which pledges commitment to improving working conditions. Primark faced coordinated protests at its stores organised by People and Plant during Fairtrade Week in 2007, and calls for consumer boycotts. However, the dilemma is that the low-price, lean supply chain business model relies on low-cost suppliers. This dilemma is shared by other low-price fashion retailers like Tesco and Asda.

The logic we are developing provides the basis for examining the linkages between CSR and competitive advantage and strategic positioning in the marketplace, in ways which have not been fully recognised in earlier stages of the consideration of CSR initiatives as social obligations with a possible 'public relations' benefit to company reputation. In particular, we distinguish between CSR as a *defence* against attacks that can undermine competitive position, and as a *strategy* which can provide new business opportunities.

<table>
<tr><td>18.4</td><td></td></tr>
</table>

18.4 Defensive corporate social responsibility initiatives

If a firm is essentially defensive or accommodative in its stance to social responsiveness then its primary concerns with CSR will be the protection of relationships, for example, with consumers, business-to-business customers, influential lobby or pressure groups, suppliers, employees and managers, and relative position against competitors. Currently, the evidence is that most firms concentrate their communications regarding CSR with their consumers, employees and shareholders (Snider *et al.*, 2003), showing some neglect of their competitors and alliance partners (Robertson and Nicholson, 1996).

One example of defensive moves in this area is the 2007 appointment by the brokerage firm Cantor Fitzgerald of a chief ethics officer. Inter-dealer broking is known for its rough-and-tumble rivalry, but faced with shareholder activism criticising the company's governance, and a court ruling where a judge pointed to the company's 'deceptive statements', a defensive response was required. The chief ethics officer was appointed to reaffirm the company's 'strong commitment to business ethics and integrity' (Mackensie and Beales, 2007).

Porter and Kramer (2006) identify an important warning regarding defensive forms of CSR, particularly in terms of responding to the challenges of pressure groups – they warn that companies seeing CSR only as a way to placate pressure groups often find that this approach turns into a series of short-term public relations actions, with minimal social benefit and no strategic benefit for the business. They suggest the most common corporate responses to CSR have not been strategic and are often little more than cosmetic. Nonetheless, the risks in remaining inactive when social demands become severe are considerable.

The changing policies at Coca-Cola are illustrative. Coke has attracted a barrage of negative publicity over recent years: the alleged mistreatment of workers in Columbia; the use of water in drought-stricken parts of India; delaying acceptance of responsibility for contaminated product in Belgium in 1999; violently ejecting shareholder activists from the AGM; and playing a major role in fuelling the childhood obesity epidemic sweeping the developed world. Coke has been actively boycotted on university campuses throughout North America and in parts of Europe. The company was in danger of replacing Nike and McDonald's as the chief corporate villains for the anti-globalisation movement. The problem recognised by management was negative perceptions of the company progressively undermining the value of the brand. The new CEO of Coke has mandated a proactive company approach to social issues, with a goal of making Coke the 'recognised global leader in corporate social responsibility'. The company has undertaken an audit of labour practices throughout its supply chain, launched several water conservation projects, embraced industry guidelines restricting the sale of sugary drinks in schools, and supported initiatives to encourage physical exercise among children. Critics claim the company is pursuing these initiatives under pressure, not because they believe they are the right things to do (Ward, 2006).

In fact, the managerial goal in a defensive CSR mode should be to anticipate and develop appropriate responses to social demands from any source that threatens to undermine the value and credibility of brands, the attractiveness of the competitive position upon which the company's strategy depends, and the viability of the marketing strategy itself. However, it is important that social initiative responses to these pressures should be carefully evaluated for likely effects, rather than constitute an unthinking 'knee-jerk' reaction by management.

Management attention can usefully be given to examining the links between CSR stance and the impacts on consumers, business-to-business customers, lobby groups, suppliers, employees and managers, and competitors. The goal should be to carefully evaluate the possible positive and negative impacts of CSR efforts on each of these groups.

Consumers and CSR

The adoption of social causes by organisations has often been based on the assumption that consumers will reward this behaviour (Levy, 1999). Nonetheless, there is a risk that it is unlikely that consumers will blindly accept social initiatives as sincere, and so may or may not reward the firm with positive attitudes and purchases (Becker-Olsen *et al.*, 2006). Indeed, research suggests that consumers will 'punish' firms that are perceived as insincere or manipulative in their social involvement (Becker-Olsen *et al.*, 2006). Nonetheless, there have been some research findings suggesting that there is a link between a company's social initiatives and positive consumer responses in attitudes, beliefs and behaviours (Brown and Dacin, 1997; Creyer and Ross, 1997; Ellen *et al.*, 2000). Positive associations have been found between social initiatives and price, perceived quality, corporate attitudes and purchase intentions (Becker-Olsen *et al.*, 2006).

However, there is a strong argument that, to be effective, social initiatives must be consistent with a firm's operating objectives and values (Levy, 1999). Indeed, there is some evidence that, when social initiatives are not aligned with corporate objectives and values, CSR initiatives may become a liability and diminish previously held beliefs about the firm. There is some priority for social initiatives and responses to be chosen carefully to reflect the firm's values and domain, so that consumers perceive initiatives as proactive and socially motivated (Becker-Olsen *et al.*, 2006).

Business-to-business customers and CSR

The escalating demands of business-to-business customers for their suppliers to implement CSR policies and initiatives that are acceptable to the customer organisation have already been noted.

The 'vendor compliance' programme at Target Corporation is illustrative. Target Corporation is a successful US retailer with more than 1,500 Target stores and nearly 200 upmarket SuperTarget outlets. Target prides itself on its high ethical standards and business principles, emphasising the protection of human rights, and extends these principles and standards to its suppliers. Target sources its purchases globally through its Associated Merchandising Corporation subsidiary. Purchasing officers are required to uphold Target Corporation social responsibility standards wherever they buy in the world, even when these exceed the requirements of local laws – Target engineers do not just inspect suppliers' factories for product quality but also for labour rights and employment conditions. Target operates a formal 'compliance organisation' for its purchasing, to enforce its vendor standards, focusing on vendor education and verification, with the following components:

- Implementation of a compliance audit programme, where audit staff conduct random visits to supplier manufacturing facilities, following which compliance violations are subject to administrative probation or severance of the relationship.
- Limitation of subcontractors used by suppliers to those approved by Target.
- Regular vendor evaluations as well as formal audits.

Target is not unusual in its attention to the ethical and social responsibility standards it demands of its suppliers throughout the world. The introduction of formal social responsibility dimensions to supplier relationships is becoming the norm rather than the exception with large customers. These social responsibility mandates impact on supplier selection, and on the continuation of relationships with existing suppliers.

Organisational customers' evolving social responsibility mandates require effective responses. Certainly, one response may be that a customer's social responsibility demands reduce the attractiveness of that customer to the seller, and the business should be sacrificed. Nonetheless, the spread of vendor evaluation approaches which make CSR demands on suppliers requires continuous and systematic evaluation as the basis for an appropriate response.

Lobby groups and CSR

There is some evidence also that companies with poor CSR records may experience serious negative consequences, such as large-scale consumer boycotts, weaker brand image or reduced sales. Part of this effect may be accounted for by the growth of consumer groups that actively promote awareness of what they believe to be company wrongdoing, and actively promote consumer boycotts (Snider *et al.*, 2003).

Certainly it appears that activist organisations have become much more aggressive and effective in bringing public pressure to bear on companies. They may target the most visible companies, to draw attention to the issue, even if the company in question has little impact on the problem. Nestlé is the world's largest seller of bottled water, and has become a major target in the global dilemma about access to fresh water. In fact, Nestlé's impact on world water usage and availability is trivial – but it is a convenient target (Porter and Kramer, 2006).

One outcome of scoping CSR issues in the way we proposed earlier is to identify the issues which are likely to become high profile with different types of pressure groups. This at least provides some basis for responding effectively when they become live issues. Nonetheless, responses to external pressure groups have to be evaluated carefully for their potential 'unintended consequences' (Fry and Polonsky, 2004).

Nonetheless, in some cases a defensive stance may be all that is available on some social issues. In such cases, initiatives should be carefully evaluated and implemented to avoid the risks of making the situation worse, being perceived as insincere and cynical, or undertaking actions with broader and undesirable consequences for the company or for society.

18.5 Corporate social responsibility and competitive advantage

Important, from the perspective of marketing strategy, is the emerging argument that corporate social responsibility (CSR) provides a source of competitive advantage which is of increasing significance. For example, Michael Porter and Mark Kramer (2006) have recently made a strong case for the position that businesses should not simply be taking corporate social responsibility seriously as an end in itself, but should be embedding it into their strategy to help build competitive advantage. They argue that conventional CSR approaches have often resulted in a mix of uncoordinated CSR initiatives and philanthropic activities that neither make meaningful social impact, nor strengthen the firm's long-term competitiveness. (We have earlier suggested the converse of this case: that companies neglecting issues of corporate social responsibility and ethical or moral standards may find themselves wrong-footed by competitors who position themselves partly on the basis of these resources.) While the Porter and Kramer model is relatively new and untried, it is likely to be highly influential in management thinking and it provides the underlying structure for this section of the chapter. Above all, Porter and Kramer link CSR directly to creating competitive advantage.

The logic linking corporate responsibility to competitive advantage follows these lines. Porter and Kramer argue that many prevailing approaches to CSR are fragmented and disconnected from business and strategy, while in fact the real challenge is for companies to analyse their social responsibility prospects using the same frameworks that guide their core business choices. The goal is to establish CSR not simply as corporate altruism but as a source of opportunity, innovation and competitive advantage.

Porter and Kramer argue that companies should make choices about which social issues to address, from:

- **Generic social issues** – things that are not affected by the company's operations, not impacting on its long-term competitiveness.
- **Value chain social impacts** – social issues that are affected by the company's activities in the normal course of business.
- **Social dimensions of competitive context** – social issues in the external environment that significantly affect the underlying drivers of the company's competitiveness.

They suggest that a company should sort social issues into these three categories for each business unit and location, and then rank them in terms of potential impact. The category into which a given issue will fall will depend on the business and its location. For example, the AIDS pandemic in Africa might be a generic social issue for a retailer in the US or Europe, a value chain impact for a pharmaceutical company, and a competitive context issue for a mining company depending on local labour in Africa for its operations.

The purpose of this ranking is to create an explicit corporate social agenda for a company that 'looks beyond community expectations to achieve social and economic benefits simultaneously. It moves from mitigating harm to finding ways to reinforce corporate strategy by advancing social conditions' (p. 85). Porter and Kramer introduce a critically important distinction between responsive CSR and strategic CSR, suggesting it is through strategic CSR that a company can make the greatest social impact while also achieving the greatest competitive benefits. Their distinction is between two levels of CSR:

- **Responsive CSR** – involves acting as a good corporate citizen, reflecting the social concerns of stakeholders in the company, and also mitigating the existing or predicted adverse effects of business activities. The domain is generic social impacts and value chain social impacts. The limitation of many citizenship initiatives remains that, however beneficial the social effects, such programmes tend to remain incidental to the company's business. The key to mitigating value chain social impacts is best practice, though competitive advantage through such endeavours is likely to be temporary.

- **Strategic CSR** – moves beyond good citizenship and value chain impacts to initiatives with large and distinctive effects. The goals are the transformation of value chain activities to benefit society while at the same time reinforcing the company's strategy, and strategic moves that leverage corporate capabilities to improve areas of competitive context. Strategic CSR may involve the introduction of radically different new products – the Toyota Prius hybrid car responds to consumer concerns about car emissions pollution, and provides both competitive advantage for Toyota and environmental benefits. However, the broader goal of strategic CSR is to invest in social aspects of the company's context to strengthen company competitiveness. This is achieved, in part, by adding a social dimension to the company's value proposition and ways of doing business. Only a small number of the social issues that could be addressed have this potential to make a real difference to society and build competitive advantage.

As a framework for examining these distinctions and differences, the Porter and Kramer logic is summarised in Figure 18.2.

Further, using the example of Whole Foods Market in the USA, Porter and Kramer underline the competitive strength achieved by adding a social dimension to the value proposition. They suggest that the heart of strategy is a value proposition that rests on the set of needs that a company can uniquely meet for its chosen customers. The most strategic CSR adds a dimension to the value proposition, such that social impact is central to strategy. The value proposition at Whole Food Market is to sell natural, organic, healthy food products to consumers who are oriented to healthy eating and the environment. The company's stance on social issues is central to what makes them unique in food retailing and able to ask premium prices. For example, sourcing emphasises purchasing at store level from local farmers; buyers screen out ingredients considered unhealthy or environmentally damaging; the

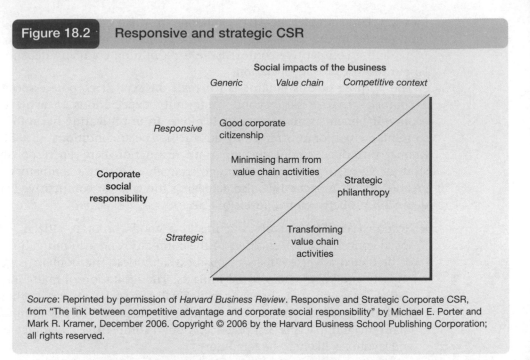

Figure 18.2 · Responsive and strategic CSR

company offsets its electricity consumption; spoiled produce goes to regional centres for composting; vehicles are being converted to run on bio-fuels; cleaning products in stores are environmentally friendly. The effect is that every aspect of the company's value chain reinforces the social dimensions of its value proposition, and provides strong differentiation from its competitors.

Porter and Kramer conclude that, while not every company can be a Whole Foods, adding a social dimension to the value proposition adds a new frontier for our thinking about competitive positioning. They also note that the number of industries and companies whose competitive advantage can involve social value propositions is rapidly growing. Their conclusion is important to how we consider the resource profile of an organisation and the ways in which it can leverage and strengthen that profile:

> *Organizations that make the right choices and build focussed, proactive, and integrated social initiatives in concert with their core strategies will increasingly distance themselves from the pack . . . Perceiving social responsibility as building shared value rather than as damage control or as a PR campaign will require dramatically different thinking in business. We are convinced, however, that CSR will become increasingly important to competitive success. (pp. 91–2)*

A similar viewpoint is adopted by Andrew Savitz, who created the environmental practice at PwC and has worked on environmental issues with some of America's largest companies. Savitz and Weber (2006) share the view that it makes financial sense for companies to anticipate and respond to society's emerging demands – anticipating reciprocal advantages in the longer term, i.e. the sustainable company will be more profitable as a result of its responsiveness. In their terms, sustainability is about conducting business in such a way that it benefits employees, customers, business partners, communities and shareholders at the same time – it is 'the art of doing business in an interdependent world' (Savitz and Weber, 2006). They suggest that the best-run companies have identified 'sustainability sweet spots' – areas where shareholders' long-term interests overlap with those of society. They point, for example, to Unilever's Project Shakti in India, where 13,000 females have been employed and trained to distribute Unilever products to rural communities, providing economic income in a deprived area, but at the same time gaining market access and penetration in a difficult market.

Nonetheless, on occasion, there may be major questions surrounding the balance between business and social benefits in some CSR initiatives of this kind. For example, some companies are benefiting commercially by asking 'green' consumers to pay them for cleaning up their own pollution. Chemicals company DuPont invites consumers to pay $4 to eliminate a tonne of carbon dioxide from the Kentucky plant where it manufactures a potent greenhouse gas called HFC-23. In fact, the equipment required to reduce such gases is relatively inexpensive. Similarly, Blue Source, a US offsetting company, invites consumers to offset their carbon emissions by investing in enhanced oil recovery (pumping carbon dioxide into depleted oil wells to bring up the remaining oil). In fact, Blue Source admits that because of the high price of oil this process is often profitable in itself, and the 'carbon credit' represents additional revenue (Harvey and Fidler, 2007). It is likely that such schemes will fail to deliver more than short-term financial benefits rather than synergy between business and social benefits.

One example of the possibilities for large-scale competitive change around social benefit initiatives is provided by the MIT team who said in 2004 they were going to overcome the digital divide between the rich and poor by making a $100 laptop for the poor children of the world – the One Laptop Per Child (OLPC) project. While initially dismissed simply as a charitable project, the MIT team's vision has underlined to the commercial IT sector the market power of the poor – the fact that the majority of the world's population does not have a computer will be one of the main drivers of growth for the sector. The effects on hardware and software companies have been dramatic.

- Intel (initially one of the fiercest critics of OLPC) has developed low-cost computers aimed at students in developing countries.

- Intel's rival, AMD, has pledged to get half the world's population online by 2015 with a device called the Personal Internet Communicator.

- Microsoft is supporting the establishment of computer kiosks in villages in developing countries to allow shared online access.

- Quanta Computer, the world's largest contract manufacturer of notebook computers, will start making laptops selling for $200, and will make the first OLPC to ship in 2007.

The OLPC project underlines the social benefits and the commercial opportunities in a cheap laptop, which was relatively easy to make using newer technologies, open source software, and stripping out unneeded functions (Hille, 2007).

Relatedly, in this sector, an interesting example of a company's leveraging its distinctive competitive competencies to further initiatives with both business and social benefits is provided by Dell Inc. – the leading computer supplier. Dell is using the strengths of its direct business model to generate collective efforts to reduce energy consumption and protect the environment. The initiative centres on improving the efficiency of IT products, reducing the harmful materials used in them, and cooperating with customers to dispose of old products. Michael Dell's environmental strategy focuses on three areas:

- Creating easy, low-cost ways for businesses to do better in protecting the environment – providing, for example, global recycling and product recovery programmes for customers, with participation requiring little effort on their part.

- Taking creative approaches to lessen the environmental impact of products from design to disposal – helping customers to take full advantage of new, energy-saving technology and processes, and advising on upgrades of legacy systems to reduce electricity usage.

- Looking to partnership with governments to promote environmental stewardship – for example, in Dell's 'Plant a Tree for Me' programme, offering customers the chance to offset emission from the electricity their computers use by making a contribution to buying a tree when they buy a PC.

As a company, Dell is also committing efforts to enhancing operational efficiencies and reducing its carbon footprint through the use of renewable energy (Dell, 2007). Importantly, Dell's initiative starts with the distinctive strengths of the company (the direct business-to-business model with corporate customers, and market leadership), applies these strengths to address an environmental issue (reduced pollution, lower energy use), but at the same time achieves business goals (reinforcing the company's leadership, strengthening customer relationships, faster take-up of newer, more efficient products and technologies). The link between this CSR initiative and the company's business model and value proposition is clear.

Similarly, 2007 saw Microsoft partnering with governments in less developed countries to offer Microsoft Windows and Office software packages for $3 to governments that subsidise the cost of computers for schoolchildren. The potential business benefit for Microsoft is to double the number of PC users worldwide, and reinforce the company's market growth. The social benefit is the greater investment in technology in some of the poorest countries in the world, with the goal of improving living standards and reducing global inequality (*Financial Times*, 2007).

On the environmental front, 2005 saw General Electric – the largest company in the world – launch its Ecoimagination initiative. Ecoimagination has grown out of GE's long-term investment in cleaner technologies, and places these technologies under a single brand. To qualify for Ecoimagination branding, products must significantly and measurably improve customers' environmental and operating performance. However, the Ecoimagination vision is driven by the principle that its green initiatives will have a positive impact on GE's competitive position and financial performance (Harvey, 2005; Hart, 2005).

CSR strategy at companies like Dell Inc., Microsoft and GE may provide a prototype of the linking of CSR to competitive advantage which will influence management thinking.

Summary

This chapter sets out to establish the impact of corporate social responsibility on marketing strategy. This is an area which is evolving rapidly, and one which is turning out to be highly significant to the ability of a company to maintain its chosen competitive position and to compete effectively. Nonetheless, it is an area where precise definitions and analytical methodologies do not yet exist. Our approach suggests that companies should devote efforts to understanding better the social pressures – which are likely to affect their ability to compete – through scoping or issue analysis. Company responses to social issues fall into several categories, ranging from altruistic company philanthropy and the concept of 'social enterprise', to defensive moves to protect competitive position, to strategic moves that aim to create competitive advantage through CSR initiatives. Our attention focuses on the latter areas: defensive CSR and creating competitive advantage through CSR.

Ballantyne, Smythson and others Case study

Getty Images Entertainment

The hold music on the telephone system at Ballantyne headquarters in Italy says it all: a constant refrain of chirpy Scottish bagpipes. Very Highlands. Very heritage. Molto strange. But for Matteo Montezemolo, managing director of Charme Investments, the private equity firm that bought the cashmere company in 2005, the Scottish link is fundamental. It is about adhering to a set of ethics that he believes should be at the heart of a modern luxury company: supporting domestic industry and expertise. 'When we bought Ballantyne, we were very impressed by how it was able to transfer on to the market such a luxury product in cashmere,' he explains. 'Then,

when we went to visit the factory in Innerleithen, we immediately realised that this luxury principle was starting exactly from there in what is the most prestigious district in the world for cashmere: the Scottish Borders.' All of the brand's knitwear is made at its Scottish factory and accounts for 60 per cent of the business (jackets and trousers are made in Italy). 'If customers pay such high amounts of money for a cashmere product,' he continues, 'they need to know what is behind the pricing. They need to know it is handmade, made with excellent materials, that it is not made in low-cost countries.' Keeping production in Scotland 'is first of all a business decision – in our view, the core business of Ballantyne is the knitwear and all this knitting needs to be made in our factory in Scotland – and secondly, it is about ethics, because my vision is that today you need to be very careful on the market. You cannot sell a luxury product at such high prices and then turn round the label and see it's made in Hong Kong, Taiwan or Korea. This is not fair, and you need to have a fair approach to your client; things need to be priced in the proper way, made in the right country, in your factory and handmade.' Montezemolo admits that this could be a financial disadvantage, though with revenue leaping from $17m to

$40m since he took over, perhaps not a significant one. Indeed, that companies should be seen to be supporting local business is of increasing importance, as Burberry discovered recently when it closed a Welsh factory. The decision to take production off-shore prompted a rash of political point-scoring and even employee demonstrations outside its store in London. All this despite the fact that the company had announced it was donating the Treorchy site to the local community and had offered retraining and an on-site resource centre to employees.

Samantha Cameron, director of stationery company Smythson, agrees that ethical matters, especially those of where you manufacture, are increasingly important in the marketplace. 'It definitely has a bearing,' she explains. 'And people do think about what they're doing and if they leave a carbon footprint – and that's as much about what you buy as how you're travelling. But we are international, so we can't get away from that: we sell product in the US and [east Asia].' Cameron does, however, feel it's important to support home talent. 'We're a British company and as long as we can get the quality, we would definitely prefer British.' The company recently bought two UK factories – one for bookbinding and one for gold stamping in order to protect its domestic manufacturing base and has invested in gold stamp training to protect the skill from dying out entirely. Buying local factories also made sense 'as we wanted to protect our source.' Nonetheless, Cameron admits that the ethical dimension is often a 'side effect, in a way' to decisions that are based on good business sense, such as the value of being UK made. 'We think the quality is best and we feel it is important to be made in England as that is the core of our brand.' 'We'd all like to hang high moral standards and ethics to our chests, but it's just what we're selling – Englishness,' says Ian Eastwood, managing director of Swaine Adeney Brigg, the traditional leather makers. For them to use anything other than English leather, tanneries and manufacturers 'would be alien. We're

quintessentially English and if we lost that niche we'd lose our identity.' It's a similar story at knitwear maker John Smedley, which launched a 'Made in England' campaign last year to focus on its commitment to UK manufacturing. 'Made in England is what we are, it defines us and what we stand for,' explains Drew Walker, managing director.

'I think there are always pressures to go off-shore, but our philosophy is that it would destroy the whole ethos of the brand, and that ethos is that things should be made from the best raw materials, in the best way, by the best. I think the UK workforce is the best.' Walker, of course, does recognise that there is a case for moving off-shore. 'But the only thing you save,' he argues, 'is [the cost of] direct labour, and even in a high-cost economy such as ours, that is about 12 per cent of the final goods selling price. So, to get it 5 per cent cheaper in China or add 5 per cent and have it made in England – there's no argument.' Walker believes consumers are increasingly concerned about where and how goods are made – at Smedley, they even know which New Zealand pastures their wool-producing sheep have grazed in. 'I think, for a while, [this concern] deserted us in pursuit of volume and cheapness. But I think there's a move towards more ethical trading and knowing there's no point in capitalising on other people's misfortunes.'

Source: Edwina Ings-Chambers, 'Location, location, location', *The Financial Times*, 2 March 2007.

Discussion questions

1 What is the key impact of CSR on marketing strategy?

2 What has location got to do with CSR? What views of CSR do Ballantyne, Smythson etc. appear to adhere to? Do they contribute to creating a sustainable competitive advantage for these companies?

3 What is the dilemna faced by fashion manufacturers in trying to reconcile modern business practices with CSR?

part six

Conclusions

Chapter 19 concludes the book by looking ahead to marketing strategies for the twenty-first century. Significant environmental changes are highlighted and a number of building blocks are suggested for developing adaptive strategies for a changing world. These include the need to become learning organisations, capturing, internalising and utilising knowledge; the need for a clear market orientation and focus on creating superior value and greater levels of satisfaction for customers; the need to base positioning strategies firmly on marketing assets and competencies; the need to establish closer relationships with key customers; and, finally, the need to rethink the role of marketing within the organisation. A number of dimensions are discussed that can provide keys to positioning in the future. Price, quality, innovation, service, benefit differentiation and customisation are compared as fundamental positioning dimensions and strategies, and the competencies and assets required for each explored.

The chapter, and indeed the book, concludes by predicting that marketing in the future will be seen more as a process for achieving a close fit between market requirements on the one hand and company competencies and assets on the other, than as a functional department within the firm. It is how this strategic, rather than operational, role for marketing is fulfilled in the future that holds much excitement for the discipline of marketing.

chapter nineteen

Twenty-first century marketing

It is not the strongest of the species that survive, nor the most intelligent, but the ones most responsive to change

Charles Darwin
Origin of Species (1853)

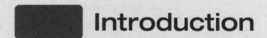 **Introduction**

The emphasis throughout this book has been on developing robust marketing strategies to enable organisations to survive and prosper in the turbulent, competitive and frequently hostile markets they face. From the outset we have stressed the critical need to develop effective ways in which to cope with the change in both customer markets and the ways in which companies go to market. However, we can go further – what of the new century we are entering? As markets and marketing continue to change, what strategies will make most sense in the third millennium AD? This chapter attempts to review some of the major trends which are already apparent, and to propose ways in which new competitive strategies can be fashioned to exploit the opportunities to emerge. As Drucker (1997) has said:

In human affairs – political, social, economic, or business – it is pointless to try and predict the future . . . But it is possible – and fruitful – to identify major events that have already happened, irrevocably, and that will have predictable effects in the next decade or two. It is possible, in other words, to identify and prepare for the future that has already happened.

19.1 The changing competitive arena

Chapter 3 reviewed some of the significant changes taking place in today's markets. Here we briefly summarise those changes.

19.1.1 Changes in the business environment

To claim that 'the only constant is change' is trite but true in today's business environment. The Royal Society for the Encouragement of Arts, Manufactures & Commerce (RSA) inquiry into Tomorrow's Company (1994) identified a number of major changes taking place in business markets.

- The pace of economic change is accelerating. During the Industrial Revolution it took 60 years for productivity per person to double. China and South Korea have done the same in 10 years.

- There is an explosion in innovation and new knowledge generation that is also accelerating. Every year as much new knowledge is generated through research and development as the total sum of all human knowledge up to the 1960s.

- Competitive pressures are intensifying. Computer manufacturers, for example, need to reduce costs and improve product performance by around 30 per cent per annum to remain competitive.

- Manufacturing can now take place almost anywhere. Companies are constantly seeking more efficient manufacturing options, and that typically means sourcing from wherever makes economic sense. 1993 figures show UK manufacturing labour costs at half those of Germany but twice those of Korea and Taiwan. Labour costs in Poland, Thailand, China and Indonesia are significantly lower still. In early 2002 the production of Dyson vacuum cleaners was switched from the UK to the Far East to benefit from just such cost advantages.

- New organisational structures are emerging as firms seek to make themselves more competitive. Firms have reorganised, reduced overheads, de-layered, merged, created alliances and partnerships in attempts to create advantage in the marketplace.

- International trade is being liberalised through the World Trade Organization, but there are still massive regional trading blocs within which regional, national, ethnic and religious groupings seek to retain individual identity.

- Company actions are becoming increasingly visible, especially their effects on the environment. Customers are demanding more both economically and environmentally.

At the macro-level these changes can be grouped into economic, technological, social, legal and political issues. Just as water supply companies cannot change weather patterns, most macro-environmental factors are outside the control of individual firms. Few companies have the ability to influence political, economic, social and technological processes significantly. Most need to ensure they understand and predict the changes going on. Water companies need to predict both weather patterns (supply of water) and demand (water usage) so that they can then put strategies in place to meet that demand.

In a keynote address to the British Academy of Management (annual conference, Aston University 1996), David Cravens cited an example of a well-known firm that had failed to grasp the significance of technological change on its market (see Sammuels, 1994; Evans and Wurster, 1997). Encyclopaedia Britannica (EB) went from peak US profits in 1990 to severe difficulties in 1996 as it failed to anticipate the impact of computer technology, particularly the CD-ROM, on its business. In that period sales plummeted by more than 50 per cent. The business had been built through a highly motivated and successful salesforce selling encyclopaedias to middle-class families (often bought by parents for their children's education) at around $1,500 each.

Then along came home computers, with CD-ROM players and encyclopaedias such as Encarta at around $50. The new entrants may not have had the depth of coverage of EB but they were in a format the children enjoyed using, offered the opportunities for multimedia display (video and audio clips, animations), could be more easily updated and, perhaps most crucially, offered middle-class parents a justification for the purchase of often expensive home computer systems which in many cases were used primarily for games purposes!

With the advent of the 'information superhighway', the World Wide Web and Internet, the holding of large amounts of data on individual PCs may become a thing of the past, posing potential problems (and, of course, opportunities) for the marketers of CD-ROM-based encyclopaedias. In particular, the advent of open access, user-built encyclopaedias such as Wikipedia have significantly impacted on the CD-based products. Rapidly updated, and relying on users to submit, update and expand on the content, these are essentially free at the point of use (making their money out of advertising links), rapidly expanding in content and do not take up local storage space on hard disk or other media (see www.wikipedia.com).

The experiences of EB are a prime example of the critical importance of market sensing, continuous listening and learning rather than being surprised and wrong-footed when a competitor 'reinvents' the business. By 1997, EB was marketing a CD-ROM version of its encyclopaedia, but by then in a crowded market dominated by Microsoft's Encarta. More recently EB has made its encyclopaedia available online to subscribers at www.eb.com, perhaps recognising that updating is critical and far easier online than via discs.

Similarly, Hoover and Electrolux were surprised strategically by the success of the Dyson bagless vacuum cleaner and have lost share to the innovation (see below). And yet Dyson offered both the rights to the product before launching it himself. The problem was not that Hoover and Electrolux did not know about the new Dyson technology, rather they had a vested interest in preserving the status quo.

It is also easy to underestimate the practical realities of rapid accelerations in the speed and disruptive impact of change. For example, consider the unfolding impact of Internet telephony. While it took 50 years for the telephone to gain widespread diffusion, it took less than a decade for the mobile phone to do the same. It is expected that Internet telephony will reach critical mass in only a few years. Similarly, in the photography market, the disruptive and pervasive impact of digital technology demanded rapid transformation in business models by existing players like Kodak. The failure of Kodak to understand the speed of change and rapid decline in demand for traditional cameras and film has led to major financial losses, extensive lay-offs and plant closures. Kodak is now a major seller of digital cameras (with very low margins compared with conventional cameras), but is not well positioned to exploit the rapid transition of mass-market photography to the mobile phone and music player.

It is also easy to overestimate how long a competitive advantage will last in converging markets. While Apple's iTunes/iPod strategy has revolutionised the recorded music business, 2005 saw telephone operator Sprint's attack on Apple's position with the launch of the Sprint Music Stores, allowing subscribers to download music to their cell phone (and a copy to the PC). Sprint's new generations of cell phone will be capable of downloading movies and television as well as music, and even offer shopping services (such as online price comparisons triggered by the phone user capturing an in-store barcode).

While companies need to operate within the bounds and conditions of the macro-environment, they may have some (limited) ability to influence it. The UK government's Private Finance Initiative (PFI), for example, designed to introduce private sector financing into public investment and infrastructure projects, is administered by a steering board including representatives of the construction and other industries. Similarly, most expenditure on scientific research is applied in nature and conducted in commercial companies such that their efforts will directly affect the technological environment in which they, and other firms, operate in the future.

No company can ever hope to predict every aspect of the macro-environment in which it operates. But organisations should aim to achieve profound understanding of their core markets. There will always be surprises and shocks as new technological breakthroughs emerge or political discontinuities occur. What is important, however, is to spot and act on more of the trends and changes than competitors. Shocks are less for companies prepared to think the 'unthinkable' and to challenge the status quo in their strategising. For example, the UK brewers and cigarette companies are quite open in admitting that they have contingency plans should cannabis be legalised.

Importantly, disruptive changes have the potential to make deep changes in the structure of a market, which may disadvantage existing competitors but offer important opportunities to others. For example, the dominance of the personal computer (PC) market by the 'Big Three' – Microsoft, Intel and Dell – is shifting in ways these companies can no longer control. The emphasis by Microsoft on software upgrades, by Intel on faster chips, and by Dell on supply-chain efficiency is increasingly seen by users as resulting in bloated software packages with too many functions, faster but inefficient chips, and poor service. Microsoft struggled for several years to get the latest version of Windows to the market, and is trying to imiate Google's approach to software development. Intel's strategy has been undermined by AMD's better designed chips, which Intel now has to equal, and Dell is looking at additional,

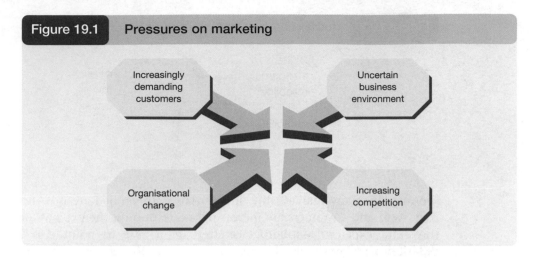

Figure 19.1   Pressures on marketing

conventional distribution channels to access consumer buyers. Remarkably, others have found ways to make money from the PC – a computing platform that Microsoft, Intel and Dell believed to be securely in their control (Waters, 2006). There are sound strategic reasons why IBM has sold its PC business to Lenovo, the leading Chinese PC business.

19.1.2   Changes in markets

A number of trends can be seen in modern markets that are likely to continue into the future (Figure 19.1).

First, customers are becoming increasingly demanding of the products and services they buy. Customers demand, and expect, reliable and durable products with quick efficient service at reasonable prices. They also expect the products and services they buy to meet their needs. Different customers have different wants and needs, and hence companies have an opportunity to select segments where their offerings most closely align with those needs and where they can focus their activities to create a competitive advantage. What is more, there is little long-term stability in customer demands. Positions may be achieved through offering superior customer value, and yet the evidence is that without constant improvement 'value migration' will occur – buyers will migrate to an alternative value offering (Slywotzky, 1996).

For example, an executive in a computer company producing laptop computers complained in 1997: 'First they wanted the notebook with a colour screen – we gave it to them. Then, last year, it had to have a Pentium chip, so we gave them that. Now they tell us they still want all that, but the thing that really matters is that the computer has to have the weight of a feather . . .'

A second major trend, one that particularly differentiates the early 2000s, is that customers are less prepared to pay a substantial premium for products or services that do not offer demonstrably greater value. While it is undeniable that well-developed and managed brands can command higher prices than unbranded

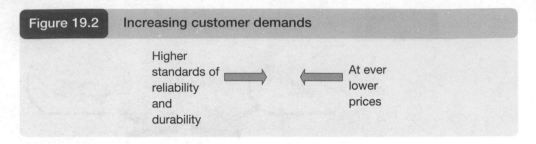

Figure 19.2	Increasing customer demands

products in many markets, the differentials commanded are now much less than they were and customers are increasingly questioning the extra value they get for the extra expense. Marlboro cigarettes are a case in point. On 2 April 1993 ('Marlboro Friday') Philip Morris announced a 20 per cent reduction in price of its market-leading brand of cigarettes to defend market share against aggressive US rivals. The brand had lost substantial market share to lower-priced competitors. Customers were simply not convinced that Marlboro was worth the premium price it had been charging. New strategic thinking has to accommodate the fact that customers are becoming more sophisticated and more marketing literate. The sophisticated customer is less likely to be attracted to cheap products with low quality, and yet neither can be won by image-based advertising. The implications are clear. Differentiation needs to be based on providing demonstrably superior value to customers (Figure 19.2).

A third major trend is in both the level and nature of competition. Competition is becoming more intense and more global in nature. As international trade becomes more liberalised under the aegis of the World Trade Organization (WTO), so firms face tougher international competition at home and increased opportunities abroad. Time and distance are shrinking rapidly as communications become near instantaneous. Millions around the world watched with disbelief on their televisions sets as the Twin Towers of the World Trade Center in New York were hit by terrorist-piloted planes on 11 September 2001. When Deng Xiaoping, the Chinese Paramount Leader, died on 18 February 1997 news of his death reached London, Washington and Bonn before many in Beijing knew about it. Firms are increasingly thinking global in their strategies, especially as cross-national segments are beginning to emerge for products and services from fast foods through toys to computers and automobiles. The increasingly widespread use of the Internet for promoting and marketing both products and services now means that communications know no national borders. Ohmae's 'borderless world' (Ohmae, 1990) exists in cyberspace at least.

Not only are markets becoming more competitive through more players emerging in them. Those firms that survive and thrive in these more competitive conditions are, by their very nature, tougher competitors. Weak firms are being shaken out of markets where they do not have clear positions and attendant capabilities. The implications of heightened, more aggressive competition, both domestic and international, are that firms will need to look even more closely at their scope of operations and targeting in the future.

And yet the executive must confront the central paradox in all this. As markets become harsher in their judgements and in the level of competitiveness faced, companies are under growing pressure to collaborate with and partner others. Increasingly, collaboration is taking place with suppliers, customers and even competitors. The clear demarcation lines of the past have gone and executives are having to deal with highly ambiguous new roles. As we have seen, the demands of customers for suppliers to demonstrate their ethical credentials and to undertake social responsibility initiatives emerged at just the same time as those same customers demanded lower prices and higher quality. Not least among the unprecedented yet exciting challenges facing executives is to achieve economic efficiency at the same time as a socially responsible organisation that creates competitive advantage from its integrity.

19.1.3 Organisational change

The 1990s saw a major emphasis in many organisations on corporate 'downsizing' or 'restructuring'. In attempts to deal with the difficult economic conditions of the early 1990s in Western, developed markets, costs came under increasing pressure and layers of both workers and managers were removed.

While 'downsizing' is now less fashionable, as firms have realised that there is only so much fat that can be cut before you damage the muscle and too aggressive slimming can lead to *anorexia industrialis* (the excessive desire to be leaner and fitter leading to total emaciation and eventual death), its impact on organisational structures for the new millennium has been far broader. These are manifest in two main directions. First, the impact within the firm; second, the impact on inter-firm relations.

Within firms the boundaries between functional areas are becoming more blurred. Where firms were once organised with clear-cut divisions between marketing, finance and operations it is now recognised that 'functional silos' can result in myopic operations and suboptimal strategies. In leading firms the functional boundaries have long since been replaced by process teams that can view the operations of the organisation in holistic terms and will not be hampered by petty rivalries between functions.

At the same time, the role of marketing *per se* in the organisation has been challenged (Brady and Davis, 1993; Doyle, 1995). In 1994 Lever Brothers abolished the job of marketing director, and merged sales and marketing departments into business groups focusing on consumer research and product development. They also created 'customer development teams' responsible for relationship building with key retail customers (*The Economist*, 9 April 1994). Similarly, in 1997 IBM announced a new approach to its global marketing activities. This took the form of the customer relationship management (CRM) initiative, working through core processes such as market management, relationship management, opportunity management, information management and skills management. This is very different from conventional views of how marketing operates (Mitchell, 1997).

Marketing departments can get in the way of serving customers for two main reasons. The first is territorial. They may see dealing with customers as their preserve and wish to retain the power and influence that goes with that. Second, however, they may encourage others in the organisation to off-load responsibility for customer building to the marketing department. This creates the dangerous view that others do not need to concern themselves with customers; someone else will take care of it. Indeed, one view is that the days of conventional marketing have long since finished, and the challenge now is to design and implement better ways of managing the process of going to market. That process cuts across traditional functional boundaries as well as external boundaries with partners.

Some writers go further in criticising the performance of marketing in organisations. Webster (1997) concludes that marketing has been effective in tactics (selling and promotional programmes), somewhat effective in advocating a customer viewpoint, but ineffective in developing robust value propositions and competitive positioning. Doyle (1997) sees marketing departments as the source of radical expansion strategies which can achieve spectacular growth in sales and profit, but which ultimately fail because they do not create customer value. In Doyle's view robust growth strategies come from providing superior customer value and from continuous learning and innovation, based on long-term investments in relationships. A compelling case begins to emerge for radically rethinking the role of marketing as a strategic force in companies.

Between firms the boundaries of where one finishes and the next starts are also increasingly blurred. Boundaries with suppliers, distributors and customers are changing as more businesses understand the need to manage the entire value chain from raw materials through to customers, and work more closely with partner firms to achieve added value through the chain. A number of authors now refer to the 'virtual organisation' (Piercy and Cravens, 1995) as networks and alliances create supra-organisational entities.

Successful strategy initiatives may increasingly rely on finding ways around the lack of responsiveness and slow movement of traditional functional bureaucracies. For example, faced with the mission of finding market areas that were totally new to IBM and capable of growing profitable billion-dollar-plus businesses in five to seven years, the company launched its Emerging Business Opportunities (EBO) programme (Baghai et al., 2000). The challenge was to break away from a culture where the most prestigious executive assignments were to run large, established IBM businesses to one where the most talented and experienced executives worked on new opportunities, not focused on short-term results in existing markets. EBOs have frequently cut across IBM's organisational structure, and challenged the IBM culture. In the first five years of the initiative, IBM launched 25 EBOs. Two were closed after the pilot stage, but the remaining 23 produced annual revenue of $15 billion, and were growing at more than 40 per cent a year. The IBM initiative recognises the need to break free from existing structures to manage multiple strategic horizons – EBO businesses are speculative and visionary and may not pay off for 5 to 10 years or longer.

In fact, the above major trends and changes taking place in both markets and organisations lead to a need to reassess business strategy in general and marketing strategy in particular. The strategies that will be successful in the future will need to be responsive and adaptive rather than rigid and fixed. Key will be creating an organisational context in which learning can take place, market changes can be

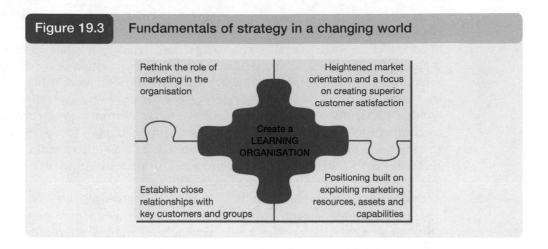

Figure 19.3   Fundamentals of strategy in a changing world

identified and capabilities can be fashioned to ensure a strategic fit between market and firm. In short, the development of dynamic capabilities will become more critical.

19.2   Fundamentals of strategy in a changing world

Figure 19.3 shows a number of factors that are increasingly essential in dealing with complex and changing circumstances.

19.2.1   The learning organisation

Central to developing a sustainable competitive advantage in rapidly, and often unpredictably, changing circumstances is the dynamic capability to learn and adapt (Fiol and Lyles, 1985; Huber, 1991; Sinkula, 1994; Kilmann, 1996; Evans and Wurster, 1997; Prokesch, 1997; Sinkula *et al.*, 1997; Morgan *et al.*, 1998). The competitive dynamics of markets with new entrants, substitute technologies and shifts in customer preferences can swiftly erode static advantages built on the 'generic' strategies of cost leadership or product differentiation (McKee and Varadarajan, 1995). Organisational learning, however, offers the potential both to respond to and act on opportunities in the markets of the firm. Indeed, Dickson (1992) suggests that the ability to learn faster than competitors may be the *only* real source of sustainable competitive advantage.

Learning is manifest in the knowledge, experience and information held in an organisation (Mahoney, 1995). It resides in both people and technical systems. Learning involves the acquisition, processing, storing and retrieval (dissemination) of knowledge. A major challenge for many organisations is to create the combination of culture and climate to maximise learning (Slater and Narver, 1995). At the human level managerial systems need to be established to create and control knowledge. At the technical level systems need to be established to facilitate the accumulation and storage of relevant information in a manner that makes it readily accessible to those who need to access it.

Much of an organisation's knowledge base typically resides in the heads of managers and workers. When personnel leave through retirement, 'downsizing' or recruitment by competitors, that knowledge may be lost or, more damagingly, gained by a competitor. Employment contracts of key personnel are increasingly including 'golden handcuffs' which prohibit critical managers from taking their knowledge to competitors. Organisations are also increasingly looking for ways of extracting the knowledge of their key people and transmitting it to others in the organisation, through expert systems and training processes, so that the knowledge is more secure and embedded in the fabric of the organisation.

Of particular importance in the context of marketing strategy is the development of knowledge and skills in how to create superior customer value. Slater and Narver (1995) show that a primary focus of market orientation is to create superior customer value, and that in turn needs to be based on knowledge derived from customer and competitor analysis, together with knowledge gleaned from suppliers, businesses in different industries, government sources, universities, consultants and other potential sources. They conclude that learning organisations continually acquire, process and disseminate knowledge about markets, products, technologies and business processes based on experience, experimentation, information from customers, suppliers, competitors and other sources. This learning enables them to anticipate and act on opportunities in turbulent and fragmented markets.

And yet developing learning capabilities need not be complex and sophisticated. Inuit's improvements to Quicken software come from a form of organised 'customer stalking' where employees follow customers home and watch their every move and reaction to the product. The development by Kimberly-Clark of Huggies (training pants for children coming out of nappies) came from sending employees to the homes of customers with small children and both watching and listening. They learned essentially that the market is driven by parental guilt about how long a child stays in nappies, not the child's waste disposal problems! Superior learning capabilities may be as much about market sensing and understanding as it is about utilising technology. Indeed, research at the Marketing Science Insitute has found that, of ten market-based capabilities, market sensing displayed the strongest impact on business process performance (Ramaswami *et al.*, 2004).

While the central requirement for competing in the future is learning, a number of other more specific building blocks can be suggested as important ingredients in fashioning competitive strategy.

19.2.2 Heightened market orientation and focus on creating superior customer value

In increasingly crowded and competitive markets there is no substitute for being market oriented. Put simply, a market orientation focuses the firm's activities on meeting the needs and requirements of customers better than competitors. This in turn requires finding out what will give customers value and ensuring that the firm's energies are directed towards providing that. Identifying ways of providing superior customer value is one of the central challenges of management for the new millennium.

A market orientation does not imply over-sophisticated marketing operation. Indeed, it has been argued by some that marketing departments can themselves get in the way of providing superior customer value.

As Simon (1996) shows, successful medium-sized German firms (he calls these 'hidden champions') demonstrate a clear focus on providing solutions for their customers. These companies go deep rather than broad (they specialise in narrow niches of the market), but operate across global markets. Their success is based on understanding their customers' needs and being highly responsive to delivering solutions to customers' problems. They typically have dominant market shares of their chosen niches worldwide. For example, Krones had 80 per cent worldwide market share in bottle-labelling machines, Hauni was world market leader in cigarette machines with 90 per cent share of high-speed machines, Brita had 85 per cent of the world market for point-of-use water filters, and Baader's share of the world market for fish-processing equipment was 90 per cent. All had a narrow focus, but operated across global markets (Simon, 1996).

Winterhalter Gastronom makes dishwashers for commercial use. There are many markets for these products, including hospitals, schools, companies, hotels, military institutions, etc., each with different product requirements. Many products are on the market and Winterhalter found that, globally, it commanded only 2 per cent of the market. This led to a refocusing of the firm's strategy. First, it decided to focus solely on hotels and restaurants (the second part of the company name was added after this decision was made). The business was redefined as the supplier of clean glasses and dishes for hotels and restaurants. In addition to designing the dish-washers to meet the specific requirements of the hotel and restaurant market the company extended its product line to include water-conditioning devices, an own-brand of detergent and round-the-clock service. Thus they were taking full responsibility for the provision of the clean glasses and dishes, going into depth with the chosen segment, rather than simply offering dishwashers across the market and leaving the provision of services and detergent to others. The company had climbed to a 20 per cent world market share of its chosen segment by the mid 1990s (Simon, 1996).

In the quest to provide superior customer value no firm can stand still. What offers better value than competitors today will be standard tomorrow. Innovation, the constant improving of the offering to customers, is essential for sustained competitive advantage. Again, Simon's hidden champions demonstrate this clearly. Many of these firms created their own markets through technological breakthroughs but then continued to innovate to stay ahead of further industry entrants. They typically hold relatively large numbers of patents and derive disproportionate amounts of profits from new products. Critically, however, they achieve a balance between being technology-driven and market-led. While they are determined to exploit their technological advantages they also ensure that these are aligned with changing market requirements. W.L. Gore Inc., for example, an American 'hidden champion', maker of semi-permeable Gore-Tex fabrics, has exploited its technological lead in fabric manufacture to develop products suitable for its customers in the garment and shoe industries (Simon, 1996).

The focus of activities in firms that are truly market oriented and intent on creating superior value for their customers is on finding solutions to those customers' problems. Rather than a focus on selling the firm's own existing products it sets out first to identify current and future customer problems and then to find solutions to them. Solutions may involve creating new products and services, integrating the offerings of other providers (through alliances), and even in some instances accepting that customers cannot be well served and recommending alternative suppliers. After exhausting all other options a truly market-oriented firm can gain more customer goodwill (and ultimately more long-term business) by admitting that it cannot provide exactly what the customer wants rather than trying to persuade the customer to accept second best, or even pretending that the solution offered is appropriate.

19.2.3 Positioning built on marketing assets, capabilities and competencies

Much of the emphasis in the strategy literature today has focused on the 'resource-based theory' of the firm (see Chapter 6). This theory emphasises the need for strategies to be based on the resources and capabilities of the firm, rather than merely chasing customers irrespective of the ability of the firm to serve them. Resource-based theorists, however, are in danger of losing sight of the fact that resources are valuable only when they are translated into providing something that customers want. This is the essence of the 'resource-based marketing' approach espoused in this book.

Markets change, and so too must resources such as assets and competencies. They need to be constantly improved and developed if the firm is to thrive. An essential task for marketing management is to identify the competencies and assets that will be needed in the future, as well as those that are needed today, so that they can be built or acquired in advance.

This may be far from easy, and freedom of manoeuvre may be limited. For example, IBM's core capability in mainframe computers became irrelevant to the PC-dominated market of the 1980s, and the company's performance across the world suffered dramatically. In the 1990s, however, the new head of IBM Lou Gerstner's strategic goal was to dominate the global network marketplace, where those mainframe capabilities are critical.

As discussed in Chapter 6, marketing resources are any properties or processes that can be exploited in the marketplace to create or sustain a competitive advantage. They range from recognised brand names, through unique use of distribution channels, to information and quality control systems. These assets are the resource endowments the business has created or acquired over time and now has available to deploy in the market. Competencies are the skills that are used to deploy the assets to best effect in the market.

These definitions are in line with resource-based theorists such as Barney (1991), who suggest that it is management that is the most important resource because they make use of the assets and other resources available to them based on their knowledge of the market acquired through their previous learning.

As we saw in Chapter 6, Day (1994) goes on to identify three main types of competencies: outside-in; inside-out; and spanning and integrating competencies. Outside-in competencies are those skills and abilities that enable a business to understand its customers and create closer linkages with them. Inside-out competencies are the internal capabilities of the firm and its employees that can be deployed in the marketplace to provide better products and services to customers. Spanning and integrating competencies bring together the inside-out and the outside-in to ensure delivery of appropriate products and services to customers.

More recently RBV theorists have emphasised the need for dynamic capabilities (Menguac and Auh, 2006; Helfat *et al.*, 2007). A dynamic capability is *'the capacity of an organisation to purposefully create, extend, or modify its resource base'* (Helfat *et al.*, 2007, p. 4). Menguac and Auh (2006) show how dynamic capabilities can be built through capitalising on market orientation and innovativeness. They demonstrate empirically how the effect of market orientation on firm performance is enhanced when firms demonstrate a high degree of innovation.

Not all assets and capabilities may be vested in the focal firm. Increasingly, companies are creating alliances and networks with others that enable them to leverage further assets and competencies of partner firms (see Chapter 16). Alliances can offer four main sets of assets and competencies: access to new markets; access to managerial competence; access to technological competence; and economic benefits. For example, we discussed earlier the problems faced by Kodak in the traditional camera and film marketplace, which is being displaced by digital photography. Part of the company's response to realign its deeply engrained model of film photography includes partnership with Motorola to extend camera-based imaging, partnership with Skype to create 'digital storytelling' combining live voice with online photo-sharing, and other collaborations in medical imaging and facial recognition software initiatives.

There are, however, problems in realising the advantages offered by alliances and networks of collaborating firms. Many of the alliances established in the early 1990s have failed. Understanding of the dynamics of alliances and the critical executive skills required by these new organisations are sadly limited (see Chapter 16).

Taken together, marketing assets and competencies/capabilities are the basis on which any competitive positioning is built. Ideally firms should seek to build their positions on the basis of assets and competencies which are superior to those of their competitors and difficult to duplicate. They should also seek to create or acquire assets and competencies that can be exploited in many other situations (e.g. extend their brand name into new markets, exploit their technology in new industries, use their networks in different ways). A critical issue for the future is how different assets and competencies can be combined to create new products and services (Hamel and Prahalad, 1994).

19.2.4 Establishing closer relationships with key customers

In Chapter 15 we discussed the ways in which firms can build closer relationships with their customers. Fundamental issues include which customers to build those relationships with and how to build them.

Relationship marketing (Payne and Frow, 2005) has been one of the most significant developments in marketing thought of recent years. While it has been recognised as important in some markets for some time and under different labels (e.g. the personal account managers in financial services), it is now generally agreed that customer retention, through superior service and relationship building, is applicable in far wider markets.

In consumer markets relationships can be built initially through branding and reputation creation. In the past, relationships in business markets have been stereotyped as between individuals – salesperson and purchasing officer. However, in modern business-to-business markets the pressure is for team-based selling and relationship building across the whole spectrum of internal departments. The challenge is to become the 'outsource of preference' by understanding the customer's business and adding value in excess of cost (H.R. Challey, 2007). Similarly, Simon (1996) stresses that the relationships which endure in business markets are those based on sound economic and business grounds rather than, perhaps ephemeral, personal/social bases. Relationships and reputations can be far harder for competitors to copy than possibly transitory product features, special offers or deals.

Zielke and Pohl (1996) show that key factors for success in the machine tool industry have changed since the early 1990s. In 1990 the keys to success were cross-functional teams, single sourcing and group working. These factors were seen to differentiate the better performing firms from the weaker ones. By 1996, however, these operational characteristics had become standard in the industry and no longer differentiated winners from losers. What now differentiates the more successful companies is their relationships with customers and suppliers. The market leaders are now managing the complete value chain, with suppliers becoming increasingly concerned with new product development and quality improvement. They are also linking pay and other rewards with customer-related performance targets. While efficiency has been the focus at the start of the decade, the emphasis has now shifted to customer and supplier relationship management.

Not all customers, however, place great value on ever closer relationships with their suppliers. Similarly, the costs of creating closer relationships with some customers (in terms of time, effort and financial resource) may well outweigh the long-term commercial benefits. What will become increasingly important will be for firms to decide the optimum intensity of relationship with each customer or customer group and then find effective and efficient means of establishing that level. It is likely that any firm will be operating in a number of different marketing modes depending on the customers served. For some key accounts a heavy emphasis on one-to-one close relationship building to create 'partners' might be applicable, while at the same time other groups are marketed less intensively so as to create 'advocates' rather than partners. For yet other customers of the same firm a mass marketing approach might be applicable to secure their business in the first place. *Multi-mode marketing*, the adoption of different marketing approaches for different customers or customer groups, is likely to take the place of more uniform marketing to all customers.

19.2.5 Rethinking the role of marketing in the organisation

The above lead to the inevitable conclusion that the role and function of marketing within the organisation (or within the 'virtual network') need to be redefined and reasserted.

Basic to that rethinking is to escape from the notion that marketing is essentially a business function, a department on the organisation chart. Increasingly, marketing is being seen as a process within the value chain, a process responsible for ensuring the creation of value for customers in both the short and long term. This requires a focus on marketing skills rather than on marketing titles (Brown, 1995). Structures need to be created that facilitate rapid response and flexibility rather than hinder it. Indeed, it is interesting to note that some of the successful companies, such as Virgin and The Body Shop, do not even have marketing departments, yet few would dispute that they are close to their customers and responsive to their needs (Doyle, 1995).

As Brown (1995) notes:

> There are now two types of corporation: those with a marketing department and those with a marketing soul. Even a cursory glance at the latest Fortune 500 shows that the latter are the top performing companies, while the former, steeped in the business traditions of the past, are fast disappearing.

Simon (1996) also notes that many of the firms in his sample of 'hidden champions' do not have marketing departments. They share, however, two main traits. First, they are extremely close to their customers and ensure that all employees recognise their role in serving them. Second, they focus on solving customers' problems through innovation to improve on their offerings to customers, continuously providing additional customer value. These two traits are the essence of a market orientation, but are achieved without the trappings of a marketing department.

It is important in defining the role of marketing for the future to recognise that marketing operates at two main levels: strategic and operational. At the operational level brand managers and marketing managers deal with day-to-day marketing tasks such as liaison with market research companies, advertising and public relations agencies and so on. In FMCG companies they also spend much of their time organising trade and consumer promotions, special deals, competitions, etc.

At the strategic level, however, marketing is more concerned with decisions as to which markets to operate in and how to compete successfully in them. At this level marketing is not a functional activity, but requires input from across the organisation of alternative perspectives and skills. As noted earlier, the challenge is then to manage the process of going to market to build superior customer value, through a complex of resources, capabilities and relationships that make up the offering.

Marketing needs to become and remain flexible and responsive to change. That entails distinguishing the philosophy from the trappings. At a strategic level everyone in the organisation should place customers at the forefront of their minds because, as the CEO of Xerox says in the firm's mission statement, ultimately it is customers who will decide whether the firm survives and whether employees and managers have a job in the future.

Handy (see Abrahams, 1996) talks of 'shamrock organisations' emerging for the future. These will consist of three leaves. The first will be a small core of professional senior managers on 'permanent' contracts who will run the business and make the strategic decisions such as the markets in which the firm will operate and the ways in which it will create competitive advantage (the positioning decisions discussed in this book). The second leaf will be those on fixed-term contracts providing services such as public relations, database management and advertising. These managers will be specialists in operational and implementation aspects of marketing, but will be closely directed as to where their efforts should go. The third leaf will be *ad hoc* contractors who will supply specialist expertise, such as advertising agencies, marketing research agencies, design consultancies, etc.

In the highly competitive markets envisaged for the foreseeable future, ability to assimilate and act on knowledge, to create strategies based on assets and competencies, to establish close, deep relationships with chosen market segments, and finally the ability to redefine the scope and role of marketing within the organisation will be the bases for creating competitive advantage.

19.3 Competitive positioning strategies

As has been argued above, competitive positioning is about making choices that ensure a fit between chosen market targets and the competencies and assets the firm can deploy to serve those chosen targets more effectively than competitors. While there are, in reality, an infinite number of different ways in which firms might position themselves in their markets, these can be summarised on the basis of the emphasis they give to six main dimensions of differentiation.

Figure 19.4 shows these six dimensions. Positioning could be based on: price; technical quality (or, more correctly, grade); service; customisation; benefit differentiation; or innovation. While individual firms may choose to position on more than one dimension simultaneously they often find that they are contradictory. For example, offering a higher grade of product is generally incongruent with keeping costs, and hence prices, as low as possible. Indeed, charging low prices for a high-grade product may create confusion in the minds of customers. The key to creating sustainable positions is to ensure that they are built on the marketing assets and competencies of the firm.

19.3.1 Price positioning

Costs must be kept in check – at least as low or preferably lower than competitors – for a low price position to be sustainable. If there is no cost advantage, price wars may put the instigator at a financial disadvantage and the whole positioning strategy may not be sustainable. Positioning as the low-price supplier requires strong inside-out and spanning capabilities. Effective cost-control systems (through activity-based costing) are needed not only within the firm's own operations but also within suppliers' operations. Procurement of raw materials and other factor inputs is organised

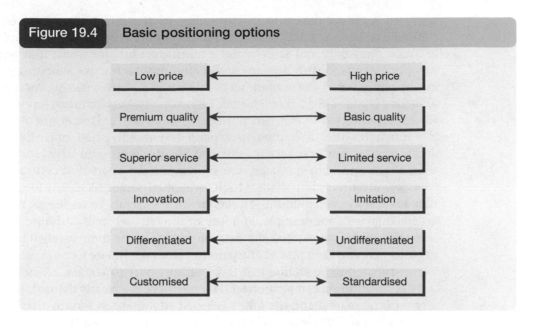

Figure 19.4   Basic positioning options

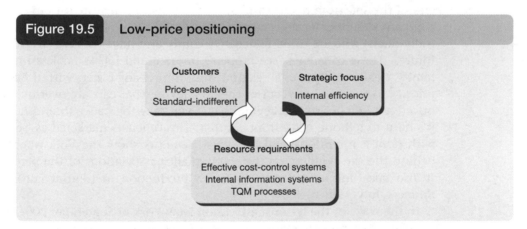

Figure 19.5   Low-price positioning

around keeping costs to a minimum. Distribution logistics are similarly managed for minimum cost (see Figure 19.5).

While the low-price position is a viable option for some firms there is a constant need to work at keeping costs down, especially when new competitors enter the market with new operating methods or unique assets that can be used to undercut the costs of incumbents.

For a price positioning strategy to be successful in the marketplace the existence of a viable, price-sensitive customer segment is also required. In most markets there are customers who will buy primarily on price. In the 1990s, however, it became clear that such customers also expect a base level of service and product quality such that rock bottom prices alone are unlikely to be good enough reasons to buy.

In November 1996, for example, the discount grocery retailer KwikSave announced the closure of 107 of its UK stores. KwikSave offered a no-frills, low-price, 'pile it high/sell it cheap' option to its customers. By the mid-1990s, however, this positioning had been eroded. KwikSave was caught between the leading multiples such as Tesco, Sainsbury and Safeway (later taken over by Morrisons) that were offering low prices coupled with superior service and more attractive shopping experiences, and newly entered discounters such as Aldi and Netto offering lower prices than KwikSave could achieve through their high-volume, very minimal service operations. KwikSave admitted that it had not been sufficiently customer-oriented, had gone too much for the deal, tried to expand too rapidly, had not offered 'modern' goods such as fresh produce, health and beauty items, and items for babies. More than 40 per cent of in-store staff were on temporary or part-time contracts, and there were few incentives to provide a high level of customer service. It was also believed that KwikSave was around 3–4 years behind its rivals in its use of technology. It accepted Switch, for example, as a way of directly debiting customer accounts, but failed to capture and analyse the data afforded to allow more detailed understanding of customers and their purchasing patterns. Sales per square foot of space at KwikSave were estimated to be around half those of Sainsbury (*Guardian*, 8 November 1996).

Price positioning can be successful where there is a clearly defined, price-sensitive sector of the market and the firm has a cost advantage in serving that market.

At £5,999 in 1995 the Skoda Felicia automobile was positioned at the low-price end of the spectrum to attract highly price-sensitive, private car buyers. Indeed, the company describes its target customers as OPTIEs (Over-mortgaged, Post-Thatcherite Individuals) who are carrying negative equity and have concern over their financial futures. These consumers see property, money and job as far less important than family, health and personal relationships. Impressing others with their cars is a low priority to them, 92 per cent of them believing that cars are over-hyped and over-priced, and 66 per cent believing that if you take the badge (brand name) off a car it's hard to tell one make from another. The Felicia is marketed as 'sensibly stylish with honest intentions' and the advertisements show the Volkswagen (VW) logo behind the car, building on the solid, quality associations of the parent company. It also takes full advantage of low-cost production in Central Europe (*Marketing Business*, July/August 1995).

In the wake of the terrorist attacks on New York in September 2001 major airline companies found a dramatic slump in passengers wishing to travel by air. The low-price operators such as Ryanair, however, were able to maintain and even increase their business. Indeed, Ryanair was performing strongly as a no-frills operator prior to September 11. The six months to 30 September 2001 saw net profits rise 39 per cent to €88 million over the same period in the previous year. Sales had risen 29 per cent to €344 million (*Fortune*, 31 December 2001). This showed that the market was clearly segmented with a significant leisure travel market highly price sensitive and happy to accept no-frills operations at low prices. The main sector of the market to be deterred from travel was the business traveller, on whom the major airlines relied.

Among the leaders in the low-price, no-frills air travel market is easyJet, launched in 1995 by Stelios Haji-Ioannou. The airline is positioned as low price, no frills, operating high frequency, point-to-point, shorthaul schedules across Europe. The firm makes extensive use of the Internet to keep costs down (around 90 per cent of bookings are made online through the airline's website). The airline has grown dramatically from 1.7 million passengers in 1998 to 7 million in 2001. Floated on the London

Stock Exchange (LSE) in November 2000, it is now among the FTSE top 200 firms, valued at over US$1 billion. Haji-Ioannou has recently extended the brand into cyber cafes (easyEverything.com), rental cars (easyRentacar.com), financial services (easyMoney.com) and online shopping (easyValue.com). All are positioned as low-price offerings, making effective use of the Internet to keep costs down (*Marketing Business*, September 2001).

Nonetheless, reliance purely on low price-based positioning can carry high risks as well. Executives are increasingly well aware of the effect of the 'China Price' threat. At the extreme, while a conventional competitor in the Triad countries might undercut your price by 10 per cent to gain business, companies in countries like China and India are more likely to offer a price which is 10 per cent of your price. It is estimated that in 2004 around 50 per cent of the merchant ships leaving Chinese ports were carrying Chinese products to Wal-Mart in the US (at that time China's eighth largest customer in the world). To attempt to compete on low price against such competition is unlikely to be effective in the absence of other competitive advantages.

Indeed, some firms position at the other end of the price spectrum. They deliberately price their products and services more highly than competitors to create an exclusivity for their offerings. High-price positions are usually accompanied by higher quality, branded offerings requiring strong reputations and clearly superior images (e.g. Harrods department store in Knightsbridge, cosmetics and designer label fashionwear). The competencies required for high-price (premium) positions to be effective are centred on the ability to create a superior, or exclusive, image that customers are willing to pay a premium to be associated with. Brand assets in particular need to be built through the use of creative promotional campaigns.

19.3.2 Quality positioning

Positioning as a high technical quality (grade) supplier also requires effective internal control systems, especially quality assessment and assurance. Beyond control, however, it also requires technical competence, particularly in engineering and manufacturing where physical products are produced. Most significantly, however, it requires a clear view of what constitutes 'quality' in the eyes of the customer. That entails the outside-in capabilities of market sensing and customer bonding (see Figure 19.6).

Also important in delivering high-quality products and services is supply-chain management, ensuring that the inputs are of the required quality, not simply the cheapest available. Marks & Spencer used to have a reputation for building long-term, demanding relationships with their suppliers to ensure that the products they put their labels on are of the required quality. M&S now sources more widely but still keeps a close eye on the quality of the fabrics used in its products.

There are four Betty's Tea Rooms in Yorkshire and one Taylor's. Together they sell 2 million cups of tea each year. They don't advertise, but people flock in their thousands and are prepared to queue for seats. The atmosphere is elegant, sophisticated. Waiters and waitresses are formally dressed in the style of Victorian servants. The tea is perfect and the cakes are delicious. The pastries range from exotic Amadeus Torte to local Yorkshire curd tarts. The company was started in Harrogate by a Swiss

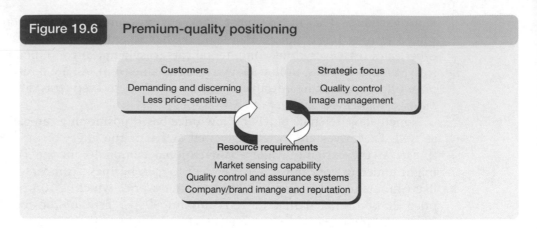

Figure 19.6   Premium-quality positioning

confectioner, Frederick Belmont, in 1919. The company's bakers and confectioners still train in Lucerne. The company has built on its brand asset by opening related gift shops on the premises, selling confectionery suited to the tourists who visit. They also sell their products by mail order. More recently they have marketed Yorkshire Tea, which has become a major brand in the beverages market (Kotler *et al.*, 1996).

Often critical to a quality positioning are the marketing assets of brand image and reputation (see above). Image and reputation can take years to create and, once established, need to be nurtured and, when necessary, defended vigorously.

To customers quality is manifest through better reliability, durability and aesthetic appearance. For quality positions to be viable customers must be prepared to pay for superior quality as there are usually, though not always, higher costs associated with offering a higher-quality product. In the automotive industry German manufacturers such as Mercedes, BMW and Audi have successfully positioned their offerings at the high-quality end of the spectrum through superior design, technical engineering skills ('Vorsprung durch Technik' – leading through technology) and attention to quality control through the manufacturing process.

We should bear in mind in all this, however, that quality and value are decided by customers in the marketplace, not by engineers in the factory, or advertising executives in the marketing department. In what may be a blueprint for other organisations, executives at Royal Mail (RM) are appraised in part by customer-perceived service levels, not actual service levels. RM received many complaints about queuing times in post offices. They reduced queuing times, but customers still complained. They redecorated some post offices and found that in these locations customers ceased complaining about queuing times although the times were the same as elsewhere. RM had learned that quality and value are only what customers perceive them to be.

19.3.3   Innovation positioning

Where markets are changing rapidly, especially as a result of technological developments, there may be opportunities to position on the basis of innovativeness, or

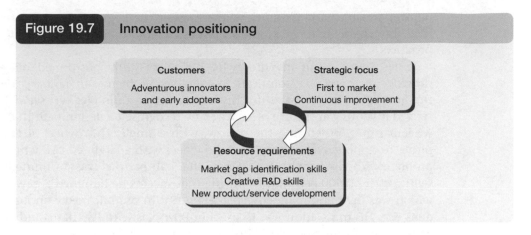

Figure 19.7 Innovation positioning

speed-to-market (see Figure 19.7). In the PC market, for example, leading firms such as Toshiba are constantly improving on their products and building in technological advances to keep their products ahead of their competitors. Hamel and Prahalad (1991) suggest that firms should encourage 'fast failure', that is, encourage the test launch of new products, in the recognition that many may fail but that some will succeed. Fast failure, they argue, is preferable to smothering new ideas at birth or delaying their launch through over-elaborate screening systems.

Similarly, the impressive success of Samsung Electronics in the 2000s is based in part on the CEO's deliberate culture of 'perpetual crisis', a powerful Value Innovation Programme, and a long-term strategic vision of controlling core technologies in an era of digital convergence. Samsung's goal of market leadership is being pursued through innovation in technology and design.

In his study of German 'hidden champions', Simon (1996) emphasises their continuous processes of product and service improvement (*Kaizen*). Constant innovation is shown to be one of the significant characteristics of these world market leaders. By the mid-1990s, however, thinking in Japan, the home of *Kaizen*, had moved on. The challenge for many Japanese firms is now believed to be radical and major change, rather than incremental improvement, to enable them to compete in the future.

The key competencies required include excellent new product development skills together with technical and creative abilities. These are combinations of inside-out and spanning competencies. Once new product ideas have been crystallised, however, it is important to test them out on customers (through fast failure or more conventional means) to avoid the launch of highly innovative, but essentially unwanted, products, such as the Sinclair C5 electric car.

Tellis and Golder (1996), in a study of first-to-market firms, concluded that for many firms a more successful strategy is to be a fast follower. Under this approach firms learn from the mistakes of the pioneers and capitalise on the growth phase of the market without incurring the costs of establishing the market in the first place. Moore (1991), in his study of innovation in high-technology markets, concludes that the critical aspect of new product success is bridging the 'chasm' between innovators (those who will be attracted to an innovation because of its innovative nature) and the early majority who represent the beginnings of the mass market. It is this chasm that, in Moore's opinion, accounts for the failure of many new products.

James Dyson is an inventor who has successfully positioned his firm as the provider of innovative solutions to everyday problems. In January 1997 he won the European Design Award for his innovative vacuum cleaner (see below). Dyson started inventing at the age of 28 when he recognised a design fault in conventional wheelbarrows. When full, the barrow, with a single, thin wheel at the front, was prone to tipping over. He replaced the wheel with a large red ball which solved the problem. When he set up in business the 'ball barrow' was an immediate success, selling over 60,000 per year. Following that success he designed a new garden roller which was light and manoeuvrable when not in use but heavy enough to roll gardens flat. His innovation was to use a hollow plastic roller that could be filled with water when in use but drained when not in use. The bagless vacuum cleaners followed and in 2002 he launched the Dyson washing machine. He is now considering modernising other household items such as dishwashers and fridges as well as marketing a diesel exhaust cleaner that reduces toxic emissions. The success of the £100 million turnover company has been based on innovation, first to market with revolutionary designs of everyday products, offering superior value to customers.

In the early 1990s Dyson's new vacuum cleaner was launched on to the UK market. The Dyson Dual Cyclone operates in a different way from conventional cleaners in that it creates a cyclone of air (faster than the speed of sound) and does away with the conventional bags to collect the dust. On conventional cleaners the pores of the bags gradually fill so that the cleaner works less well when half full. The Dyson cleaner claims three times the performance of conventional vacuum cleaners but, at around £200, costs up to double the price. Manufacturers of conventional vacuum cleaners were unimpressed by the new product as they derive good ongoing profits from the sale of the disposable dust bags (that market alone being worth around £100 million per annum). They fought to keep the Dyson from conventional outlets and Dyson eventually hit on the idea of selling through mail order catalogues (a further innovation in the vacuum cleaner business). Despite the price disadvantage the Dyson had achieved 25 per cent UK market share within three years of its launch. Not content with the UK market, Dyson has also achieved the almost unique success of a British appliance manufacturer with a substantial market share in Japan, rather than vice versa.

Innovation may also come in the form of new processes or approaches to market. Dell, for example, sells PCs direct to businesses (and to a lesser extent household consumers) rather than through retail shops and resellers. Direct marketing eliminates the intermediaries and also speeds up the time to market of the computers. About 80 per cent of the cost of a PC is made up of components (such as microprocessor chips), the price of which is falling at around 30 per cent per annum. Too much inventory, therefore, means high-cost products waiting to be sold at high prices. Similarly, when technology changes (e.g. from 486 to Pentium-based processors) a company can be left with large stocks of out-of-date computers. By selling direct, Dell turns over its inventory every 14 days, compared with 50 days for Compaq, its rival. That has been estimated to give Dell a 3 per cent cost advantage. As important, however, has been the market advantage that has been conveyed through the switch from reseller to direct marketing. Dell has been growing at 50 per cent per annum in a market growing at 20 per cent: it is now the fifth largest manufacturer of computers (*The Economist*, 5 October 1996). Nonetheless, the dramatic slowing of Dell's growth in 2005/6 raises the question of whether Dell will be displaced by new competitors with their own innovations, especially in markets like China where the direct business model fits poorly with purchasers' preferences for personal selling and face-to-face advice.

19.3.4 Service positioning

Positioning on the basis of offering superior service, or rather service clearly tailored to the needs of the target market, is increasingly being used. Variations in the nature and level of service offered, coupled with differences in requirements across customer groups, mean that service positioning can be viable and attractive for more than one company in a market. Critical to providing superior service are market sensing skills which can identify what level/type of service is required; customer bonding skills that build closer relationships with key customers; service systems that assist the service providers in delivering service to customers, and monitoring skills that can regularly assess the customer satisfaction with the level and type of service provided. Most critical of all to providing superior service are the people, or staff, that actually provide the service. Selection, training, motivation and reward of service staff are areas that need high priority in firms seeking to establish a competitive edge through service provision (see Figure 19.8).

Firms seeking to create a service edge to position themselves as offering superior service to that of competitors need first to understand how their customers judge service, what dimensions are important to them and how they are manifest. They then need to put in place strategies and systems to ensure their staff can deliver superior service (see Chapter 15).

Otis Elevator recognised the importance of providing excellent service in the elevator business. Customers preferred to deal directly with Otis rather than go through an intermediary, and hence the company set up the OTISLINE through which customers can contact the firm's service centre 24 hours a day. The service has been used to market the firm's offerings and to give customers confidence in them. It also

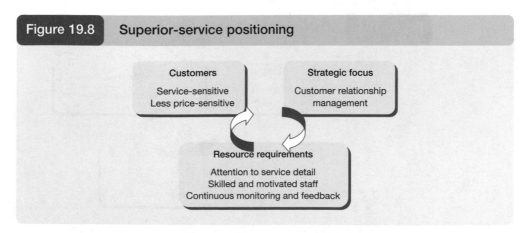

Figure 19.8   Superior-service positioning

Customers
Service-sensitive
Less price-sensitive

Strategic focus
Customer relationship management

Resource requirements
Attention to service detail
Skilled and motivated staff
Continuous monitoring and feedback

formed the basis for the company's making further improvements in information systems, including REM (remote elevator monitoring) identifying problems before lifts break down. The system improved response times through better call management, improved diagnostic capabilities and strengthened the service team by providing them with better communications. The result has been significant increases in customer satisfaction levels (Armistead and Clark, 1992).

In summer 1996 IBM, under its new head Lou Gerstner, shifted the emphasis of its positioning away from physical products towards service offered to clients. Branded 'IBM Global Service', the new focus on service included an advertising campaign featuring IBM personnel and the services they provide to their customers (*Marketing Business*, November 2001).

19.3.5   Differentiated benefits positioning

Differentiated benefits positioning rests on clearly identifying alternative benefit segments within markets and then focusing on providing what they want (Yanklovich and Meer, 2006) (see Figure 19.9). As discussed in Chapter 10, segmenting markets on the basis of the benefits customers are seeking can often help identify new market opportunities and suggest ways in which marketing effort can be more effectively targeted.

Positioning on this basis is dependent on having well-developed outside-in competencies to identify the benefits customers are seeking in the first place and to segment the market creatively into meaningful but commercially viable sectors. It can also require effective new product/service development skills to ensure that the benefits sought are actually delivered to customers through building in the relevant features.

In the US mouthwash market, for example, P&G successfully challenged market leader Listerine with their good-tasting Scope brand. Previously mouthwashes had tasted bad (Listerine was 'the taste you hate two times a day') and customers assumed this was necessary for them to be effective. Scope was launched offering the additional benefit of good taste ('a mouthwash doesn't have to taste bad to be effective'). Within a few years Scope was level with Listerine in market share (*Marketing Insights*, September 2001).

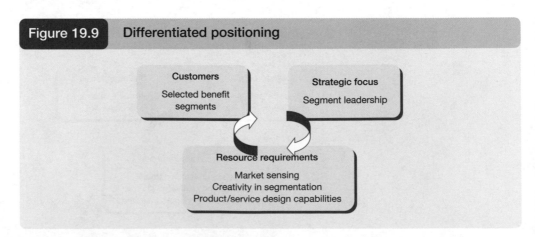

Figure 19.9   Differentiated positioning

Fairy Liquid is a washing-up liquid that has been consistently positioned on the basis of the twin benefits it provides to users: clean dishes but smooth hands for the washer-up. The product was test launched in Birmingham, UK, in 1959 when the market was in its infancy, with only 17 per cent of consumers using washing-up liquid, the remainder relying on soap powders or household soap to wash their dishes. The national launch in 1960 involved a massive door-to-door programme, which delivered 15 million sample bottles to 85 per cent of houses in the UK. The launch platform stressed that the product was strong enough to remove dirt and grease from plates and dishes but was mild on hands.

By 1980, 1 billion bottles of Fairy Liquid had been sold. Product improvements in 1982 enabled the advertisements to demonstrate a 20 per cent improvement in the volume of dishes that could be washed with one bottle (a 20 per cent 'mileage' improvement) and the brand had reached 27 per cent market share. Further continuous product improvement followed with the launch of a lemon-scented variant in 1984/5 (share climbed to 32 per cent) and further increased mileage in 1988 (by 15 per cent) and 1992 (by a further 50 per cent and signalled by a change of name to Fairy Excel), taking market share above 50 per cent for the first time. In 1993 Fairy Excel Plus replaced Fairy Excel, offering yet a further 50 per cent mileage improvement but still retaining the mildness to hands. One manager was quoted as saying, 'the heritage of the brand is so linked with mildness it [putting anything less mild on the market] would be regarded as treachery by the consumer.'

In the overcrowded beer market Boddingtons Draught Bitter has been successfully positioned on the basis of the benefit of 'smoothness'. In a market where most beers have emphasised the sociability of beer drinking, or the personal (generally macho) characteristics of beer drinkers, Boddington advertising has focused on conveying the 'cream of Manchester' attribute through poster and press advertising. Indeed, the advertising campaign won the 1994 IPA Advertising Awards Gold Medal.

Automobile manufacturers have been particularly effective at positioning their offerings to convey particular benefits. Estate cars offer additional carrying capacity, sports cars offer performance benefits, and four-wheel drive cars offer off-road capabilities (though many purchasers never test this out in reality!). Most recently, manufacturers have been developing small cars for city use in anticipation of legislation concerning pollution levels. The Ford Ka, the Renault Twingo, the Mercedes Smart and the Volkswagen Lupo are examples. These cars are typically compact and fuel economical (the Lupo claims 99 mpg) to reduce noxious emissions in city centres. BMW has also launched into the compact car market with its Mini, a brand retained after its brief ownership of Rover. In the second half of 2001 it sold 25,000 in Europe and it was launched in the USA in spring 2002.

Yamaha was world market leader in fine upright and grand pianos. Globally the company held 40 per cent of the market, but the market was in decline at around 10 per cent per annum. Market research showed that many pianos were seldom played, gathered dust and were out of tune. Using its competencies in digital music technology (the firm had pioneered electronic keyboards), the firm set about offering additional benefits in the pianos it sold. They developed the 'disklavier', which was a traditional piano (upright and grand) which could be played normally but also had an additional feature. Attached to the piano was an electronic device that enabled the owner to play pre-recorded music on their own piano. The device accepted a 3.5-inch disk, similar to a computer floppy disk, which contained the recorded music and played it on the piano. On its launch in Japan the product was an immediate success, rising to 20 per cent market share within three years. The firm also worked on the possibilities of retro-fitting existing pianos with the device to expand the market potential even further.

The 1996 Harrods catalogue carried an advertisement for a digital grand piano:

> *Yamaha DC11 Digital Piano – the perfect choice for real music lovers, the DC11 disklavier is a high quality acoustic piano with an added disc drive. Play as a normal instrument or use the computer facility to play back the disc of your choice. In addition record your own music directly onto disc while you play. Usual price £18,099, SALE PRICE £15,299.*

Interestingly, the concept was not completely new. In 1930s America, pianolas (pianos that could play rolls of punched paper when pedalled) were very popular!

The yellow fats market has also been extensively segmented on the basis of benefits sought and individual products positioned to appeal to specific benefit segments (see Chapter 12). In the 1960s, butter dominated the market, with margarine seen as a cheap, downmarket substitute. In the 1970s, however, concerns over healthy eating led to the launch of Flora by Van den Bergh and Vitalite by Kraft, both positioned as more healthy alternatives to butter. The features included polyunsaturated fat rather than the saturated fat of butter (which had been linked with cholesterol and heart disease). Van den Bergh also launched Outline, aimed at the weight-conscious sector, conveying low calories as its prime benefit. The competition to offer yet more healthy spreads led to lower fat levels in 'extra light' and 'reduced salt' versions. During the 1980s, however, some consumers began to crave the benefit of a 'real butter taste' once again, but without the health concerns of full fat butter. In the early 1980s Van den Bergh launched Krona, and in 1983 Dairy Crest launched Clover. In 1991 Van den Bergh launched its new butter substitute 'I Can't Believe It's Not Butter' with one of the most innovative brand names to date. The name, though clumsy, was certainly memorable and clearly conveyed the benefit it was designed to offer – butter taste. St Ivel followed the same positioning in 1995 with 'Utterly Butterly'.

Positioning based on benefits sought by customers is conventionally associated with consumer markets. In fact, the same is true of the strategies of successful firms in business-to-business markets. In both cases, benefit segments provide a powerful basis on which to build positioning directly related to the requirements of customers.

19.3.6 Customised positioning (one-to-one marketing)

Perhaps the ultimate in targeting and positioning is the attempt to offer products customised to the requirements of individual customers. While this has been practised in many business-to-business markets for some time, it is now coming to others and consumer markets too (see Figure 19.10).

The 1996 Paris motor show saw the launch by Mercedes-Benz of its 'Smart Car', a two-seater bubble car jointly developed with MCC (Micro Compact cars), a joint venture with SMH, the Swiss makers of the Swatch ('Smart' stands for Swatch, Mercedes and Art). The Smart Car had a small petrol engine (future versions are

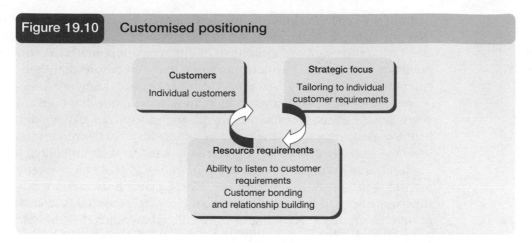

Figure 19.10   Customised positioning

intended to be battery-driven), seated only two and was aimed at couples living in cities who want a second car. To create the car, innovative production methods were used. It was produced in France at Hambach, where clusters of suppliers around the main factory each produce sub-assemblies, which were then 'snapped' together, giving major savings in production time (only around 4.5 hours are needed per car) and costs, but also making it possible to customise the fittings to individual customer requirements even after delivery. The customer could simply return the car and have additional components added (such as air conditioning), current options changed, or even change colours by swapping individual panels. In addition, MCC offered customers a leasing package by which they can rent a larger car for a couple of weeks for annual vacations, etc. (*The Economist*, 9 November 1996).

The car went on sale in Paris in 1998 but was initially priced too high for its market at US$11,000. It also failed the 'elk test' on manoeuvrability. First-year sales were disappointing at 80,000 (original estimates had been around 200,000). The strategic alliance between MCC and Mercedes was short-lived and Mercedes bought out MCC. Smart is now marketed as a cheap runabout (priced at US$8,000) but customers can still purchase an extra set of coloured body panels which can be easily fitted for $1,275. Sales reached 100,000 in 2000 and were expected to reach 250,000 by 2005. The company is also planning a four-seater version (*Fortune*, 30 April 2001). The website for Smart in the UK now offers customers the opportunity to customise online by choosing colours, interiors, options and accessories through the site (www.thesmart.co.uk, March 2002).

At the other end of the car market German manufacturer Porsche produces around 150 cars a day from its assembly line in Stuttgart. Each car is customised so that customers have more than 1 billion combinations to choose from. They can choose interiors, seats, dashboards, engine types, body styles and colours. In fact, Porsche will paint the car any colour the customer desires. One Texan had his car painted the same colour as his wife's favourite lipstick (*Fortune*, 11 March 2002).

The important skills for customised positioning are a combination of outside-in competencies to enable the firm to identify what the customer wants, and to establish relationships with customers, with inside-out competencies of flexible production capability. Recent advances in 'mass customisation' (Pine, 1993) make it increasingly possible for firms to enjoy the cost and efficiency advantages of mass production while at the same time tailoring their offerings to individual customer requirements. Dell, for example, builds products to order. Over the phone or the web customers select what they want from hundreds of different components to configure the computers of their choice. Business purchasers can also ensure that their purchases are compatible with existing systems in the firm (Agarwal, Kumaresh and Mercer, 2001).

In some markets mass customisation, by another name, has been around for many years. Supermarkets, for example, provide such a wide range of goods on display and 'employ' customers to do their own selection such that each customer leaving the store has a unique collection of groceries tailored to their individual needs.

The clearest examples of customised positioning, however, are generally found in services, both consumer and business, where a customised service can be tailored to the requirements of individual customers. Financial consultants offer tailored analysis of investment needs, accountants offer tailored accounts, hairdressers offer tailored haircuts, and architects can offer (if the customer can pay) individual house designs.

Customised positioning rests on understanding individual, rather than market segment, needs and having the flexibility to provide for them at a price the customer is willing to pay. While technology, such as the use of the Internet, can play an important role in enabling economically viable customisation, the process needs to be market-led rather than technology-driven. Increasingly, companies are looking to create synergies through the use of new technology to respond to customer demands.

Levi Strauss now offers customised blue jeans – tailored to the tight fit required by customers – by taking measurements in the shop which are sent electronically to the factory to produce a unique garment (and store the data for repeat purchases). The same type of customer offer is made by some shoe suppliers in the US, who respond to customer preferences for unique products by using technology to achieve this at a reasonable cost.

Amazon.com has around 5 million customers but manages to practise one-to-one marketing in a highly effective manner. The firm is very successful at tracking what customers do and, using that information, sends e-mails to them with information about new books and videos similar to those they have purchased, or by the same authors, or in the same genre. This customised information service has helped Amazon achieve good levels of customer retention.

The above alternative approaches to positioning are not necessarily exclusive of each other. They do constitute, however, the main basic alternatives open to firms. The creative application of those alternatives offers an almost infinite variety of ways that firms might build competitive advantage for the new millennium. The task of marketing is to select among the alternatives, basing the choice firmly on the competencies and capabilities of the firm.

Summary

Business is changing and so must marketing. Successful strategies for the future will be based on creating a fit between the requirements of the chosen market and the resources of the firm, its ability to meet those requirements.

Marketing will be seen more as a process for achieving this type of matching, rather than a functional specialisation or department. To focus on the process of going to market, rather than conventional marketing structures, offers the chance to enhance the role of the customer as a driving force for the company and to finally achieve operationally the goal that 'marketing's future is not as *a* function of business but as *the* function of business' (Haeckel, 1997). The new processes of marketing will require us to learn new ways of doing business in unfamiliar organisations.

Neither resources nor markets are fixed. We may by now be well used to the notion of market requirements changing over time and the need to monitor those changes. We are perhaps less aware of the need, explicitly and constantly, to examine and develop our resources and capabilities over time. New dynamic capabilities must be built or otherwise acquired (e.g. through alliances, mergers or acquisitions) to enable the company to compete in the future. At the same time, the firm should examine how it can use its current set of capabilities and assets in different markets or combine its existing capabilities in innovative ways to create new opportunities (as Yamaha did with their digital pianos).

Fundamentally we can expect firms to be more selective and narrower in their choice of markets and customers to serve, but to concentrate their efforts on creating deeper relationships with those chosen to ensure long-term value creation through long-term relationships. There is, of course, an infinite number of ways in which firms can create relationships with their customers. This new millennium is an exciting period for competitive marketing!

Trend-spotting at the Henley Centre and elsewhere Case study

Mark Sunderland Photographers Direct

Welcome to the future, where energy, space and information will be crucial, consumers increasingly irrational, sales of bottled water will soar and a party at home dancing to your old LPs will be the height of fashion.

In the run-up to the millennium, trend-spotting was big business. Most of the big advertising agencies and branding consultants had an in-house futurologist who would assure anxious clients that wristwatch phones, oxygen bars and functional foods were the next big thing.

Leo Burnett, Young & Rubicam and Bartle Bogle Hegarty were among those providing corporate soothsaying. Some planning departments and research departments were re-branded as 'consumer insight' teams or given other grand titles. However, as the economy has slumped, clients have made it clear that they are unwilling to pay extra for information that they believe the planning department should provide for free, or to pay for some of the futurologists' more tenuous predictions. As a result, most agencies have returned to concentrating on their core business – making ads.

However, there are still specialists providing clients with insights into the future. The doyen is

Faith Popcorn, whose US-based Brain-Reserve company has advised, among others, IBM, BMW and Nabisco. Popcorn is perhaps best known for identifying 'cocooning' – protecting oneself from the harsh realities of an unpredictable world by retreating into our homes. Popcorn says that 'cocooning' is responsible for the rise in interest in DIY and presumably TV makeover shows.

In the UK, the Henley Centre continues to provide clients, who include retail, financial services and government departments, with strategic insights into consumer behaviour. Chairman Martin Hayward says consumers will be taking a long-term view in 2003. 'In the past few years consumers have lived for today and thought "sod the consequences" but with high levels of debt and job insecurity they will have to consider the future.'

However, he says this will lead to greater irrationality. 'It is very contradictory behaviour but we may well see them spending lots of money on something completely meaningless like a designer handbag and then scrimping on everything else.'

A few years ago the Henley Centre identified cash-rich but time-poor consumers. Now it has gone a step further and says consumers will look for products and services that save energy, provide information and don't take up too much space in our cluttered homes and lives. 'Companies that can provide these will meet a real consumer need,' says Hayward.

Meanwhile, Marian Salzman, who has worked in trend identification for TBWA, Y&R and now for Euro RSCG Worldwide, says: 'So much of what we're seeing in trends is a response to our heightened feelings of insecurity. Even as we go about our daily business, we are aware that things are not quite normal. This is why we're turning to products and services that help us keep some sense of control.'

Salzman predicts that sales of bottled water and water filtration systems, for example, will boom due to fears of terrorism. In the US, she says, the desire to feel safe will result in a growth in 'personal weaponry' and panic rooms in people's homes.

She says that in Europe and the US people are taking comfort in all that is genuine. 'Our research shows that consumers think companies owned and managed by families are more likely to make products they can trust and to treat their employees well. We'll see more companies follow the lead of cleaning products company SC Johnson, which last year re-branded itself as SC Johnson: A Family Company. We will also start to see companies use real people in their marketing communications.'

Home will also become increasingly important, says Salzman, and there will be continued interest in DIY, furnishings, home-cooked meals and even home schooling. The dinner party or dancing round the coffee table in your own home will become increasingly fashionable because it's safer than venturing out to a city centre restaurant or club.

Salzman's focus on security is echoed by Crawford Hollingworth, chief executive of strategic consultancy Headlight Vision. He predicts that consumers will demand a paradoxical combination of openness and protection. 'People will want their own personal space and privacy and don't like the idea of anyone being able to track their e-mails but they will still want protection whether it's from terrorism or corporate scandals like Enron,' he says.

Hollingworth also believes that we will see an end to 'No Logo' and that consumers will instead become 'Pro Logo', as, he explains, 'our trust in traditional institutions such as the government and the church declines, consumers will look for brands that they can trust to fulfil that role'.

But do clients actually take much notice of the predictions? Martin Hayward at the Henley Centre says they do: 'Clients increasingly realise that markets are driven by consumers and that you really have to understand their behaviour and motivation.'

Salzman admits that the thrust of her work has changed dramatically in the past couple of years. 'The percentage of work that is trend-spotting versus strategic planning is different. Once it was 90–10 and today it is 20–80.'

Euro RSCG provides basic trend-spotting as part of all account planning on big accounts. 'We also provide innovations-related consulting on a paid-for basis, which leans heavily on future forecasting and creating products and services that will suit future consumers,' says Salzman.

She says clients have become increasingly future-focused. 'However, they want "actionable" insights – trends they can manage and make money from. They also seek ideas that they can tweak uniquely to ensure competitive advantage.'

Salzman claims to have helped clients spot a number of trends before they became mainstream. 'We identified "wiggers" – white teenagers who adopted black street fashion styles, which spawned a whole industry for baggy clothing. We also spotted the fact that single women are the new yuppies, and the rise of nostalgia for the 1970s.

'Clients were able to act on these insights early and get a head start over the competition, so they obviously think that what we do is valuable.'

Source: Helen Jones, 'It's scary out there', *Financial Times*: Media Business: Special Report, 3 January 2003, p. 15,

Discussion questions

1 To what extent do you accept or reject the trends forecast by the experts?

2 What other major trends do you see influencing markets in the early years of the new millennium? Structure these under the headings of Political, Economic, Social and Technological trends and give reasons for your belief in the projected changes.

3 How are the trends in questions 1 and 2 likely to influence the demand and design of the following: automobiles, homes, home-delivered services, entertainment?

References

Aaker, D.A. (1982), 'Positioning your product', *Business Horizons*, 25 (3), 56–62.

Aaker, D.A. (1991), *Managing Brand Equity*, New York: The Free Press.

Aaker, D.A. (1995), *Strategic Market Management*, 4th edn, New York: Wiley.

Aaronson, S.A. (2005), '"Minding Our Business": What the United States Government Has Done and Can Do to Ensure that US Multinationals Act Responsibly in Foreign Markets', *Journal of Business Ethics*, 59, 175–98.

Abell, D.F. (1978), 'Strategic windows', *Journal of Marketing*, 42 (3), 21–6.

Abell, D.F. and Hammond, J.S. (1979), *Strategic Market Planning: Problems and analytical approaches*, Hemel Hempstead: Prentice Hall International.

Abrahams, B. (1996), 'Life after downsizing', *Marketing*, 30 May, 26–7.

Achrol, R. (1991), 'Evolution of the marketing organization: New forms for turbulent environments', *Journal of Marketing*, 55 (October), 77–93.

Achrol, R. (1997), 'Changes in the theory of interorganizational relations in marketing: Toward a network paradigm', *Journal of the Academy of Marketing Science*, 25 (1), 56–71.

Ackerman, R.W. (1975), *The Social Challenge in Business*, Cambridge, MA: Harvard University Press.

Adams, J.L. (1987), *Conceptual Blockbusting: A guide to better ideas*, Harmondsworth, Middlesex: Penguin Books.

Agarwal, V., Arjona, L.D. and Lemmens, R. (2001), 'e-Performance: the path to rational exuberance', *McKinsey Quarterly*, (1), 31–43.

Agrawal, M., Kumaresh, T.V. and Mercer, G.A. (2001), 'The false promise of mass customization', *McKinsey Quarterly*, (3), 62–71.

Ahuja, G. and Katila, R. (2004), 'Where do resources come from? The role of idiosyncratic situations', *Strategic Management Journal*, 25, 887–907.

Airline Industry Information (2007), 'Boeing and Lockheed Martin Form Strategic Alliance', 23 January, 1.

Al Bawaba (2006a), 'Dell/EMC Extend Multi-Billion Dollar Strategic Alliance Until 2011', 18 September, 1.

Al Bawaba (2006b), 'Standard Chartered Leading the Way in Asia, Africa and Middle East', 21 August, 1.

Alexander, L.D. (1991), 'Strategy Implementation: Nature of the Problem', in D. Hussey (ed.) *International Review of Strategic Management*, 2 (1), Chichester: Wiley, p. 74.

Alpert, M.I. (1972), 'Personality and the determinants of product choice', *Journal of Marketing Research*, 9 (1), 179–83.

Alsem, K.J., Leeflang, P.S.H. and Reuyl, J.C. (1989), 'The forecasting accuracy of market share models using predicted values of competitive marketing behavior', *International Journal of Research in Marketing*, 6 (3), 183–98.

Ambler, T. (2000), *Marketing and the Bottom Line: The New Metrics of Corporate Wealth*, Hemel Hempstead: Prentice Hall.

Ambler, T. (2001), 'Are brands good for Britain?' *British Brands* 13, 4–5.

Ambler, T. (2003), *Marketing and the Bottom Line*, 2nd edn, Hemel Hempstead: Prentice Hall.

American Salesman (2002), 'Shift to Value-Added Selling is Biggest Challenge in Sales', November, 13.

Amit, R. and Shoemaker, P.J.H. (1993), 'Strategic assets and organizational rent', *Strategic Management Journal*, 14, 33–46.

Anderson, E. and Trinkle, B. (2005), *Outsourcing the Sales Function: The Real Costs of Field Sales*, Mason OH: Thomson.

Anderson, E.W. and Sullivan, M.W. (1993), 'The antecedents and consequences of customer satisfaction for firms', *Marketing Science*, 12 (2), 125–43.

Anderson, J.C., Håkansson, H. and Johanson, J. (1994), 'Dyadic business relationships within a business network context', *Journal of Marketing*, 58 (October), 1–15.

Anderson, J.C. and Narus, J.A. (1993), 'A model of distributor firm and manufacturer firm working partnerships', *Journal of Marketing*, 57 (January), 42–58.

Anderson, J.C., Narus, J.A. and van Rossum, W. (2006), 'Customer Value Propositions in Business Markets', *Harvard Business Review*, March, 91–99.

Andreasen, A.R. (1994), 'Social Marketing: Its Definition and Domain', *Journal of Public Policy and Marketing*, 13, Spring, 108–114.

Anfuso, D. (1994), 'Coca-Cola's staffing philosophy supports its global strategy', *Personnel Journal*, 73 (11), 116.

Anfuso, D. (1995), 'Colgate's global HR unites under one strategy', *Personnel Journal*, 74 (10), 44–8.

Anon. (1993), 'Quality through customer care', *Industrial Relations Review and Report*, September, 2–5.

Ansoff, H.I. (1984), *Implanting Strategic Management*, London: Prentice Hall.

Anthony, S.C., Eyring M. and Gibson, L. (2006), 'Mapping your Innovation Strategy', *Harvard Business Review*, 84 (5), 104–13.

Armistead, C.G. and Clark, G. (1992), *Customer Service and Support*, London: Pitman Publishing.

Armstrong, J.S. (1985), *Long-range Forecasting: From crystal ball to computer*, New York: Wiley.

Armstrong, J.S. and Collopy, F. (1996), 'Competitor orientation: effects of objectives and information on managerial decisions and profitability', *Journal of Marketing Research*, 33 (May), 188–99.

Armstrong, J.S. and Hutcherson, P. (1989), 'Predicting the outcome of marketing negotiations: role playing versus unaided opinions', *International Journal of Research in Marketing*, 6 (3), 227–39.

Arndt, J. (1983), 'The political economy paradigm: Foundation for theory-building in marketing', *Journal of Marketing*, 47, 44–54.

Arrington, M. (2007), 'AT&T Piles on Yahoo', www.TechCrunch.com, 9 March.

Arruñada, B. and Vázquez, X.H. (2006), 'When Your Contract Manufacturer Becomes Your Competitor', *Harvard Business Review*, September, 135–44.

Ashton, J. (2005), 'Marconi Up For Grabs', *Daily Mail*, 4 May, 64.

Aufreiter, N.A., Lawler, T.L. and Lun, C.D. (2000), 'A New Way To Market', *The Mckinsey Quarterly*, (2), 52–61.

Baghai, M., Coley, S. and White, D. (2000), *The Alchemy of Growth: Practical insights for building the enduring enterprise*, Perseus Books.

Baker, M.J. (1992), *Marketing Strategy and Management*, 2nd edn, London: Macmillan.

Baldauf, A., Cravens, D.W. and Piercy, N. (2001), 'Examining Business Strategy, Sales Management, and Salesperson Antecedents of Sales Organization Effectiveness', *Journal of Personal Selling & Sales Management*, 21, 123–34.

Baldauf, A., Cravens, D.W. and Piercy, N. (2005), 'Sales Management Control Research – Synthesis and an Agenda for Future Research', *Journal of Personal Selling & Sales Management*, 25 (1), 7–26.

Baldauf, A., Piercy, N. and Cravens, D.W. (2001), 'Examining the Consequences of Sales Management Control Strategies in European Field Sales Organizations', *International Marketing Review*, 18, 474–508.

Bamford, J., Ernst, D. and Fubini, D.G. (2004), 'Launching a World-Class Joint Venture', *Harvard Business Review*, February, 90–100.

Barnes, S. and Hunt, B. (2001), *e-Commerce and v-Business*, Oxford: Butterworth-Heinemann.

Barnes, S.J., Bauer, H.H., Neumann, M.M. and Huber, F. (2007), 'Segmenting cyberspace: A customer typology for the internet', *European Journal of Marketing*, 41 (1/2), 71–93.

Barnett, F.W. (1988), 'Four steps to forecast total market demand', *Harvard Business Review*, 66 (4), 28–34.

Barney, J.B. (1991), 'Firm resources and sustained competitive advantage', *Journal of Management*, 17 (1), 99–120.

Barney, J.B. (1997), 'Looking inside for competitive advantage', in A. Campbell and K.S. Luchs (eds), *Core Competency-Based Strategy*, London: International Thomson Business Press.

Barone, M.J., Miyazaki, A.D. and Taylor, K.A. (2000), 'The Influence of Cause-Related Marketing on Consumer Choice: Does One Good Turn Deserve Another?', *Journal of the Academy of Marketing Science*, 28 (2), 248–62.

Bartlett, C.A. and Ghoshal, S. (1994), 'Changing the role of top management: Beyond strategy to purpose', *Harvard Business Review*, 72 (6), 79–88.

Bass, F.M. (1969), 'A new product forecasting model for consumer durables', *Marketing Science*, 15 (2), 215–27.

Baumwoll, J.P. (1974), 'Segmentation research: the Baker vs the Cookie Monster', in Proceedings, American Marketing Association Conference, 3–20.

BBC News Service (28 June 2006), Global Fairtrade sales taking off. Cited on Wikipedia.

Beamish, P.W. and Killing, J.P. (eds) (1997), *Co-operative Strategies: European Perspectives*, San Francisco: The New Lexington Press.

Becket, M. (1997), 'Top brands to share research on consumers', *The Daily Telegraph*, 21 July, 23.

Becker-Olsen, K.L., Cudmore, B.A. and Hill, R.P. (2006), 'The Impact of Perceived Corporate Social Responsibility on Consumer Behavior', *Journal of Business Research*, 59, 46–53.

Bell, E. (1996), ' "Bastards" are losing out to Mr. Clean', *Observer*, 30 June.

Bell, S.J., Menguc, B. and Stefani, S.L. (2004), 'When Customers Disappoint: A Model of Relational Internal Marketing and Customer Complaints', *Journal of the Academy of Marketing Science*, 32 (2), 112–26.

Bensimon, S. (1999), 'Strategic Alliances', *Executive Excellence*, 16 (10), 9.

Bergen, M. and Peteraf, M.A. (2002), 'Competitor Identification and Competitor Analysis: A Broad-Based Managerial Approach', *Managerial and Decision Economics*, 23 (4–5), 157–69.

Bernhardt, D. (ed.) (1993), *Perfectly Legal Competitor Intelligence*, London: Pitman Publishing.

Bernoth, A. (1996), 'Companies show they care', *Sunday Times*, 8 December.

Berry, L.L. (1981), 'The employee as customer', *Journal of Retail Banking*, 3 (1), 271–8.

Berry, L.L. and Parasuraman, A. (1991), *Marketing Services: Competing Through Quality*, New York: The Free Press.

Berry, L.L., Conant, J.S. and Parasuraman, A. (1991), 'A framework for conducting a services marketing audit', *Journal of the Academy of Marketing Science*, 19 (3), 255–68.

Berstell, G. and Nitterhouse, D. (2005), 'Letting the Customer Make the Case', *Strategy and Innovation*, Harvard Business School Publishing, March–April, 3–6.

Birchall, J. (2007), 'Makers of Pet Foods Take Bite Out of Crisis', *Financial Times*, Tuesday 27 March, 12.

Blackwell, D. (1997), 'ICI set for bulk chemicals deal', *Financial Times*, 14 July, 19.

Blattberg, R.C. and Hoch, S.J. (1992), 'Database models and managerial intuition: 50% model + 50% manager', *Management Science*, 36 (6), 887–99.

Bogner, W.C., Thomas, H. and McGee, J. (1999), 'Competence and competitive advantage: Towards a dynamic model', *British Journal of Management*, 10, 275–90.

Bonoma, T.V. (1985), *The Marketing Edge: Making strategies work*, New York: Free Press.

Bonoma, T.V. (1990), 'Employees can free the hostages', *Marketing News*, 19 March.

Booz, Allen and Hamilton (1982), *New Products Management for the 1980s*, New York: Booz, Allen and Hamilton Inc.

Borden, N. (1964), 'The concept of the marketing mix', *Journal of Advertising Research*, 4, June 1964, 2–7.

Boston Consulting Group (1979), *Specialization*, Boston: BCG.

Bowen, D.E. and Lawler, E.E. (1992), 'The empowerment of service workers: what, why, how and when', *Sloan Management Review*, Spring, 31–9.

Bowman, C. and Ambrosini, V. (2003), 'How the resource-based and dynamic capabilities views of the firm inform corporate-level strategy', *British Journal of Management*, 14, 289–303.

Bradley, U. (1987), *Applied Marketing and Social Research*, 2nd edn, Chichester: John Wiley.

Brady, J. and Davis, I. (1993), 'Marketing's mid-life crisis', *The McKinsey Quarterly*, 2 (2), 17–28.

Branco, M.C. and Rodrigues, L.L. (2006), 'Corporate Social Responsibility and Resource-Based Perspectives', *Journal of Business Ethics*, 69, 111–32.

Brand Strategy (2006), 'Marketing Capability – Blend for Flexibility', 17 July, 30.

Brierley, S. (1996), 'Shell pours oil on employee relations', *Marketing Week*, 29 November.

Brittan, Sir L. (1990), 'A compelling reality', *Speaking of Japan*, February, 10 (110), 18–24.

Broadbent, S. (ed.) (1983), *Advertising Works 2*, London: Holt, Reinhart and Winston.

Brodie, R.J. and de Kluyver, C.A. (1987), 'A comparison of the short-term accuracy of econometric and naive extrapolation models of market share', *International Journal of Forecasting*, 3 (3), 423–37.

Brown, A. (1995), 'The fall and rise of marketing', *Marketing Business*, February, 25–8.

Brown, S. (1995), *Postmodern Marketing*, London: Routledge.

Brown, T.J. and Dacin, P.A. (1997), 'The Company and the Product: Corporate Associations and Consumer Product Responses', *Journal of Marketing*, 61, January, 68–85.

Brownlie, D. (1996), 'Marketing audits and auditing: diagnosis through intervention', *Journal of Marketing Management*, 12 (1–3), 99–112.

Brugmann, J. and Prahalad, C.K. (2007), 'Co-creating Businesses' New Social Compact', *Harvard Business Review*, February, 80–90.

Brummer, A. (2005), 'Marconi Crisis is a Disaster for UK PLC', *Daily Mail*, 11 May, 67.

Bucklin, L.P. and Sengupta, S. (1993), 'Organizing successful co-marketing alliances', *Journal of Marketing*, April, 32–46.

Buffington, B.I. and Frabelli, K.F. (1991), 'Acquisitions and alliances in the communications industry', in H.E. Glass (ed.), *Handbook of Business Strategy*, 3rd edn, New York: Warren Gorman and Lamont.

Bultez, A. and Parsons, L. (eds) (1998), *Retail Efficiency*, special issue of *International Journal of Research in Marketing*, 15 (5).

Burack, E.H., Burack, M.D., Miller, D.M. and Morgan, K. (1994), 'New paradigm approaches in strategic human resource management', *Group and Organizational Management*, 19 (2), 141–59.

Business Week (1993), 'The virtual corporation', 8 February, 98–102.

Business Week (2006), 'Fixing Ford is Now Job One', *Business Week*, 4 September, 30.

Buzzell, R.D. and Gale, B.T. (1987), *The PIMS Principles*, New York: The Free Press.

Buzzell, R.D. and Ortmeyer, G. (1994), *Channel Partnerships: A new approach to streamlining distribution*, Cambridge, MA: Marketing Science Institute.

Buzzell, R.D. and Wiersema, F.D. (1981), 'Successful share building strategies', *Harvard Business Review*, 59 (1), 135–44.

Calder, B.J. (1994), 'Qualitative marketing research' in Richard P. Bagozzi (ed.), *Principles of Marketing Research*, Boston, MA: Blackwell.

Calfee, D.I. (1993), 'Get your mission statement working', *Management Review*, January, 54–7.

Capizzi, M.T. and Ferguson, R. (2005), 'Loyalty trends for the twenty-first century', *Journal of Consumer Marketing*, 22 (2), 72–80.

Capon, N. (2001), *Key Account Management and Planning*, New York: The Free Press.

Cappelli, P. and Crocker-Hefter, A. (1996), 'Distinctive human resources are firms' core competencies', *Organizational Dynamics*, 24 (3), 7–22.

Cardozo, R.N. (1979), *Product Policy*, Reading, MA: Addison-Wesley.

Carey, T. (1989), 'Strategy formulation in banks', *International Journal of Bank Marketing*, 7 (3), 4–44.

Carroll, A.B. (1979), 'A Three-Dimensional Model of Corporate Performance', *Academy of Management Review*, 4 (4), 497–505.

Carroll, D.J., Green, P.E. and Schaffer, C.M. (1986), 'Interpoint distance comparisons in correspondence analysis', *Journal of Marketing Research*, 23, 271–80.

Carroll, D.J., Green, P.E. and Schaffer, C.M. (1987), 'Comparing interpoint distances in correspondence analysis: a clarification', *Journal of Marketing Research*, 24, 445–50.

Cascino, A.E. (1969), 'Organizational implications of the marketing concept', in E.J. Kelley and W. Lazar (eds), *Managerial Marketing: Perspectives and viewpoints*, Homewood, IL: Irwin.

Cassino, K.D. (1984), 'Delphi method: a practical "crystal ball" for researchers', *Marketing News*, 16 January, 705–6.

Cattin, P. and Wittink, D.R. (1992), 'Commercial use of conjoint analysis: a survey', *Journal of Marketing*, 46 (1), 44–53.

Cave, F. (2005), 'Surging Costs Put More pressure on Manufacturers', *Financial Times*, 12 July, 4.

Central Statistical Office (1995), *Annual Abstract of Statistics*, London: HMSO.

Cespedes, F.V. (1993), 'Coordinating Sales and Marketing in Consumer Goods Firms', *Journal of Consumer Marketing*, 10 (2), 37–55.

Cespedes, F.V. (1994), 'Industrial Marketing: Managing New Requirements', *Sloan Management Review*, Spring, 45–60.

Cespedes, F.V. (1995), *Concurrent Marketing: Integrating Product, Sales and Service*, Cambridge, Mass: Harvard Business School Press.

Cespedes, F.V. (1996), 'Beyond Teamwork: How the Wise Can Synchronize', *Marketing Management*, 5 (1), 25–37.

Cespedes, F.V. and Piercy, N.F. (1996), 'Implementing Marketing Strategy', *Journal of Marketing Management*, 12, 135–60.

Chally Group H.R. (1996), *The Customer Selected World Class Sales Excellence Report*, Ohio: H.R. Chally Group.

Chally, H.R. (2006), *The Chally World Class Sales Excellence Research Report*, Dayton, OH: The H.R. Chally Group.

Chang, J.J. and Carroll, J.D. (1969), 'How to use MDPREF: a computer program for multidimensional analysis of preference data', unpublished paper, Murray Hill, NJ: Bell Laboratories.

Chang, J.J. and Carroll, J.D. (1972), 'How to use PREFMAP and PREFMAP 2 – Programs which relate preference data to multidimensional scaling solutions', unpublished paper, Murray Hill, NJ: Bell Laboratories.

Chang, J. (2005), 'From The Inside Out', *Sales & Marketing Management*, August, 8.

Chatterji, A. and Levine, D. (2006), 'Breaking Down the Wall of Codes: Evaluating Non-Financial Performance Measurement', *California Management Review*, 48 (2) Winter, 29–51.

Chattopadhyay, A., Nedungadi, P. and Chakravarti, D. (1985), 'Marketing strategy and differential advantage – a comment', *Journal of Marketing*, 49 (2), 129–36.

Chesbrough, H.W. and Teece, D.J. (1996), 'When virtual is virtuous', *Harvard Business Review*, 74 (1), 65–73.

Chimhanzi, J. (2004), 'The Impact of Marketing/HR Interactions on Marketing Strategy Implementation', *European Journal of Marketing*, 38 (1–2), 73–98.

Chisnall, P.M. (1985), *Strategic Industrial Marketing*, Hemel Hempstead: Prentice Hall International.

Christensen, C. and Bower, J. (1996), Customer power, strategic investment and the failure of leading firms', *Strategic Management Journal*, 17 (3), 197–218.

Christensen, C.M., Anthony, S.D., Berstell, G. and Nitterhouse, D. (2007), 'Finding the Right Job for your Product', *MIT Sloan Management Review*, 6 (38), 2–11.

Christopher, M., Payne, A. and Ballantyne, D. (1991), *Relationship Marketing*, Oxford: Butterworth-Heinemann.

Chu, J. (2002), 'What top-performing retailers know about satisfying customers: Experience is key', IBM Institute for Business Value.

Clark, M. and Payne, A. (1995), 'Customer retention: does employee retention hold a key to success?', in A. Payne (ed.), *Advances in Relationship Marketing*, London: Kogan Page.

Clark, P. (1986), 'The marketing of margarine', *European Journal of Marketing*, 20 (5), 52–65.

Clarkson, M.B.E. (1995), 'A Stakeholder Framework for Analysing and Evaluating Corporate Social Responsibility', *Academy of Management Review*, 20 (1), 92–117.

Clausewitz, C. von (1908), *On War*, London: Routledge & Kegan Paul.

Clavell, J. (ed.) (1981), *The Art of War by Sun Tzu*, London: Hodder and Stoughton.

Clemen, R.T. (1989), 'Combining forecasts: a review and annotated bibliography', *International Journal of Forecasting*, 5 (4), 559–83.

Clover, C. (1996), 'The green shopper is alive and well', *Daily Telegraph*, 11 December.

Coad, T. (1989), 'Lifestyle analysis – opportunities for early entry into Europe with effective customer targeting', Institute of International Research Conference on *Customer Segmentation and Lifestyle Marketing*, London, 11–12 December.

Colletti, J.A. and Chonko, L.B. (1997), 'Change Management Initiatives: Moving Sales Organizations from Obsolescence to High Performance', *Journal of Personal Selling & Sales Management*, 17 (Spring), 1–30.

Collier, J. and Esteban, R. (2007), 'Corporate Social Responsibility and Employee Commitment', *Business Ethics*, 16 (1), 19–29.

Collis, D.J. and Montgomery, C.A. (1995), 'Competing on resources: strategy for the 1990s', *Harvard Business Review*, 73 (4), 118–28.

Collis, D.J. and Montgomery, C.A. (1997), *Corporate Strategy: Resources and the scope of the firm*, Chicago: McGraw-Hill.

Commission of the European Communities (2001), *Green Paper: Promoting a European Framework for Corporate Social Responsibility*, COM, July, p. 6.

Cook, V.J. (1983), 'Marketing strategy and differential advantage', *Journal of Marketing*, 47 (2), 68–75.

Cook, V.J. and Mindak, W.A. (1984), 'A search for constants: the heavy user revisited', *Journal of Consumer Research*, 1 (4), 80.

Cooper, R. and Kleinschmidt, E. (1990), 'New product success factors: A comparison of kills versus successes and failures', *R&D Management*, 17 (3), 47–63.

Cooper, R. and Kleinschmidt, E. (1993), 'New product success in the chemical industry', *Industrial Marketing Management*, 22 (1), 85–99.

Cooper, R. and Kleinschmidt, E. (1995), 'New product performance: Keys to success, profitability and cycle time reduction', *Journal of Marketing Management*, 11, 315–37.

Coye, R.W. (2004), 'Managing Customer Expectations in the Service Encounter', *International Journal of Service Industry Management*, 15 (4), 54–71.

Coyles, S. and Gokey, T.C. (2005), 'Customer retention is not enough', *Journal of Consumer Marketing*, 22 (2), 101–05.

Cramp, B. (1996), 'Neighbourhood watch', *Marketing Business*, May, 44–7.

Cravens, D.W. (1991), *Strategic Marketing*, 3rd edn, Chicago: Irwin.

Cravens, D.W. (1995), 'The Changing Role of the Sales Force', *Marketing Management*, Fall, 17–32.

Cravens, D.W., Greenley, G., Piercy, N.F. and Slater, S. (1997), 'Integrating contemporary strategic management philosophy', *Long Range Planning*, 30 (4), 493–506.

Cravens, D.W. and Piercy, N.F. (1994), 'Relationship marketing and collaborative networks in service organizations', *International Journal of Service Industry Management*, 5 (5), 39–53.

Cravens, D. W. and Piercy, N.F. (2006), *Strategic Marketing*, 8th edn, New York: McGraw-Hill/Irwin.

Cravens, D.W., Piercy, N.F. and Shipp, S.H. (1996), 'New organizational forms for competing in highly dynamic environments: The network paradigm', *British Journal of Management*, 7, 203–18.

Cravens, D.W., Shipp, S.H. and Cravens, K.S. (1993), 'Analysis of co-operative interorganizational relationships, strategic alliance formation, and strategic alliance effectiveness', *Journal of Strategic Marketing*, March, 55–70.

Cravens, D.W., Shipp, S.H. and Cravens, K.S. (1994), 'Reforming the traditional organization: The mandate for developing networks', *Business Horizons*, July–August, 19–28.

Cravens, K., Piercy, N. and Cravens, D.W. (2000), 'Assessing the Performance of Strategic Alliances: Matching Metrics to Strategies', *European Management Journal*, 18 (5), 529–41.

Creyer, E. and Ross, W.T. (1997), 'The Influence of Firm Behavior on Purchase Intention: Do Consumers Really Care About Business Ethics?' *Journal of Consumer Marketing*, 14 (6), 421–8.

Crimp, M. (1990), *The Marketing Research Process*, 3rd edn, Hemel Hempstead: Prentice Hall.

Crimp, M. and Wright, L.T. (1995), *The Marketing Research Process*, 4th edn, Hemel Hempstead: Prentice Hall.

Cripe, E.J. (1994), 'Upgrading the service level of HR', *Human Resources Professional*, 7 (3), 7–11.

Croft, M. (2007), 'Training and Development: Brand Ambassadors', *Marketing Week*, 8 March, 39.

Crosby, L.A., Evans, K.R. and Cowles, S. (1990), 'Relationship quality in services selling: an interpersonal influence perspective', *Journal of Marketing*, 54, 68–81.

Cross, J., Hartley, S.W., Rudelius, W. and Vassey, M.J. (2001), 'Sales Force Activities and Marketing Strategies in Industrial Firms: Relationships and Implications', *Journal of Personal Selling & Sales Management*, 21 (3), 199–206.

Crouch, S. and Housden, M. (1996), *Marketing Research for Managers*, 2nd edn, Oxford: Butterworth-Heinemann.

Culliton, J. (1948), *The management of marketing costs*, Graduate School of Business Administration, Research Division, Harvard University, Boston, 1948.

Cunningham, M.T. and Clarke, D.C.J. (1976), 'The product management function in marketing', *European Journal of Marketing*, 9 (2), 129–49.

Czaplewski, A.J., Ferguson, J.M. and Milliman, J.F. (2001), 'Southwest Airlines: How Internal Marketing Pilots Success', *Marketing Management*, Sept/Oct, 14–17.

Daily Telegraph (1997), 'Laura Ashley may defeat superman', 27 August.

d'Astous, A. and Boujbel, L. (2007), 'Positioning countries on personality dimensions: Scale development and implications for country marketing', *Journal of Business Research,* 60, 231–9.

Danneels, E. (1996), 'Market segmentation: Normative model versus business reality', *European Journal of Marketing*, 30 (6), 36–51.

Dartnell's 30th Sales Force Compensation Survey: 1998–1999, Chicago: Dartnell Corporation.

Davey, J. and Laurance, B. (2007), 'Trading Bright Green Ideas', *The Sunday Times*, 21 January, 3.5.

Davidson, H. (1983), 'Putting assets first', *Marketing*, 17 November.

Davidson, H. (1987), *Offensive Marketing*, London: Penguin Books.

Davidson, H. (2002), *The Committed Enterprise*, Oxford: Butterworth-Heinemann.

Dawson, L.M. (1969), 'The human concept: New philosophy for business', *Business Horizons*, December, 29–38.

Day, G.S. (1977), 'Diagnosing the product portfolio', *Journal of Marketing*, 41 (2), 29–38.

Day, G.S. (1992), 'Marketing's contribution to the strategy dialogue', *Journal of the Academy of Marketing Science*, 20 (4), 37–52.

Day, G.S. (1994), 'The capabilities of market-driven organizations', *Journal of Marketing*, 58 (3), 37–52.

Day, G.S. (1994), *Market Driven Strategy: Processes for creating value*, New York: Free Press.

Day, G.S. (1997), 'Aligning the organization to the market', in D.R. Lehmann and K.E. Jocz, (eds), *Reflections on the Futures of Marketing*, Cambridge, MA: Marketing Science Institute.

Day, G.S. (1999), 'Misconceptions about market orientation', *Journal of Market Focused Management*, 4 (1), 5–16.

Day, G.S., Shocker, A.D. and Srivastava, R.K. (1979), 'Customer-oriented approach to identifying product markets', *Journal of Marketing*, 43 (4), 8–19.

De Boer, L., Labro, E. and Morlacci, O. (2001), 'A Review of Methods Supporting Supplier Selection', *European Journal of Purchasing and Supply Management*, 7 (2), 75–89.

de Chernatony, L. and MacDonald, M.H.B. (1992), *Creating Brands*, Oxford: Butterworth-Heinemann.

Deise, M.V., Nowokow, C., King, P. and Wright, A. (2000), *Executive's Guide to e-Business*, New York: John Wiley & Sons.

Delios, A., Inkpen, A.C. and Ross, J. (2004), 'Escalation in International Strategic Alliances', *Management International Review*, 44 (4), 457–79.

Dell, M. (2007), 'Everyone Has A Choice', *Financial Times Digital Business – Special Report*, Wednesday 18 April, 1.

Deloitte Touche (2005), *Strategic Sales Compensation Survey*, New York: Deloitte Touche Development LLC.

de Kare-Silver, M. (1998), 'Shopping on the Net is poised to change face of retailing', *Sunday Times*, November 8.

Deshpandé, R. (1982), 'The organizational context of marketing research use', *Journal of Marketing*, 46 (3), 91–101.

Deshpandé, R. and Zaltman, G. (1984), 'A comparison of factors affecting researcher and manager perceptions of market research use', *Journal of Marketing Research*, 21 February, 32–8.

Deshpandé, R. and Webster, F.E. (1989), 'Organizational Culture and Marketing: Defining the Research Agenda', *Journal of Marketing*, 53 (January), 3–15.

Deshpandé, R., Farley, J.U. and Webster, F.E. (1993), 'Corporate culture, customer orientation and innovativeness in Japanese firms: a quadrad analysis', *Journal of Marketing*, 57, 23–27.

Dewar, R. and Schultz, D. (1989), 'The product manager: An idea whose time has gone', *Marketing Communications*, May, 28–35.

Dewsnap, B. and Jobber, D. (2000), 'The Sales–Marketing Interface in Consumer Packaged-Goods Companies: A Conceptual Framework', *Journal of Personal Selling & Sales Management*, 20 (2), 109–119.

Diamantopoulos, A. and Schlegelmilch, B.B. (1997), *Taking the Fear out of Data Analysis*, London: The Dryden Press.

Dibb, S. and Simkin, L. (1994), 'Implementation problems in industrial market segmentation', *Industrial Marketing Management*, 23, February, 55–63.

Dickson, P.R. (1992), 'Towards a general theory of competitive rationality', *Journal of Marketing*, 56, January, 69–83.

Dierickx, I. and Cool, K. (1989), 'Asset stock accumulation and sustainability of competitive advantage', *Management Science*, 35, 1504–51.

Divita, S. (1996), 'Colleagues are customers, market to them', *Marketing News*, 21 October.

Dixon, N.F. (1976), *On the Psychology of Military Incompetence*, London: Futura.

Donaldson, T. and Preston, L.E. (1995), 'The Stakeholder Theory of the Corporation: Concepts, Evidence and Implications', *Academy of Management Review*, 29, January, 65–91.

Donath, R. (1997), 'Marketers of Technology make Promises They Can't Keep', *Marketing News*, 13 October, 5.

Dorsch, M.J., Scott, R., Swanson and Kelley, S.W. (1998), 'The Role of Relationship Quality in the Stratification of Vendors as Perceived by Customers', *Journal of the Academy of Marketing Science*, 26 (2),128–42.

Dowdy, C. (2001), 'Internal Branding', *Financial Times*, 6 November, 4.

Doyle, P. (1994), *Marketing Management and Strategy*, Hemel Hempstead: Prentice Hall International.

Doyle, P. (1995), 'Marketing in the new millennium', *European Journal of Marketing*, 29 (13), 23–41.

Doyle, P. (1997), 'Go for robust growth', *Marketing Business*, April, 53.

Doyle, P. (2000), *Value Based Marketing*, Chichester: John Wiley & Sons.

Doyle, P. (2002), *Marketing Management and Strategy*, 3rd edn, London: Pearson Education Ltd.

Doyle, P. and Bridgewater, S. (1998), *Innovation in Marketing*, Oxford: Butterworth-Heinemann.

Doyle, P. and Wong, V. (1996), 'Marketing and international competitiveness: An empirical study', Proceedings of the 25th annual conference of the European Marketing Academy, May, Budapest, Hungary, 351–70.

Doyle, P., Saunders, J.A. and Wong, V. (1986), 'A comparative study of Japanese and British marketing strategies in the UK market', *Journal of International Business Studies*, 17 (1), 27–46.

Doyle, P. and Stern, P. (2006), *Marketing Management and Strategy*, 4th edn, Harlow: Pearson Education.

Doz, Y.L. (1988), 'Technology partnerships between larger and smaller firms: Some critical issues', *International Studies of Management and Organization*, 17 (4), 31–57.

Drake, S.M., Galman, M.J. and Roberts, S.M. (2005), *Light Their fire: Using Internal Marketing to Ignite Employee Performance and Wow Your Customers*, Kaplan Business.

Drucker, P. (1954), *The Practice of Management*, New York: Harper & Row.

Drucker, P.F. (1973), *Management: Tasks, Responsibilities and Practices*, New York: Harper & Row.

Drucker, P. (1997), 'The future that has already happened', *Harvard Business Review*, 75 (5), 20–4.

Drumwright, M.F. (1989), 'Socially Responsible Organizational Buying: Environmental Concerns as a Noneconomic Buying Criterion', *Journal of Marketing*, 58, July, 1–19.

Durman, P. and Box, O. (2005), 'Cut Off', *Sunday Times*, 1 May, 3.5.

Dwek, R. (1997), 'Losing the race', *Marketing Business*, March.

Economist (1994a), 'Death of the brand manager', 9 April, 79–80.

Economist (1994b), 'Furnishing the world', 19 November, 101.

Economist (1997), 'Dr Gallup's finger on America's pulse', 17 September, 133–4.

Economist (2001), 'Internet Pioneers: we have lift off', 3 February, 79–81.

Egan, C. (1995), *Creating Organizational Advantage*, Oxford: Butterworth-Heinemann.

Eisenstat, R.A. (1993), 'Implementing strategy: Developing a partnership for change', *Planning Review*, 21 (5), 33–6.

Eisenstat, R., Foote, N., Galbraith, J. and Miller, D. (2001), Beyond the business unit, *McKinsey Quarterly*, (1), 54–63.

Eisenhardt, K.M. and Martin, J.A. (2000), 'Dynamic Capabilities: What are they?' *Strategic Management Journal,* 21, 1105–21.

Elgie, S.S. (1990), *Travel Problems and Opportunities – Turning adversity to advantage in the 1990s*, London: Elgie Stewart Smith.

Ellen, P.S., Mohr, L.A. and Web, D.J. (2000), 'Charitable Programs and the Retailer: Do They Mix?', *Journal of Retailing*, 76 (3), 393–406.

English, J. (1989), 'Selecting and analyzing your customer/market through efficient profile modeling and prospecting', *Institute of International Research Conference on Customer Segmentation and Lifestyle Marketing*, London, 11–12 December.

Ernst, D. and Bamford, J. (2005), 'Your Alliances are too Stable', *Harvard Business Review*, June, 133–41.

Evans, F.B. (1959), 'Psychological and objective factors in the prediction of brand choice', *Journal of Business*, 32, October, 340–69.

Evans, P.B. and Wurster, T.S. (1997), 'Strategy and the new economics of information', *Harvard Business Review*, 75 (5), 71–82.

Evans, P.B. and Wurster, T.S. (1999), *Blown to Bits: how the new economics of information transforms strategy*, Cambridge, MA: Harvard Business School Press.

Fahy, J. and Hooley, G.J. (2002), 'Sustainable competitive advantage in e-business: towards a contingency perspective on the resource based view', *Journal of Strategic Marketing*, 10 (4), 1–13.

Farley, J.U. (1997), 'Looking ahead at the marketplace: It's global and it's changing', in D.R. Lehmann and K.R. Jocz (eds), *Reflections on the Futures of Marketing*, Cambridge, MA: Marketing Science Institute.

Farris, P.W., Bendle, N.T., Pfeifer, P.E. and Reibstein, D.J. (2006), *Marketing Metrics: 50+ Metrics Every Executive Should Master*, Upper Saddle River, NJ: Wharton School Publishing.

Felton, A.P. (1959), 'Making the marketing concept work', *Harvard Business Review*, 37 (4), 55–65.

Ferrell, O.C. and Lucas, G.H. (1987), 'An evaluation of progress in the development of a definition of marketing', *Journal of the Academy of Marketing Science*, 15 (3), 12–23.

Financial Times, 'Footing the Bill: Gates Offers $3 Software to Poor', Friday 20 April 2007, 1.

Financialwire (2006), 'AT&T, Yahoo Hit 5-Year Mark With Broadband Partnership', 22 November, 1.

Fink, R.C., Edelman, L.F. and Hatten, K.J. (2007), 'Supplier Performance Improvements in Relational Exchanges', *Journal of Business and Industrial Marketing*, 22 (1), 29–40.

Fiol, C.M. and Lyles, M.A. (1985), 'Organisational learning', *Academy of Management Review*, 10, 803–13.

Fishburn, D. and Green, S. (eds) (2002), *The World in 2003*, London: Economist Newspapers Ltd.

Fisher, J.C. and Pry, R.M. (1978), 'A simple substitution model of technological change', *Technological Forecasting and Social Change*, 3 (1), 75–88.

Fitzgerald, L., Johnston, R., Brignall, S., Silvestro, R. and Voss, C. (1991), *Performance Measurement in Service Businesses*, London: Chartered Institute of Management Accountants.

Fitzhugh, K.L.M. and Piercy, N.F. (2006), 'Integrating Marketing Intelligence Sources: Reconsidering the Role of the Salesforce', *International Journal of Market Research*, 48, 699–716.

Fletcher, K. (1996), *Marketing Management and Information Technology*, 2nd edn, London: Prentice-Hall International.

Flipo, J.-P. (1986), 'Service firms: Interdependence of external and internal marketing strategies', *European Journal of Marketing*, 20 (8), 5–14.

Forbis, J.L. and Mehta, N.T. (1981), 'Value-based strategies for industrial products', *Business Horizons*, 24 (3), 32–42.

Foster, R.N. (1986a), *Innovation: The attacker's advantage*, London: Macmillan.

Foster, R.N. (1986b), 'Attacking through innovation', *The McKinsey Quarterly*, Summer, 2–12.

Frank, R.E., Massey, W.F. and Wind, Y. (1972), *Market Segmentation*, Englewood Cliffs, NJ: Prentice-Hall.

Franks, J.R. and Broyles, J. (1979), *Modern Managerial Finance*, Chichester: Wiley.

Friedman, L.G. (2002), *Go To Market Strategy*, Woburn MA: Butterworth-Heinemann Business Books.

Friedman, M. (1970), 'The Social Responsibility of Business is to Increase its Profits', *New York Times Magazine*, 12 September, 122–6.

Freedman, M. (2003), 'The Genius is in the Implementation', *Journal of Business Strategy*, March/April, 26–31.

Frosch, R. (1996), 'The customer for R&D is always wrong!' *Research-Technology Management*, (Nov–Dec), 22–7.

Fry, M-L. and Polonsky, M.J. (2004), 'Examining the Unintended Consequences of Marketing', *Journal of Business Research*, 57, 1303–6.

Fulmer, W.E. and Goodwin, J. (1988), 'Differentiation: Begin with the customer', *Business Horizons*, 31 (5), 55–63.

Galea, C. (2006), 'The Rising Tide Does It Again', *Sales and Marketing Management*, May, 30–35.

Gapper, J. (2007), 'The Sober Side of Corporate Hospitality', *Financial Times*, Monday 26 March, 17.

Gardner, E.S. (1985), 'Exponential smoothing: The state of the art', *Journal of Forecasting*, 4 (1), 1–28.

Gardner, N. (1997), 'Defining your class is as easy as ABC', *The Sunday Times*, 9 February, 7.

Gerlach, M.L. (1992), *Alliance Capitalism*, Berkeley: University of California Press.

Gershman, M. (1991), *Getting it Right the Second Time*, London: Mercury Books.

Gilly, M.C. and Wolfinbarger, M. (1996), *Advertising's Second Audience: Employee reactions to organizational communications*, Cambridge, MA: Marketing Science Institute.

Glassman, M. and McAfee, B. (1992), 'Integrating the personnel and marketing functions: The challenge of the 1990s', *Business Horizons*, 35 (3), 52–9.

Gluck, F. (1986), 'Strategic planning in a new key', *McKinsey Quarterly*, Winter, 173–83.

Godfrey, P.C. and Hatch, N.W. (2007), 'Researching Corporate Responsibility: An Agenda for the 21st Century', *Journal of Business Ethics*, 70, 87–98.

Gordon, W. and Langmaid, R. (1988), *Qualitative Research: A practitioners' and buyers' guide*, London: Gower.

Gounaris, S.P. (2006), 'Internal-Market Orientation and Its Measurement', *Journal of Business Research*, 59 (4), 432–48.

Grande, C. (2005), 'Marconi's Technology Fails the Price Test', *Financial Times*, 4 May, 23.

Grande, C. (2007a), 'Ethical Consumption Makes Mark on Branding', *Financial Times*, Tuesday 20 February, 24.

Grande, C. (2007b), 'Businesses Behaving Badly, Say Consumers', *Financial Times*, Tuesday 20 February, 24.

Grant, J. (2005), 'Mr Daley's Mission: To Reach 6Bn Shoppers and Make Money', *Financial Times*, 15 July, 32.

Grant, R. (1996), 'Message from a bottle', *Financial Mail on Sunday*, 15 December, 12.

Grant, R.M. (1995), *Contemporary Strategy Analysis*, 2nd edn, Cambridge, MA: Basil Blackwell.

Grant, R.M. (2005), *Contemporary Strategy Analysis*, 5th edn, Blackwell.

Gratton, L. (1994), 'Implementing strategic intent: Human resource processes as a force for change', *Business Strategy Review*, 5 (1), 47–66.

Green, P.E. and Wind, Y. (1975), 'New way to measure consumers' judgements', *Harvard Business Review*, 53 (4), 107–17.

Green, P., Carroll, J. and Goldberg, S. (1981), 'A general approach to product design optimization via conjoint analysis', *Journal of Marketing*, 43, summer 1981, 17–35.

Green, P.E., Carmone, F.J. and Smith, S.M. (1989), *Multidimensional Scaling: Concepts and applications*, Boston, MA: Allyn and Bacon.

Green, P.E., Tull, D.S. and Albaum, G. (1993), *Research for Marketing Decisions*, 6th edn, Englewood Cliffs, NJ: Prentice Hall International.

Greenley, G.E. and Foxall, G.R. (1996), 'Consumer and non-consumer stakeholder orientation in UK firms', *Journal of Business Research*, 35, 105–16.

Greenley, G.E. and Foxall, G.R. (1997), 'Multiple stakeholder orientation in UK companies and the implications for company performance', *Journal of Management Studies*, 34, 259–84.

Greyser, S.A. (1997), 'Janus and marketing: The past, present and prospective future of marketing', in D.R. Lehmann and K.R. Jocz (eds), *Reflections on the Futures of Marketing*, Cambridge, MA: Marketing Science Institute.

Gribben, R. (1997), 'BA has secret global deal, claims Branson', *The Daily Telegraph*, 20 August, 6.

Gronhaug, K. and Gilly, M.C. (1991), 'A transaction cost approach to consumer dissatisfaction and complaint actions', *Journal of Economic Psychology*, 12, 165–83.

Grönroos, C. (1984), *Strategic Management and Marketing in the Service Sector*, London: Chartwell-Bratt.

Grönroos, C. (1985), 'Internal marketing – theory and practice', in T.M. Bloch, G.D. Upah and V.A. Zeithaml (eds), *Services Marketing in a Changing Environment*, Chicago: American Marketing Association.

Grönroos, C. (1994), 'From marketing mix to relationship marketing: Towards a paradigm shift in marketing', *Management Decision*, 32 (2), 4–32.

GroupFMI (2001), *Website Visitor Analysis – Statistics or Intelligence?* www.groupfmi.com, November.

Gubman, E.L. (1995), 'Aligning people strategies with customer value', *Compensation and Benefits Review*, 27 (1), 15–22.

Gulati, R., Sytch, M. and Mehotra, P. (2007), 'Preparing for the Exit: When Forming a Business Alliance, Don't Ignore One of the Most Crucial Ingredients: How To Break Up', *Wall Street Journal (Special Report)*, 3 March, R1.

Gummesson, E. (1987), 'The new marketing – developing long-term interactive relationships', *Long Range Planning*, 20 (4), 10–20.

Gummesson, E. (1987), 'Using internal marketing to develop a new culture – the case of Ericsson quality', *Journal of Business and Industrial Marketing*, 2 (3), 23–8.

Gummesson, E. (1990), *The Part-Time Marketer*, University of Karlstad, Research Report. 90:3.

Gummesson, E. (1994), 'Service management: An evaluation and the future', *International Journal of Service Industry Management*, 5 (1), 77–96.

Gummesson, E. (1999), *Total Relationship Marketing*, Oxford: Butterworth-Heinemann.

Gupta, A.K., Raj, S.P. and Wilemon, D. (1986), 'A model for studying R&D/Marketing interface in the product innovation process', *Journal of Marketing*, 50, 7–17.

Haeckel, S. (1997), 'Preface', in D.R. Lehmann and K.R. Jocz (eds), *Reflections on the Futures of Marketing*, Cambridge, MA: Marketing Science Institute.

Hair, J.F., Anderson, R.E., Tatham, R.L. and Black, W.C. (1998), *Multivariate Data Analysis*, 5th edn, London: Prentice Hall International.

Haley, R.I. (1968), 'Benefit segmentation: A decision-oriented tool', *Journal of Marketing*, July, 30–5.

Haley, R.I. (1984), 'Benefit segmentation – 20 years on', *Journal of Consumer Marketing*, 5–13.

Hall, R. (1992), 'The strategic analysis of intangible resources', *Strategic Management Journal*, 13, 135–44.

Hall, R. (1993), 'A framework for linking intangible resources and capabilities to sustainable competitive advantage', *Strategic Management Journal*, 14, 607–18.

Hall, W. (1995), *Managing Cultures: Making strategic relationships work*, Chichester: John Wiley.

Hall, W.A.K. (1980), 'Survival strategies in a hostile environment', *Harvard Business Review*, 58 (5), 75–85.

Hamel, G. (1996), 'Strategy as revolution', *Harvard Business Review*, 74 (4), 9–82.

Hamel, G. and Prahalad, C.K. (1989), 'Strategic intent', *Harvard Business Review*, 67 (3), 63–76.

Hamel, G. and Prahalad, C.K. (1991), 'Corporate imagination and expeditionary marketing', *Harvard Business Review*, 69 (4), 81–92.

Hamel, G. and Prahalad, C.K. (1994), *Competing for the Future*, Boston, MA: Harvard Business School Press.

Hammermesh, R.G., Anderson, M.J. and Harris, J.E. (1978), 'Strategies for low market share businesses', *Harvard Business Review*, 50 (3), 95–102.

Han, J.K., Kim, N. and Srivastava, R.K. (1998), 'Market orientation and organizational performance: is innovation the missing link?', *Journal of Marketing*, 62, 30–45.

Harris, L.C. (1996), 'Cultural obstacles to market orientation', *Journal of Marketing Practice: Applied Marketing Science*, 4 (2), 36–52.

Harris, L.C. (1998), 'Cultural domination: The key to a market oriented culture', *European Journal of Marketing*, 32 (3/4), 354–73.

Harrison, J.S. and St John, C.H. (1994), *Strategic Management of Organizations and Stakeholders*, St Paul: West.

Hart, C.W.L., Heskett, J.L. and Sasser, W.E. (1990), 'The profitable art of service recovery', *Harvard Business Review*, 68 (2), 148–56.

Hart, S. (2005), *Capitalism at the Crossroads: The Unlimited Business Opportunities in Solving the World's Most Difficult Problems*, Wharton School Publishing.

Harvey, F. (2005), 'GE Looks Out for a Cleaner Profit', *Financial Times*, Friday 1 July, 13.

Harvey, F. and Fidler, S. (2007), 'Industry Caught in "Carbon Credit" Smokescreen', *Financial Times*, Thursday 26 April, 1.

Haspeslagh, P. (1982), 'Portfolio planning: Uses and limits', *Harvard Business Review*, 60 (1), 58–73.

Hathi, S. (2007), 'Using Blogs to Involve', *Strategic Communication Management*, Feb/Mar, 8.

Hayes, R. and Abernathy, W. (1980), 'Managing our way to economic decline', *Harvard Business Review*, 1 July.

He, H-W and Balmer, J.M.T. (2006), 'Alliance Brands: Building Corporate Brands Through Strategic Alliances?', *Journal of Brand Management*, 13 (4/5), 242–56.

Hedley, B. (1979), 'Strategy and the business portfolio', *Long Range Planning*, 10 (1), 9–15.

Heineman, R.W. Jnr (2007), 'Avoiding Integrity Land Mines', *Harvard Business Review*, April, 100–108.

Helfat, C.E. and Peteraf, M.A. (2003), 'The dynamic resource-based view: Capability lifecycles', *Strategic Management Journal*, 24, 997–1010.

Helfat, C.E., Finkelstein, S., Mitchell, W., Peteraf, M.A., Singh, H., Teece, D.J. and Winter, S.G. (2007), *Dynamic Capabilities: Understanding Change in Organisations*, Oxford: Blackwell Publishing.

Henderson, B. (1970), *The Product Portfolio*, Boston, MA: The Boston Consulting Group.

Henriques, I. and Sadorsky, P. (1999), 'The Relationship Between Environmental Commitment and Managerial Perceptions of Stakeholder Importance', *Academy of Management Journal*, 42 (1), 89–99.

Hill, R. (1979), 'Weak signals from the unknown', *International Management*, 34 (10), 55–60.

Hille, K. (2007), 'The Race for the $100 Laptop', *Financial Times*, 9 April, 8.

Hindle, T. and Thomas, M. (1994), *Pocket Marketing*, 2nd edn, Harmondsworth: The Economist Books.

Hogarth, R.M. (1978), 'A note on aggregating opinions', *Organizational Behavior and Human Performance*, 21 (1), 40–6.

Homburg, C. and Pflesser, C. (2000), 'A multiple layer model of market-oriented organizational culture: measurement issues and performance outcomes', *Journal of Marketing Research*, 37, 449–62.

Homburg, C., Workman, J.P. and Jensen, O. (2000), 'Fundamental Changes in Marketing Organization: The Movement Toward A Customer-Focused Organizational Structure', *Journal of the Academy of Marketing Science*, 28 (4), 459–78.

Homburg, C., Workman, J.P. and Jensen, O. (2002), 'A Configurational Perspective on Key Account Management', *Journal of Marketing*, April, 38–60.

Hooley, G.J. (1980), 'Multidimensional scaling of consumer perceptions and preferences', *European Journal of Marketing*, 14 (7), 436–80.

Hooley, G.J. (1982), 'Directing advertising creativity through benefit segmentation', *Journal of Advertising*, 1, 375–85.

Hooley, G.J. (1994), 'The life cycle revisited – aid or albatross?', *Journal of Strategic Marketing*, 3 (1), 23–40.

Hooley, G.J., Cox, A.J. and Adams, A. (1992), 'Our five year mission – to boldly go where no man has gone before', *Journal of Marketing Management*, 8 (1), 35–48.

Hooley, G.J., Greenley, G., Cadogan, J.W. and Fahy J. (2005), 'The performance impact of marketing resources', *Journal of Business Research*, 58 (1), 18–27.

Hooley, G.J. and Beracs, J. (1997), 'Marketing strategies for the 21st century: Lessons from the top Hungarian companies', *Journal of Strategic Marketing*, 5 (3), 143–65.

Hooley, G.J., Lynch, J.L. and Shepard, J. (1990), 'The marketing concept: Putting the theory into practice', *European Journal of Marketing*, 7–23.

Hooley, G.J., Möller, K. and Broderick, A.J. (1998), 'Competitive Positioning and the Resource Based View of the Firm', *Journal of Strategic Marketing*, 6 (2), 97–115.

Hooley, G.J., Greenley, G.E., Attia, S. and Fahy, J. (2001), 'Creating sustainable competitive positions in e-business: up the Amazon.com without a paddle?', Proceedings European Marketing Academy Conference, Bergen, Norway.

Hooley, G.J., Cox, A.J., Shipley, D., Fahy, J., Beracs, J. and Kolos, K. (1996), 'Foreign direct investment in Hungary: Resource acquisition and domestic competitive advantage', *Journal of International Business Studies*, 27 (4), 683–709.

Hooley, G.J., Fahy, J., Cox, A.J., Beracs, J., Fonfara, K. and Snoj, B. (2000), 'Market orientation in the transition economies of central Europe', *Journal of Business Research*, 50 (3), 273–85.

Hooley, G.J. and Hussey, M.K. (eds) (1999), *Quantitative Methods in Marketing*, 2nd edn, London: Thomson Press.

Hrebiniak, L.G. (2006), 'Obstacles to Effective Strategy Implementation', *Organizational Dynamics*, 35 (1), 12–31.

Huber, G.P. (1984), 'The nature and design of post-industrial organizations', *Administrative Science Quarterly*, August, 928–51.

Huber, G.P. (1991), 'Organisational learning: the contributing processes and the literatures', *Organizational Science*, 2, 88–115.

Hulbert, J.M. and Pitt, L. (1996), 'Exit left centre stage', *European Management Journal*, 14 (1), 47–60.

Hulbert, J.M., Capon, N. and Piercy, N.F. (2003), *Total Integrated Marketing: Breaking the Bounds of the Function*, New York: The Free Press.

Hussey, M.K. and Hooley, G.J. (1995), 'The diffusion of quantitative methods into marketing management', *Journal of Marketing Practice: Applied Marketing Science*, 1 (4), 13–31.

IBM (2005), *The Strategic Agenda for Customer Management in the Consumer Products Industry*, New York: IBM Institute for Business Value Executive Brief.

Imai, M. (1986), *KAIZEN: The key to Japan's competitive success*, Maidenhead: McGraw-Hill.

Imparato, N. and Harari, O. (1994), *Jumping the Curve: Innovation and strategic choice in an age of transition*, San Francisco: Jossey-Bass.

Ingram, T.N., LaForge, R.W. and Leigh, T.W. (2002), 'Selling in the New Millennium: A Joint Agenda', *Industrial Marketing Management*, 31, 559–67.

IRS Employment Review (1996), 'HRM is not part of strategic decision making', September, 4.

Jack, A. (2007), 'Beyond Charity? A New Generation Enters the Business of Doing Good', *Financial Times*, Thursday 5 April, 13.

Jackson, S. (2007), 'Market share is not enough: Why strategic market positioning works', *The Journal of Business Strategy*, 28 (1), 18–25.

Jackson, T. (1997), 'Dare to be different', *Financial Times*, 19 June.

Jain, S.C. (1985), *Marketing Planning and Strategy*, 2nd edn, Cincinatti, OH: South Western.

Jain, S.C. (1990), *Marketing Planning and Strategy*, 3rd edn, Cincinatti, OH: South Western.

James, B.J. (1984), *Business Wargames*, London: Abacus.

James L., Heskett J.L., Sasser W.E., Jr and Schlesinger L.L. (2007), *The Value Profit Chain: Treat Employees Like Customers and Customers Like Employees*, New York: The Free Press.

Janal, D. (2000), *Dan Janal's Guide to Marketing on the Internet*, New York: Wiley.

Janda, S. and Seshandri, S. (2001), 'The Influence of Purchasing Strategies on Performance', *Journal of Business and Industrial Marketing*, 16 (4), 294–306.

Japan Corporate News Network (2006), 'Honda and Hong Kong Disneyland Form Strategic Alliance', 12 July, 1.

Jaworski, B.J. and Kohli, A.K. (1993), 'Market Orientation: Antecedents and Consequences', *Journal of Marketing*, 57, July, 53–70.

Jobber, D. (2001), *Principles and Practice of Marketing*, 3rd edn, London: McGraw Hill.

Jobber, D., Saunders, J.A., Hooley, G.J., Guilding, B. and Hatton-Smooker, J. (1989), 'Assessing the value of a quality assurance certificate for software: An exploratory investigation', *MIS Quarterly*, March, 18–31.

John, G. and Martin, J. (1984), 'Effects of organizational structure of marketing planning on credibility and utilization of plan output', *Journal of Marketing Research*, 21 May, 170–83.

Johnson, G. and Scholes, K. (1988), *Exploring Corporate Strategy*, 2nd edn, Hemel Hempstead: Prentice Hall International.

Johnson, L.K. (2006), 'Harnessing the Power of the Customer', *Harvard Management Update*, November.

Jones, T.M. (1995), 'Instrumental Stakeholder Theory: A Synthesis of Ethics and Economics', *Academy of Management Review*, 20 (2), 404–37.

Jones, T.O. and Sasser, W.E. (1995), 'Why satisfied customers defect', *Harvard Business Review*, 73 (6), 88–99.

Jones, E., Brown, S.P., Zoltners, A.A. and Weitz, B.A. (2005), 'The Changing Environment of Selling and Sales Management', *Journal of Personal Selling & Sales Management*, 25 (2), 105–111.

Kale, P., Singh, H. and Perlmutter, H. (2000), 'Learning and Protection of Proprietary Assets in Strategic Alliances: Building Relational Capital', *Strategic Management Journal*, 21, 217–37.

Kalligianis, K., Iatrou, K. and Mason, K. (2006), 'How Do Airlines Perceive That Strategic Alliances Affect Their Individual Branding?', *Journal of Air Transportation*, 11 (2), 3–21.

Kanner, B. (1996), 'In search of brand loyalty', *Sunday Business*, 30 June, 11.

Kapelianis, D., Walker, B.A., Hutt, M.D. and Kumar, A. (2005), 'Those Winning Ways: The Role of Competitive Crafting in Complex Sales', Working Paper, Arizona State University.

Kaplan, R.S. and Norton, D.P. (1996), *Translating Strategy Into Action: The Balanced Scorecard*, Boston MA: Harvard Business School Press.

Kay, J. (1993), *Foundations of Corporate Success*, Oxford: Oxford University Press.

Keegan, J. (1993), *A History of Warfare*, London: Hutchinson.

Keith, R.J. (1960), 'The marketing revolution', *Journal of Marketing*, 24 (1), 35–8.

Keller, S.B., Lynch, D.F., Ellinger, A.E., Ozment, J. and Calantone, R. (2006), 'The Impact of Internal Marketing Efforts in Distribution Service Operations', *Journal of Business Logistics*, 27 (1), 109–139.

Kelly, K. (1998), *New rules for the new economy: 10 radical strategies for the connected world*, New York: Viking Press.

Kerrigan, R., Roegner, E.V., Swinford, D.D. and Zawada, C.C. (2001), 'B2Basics', *McKinsey Quarterly*, (1), 45–53.

Khoo, P.C. (1992), *Sun Tzu and Management*, Petaling Jaya, Malaysia: Pelanduk.

Khosla, V., quoted in Taylor, R. (1999), 'Shaping the Future with Nothing but Ideas', *Financial Times*, July 19.

Kilmann, R.H. (1996), 'Management learning organisations: enhancing business education for the 21st Century', *Management Learning*, 27, 203–38.

King, S. (1985), 'Has marketing failed or was it never really tried?', *Journal of Marketing Management*, 1 (1), 1–19.

Kinnear, T.C., Taylor, J.R. and Ahmed, S.A. (1974), 'Ecologically concerned consumers: Who are they?', *Journal of Marketing*, 38 (2), 20–4.

Knight, R. (2006), 'Business Students Portrayed as Ethically Minded in Study', *Financial Times*, Wednesday 25 October, 9.

Koerner, LaVan (2005), 'Conducting an Organizational Assessment of your SAM Programme', Presentation at Strategic Account Management Association Conference, Paris.

Kohli, A.K. and Jaworski, B.J. (1990), 'Market orientation: The construct, research propositions and managerial implications', *Journal of Marketing*, 54 (2), 1–18.

Kotha, S. (1998), 'Competing on the Internet: the case of Amazon.Com', *European Management Journal*, 16 (2), 212–22.

Kotler, P. and Levy, S. (1969), 'Broadening the Concept of Marketing', *Journal of Marketing*, 33, January, 10–15.

Kotler, P.C. (1978), 'Harvesting strategies for weak products', *Business Horizons*, 21 (4), 15–22.

Kotler, P.C. (1997), *Marketing Management: Analysis, planning, implementation and control*, 9th edn, Hemel Hempstead: Prentice Hall International.

Kotler, P.C. and Singh, R. (1981), 'Marketing warfare in the 1980s', *Journal of Business Strategy*, 1 (3), 30–41.

Kotler, P.C., Fahey, L. and Jatusritpitak, S. (1985), *The New Competition*, Hemel Hempstead: Prentice Hall.

Kotler, P.C., Gregor, W. and Rogers, W. (1989), 'The marketing audit comes of age', *Sloan Management Review*, 18 (2), 49–62.

Kotler, P.C., Armstrong, G., Saunders, J.A. and Wong, V. (1996), *Principles of Marketing: the European Edition*, Hemel Hempstead: Prentice Hall.

Kotler, P. and Keller, K.L. (2007), *A Framework for Marketing Management*, 3rd edn, Pearson/Prentice Hall.

Krohmer, H., Homburg, C. and Workman, J.P. (2002), 'Should Marketing Be Cross-Functional? Conceptual Development and International Empirical Evidence', *Journal of Business Research*, 35, 451–65.

Kruskal, J.B., Young, F.W. and Seery, J.B. (1973), 'How to use KYST: A very flexible program to do multidimensional scaling', Multidimensional Scaling Program Package of Bell Laboratories, Murray Hill, NJ: Bell Laboratories.

Lafferty, B.A. and Hult, G.T.M. (2001), 'A synthesis of contemporary market orientation perspectives', *European Journal of Marketing*, 35 (1/2), 92–109.

Laing, H. (1991), *Brand Advertising Targeting System*, London: Laing Henry.

Lambert, D.M., Marmorstein, H. and Sharma, A. (1990), 'Industrial Salespeople As A Source of Market Information', *Industrial Marketing Management*, 17, May, 111–8.

Lambert, D.M., Emmelhainz, M.A. and Gardner, J.T. (1996), 'So you think you want to be a partner?', *Marketing Management*, Summer, 25–41.

Langerak, F. (2001), 'Effects of Market Orientation on the Behaviours of Salespersons and Purchasers, Channel Relationships and the Performance of Manufacturers', *International Journal of Research in Marketing*, 18, 221–34.

Lattice, J. (1996), 'Blue's legend', *Sunday Business*, 21 April.

Lawrence, M.J., Edmundson, R.H. and O'Connor, M.J. (1985), 'An examination of the accuracy of judgmental extrapolation of time series', *International Journal of Forecasting*, 1 (1), 23–35.

Lehmann, D.R. and Jocz, K.E. (eds) (1997), *Reflections on the Futures of Marketing*, Cambridge, MA: Marketing Science Institute.

Lehmann, D.R. and Winer, R.S. (1991), *Analysis for Marketing Planning*, 2nd edn, Homewood, IL: Irwin.

Leigh, T.W. and Marshall, G.W. (2001), 'Research Priorities in Sales Strategy and Performance,' *Journal of Personal Selling & Sales Management*, 21, Spring, 83–94.

Leonard-Barton, D. (1992), 'Core capabilities and core rigidities: A paradox in managing new product development', *Strategic Management Journal,* 13 (Summer Special Issue), 111–25.

Leppard, J. and McDonald, M.H.B. (1987), 'A reappraisal of the role of marketing planning', Proceedings: Marketing Education Group Conference, Warwick, July.

Levitt, T. (1960), 'Marketing Myopia', *Harvard Business Review*, July–August, 45–56.

Levitt, T. (1975), 'Marketing myopia – Retrospective commentary', *Harvard Business Review*, 53 (5), 177–81.

Levitt, T. (1986), *The Marketing Imagination*, New York: The Free Press.

Levy, R. (1999), *Give and Take*, Cambridge, MA: Harvard Business School Press.

Lewis, B. (1989), 'Customer care in service organizations', *Marketing Intelligence and Planning*, 7 (5/6), 18–22.

Liddell Hart, B.H. (1972), *History of the First World War*, London: Pan.

Liddell Hart, B.H. (1973), *History of the Second World War*, London: Pan.

Lilien, G.L. and Kotler, P.C. (1983), *Marketing Decision Making: A model-building approach*, London: Harper & Row.

Lilien, G.L., Kotler, P. and Moorthy, K.S. (1992), *Marketing Models*, Hemel Hempstead: Prentice Hall International.

Lim, K. (2006), 'Gap to Open First Stores in Asia Outside Japan by End of the Year', *Wall Street Journal*, 2 August.

Lin, Y.S.L. (1990), 'Comparison of survey response among Asian, European and American consumers and their interpretations', *ESOMAR Conference Proceedings*, Venice, June, 120–32.

Lings, I.N. and Greenley, G.E. (2005), 'Measuring Internal Market Orientation', *Journal of Service Research*, 7 (3), 290–305.

Lippman, S. and Rumelt, R.P. (1982), 'Uncertain inimitability: an analysis of inter-firm differences in efficiency under competition', *Bell Journal of Economics*, 13, 418–53.

Little, J.D.C. (1979), 'Decision support systems for marketing management', *Journal of Marketing*, 43 (3), 9–26.

Lombardi, L.J. (2005), 'Managing Strategic Customer Relationships as Assets', *LIMRA'S Market Facts Quarterly*, 24 (1), 23–5.

Lusch, R.F., Vargo, S.L. and Malter, A.J. (2006), 'Marketing as Service Exchange: Taking a leadership role in global marketing management', *Organisational Dynamics*, 35 (3), 264–78.

MacDonald, M. (1984), *Marketing Plans*, London: Heinemann.

Mackintosh, J. (2005), 'VW Takes a Hard Line With Parts Suppliers', *Financial Times*, 24 June, 30.

Mackintosh, J. and Simon, B. (2005), 'Ford to Focus on Business from "Key Suppliers"', *Financial Times*, 30 September, 32.

Mackensie, M. and Beales, R. (2007), 'Cantor Fitzgerald Appoints Ethics Czar', *Financial Times*, 14/15 April, 13.

Magretta, J. (1999), *Managing in the New Economy*, Cambridge MA: Harvard Business School Press.

Mahadevan, B. (2000), 'Business models for internet-based e-commerce: an anatomy', *California Management Review*, 42 (4), 55–69.

Mahoney, J.T. (1995), 'The management of resources and the resource of management', *Journal of Business Research*, 33 (2), 91–101.

Mahoney, J.T. and Pandian, J.R. (1992), 'The resource based view of the firm within the conversation of strategic management', *Strategic Management Journal*, 13, 363–80.

Maier, J. and Saunders, J.A. (1990), 'The implementation of segmentation in sales management', *The Journal of Personal Selling and Sales Management*, 10 (1), 39–48.

Maignan, I., Ferrell, O.C. and Hult, G.T.M. (1999), 'Corporate Citizenship: Cultural Antecedents and Business Benefits', *Journal of the Academy of Marketing Science*, 27 (4), 455–69.

Maignan, I. and Ferrell, O.C. (2004), 'Corporate Social Responsibility and Marketing: An Integrative Framework', *Journal of the Academy of Marketing Science*, 32 (1), 3–19.

Maignan, I., Ferrell, O.C. and Ferrell, L. (2005), 'A Stakeholder Model for Implementing Social Responsibility in Marketing', *European Journal of Marketing*, 39 (9/10), 956–77.

Maitland, A. (2006), 'The Frustrated Will to Act for Public Good', *Financial Times*, Wednesday 25 January, 15.

Makridakis, S., Chatfield, C., Hibon, M., Lawrence, M., Mills, T., Ord, K. and Simmons, L. (1993), 'The M2 competition: A real-time judgmentally based forecasting study', *International Journal of Forecasting*, 9 (1), 5–22.

Market Research Society (annual), *Organisations Providing Marketing Research Services in the UK*, MRS.

Marketing Business (1997a), 'Marketing prefers navel gazing to NPD', March, 6.

Marketing Business (1997b), 'Marketplace', March.

Marketing Week (2001), 'Sorrell Starts Internal Marketing Acquisitions Drive', 12 July, 10.

Marketing Week (2003), 'Survey Reveals "Inadequate" State of Internal Marketing', 3 July, 8.

Markowitz, H. (1952), 'Portfolio selection', *Journal of Finance*, 7 (2), 77–91.

Maunder, S., Harris, A., Bamford, J., Cook, L. and Cox, A. (2005), 'O$_2$: It only Works if it Works – how troubled BT Cellnet was transformed into thriving O$_2$', in Hoad, A. (ed.) *Advertising Works 13: Proving the Effectiveness of Marketing Communications*, Henley-on-Thames: World Advertising Research Centre.

Mazur, L. (1996), 'Brands', *Marketing Business*, November, 16.

Mazur, L. (2000), 'The Changing Face of Sales', *Marketing Business*, May, 31.

McDowell, C. (1996), 'Aligning work force capabilities with business strategies', *Human Resource Professional*, 9 (5), 3–5.

McKee, D. and Varadarajan, P.R. (1995), 'Introduction: Special issue on sustainable competitive advantage', *Journal of Business Research*, 33 (2), 77–9.

McKitterick, J.B. (1957), 'What is the marketing management concept?', Proceedings: AMA Teachers' Conference, Philadelphia.

McLeod, J. (1985), 'Marketing information systems: A review paper', *Quarterly Review of Marketing*, 10 (3).

McNerney, D. (1994), 'Competitive advantage: Diverse customers and stakeholders', *HR Focus*, 71 (6), 9–10.

Menguc, B. and Auh, S. (2006), 'Creating firm-level dynamic capability through capitalising on market orientation and innovativeness', *Journal of the Academy of Marketing Science*, 34 (1), 63–73.

Menon, A. and Menon, A. (1997), 'Enviropreneural Marketing Strategy: The Emergence of Corporate Environmentalism as Marketing Strategy', *Journal of Marketing*, 61, January, 51–67.

Micolo, A.M. (1993), 'Suggestions for achieving a strategic partnership', *HR Focus*, 70 (9), 22.

Miles, R.E. and Snow, C.C. (1984), 'Fit, failure, and the Hall of Fame', *California Management Review*, Spring, 10–28.

Miller, A.I. (1996), *Insight of Genius*, New York: Springer-Verlag.

Miller, D. (2002), 'Successful Change Leaders: What Makes Them? What Do They Do That Is Different?' *Journal of Change Management*, 2 (4), 359–68.

Millman, T. and Wilson, K. (1989), 'Processual Issues in Key Account Management: Underpinning the Customer-Facing Organization', *Journal of Business & Industrial Marketing*, 14 (4), 328–37.

Mingo, J. (1994), *How the Cadillac Got its Fins*, New York: HarperCollins.

Mintzberg, H. (1994), 'The fall and rise of strategic planning', *Harvard Business Review*, 72 (1), 107–14.

Mitchell, A. (1994a), 'The people factor', *Marketing Business*, October, 24–7.

Mitchell, A. (1994b), 'The revolution within', *Marketing Business*, December, 22–5.

Mitchell, A. (1995), 'Changing channels', *Marketing Business*, February, 10–13.

Mitchell, A. (1997a), 'Speeding up the process', *Marketing Business*, March.

Mitchell, A. (1997b), 'Stargazing', *Marketing Business*, June, 32–5.

Mitchell, R.K., Agle, B.R. and Wood, D.J. (1997), 'Toward a theory of stakeholder identification and salience: defining the principle of who and what really counts', *Academy of Management Review*, 22, 853–86.

Möller, K. and Anttila, M. (1987), 'Marketing capability: A key success factor in small business?', *Journal of Marketing Management*, 3 (2), 185–203.

Montgomery, D.B. and Webster, F.E. (1997), 'Marketing's Interfunctional Interfaces: The MSI Workshop on Management of Corporate Fault Zones', *Journal of Market-Focused Management*, 2, 7–26.

Moon, Y. (2005), 'Break Free from the Product Life Cycle', *Harvard Business Review*, May, 87–94.

Moore, G.A. (1991), *Crossing the Chasm*, New York: HarperCollins.

Moore, G.A. (2004), 'Innovating within established enterprises', *Harvard Business Review*, July–August, 86–92.

Moore, G.A. (2006), *Dealing with Darwin: How great companies innovate at every phase of their evolution*, Chichester: Capstone.

Moores, B. (1986), *Are They Being Served?*, Oxford: Philip Alan.

Morgan, R.E., Katsikeas, C.S. and Appiah-Adu, K. (1998), 'Market orientation and organizational learning', *Journal of Marketing Management*, 14, 353–81.

Morgan, R.E. (2004), 'Business Agility and Internal Marketing', *European Business Review*, 16 (5), 464–72.

Morgan, R.M. and Hunt, S.D. (1994), 'The commitment–trust theory of relationship marketing', *Journal of Marketing*, 58 (3), 20–38.

Morrison, A. and Wensley, R. (1991), 'Boxing up or boxed in?: A short history of the Boston Consulting Group Share-Growth Matrix', *Journal of Marketing Management*, 7 (2), 105–30.

Morrison, S. and Waters, R. (2005), 'Time Comes to "Think Different"', *Financial Times*, 7 June 2005, *25*.

Moutinho, L. (1991), *Problems in Marketing*, London: Paul Chapman Publishing.

Murphy, J. (1991), *Brand Valuation*, 2nd edn, London: Business Books Ltd.

Murphy, P.E. and Staples, W.A. (1979), 'A modernized family life cycle', *Journal of Consumer Research*, June, 12–22.

Narayanda, D. (2005), 'Building Loyalty in Business Markets', *Harvard Business Review*, September 2005.

Narver, J.C. and Slater, S.F. (1990), 'The effect of a market orientation on business profitability', *Journal of Marketing*, 54 (4), 20–35.

Norusis, M.J. (1992), *SPSS for Windows*, Release 5.0, Chicago: SPSS Inc.

O'Brien, N. and Ford, J. (1988), 'Can we at last say goodbye to social class?', *Journal of Market Research Society*, 16 (2), 43–51.

O'Shaughnessy, J. (1992), *Explaining Buyer Behavior*, Oxford: Oxford University Press.

O'Shaughnessy, J. (1995), *Competitive Marketing*, 3rd edn, London: Routledge.

Ogbuchi, A.O. and Sharma, V.M. (1999), 'Redefining Industrial Salesforce Roles in a Changing Environment', *Journal of Marketing Theory and Practice*, 7 (1), 64–71.

Ogden, S. and Watson, R. (1999), 'Corporate performance and stakeholder management: balancing shareholder and customer interests in the UK privatized water industry', *Academy of Management Journal*, 42, 526–38.

Ohmae, K. (1982), *The Mind of the Strategist*, Harmondsworth: Penguin Books.

Ohmae, K. (1990), *The Borderless World*, New York: Harper Business.

Olins, R. (1997a), 'Wilting', *The Sunday Times*, 24 August, 3.

Olins, R. (1997b), 'W.H. Smith stalls on the road to nowhere', *The Sunday Times*, 31 August, 5.

Olson, E.M. (1993), 'The marketing/manufacturing relationship within the new product development process', Proceedings, American Marketing Association Educators' Conference, Chicago, 4, 280–6.

Olson, E.M., Cravens, D.W. and Slater, S.F. (2001), 'Competitiveness and Sales Management: A Marriage of Strategies', *Business Horizons*, March/April, 25–30.

Oxx, C. (1972), 'Psychographics and life style', *Admap*, October, 303–5.

Ozretic-Dosen, D., Skare, V. and Krupka, Z. (2007), 'Assessments of country of origin and brand cues in evaluating a Croation, western and eastern European food product', *Journal of Business Research,* 60 (2), 130–6.

Palazzo, G. and Richter, U. (2005), 'CSR Business As Usual? The Case of the Tobacco Industry', *Journal of Business Ethics*, 61, 387–401.

Pansiri, J. (2005), 'The Influence of Managers' Characteristics and Perceptions in Strategic Alliance Practice', *Management Decision*, 43 (9), 1097–1113.

Parasuraman, A. and Colby, C.L. (2001), *Techno-Ready Marketing: How and Why Your Customers Adopt Technology*, New York: Free Press.

Parasuraman, A., Zeithaml, V.A. and Berry, L.L. (1985), 'A conceptual model of service quality and the implications for further research', *Journal of Marketing*, Fall, 41–50.

Parasuraman, A., Zeithaml, V.A. and Berry, L.L. (1988), 'SERVQUAL: A multiple-item scale for measuring customer perceptions of service quality', *Journal of Retailing*, 64 (1), 12–40.

Parasuraman, A., Zeithaml, V.A. and Berry, L.L. (1994), 'Reassessment of expectations as a comparison standard in measuring service quality: implications for further research', *Journal of Marketing*, 58 (1), 111–24.

Pardo, C. (1997), 'Key Account Management in the Business to Business Field: The Key Account's Point of View', *Journal of Personal Selling & Sales Management*, 17 (4), 17–26.

Payne, A. (1993), *The Essence of Services Marketing*, London: Prentice Hall.

Payne, A. (ed.) (1995), *Advances in Relationship Marketing*, London: Kogan Page.

Payne, A., Christopher, M., Clark, M. and Peck, H. (1995), *Relationship Marketing for Competitive Advantage*, Oxford: Butterworth-Heinemann.

Payne, A. and Frow, P. (2005), 'A strategic framework for customer relationship management', *Journal of Marketing*, October, 167–76.

Peppers, D. and Rogers, M. (1993), *The One-to-One Future*, London: Piatkus.

Perrien, J. and Ricard, L. (1995), 'The meaning of a marketing relationship', *Industrial Marketing Management*, 24 (1), 37–43.

Perrien, J., Filiatraut, P. and Line, R. (1993), 'The implementation of relationship marketing in commercial banking', *Industrial Marketing Management*, 22 (2), 141–8.

Peters, T. (1987), *Thriving on Chaos*, London: Macmillan.

Peters, T. and Waterman, R. (1982), *In Search of Excellence*, New York: Harper and Row.

Pfeffer, J. (1994), 'Competitive advantage through people', *California Management Review*, 36 (2), 9–28.

Piercy, N.F. (1995), 'Customer satisfaction and the internal market: Marketing our customers to our employees', *Journal of Marketing Practice: Applied Marketing Science*, 1 (1), 22–44.

Piercy, N.F. (1997), *Market-Led Strategic Change: Transforming the process of going to market*, 2nd edn, Oxford: Butterworth-Heinemann.

Piercy, N.F. (2002), *Market-Led Strategic Change: A Guide To Transforming the Process of Going To Market*, 3rd edn, Oxford: Butterworth-Heinemann.

Piercy, N.F. and Cravens, D.W. (1996), 'The network paradigm and the marketing organization', *European Journal of Marketing*, 29 (3), 7–34.

Piercy, N.F. and Lane, N. (1996), 'Marketing Implementation: Building and sustaining a real market understanding', *Journal of Marketing Practice: Applied Marketing Science*, 2 (3), 15–18.

Piercy, N.F. and Morgan, N.A. (1991), 'Internal marketing strategy: Leverage for managing market-led strategic change', *Irish Marketing Review*, 4 (3), 11–28.

Piercy, N.F. and Morgan, N.A. (1993), 'Strategic and operational market segmentation: A managerial analysis', *Journal of Strategic Marketing*, 1, 123–40.

Piercy, N.F., Cravens, D.W. and Morgan, N.A. (1997), 'Sources of effectiveness in the business-to-business sales organization', *Journal of Marketing Practice: Applied marketing science*, 3 (1), 43–69.

Piercy, N.F., Harris, L.C. and Lane, N. (2002), 'Market orientation and retail operatives' expectations', *Journal of Business Research*, 55 (4), 261–73.

Piercy, N., Low, G.S. and Cravens, D.W. (2004a), 'Consequences of Sales Management's Behavior- and Compensation-Based Control Strategies in Developing Countries', *Journal of International Marketing*, 12, 30–57.

Piercy, N., Low, G.S. and Cravens, D.W (2004b), 'Examining the Effectiveness of Sales Management Control Practices in Developing Countries', *Journal of World Business*, 39, 255–67.

Piercy, N. (2006), 'The Strategic Sales Organization', *The Marketing Review*, 6, 3–28.

Piercy, N.F. and Lane, N. (2006a), 'The Underlying Vulnerabilities in Key Account Management Strategies', *European Management Journal*, 24 (2–3), 151–82.

Piercy, N.F. and Lane, N. (2006b), 'The Hidden Risks in Strategic Account Management Strategy', *Journal of Business Strategy*, 27 (1), 18–26.

Piercy, N.F. and Lane, N. (2007), 'Ethical and Moral Dilemmas Associated With Strategic Relationships Between Business-to-Business Buyers and Sellers', *Journal of Business Ethics*, 72, 87–102.

Pine, B.J. (1993), *Mass Customization: The new frontier in business competition*, Boston, MA: Harvard Business School Press.

Pitt, L.F. (2001), 'Total e-clips: new strategic forces', *Journal of General Management*, 26 (4), 1–15.

Pitt, L.F., Berthon, P., Watson, R.T. and Ewing, M. (2001), 'Pricing Strategy on the Net', *Business Horizons*, 44 (2), 45–54.

Plank, R.E. (1985), 'A critical review of industrial market segmentation', *Industrial Marketing Management*, 14, 79–91.

Plevel, M.J., Martin, J., Lane, F., Nellis, S. and Schuler, R.S. (1994), 'AT&T global business communications systems: Linking HR with business strategy', *Organizational Dynamics*, 22 (3), 59–72.

Pollock, R.B. (1995), 'Linking marketing and human resources in the new employment contract', *Employment Relations Today*, 22 (1), 7–15.

Porter, M.E. (1980), *Competitive Strategy*, New York: The Free Press.

Porter, M.E. (1985), *Competitive Advantage*, New York: The Free Press.

Porter, M.E. (1987), 'From competitive advantage to corporate strategy', *Harvard Business Review*, 65 (3), 43–59.

Porter, M.E. (1996), 'What is strategy?', *Harvard Business Review*, 74 (6), 61–78.

Porter, M.E. (2001), 'Strategy and the Internet', *Harvard Business Review*, 79, 63–78.

Porter, M.E. and Kramer, M.R. (2002), 'The Competitive Advantage of Corporate Philanthropy', *Harvard Business Review*, December, 57–68.

Porter, M.E. and Kramer, M.R. (2006), 'Strategy and Society: The Link Between Competitive Advantage and Corporate Social Responsibility', *Harvard Business Review*, December, 78–92.

Pounsford, M. (1994), 'Nothing to lose: Is internal communications adding value in today's organizations?', *Internal Communication Focus*, September, 6–8.

Powell, W.W. (1990), 'Neither market nor hierarchy: Network forms of organization', *Research in Organizational Behavior*, 12, 295–336.

Prahalad, C.K. and Hamel, G. (1990), 'The core competence of the corporation', *Harvard Business Review*, 68 (3), 79–91.

Prokesch, S.E. (1995), 'Competing on customer service', *Harvard Business Review*, 73 (6), 101–12.

Prokesch, S.E. (1997), 'Unleashing the power of learning: An interview with British Petroleum's John Browne', *Harvard Business Review*, 75 (5), 146–68.

Punj, G. and Stewart, D.W. (1983), 'Cluster analysis in marketing research: Review and suggestions for applications', *Journal of Marketing Research*, 20, May, 135–48.

Quinn, J.B. (1985), 'Managing innovation: Controlled chaos', *Harvard Business Review*, 63 (3), 73–84.

Quinn, J.B. (1992), *Intelligent Enterprise*, New York: Free Press.

Quinn, J. (2005), 'Gillette Deal to Put P&G Ahead by a Close Shave', *Daily Mail*, 29 January, 105.

Quinn, J. (2005), 'Suppliers Turn the Screw on Rover', *Daily Mail*, 8 April, 89.

Rackham, N. and DeVincentis, J. (1999), *Rethinking the Sales Force: Redefining Selling to Create and Capture Customer Value*, New York: McGraw-Hill.

Ramsdell, G. (2000), 'The real business of B2B', *McKinsey Quarterly*, (3), 174–84.

Ramaswami, S., Bharghava, M. and Srivasta, R. (2004), *Market-based Assets and Capabilities, Business Processes, and Financial Performance*, Cambridge MA: Report No. 04-102, Marketing Science Institute.

Rankine, K. (1996), 'Not a happy house', *The Daily Telegraph*, 5 October, B2.

Reed, R. and DeFillippi, R.J. (1990), 'Causal ambiguity, barriers to imitation and sustainable competitive advantage', *Academy of Management Review*, 15, 88–102.

Reed, J. and Milne, R. (2007), 'An Embattled Industry Tries to Engineer Itself out of a Hole', *Financial Times*, 27 April, 11.

Regan, G. (1992), *Military Blunders*, London: Guinness.

Reichheld, F. (1993), 'Loyalty-based management', *Harvard Business Review*, 71 (2), 64–73.

Reichheld, F. and Sasser, W.E. (1990), 'Zero defections: Perfecting customer retention and recovery', *Harvard Business Review*, 68 (5), 105–11.

Reicheld and Schefter (2000), 'e-loyalty: your secret weapon on the Web', *Harvard Business Review*, July–August 2000.

Ries, A. and Trout, J. (1982), *Positioning: The battle for your mind*, New York: McGraw-Hill.

Ries, A. and Trout, J. (1986), *Marketing Warfare*, New York: McGraw-Hill.

Rifkin, J. (2000), *The Age of Access: How the Shift from Ownership to Access is Transforming Capitalism*, London: Allen Lane.

Rigby, E. and Wiggins, J. (2005), 'Dixons Closes Shutters in Film Cameras', *Financial Times*, 9 August, 5.

Rigby, E. (2007), 'Shopping gets Tougher for Online Supermarkets', *Financial Times*, Monday 9 April, 19.

Ring, P.S. and Van de Ven, A.H. (1992), 'Structuring co-operative relationships between organizations', *Strategic Management Journal*, 13 (7), 483–98.

Robertson, D.C. and Nicholson, N. (1996), 'Expressions of Corporate Social Responsibility in UK Firms', *Journal of Business Ethics*, 15 (10), 1095–1106.

Robinson, S.J.Q., Hichens, R.E. and Wade, D.P. (1978), 'The directional policy matrix – tool for strategic planning', *Long Range Planning*, 11 (3), 8–15.

Rogers, E. (1962), *Diffusion of Innovations*, New York: The Free Press.

Rouzies, D., Anderson, E., Kohli, A.K., Michaels, R.E., Weitz, B.A. and Zoltners, A.A. (2005), 'Sales and Marketing Integration: A Proposed Framework', *Journal of Personal Selling & Sales Management*, 25 (2), 113–22.

Rowe, A.J., Mason, R.D., Dickel, K.E. and Synder, N.H. (1989), *Strategic Management: A methodological approach*, 3rd edn, Wokingham: Prentice Hall.

Rowley, T.J. (1997), 'Moving beyond dyadic ties: a network theory of stakeholder influences', *Academy of Management Review*, 22, 887–910.

RSA (1994), *Tomorrow's Company: The role of business in a changing world*, London: RSA (Royal Society for the Encouragement of Arts, Manufactures and Commerce).

Rubel, C. (1996), 'Treating co-workers right is the key to Kinko's success', *Marketing News*, 29 January.

Ruekert, R. and Walker, O. (1987), 'Marketing's interaction with other functional units: A conceptual framework and empirical evidence', *Journal of Marketing*, 51, 1–19.

Rushe, D. (2007), 'Starbucks Stirs up a Storm in a Coffee Cup', *The Sunday Times*, 2 March, 3.7.

Rust, R.T. and Zahorik, A.J. (1993), 'Customer satisfaction, customer retention and market share', *Journal of Retailing*, 69 (2), 193–215.

Salmon, A.-M. (1997), 'Transforming a brand with energy: Lucozade in sickness and in health', *British Brands*, 4, Summer, 3.

Sammuels, G. (1994), 'CD Rom's first big victim', *Forbes*, 28 February, 42–4.

Sanders, N.R. and Ritzman, L.P. (1992), 'The need for contextual and technical knowledge in judgmental forecasting', *Journal of Behavioral Decision Making*, 39–52.

Saunders, J.A. (1990), 'Brands and valuations', *International Journal of Forecasting*, 8 (2), 95–110.

Saunders, J.A. (1994), 'Cluster analysis', in G.J. Hooley and M.K. Hussey (eds), *Quantitative Methods in Marketing*, London: Academic Press.

Saunders, J.A. (1999), Cluster Analysis. In Hooley, G.J. and Hussey, M.K. (eds), *Quantitative Methods in Marketing*, 2nd edn, London: International Thomson Business Press.

Saunders, J.A. and Saker, J. (1994), 'The changing consumer in the UK', *International Journal of Research in Marketing*, 11, 477–89.

Saunders, J.A., Sharp, J. and Witt, S. (1987), *Practical Business Forecasting*, Aldershot: Gower.

Saunders, J., Stern, P., Wensley, R. and Forrester, R. (2000), 'In Search of the Lemmus, Lummus: An Investigation Into Convergent Competition', *British Journal of Management*, 11, S81–S94.

Savitz, A. and Weber, K. (2006), *The Triple Bottom Line: How Today's Best-Run Companies are Achieving Economic, Social and Environmental Success and How You Can Too*, San Francisco, CA: Pfeiffer Wiley.

Schultz, D.E. (2002), 'Study Internal Marketing for Better Impact', *Marketing News*, 14 October, 8.

Schultz, D.E. (2004), 'Building An Internal Marketing Management Calculus', *Interactive Marketing*, 6 (2), 111–29.

Sculley, J. (1992), Chairman of Apple Computer, quoted in *Forbes ASAP*, Technical Supplement, 7 December.

Segnit, S. and Broadbent, S. (1973), 'Life-style research: A case history in two parts', *European Research*, January, 6–13, March, 62–8.

Seidenschwartz, W. (2005), 'A Model for Customer Enthusiasm: Connecting the Customer with Internal Processes', Strategic Account Management Association Conference, February, Paris.

Self, A. (1997), 'Hello Johann, got a new motor?', *The Mail on Sunday*, 12 April, 26.

Selnes, F., Jaworski, B.J., Kohli, A.J. (1996), 'Market orientation in the United States and Scandinavian companies: a cross-cultural view', *Scandinavian Journal of Management*, 12 (2), 139–57.

Sen, S. and Bhattacharya, C.B. (2001), 'Does Doing Good Always Lead to Doing Better? Consumer Reactions to Corporate Social Responsibility', *Journal of Marketing Research*, 38, May, 225–43.

Sengupta, S. and Bucklin, L.P. (1994), *To Ally or Not to Ally*, Cambridge, MA: Marketing Science Institute.

Shameen, A. (2007), 'Volkswagen Nears Proton Deal', *Financial Times*, 19 March, 27.

Shapiro, B.P. and Bonoma, T.V. (1990), 'How to segment industrial markets', in R.J. Dolan (ed.), *Strategic Marketing Management*, Cambridge, MA: Harvard Business School Press.

Shapiro, B.P., Slywotsky, A.J. and Doyle, S.X. (1998), *Strategic Sales Management: A Boardroom Issue*, Note 9–595–018, Cambridge MA: Harvard Business School.

Shapiro, B.P. (2002), *Creating the Customer-Centric Team: Coordinating Sales and Marketing*, Harvard Business School, Note 9-999-006.

Shermach, K. (1995), 'Portrait of the world', *Marketing News*, 28 August, 20.

Sherwood, R. (2007), 'Stores Compete to Prove Their Green Credentials are in the Bag', *Financial Times*, 26 April.

Sheth, J.N. (1994), 'Relationship marketing: A customer perspective', Keynote address, Relationship Marketing Conference, Emory University.

Sheth, J.N. and Mittal, B. (1996), 'A framework for managing customer expectations', *Journal of Market-Focused Management*, 1, 137–58.

Sheth, J.N., Eshghi, A. and Krishnan, B.C. (2001), *Internet Marketing*, Fort Worth: Harcourt College Publishers.

Siguaw, J.A., Brown, G. and Widing, R.E. (1994), 'The influence of the market orientation of the firm on sales force behavior and attitudes', *Journal of Marketing Research*, 31, 106–16.

Simon, B. (2005), 'Suppliers Reorder Priorities for Survival', *Financial Times*, 10 June, 28.

Simon, H. (1992), 'Lessons from Germany's midsize giants', *Harvard Business Review*, 70 (2), 115–23.

Simon, H. (1996), *Hidden Champions*, Boston, MA: Harvard Business School Press.

Simms, J. (1996), 'Mission control', *Marketing Business*, July/August, 18–21.

Simms, J. (2003), 'HR or Marketing: Who Gets Staff on Side?', *Marketing*, 24 July, 23.

Sinkula, J.M. (1994), 'Market information processing and organizational learning', *Journal of Marketing*, 58 (1), 35–45.

Sinkula, J.M., Baker, W.E. and Noorewier, T. (1997), 'A framework for market-based organizational learning: linking values, knowledge and behaviour', *Journal of the Academy of Marketing Science*, 25, 305–18.

Slater, S.F. (1997), 'Developing a customer value-based theory of the firm', *Journal of the Academy of Marketing Science*, 25 (2), 162–7.

Slater, S.F. (1998), 'Customer-led and market-oriented: let's not confuse the two', *Strategic Management Journal*, 19, 1001–6.

Slater, S.F. and Narver, J.C. (1994), 'Does competitive environment moderate the market orientation-performance relationship?', *Journal of Marketing*, 58 (1), 46–55.

Slater, S.F. and Narver, J.C. (1995), 'Market orientation and the learning organisation', *Journal of Marketing*, 59, July, 63–74.

Slywotzky, A. (1996), *Value Migration*, Boston, MA: Harvard Business School Press.

Smith, A. (1997), 'Brand-builders perceive pattern', *Financial Times*, 23 June, 14.

Smith, D.J. (2003), 'Strategic Alliances and Competitive Strategies in the Aerospace Industry: The case of BMW and Rolls-Royce GmbH,' *European Business Review*, 15 (4), 262–76.

Smith, N.C. and Ward, H. (2007), 'Corporate Social Responsibility at a Crossroads?', *Business Strategy Review*, 18 (1), March, 16–21.

Smith, S.M. (1990), *PC MDS Version 5.1: Multidimensional scaling package*, Provo, UT: Brigham Young University.

Smith, W.R. (1956), 'Product differentiation and market segmentation as alternative marketing strategies', *Journal of Marketing*, July, 3–8.

Snider, J., Hill, R.P. and Martin, D. (2003), 'Corporate Social Responsibility in the 21st Century: A View from the World's Most Successful Firms', *Journal of Business Ethics*, 48 (2), 175–87.

Snow, C.C. (1997), 'Twenty-first century organizations: Implications for a new marketing paradigm', *Journal of the Academy of Marketing Science*, 25 (1), 72–4.

Snyder, A.V. and Ebeling, W.H. (1997), 'Targeting a company's real core competencies', in A. Campbell and K.S. Luchs (eds), *Core Competency-Based Strategy*, London: International Thomson Business Press.

Sorrell, J. (1989), 'Power tools', *Marketing*, 16 November, 45.

Spackman, A. (2001), 'Smart housing for high-tech future', Survey (Residential Supplement), 19 May 2001.

Spanos, Y.E. and Lioukas, S. (2001), 'An examination into the causal logic of rent generation: Contrasting Porter's competitive strategy framework and the resource-based perspective', *Strategic Management Journal*, 22, 907–34.

Sparks, D.L. and Tucker, W.T. (1971), 'Multivariate analysis of personality and product use', *Journal of Marketing Research*, 8 (1), 67–70.

Spethman, B. (1992), 'Category management multiples', *Advertising Age*, 11 May, 42.

Stalk, G. (1988), 'Time – the next source of competitive advantage', *Harvard Business Review*, 66 (4), 41–51.

Steffens, J. (1994), *Newgames: Strategic competition in the PC revolution*, Oxford: Pergamon Press.

Stephens, H. (2003), CEO, The H.R. Chally Group, Presentation at the American Marketing Association summer Educators' Conference, August.

Stewart, T.A. (2006a), 'Corporate Social Responsibility: Getting the Logic Right', *Harvard Business Review*, December, 14.

Stewart, T.A. (2006b), 'The Top Line', *Harvard Business Review*, July–August, 10.

Stonich, P.J. (1982), *Implementing Strategy*, Cambridge, MA: Ballinger.

Storbacka, K., Strandvik, T. and Grönroos, C. (1994), 'Managing customer relationships for profit', *International Journal of Service Industry Management*, 5 (5), 21–8.

Story, J. (1992), 'HRM in action: The truth is out at last', *Personnel Management*, 24 (4), 28–31.

Strahle, W.M., Spiro, R.L. and Acito, F. (1996), 'Marketing and Sales: Strategic Alignment and Functional Implementation', *Journal of Personal Selling & Sales Management*, 16 (Winter), 1–20.

Straub, D. and Klein, R. (2001), 'e-Competitive transformations', *Business Horizons*, 44 (3), 3–12.

Strelsin, S.C. and Mlot, S. (1992), 'The Art of Strategic Sales Alignment', *Journal of Business Strategy*, 13 (6), 41–7.

Svendsen, A. (1997), 'Building relationships with microcommunities', *Marketing News*, 9 June, 13.

Swain, C.D. (1993), 'Competitive benchmarking', in D. Bernhardt (ed.), *Perfectly Legal Competitor Intelligence*, London: Pitman Publishing.

Swanson, D.L. (1995), 'Addressing a Theoretical Problem by Reorienting the Corporate Social Performance Model', *Academy of Management Review*, 20 (1), 43–64.

Szulanski, G. (1997), 'Intra-firm transfer of best practices', in A. Campbell and K.S. Luchs (eds), *Core Competency-Based Strategy*, London: International Thomson Business Press.

Tallman, S. (2003), 'Dynamic Capabilities', in Faulkner, D.O. and Campbell, A. (eds), *The Oxford Handbook of Strategy: Volume 1: A Strategy Overview and Competitive Advantage*, Oxford: Oxford University Press.

Talluri, S. and Narasimhan, R. (2004), 'A Methodology for Strategic Sourcing', *European Journal of Operational Research*, 154 (1), 236–50.

Tapscott, D. and Castor, A. (1993), *Paradigm Shift: The new promise of information technology*, New York: McGraw-Hill.

Taylor, R. (1999), 'Shaping the Future with Nothing but Ideas', *Financial Times*, July 19.

Taylor, A. (2005), 'An Operations Perspective on Strategic Alliance Success Factors', *International Journal of Operations & Production Management*, 25 (5), 469–90.

Taylor, A. (2007), 'Microsoft Drops Supplier Over Diversity Policy', *Financial Times*, March 24/25, 5.

Teece, D.J., Pisano, G. and Shuen, A. (1992), *Dynamic Capabilities and Strategic Management*, Working Paper, University of California, Berkeley.

Teece, D.J., Pisano, G. and Shuen, A. (1997), 'Dynamic Capabilities and Strategic Management', *Strategic Management Journal*, 18, 509–33.

Teinowitz, I. (1988), 'Brand managers: 90s dinosaurs?', *Advertising Age*, 19 December, 19.

Tellis, G. and Golder, P. (1996), 'First to market, first to fail: Real causes of enduring market leadership', *Sloan Management Review*, 37 (2).

The Sales Educators (2006), *Strategic Sales Leadership: Breakthrough Thinking for Breakthrough Results*, Mason, OH: Thomson.

Thomas, M.J. (1987), 'Customer care: The ultimate marketing tool', *Proceedings*: Marketing Education Group Conference, Warwick.

Tighe, C. (1997), 'Lean sales machine', *Financial Times*, 25 June, 26.

Timmers, P. (1999), *Electronic Commerce*, Chichester: John Wiley & Sons.

Todeva, E. and Knoke, D. (2005), 'Strategic Alliances and Models of Collaboration', *Management Decision*, 43 (1), 123–48.

Toffler, A. (1981), *The Third Wave*, William Collins/Pan Books.

Townsend, J. and Favier, J. (1991), *The Creative Manager's Pocketbook*, Alresford, Hants: Management Pocketbooks.

Trai, C.C. (1991), *Chinese Military Classic: The art of war*, Singapore: Asiapac Books.

Treacy, M. and Wiersema, F. (1995), 'How market leaders keep their edge', *Fortune*, February, 88–9.

Treacy, M. and Wiersema, F. (1995), *The Discipline of Market Leaders*, London: HarperCollins.

Tull, D.S. (1967), 'The relationship of actual and predicted sales and profit in new product introductions', *Journal of Business*, 40 (3), 233–50.

Tull, D.S. and Hawkins, D.I. (1993), *Marketing Research: Measurement and method*, 6th edn, Englewood Cliffs, NJ: Prentice Hall.

Tyebjee, T.T. (1987), 'Behavioral biases in new product forecasting', *International Journal of Forecasting*, 3 (4), 393–404.

Tzokas, N., Saren, M. and Brownlie, D. (1997), 'Generating Marketing Resources by Means of R&D Activities in High Technology Firms', *Industrial Marketing Management*, 26, 331–40.

Ulrich, D. (1989), 'Tie the corporate knot: Gaining complete customer commitment', *Sloan Management Review*, Summer, 19–27.

Ulrich, D. (1992), 'Strategic and human resource planning: Linking customers and employees', *Human Resource Planning*, 15 (2), 47–62.

Varadarajan, P.R. (1992), 'Marketing's contribution to the strategy dialogue: The view from a different looking glass', *Journal of the Academy of Marketing Science*, 20 (4), 335–44.

Varadarajan, P.R. and Menon, A. (1988), 'Cause-Related Marketing: A Coalignment of Marketing Strategy and Corporate Philanthropy', *Journal of Marketing*, 52, July, 58–74.

Vargo, S.L. and Lusch, R.F. (2004), 'Evolving to a new dominant logic for marketing', *Journal of Marketing*, 68 (January), 1–17.

Varianinin, V. and Vaturi, D. (2000), 'Marketing lessons from e-failures', *McKinsey Quarterly*, (4), 86–97.

Walker, J.W. (1994), 'Integrating the human resource function within the business', *Human Resource Planning*, 17 (2), 59–77.

Wall, M. (1997), 'Boots to offer health cover', *The Sunday Times*, 1 June, Section 4, 1.

Walsh, J. and Godfrey, S. (2000), 'The Internet: a new era in customer service', *European Management Journal*, 18 (1), 85–92.

Wang, C.L. and Ahmed, P.K. (2007), 'Dynamic Capabilities: A review and research agenda', *International Journal of Management Reviews*, 9 (1), 31–51.

Ward, A. (2006), 'Coke Joins the Battle for the Brand Corporate Responsibility', *Financial Times*, 21 November, 10.

Ward, J. (1963), 'Hierarchical grouping to optimize an objective function', *Journal of the American Statistical Association*, 58, 236–44.

Warner, W.L. (1960), *Social Class in America*, New York: Harper and Row.

Waters, R. (2006), 'Computer pack top dogs lose their bite', *Financial Times*, 5 June, 19.

Webster, F.E. (1992), 'The changing role of marketing in the corporation', *Journal of Marketing*, 56 (4), 1–17.

Webster, F.E. (1994), *Market Driven Management*, London: Wiley.

Webster, F.E. (1997), 'The future role of marketing in the organization', in D.R. Lehmann and K.E. Jocz (eds), *Reflections on the Futures of Marketing*, Cambridge, MA: Marketing Science Institute.

Wells, K. (1994/5), 'The road ahead', *Marketing Business*, Dec.-Jan., 18–20.

Wells, W.D. and Gubar, G. (1966), 'Life cycle concepts in marketing research', *Journal of Marketing Research*, 3 (4), 355–63.

Wensley, R. (1981), 'Strategic marketing: Boxes, betas or basics', *Journal of Marketing*, 45 (3), 173–82.

Wernerfelt, B. (1984), 'A resource-based view of the firm', *Strategic Management Journal*, 5 (2), 171–80.

Wernerfelt, B. (1995), 'The resource-based view of the firm: Ten years after', *Strategic Management Journal*, 16, 171–80.

Weyer, M.V. (1997), 'The shop that time forgot', *The Daily Telegraph*, 30 August, 16.

Wheatcroft, P. (1997), 'Bright new look from Persil man', *Financial Mail on Sunday*, 9 February, 9.

Wilmott, M. (1989), 'Whose lifestyle is it anyway?', Institute of International Research Conference on *Customer Segmentation and Lifestyle Marketing*, London, 11–12 December.

Wind, Y. (1978), 'Issues and advances in segmentation research', *Journal of Marketing Research*, 15 (3), 317–37.

Wind, Y. and Mahajan, V. (1981), 'Designing product and business portfolios', *Harvard Business Review*, 59 (1), 155–65.

Winter, S.G. (2003), 'Understanding Dynamic Capabilities', *Strategic Management Journal*, 24, 991–5.

Wissema, J.G., Van der Pol, H.W. and Messer, H.M. (1980), 'Strategic management archetypes', *Strategic Management Journal*, 1 (1), 37–47.

Witzel, M. (2005), 'An Alliance that Can Supply a Competitive Edge', *Financial Times*, 13 June, 14.

Witzel, M. (2005), 'Big Spenders are a Boon – But Don't Forget the Little Guy', *Financial Times*, 8 August, 14.

Womack, J.P. and Jones, D.T. (1996), *Lean Thinking: Banish Waste and Create Wealth in Your Organization*, New York: Simon & Schuster.

Wong, V. (1993), 'Ideas generation', in *Identifying and Exploiting New Market Opportunities*, London: Department of Trade and Industry.

Wong, V., Saunders, J.A. and Doyle, P. (1992), 'Business orientations and corporate success', *Warwick Business School Research Papers*, No. 52, 41 pp.

Wood, D.J. (1991), 'Corporate Social Performance Revisited', *Academy of Management Review*, 16 (4), 691–718.

Woodhead, M. (2007), 'Dirty Rotten Business', *The Sunday Times*, 28 January, 3.5.

Workman, J.P., Homburg, C. and Gruner, K. (1998), 'Marketing Organization: An Integrative Framework of Dimensions and Determinants', *Journal of Marketing*, 62, July, 21–41.

Workman, J.P., Homburg, C. and Jensen, O. (2003), 'Intraorganizational Determinants of Key Account Management Effectiveness', *Journal of the Academy of Marketing Science*, 31 (1), 3–21.

Wright, P., Kroll, M., Pray, B. and Lado, A. (1990), 'Strategic orientations, competitive advantage and business performance', *Journal of Business Research*, 33, 143–51.

Yanklovich, D. and Meer, D. (2006), 'Rediscovering market segmentation', *Harvard Business Review*, 84 (2), 122–31.

Yeh, A. (2006), 'McDonald's Seeks Heavy Traffic Fast-Food Expansion', *Financial Times*, 21 June, 12.

Yoshino, M.Y. and Rangan, U.S. (1995), *Strategic Alliances: An entrepreneurial approach to globalization*, Boston, MA: Harvard Business School Press.

Young, D. (1996), 'The politics behind market segmentation', *Marketing News*, 21 October, 17.

Young, S., Off, F. and Fegin, B. (1978), 'Some practical considerations in market segmentation', *Journal of Marketing Research*, 15, August, 405–12.

Zander, I. and Zander, U. (2005), 'The inside track: On the important (but neglected) role of customers in the resource-based view of strategy and firm growth', *Journal of Management Studies,* 42 (8), 1519–48.

Zeithaml, V.A., Parasuraman, A. and Berry, L.L. (1990), *Delivering Service Quality*, New York: The Free Press.

Zeithaml, V.A., Parasuraman, A. and Malhotra, A. (2000), *A Conceptual Framework for Understanding e-Service Quality: Implications for Future Research and Managerial Practice*, MSI Report 00-115, Boston, MA: Marketing Science Institute.

Zielke, A. and Pohl, M. (1996), 'Virtual vertical integration: The key to success', *McKinsey Quarterly*, (3), 160–3.

Zollo, M. and Winter, S.G. (2002), 'Deliberate learning and the evolution of dynamic capabilities', *Organization Science,* 13 (3), 339–51.

Zoltners, A.A., Sinha, P. and Lorimer, S.E. (2004), *Sales Force Design for Strategic Advantage*, New York: Palgrave Macmillan.

Index

segmentation research (*continued*)
  in internal marketing 502
  post-hoc/cluster based approaches 248–56
    boundary setting 248–50
    data analysis 251–4
    data collection 250–1
    implementation 255
    tracking 255–6
    validating segments 254–5
  see also business *and* consumer market segmentation
Seiko 48
selling capabilities 165
service development capabilities 168
service in value chain analysis 128
service management capabilities 164–5
service positioning 563–4
services spectrum 395–7
Shapiro, B.P.
  on customer management 422, 425, 427, 432–3
  on internal marketing 506–7, 509
  on segmentation 226, 234
shared research 101–2
shareholders
  as stakeholders 16
Sheila's Wheels 33
Sheth, J.N. 478, 505
Siemens 516
Simon, H. 551–2, 554, 555, 561
simple exponential smoothing 199
Sinclair 84, 375
Singh, R. 319, 320–1
Sinopec 462
Skandia 17
Skoda 124, 558
Slater,S.F. 9, 14, 20, 21, 70, 144, 549–50
sleepers 37, 170
sloths 340
Slywotzky, A. 65, 545
Smythson (case study) 538
Snider, J. 527, 529
successful idealists 246
social acceptability 285
social environment 63–7
  and organisations 65–7
societally conscious 246
socio-economic characteristics and market
    segmentation 215–17
Sock Shop 5
Sony Corporation 41, 341, 376
Southwest Airlines 491–2
SPACE analysis 98–89
spanning competencies 553
special events as promotions 353

specialised markets 90–1
spin-out approach to innovation 389
sponsorship as communication tool 358
Spring Ram Corporation 374
Sprint 544
stakeholder objectives 19–21
stakeholders and CSR 522
stalemate markets 89–90
Standard Chartered Bank 458
Starbucks 53, 517
statistical demand analysis 190
stealth positioning strategy 345–6
Stephens, H. 423, 429
Stern, P. 349, 351
strategic account management (SAM) 440–1
  case for 441–2, 450–1
  vulnerabilities in 442–9
    balance of power 442–3
    buyer-seller relationship 443–4
    and competition intensity 445
    and customer loyalty 447
    dependence, risk of 444
    key account investment 445
    and major customers 446–7
    and rate of change 448–9
    regulation 449
    requirements 445–6
    weaknesses 442–3
strategic account partnership 440
strategic accounts in customer portfolio 437–40
strategic alliances 73, 467–9, 470
  competing through 475–81
  as competitive force 471–2
  disengaging from 480–1
  facilitators 476
  outsourcing 468–9
  performance assessment 479–80
  priorities 475–6
  risks in 472–5
  vigilance in 478–9
strategic collaboration 458–9
  customer diversity 460
  drivers of 459–63, 476
    market complexity and risk 460–1
    skills and resource gaps 461–2
    supply chain management 462–3
  market boundaries 460
strategic CSR 533
strategic customer management (SCM)
  customer perspective 435
  customer portfolio 436–8
  dominant customers 436, 438–51
  sales alignment 434–5